THE
SECOND
WORLD
WAR
IN THE
AIR

THE
SECOND
WORLD
WAR
IN THE
AIR

THE STORY OF AIR COMBAT IN EVERY

THEATRE OF WORLD WAR TWO

MERFYN BOURNE

Matador
9 Priory Business Park,
Wistow Road, Kibworth Beauchamp,
Leicestershire. LE8 0RX
Tel: (+44) 116 279 2299
Fax: (+44) 116 279 2277
Email: books@troubador.co.uk
Web: www.troubador.co.uk/matador

ISBN 9781780884417

British Library Cataloguing in Publication Data.
A catalogue record for this book is available from the British Library.

Printed and bound in the UK by TJ International, Padstow, Cornwall
Typeset in 10pt Aldine401 BT Roman by Troubador Publishing Ltd, Leicester, UK

Matador is an imprint of Troubador Publishing Ltd

For Vanessa

Contents

Introduction

The origin of my interest in the aviation of World War Two lies in the fact that my first school was situated at the end of the runway of Croydon Airport, then the principal London airport. No small boy could fail to be impressed by the sight of silver-bellied passenger planes wobbling slowly over the school playground as they came in to land. The origin of this book was my unavailing search for a history of air combat in World War Two that covered the whole war rather than the part the author knew best and which was a narrative history rather than an analytical assessment.

This book makes no pretensions to deep scholarship: its use of original sources is limited and it boasts no historical discoveries. Its aim is to tell the story of the Second World War in the air in a straightforward consecutive manner in a single volume. It is designed for any general reader with an interest in the history of the period and for aviation enthusiasts as well, though experts in the field may find it simplistic in places. It is bound to be so in the light of the amount of information that has to be packed into a single volume.

I have resisted the temptation to describe one theatre from first to last and only then move on to another, simply because the reality is that events all over the world happen together at the same time and not in conveniently watertight sections. The result is that the second half of the book jumps back and forth between various theatres of war in a staccato fashion but I make no apology for this. The men taking the important decisions at the time had to turn their minds from one theatre of war to another in rapid succession and if the reader has to do the same then this only adds to his appreciation of the difficulties they faced and, it is to be hoped, will add to the immediacy of its impact. Of course there is nothing to stop you tackling the chapters out of sequence in order to follow developments in one theatre of war at a time.

Whichever way it is approached there is no getting away from the fact that this book is not a thriller and it includes a considerable number of statistics and administrative details that are essential to give a full picture of the subject though some readers may find them heavy going. At the end of the day air warfare at this time was a numbers game, perhaps more than at any other period of aviation. As a general rule in World War Two, if you had more aircraft you won and if you had less you lost. It took a big imbalance of training or equipment quality to defeat that rule.

One surprising problem that I have encountered is the unexpected difficulty of obtaining accurate facts. Much that might appear straightforward and factual turns out to be obscure and controversial. How many aircraft were shot down on 15th

September 1940, the climactic day of the Battle of Britain? The exact answer is unclear and is not very important anyway but other details are more significant. For instance the bomb-carrying capacity of the B-17 Flying Fortress is often wildly exaggerated even in the most reputable writing and this *does* matter because the whole course of the strategic war in the West was influenced by the fact that American heavy bombers carried substantially smaller bomb loads than their British counterparts. It seems to be a problem intrinsic to the subject that aircraft with an outstanding reputation are awarded inflated qualities by commentators and their shortcomings ignored. Equally, events that reflect poorly on the air forces of a particular country, are glossed over or selectively reported by the historians of that country and battles where the country excelled, are awarded excessive importance. For many years the Soviet Union led the field in this kind of disinformation and its official history of the Soviet Air Force in World War Two must be considered misleading at best.

The worst fields for technical errors are the details relating to the construction and performance of the aircraft themselves. There are many books filled with pages of specifications and columns of performance figures, but for a book concerned with the larger picture the figures are next to irrelevant and much of the time misleading as well. One reads that the such-and-such plane had a maximum speed of 350 mph. but this is quite divorced from reality.

The figure was derived from a test flight in ideal weather with a new aircraft in perfect condition carrying as little fuel as it could get away with, no ammunition or camouflage paint and flown by a highly skilled test pilot. In the front line these conditions were never repeated so the maximum speed figure is, in effect, a fantasy. Equally, bomb loads are a minefield of dubious information because the weight of bombs a given bomber could carry varied, according to the distance to the target, the further the target the smaller the bomb load. On the other hand most books list the maximum bomb load even though the bomber may never be sent against a target close enough for that figure to apply.

For these reasons I have in general tried to avoid giving too many figures relating to the capabilities of individual aircraft and contented myself with a short portrait of their worth in general terms. This does not mean that all technical detail has been abandoned and for those who find the figures dull I can only say that I understand their complaint, but they must content themselves with the thought that it could have been much worse.

I have tried to deal with everything of importance in the air war though, clearly, some subjects must receive more thorough coverage than others. At the end of the day this is a question of subjective judgement. Inevitably not everyone will agree with my decisions. I have kept coverage of the Battle of Britain under strict control because it has been covered so thoroughly in so many books and because its historical importance is, in my opinion, over-emphasized by British historians though one can understand why. It is only one of several crucial episodes in a six year war. Similarly the campaign against the U-boat threat has been pared down to the minimum, not because it is unimportant but because it was a relatively minor part of the air war as such, engaging relatively few men and aircraft compared to strategic bombing or ground attack.

I took the view that it would be misleading to ignore the build-up to the war because so much of what was done during the fighting was governed by attitudes and experiences formed or undergone in the pre-war years and the uses and limitations of aircraft were determined by design features of an evolutionary nature whose origins went back to the dawn of flight. I have therefore briefly summarized the history of flight from that very dawn to the outbreak of the Second World War.

I think this is important for a full understanding of what happened during the war and why events fell out as they did. I admit though, that this approach has led to a fairly lengthy overture before we arrive at Act One and if you cannot bear the delay you can cut straight to Chapter Five and the invasion of Poland.

Covering such a large field in a single volume inevitably means that some subjects must be omitted altogether or earn only a sentence or two. I have written largely about the front line and therefore subjects such as training, industrial production, scientific developments, weapons, civilian involvement, anti-aircraft and fire services, amongst others, have received only a mention here and there as the narrative demands rather than the full exploration they deserve. In addition some of the major issues arising out of the fighting itself, such as the developing efficacy of air attack, on armoured vehicles and ships, have not been given detailed coverage simply for lack of space. I have been constantly aware too of the further danger that compression may lead to distortion. A generalization may ignore small exceptions because there is not the space to elaborate and so there is the danger that brevity can be misleading. I hope that I have not fallen into this trap too often.

One area where I have digressed to go into some detail is the design of warplanes and the mechanics of their use in battle. This would so slow the flow of the narrative however, that I have banished the discussion to an appendix that the reader can tackle at leisure or not at all, according to his fancy. If it is to be read, it should be read earlier rather than later.

The war in Russia is a subject that I have covered at length and I believe I am the first author of a general history of the air war to do so. This is essential because it was arguably the most important part of the whole air war. This was the theatre where the war was won or lost and until now it has been very difficult to describe because of the paucity of English language writing on the subject. In recent years the situation has changed and it is possible to give the eastern front the coverage it deserves. It must be said in passing that this is in no small part thanks to the publication of Christer Bergstrom's outstanding four volumes on the subject. I owe this work a substantial debt of scholarship when it comes to the chapters on the war in Russia and I recommend it to anyone who wishes to know more about that theatre of war.

One difficulty inherent in writing about the air war in Russia and in other theatres where the air fighting accompanies a moving ground campaign, is that it is impossible to separate the air campaign from the ground. The result is that the book can very easily become a general history of the war with merely an emphasis on the aerial element. Description of the ground fighting must therefore be kept to a minimum but must be detailed enough that the reader understands what is going on. Much of the time the measure of aerial success is the degree of advance achieved on the ground and so the two are intimately connected. I must ask the reader to bear this in mind if he or she finds the narrative sometimes straying too far from the air war itself.

Because of the forgoing it is much easier to write about the Battle of Britain or the strategic bombing campaign in the West because they are not accompanied by any significant land warfare. The most agreeable subjects of all are found in the Pacific War where air/sea battles fought in a day changed the course of the war and constitute high drama in themselves. The Battle of Midway stands out as the exemplar of this kind of history: it is only a small exaggeration to say that a morning's fighting ensured Japan would lose the war.

I can only hope that the emphasis I have placed on one subject and not on another has not led to distortion of history beyond what is inevitable in any piece of historiography. One area where I am aware of coming close to distortion is in the strategic air war in the West. I have devoted considerably more space to the less important R.A.F. offensive and less to the more important American offensive. The reason for this is the continuing controversy over the morality of British area bombing. No one seriously criticizes the Americans for their bombing of military targets in Germany despite the collateral damage done. In the terrible business of war there seems to be general agreement that air power can be used this way. Even their saturation bombing of Japanese cities can be seen as an effective way to destroy industry in the particular circumstances of the case. On the other hand R.A.F. carpet bombing remains controversial and it therefore seems reasonable to look at it in rather more detail and take a view on the moral issues raised.

One gratuitous inaccuracy is my use of the term 'Great Britain' when what I am really referring to is the United Kingdom. I have done this deliberately because that was the usage of the time, and the phrase 'United Kingdom' seems to me to be something of an anachronism in this context. I must beg the forgiveness of the good people of Ulster.

In general I have not hesitated to take sides and to criticize where it seems to me that criticism is due. I am aware that this is all too easy to do with hindsight and so I have tried to restrain my critical instincts except when dealing with an issue such as R.A.F. carpet bombing which is so controversial that refusing to take a position would be sheer evasion. I have also expressed strong views in cases where the negligence, stupidity or malice were gross and exceptional such as the failure properly to defend the Philippines immediately after Pearl Harbour or the treatment of Dowding and Parke after the Battle of Britain.

Some may feel that I have let Germany and Japan off too lightly. If that is so, then one reason for it is that they lost and thus are all too easy to censure and, in Germany's case, the military men indeed fought a generally skillful war against increasingly powerful opponents. The mistakes were largely those of the politicians, a category in which I include Hermann Goering. In the case of Japan the fact that its whole war against the United States was suicidal from the start and its approach to fighting governed largely by cultural attitudes wholly alien to the western mind makes objective criticism very difficult.

The views expressed in this book are mine and mine alone as is the responsibility for mistakes of which I am sure there are a number despite my zealous search for accuracy and truth.

I offer my thanks to Laura Wilkins, Christopher Wilkins, David Hooper, Michael Dover, Gordon Bourne, Georgina Bourne, Diana Evans, Angharad Williams and the staff of the National Museum of Grenada who helped me in various ways in the production of this book and to my wife Vanessa who gave me her unfailing support in the two years it took to write it – not to mention the thirty-six years before that.

CHAPTER ONE

The First World War and its Legacy

From the very moment of the Wright brothers' first flight at Kittyhawk, North Carolina in 1903, the military potential of the aeroplane was apparent to all. If governments were slow to involve themselves in the early years of the aeroplane's development, that was not due to lack of interest so much as caution in the face of exaggerated claims and under-performance on the part of the early aviation pioneers. Truly the aeroplanes of the early years of the twentieth century were flimsy contraptions not calculated to inspire confidence in anyone. In 1909 Louis Bleriot crossed the English Channel in one of these machines, but you have only to look at pictures of his aircraft to wonder that it ever took to the air or that he had the courage to ride in it.

Nonetheless when the world went to war in 1914 all the major combatants included aircraft in their armoury. The French had the Farman, the Austrians had the Hansa-Brandenburg and the British had the B.E.2. All were given the job of reconnaissance. In these early days this was the job that aircraft were manifestly fitted to carry out and it was, for a while, the only one they were capable of carrying out. In fact the aeroplane, coupled with photography, revolutionized the business of reconnaissance. Hitherto cavalry had been the means of scouting ahead of an army and they had had that role for millennia. But when it comes to scouting, anything a horse and rider can do, an aeroplane can do better. The armies were able to attack with the benefit of detailed maps of the enemy's positions built up from aerial photographs and artillery fire could be directed from the air with speed and accuracy. That the attacks so often came to nothing was not the fault of the aeroplane.

In 1915 Lieutenant Sholto Douglas, flying one of these missions, passed a German machine on a similar task. The two pilots waved to one another and flew on.[i] Such courtesy did not last long. The efficacy of the aircraft at spotting soon led to the consideration of how to counteract it. The obvious answer was to destroy the scouting plane. At first this was attempted by a pilot carrying a pistol and attempting to shoot the enemy pilot, but this was hopelessly impractical. In due course it was discovered that the only effective way to arm an aeroplane so that it had a reasonable chance of stopping another aeroplane was to bolt on a machine-gun. At first this was a moveable gun manned by a gunner and not the pilot, but it soon emerged that a fixed gun fired by the pilot worked better even though aiming it involved turning the whole aeroplane.

The obvious place to put such a machine-gun was on top of the fuselage right in front of the pilot. He could deal with jams and reloading because the breech of the gun was within easy reach and it was handily placed for him to take aim. (Guns in the wings were never an option at this stage of the aeroplane's development because the wings were not strong enough to bear the weight.) The big problem with any centrally placed gun was that it had to fire through the arc of the spinning propeller. Some bullets would miss the propeller blades but others would hit them and so the aircraft would, in effect, shoot itself down. One solution was to develop an aircraft with a pusher engine: that is, with an engine mounted behind the pilot and pushing the aircraft forward rather than pulling it from in front, in the more conventional setting with the propeller attached to the nose of the plane.

This was tried but it turned out to have a number of drawbacks. The aircraft in front of the propeller obstructed the airflow and made the engine less efficient. Secondly, this configuration presented problems of directional stability as will be appreciated by anyone who has worked with a wheelbarrow. Most of the time you push a wheelbarrow but you must be careful how you do so or it will tip over, particularly if you try to turn too sharply. If you simply pull it, the task is much easier as the wheelbarrow follows your every move in a docile fashion. The problem, of course, is that you can't see where you are going. But in an aircraft, that does not apply as the pilot faces forward whatever kind of propeller he has. The third problem was that the engine was the heaviest part of the plane and maintained considerable momentum. If the pilot had to crash-land, as was common with these primitive aircraft in wartime, the engine would tear out of its mountings, bound forward and crush the pilot. Quite apart from the question of gunnery, these drawbacks explain why 'pusher' aircraft have never found much favour throughout the history of aviation.

Various experiments were tried. The French pilot, Roland Garros, attached hardened wedges to the blades of the propeller at the point where the bullet would strike. The idea was that these would deflect the bullet and so save the propeller. The idea worked after a fashion but was no real solution because the strain imposed on the propeller blades by repeated bullet strikes did not take much time to cause structural failure. Before long the interrupter gear was invented. This was a simple mechanical system whereby, once the trigger was pulled, each time a propeller blade cleared the muzzle of the machine-gun it pushed a rod that activated the firing mechanism of the gun. In effect the propeller was firing the gun. This was an inefficient system because the engine was usually turning at a slower speed than the gun could fire so that the gun's full power was not being utilized. Moreover, the mechanical linkages required were prone to failure. Nevertheless it revolutionized aerial warfare.

It was the Germans who invented this system and it gave them a short-lived but distinct advantage. They fitted this arrangement to an aircraft called the Fokker E1,

Merfyn's book is a comprehensive history including the lesser known campaigns such as fighting in Burma, Italy and East Africa as well as the air offensive in Western Europe and the struggle in the Pacific. It also re-examines the RAF bombing of German cities and the moral issues raised. The key feature of this work is that it is the first history of air war to give full and proportionate coverage to the war in Russia, which until now has been largely ignored.

'My interest in the aviation of WWII lies in the fact that my first school was situated at the end of the runway of Croydon Airport, then the principal London air hub. No small boy could fail to be impressed by the sight of silver-bellied passenger planes wobbling slowly over the school playground as they came in to land,' observes Merfyn, who now lives in Carmarthenshire.

The Second World War in the Air is a comprehensive review of the air war. It's meticulously researched and highly readable.

PUBLICATION DATE 1ST APRIL 2013

ISBN: 9781780884417 PRICE: £15.99

PRESS PACK

FOR AUTHOR INTERVIEWS, REVIEW OR COMPETITION COPIES, ARTICLES, PHOTOS OR EXTRACTS PLEASE CONTACT JANE ROWLAND

TEL: 0116 279 2299   EMAIL: MARKETING@TROUBADOR.CO.UK
TROUBADOR PUBLISHING, 9 PRIORY BUSINESS PARK, WISTOW ROAD, KIBWORTH, LEICESTER LE8 0RX

THE SECOND WORLD WAR IN THE AIR

Merfyn Bourne tells the story of air combat in every theatre of World War Two

This book is a complete narrative history of the Second World War in the air, which starts by describing the early days of flight in order to put military air power in context when WWII began. It then moves on to a step-by-step coverage of the air combat in each theatre of war.

'I wanted to write a history of air combat in WWII that covered the whole war,' says Merfyn. 'My aim was to tell the story in a straightforward manner and in a single volume. I hope it will appeal to general readers, with an interest in the history of the period, and aviation enthusiasts too.'

generally known as the Fokker Eindecker because it had only a single wing when almost every other plane of this time was a biplane. In 1915, the Eindeckers patrolled the front, shooting down Allied planes more or less at will and became known as the 'Fokker Scourge'. In recent years a replica Fokker E1 has been built and those who have flown it bear witness to the difficulty of controlling it, let alone shooting anything down with it. If roughly handled it falls into a spin and it manoeuvers in slow and ponderous fashion because its means of control is the 'wing warping' system.

Wing warping was the control system devised by the Wright brothers and used on most of the early aircraft. Wires attached to the flat surfaces of the wings and tail could be pulled by the pilot to twist part of the surface up or down. This was a very primitive and imprecise system but, at first, nothing better could be devised.

The interrupter gear soon fell into the hands of the Allies who, in any event, were well aware of the principles involved which were no secret in aeronautical circles. By 1916, the Allies had developed their own version and the Sopwith 1½ Strutter and early Nieuports drove the Fokkers from the sky. These latter aircraft were a significant improvement in design on the Fokker. They were biplanes which, given the low power of these early aircraft, was a more practical design. They had also developed separate control surfaces for controlling the aircraft and this system is still in use today. It involves having hinged sections at the rear of the wings and the tail that can move up or down under the pilot's control. In the era we are considering, this control was always done by rods or wires, though nowadays it is more usually electronic. When the hinged sections were raised or lowered they cut into the airflow and caused an obstruction on which the air pressed, pushing it in the other direction. Thus if you raised the elevators on the tailplane, the pressure of the air on them pushed the tail down and the nose up. By this means you could point the aircraft in any direction and control it with some precision. The big drawback was that it was a system with a number of moving parts subjected to constant strain and thus liable to fail.

The remainder of the First World War witnessed a technology race of unprecedented intensity. It appears to be a sad fact of life that there is nothing like a war to propel research forward. By 1917, the Germans had the lead again and enjoyed a second period of supremacy with their Albatross aircraft. This boasted the advantage of greater speed and ruggedness of construction than its contemporaries together with a heavier armament. It also showed an early appreciation of the value of streamlining. The Allies countered with several aircraft of improved design: the Spad 13, SE5A, Sopwith Camel and Nieuports 17 and 28. These tipped the balance in their favour during late 1917 and early 1918. Then Germany jumped ahead again with the Fokker D7, a quite remarkable aircraft of unmatched speed and agility. So advanced was it, that when the war ended it was specifically mentioned in the armistice agreement which required every Fokker D7 to be handed over to the Allies.

It should be emphasized again just how dangerous flying was in this era. If you dived too steeply the wings fell off. If you turned upside down you were liable to fall out because there were no safety harnesses. Pilots were not generally issued with parachutes. The engine often caught fire and since it was right in front of the pilot the wind blew the flames onto him. Many pilots flew with a loaded gun so that if this happened they could shoot themselves rather than be burned to death.

A popular song of the time, sung in every British squadron mess to the tune of 'My Bonnie Lies Over the Ocean,' was 'The Young Aviator Lay Dying.'[ii] It began as follows:

'The young aviator lay dying
And as in the hangar he lay
To the mechanics who round him were standing
These last parting words he did say

Take the cylinders out of my kidneys
The connecting rod out of my brain
The cam box from under my backbone
And assemble the engine again.'

The song continues for many verses but that is enough to give the reader the flavour of its dark humour. What is most significant is that the aviator hero of the song has not been shot down by the enemy but crashed in an accident on landing due to 'pilot error'.

The two key components of any aircraft are the wings and the engine. The wings generate the lift and the engine drives the plane forward so that there is an air flow over the wings to cause that lift. At its simplest, developing the plane means having more of both. The subtleties of aerodynamics were little comprehended at this time but the basic shape of a wing required to create lift is not complicated and was well understood by World War One's engineers who struggled to get more lift from less weight. The simplest design is to have one wing but unless you brace it firmly somehow, the forces acting on it will soon cause it to snap. For this reason the monoplanes that saw service during the war often had a bracing system whereby wires ran from the wing to a post on top of the fuselage and these took some of the strain. The alternative was to build the wing stronger but that would have made it too heavy to be practical. The designers of the time found that a much easier answer was to have two wings held together with struts and cross-wires. This configuration had the added advantage that you had much more lifting area and the upper wing was not interrupted by the body, but was a clean lifting area from one end to the other. The disadvantage was that all the bracing and the struts and wires created a great deal of drag. Given the limitation of the engines of the time the biplane solution probably was the sensible one: certainly the vast majority of aircraft built at this time were of the biplane type.

The big challenge presented by engines was to develop more power without more weight: that is, to develop a better power-weight ratio. The engine of the original Wright Flyer that took to the air in 1903, weighed 170 lbs, and developed 12 horsepower. That is a little over 14 lbs per horsepower. By 1916 the French Rhone engine that powered various Nieuports generated 113 horsepower and weighed 330 lbs. That is a little under 3 lbs per horsepower. By the last year of the war, the Sopwith Camel was powered by a Bentley-Clerget producing 150 horsepower from 397 lb. The relevant figure is 2.6 lbs per horsepower. By way of comparison the Daimler Benz 601 that was to power many German aircraft in the early years of World War Two produced 1360 horsepower from 1540 lbs. You can see at once that the ratio has come down to something approaching 1 lb per horsepower.

Even by the end of World War One engines were five times more efficient than they had been when aviation started. It should be born in mind that at this time, and for most of subsequent history, the engine was more expensive than the rest of the aircraft put together. For this reason, as much as for aerodynamic ones, aircraft designers tended to design their aircraft around an available and affordable engine rather than creating a design to do a particular job and then looking for an engine to power it.

During the war, engine development took an avenue that appeared promising but turned out ultimately to be a dead end. That avenue was the rotary engine. (This engine, it should be made clear, was quite unrelated to the modern rotary car engine, sometimes called the Wankel engine.) A rotary engine was a strange design in which the propeller was fixed to the engine and the whole assembly revolved around a hollow shaft. The fuel was piped along the shaft and into each cylinder as it passed, via a tube. This design generated a lot of power for its weight and was simpler than most other engines to build.

Unfortunately the fuel feed arrangement did not readily lend itself to regulation by a throttle and control had to be exercised by varying the strength of the fuel mixture and by switching the engine on and off. Even worse, the spinning engine developed a huge degree of torque and was effectively a gyroscope, and this made aircraft, powered by these engines very difficult to control. In an age of dangerous aircraft, these were veritable death-traps. In fact the scope for development of the rotary engine was limited by this torque because, beyond a certain power, it was literally, uncontrollable. Moreover, beyond a certain speed the engine moved too fast for the fuel to be injected into the cylinders. These limits had been reached by the end of the war and thereafter use of rotary engines rapidly faded away.

A pilot who is busy flying his aeroplane and/or shooting at another plane is not free to take photographs and so almost from the war's outset there was a divergence of function and the development of specialization in aircraft design. The basic design was the spotter because that was the perceived role of an aircraft. This was a two-seater plane with a pilot and an observer who did the spotting. The fighter plane emerged almost simultaneously and was a single seat plane. Fighter planes not only attacked the spotters they also attacked each other, and in increasing numbers as the war progressed. By 1918 there were regular combats of dozens of aircraft at a time and a curious paradox was developing. The point of a military aircraft is either to observe or to attack things on the ground. Fighter aircraft make no direct contribution to this: they either protect or hunt the aircraft doing the observing and attacking. Their entire usefulness is thus indirect, at one remove from the true objective of the air force to which they belong. However, it is often the case that fighter to fighter battles are among the most significant to occur. The reason for this is that if your side loses the fighter battle, then the enemy will be free to destroy your spotter and bomber aircraft at will. You therefore must contest the fighter battle with all your might.

The last of the three main types of aircraft to emerge was the bomber which did the aforementioned attacking. It is a short step from flying over your enemy and watching him to dropping things on him. Aviators soon took to carrying a variety of disagreeable items in their planes which they heaved over the side while on a spotting patrol over the enemy lines. Inevitably they began to drop explosive devices and soon developed the purpose-built aerial bomb. At first these were carried inside the body of the aircraft and dropped manually by the observer, but as the bombs became larger this was no longer possible and they were now attached to hard points under the wings and dropped by means of an electrical release switch.

Development in the field of aerial bombing is a matter of carrying more and larger bombs and dropping them ever more accurately. Bombing never really developed into anything more than a nuisance weapon in World War One, though large aircraft such as the British Handley Page V/1400 could fly from Norfolk to Berlin and back, with bombs weighing more than a whole 1914 aircraft[iii] and quite sophisticated sights were developed that took into account factors such as the aircraft's height, speed and drift due to wind. One of the problems was that nobody quite knew in which direction to go. You could bomb the enemy's troops and his supply dumps close behind the lines or, if you had planes with the necessary range, you could fly deep into his country and bomb targets such as factories but that was a long-term strategy promising no quick results. Each nation faced different problems and adopted a different solution.

For the French in particular, there was the drawback that many of the likely targets were in France, albeit behind the German lines and they were understandably reluctant to bomb their own country and their own people. The same problem constrained the British since France was their ally but they developed large bombers such as the Handley Page and the Vickers Vimy and used them to a limited degree against German held territory anyway. They did not produce enough planes to make a significant impact however. More important to them was the exploitation of short range bombing and what would today be called close air support or ground-attack. Existing fighter planes could double up in this role machine-gunning enemy troops and dropping small bombs.

The same constraints applied to the Russians as well, and to an even greater degree. They produced the world's first four-engine bomber in the Murometz, designed by Igor Sikorsky before the war as a passenger plane and converted to bomber status. But they only produced 73 of them altogether and never more than 40 were in the front line together at the same time. The distances on the eastern front coupled with the weakness of Imperial Russia's industrial base, meant that the Russians were never likely to be serious competitors in the bombing field.

The Germans developed an excellent bomber by the standards of the time in the Gotha but they never devoted the resources to aerial bombing which would have made it a significant factor. Their industry was stretched by all the conflicting demands of a war against several other giant economies and they had also adopted a defensive mind-set when it came to the war in the air. One tempting target for them was the United Kingdom. Until the coming of the aeroplane the U.K. had been safe behind the waves of the channel. No army could touch her without an actual invasion. The aeroplane changed all that. The Germans used aeroplanes and Zeppelins to bomb London and other targets though the material effect of these raids was minimal. There was however, another outcome of these raids which will be further explored shortly.

Austria-Hungary scarcely developed a bombing campaign for much the same reason as Russia.

All the nations faced the question of cost. Bombing in the tactical form was embraced by all the combatants to varying degrees but deep penetration bombing, or strategic bombing as it came to be known, required large numbers of big, long range bombers and the costs were huge. Moreover, by its very nature, strategic bombing was not going to produce any short-term results. The long-term results promised much: just how much, was to become one of the major controversies of the Second World War.

A few words must be said about Zeppelins and other lighter-than-air craft. Aeroplanes offer one means of defeating gravity; balloons offer another. Germany was the great experimenter in the lighter-than-air field. Count Ferdinand von Zeppelin made it his life's work to produce a viable weapon out of the humble balloon and he succeeded, up to a point. Certainly Zeppelins were imposing craft over 600 feet long and capable of carrying three to four tons of bombs (which was far more than aeroplanes could carry). Unfortunately they proved to be very vulnerable to fighter planes and anti-aircraft fire: their sheer size was their enemy in that they presented a gigantic, slow-moving target that it was hard to miss. Moreover they were at the mercy of high winds and bad weather. Fully half the

Zeppelins lost in world War One were lost due to accidents as opposed to enemy action. Germany was the only country to use airships, as they were known, as weapons of war but both Britain and the U.S.A. experimented with them in the inter-war years with conspicuous lack of success. One after another they succumbed to accidents and enthusiasm waned. The culminating moment was the docking of the Hindenburg at Lakehurst New Jersey in 1937, when the great airship burst into flames and crashed to the ground killing thirty-six people. This occasion, which degenerated into disaster, was being broadcast live on radio and was thus the worst publicity that airships could have. Shortly afterward the Second World War took them out of service and by its end the future clearly lay with the aeroplane and not the airship.

Zeppelins bombed London during World War One and after they had been withdrawn because of excessive casualties, Gotha bombers continued the job. The Germans were aware that the material damage they were going to cause would be slight, but they hoped that the bombing would have a serious impact on British morale contributing to a war weariness that might drive Britain out of the conflict. This did not happen but the raids did create an atmosphere approaching panic in London and heavy criticism of the government for not adequately protecting its people. Reports suggested that industrial production in the London area had dropped dramatically as a result of the raids. Steps were taken to improve the defences and the crisis, if that was what it was, passed. Analysts, however, drew inferences about the achievements of strategic bombing that were to be central to the strategy of the next war.

During World War One the basic tactics for carrying out the three main tasks of the military aeroplane were hammered out by bitter experience. The key to spotting was to fly high and fast to avoid the enemy. The Germans realized this quicker than the Allies. The British and the French kept up an offensive stance in their aerial operations as a matter of policy and therefore ignored the tactics of evasion and tried to fly spotter missions in the face of fighter opposition, sometimes with escort and sometimes without.

The Germans were, in general, happy to let this situation continue and stay on the defensive. Defensive aerial battles are easier, particularly if you are outnumbered, and they carry advantages such as the fact that you tend to recover most of your downed pilots because you are fighting over your own territory, whereas the aggressor loses his, because they are taken prisoner. For most of the war Allied losses of aircraft were substantially higher than German. The fact that parachutes were not generally in use, particularly on the Allied side, might lead one to think that any pilot shot down in combat must be killed. In fact this was far from universally so. The aeroplanes of this time flew at a speed low enough to make many crashes surprisingly survivable. Captain Ira Jones, a British ace pilot with 40 victories to his credit, survived numerous crashes.[iv] Obviously, if you survive a crash but are captured, you are still a write-off for the air force you are flying for. Many aircraft that are shot down are, in fact, damaged and are able to fly for a short distance before they have to crash-land. Once again there are obvious advantages to being over, or near, your own territory.

Bombing must be divided into two categories: 'level' and 'ground attack.' Level bombing was fairly straightforward at this time. You flew to your target, dropped your bombs and flew home again. Bombsights were in their infancy and most of the time you flew low enough to dispense with such aids. If the weather was bad you did not fly at all. Level Bombing was the branch of air warfare that probably had the most developing to do.

Ground attack was always a low level business and did not involve the use of a bombsight at all. If bombs were dropped they were dropped by the pilot 'by eye'. If rockets were used the pilot fired them like the guns and used the gun sight. Air-to-ground rockets were developed in World War One and have gone from strength to strength ever since. If the guns were used against ground targets (what was called 'strafing',) then it was done by any member of the crew whose gun could bear and naturally the gun sight was used. The key to this kind of attack (as with all bombing) was, quite simply, accuracy. This was achieved by experience and by getting in close. The problem was defensive fire from the ground and there was not much the pilot could do to avoid it if he was to fulfill his mission. For this reason ground attack was feared by pilots and with good reason: losses were high. The tactics of ground attack have not changed much over the decades.

Lastly there is the question of fighter tactics. Fighter planes enter combat with enemy bombers, or spotters, or fighters but which ever it is, they have to get into a firing position first and then fire accurately and with sufficient power to bring down the enemy plane.

Obviously you can approach another plane from any angle, but if you are both travelling at speed you will not be near each other for very long, unless you both travel in the same direction. You can do that either side by side or one behind the other. Since a fighter plane of that time, or any other for that matter, was usually armed with guns facing forward, the place to be was behind the enemy plane. There was an additional reason to take up that position and that was the problem of deflection. If a plane crossed in front of you, you could fire at it but by the time your bullets reached it, it had moved on. The average bullet travels at about 700 mph and the planes of the World War One era, let alone those of a later time, could easily do 100 mph so if our fighter opens fire at 250 yards the bullet is only going at seven times the speed of the target plane. In the time it takes to cross the 250 yards the target plane has gone one seventh of that distance or, roughly, 35 yards which is quite enough to take it out of harm's way. To hit it you must aim ahead of it. On the other hand, if you shoot from behind, the plane may move but it remains in the path of

9

the bullets which will rapidly catch it up. Much the same rules apply if you fly head to head, but you have only a very short time to fire because your two planes are closing fast and the enemy can also fire at you. Moreover there is a serious danger of collision.

For fighter planes therefore, the key was to get behind the enemy, 'on his tail.' Then you had to shoot accurately. One must remember that while you are lining up on your enemy's tail, he is making every move possible to stop you doing so and thus, when you are in a position to take a shot at him it may well be for only a second or so and it is unlikely to be from absolutely dead behind so you may well have to take into account some degree of deflection as well.

Here there occurs another problem of aerial gunnery. If you throw a ball as hard as you can in front of you and immediately turn right, the ball will not be in front of you when it lands, it will be to your left and probably out of sight. The ball has not changed direction, you have. Similarly the pilot who fires his guns while turning will find that the bullets appear to turn back the way he has come and thus vanish under the nose of the plane (because a plane tips over in the direction it is turning.) It was not unusual therefore for a pilot to be firing at a target that he could not see because it was under his nose.

If all this seems unduly technical, all one has to remember is that you generally fire from behind and the chance to do so is fleeting. Only at the very end of World War Two was a sight invented that helped the pilot make the calculations involved in deflection shooting. The overwhelming majority of pilots had to aim by eye, aided by a simple ring sight. This was a critical skill. All the great aces had a natural gift for this skill or learned it on the job. Ira Jones who flew with Micky Mannock, the leading ace of Great Britain in the Great War, observed that it was his shooting that made Mannock so deadly. Where other pilots would spray bullets in the general direction of the enemy Mannock would fire a short burst and the enemy plane would go down because he understood deflection shooting.[v]

It is no coincidence that many of the famous aces of the air fighting in the World Wars were country boys with experience of game shooting, particularly shooting at birds. Shooting game birds presents almost all the same ballistic problems as shooting at aircraft. Johnnie Johnson, Britain's top scoring ace in World War Two, said that his interest in game-shooting was essential to his skill as an aerial marksman. Indeed, so keen was he on game-shooting that he was out with his shotgun as soon as the flying action died down.[vi] Bob Johnson, one of the top U.S. aces of that war was a farm boy from Oklahoma who grew up shooting game with a .22 calibre rifle and he too was confident that it was this that was the cause of his deadly accuracy in the skies.[vii]

Some adjustment must be made to the above in the case of the fighter attacking the heavy bomber. The bomber is too large and unwieldy to dart out of the way and therefore is an easy target for the fighter. The fighter simply bores in from the rear and pours fire into the bomber. The answer for the bomber is to have guns facing to the rear and by the end of World War One the larger bombers had guns covering not only the rear but every possible angle of approach. There did not appear to be a great deal that the fighters could do about this, particularly if several bombers flew together in formation and presented a target bristling with defensive fire. The fighter was especially vulnerable because its engine was at the front and thus an easy target for the defensive gunners and the pilot also was very much in the way of defensive fire. The fighter could jink around to put the gunners' aim off but jinking put his own aim off too.

The final element of air combat is to ensure that you have the offensive power to shoot your enemy down. At first fighter planes carried a single machine-gun and then two. Spotters carried a single gun firing in an arc to the rear. Later in the war, bombers carried a variety of machine-guns as noted above. No fighter in service in any numbers carried more than the two guns in front of the pilot. This was adequate to shoot down another fighter plane but by the war's last year it was clear that it was not enough to bring down a large bomber without the exercise of great skill and a slice of luck.

By the end of the war it appeared that there was a big future for bombing with large aircraft of increasing range and armament that would be very hard to stop.

If there was a popular hero who emerged from this new field of conflict it was the fighter pilot. Compared to the squalor of the trenches the aerial conflict seemed clean and almost ethereal; it invited comparison with mediaeval jousts. The deeds of men such as Albert Ball, Georges Guynemer and Manfred von Richthofen inspired the public and they became national heroes. Even today there is hardly a household in the Western World where the name of the 'Red Baron' is not known. The whole business of flying and aerial combat came to seem glamorous and exciting.

It is worth recalling that from the point of view of the aviators the war ended very suddenly. One day they were flying missions and the next the war was over. The German air force was by no means beaten in November 1918 and there was a feeling of unfinished business in the air. Aerial warfare had developed out of all recognition in four years and it was clear to most senior officers and designers what the next improvements must be, but suddenly it was all over and the pace of development slowed to a peacetime crawl.

In the early days of the War aerial battles involved first a pair of aircraft and then groups of two or three, but by 1918, there were aerial battles taking place involving one hundred or more aircraft at a time, all wheeling and looping all over the sky. Each major combatant country had an air force of thousands of planes. The world was in love with flying.

CHAPTER TWO

The Inter-War Years

It need hardly be said that no one at the time thought of them as the inter-war years, at least, not at first; in fact, quite the reverse. The First World War was the war 'to end all wars' and now there was going to be peace forever. An international organization, the League of Nations was set up to resolve international conflicts without recourse to war and there seemed a real possibility that there might be peace, if not forever, then for decades. After all, the close of the Napoleonic period saw peace in Europe for nearly fifty years and no general war for a hundred. There was universal revulsion against the last four years that had seen the death of millions of young men across Europe.

Of the war's major combatants Austria-Hungary had ceased to exist, Russia was out of the running, at least for the time being, while it coped with revolution and internal chaos and Germany was banned from having any air force at all (which just goes to show how much importance the great powers attached to aircraft). The other powers were busy getting rid of unwanted aeroplanes and servicemen as fast as possible. The R.A.F. had 188 squadrons in 1918 and employed 290,000 men. In 1920 it had 12 squadrons and 30,000 men. There were similar reductions in France, Italy and the U.S.A., though the latter had not had the time to develop a very large air corps. The U.S.A. also had not developed a military aircraft industry on the same scale as the European powers, but had used French planes in the conflict. Accordingly it suffered no large-scale industrial dislocation caused by cancelled orders for military hardware.

Aircraft were sold off or scrapped by the thousands and the great aces of the war had to find something else to do. Charles Nungesser, France's number three ace, started a flying school and when that failed he sailed for Hollywood to try to make his name in the movies. Ernst Udet of Germany became a stunt pilot, making several movies with Leni Riefenstahl; then he ran his own aircraft construction company and tried to start an airline. In between times he had numerous affairs and drank and gambled. Women apparently found him enchanting though he was only five foot three inches tall. Godwin Brumowski, Austria-Hungary's leading ace, took to farming in Transylvania. Transylvania was then part of Hungary and he was surrounded by Hungarians, yet spoke no Hungarian. It is not surprising that he was not a success. He then started a flying school and was killed in a flying accident in the 1930s.

Not all the retired pilots were failures. Reuben Fleet who had been a flying instructor for the U.S. Army, started the U.S. air mail service and then went on to start his own aircraft manufacturing company. This company, Consolidated Aircraft, grew to be one of the largest aircraft companies in the United States.

Charles Kingsford Smith was an Australian who fought at Gallipoli and then joined the Royal Flying Corps. In 1917, he was shot down and seriously injured but his enthusiasm for flying was not dented. When the war was over he became one of the early 'barnstormers' in the U.S.A. In the American prairies there are large barns that have doors at both ends and 'barnstorming' involved flying in one end and out the other. That and other tricks were performed by aviators in front of large crowds who paid a small sum to attend. There was an almost limitless demand for this kind of entertainment in the U.S.A. in the 1920s and an almost limitless supply of out-of-work aviators to meet that demand. In Europe the demand was more for rides in an aeroplane and that was provided for too. In fact, biographies of leading World War Two pilots repeatedly describe how the subject's interest in flying was fired by taking such a joy ride.

In 1928, Kingsford Smith became the first man to fly the Pacific, going from California to Brisbane. In 1929, he was forced to crash-land in the Australian desert when his aircraft developed a fault. He had to survive for a fortnight before rescuers could reach him. He went on to become the first man to fly across Australia and then the first man to fly from Australia to New Zealand. In 1930, he entered the London to Australia air race and won it, setting a new record. In 1932, he was knighted but in 1935, he disappeared over the Andaman Sea while trying to improve on his London-Australia record. He was a household name in Australia and famous throughout the world. His kind of romantic daring and not least his tragic death, added immeasurably to the glamour of the aeroplane and of flying generally.

The inter-war years were a great time for setting flying records. As early as 1919, John Alcock and Arthur Brown became the first to fly the Atlantic non-stop. They were competing for a prize offered by the Daily Mail for the first direct, non-stop transatlantic flight. They took off from Labrador in a Vickers Vimy, a converted wartime bomber, and landed in Ireland fifteen hours later after a hair-raising flight during which their radio failed and they nearly flew into the sea. For much of the journey they flew through fog. The noise of the engines was so great that they could only communicate by passing notes. They were, of course, in open cockpits.

In 1927, Charles Nungesser and a colleague, Francois Coli, tried to fly the Atlantic the other way, which is more difficult because you fly against the prevailing winds. They disappeared over the vast stretches of the ocean never to be seen again. Two years later the feat was accomplished by Baron von Hunefeld and his crew. Their feat never received the acclaim it deserved and it is hard to resist the conclusion that this was partly because Hunefeld and his pilot were German at a time when Germans were unpopular. It also came after the flight of Charles Lindbergh and was therefore, illogically, seen as a second and not a first.

Perhaps the most famous of all these pioneering flights was the transatlantic crossing by Charles Lindbergh in 1927. A New York hotelier called Raymond Orteig offered a prize of $25,000 for the first non-stop flight between New York and Paris in 1919. By 1927, the prize was still unclaimed. Nungesser and half a dozen other famous aviators had died in unsuccessful attempts to win it. Lindbergh, an unknown young pilot, took on the challenge. He made the flight in a Ryan monoplane specially designed for the occasion and called 'Spirit of St. Louis' in honour of his financial backers who came from that city. As aeroplanes go, this was one of the strangest ever seen, for it had no forward view. The space where a windshield would have fitted was taken up by a fuel tank. A periscope gave the pilot some kind of idea of what lay ahead. Perhaps this is not quite as surprising as it seems since the aircraft was only ever intended to make one landing (though, in the event it made considerably more). Less remarked on but equally remarkable is the fact that it had only a single engine. Lindbergh's reasoning was that if he had two engines and one failed in mid-Atlantic he was doomed anyway because a plane large enough to house two engines would never complete the journey on one, and two engines meant twice the chance of engine failure. (More than two engines was never a realistic possibility for reasons both of cost and the engineering limitations of the time.)

He took off from Roosevelt Field, New York on 20th May 1927, at ten minutes to eight in the morning and arrived at Le Bourget late in the evening of 21st. He was met there by an excited crowd estimated at 150,000 who carried him shoulder high. Back home in the U.S.A. he was honoured with a ticker-tape parade down Fifth Avenue and awarded the Congressional Medal of Honor. From then on he was an international hero. He toured the United States promoting aviation and his efforts transformed the attitude of the American public to flight. Where it had been seen as exotic and too dangerous to be a realistic means of travel, it was now accepted as the travel mode of the future. In later years Lindbergh's life was darkened by the kidnap and murder of his baby son. He became an ardent isolationist and mildly eccentric but once the Second World War started he supported it wholeheartedly. He tried to enlist but this was vetoed by the President who realized that his death in action would be a much greater blow to the country than any benefit gained by his enlistment. Instead he became a civilian consultant on aviation which gave him the excuse to travel to the Pacific and fly unofficial combat missions in defiance of the ban.

No consideration of the heroes of early aviation would be complete without mention of the female flyers. Amelia Earhart is premiere among them. In 1932, she became the first woman to fly the Atlantic solo: she had already made the trip once as a member of the crew of a pilot named Wilmer Stultz. In 1936 she too disappeared during an attempt to fly round the world.

Amy Johnson achieved fame in 1930 by being the first woman to fly solo from England to Australia. She also set a number of other records in the 1930s and when the Second World War broke out, became a transport pilot with the R.A.F., Air Transport Auxiliary. She died in 1941 when she became lost in bad weather and had to bail out over the Thames estuary. She drowned before she could be rescued.

As well as these two pre-eminent figures there were a number of less well remembered female pioneers such as the Stinson sisters in the United States, Jean Batten of New Zealand and the Honourable Mrs. Victor Bruce who not only flew round the world, but set powerboat records and won the Monte Carlo Rally in 1927.

So many of these early aviators met a premature death that one is tempted to wonder what it was that drove them on. It must have been clear to them all that if they kept on trying to break records and go faster and faster and cross remote regions of the globe, death would catch up with them sooner rather than later. Charles Lindbergh was a rarity in that once he had captured one big record he stopped tempting fate.

As has been mentioned, many of these records were set in the course of seeking to win prizes or races and in that context the most famous of all these contests was the Schneider Trophy. This was an annual race designed to find the fastest seaplane in the world. It was created in 1913 by Jacques Schneider, heir to a fortune derived from the Schneider Creusot armament combine. The trophy itself was a fine silver statue of a winged goddess touching a billowing wave. One of the rules was that if any country should win the race for three consecutive years it would keep the trophy in perpetuity. The first race was won by France and the second by Great Britain; the race was then suspended for the duration of the First World War. It was resumed at Bournemouth in 1919, but foggy conditions made it a fiasco in which only one plane finished the race and that was disqualified when it was discovered that it had not followed the correct course. The race was declared void and interest in it flagged as a result. The next two races were held in Venice and were won by the Italians by default as no other country's planes competed. In 1922, Britain and France entered the race as well as Italy and the British entry won the race by a narrow margin. This was very much against expectations as the Italians were the acknowledged world leaders in aero-design at the time.

The 1922 race rejuvenated the Schneider Trophy and there was widespread international interest. The 1923 race was won by the United States who dominated it for a period but without winning for the crucial three consecutive years. In 1927 Britain won again. By now the government was backing the British entry and the pilots were from the R.A.F.. It was then decided to hold the race every two years in order to provide more time for development of the aircraft and in 1929, Britain won again. In 1931 the Labour Government of the time withdrew its financial support from the Schneider race team but a private donation ensured that Britain was still able to compete. On Southampton Water, in front of a crowd of half a million people lining the coast, Britain won the race again and retained the trophy for good. The winning plane shortly afterward set a new world speed record. The trophy is currently on display in the Science Museum in London

This winning plane was the Supermarine S6B designed by R.J. Mitchell who was later to design the Spitfire. It is often said that the S6B was the fore-runner of the Spitfire but this is not strictly true since it was a completely different kind of aeroplane. What *was* true was that taking part in this competition and designing seaplanes to compete in it, particularly the S6B, gave Supermarine and Mitchell the experience and the reputation to enable them to compete for Air Ministry fighter contracts with the famous result. Indeed the Schneider Trophy gave a tremendous boost to aerial research in all the countries that took part.

The S6B was a world away from the aeroplanes of the First World War. It was a monoplane with a racing engine made by Rolls Royce, known as the 'R' model and developing 2,300 horsepower. It will be remembered that the Sopwith Camel at the end of the first war developed 150 horsepower: this shows how far engine development had come. In fact the Rolls Royce R was an exceptional engine built for racing and impractical in other contexts. The Spitfire Mark I that fought the Battle of Britain was powered by a Rolls Royce Merlin engine of fractionally over 1,000 horsepower, but this is still seven times the power deployed by the Sopwith.

One can think of this as the gold standard of aero-engines: 1,000 horsepower in 1940 bought you a premier fighter plane capable of taking on anything in the world. By way of comparison the Messerschmitt Me109, which was the Spitfire's German opposite in the Battle of Britain was powered by an engine of 1,175 horsepower and the contemporary American P-36 Hawk also boasted a little over 1,000 horsepower.

In fact, compared with the frantic pace of development in World War One, aviation advanced comparatively slowly in the inter-war years. Not surprisingly the real emphasis was on the commercial uses of the aeroplane. In the 1920s, aeroplane designs were not yet ready to carry passengers in any numbers nor was the public ready to use flight as a means of transport. One of the main uses for aeroplanes in the 1920s was carrying mail. Government contracts to do this greatly assisted the development of commercial flying, particularly in the United States.

By the 1930s commercial passenger flights were a viable proposition and economic realities dictated that bigger aircraft were better because they carried more people and earned more money. Simple engineering restrictions prevented land-based passenger planes from growing too large. From the very early days of flight, however, it had been apparent that aeroplanes could just as easily take off from and land on water. It soon became clear that it was easier to build a big aircraft if it used the water rather than the land. Such water craft are usually divided into two categories: seaplanes and flying boats. The former have floats instead of wheels but the body of the plane is out of the water while the latter rest their bellies in the water and have small floats under the wings to hold them level when the plane is on the surface. Where size is concerned seaplanes faced many of the same restrictions as land-based planes but flying boats were another matter. Different companies were soon vying with one another to build bigger and bigger planes. In America Curtiss and Sikorsky led the field, in Britain there were Short Brothers and Supermarine and in Germany there was Dornier. (This is the same Sikorsky we encountered designing the Murometz for the Imperial Russian Air Force. He emigrated to The U.S.A. after the revolution.)

A flying boat did not have to bother with an undercarriage, always a weakness with large planes because of the weight it had to carry, particularly at the moment of impact on landing. Most land based aviation was carried out from grass fields but that was not possible with a large aircraft. Beyond a certain weight you had to have a proper concrete or metaled runway and that was very expensive to install. A flying boat dispensed with this requirement too. All it needed was a stretch of clear water and there was an abundance of those. Almost overnight these large aircraft opened up the possibility of long distance, even inter-continental travel.

Great Britain's Imperial Airways flew routes to South Africa and to India with the Short Empire flying boat and Pan American Airways pioneered routes in South America and the Pacific first with the Sikorsky S42 and later with the Boeing 314. These were large aircraft even by today's standards. The Empire had a wingspan of 114 feet and was 88 feet long and had two floors. It is then a surprise, perhaps, to discover that it carried only seventeen passengers. The reason was that those seventeen flew in great luxury with a separate lounge and dining room. Meals were prepared by a chef in a roomy kitchen. There was no mass market in long distance air travel and the clientele of these flying boats were the rich and those flying for business or government reasons.

The crew of these machines were minutely trained in every detail of their business and a man could not become the captain of a passenger flying boat until he had worked his way up through the ranks, often starting as mechanic toiling on their engines. The result was quite exceptional, pilots with a breadth of knowledge unparalleled in the industry. One of these was a young Australian named Donald Bennett who was another in love with flying. He became a master of every facet of the business from piloting to navigation to engineering to radio and anything else that might be involved. In the coming war he was to play a most distinguished, if flawed, part in the R.A.F. and become its youngest ever Air Vice Marshal.

On land the biggest competition to these giants of the business was the Douglas DC3 Dakota. This aircraft was half their size but compared favourably in terms of range. As it turned out the future belonged to the land based transport plane and the DC3 was a leader of its class. In fact it must be rated as one of the greatest aircraft ever designed. Versatile, simple to build and maintain and easy to fly, it was nothing less than a masterpiece. It first flew in 1935 and some hundreds of DC3s were still in service around the world at the dawn of the new millennium.

That flying boats fell out of favour was partly due to their own failings and partly due to the advent of war, to which they were ill-suited. When the war was over, all those expensive paved runways had been built and flying boats had lost one of their crucial advantages. But they always had their drawbacks. They needed dead calm water on which to operate so there were some regions of the world where they were not a realistic alternative: either there was no water or the weather froze it. Moreover they could not fly even in clear weather if there was a wind creating choppy water let alone a heavy swell. In this respect they were even less versatile than land planes. Any obstruction in the water, even a small piece of driftwood, would cause a calamitous accident. In wartime their use was limited. In theory they would make good bombers, but large bombers carry their bombs internally and drop them out through bomb bay doors in the belly. A flying boat puts that belly in the water so bomb bay doors would have had to be waterproof and that was not practical. Moreover bombers tend to collect shrapnel holes in their skin as they go about their business. In a land plane this is not fatal, so long as no vital part of the structure is hit, but with a flying boat, a hole in the wrong place will cause it to sink in double quick time as soon as it lands. Finally, flying boats and seaplanes were slow when aerial warfare increasingly demanded speed.

This does not mean that World War Two had no use for flying boats but they played a far smaller part than their pre-war popularity would have led one to suppose. Reconnaissance, transport and air-sea rescue were their forte. Few took an active part in the fighting. Two honourable exceptions were the Short Sunderland used by R.A.F. Coastal Command as an anti-U-boat weapon and the versatile Consolidated PBY Catalina used by the U.S. Navy for air-sea rescue, for night-time hit-and-run raiding in the Pacific and as a sub-hunter both there and in the Atlantic.

Peace in the years after 1918 and the great number of surplus military aircraft available, meant that interest in and budgets for further development of military aircraft were at a low ebb. In the 1920s there was really only one significant improvement in design. Where military aircraft of World War One had been constructed with canvas stretched over a wooden frame, now there was a switch to a metal frame which was both stronger and lighter. Such new aircraft as there were tended to be unsophisticated, multi-role designs calculated to get the maximum utility from a limited expenditure. One such was the British Vickers Vernon. Intended as a transport plane it could double as a bomber if necessary.

From the early 1930s, the illusion that there would be a lengthy peace began to fall apart and interest in improving the design of military aircraft revived accordingly.

The Spitfire of 1940 was the last word in aero design at the time and it was a world away from the open cockpit planes of 1918. It was a monoplane which was essential for speed. The impedimenta of struts and wires required for a biplane were abandoned at last. Its pilot sat in an enclosed cockpit which not only made his work much easier but also improved streamlining. He was provided with oxygen for high altitude flight and this greatly extended the height at which air war could be carried on. He also had a radio with which he could talk both to a controller on the ground and to other aircraft.

The Spitfire had eight guns instead of two, and in this respect alone, it was perhaps not at the forefront of design. These guns were of .303 calibre which was the same as the standard rifle bullet of that time. It soon became apparent once hostilities commenced that this was not enough to bring down an enemy bomber of any size. The U.S.A. was already using .5 calibre bullets which had much more of a punch and other air forces were looking at the aerial cannon. This fired cannon shells instead of bullets and these were a thin metal shell around a core of explosive. The shell exploded on impact with the enemy plane and caused much more damage than a bullet. This was a large, heavy gun however and its ammunition was bulky.

Most cannon were of the 20 mm variety. The 20 mm shell was 6 1/2 inches, or 17 centimetres, long and an inch, or 30 mm wide at the base of the cartridge. (Cartridges are always substantially wider than the bullet or shell they fire.) It weighed 9 ½ ounces. A full load of ammunition weighed as much as having another person on board. The R.A.F. did try to fit cannons into its Spitfires but the wing was too thin to hold them, unless they were installed lying on their side, and it transpired that this interfered with the smooth flow of the ammunition into the gun on its belt and the cannon repeatedly jammed. It was 1941, and after the Battle of Britain before the Spitfire was redesigned to accommodate cannon.

When firing those guns, the pilot now had available the reflector sight which was a great advance on the old ring and bead of World War One. This was, in effect, a small torch that projected a circle of light with a dot in the middle onto a small glass plate in front of the pilot. Brightness could be adjusted to suit the light conditions and many sights actually had several circles, thus helping the pilot to judge the range of his target, but the big advantage of the sight was that if the pilot's head was not in the right place the circle(s) did not appear on the glass at all. In effect this was a much simpler and easier way to achieve the lining up required by the ring and bead.

The retractable undercarriage fitted to the Spitfire was one of the greatest improvements in aircraft design of the inter-war years. A fixed undercarriage was a great handicap for any aircraft because of the drag which it generated. On the other hand, making it retract was a considerable engineering challenge and necessarily added weight to the plane. A few aircraft that did not need speed to do their jobs achieved a measure of fame despite having fixed wheels. The German 'Stuka' was one such and the British Fairey Swordfish another. That is not to say they would not have been better planes had their undercarriages retracted. With the quest for higher speeds came an awareness of the importance of streamlining in all aircraft design.

For retraction of the undercarriage to work, you have to have flexible joints which can straighten out and be strong enough to take the weight of the aircraft and particularly the shock of landing. You also have to have some kind of winding gear to haul the wheels up and down. For a short while this was done by hand. The pilot had a handle in his cockpit which he pumped up and down until the wheels were up, or down, as the case may be. Some of the earliest Spitfires worked this way, as did the Russian Polikarpov I-16 which was used in thousands by the Soviet Air Force. The disadvantages of this system need hardly be specified. Hydraulic power soon became the standard method of retracting and extending landing gear.

The other big difficulty was where to put the landing gear. This was not a new problem but higher speeds and heavier planes were making it more acute. The main weight of a plane lies in the fuselage, so you want to have the landing gear directly underneath it in order to bear the weight directly. This has the advantage that all the machinery for winding the gear up and down can be in the fuselage too. When retracted, the wheels and their undercarriage legs fold outward and upward into the underside of the wing. The big drawback with this system is that the wheels are set very close together under the plane which makes it unstable laterally and hard to land safely. Both the Spitfire and its German opposite, the Me109 used this system. The 109 was hard to land for other reasons as well, with the result that 5 to 10% of all the 109s built were destroyed in landing accidents.[i] The alternative was to put the wheels under the wings and fold them inward into the fuselage. This was a much more stable arrangement and became the favoured design for fighter planes, despite the disadvantages of making the wings carry the whole weight of the plane and putting the winding gear for the undercarriage in the wings where there was precious little space. The Spitfire and the 109 had been built with wings too thin to bear the weight. It was thought, wrongly as it turned out, that a thin wing was essential to give a plane speed.

Just as the Spitfire and Hurricane were entering service there came another advance: the variable pitch propeller. This enables the pilot to alter the angle at which the propeller blades strike the air. The effect of this is much like the effect of the gears in a car. Its use greatly increases the efficiency of the engine as a machine for driving the plane forward.

Now the whole aircraft was fabricated using a new technique: monocoque design, often called 'stressed skin' construction. The idea here was that the skin of the aircraft consisted of thin metal plates, made of aluminium or one of its alloys which were riveted to the skeleton and became part of the structural strength of the machine in a way that canvas obviously could not. Most of these innovations appeared, at least in the R.A.F., at the very last minute.

As late as World War Two itself there were still elegant Hawker biplanes in service, with open cockpits and fixed undercarriages. Even the Hurricane, the Spitfire's stable-mate was still built with the old style canvas skin over most of the aircraft. Many of the improvements that went into the design of the Spitfire and other advanced fighter planes of the late 1930s were the direct result of lessons learned from the Schneider Trophy races.

This discussion of technical advances has concentrated on the Spitfire, but that is only because it is a plane familiar to most readers. All of the major powers had incorporated at least some of these advances into their latest fighter aircraft. The Germans had the Messerschmitt Me109 which had all the same refinements. This and other early Messerschmitt aircraft are often referred to with the prefix letters Bf, e.g. Bf109, which stands for Bayerische Fluzeugwerke. The company that built them and was taken over by Messerschmitt in 1938. He had designed them however, and the company was 'Messerschmitt' throughout the Second World War, and so it seems unnecessary and confusing, if pedantically accurate, to use the 'Bf' prefix. The Americans had the Curtiss P-40, the French, the Morane Saulnier and the Russians, the Yak. These planes even looked similar.

This may be the moment for a word of caution about the names and numbers applied to military aircraft of the World War Two era. One must be aware that those names and numbers follow almost no logic. You might think that the Focke Wulf FW190 was a development of the FW189, but in fact they were aircraft of quite different types, having almost nothing in common at all except being made by the same company. The FW190A and the FW190D were different models of the same aircraft but they were, in fact, so different that in a world with any logic, the 190D would have another number.

On the other hand the Hawker Typhoon and the Hawker Tempest have different names, yet the one was a development of the other and they were so similar that they were hard for the layman to tell apart. The Tempest was originally to be called the Typhoon Mark II. Any idea that companies tended to specialize in particular types of aircraft is dangerous too. Supermarine who made the Spitfire, also made lumbering flying boats. Boeing, famous for its heavy bombers, made a fighter in the 1930s and so on.

Naturally there was a parallel development in the field of bomber aircraft. All the advances mentioned above were adopted for bombers and the U.S. produced the ground-breaking Martin B-10 in 1932 which, in addition, was the first bomber to have a power operated gun turret and an internal bomb bay. It was also the first bomber to have a speed in excess of 200 mph which made it faster than most fighter planes of the time. The U.S. government was so impressed by its success as a design, that it promptly invited three aircraft manufacturers to design an even larger successor plane. This led to the development of the Boeing B-17 which was to become the U.S. Army Air Force's first four-engine strategic bomber and was to earn fame in World War Two as the 'Flying Fortress'.

Once again the advances were applied world-wide and though the R.A.F. had no four-engine bombers at the start of the war, it had plenty of planes with two engines and they were just as technologically advanced as the American machines. France had no true strategic bombers, but it had at least one modern type of medium bomber. Japan, Germany and Russia were equally advanced but their situation was rather different in each case and we shall consider them in more detail in the next chapter.

CHAPTER THREE

Approaching Conflict:
Japan, Russia and Italy

In 1921, a retired Italian general named Giulio Douhet, wrote a book about the use of air power called, 'The Command of the Air'. Douhet was a fervent advocate of air power to the extent that he underwent court-martial in the First War because of immoderate criticism of his superiors, for their failure to use aircraft to his satisfaction. Douhet's book had immense influence in aviation circles around the world.

He argued that strategic bombing was all that mattered and the rest was a waste of time. Strategic bombing, he said, could not be stopped because of the width of the skies and the speed of the attack. Large numbers of fast bombers would be irresistible. The only defence was to be the first to launch the attack for then you could destroy the enemy's air force on the ground. Strategic bombing, he emphasized, must concentrate on industry, transport, communications, government and the will of the people. The last was particularly important because heavy bombing would cause a collapse of the enemy citizens' will to fight, whereupon there would be a revolt and the people would force their government to make peace. This would all occur long before conventional armies could decide the issue and so armies would become superfluous and strategic bombing would in fact, save lives in the long run. If armies were irrelevant then so were ground attack planes, not to mention fighters, though Douhet was eventually to concede grudgingly that an escort fighter might be a worthwhile investment.

Meanwhile he did not believe in doing things by halves. Bombing should start with high explosive bombs to smash buildings and follow with incendiaries to set fire to the exposed combustible wreckage. Finally poison gas should be dropped to prevent fire-fighting efforts. An air force, he wrote, should be an independent military organization and not simply an adjunct to the army and navy.

There was a certain amount of evidence at the time to suggest that Douhet was broadly right. Bombing on a fairly small scale had caused unrest in England in the First World War and in 1918 there were signs that it was very hard to stop large bombers from reaching their target. Moreover, his argument was just what the senior officers in air ministries in all the major powers wanted to hear because it gave them a compelling reason to demand a large and expensive air force. The first country to have the chance to try out his theories in real conflict was Japan.

Japan took a minimal part in World War One and so did not suffer the death of a generation of its young men. It therefore approached the following decades with a quite different viewpoint from the Allied powers of Western Europe. In particular, and from the very start, it always viewed aeroplanes from the point of view of their military significance.

Ever since Japan opened its doors to the West in the mid-nineteenth century, it had watched the development of western technology with a discriminating eye and it did not take the Japanese long to exploit the military potential of the aeroplane. The first aircraft factory, Nakajima Hikoki was established in 1916. At first this factory built European aircraft under licence and with the end of World War One, Japan imported large numbers of the cheap European warplanes then on the market. Mitsubishi Industries began aircraft production about this time producing Sopwith aeroplane types under a licence from that company.

By the end of the 1920s Japan was beginning to produce her own aircraft. In 1929 the Nakajima Type 90 first flew. This was a biplane fighter designed for use on aircraft carriers and built for the Japanese Navy. Japan, along with most of the world's larger states, effectively had two air forces: army and navy. In Japan the two services were empires within an empire. They competed for resources and influence and had their own ministers in the cabinet. Quite unlike western powers Japan was, in part, run by its armed services.

Japanese policy was expansionist and accordingly there was plenty of scope for the development and use of military aircraft. In 1931 Japan occupied Manchuria. Ever since the Russo-Japanese War at the start of the century, Japan had enjoyed the right to run the only railway in Manchuria. In 1931 she used the excuse of alleged sabotage of the railway by local nationalists to occupy the whole country. In 1937 she began the invasion of China. She had enjoyed a similar right to guard the railway to Beijing and, in 1937, Chinese troops supposedly fired on the guards in what became known as the 'Marco Polo Bridge incident.' This became the excuse for a full-scale invasion of China. This latter military exercise was to become a long-lasting campaign that only ended with the conclusion of World War Two in 1945. To pursue this war the Japanese Army wanted an air force geared to ground support that would back up the soldiers on the ground at all times. They were only marginally interested in strategic bombing: China was too large and had too little industry to make strategic bombing very rewarding. In addition the cost of large bomber planes was something the Japanese Army did not wish to burden itself with. The fact that Douhet thought ground support planes were unnecessary cut no ice with them.

Ground attack in support of your army had been shown in World War One to be one of the most effective uses of air power and they were not going to abandon it on the off-chance that Douhet's theories about strategic bombing would be proved right. Such strategic bombing as there was, was left to the Navy. All the Japanese military, both Army and Navy, were always very conscious of their country's limited resources and such an expenditure was never likely to be undertaken unless it could be seen that it would bring a clear benefit.

The Japanese Navy had different factors to take into account. The most important was the sheer size of the theatre in which their operations would have to take place. This led them always to think in terms of aircraft with a long range and it led them to think in terms of aircraft carriers. Long range bombers are usually big aircraft and that was why they assumed the strategic role in China, such as it was.

In 1920 the Japanese Navy laid down a battleship and a battle-cruiser, but plans for them were changed halfway through construction as the navy realized that battleships and battle-cruisers were becoming obsolete and they were completed as aircraft carriers. They were the Kaga and the Akagi respectively and they were mighty ships of 27,000 tons each and carrying 90 aircraft apiece. They were two of the carriers that were to conduct the attack on Pearl Harbour. The Japanese were very quick to appreciate the value of the aircraft carrier for an island race with expansionist ambitions on the rim of a vast ocean.

Both army and navy were now equipped with Japanese-made aircraft. The army principally relied for fighters on the Nakajima Type 97 Ki-27b. This was a small, light monoplane with a fixed undercarriage and an open cockpit. Its armament was just a pair of machine-guns. Its range was a thousand miles however. (By comparison, the Spitfire could barely manage 400.) Plainly this was an aircraft that was halfway between the designs of the two world wars. It was slow and it was under-armed but it was remarkably agile and was to remain in service well into the Second World War.

It will be noticed that its name was more than usually cumbersome, as was the case with all Japanese aircraft. The Americans came up with a solution to this problem, which was to give all Japanese aircraft a simple human name, boys for fighters and girls for bombers. It is proposed to follow this useful expedient except for the first mention of an aircraft type when it will be given its formal designation, or at least, enough of it to allow proper identification of the plane. The Nakajima Type 97 was called 'Nate'.

The navy's fighter was the Mitsubishi Type 96 A5M4 'Claude'. Despite the antagonism of the two Japanese services the design of the Claude was almost identical to that of the Nate save that it had an even greater range of 1,200 miles.

Bombers were the army's Ki-21 'Sally' and the navy's G3M 'Nell'. Both were twin-engine aircraft of comparatively light construction and the familiar long range. The Navy also had carrier-borne attack planes but we will deal with them in more detail later.

Both Imperial air forces were efficient, disciplined bodies with high standards of operation and training. The navy, in particular, demanded almost impossibly high standards of its pilots and these men were to be at the forefront of the great expansion across the Pacific in 1941 and 1942. Their skill was no small part of Japanese success in this endeavour.

The war in China was a constant stream of Japanese successes. The army's aircraft proved invaluable in supporting its operations and the navy's aircraft pounded cities. This did not lead to a collapse of morale and Chinese pleas for peace, but the Japanese never really thought it would. Bombing cities usually had more immediate tactical aims such as hindering transport and communications and any effect on civilian morale was a useful, if unquantifiable, bonus. Such bombing did, however, cause international concern and the Japanese were strongly criticized for their conduct.

China's air force was a ramshackle affair. An American training mission had visited China in 1932, but left two years later and was replaced by the Italians. Chinese aircraft were a whole kaleidoscope of types from all over the world: there was no indigenous aircraft industry. It would be fair to say however, that the backbone of Chinese airpower was the Curtiss Hawk III, a biplane fighter originally designed for the U.S. Navy.

When Japan invaded, the Chinese air force could probably have mustered not more than 150 airworthy front line aircraft. There was also a squadron of foreign volunteer pilots and as from the end of 1937, there were two bomber and four fighter squadrons provided by Russia. In 1936 a chance meeting led to an American officer, Captain Claire Chennault being offered the post of advisor to the Chinese government on aviation affairs. He devoted himself to getting the best out of China's limited air assets and, sometime later, was instrumental in establishing the American Volunteer Group, popularly known as the 'Flying Tigers', which was a force of U.S. pilots and aircraft flying as mercenaries for China with unofficial U.S. government backing.

Chinese pilots did not lack bravery but their standard of training was low and the multiplicity of different aircraft types made maintenance a nightmare. They defended Shanghai heroically but unsuccessfully, and they sometimes inflicted serious losses on unescorted bomber formations, forcing the Japanese to use fighter escorts and thus, interestingly, casting doubt on Douhet's theory that the only way to defeat bombers was by your own bombing and vindicating his critics' claims that an escort would be necessary. The threat could not be maintained however, because of maintenance problems and the gradual attrition of experienced pilots. The best consistent results were achieved by the Russians, until their withdrawal in 1939 after the Molotov-Ribbentrop pact made Germany and Russia allies. Germany was allied to Japan too and lobbied for the Russians in China to be sent home.

Shortly thereafter occurred a curious, brief, undeclared war between Japan and Russia that was to have far-reaching implications for the conduct of the whole war in the Pacific. This episode was known as the 'Nomonhan Incident' (sometimes also called the 'Khalkin-Ghol' incident). This was a border dispute over a mere ten mile strip of land between Manchuria, which was by now a Japanese puppet state and

Mongolia, which was a Russian one. In a series of battles between May and September of 1939, the Japanese were at first successful and then soundly defeated. The Army Air Force performed well. For part of the time it was deliberately withheld from action on orders from Tokyo as a reaction to its use by local commanders without authority and its absence noticeably affected operations. The incident strengthened the Army's faith in its air arm but, much more importantly for the big picture it persuaded Japan not to pick a fight with Russia by trying to expand at Russia's expense. This had been the Army's long-term plan. Instead it was resolved to follow the Navy's preference for expansion southward into Southeast Asia and the Pacific.

Russia had suffered in World War One though her casualties compared to her population were nowhere near as grievous as those of, say, France. On top of that, she had undergone a revolution and was a new state with no ties to the past. Her government was determined that she should be heavily armed as fast as an expanding industrial base could handle. The purpose of this was to defend the 'Revolution' and, as the next step, to spread it to the other nations of Europe, by force if necessary.

In 1935 the Russian Air Force had the largest force of bombers of any air force in the world. Its leader, Yakov Alksnis, was inspirational and the Air Force was principally his creation. Unfortunately he was a victim of the purges, being shot in 1938. Most of the best aircraft designers also fell foul of the purges. Tupolev, Petlyakov and Polykarpov were all arrested and charged with political crimes of a fantastical nature. But they all managed to continue their work. Stalin's Russia had an extraordinary scheme whereby scientists were put in special prisons equipped for research where they carried on their normal work in conditions much above the usual prison level. No doubt such strange goings on did nothing to improve the quality of the Air Force and they certainly caused the casual observer to give thanks that their experience of 1930s Russia is confined to reading about it.

Russian industry began to produce modern aircraft at the end of the 1920s, at the time of the first Five Year Plan.[i] The TB-1 was an all-metal monoplane, medium bomber produced at a time when most other countries were still building fabric covered biplanes to fill this role. The TB-3 was a heavy bomber and a quite remarkable aircraft. It was the first four-engine bomber to go into mass production anywhere and it was well ahead of its time. It was constructed of corrugated metal (corrugation gives metal sheeting additional strength), had a crew of six and wings so thick that there were crawl-ways inside to allow the crew access to the engines during flight. Its undercarriage was fixed and the exceptionally large wheels embodied long spokes so that the whole assembly resembled a bicycle wheel. This machine drew a great deal of international attention at the time and stunts were performed involving paratroops sitting in large numbers on the wings and fuselage while it was in the air. It first flew in 1930 and some 500 were still in service in 1941 at the time of the German attack. It was used as a night bomber for the first year of the war and then as a transport for the remainder. Prior to that, it had taken part in the Finnish Winter War in 1939.

Other Russian bombers of this period were not so distinguished. The main medium bomber was the SB-2. This entered service in 1935 and was fast for its time, but its speed was bought at the cost of robust construction. Russia used it in China and in the Nomonhan Incident as well as in Finland and Spain. It was the staple bomber of the late 1930s but as the Second War grew near it was showing its age. There was also the DB-3 that was designed to be a heavy, long range bomber but was only a medium bomber by World War Two standards and not of exceptional range either. It was, nonetheless, a fine aircraft that gave reliable service throughout the Russo-German War.

Another outstanding aircraft of this vintage was the Polikarpov Po-2. This was a simple two-seater biplane that was about as rudimentary as planes come. However its simplicity and its hardiness made it ideal for all kinds of work in the harsh backwoods of 1930s Russia. It went on to find work in World War Two as a trainer and night nuisance bomber, in which role it was often flown by women. After the war, production continued, mainly in Warsaw Pact countries, until the 1960s. Altogether some 40,000 of them were built, making it the second most popular aircraft of all time. (The most popular is the Cessna 172 an American small private plane first built in 1955 and still in production. Over 43,000 have been built so far.)

In 1936 occurred the first flight of the Petlyakov Pe-8. This was a four-engine bomber that carried on the tradition of Russian heavy bombers embodied in the Murometz and the TB-3. It was similar in appearance to the American Flying Fortress and carried a slightly larger bomb load but less far. The prototype had the strange set-up of a fifth engine inside the fuselage to drive the superchargers for the other four engines. This cumbersome arrangement was dropped for the production versions which used superchargers driven by the main engines themselves in the conventional arrangement.

Oddly, only a small number of these planes were built. Estimates vary but it was probably about one hundred. The reason usually given for this is that there were continuing troubles with powering the machine, various engines being tried and rejected. This is hard to accept however. What Pe-8s there were, seem to have given satisfactory service including a raid on Berlin. A Pe-8 was trusted to carry Molotov, the foreign minister of the U.S.S.R. to London and Washington for conferences. It is hard to believe that Soviet industrial ingenuity could not overcome the power plant problem: there were plenty of well-designed Russian engines available and though Russian manufacturing quality was indifferent they managed to power all their other planes. It is surely more likely that this was a policy decision based on the desire to use air power as a tactical tool in support of the army. After all, the Red Army's plans for a European war with Poland and/or Germany were wholly offensive. If those plans worked well Russian motorized units would be in Berlin within a week and that was far too soon for any strategic bombing campaign to have yielded results. After the partition of Poland in the autumn of 1939, Soviet territory extended to Brest Litovsk only some 350 miles of easy marching from Berlin. Pe-8s entered service in 1940 so the timescale fits this reasoning.

Russian fighters in the late 1930s were principally the I-15 and its derivative the I-153 followed by the I-16. The first of these was a fixed undercarriage biplane of traditional and uninspired design. The I-153 was an improvement of this design with a retractable undercarriage and an upper wing that joined onto the top of the fuselage rather than stretching over it. This gave the wing greater strength and improved the pilot's view. The I-16 was one of the best fighters of the late 1930s. It was a monoplane of the very latest kind and an interesting design that kept the fuselage to the minimum behind a large radial engine. The result was a small plane with a front-heavy appearance. The appearance was indeed reminiscent of a U.S. racing plane called the Gee Bee Racer of a few years earlier, though Russian sources have always denied any direct design connection.[ii]

The I-16 was unstable and delicate to fly, had a short range and an undercarriage the pilot had to pump up and down by hand but it was well armed and extraordinarily agile and was one of the world's best at the time. It was used in the Nomonhan incident where it acquitted itself well and in the Finnish Winter War where things did not go quite so well. It was also the principle fighter of the Republican Air Force in the Spanish Civil War

Clearly, ideas in aircraft design are international. Shortly after the time we are considering the Russians produced one of their most successful planes: the Petlyakov Pe-2. This was designed to be a twin-engine long range fighter and reconnaissance aircraft but it was increasingly used as a light bomber with great success. Its design featured a long cockpit with pilot in front and gunner behind, facing to the rear, together with a double tail unit, that is two rudders, one at each end of the horizontal tail-plane. It had in-line, liquid cooled engines. The design was almost identical to the German Me110 and the French Potez 631 and all three were more or less the same size. In France in 1940, a number of Potez 631s were accidentally shot down by their own side because they were almost indistinguishable from the Me110. All these planes were being designed at much the same time and cannot be identical by chance. Someone, somewhere, had the original idea and two other designers in different countries copied it with only slight variations. Indeed the Russian designer Tupolev was imprisoned for allegedly selling to Germany blueprints for an aircraft that was to become the Me110. Since this occurred at the height of the purges little faith can be placed in the justice of the charge however.

In 1939 Russia's part in the main European conflict was confined to the occupation of half of Poland which was just as well since her air force was stocked with planes coming to the end of their useful life. This point was made by the Winter

War against Finland at the end of the year. By the time that the Germans invaded in 1941 there would be a raft of new designs that would transform the 'V.V.S.' as the Soviet Air Force was known. The initials stand for Voenno-Vozdushnye Sily or 'Military Air Forces'.

Russia became involved in the Spanish Civil War but only to the extent that she provided armaments to the Republican side. These armaments included some 800 aircraft. Indeed they were the only aircraft available to the Republicans. They were flown partly by Spaniards and partly by Russians who were in Spain as 'advisers'. The number of Russian pilots was not large and so their performance is of limited value in assessing the history of the Soviet Air Force. The I-16 did particularly well in Spain but this was really its finest hour and from then on its performance declined as its opponents improved.

The Molotov-Ribbentrop Pact of 1939, whereby Germany and Russia became allies, gave Russia a free hand to pursue her territorial ambitions in eastern Europe and one of the victims was Finland. Finland had only existed for twenty years having been a part of the empire of Tsarist Russia. She achieved independence in 1918 and had prospered since then but Stalin decided to lay claim to certain parts of the country and when negotiation failed he declared war.

The Soviet Air Force supported the attack with 2,500 aircraft including large numbers of the SB-2 bombers which proved disappointingly ineffective. Their bomb load was too small and in the wilds of Finland there were not enough concentrated targets. Railways were the principal transport targets but it soon became apparent that cutting a rail track was next to useless because it was so easily and quickly repaired. This was a lesson all the powers took to heart and bombing thereafter usually left railway lines, as such, strictly alone. That is not to say that railway *systems* were ignored: far from it, but bombing concentrated on vulnerable, hard-to-repair targets such as bridges and marshaling yards where rolling stock was kept and put together into trains. The Red Air Force bombed cities but not in any systematic way except in the case of the city of Vyborg close to the front which was devastated by repeated attacks. The years just prior to the Second World War and the early years of the war show repeated examples of strategic bombing attacks on cities where it is hard to discern what exactly the aggressor thought he was achieving. Guernica, Rotterdam and Warsaw are other examples. There seems to have been a kind of generalized feeling, born of the Douhet doctrine, that such bombing would both cause direct damage to the war effort by destroying communications and hindering transport and also undermine that effort by terrorizing the local population. The transport and communication argument is valid but it is hard to resist the impression that the main inspiration for these attacks was simply the fact that there were now aircraft that made them possible and that was enough. You bombed because you could.

Finland had a tiny air force. At the start of the conflict in November 1939, its front line strength was just over 100 aircraft including reconnaissance and army co-operation aircraft.[iii] The main fighter in use was the Dutch-built Fokker D-21, a semi-modern design but with a fixed undercarriage. The big Finnish advantage lay in the fact that they were one of the few nations to have studied fighter tactics with some care between the wars, with the result that they had discovered the advantages of the so-called 'finger four' formation. They had also discovered that fighter combat tended to break down into one-against-one contests which were almost always won by the best pilot even if he was in a slightly inferior plane. They therefore concentrated on making sure that their fighter pilots were as well trained as possible. They also were careful to make sure their air force was independent of the other armed services and it was officially founded on March 6th 1918, making it the world's first independent air force, three weeks ahead of the R.A.F.[iv] This policy paid dividends because although they were always outnumbered, often by ten to one, Finnish fighter pilots consistently shot down large numbers of Soviet planes at a rate of three and a half enemy kills for every loss of their own. On top of that the Russians lost 300 planes to efficient Finnish anti-aircraft fire and another four hundred to wastage, that is, aircraft lost due to the weather, poor maintenance, accidents etc.

There was considerable sympathy for Finland in the international community with the result that she was given some replacement aircraft by several countries and bought others. The result was that she had more fighter planes at the end of the conflict than she had had at the beginning.[v]

In the end the large numbers told, however, and in March 1940 Finland had to accept a peace that ceded crucial parts of her territory to Russia. Her numerical inferiority in the air had meant that although she had defended well, she had never been able to mount a serious bombing campaign herself.

Despite its losses in the campaign in Finland the Soviet Air Force remained, by some way, the largest in the world.

Italy was in the forefront of aeronautical thinking in the 1920s and in the forefront of aeronautical design, but she began to lose her lead as the Second World War approached. Her air force, named the Regia Aeronautica, was created as a separate command in 1928 with a developed aviation industry behind it, not least the industrial giant Fiat. The problem was that Italian industry had not developed sufficiently powerful aero-engines. It was determined that radial engines were best for the air force because they were rugged and easy to maintain but the three main engines, produced by Fiat, Alfa Romeo and Piaggio were less powerful than contemporary engines in use in other air forces and so Italian planes were at a disadvantage. For example the Fiat G50, which was the premier Italian fighter in 1939, a monoplane with all-metal construction and retracting undercarriage only had an 840 horsepower engine and it will be recalled that the Spitfire had an engine of 1,000 and the Me109 an engine of 1,100 horsepower and more. The need to save weight because of low power, coupled with the innate conservatism of the Italian military establishment of that time, not least the pilots, meant that Italian fighters were under-armed with merely two machine guns. Moreover the biplane configuration and the open cockpit were retained long past their useful life. The other standard fighter, the Fiat CR42 was a biplane that would have been at home on the Western Front in 1918.

The Italian bomber arm was distinctive for the use of tri-motor types shunned by other nations. This design had certain advantages: principally the added survivability granted by three engines rather than two, particularly in an air force that was going to be doing a lot of flying over water. It was also a useful configuration where each of those engines was not individually very powerful. The penalties to be paid were that the design made bomb-aiming difficult because this was usually done from a position in the nose of the plane, but you had an engine there instead. You also could not have guns in the nose and so you were vulnerable to frontal attacks by fighters. With their slightly hunched backs and flowing lines these bombers had an animal look that at least made them aesthetically pleasing.

There was the Savoia Marchetti SM79 Sparviero and the Cantieri Z 1007 Alcioni. The names respectively mean 'Sparrow Hawk' and 'Kingfisher'. The first was the pillar of the Regia Aeronautica and some 1,300 were built. It was also bought by air forces in the Balkan countries. Unfortunately both planes had only a modest range of a little over a thousand miles and the SM79 an even more modest bomb load.

In 1935 Italy fought and conquered Abyssinia (modern Ethiopia) and the air force played its part but Abyssinia had no air force and no anti-aircraft defences and the exercise proved nothing and amounted to little more than a training opportunity for the pilots.

Italy sent 600 aircraft to Spain to take part in the Spanish Civil War on the Nationalist side and in the ultimate test of front line service their weaknesses betrayed them. Italian Fiat fighters were outfought by Russian Polikarpovs and Savoia Marchettis suffered grievously from the attentions of those same Russian fighters. Italian planes were simply too lightly constructed and, as already noted, they were underpowered. It was however, too late for many changes to be made before the Second World War: Italy's limited industrial base was simply under too much pressure. Efforts were put in hand to provide a superior fighter plane but even that retained many of the old faults such as inadequate armament.

No discussion of the Regia Aeronautica in this period would be complete without mention of Marshal Italo Balbo. Born in 1896 near Ferrara, he fought in the First World War during which he applied for pilot training, but the war ended before this could begin. After the war he entered politics as an enthusiastic Fascist and follower of Mussolini. In 1926 he was appointed Secretary of State for Air despite his lack of any experience in aviation matters and was surprisingly competent in the job. His energy and charisma were exactly what the young Italian air force needed. He was not just an administrator but thought deeply about aerial tactics and became convinced that the key to success in the air was to employ aircraft in large formations. In 1933 he led a flight of twenty-four flying boats that flew from Italy to Chicago and back. This caused a sensation in the United States and during his stay there he was invited to a meeting with President Roosevelt and was made an honorary chief of the Sioux tribe. Across the world the word 'Balbo' became the name for a large formation of aircraft.

At the end of 1933 Balbo was made governor of Libya. Partly this was done so that he could become the flag-carrier for Italian imperialist ambitions in North Africa and partly so that he was sent away from Rome where Mussolini was beginning to see him as a political threat. In 1939 he publicly criticized Italy's alliance with Germany saying that it was Great Britain that they should be allied to, as in the First War. Shortly after Italy entered the Second War in 1940, Balbo's plane was accidentally shot down by anti-aircraft gunners at Tobruk where he was about to land, and he was killed. There were persistent rumours that he had been assassinated by Mussolini but it seems unlikely. Tobruk had just suffered a British air raid and the gunners were nervous and trigger-happy. The coming war was to provide many examples of friendly-fire accidents. Whatever its cause Balbo's death was a great blow to the Italian Air Force and to Italy.

On the eve of the war Italy possessed an air force of some 2,000 front line aircraft with the deficiencies already discussed. The Regia Aeronautica was still a force to be reckoned with however, and the quality of its pilots was high.

CHAPTER FOUR

Approaching Conflict: The Western Powers

Under the Treaty of Versailles in 1918 Germany was not allowed to have an air force at all. Not surprisingly she began almost immediately to seek ways of circumventing this proscription. She was allowed civil aviation so a program began of training men to be civilian pilots who were really training for the military. Aircraft were designed for use as civilian airliners that could be easily converted to military use. Most of the German bombers in the early years of the Second World War started their career in this guise. Flying clubs of all kinds abounded.

In 1922 Germany and Russia signed the Treaty of Rapallo by which they renounced territorial claims on one another and promised co-operation. This might seem an odd alliance but both countries were effectively outcasts from the international community and this unhappy status threw them together with a good deal to gain by co-operation. A secret addendum to the treaty called for Russia to provide training facilities for German military pilots in Russia. A training airfield was set up at Lipetsk which lasted until Hitler came to power in 1933, when it was closed down because of his anti-Soviet inclinations, and the fact that the military restrictions imposed by the Treaty of Versailles were by then moribund and he intended to train pilots openly in Germany. The government of Germany had announced in 1932 that it no longer intended to be bound by these military restrictions and Hitler was actively and openly re-arming by 1935. In that year the Luftwaffe was formally established as a force independent of the army or navy and its commander was Hermann Goering.

Goering was such a vibrant character and led such an extraordinary life that if he were invented in a novel no one would believe he could really exist. He was born in 1893, his father being a colonial administrator who had been governor of German Southwest Africa (Namibia). He grew up in a castle in Bavaria owned by his godfather who was of Jewish background and who was having an affair with his mother. He became a cadet and joined the German army. During the First World War he applied to join the Air Force and was turned down but he began flying as observer for a friend anyway. Eventually he rose to become one of Germany's leading aces and the last commander of the Richthofen Circus, that is, the wing that von Richthofen had commanded.

After the War, Goering was one of the many disaffected ex-servicemen who existed in many of the combatant countries, but were a most serious problem in

Germany. (Hitler himself was another such). He supported himself as a civil pilot and while carrying out one such job he met a Swedish baroness with whom he fell in love. Unfortunately she was married to someone else, albeit unhappily. Before long she divorced her husband and married Goering and this transformed his fortunes because she was a rich woman. He became a student in Munich and there met Hitler. He succumbed to Hitler's magnetism and for Hitler, Goering, as a national war hero, was a very useful and high profile ally. Goering was at Hitler's side and was seriously wounded in the Munich Beer Hall Putsch, the latter's abortive attempt in 1923 to topple the German government by a coup. He was smuggled out of Germany where he was now a wanted man and taken to Austria for treatment and then on to Italy. From there he eventually made his way to Sweden but by now he was addicted to morphine which he had taken to combat the pain of his wound. There followed a period in a clinic in Sweden while he was cured, at least temporarily, of his addiction.

Goering returned to Germany in 1927 when President Hindenburg declared an amnesty for those involved in the 1923 Putsch. All this preceded the events that were to make him famous as a politician. By this time he had become portly and since he was an egoist fond of making an exhibition of himself in fancy uniforms, he could very easily be a figure of fun for his enemies.

Goering proved to be a very adroit politician and with his close association with the Fuehrer, he was bound to do well as the party prospered. When the Nazis became the government of Germany it was inevitable that he would be the head of the new Luftwaffe. Despite this titular command he was not the main person behind that institution's growth in the 1930s. He was never a man for the administrative hard grind: he liked to make grand policy decisions and leave others to see them put into effect. To be fair to him, he was also the Prussian interior minister and head of the Four Year Plan by which Germany was to be re-armed. On top of that he was Hitler's chosen successor and was at the very centre of high politics in Berlin so that his time was fully taken up.

The real creator of the Luftwaffe was Erhard Milch. Curiously, Milch too had more than a slight Jewish connection in that his father was Jewish. When this was brought to Goering's attention he chose to ignore it with the memorable remark: 'I decide who is a Jew.'[i]

Milch came to the Luftwaffe from civil aviation , having been the chief executive of Lufthansa, the German airline. He was made State Secretary at the Air Ministry in 1933 and at once began to build up Germany's air arm. The technical side of the work became the province of Ernst Udet who had been sucked into Nazi politics through his friend Goering. What needs to be stressed about the growth of the Luftwaffe is the short time frame in which it was achieved. The Nazis only came to power in 1933 and yet a short six years later, they had probably the best air force in the world and the second largest. Their plan, of course, was not to go to war in 1939 but several years later by which time they might have developed a long range strategic bomber, the lack of which was to hamstring the Luftwaffe's efforts in World War Two on more than one occasion.

Udet became fascinated with the technique of dive bombing which he had seen in America. He commissioned the development of a dive bomber for the Luftwaffe and the result was the Junkers Ju87 known as the 'Stuka.' The word 'stuka' is an abbreviation for 'sturzkampfbomber' which means dive-bomber in German. It did not originally refer to the Ju87 specifically but since the Ju87 was the Luftwaffe's only really effective dive-bomber and earned itself such a world-wide reputation it was not long before it became synonymous with the term 'stuka'. This commitment to dive bombing was a bold and radical step since it was a new and largely unproven technique.

The Ju87 was a truly iconic plane whose silhouette is recognized to this day. It was a single-engine plane with a crew of two: a pilot and an observer/gunner who sat behind the pilot and manned a rear-firing gun. Its wings were of inverted gull shape which means that they started angled down and then turned up at a joint halfway along their length. This gave the plane a 'W' profile in fore-and-aft view. The fixed undercarriage was covered by distinctive large spats. It had a 1,200 horsepower Junkers Jumo engine which gave it a very modest cruising speed of just over one hundred miles per hour. It was 50 percent heavier than a Spitfire but its engine was only 20 percent more powerful: and we are talking about the weight before it carried its 1,100 lb bomb load. It was fairly large for a single-engine plane and accordingly its manoeuverability was limited but it was easy to fly and was liked by its pilots. Given that it would have to operate from many primitive airfields in the Mediterranean and Russia, its simple and tough undercarriage was an advantage.

The attack technique with the Stuka was to approach the target until it was obscured by the nose of the aeroplane. The pilot then held to the same course and the target would, in due course, appear in a glass panel set in the floor of the cockpit between his feet. When he saw it there the pilot would cut his throttle to minimum, apply the dive-brakes, roll the aircraft over and dive straight down vertically. The dive brakes were structures somewhat like Venetian blinds that were extended under each wing and slowed the speed of the dive enough to make the aircraft manageable, as it descended vertically so that the target could be kept in the crosshairs. The dive-brakes also automatically activated the siren which was driven by a small propeller on the wing and made the familiar whining sound as the aircraft dived. The siren had no practical purpose and was simply designed to cause fear which, apparently, it did quite efficiently. At about 2,000 feet the bomb was released and the pilot pulled out of his dive and raced away at low level. Since this was a slow aeroplane 'racing away' was done in stately fashion and a Stuka could easily be caught by almost any contemporary fighter. Despite its vulnerability, the Ju87 Stuka was a most successful design because it could drop bombs with unparalleled accuracy.

The Luftwaffe developed two medium bombers, the Dornier Do17 and the Heinkel He111. Both were of civil airliner origin which accounted for some oddities of design such as the fact that bombs were loaded into the Heinkel vertically with the nose upward, a unique arrangement. By the time World War Two began the Do17 was showing its age. When first adopted by the Luftwaffe in 1935 it was faster than most contemporary fighters, but by the time of the Battle of Britain five years later the position was reversed. The He111 was not an especially outstanding design but it was a large and rugged aircraft that could carry a big bomb load. It was also suitable for a number of roles besides bombing such as transport, reconnaissance and torpedo attack. For this reason it was used throughout the War. It is perhaps best known for its completely glazed and unstepped nose resembling some kind of flying greenhouse.

As the outbreak of the conflict grew close in 1939, the Luftwaffe were bringing a third medium bomber into service designed to replace the Do17 in due course. This was the Junkers Ju88. The Ju88 looked much like the Do17 with all the crew sitting in the nose but its performance was far better. Its maximum speed of 280 mph was almost a match for the fighters of the time and its bomb load of 8,000 lbs was almost double that of its British counterpart the Vickers Wellington. So good was it that it was used in almost every role in the course of its career from heavy fighter to torpedo bomber and dive bomber. It was one of the great aircraft of World War Two.

In fact the Ju88 was better as a level bomber than a dive bomber but so obsessed was the Luftwaffe with dive bombing, particularly after the War's early Stuka successes that all future bomber development was hamstrung by a desire to make all and every design capable of dive-bombing irrespective of practicality.

There was even a strategic bomber of a kind. The Focke Wulf 200 Condor was a four-engine plane, once more of civil airliner provenance, with a range in excess of two thousand miles. Unfortunately it was lightly built and fragile and carried a small bomb load so that although it looked the part, it was never a serious contender for a major strategic bomber role. It found its niche as a convoy raider on long patrols far out over the Atlantic and as such it was extremely effective. Had they been given more time, the Luftwaffe would undoubtedly have produced a first class strategic bomber and they did try, but they were so hampered by the obsession with giving it a dive-bombing capability and by a multiplicity of research projects competing for the limited resources available, that the aircraft they finally produced was a mediocrity at best.

The Luftwaffe could see the need for two kinds of fighter: a short range interceptor and a long range escort fighter that would accompany and protect bombers on long forays into enemy territory. Tenders were invited for an aircraft to operate in the interceptor role and in 1936 there was a competitive demonstration of the two leading contenders: the Messerschmitt Me109 and the Heinkel He112. The Me109 won the competition and was chosen for development. There are varying reports of this competition and some suggest that the He112 should have won but Willy Messerschmitt, designer of the 109, was a friend of Goering and Rudolf Hess and, hence, political influence swung the decision his way. Undoubtedly the He112 was a good design but the 109 was certainly faster and handled more smoothly and this weighed heavily with the German Air Ministry. In addition the Me109 was a simpler aircraft and so easier and quicker to put into mass production.[ii] Time was always a critical factor in Luftwaffe development plans and in this case it was a particularly acute one because the Germans were aware that the British had already placed an order for Spitfires which outclassed anything the Luftwaffe possessed at the time.

Messerschmitt also built their long range fighter, the Me110, but it was not as successful as the 109 nor was it as well known. All the major powers were developing a long range fighter in the late 1930s and almost all of them were failures in their intended task. The problem was that for long journeys they needed to be able to carry a great deal of fuel and they needed more than one engine so that they could pull the extra weight and to provide a measure of reliability in an age when engine breakdown was common. The end result was a large aircraft that did not have the manoeuverability to match the short-distance interceptors that it was bound to meet. There is no point in a fighter plane that can fly long distances to its target if it is going to be shot down when it gets there.

On the other hand the Me109 proved to be another of the great aircraft of the war. To look at, it was much like a Spitfire but with straight edges instead of curves and its performance was much the same. Although quirky and difficult to fly, it was deadly in the hands of an experienced pilot and Luftwaffe veterans loved it.

The new Luftwaffe was able to provide itself with real-life battle training in the Spanish Civil War. Germany sent aircraft and pilots as part of the Condor Legion to take part in the war on the Nationalist side. This provided an invaluable testing ground for aircraft and tactics and a chance to give aircrew front line experience. It vindicated the decision to use dive-bombers and proved the superiority of the modern monoplane fighters. It also allowed German pilots to develop fighter tactics that were much superior to anything in use in any other country. Moreover it led to the development of close co-operation between Luftwaffe and army units on the ground which was one of the key ingredients of the blitzkrieg that Hitler was about to unleash on Europe. Because it was a young organization starting from scratch, the Luftwaffe was willing to learn from its experiences in Spain in a way that other air forces, more influenced by tradition, were not.

There was also one lesson that was not learned, or more accurately, was misinterpreted. This was the effectiveness of the bombing of cities. The Spanish town of Guernica was heavily bombed and severely damaged in the Spanish Civil

War, an episode that became notorious and was the subject of a famous painting by Picasso. This appeared to be an efficient, if ruthless use of airpower destroying the economic value of the town and terrifying the inhabitants as prescribed by Douhet. In fact, although the damage always looked impressive everyone at the time wildly underestimated the ability of a town to recover from bombing and of its people to recover from their terror. Moreover Guernica was a town of modest size in a country district of a land torn by civil war and it was thus not a good indicator of how strategic bombing would fare against a major city such as London or Berlin.

The Luftwaffe was not alone in this error of interpretation: it was almost universal but did not alter the fact that by September 1939, Germany had some 2,900 combat aircraft in the best air force in the world, well trained, well equipped and ready to take anyone on.

The Royal Air Force came out of the First World War as the world's leading air force. It was the first air force to become independent of the other armed services amongst the major powers and had its official birth on 1st April 1918. As already noted, as soon as the war was over it was promptly slashed to the bone by governments determined, not unreasonably, to spend money on peaceful objects rather than weapons of war.

Between 1919 and 1930 the Chief of the Air Staff, the man who ran the R.A.F., was Hugh Trenchard a remarkable figure who probably had more influence on its development than any other single individual. Trenchard was an infantry officer who came to flying rather late in life: he was first commissioned in 1893 and had had a full military career including grievous injury in the Boer War that at one stage threatened to leave him disabled. He seems to have been recognized as a natural leader at an early stage. As Chief of the Air Staff he fought the cause of the R.A.F. at every turn and it is thanks to him that it did not revert to the status of a subsidiary of the other forces. Constantly struggling with miserly budgets Trenchard could not afford the luxury of substantial expansion and his development of new aircraft was conservative to the point of putting the United Kingdom in the second division so far as equipment was concerned. On the other hand he looked to the future and sought to lay solid foundations on which the R.A.F. could expand in due course.

He made sure that the R.A.F. had a network of well-built, permanent bases. He set up a training scheme for the mechanics and fitters that it needed and a military college to produce pilots as well as a staff college to instruct more senior officers. He found economical ways of expanding the R.A.F. within a limited budget such as the University Air Squadrons and the Auxiliary Air Force which was an organization of part-timers who learned to fly in their spare time. He was also a disciple of Douhet and his strategic bombing doctrine. During his time in charge of the R.A.F. the resources were not there to make any practical progress in this direction but his championship of the cause made sure that strategic bombing was accepted by all senior British officers as the key to the use of air power. Politicians were persuaded too, hence Prime Minister Stanley Baldwin's comment: 'The bomber will always get through.'

When this remark was made in the early 1930s, there was plenty of evidence that it was true. The bombers of the time had developed further than the fighters and were in many cases faster. British experience in the Empire had shown that tribesmen could be effectively cowed by air attack on their villages (though under conditions so different from any that would obtain in a European war that the lesson was less than clear). This presented the real possibility that enemy bombers could violate your airspace, bomb large cities and fly away again before your fighters could catch them. The orthodox Douhet solution, of course, was that you bombed your enemy first.

By the end of the 1930s the situation was radically changed by two developments. The first was the fact that fighter development leapfrogged ahead of bomber so that Spitfire and Messerschmitt had the speed and armament to be a real threat to bombers. The second was radar. Radar (which is a contraction of 'radio detection and ranging') was under development in several countries in the late 1930s. However it was in the U.K. that it was to have its first big test as a practical military system and there its chief researcher was Sir Robert Watson-Watt. He is often stated to be the inventor of radar but this is an honour that he must share with other scientists in other countries. So important were the implications of the use of radar that all development of it was carried on in utmost secrecy. Its key use in air warfare was that you could detect the approach of enemy aircraft at a distance. For a small island like Britain this was vital because if bombers were not spotted until they reached the coast they could bomb London and get away again before fighter planes could catch them. With advance warning the fighters could be up in the sky in time to meet the bombers coming in. There was another solution which was that standing patrols be kept over the Channel at all times to give advance warning of incoming bombers, but this was only marginally practical because of the wear and tear on aircraft and pilots and the fact that such patrols would not go undisturbed by the enemy's fighter planes.

From the time of Adolph Hitler's accession to power in Germany and his decision to re-arm, it became increasingly apparent to the British government that their armed forces, and particularly their air forces, were insufficient for national security. Budgets increased accordingly and the R.A.F. expanded. Despite the conviction of the R.A.F. hierarchy that the future of air warfare lay with strategic bombing, there was a huge expansion of fighter squadrons because it was beginning to look as though fighter planes might after all be effective against bombers and because, even if they were not, no government could afford to let hostile bombers roam its skies unchallenged and fighters were much cheaper to build than bombers. As the outbreak of war began to appear more and more inevitable the expansion gathered pace.

By the summer of 1939 the R.A.F. could muster nearly 1,700 aircraft including 39 squadrons of fighters and 22 of bombers. There were also ground attack aircraft and a substantial number of squadrons devoted to watching the coast and the seas around Britain to protect the country's vital sea lanes.

Shortly after the war broke out the R.A.F. arranged the Empire Air Training Scheme whereby aircrew for the R.A.F. could be trained overseas in Australia, Canada or New Zealand. A parallel agreement provided for training in South Africa as well. These arrangements allowed young men to receive their initial training in places where the weather was good and the airspace unlimited. It was of inestimable value in the years to come in providing a steady flow of trained airmen without straining overstretched British resources. It was an example of forward strategic thinking at its best.

There were three kinds of heavy bomber, all modern monoplanes with two engines but barely of a size to be truly strategic bombers. The Vickers Wellington was soon to show itself clearly superior to the other types, the Hampden and the Whitley which were replaced with Wellingtons as fast as circumstances allowed once the war made this superiority apparent. More Wellingtons were produced than any other British heavy or medium bomber. It is often thought that this honour belongs to the famous Avro Lancaster but this is not the case. The Wellington was the backbone of bomber command until 1943 and it continued in a variety of roles in all the major theatres of war in which Britain was involved throughout the conflict. It was built in a unique way with a design known as 'geodetic construction' that was the brainchild of a gifted aero-engineer called Barnes Wallis. Geodetic construction consisted of a metal skeleton of a diamond pattern somewhat resembling fishnet covered by stretched canvas. It was extremely strong for its weight and ideal for aeroplane construction. Only difficulty of manufacture prevented its more widespread use.

There was a medium bomber with a strange pedigree. In 1934 Lord Rothermere, a newspaper magnate, ordered a private plane for his own use as a deliberate boost to the aircraft industry. The result was a twin-engine aircraft built by the Bristol aircraft company that first flew in 1935 and whose performance was so startling that it was immediately adopted by the Air Ministry for military purposes. Named the Bristol Blenheim, it became a mainstay of the R.A.F. in the early years of the war. When it first flew it was faster than any fighter then in service and so it was used as a heavy fighter as well as a bomber. By the time the war came improvements in aircraft design had overtaken it and its performance was now mediocre but Britain lacked anything better and the capacity of the air manufacturing industry was fully taken up producing aircraft of higher priority. So the Blenheim soldiered on for half the war because it could do a number of different tasks fairly well and was a relatively simple piece of machinery by contemporary standards of aero-design.

For ground attack the R.A.F. used an aeroplane called the Fairey Battle. This was a single-engine monoplane with a crew of three. It filled much the same role as the Ju87 though it was not a dive-bomber. Like the Ju87 it was slow and vulnerable and it duly suffered terrible casualties in the fighting in France in 1940. The R.A.F. promptly withdrew it from front line service and assigned it to training and other support activities. This aircraft has always had a very poor reputation because of its short and tragic career but this is somewhat unfair. Certainly it was not in the first division of design and was not new when it was used but no one at this time had quite appreciated how vulnerable all ground attack aircraft were in the absence of complete air superiority.

Air Ministry planning called for two heavy fighters and two interceptors. The first of the heavy fighters was the Westland Whirlwind and it was a complete failure. It was fast but its range was hardly any greater than that of an interceptor and having two engines it was not especially agile. The engine was a new design from Rolls Royce with which there were constant teething problems and the plane had too high a landing speed to use many of the fighter bases available. It was soon abandoned and only 100 or so were made. The other heavy plane was the Bristol Beaufighter a sound, twin-engine design with very heavy armament that was used as a night fighter and anti-shipping plane, but not as a day fighter as originally intended. By the time it was ready for mass production the R.A.F. had seen that heavy fighters could not compete with interceptors in day battles.

The two interceptor fighters were both to become famous. They were the Hawker Hurricane and the Supermarine Spitfire. In many ways they were similar aircraft in that both were low-wing monoplanes powered by Rolls Royce Merlin engines and armed with eight .303 machine guns. In basic construction however, they were far different. The Hurricane was the last of the line of Hawker designs for the R.A.F. that stretched back almost to the First War and it was very traditional being built in the old canvas-over-metal-frame method. Indeed, the first draft of the design was a biplane. Although it was very manoeuverable its speed was not outstanding.

The Spitfire was smaller, lighter and faster and everyone who flew it said it was the most responsive aircraft they had ever known. Its construction was the modern metal stressed skin design. Its beautiful curves made it aesthetically pleasing to look at but difficult to manufacture. It was generally agreed that this was a 'winner' and it has remained a household name to the present time. The government wanted more of them than Supermarine, which was not a very large enterprise, could produce. To solve the problem a giant new factory to mass-produce them was built at Castle Bromwich near Birmingham, but it took some time for this to come on line. The Spitfire was only being introduced as the war began and it was the Hurricane that would have to bear the brunt of the early fighting. In the Battle of Britain it outnumbered the Spitfire by two to one. Moreover, in the R.A.F. outside Great Britain itself even the Hurricane had not penetrated and the principle fighter in the British Empire was the Gloster Gladiator, an old-fashioned biplane with fixed undercarriage.

The story of the French air force in the build-up of the 1930s is a lamentable one. The French air force became an independent body in 1934 known as the Armee de L'Air, but the aircraft industry was really inadequate to its needs. The decline in the demand for fighting aircraft at the end of the First World War had hidden the fact that the industry was composed of too many small firms operating with outdated production techniques. The only real exception was a combine called S.A.S.O. put together by Marcel Bloch and Henri Potez that would later become the Dassault aircraft company of modern times. Each year the Air Force had to compete strenuously with the army and navy for its share of the military budget. The degree of competition between the forces was quite unlike anything in Britain or Germany. Despite its independence the army saw the air force as existing merely to meet army needs. A brief flirtation with the idea of strategic bombing was quickly abandoned and the army's influence increased to the point where it had an active say in the tasks given to air units in the event of war. When expansion was called for after 1933 the industry simply did not have the capacity to meet the demands made on it. In 1936 a socialist government took over in France and nationalized the aircraft industry which it adjudged, rightly, to be incapable of meeting the needs of the nation under private ownership. Unfortunately this was done by dividing France arbitrarily into six geographical districts and combining all the aircraft construction facilities in each district into one single, state-run concern. Far from improving output this bureaucratic exercise caused the industry to descend into chaos. So strong were the conflicting political convictions in France at the time that there were instances of sabotage within aircraft factories by their own workers.

Arthur Harris, who later led R.A.F. Bomber Command and had served five years on the Committee of Imperial Defence, described the Armee de L'Air as 'deficient in every way'.[iii] He said that French planners saw their air force as purely a form of long range artillery for the army.

By the time that war broke out the Armee de L'Air was plagued by obsolete aircraft and a multiplicity of types. It had one reasonably modern bomber in the Lioret-et-Olivier LeO 451 a twin-engine plane that was fast and carried an effective bomb load but it was still using the extraordinary Amiot 143 designed as long ago as 1925 though built later. This was one of aviation's uglier offspring, resembling a conservatory with wings and wholly out of date by 1939. Yet when the invasion of France began in May 1940, four French bomber groups went to war equipped with it and suffered accordingly. Increasingly aware that their bomber force was quite inadequate for its task, the French Air Ministry bought first one hundred and then another 270 Douglas A-20s from the U.S.A. before the U.S. air force had even finished evaluating the plane. This was a first class aircraft but only the first hundred were delivered before the fall of France, the remainder being diverted to Great Britain. It is uncertain whether any of the French consignment ever saw active service. If so, only minimal use was ever made of them before the armistice. Britain certainly used them and this gave them the odd distinction of flying for two foreign air forces before they flew for their own.

The situation with fighter aeroplanes was equally unsatisfactory. The mainstay of the Armee de L'Air was the Morane-Saulnier 406 an aircraft of average capability. Its top speed fell slightly short of that of the Hurricane at 302 mph and was far inferior to that of the Spitfire or the Me109 by 50 mph or more. Another fighter was the Bloch 151 but that was clearly underpowered and under-armed. Bloch designed the 152 to cure these problems and it was delivered to the front line squadrons from the beginning of 1940 but of the first 300 delivered, none could be used because two thirds had been supplied with the wrong propellers and they all lacked gun-sights.[iv] In May 1940 the first examples of the Dewoitine D520 were entering service. This was a good aeroplane but it came too late: only some thirty were in service on May 10th. To make up the deficiency in French production the Armee de L'Air was again forced to buy abroad and four fighter groups were equipped with the Hawk 75 an American aircraft built by Curtiss-Wright and widely exported in the 1930s. They were already fighting in China and did so in the Winter War in Finland too. These were good aircraft in their time but, once again, they were an obsolete model by 1939/40. The French fighter force thus effectively had five different types of single engine fighter aircraft using three different engines to be catered for, with all the servicing complications that that involved. By comparison the Germans had one type of aircraft and the British two. In each case there was only one engine type.

French military thinking had not reached a conclusion on the right way to use an air force and accordingly there was no strategic plan other than the default idea of support for the army. Worse than this there was really no flexibility of thought so that when France was faced with blitzkrieg, no one had any idea how the Armee de L'Air should counter it.

The United States was in a quite different situation from the other powers. Geographically it was isolated with no other major state nearby, so it did not have to concern itself with any threat to its national security. Even the advent of the Nazis in Germany and their bellicose noises from the mid-1930s did not concern Americans unduly. They certainly had no intention of involving themselves again in Europe's problems. In this climate there was never going to be very active development of military aircraft but the restless and inventive American spirit was not likely to forsake aviation research completely. The aeroplane was, after all, their invention.

The fact that The U.S.A. bordered two great oceans naturally set military minds to thinking in terms of flying boats and long range aircraft generally. So it is no surprise that they were the first power to develop a really effective modern four-engine strategic bomber. This was the Boeing B-17, a huge aircraft for its time with a wingspan of over one hundred feet, a range of 2,000 miles and a heavy armament that was increased further with time and led to it being called the 'Flying Fortress'. It flew for the first time in 1935. Early models of the plane had a stability problem when fully loaded because the centre of gravity was too high but this was cured in the 'E' and later versions by the addition of a great sail-like tail fin that gave the whole aircraft a most pleasing appearance. Its majestic outline is familiar from a thousand photographs and it has entered the aviation hall of fame.

One of the obvious uses for such an aircraft would be to attack enemy ships threatening the United States or her possessions. At this time the effectiveness of aircraft against ships was something of an unknown quantity because World War One had not produced any air/sea battles of note. In 1921 a thrusting air force officer, Colonel Billy Mitchell, arranged a demonstration in which aircraft attacked and bombed an old German battleship given to the U.S. as part of war reparations. The aircraft sank the battleship very efficiently but critics scoffed that the trial had not been realistic since the ship was stationary and had no anti-aircraft defence. Nonetheless this demonstration gained great publicity and was an important step in the growth of airpower. Mitchell himself was a follower of Douhet and called with increasing stridency for the expansion of the air force at the expense of the other services. Eventually he described the conduct of the senior officers of the armed services as 'almost treasonable' in their disregard of air power.[v] This was too much and he was court-martialed and sentenced to suspension without pay for five years. He promptly resigned and made an even greater nuisance of himself as a civilian. In fact much informed opinion was on his side and undoubtedly the time was shortly to come when the aircraft would sign the death warrant of the conventional warship.

Partly because of Mitchell and partly because of the geographical position of the United States the Douhet doctrine was very popular there and when World War Two finally reached American shores Air Force doctrine was founded on the primacy of strategic bombing.

Another feature of American geography was the need for good reconnaissance planes to spot enemies in those waters surrounding her coasts. In 1936 the U.S. Navy deployed the Consolidated PBY flying boat perhaps better known by its other name: Catalina. This versatile aircraft was used throughout the war by Britain as well as the U.S.A. and was the most successful flying boat to see service anywhere in World War Two. It had a range of 1,900 miles and could be used for bombing, mine laying, reconnaissance, transport, air/sea rescue and anti-submarine work. Its wing and two engines stood above the fuselage on a kind of pylon so that the wing could give maximum lift and the engines were kept well clear of sea spray. It was an old design when the war started but, like the B-17, it was such a good design that it wore its age lightly and was still in service in 1945.

The year of 1939 saw the introduction of two fighter planes: one interceptor and one long range. The interceptor was the Bell P-39 Airacobra. This was an eccentric design with the engine in the fuselage behind the pilot. This arrangement allowed it to have a tricycle undercarriage with a nose wheel instead of a tail wheel which made for much easier landing and handling on the ground. It also allowed it to mount a 37mm cannon in the nose. One single hit from this cannon could shoot down an enemy aircraft but it was slow firing and difficult to aim. Such firepower gave the P-39 a role as a ground attack aircraft as well as a fighter. The unusual position of the engine made it less vulnerable to ground fire than the usual nose position but, conversely, more vulnerable to fire from other fighter planes which tended to come from behind. The P-39 had no supercharger and so poor performance at high altitude which was to prove a severe handicap when it was used against the Japanese in the Pacific. American pilots generally disliked flying it: some called it the 'iron dog'. On the other hand many P-39s were given to the U.S.S.R. under lend-lease and the Russians loved them because Russian air battles tended to be fought at much lower levels. Bell produced an improved version of this aircraft in the middle of the war, called the Kingcobra, mainly because of Russian demand and almost all the planes built went to Russia.

The long range fighter was the Lockheed P-38 Lightning which was another eccentric design. It had two fuselages and two engines joined by the wing with a nose and cockpit fitted to the wing between them. It had a range of 2,200 miles and of all the long range fighters produced in the early years of the war this was the only one to achieve a measure of success. It was widely used and was probably at its best in the Pacific theatre where its long range was a great advantage and it had a wide speed margin over contemporary Japanese fighters.

Had the United States entered the war in 1939 it would have found itself relatively poorly equipped. The two fighters just mentioned were not yet in front line squadrons and its main fighter was the P-36, known as the Hawk 75 in its export version, outclassed by Spitfires and Messerschmitts. It had no modern medium bomber though it was on the verge of acquiring several. The fact was that it had another two years to prepare itself before it became involved and it addressed the task of arming its air force with characteristic energy as we shall see in due course.

CHAPTER FIVE

Blitzkrieg

On 1st September 1939 Germany invaded Poland.

Poland was a young country only twenty-one years old. It had been created at the end of the First World War out of parts of Germany, Russia and Austria-Hungary. Almost immediately it was at war with Soviet Russia and appeared at one point to be on the verge of extinction as Russian armies closed on Warsaw, but the Poles counterattacked and in 1920 a peace was signed and Poland was assigned the eastern border that it maintained until World War Two. Much of the western part of the country consisted of land that had been part of Germany for the last hundred years or more and with it the Poles inherited a substantial minority of disgruntled Germans. The peace of 1918 had also awarded Poland a corridor of land giving it access to the Baltic Sea. This corridor included the city of Danzig (modern Gdansk), also once part of Germany and now a free city (i.e. a self-governing city). It was a clear German foreign policy aim in the 1930s to reclaim the country's lost territory and, in particular, to re-unite Danzig with the rest of Germany. Danzig was an ancient Hansa port with a population not far short of half a million and a mixed German and Polish history. At one time it had been a stronghold of the Teutonic Knights. It was a beautiful city and, more prosaically, it was a prosperous trading port and it contained the Schichau shipbuilding yard, one of the largest in northern Europe, and an economic prize of some value.

The Poles were therefore well aware that they were threatened by their larger neighbours and that Germany, in particular, would one day seek to take Polish territory. They accordingly made sure during the 1930s that they had a large army and a substantial air force. Unusually for a country of its size Poland had its own indigenous aircraft industry rather than relying entirely on foreign imports. At the outbreak of war the Polish air force had about 750 front line aircraft. Its principal fighter plane was the PZL P.11 designed in the early 1930s. As was so often the case, this was a good aircraft when it first flew but by 1939 it was obsolete and slower than the German bombers it was supposed to attack. It was most unusual amongst fighter planes for having a high wing configuration more appropriate for bombers. The designers were working on something better but in the meantime the Polish government had ordered Morane Saulnier and Hurricane fighters from abroad but they had not yet arrived in September 1939. The main ground attack aircraft was the PZL P.23 a light bomber that was completely out of date. The best Polish aircraft was their P.37 medium bomber: one of the best of its type in the world. It was faster than

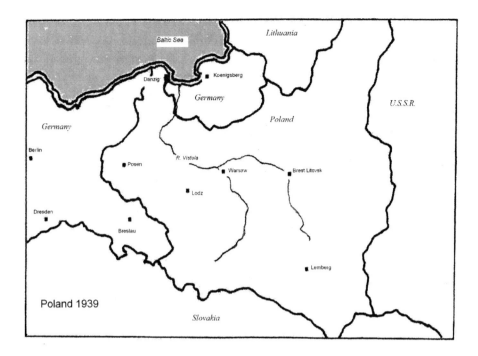

Poland 1939

the British Wellington, an equivalent aircraft, had a longer range and carried a bigger bomb load. Unfortunately the business of equipping the squadrons with this excellent plane had only just begun and a mere 36 were in service when war broke out.

This may be an appropriate moment for a small diversion about the question of counting aircraft. It is common for the figures to omit aircraft that do not have an active combat role such as reconnaissance or training aircraft. If this were not done then the fighting strength of the air force in question would appear much greater than it really is. On the other hand the training and reconnaissance aircraft are often types that are capable of a combat role and may be pressed into one, particularly if things are not going well. The other complicating issue is aircraft availability. Aircraft are complex machines and need a lot of looking after. At any one time a combat formation will have a proportion of its aircraft undergoing servicing or repair, so if it is required to fly a combat mission it will not be able to put into the air all the aircraft that it appears on paper to own. Different air forces have dealt with this problem in different ways and there is different terminology for expressing it. One often hears that a squadron has, for instance, twelve aircraft 'on hand' and nine 'available' or 'serviceable.' In fact the above figures are realistic and conservative and it can be seen that we are looking at a situation in which some 25-30 percent of an air force is not available at any one time. There may be pressures making this figure better or worse. Commanders were often reluctant to admit that an aircraft was a write-off, particularly after an accident, and it might sit for weeks in the workshops, still on the squadron roster as 'on hand' but in practice, most unlikely ever to fly again. Conversely, in the Battle of Britain the R.A.F. had a plentiful supply of aircraft most of the time but not pilots and so there was a tendency to write aircraft off that could have been repaired: it was easier and safer to get a new one.

There is no uniformity in the way historians have dealt with aircraft numbers and so, in a particular situation, one source will say there were 750 aircraft while another says there were 500. In effect both are right. It is, perhaps, more common to talk about the 'on hand' figure wherever possible and that is the policy generally followed in this book, save for strictly tactical situations. After all, if your car is in the garage for repairs you still consider yourself a car owner.

If the quality of Polish aircraft was mixed the standard of their pilots was first class. They were fired by a deep sense of patriotism and knew that there was a very real prospect of combat in a struggle for the survival of their country. Training was realistic and constant.

Each of the six Polish field armies had its own assigned fighters and bombers and there was also a special brigade of aircraft held near Warsaw to act as protection for the capital and as a flexible reserve. The Poles were well aware that in the event of a German attack their chances of survival without international help were small. Not only was Poland a much less populous and industrialized country than Germany but it was geographically near impossible to defend. There are no mountains in Poland and only one river of any size: the Vistula. The Vistula flows from north to south down the middle of the country and so a defence based on using it as a barrier involved giving up the western half of the country without a fight. This, of course, was politically impossible.

It is said that when Goering learned of Hitler's intention to attack Poland, which the Fuehrer revealed to him over dinner, he could not eat another mouthful. He was sure that Germany was not yet ready to face a general European war and that, if she invaded Poland, that was what she would provoke. He tried desperately to change Hitler's mind but without success.[i]

Certainly, as regards the limited scope of a conflict with Poland, there was every cause for confidence. The German army was much larger than the Polish and better equipped. It was also prepared to use new battlefield tactics so far untried in real combat but tested in war games with startling results. These were the tactics of motorized warfare that Germany had developed between the wars to a level far surpassing any other nation. Motorization had been studied by the German general staff and specifically by Heinz Guderian, since the early 1920s. The conclusion they had come to was that a force consisting of tanks, infantry and artillery, all motorized and acting in concert could wreak havoc with the more traditional army that relied entirely on the foot soldier. (Even the Germans though, could only afford to have a small proportion of their army motorized.) The two keys to success were, first, massing your mobile forces together in motorized or armoured divisions and, second, seizing control of the air and using it to support your troops on the ground. The invasion of Poland was to be the first large-scale test of these tactics which were shortly to earn the title 'Blitzkrieg'.

The Luftwaffe was ready to play its part. In 1939 it had at its disposal 2,900 aircraft though not all of these could be deployed against Poland as it had to guard Germany's western border lest Britain and France try to interfere. There were available to support the attack on Poland 900 bombers, 200 fighters and 470 reconnaissance and transport aircraft. The strategic plan for the invasion was for Army Group North based in East Prussia and Pomerania to strike south towards Warsaw and Army Group South based in Silesia to strike northeast, also to Warsaw. It was a giant pincer movement. Subsidiary attacks would cut the Polish corridor and occupy Danzig in the north and in the south a column would strike east to take the major city of Lemberg (Lvov or Lviv). The northern attack would be supported by Airfleet One under Albert Kesselring, a veteran of World War One and a most able man, with 807 aircraft and the southern by Airfleet Four under Alexander Loehr with 627. Loehr was an Austrian and a fighter pilot from the First World War who had risen to be commander-in-chief of the Austrian Air force before the Anschluss and continued his career with the Luftwaffe thereafter. The balance of available planes were chiefly fighters kept back for defence and under central control.

For some weeks before the campaign began, German reconnaissance aircraft had been flying in Polish airspace with increasing audacity photographing everything of military significance and taking a particular interest in airfields. In addition, there was no shortage of spies in Poland willing to provide the Germans with useful information. The air plan envisaged that the first phase of the attack would be the destruction of the Polish air force and the crucial first step toward that goal would be a surprise attack on airfields on the first day of the war. With the air force out of the way the Luftwaffe would then go on to its army support role. The plan was modified at the army's request by allocating some of the bombers to attack communications from day one. It was modified at the request of the navy by assigning some of the bombers in Airfleet One to attack the insignificant Polish navy in the Baltic. The army's idea was a good one because it was shortly to become apparent that disrupting communications was one of an air force's most useful functions. The navy's idea was a very bad one because it was a classic case of diverting vital resources to a non-essential target. The campaign would be decided on land and the Polish navy was irrelevant. Kesselring was furious at the waste of his aircraft but the instructions had the backing of Hitler so he had to comply.[ii]

A few days before the campaign began there was a tragic accident that called into doubt the whole concept of the dive bomber, a concept that was by no means universally accepted by the Luftwaffe's senior officers. A squadron of Stukas was putting on a demonstration of dive-bombing technique at a training ground at the small town of Neuhammer. A weather report indicated there was a thin layer of cloud and the pilots were told to dive through it. After the report was delivered the cloud then rapidly thickened until it virtually reached the ground by the time the demonstration took place. The Stuka pilots dived and waited to emerge from the cloud layer. When they did so they found they were too low to pull up and thirteen planes flew straight into the ground, killing their crews. One might, at first glance, think that the pilots' altimeters would have warned them of the danger they were in but the cockpit instruments of those days were easily upset by violent manoeuvres and would have been quite unreliable during the dive.[iii]

The moment for the attack to begin was set as 4.45am on 1st September. Ten minutes prior to that time three Stukas led by Senior Lieutenant Bruno Dilley roared at tree-top height through the dawn light toward the railway bridge at Dirschau (now Tczew) that spanned the Vistula. The Poles intended to blow the bridge up to prevent the German army using it: it was at a vital strategic point in the Polish corridor. The Germans knew all about the Polish intentions and Bruno Dilley's mission was to bomb the embankment behind the bridge to destroy the wires laid there that led to the demolition charges on the bridge. The Stukas had decided to come in at low level to achieve surprise. They were successful and their bombs burst on the embankment and severed the wires. This was the first aerial action of World War Two.[iv]

The Polish engineers immediately set about repairing the wires and blowing the bridge and despite another raid later in the morning they were successful, though in the long term it did them no good.

This small action set the tone of mixed fortune for the Luftwaffe's first day of war. At first there was fog and many planes could not take off at all until late in the day. Then the raids on airfields were an anticlimax because the Poles had taken the precaution of dispersing their aircraft under cover or in fields at a distance from their bases. Though propaganda claimed the Polish air force had been destroyed on the ground and this claim lived on into some post-war literature, the truth was that only some training and transport craft had been lost. However, the bombing did damage the airfield facilities and the fact of the dispersal itself hampered the response of the Polish air force.

At Deblin airfield, south of Warsaw, Captain Witold Urbanowicz was giving dogfighting instruction to a student pilot that morning when live tracer bullets streamed past his cockpit. He took desperate evasive action, cursing the mechanic who had mistakenly loaded the student's guns with live ammunition and wondering how a mere student had so efficiently got the best of an instructor. He ordered the student to land at once and then did so himself. As he climbed out of his cockpit in a foul temper ready to issue reprimands on all sides, another instructor came running over to Urbanowicz to ask if he was all right. The angry Urbanowicz asked him what the hell was going on.

The second instructor shook his head: 'You should go to church and light a candle. You have just been attacked by a German Messerschmitt.'[v]

A suburb of Warsaw burns after bombing. The view is from a German Junkers 52 transport aircraft. © Imperial War Museum (HU3218)

Although it was not immediately apparent, the raids on communications were particularly effective. Broken telephone and power lines, smashed radio stations and fallen bridges brought control of the Polish army to near paralysis. The heaviest raids were made on Warsaw and its adjoining airfields. These clashed with the Polish aircraft of the central reserve and a major air battle developed over the capital with something in the region of 150 aircraft participating. The battle did not last long and there were a half dozen losses on each side. The problem for the Poles was that they could afford their losses far less than the Germans. Moreover, as the days went by, they suffered similar losses in aerial combats time and again. In five days the central reserve had lost seventy-five percent of its strength.

There were ground attack aircraft attached to each of the Polish field armies; they were mainly the lumbering, single-engine P.23 Karas, (a bit like a Stuka's poor relations) and they flew into a wall of German anti-aircraft fire at low level and were destroyed in large numbers. All over the country the air force fought with great bravery but their cause was hopeless: they were outnumbered and were flying inferior machines. At the end of a week they were no more serious threat to German supremacy.

The Luftwaffe had already switched the emphasis of its attacks to backing up the army and this was done with great success and contributed to the remarkable speed with which the army crossed the country. The defenders began to be overwhelmed by the chaos of defeat. On 17th September the Russians invaded Poland from the East in accordance with the secret protocol of their pact with Hitler. On the 18th the last 98 serviceable Polish planes flew over the border into neutral Rumania and the air war was over. Most of the Polish pilots found their way to France and/or Great Britain to continue the fight flying for other countries.

German aircraft now gave their undivided attention to ground attack and to devastating Warsaw, which had been under siege since 13th. Some of the bombers were withdrawn from action for a rest since the end was now just a matter of time. The last Polish resistance ceased on 6th October. The whole campaign was over in little more than a month and the air war had lasted a mere two weeks and four days.

For the Luftwaffe it had been a triumph but there were lessons to be learned; 275 aircraft had been lost and the Poles had lost in the region of 330, totally destroyed. Considering the German advantage both in numbers and quality of equipment, the smallness of the margin between these two figures was surprising and a tribute to the pilots of the Polish air force. It demonstrated the extent to which an aerial battle depended on the skill and dedication of the men involved.

It was a surprise to all the speed with which the air power of a retreating army melted away. The big difficulty in this regard was that when an airfield had to be abandoned a great deal of equipment, including all aircraft under repair had to be abandoned with it. Although the airworthy aircraft could fly to another base all the ground personnel had to follow by road transport and thus became caught up in the chaos of an army in retreat. Until they reached the new base there was not much the aircraft could do without their ground support team.

The swiftly advancing armoured spearheads tended to outrun their communications and army headquarters therefore often had little idea where their leading units were to be found. Without this information bombers could hardly lend them air support. Clearly this problem would need solving for future campaigns.

The Luftwaffe soon found that it had underestimated its supply needs. In the middle of the campaign it commandeered a number of Lufthansa passenger craft to carry supplies, but even they did not entirely solve the difficulty. Indeed this was to be a recurring theme in different theatres throughout the war until the Luftwaffe was finally grounded in the closing days through lack of gasoline.

In conclusion it must be said that close air support for troops on the ground had proved its worth ten times over.

While Poland was being subdued the Western Allies did very little. As Goering had feared, the attack on Poland prompted Britain and France to declare war on Germany. Despite their commitment to aid Poland the geography of the situation was such that there was little practical aid they could give. Perhaps, with more dynamic governments, one or other country might have found some way to intervene but the timescale was such that it was unrealistic to think that Poland could be saved. The one thing that Britain and France could have done was the one thing they were not going to do and that was to launch an all-out offensive on the western front. Memories of 1914-18 were too fresh for that. It is probably not exaggerating much to say that an attempt to do so would have risked civil disorder in both countries. To be fair, the French did launch a minor offensive in the Saar area in September with the explicit intention of assisting the Poles but it was far too small an effort, easily resisted by the Germans and abandoned at the first sign of difficulty.

What did occur in this period, and indeed, all through the autumn, was aerial warfare. The western front was continually patrolled by the reconnaissance planes of both sides and there were frequent but isolated combats. All the air forces concerned were under strict instructions from the politicians not to bomb any enemy targets that might risk injury to civilians. Considering what was to come later in the war in the way of area bombing these instructions seem almost ludicrously fastidious; certainly they were quite contrary to the Douhet doctrine. It is also noticeable that the Germans had observed no such restraint in their dealings with Poland but this merely illustrates the developing schizophrenic nature of Germany's war whereby she always tried, in the West, to pay at least lip service to the conventions of war whereas, in the East, she fought total war at its most brutal from the start.

The result of these injunctions was that for both sides the only practical targets were warships.[vi] At this time the Germans obeyed their instructions rather more precisely than the R.A.F. and even kept clear of ships in harbour. They could afford to do so because their navy was achieving its own successes in this regard. A U-boat managed to penetrate the closely guarded Royal Navy anchorage at Scapa Flow in the Orkney Islands and sink the battleship Royal Oak, and another torpedoed and sank the aircraft carrier, Courageous, off the southwest coast of the British Isles. The Courageous had only two destroyers for escort at the time, which were quite inadequate for the task and it was positively negligent of the navy to risk such an important ship in this way. The Courageous was on convoy protection duty and her loss caused the Royal Navy to withdraw other carriers from this task which was in itself a singular victory for the German Navy.

The R.A.F. raided warships in and near the harbours of the north German coast. They carried out their raids in daylight and their bombers were unescorted because the targets were far beyond the range of any fighter plane. The result was the slaughter of British bombers and the decision by the R.A.F. to carry out all long range bombing by night. We will look at this episode in a little more detail later on.

The Luftwaffe used these quiet months for the gradual introduction of the Ju88 bomber into their squadrons. It was a complex aircraft and difficult to manufacture with its powerful engines and semi-automatic dive bombing system. The result was that its integration was slow and it did not finally replace the last Dorniers until Late in 1941. So good was this aircraft that it was worth the wait.

For three months the winter weather effectively ended combat flying and in the spring Hitler's onslaught on the West was scheduled to unfold, but he several times postponed it for one reason or another and in the meantime the question of Norway arose. Germany did not have adequate deposits of iron ore and imported much of its needs from Sweden. During the winter the Baltic Sea froze and the iron ships could not sail. Instead the iron ore was taken by rail to the ice-free port of Narvik in Norway and shipped from there. Its route to Germany was thereafter largely accomplished in Norwegian territorial waters. The prospect of interfering with the ore ships was a tempting one for the British who were looking for a way to strike at Germany without a major land campaign in France.

Germany was anxious to guard its iron ore supply but it was also attracted by the dazzling prospect of acquiring hundreds of miles of coastline giving directly on to the Atlantic Ocean. Possession of this coast by Britain would enable it to impose a tight blockade whereas possession by Germany would make total blockade next to impossible. Moreover the coast could be a base for U-boats and reconnaissance aircraft with easy access to the Atlantic. Of course, for German planners at this stage the occupation of France with its long Atlantic coastline was a far-off pipe dream.

On February 16th 1940 Great Britain violated Norwegian neutrality by sending a warship into her territorial waters to intercept a German supply vessel called Altmark which they knew contained British merchant seamen captured on the high seas by the German commerce raider Graf Spee. The seamen were liberated and several German sailors were killed. This incident seemed to Hitler to demonstrate that Norwegian neutrality was no protection and the British could violate it whenever they wanted. He decided there must be an invasion at the earliest possible moment.

The invasion was launched on April 9thth 1940 and included, as a preliminary, the subjugation of Denmark. It was the demands of geography rather than any political goal that made this a necessary first step. Germany needed to have the Danish coastline in safe hands and possession of her airfields so that Norway was in range for the Luftwaffe. Paratroops were dropped on Aalborg airfield and on the main bridge leading into Copenhagen and troops were landed from transport ships in the city's docks and rapidly occupied the town. Simultaneously the German ambassador presented an ultimatum to the King, Christian X. After consultation with the Government the King decided that resistance would be futile and ordered a capitulation. The occupation of Denmark was completed the next day. From a military point of view the attack on Denmark was most notable for the fact that it witnessed the first ever use of paratroops in war.

The aerial aspect of the Denmark/Norway operation was carried out by 10th Air Corps under the command of General Hans-Ferdinand Geisler. Geisler had been a naval officer throughout World War One, joining the newly formed Luftwffe in 1933, and was an expert in air/sea operations. He had some 500 combat aircraft at his

Scandinavia 1940

disposal and 500 transport aircraft, earmarked for an important part in the operation, were attached to his command.

Paratroops were also due to be dropped on airfields in Norway, in particular those outside Oslo and Stavanger. The Oslo landings were especially important because once the airfield was secured the troops were to proceed to Oslo, Norway's capital, occupy it and seize the Government and the Royal Family. The Ju52 transport planes carrying the paratroops had to turn back because of poor weather. The plan was that the paratroops should make the airfield safe and then a second wave of transports carrying more troops would land and release them in the conventional way: down the steps. These latter troops would then proceed to the capture of Oslo. When the second wave planes arrived all seemed quiet and they assumed they should land. When they tried to do so the Norwegians opened fire and Norwegian Gladiator fighters attacked. Escorting Me110 heavy fighters strafed the defenders and shot down a Gladiator and the transports were then able to land though several crashed due to the shortness of the runway.[vii] It turned out that the defenders of the airfield were too few to offer any serious resistance and they were put to flight by Me110s landing and using their cannon while on the ground. From here on events proceeded more or less in accordance with the plan though Government and King were not captured. Oslo was declared an open city and Vidkun Quisling, the leader of the Norwegian fascist party, proclaimed himself the leader of a new provisional government. King Haakon and the legitimate government refused to deal with either him or the Germans and soon retreated to the north of the country where they remained until June.

Operations at other airfields went more smoothly and Luftwaffe aircraft were soon flying in to use them as their own bases.

At the same time naval forces were approaching Oslo from the sea. Further naval task forces were sailing for Norway's other principal ports. A Royal Navy attempt to interfere was driven off by Luftwaffe bombers and all the relevant ports were eventually captured. The Norwegians, who had been taken by surprise and, in any event could muster only limited armed forces, resisted valiantly but could not alter the final outcome. However, German naval losses in this campaign, both against the Norwegians and the Royal Navy were severe. They lost one of their two heavy cruisers and ten of their twenty destroyers together with some other ships. The result was to reduce the Kriegsmarine from an effective, if second division, navy to a mere raiding force. One of their other losses was the light cruiser Koenigsberg sunk in Bergen Fjord early in April by British Fleet Air Arm Skua aircraft, flying from the Orkney Islands to the very limit of their range. This was the first significant warship in history to be sunk by air attack. It had however, been hit by shore batteries in the attack on Bergen and was awaiting engine repairs so it was a stationary target. Nevertheless it was a partial justification of the inter-war theories of Billy Mitchell. It still remained, however, to sink such a ship in the open sea, which was the real challenge.[viii]

This episode was the high point in the career of the Blackburn Skua, a dive bomber of limited capabilities supplied in small numbers to the Royal Navy pre-war. It was the Navy's first monoplane aircraft and one of the very few dive bomber types that served with the British armed forces since the British were always suspicious of the dive bomber role. The attack on the Koenigsberg seemed a vindication of the technique particularly since no aircraft were lost. A few days later, however, the Navy tried this gambit again with an attack on the battle-cruiser Scharnhorst in Trondheim fjord. No damage was done to the ship and eight out of 15 attacking planes were shot down.[ix]

Norway possessed only a tiny air force of 74 planes. Most of them were Fokker CVs, a general purpose biplane type of the 1930s with a top speed of 140 mph (200 mph slower than a Me109!). There were also a few Gladiator fighters of British origin. They were swept away by the Luftwaffe which soon established itself in Norwegian bases where it was to remain until the war's end.

Britain decided she could not let the invasion of Norway pass unchallenged. Winston Churchill, who was at this time First Lord of the Admiralty, was the driving force behind the intervention which was badly planned and worse executed. Three expeditionary forces were sent out in the middle of April, two to the area around Trondheim in the southern part of Norway and one to Narvik. The southern two made some initial progress but were severely hampered by the fact that they had no air support and Luftwaffe bombers, now based in Norway hammered them mercilessly. By the end of the month they had been brought to a halt by German ground forces and the decision was taken to bring them home. The Narvik force was given air support because the British planners had learned their lesson. This consisted of two squadrons of fighters, one of Hurricanes and one of Gladiators, that were brought in by aircraft carrier. Narvik was captured and the British dug themselves in. There was then something of a stalemate. The British force was not strong enough to challenge the German occupation of Norway as a whole and the winter was over so the importance of Narvik as an ore port was finished for another year. By late May developments in France were making the Narvik expedition seem pointless and by the 8th June all British troops had left Norway.

On 7th the aircraft carrier Glorious took on board the remaining ten Gladiators and eight Hurricanes. They flew from shore and landed on the ship. This was the first ever landing of ordinary aircraft unequipped with arrestor hooks, on an aircraft carrier and it was a complete success. Each aircraft had a large sandbag placed inside the rear of the fuselage and this enabled the pilot to brake hard on landing without making the aircraft tip over on its nose.[x] It was all to no avail however, because, on the way home the Glorious which was escorted by only two destroyers, ran into the German battleships Scharnhorst and Gneisenau and carrier and escorts were sunk in short order. Intercepted signals had suggested these battleships were in the area but had been ignored as being inherently improbable. After the Courageous episode it is hard to believe the Royal Navy would again put such a valuable ship at risk in this casual way. Part of the blame must lie with the captain of the Glorious who declined to sail in a convoy that was available because his ship was faster on its own. He went down with his command and so paid the ultimate price for his failure of judgement.

Also on 7th June the Royal Navy carried King Haakon and his Government to England and though there was never any official surrender, from this date on the Government of Vidkun Quisling was the de facto administration of the country.

The Norway campaign was a big gamble for Germany. It depended on the use of aircraft and paratroops in a way never seen before and on naval landings which are notoriously risky. It was a success but the navy suffered grievously and the collapse of France two months later gave Germany the access to the Atlantic she wanted anyway and this fact to some degree devalued the possession of Norway. The campaign was a great success for the Junker Ju52, the transport aircraft that carried all the airborne troops and supplies. This was an elderly passenger aircraft with three motors, remarkable stability and a short take-off and landing run. It first flew in 1934 and was extensively used by Lufthansa. It had been tried as a bomber in Spain but with less happy results. 500 of these aircraft were used in the Norwegian campaign and they had proved their worth. They were to serve the Luftwaffe in large numbers throughout the war. They seem to have attracted a sentimental attachment from all who dealt with them and were affectionately known as 'Tante Ju' or 'Auntie Ju'.

CHAPTER SIX

The Fall of France

The German offensive in the West finally began on May 10th 1940. This was the crucial showdown that would offer Germany the chance to reverse the verdict of history given by World War One. Approximately three million men were deployed in ninety-three divisions along her western border. Of those divisions ten were armoured and six motorized. All the rest were infantry but it was with those sixteen mobile divisions that the key to success lay. There were some 5,000 aircraft of all kinds to back up the ground offensive. Of these perhaps 3,500 were front-line types. They were divided into two Airfleets: the Second and the Third under Generals Kesselring and Sperrle respectively. (In the Polish campaign the Luftwaffe deployed the First and Fourth Air Fleets but in both campaigns it was the same aircraft being used. Airfleets were 'paper' organizations and the actual aircraft could be shuttled around between them at will.)

Albert Kesselring was a general of great talent. He was a Bavarian career army officer who fought in World War One and remained in the army after the war until forced, against his will, to resign in 1933 and accept a post as chief administrator for the organization that was to become the Luftwaffe. In due course he became the chief of staff of the Luftwaffe from 1936 to 1938 when he asked to be relieved because of friction between him and Erhard Milch. He was to rise to overall command of the Italian front later in the war.

Hugo Sperrle was from Ludwigsburg near Stuttgart in Wurttemberg. He fought in the German air force in World War One as an observer and joined the Luftwaffe in 1935. He was the officer in command of the Condor Legion of German pilots in the Spanish Civil War. He was a capable officer though not, perhaps, quite in the class of Kesselring and with an abrasive manner not to everyone's taste. He was also a somewhat eccentric figure who, besides being portly and wearing a monocle, was a keen gourmet and kept a refrigerator in his private transport aircraft to keep his wine cool.[i]

France had approximately 1,550 aircraft assigned to operations against Germany and there were 430 of the R.A.F. attached to the British Expeditionary Force in France. Most of the bombers were grouped in an ad hoc organization called the 'Advanced Air Striking Force'. In addition the R.A.F. disposed of another 1,000 aircraft in the British Isles that could interfere in the northern part of the theatre of operations. Holland had a further one hundred and forty planes, most of them built by the Fokker Company. This company had been set up by Anthony Fokker who

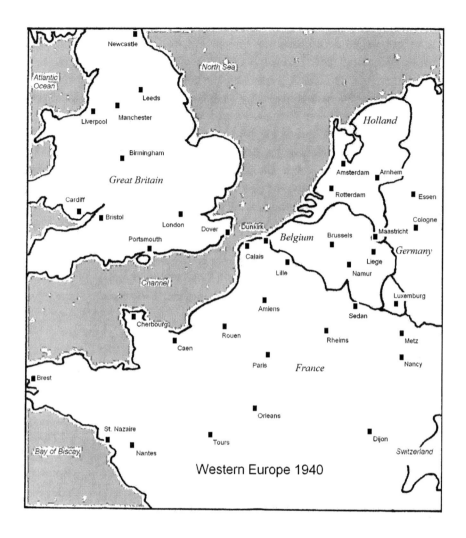

Western Europe 1940

had worked in Germany during the First World War and created famous aircraft such as the Fokker Triplane flown by Manfred von Richthofen, the Red Baron. In 1918, with Germany banned from having an air force, Fokker moved back to Holland and set up a new company. In 1940 the Fokker aircraft in use were no match for contemporary German designs.

Belgium's air force was only slightly larger. It could put around 170 aircraft into action. Having no indigenous aircraft industry its aircraft were all bought in from abroad and principally consisted of Italian Fiat CR42s and British Hurricanes and Battles. The Belgians were in the middle of a modernization program and had war come to them a year later, they would have been in a much stronger position.

The German plan of campaign was that Army Group B in the North would attack Holland and Belgium and draw the French and the British forward into those countries. Meanwhile Army Group A would attack through the Ardennes in the middle of the front. This attack would have the bulk of the armoured divisions and once they had broken through they were to drive northward to cut the allied forces in two. Army Group C would meanwhile maintain a strictly defensive stance at the southern end of the line opposite the formidable Maginot Line, a series of fortresses and redoubts linked underground and running just behind the French border all the way to Switzerland. The key to the plan was that the Allies should assume the northern thrust to be the main one and not immediately spot the advance of Army Group A who would have to negotiate the difficult country of the Ardennes to get into place for their attack. The very difficulty of the terrain would, it was hoped, convince the French that no offensive was likely in this area. The Ardennes is the area roughly bounded by Luxembourg, Sedan and Namur (see map).

The Allied right hand, or southern, wing was anchored on the Maginot Line, considered to be an impregnable series of fortifications. The position on the left was complicated by the fact that Belgium and Holland were neutral but could never resist Germany for long if attacked. The best French formations and the B.E.F. were therefore arranged along the French frontier with Belgium so that they could race to give assistance if either of the smaller countries were attacked.

Kesselring's Airfleet Two was to support the northern attack into the Low Countries. Holland's defence was based on utilizing the difficulties of its geography: the country was a mass of canals and dykes and large areas could be deliberately flooded. For this reason the German attack involved the use of paratroops to take crucial bridges and junctions and airfields and hold them until the ground forces arrived to relieve them. The first move for Airfleet Two was to attack the Dutch air force on the ground at the opening of hostilities. By way of contrast to the Polish campaign this gambit worked well: some two hundred aircraft were destroyed on the ground though probably only a third of these were front line types. The remainder of the Dutch air force fought hard but were quickly overwhelmed by superior numbers and superior equipment.

The parachute drops were successful but not without hard fighting. Nearly one hundred of the Ju52s carrying airborne troops were shot down or crashed. The Dutch had learned the lessons of Norway and made sure their airfields were well garrisoned to prevent just this kind of seizure from the air. There was extensive fighting and the defenders achieved some successes. One detachment of paratroops was detailed to take the airfield at the Hague so that transports could land airborne troops who would advance into the city and capture the Royal Family and the Government but the Dutch defenders fought the paratroops to a halt and shot down the transports when they arrived: the advance into the Hague was stillborn but in most areas the Germans eventually prevailed. Assisted by the Luftwaffe the German army carved its way into Holland and made for Rotterdam.

On 14th May the German troops were fighting in the outskirts of Rotterdam and peace negotiations were under way. An air strike was organized to hit the defenders but because the fighting was obviously on the verge of conclusion it was cancelled. Unfortunately the cancellation was too late and the bombers were already airborne. A recall message was sent but only half the planes received it and the others carried on with their bombing and left the town in ruins and eight hundred civilians dead. The effect of the bombing was magnified because Rotterdam was the world centre of the vegetable oil trade and huge stores of oil were set on fire by the bombs. This episode was widely and internationally reported as an example of terror bombing and German ruthlessness. The Germans protested that it had been an air raid with a military purpose and a mistake in any event. Their pleas were ignored. They had just bombed Warsaw without military justification and were shortly to bomb British towns indiscriminately. Moreover the basic question was: what were they doing attacking a peaceful, neutral country in the first place?

On the 15th May Dutch resistance ceased and the first part of the campaign in the West was over. One of the last casualties was General Kurt Student, the commander of the 7th Airborne Division to which all the paratroops and airborne forces used here and in Norway belonged. He was hit in the head by friendly fire and spent the next eight months recovering.

Belgian defences centered on the fortress of Eban Emael. It lay just south of Maastricht at the junction of the Meuse River and the Albert canal and it guarded three crucial bridges. This was not a fortress of the traditional kind with towers and walls: such a building would have been rapidly destroyed by artillery. Like the Maginot Line it was almost entirely underground with only gun cupolas and ventilation shafts sticking up out of the earth to be seen. Most of its roof was grassed over.

On 10th May German gliders landed right on top of it. This was the one attack against which it had no defence for its guns faced outward and the gliders landed behind them. Airborne troops threw explosives down the ventilation shafts and set charges against the gun cupolas. The result was that this supposedly impregnable fortress surrendered after a single day of fighting.

The battle against the Belgian air force was also over quickly. Much of it was caught on the ground on 10th May or destroyed in desperate battles in the air. After that first day the Belgians were no longer an effective fighting force. In the first six days of the campaign they only flew 146 operational sorties and much time was spent trying to find a safe haven on the ground where they would not be bombed.

Bombers now concentrated on assisting the advancing motorized columns below and struck targets such as bridges, marshaling yards, supply dumps, stations and troop columns up to fifty miles beyond the leading German troops who themselves carried large swastikas and fired signal rockets to identify themselves to the aircraft above. The first contact between French and Germans occurred near Namur on 12th May.

Aerial casualties were light and there was a strange absence of opposition from the French and British.

Much of the reason for the inactivity was tied up with the Byzantine complexity of the French aerial command structure which has been described as the worst in the world.[ii] The Armee de L'Air was commanded by General Vuillemin at his headquarters just outside Paris. Under him came General Tetu who was the commander of all aerial forces on the western front and was, in effect, a second supreme commander and under him again came the various air divisions but these were divided between different geographical 'Zones of Operation'. Tetu's command covered five separate zones and within each zone the local army commander had a say in how aircraft were used. In the zone covering the Belgian battlefront the army banned bombing attacks in or near urban areas for fear of civilian casualties. Given the heavily populated nature of the area where the fighting was going on this proscription virtually eliminated the use of air power altogether. It must be added that the British air contingent in this area had subordinated itself to French direction.

On the evening of the 12th General von Richthofen, commander of 8th Air Corps which was at the centre of the air support operation was settling into his new accommodation in a hotel in Maastricht when he received a telephone call to tell him that he was to move his whole corps south to the Sedan area to support the breakthrough in that area. (General von Richthofen was a distant relative of the famous Red Baron of the First World War.)

The air war in the Ardennes around Sedan got off to an uncertain start because the pre-emptive air strikes designed to knock out the Armee de L'air on the ground had gone awry. 42 airfields were attacked but only 29 were in active use and half of those were not front line fields. The Luftwaffe claimed 250-500 aircraft destroyed but the reality was closer to 40. The failure was partly due to faulty intelligence and partly to persistent cloud cover that caused a number of aircraft to miss their targets. Results from air battles were more impressive: up to 15th May, 66 British and French aircraft were shot down in this area together with another 22 that fell victim to German anti-aircraft fire.

At Sedan on the evening of the 13th May the Germans launched their crossing of the Meuse River which they had reached without, they believed, the French spotting them. In fact they had been spotted but the significance of what they were doing had not been appreciated. This crossing was the hinge on which the whole offensive hung. If they were held then the plan of campaign for the assault in the West would grind to a halt. The French army occupied the high ground on the west bank and at first poured down fire on the attackers. General Guderian, who was in charge of the assault, himself crossed the river under heavy fire to get a front line view of how the situation was progressing. When he reached the west bank he was met by the officer in charge on the spot who said to him: 'Joy-riding in canoes on the Meuse is forbidden;' a repetition of the General's own words spoken earlier during a rehearsal of the operation when he felt the attitude of his junior officers was too light-hearted![iii]

While the crossing was under way the Stukas of Sperrle's Airfleet 3 arrived, and a little later, some of von Richthofen's aircraft, and together they proceeded to pound the French defenders continuously, flying raid after raid. This was the apotheosis of the German dive bomber doctrine. The aircraft dived vertically, sirens screaming, to drop bombs with extraordinary accuracy on the troops and their trenches, blockhouses and headquarters. There was only a few minutes' respite after a raid before the next one began. Any troops would have found this treatment hard to take but the troops here were reservists of the 55th Division because the French high command had taken the view that this was a part of the front where little of moment was likely to happen. They were a mixture of older men and men of second rate medical fitness. After hours of remorseless bombardment the defenders' nerve broke and they began to flee.

Now there was a hole in the line and the German spearhead was through and into the open. Their motorized forces crossed pontoon bridges built across the Meuse and raced northwest across the French countryside. Whenever they encountered opposition, air support was called in to bomb it. Both level bombers and dive bombers took part but it was the dive bombers that took the prize. The co-operation between aircraft and ground forces was outstanding so that the Stukas were virtually flying artillery. There were occasions when only ten minutes elapsed between the time of the radio message calling for assistance and the arrival of the first aircraft.[iv] The whole operation was covered by Messerschmitt fighters to keep Allied interceptors at bay. The level bombers, Dorniers, Heinkels and Junkers 88s, also attacked targets further in the rear, in particular rail yards and junctions, in order to hinder the movement of French troops and supplies. This gave rise to one particularly tragic accident when three Heinkel 111 bombers of Bomber Wing (Kg) 51 (see Appendix One for details of aircraft unit organization) became lost in cloud and dropped their bombs on Freiburg in Germany by mistake. A primary school was hit and 22 children killed. The Propaganda Ministry promptly claimed that this was the work of Allied bombers. The pilot of the lead Heinkel was distraught and remained so until his death three months later in the Battle of Britain.[v]

From the very start of the offensive on the 10th, Allied politicians and military commanders had been shaken by the speed and ferocity of the attack. The French and British air forces at once began to take heavy casualties. One low level raid by Dorniers on the airfield at Vaux had caught the Blenheims of the R.A.F.'s 114 Squadron lined up for take-off and wiped them out. The Germans claimed 30 aircraft destroyed. That was an exaggeration but 114 Squadron was finished as a fighting force. The Advanced Air Striking Force had lost 30 of its Battle bombers in the first two days. A strange lethargy seemed to overtake the Armee de L'Air whose aircraft could barely manage one sortie per day where the R.A.F. flew two or three.

The breakthrough at Sedan caused near panic. On the morning of 15th May Churchill, who had just become Prime Minister, was woken by a telephone call from

Paul Reynaud the French Prime Minister. Reynaud was close to hysteria. 'We are beaten. We have lost the battle.' he said. 'A torrent of tanks is bursting through.' Though the phlegmatic Churchill did not take this at face value it turned out to be a stark but accurate summary of the situation.[vi]

For a short time there was a chance of halting, or at least slowing, the German advance by destroying the pontoon bridges over the Meuse. The day before the above conversation, the Allied air forces had put everything they had into doing just that. Every remaining bomber of the Advanced Air Striking Force was thrown into the attack and they were escorted by French fighters. They flew into a hornet's nest of anti-aircraft fire and defending fighters.

The anti-aircraft fire of the period came in two kinds: heavy and light. Heavy guns were intended to fire at aircraft at high altitude. The shells were large and when they burst their casing broke into shrapnel which sprayed around the bursting point. A direct hit with one of these shells was a million to one chance but near misses were common and a near miss could bring a plane down with the effect of the shrapnel damage. Light anti-aircraft fire was intended for use at low level and was produced by automatic guns firing strings of small shells that exploded on contact much like the ones carried by fighter planes. The shells could be a variety of calibres but 20, 30, 37 and 40 millimetres were the most common. The guns were often mounted together so that one gunner was firing a mounting with two or even four barrels and the volume of fire they could produce was impressive. Such guns had made great strides since World War One and one of the unpleasant surprises for all air forces in 1940 was their lethality against low flying aircraft. German anti-aircraft fire was generally called 'flak', short for 'flugabwehrkanone' and this word was frequently used for any kind of anti-aircraft fire anywhere.

Obviously the Germans were aware just how vital the Meuse bridges were and they were protected by 162 heavy guns and 135 light. They could and did put up a storm of fire. Allied bombers had to attack at low level to have any serious chance of hitting the bridges. Just over 100 attacked and 44 were shot down by flak and fighters along with 41 French fighters. There were no hits on the bridges. In addition to the aircraft shot down many more suffered varying degrees of damage and injury to their crews. This was nothing short of a disaster and when the news reached Air Marshal Barratt, the commander of the British air forces in France, he broke down in tears.[vii] He knew that in low level attacks such as this the crews had no chance of baling out and each plane lost meant a whole crew dead.

As the Germans crossed France and the Allies fell back in retreat the familiar chaos set in and the effectiveness of the Allied air forces, already severely reduced, sank to near zero. The French appealed to Churchill to send more R.A.F. fighters to France and he was at first sympathetic but the Chief of the Air Staff Sir Cyril Newall, in effect the commander of the whole R.A.F., was against this move and Sir Hugh Dowding, the chief of Fighter Command warned that to do this would compromise

Britain's ability to survive alone after the now inevitable fall of France. It was only due to the foresight and persistence of these two men that Great Britain possessed the fighters later in the summer to resist the onslaught of the Luftwaffe. As it was, the Battle of France took a terrible toll of R.A.F. fighters: by June 3rd Fighter Command's front line strength had been halved to some 470 aircraft.

Meanwhile the squadrons in France were struggling with the confusion. Paul Richey a Hurricane pilot in Number One Squadron, was shot down on the 15th May but parachuted to safety and returned to his squadron. He fell into bed exhausted that night but was woken at midnight because the squadron was moving to Vaux. He travelled by car and did not arrive until the next afternoon because the roads were choked with traffic. That night, after one hour in bed he was roused because the Germans were near and it was time to move again. After some delay it emerged the proximity of the Germans was a false alarm and he was able to go back to bed for three hours sleep before another day of duty. During the day a genuine order came through for another move and he was in his aircraft taking off at dawn the following morning.[viii] This kind of impossible existence wore pilots out very rapidly and reduced their effectiveness when they were fighting: their reactions were slowed and their judgement impaired. There were cases of aircraft landing and the pilot being fast asleep by the time it rolled to a stop. Paul Richey himself was shot down again a few days later and seriously wounded. A bullet clipped his jaw and went through his neck to lodge in the spine. He crash-landed and collapsed. The French took him to the American hospital at Neuilly-sur-Seine where his life was saved by the distinguished neuro-surgeon Professor Count Martel.[ix] Richey was evacuated to Britain, recovered and fought again. Professor Martel killed himself when the Germans captured Paris.

The Luftwaffe was now roaming the air pretty much as it pleased. Its support of the advancing armoured columns on the ground was also extremely effective. When one of these columns asked for air support by radio the Stukas always arrived in ten to twenty minutes. As soon as a counter-attack was prepared by the British or the French, Luftwaffe bombers attacked it. It was found that German fragmentation bombs, designed as anti-personnel weapons, were very effective at breaking tank tracks rendering the tanks immobile and useless even if otherwise unharmed. In addition the confusion caused by these attacks was almost as useful as the material damage done. Hans Seidemann, von Richthofen's chief of staff, commented that: 'Never again during the course of the war was such a smoothly functioning system for ….. joint operations achieved.'[x]

On 18th May Guderian's tanks had reached the old Somme battlefield only 50 miles from the coast. Two days later they took Amiens. Two days after that they reached the coast at Abbeville and the Allied forces were split in two. By then the Armee de L'Air had lost 420 aircraft on the ground alone. The R.A.F. contingent of the B.E.F. in France began withdrawing back to England on 19th. It had lost 200 aircraft including 128 destroyed on the ground since the offensive began (and this excludes the Advanced Air Striking Force).

The Germans too were having their problems. Though their level bombers had the range to remain at their bases in western Germany their Messerschmitt fighters and Stukas had to move forward from base to base in much the same way as the Allied air forces moved back. For the victor the problems are less but they are still material. The Germans found that there were few operating airfields for them to use and what there were, became grossly overcrowded. The problems of bringing forward fuel, ammunition and spare parts were the chief limiting factor on the Luftwaffe's air operations. Huge stocks of French fuel were captured but the Germans dared not use them in case they had been deliberately tampered with to damage engines, a fear that turned out to be unfounded. As the spearheads neared the coast they came within range of British fighters of 11 Group operating from bases in England and discovered that the R.A.F. was far from beaten. Between 21st and 25th May 25 percent of Luftwaffe losses from all causes were to such fighters.

As the ground forces approached Dunkirk where British and French forces were preparing for evacuation they encountered marshy land cut by canals which was difficult going for motorized forces. They were also exhausted. Goering went to Hitler on 23rd May and said: 'My Fuehrer, leave the destruction of the enemy surrounded at Dunkirk to me and my Luftwaffe.'[xi] Accordingly Hitler gave his controversial order to Guderian to halt and the Luftwaffe began an assault on the port. The bombers too were becoming exhausted and there was never any real prospect of aircraft stopping the evacuation particularly since the weather was far from ideal and the R.A.F. fought hard to protect it, setting up a rota of hourly fighter patrols over the coastal area. On 26th May they had their best day shooting down 30 German aircraft. On the other hand the Dunkirk 'miracle' was not achieved without cost. 89 merchant ships of various kinds were sunk and the Royal Navy lost 8 destroyers with a further 21 damaged.

On 29th May Alan Deere a Spitfire pilot with 54 Squadron was flying over Dunkirk when he saw a German Dornier bomber and attacked it. The bomber returned fire and hit the Spitfire's cooling system causing the engine to overheat. Deere knew he had no chance of getting back to England and had to land at once before his engine seized up. He managed to crash-land on the beach a few miles east of Dunkirk but was knocked out in the process and cut his head badly. The wound was dressed by a Belgian woman and Deere hitched a lift to Dunkirk with a British army lorry. There he saw thousands of soldiers queuing for the chance of a place on a boat for England and jumped the queue to get onto a destroyer so that he could get straight back into action. He was landed at Dover and caught a train to London. The ticket collector tried to throw him off the train because he did not have a ticket but relented when a senior army officer intervened. By 11.15pm he was back in his squadron mess at Hornchurch from where he had set out early that morning.[xii]

After Dunkirk the defeat of France was, in effect, just a matter of time. The

German armies turned west along the coast and southwest toward Paris. Although the Armee de L'Air still had plenty of aircraft on paper, the confusion of defeat and retreat had reduced its effectiveness to the extent that the Germans enjoyed near complete air superiority and were able to bomb targets such as airfields, troop columns and railway stations as far afield as Lyons and Marseilles with impunity. Their main problems remained those of supply and the wear and tear of six weeks hard campaigning. Even so, it was possible to begin winding down. The bomber wing Kg54, for instance, was withdrawn to Germany to re-equip with the Ju88.

At the end of May reports reached the Luftwaffe that the French were bringing in reinforcements from North Africa. Accordingly, on 1st June some 125 bombers from Kgs 53 and 55 carried out a raid on targets in Marseilles and the Rhone valley. The Marseilles – Lyons railway line was cut in several places and marshaling yards were hit and a liner in Marseillies harbour was sunk. This was the longest mission flown so far by German bombers and it took them over Switzerland in violation of Swiss airspace. The Swiss did not take this lying down and their fighters (Me109s) attacked and shot down several German bombers. The results of this raid were judged to be unsatisfactory insofar as factories and airfields around Marseilles that were targeted, were not hit and so another raid was carried out. This raid had a fighter escort for the section of the flight over Switzerland and they shot down one Swiss fighter without any German losses. Targets around Marseilles were bombed together with Lyons-Bron airfield. The Germans claimed 15 aircraft destroyed on the ground there but accurate information about the effect of these raids was never collected. Shortly after this, the Italians took over responsibility for the south of France and they had no motivation to collate damage records for the benefit of the Luftwaffe.

On 3rd June there was a heavy raid on targets around Paris, particularly airfields, involving virtually the Luftwaffe's whole frontline strength. Reconnaissance had revealed that there were up to 1,000 French aircraft packed into the airfields around Paris so, at the end of May, Hoffmann von Waldau, Operations Officer at OKL, the Luftwaffe High Command, had planned a major raid to hit these, together with the aircraft factories situated around the city. It was codenamed 'Paula'. It was not until 3rd June that the weather was suitable and on that afternoon 640 bombers escorted by 460 fighters took off and flew to the French capital. This was supposed to be a knockout blow against the French air force and aircraft industry. The French had foreknowledge of the attack through code-breaking but the take-off signal for their fighters was broadcast from the Eiffel Tower in order to co-ordinate the attack. The effect was the reverse since many squadrons did not hear it and only 80 fighters intercepted the raid. They shot down ten Germans for 15 losses of their own. One of the German casualties was Colonel Josef Kammhuber, commanding officer of Kg51. He was shot down, injured and captured, to be freed on France's fall. Promotion and a vital role in Luftwaffe planning were to follow. German bombing was scattered that day and though propaganda claimed 400 French aircraft destroyed on the ground the real figure was less than 50. Damage to the aircraft factories was light, though 250 people were killed.

On 10th June France's woes redoubled when Italy declared war on her and on Great Britain and attacked her Mediterranean border.

On 14th June German troops entered Paris and the end was obviously close. British troops were evacuating from ports in the West and the Luftwaffe did its best to intercept them. Since Dunkirk they had improved their skills against shipping and much damage was caused. On 17th June this work reached its terrible zenith when Ju88s sank the 16,000 ton liner Lancastria off St. Nazaire with the loss of 4-6,000 lives: no one knows exactly how many were aboard. The passengers included large numbers of soldiers and many British nationals resident in France including most of the embassy staff. The ship rolled over and spilled large amounts of oil into the sea, some of which caught fire. Many passengers in the sea were choked to death by the oil and others were reportedly machine-gunned by the attacking aircraft. Some sources say that one third of all the casualties suffered by the British army in France in 1940 were lost on this ship.[xiii] At the time this was the worst ever loss of life in a sea disaster and the British government kept the news secret until July when foreign press comment on the event made continuing secrecy futile.

The classic, glamorous fighter pilot. This is Flight Lieutenant Edgar "Cobber" Kain an early R.A.F. ace killed in France in 1940. ©Imperial War Museum (C188)

On 24th June the French government accepted terms and a ceasefire was effective the next morning. The campaign was over. The world was stunned: mighty France had been utterly defeated by Germany in six weeks and Hitler now ruled continental Europe from eastern Poland to the Atlantic.

For the Luftwaffe the campaign had been another triumph and it eclipsed Poland and Norway. They had outfought their opponents at every turn. Partly this was a matter of better equipment, partly of experience gained in Poland and Norway and partly the sheer difference in morale. The lessons of the Polish campaign had been learned save only the admittedly important, issue of supply. The Armee de L'Air had lost 574 aircraft destroyed in the air and some 700 on the ground or about 80% of the number that started the campaign. The R.A.F. lost 959 aircraft including the vast majority of those that went to France. The victory did not come cheaply however. The Luftwaffe lost 1,129 planes in action and another 300 in accidents and wastage. This was 28% of their starting force. A small compensation was the release of Luftwaffe aircrew captured by the French including Josef Kammhuber and Germany's foremost ace Werner Moelders. Other pilots had come to the fore with outstanding performances such as Adolf Galland and Helmut Wieck and the top scorer in the campaign, Wilhelm Balthasar who shot down 22 planes. The top French ace was Edmond La Meslee who shot down 16. Considering the fact that he was usually outnumbered and flew a second division Hawk 75, this was an astonishing achievement. The leading R.A.F. ace was Edgar 'Cobber' Kain who shot down 17 aircraft and was the War's first fighter pilot winner of the Distinguished Flying Cross. He died on 6th June when showing off with low level aerobatics over his own base. Trying to roll his plane when too low he crashed and was killed instantly.

The German armed forces had shown that the way to win wars in the modern age was to win control of the air and then use your air force to strike at the enemy's ground forces in close co-operation with your own. In particular, spearheads led by tanks now took the role once assigned to cavalry and aircraft could be used to knock out any obstruction the tanks encountered and to keep their flanks clear of counterattacks. This lesson was rapidly absorbed by military thinkers in all the major powers but in Germany it had something of a negative effect for two reasons. The first was the natural assumption by the inventors of the system that they were leagues ahead of their competitors and could relax and let others try to catch up. The second was the feeling that the war was won and therefore effort expended now on armaments and military thinking was effort wasted. For these reasons the Luftwaffe in particular, allowed itself to some degree, to stagnate. Aircraft production did not increase and new types were not developed. In particular, no thought was given to what would follow the Ju87 Stuka, which was already showing its age, or to how to counter enemy tanks.

Peace seemed very close. The only remaining issue was Great Britain.

CHAPTER SEVEN

The Battle of Britain

Adolf Hitler was as surprised as anyone by his swift victory in the West but he was now free to turn his attention to his real goal: the conquest of the vast spaces of Eastern Europe which would provide 'lebensraum', or living space, for the German people. The only nagging problem was that Great Britain did not open negotiations for peace as he had expected. He therefore decided that England must be subdued by invasion, or did he? There has been much argument over the years about his real intentions. One school of thought has it that he never really intended an invasion but went through a pretence designed to force Britain to the negotiating table. General Gunther Blumentritt, operations officer on Field Marshal von Rundstedt's's staff was interviewed by the British military theorist and historian Basil Liddell Hart after the war. Von Rundstedt was the man in command of the army's invasion force and Blumentritt, who was at the centre of planning for Operation Sealion, the invasion of Britain, told Liddell Hart:

'Among ourselves we talked of it as bluff and looked forward to news that an understanding with Britain had been reached'.[i]

Certainly no one had foreseen this situation and there was no detailed plan for an invasion though the German Navy had prepared an outline as far back as 1939. Not until July 16th 1940 did Hitler finally make a definite decision that there would be an invasion and numerous German military files available after the war are strong evidence that he was serious, or was taken seriously. Moreover one has to ask what the hesitation was about if the proposed invasion was only a sham. There was promptly an outburst of frenzied planning by both the army and the navy in order to be ready for the invasion while good summer weather prevailed. It was immediately apparent that this was no simple undertaking and the army and the navy disagreed about the proper approach to it. The army wanted landings on a broad front but the navy argued that it simply did not have the resources to support this. The dispute finally had to be resolved by Hitler himself who came down on the side of the navy. He was clearly not happy about the situation however. Here was a complex and critical operation that was being carried out under great time pressure and without the usual detailed and meticulous planning for which the German armed forces were justifiably famous. It is hard to resist the impression that this was one big risk too far and that he was only too glad to find an excuse to call off the invasion when his air assault did not produce the promised results. For there was one thing on which all parties were agreed: for Sealion to succeed The Luftwaffe must first achieve complete air superiority. Without it the Royal Navy, which hugely outnumbered the German Navy, would send the invasion ships to the bottom of the sea. Moreover, each German campaign so far had started with an all-out successful attack on the enemy's air force and it was an integral part of the High Command's strategic thinking.

Goering was confident that his Luftwaffe could destroy the R.A.F.. He estimated that it would take only four days to defeat it but that complete destruction would take from two to four weeks. The invasion was provisionally set for 15th September.

At the close of the Battle of France Airfleet Two occupied the low countries and the Pas de Calais and Airfleet Three, which had been further south, had swung round north-westward to reach the coast to the west of Two. The boundary between them was the mouth of the River Seine. The end of June and early July had been a time of rest and recuperation while efforts were made to fill the gaps in the ranks and bring unit strength back up to par. By the time the Germans were ready to renew the struggle they could deploy some 950 fighters, 1200 level bombers, 300 dive bombers and 150 reconnaissance aircraft. These are the gross figures: on any particular morning the number of planes actually available to take off and fly a mission would be about 20 percent less. They also had available the aircraft of Airfleet Five in Norway which could attack targets in Scotland and the North of England. These numbered 130 level bombers and some 30 fighters with adequate range. The level bombers were mainly He111s and Do17s with a sprinkling of the newer Ju88s thrown in. Two thirds of the fighters were Me109s and the balance the under-performing twin engine Me110s. The dive bombers were, of course, all Stukas although it must be recalled that the Ju88s had the capacity to dive bomb if required.

The Luftwaffe's biggest advantage was its experience. The majority of the pilots had now fought their way through three successful campaigns and knew all the tricks of survival in the air. Some of them had experience that went even further back. Johannes Fink, commanding officer of the bomber wing Kg2 had fought through the whole of World War One in the infantry. He was 45 years old in 1940 and was promoted to general immediately after the battle. Otto Hoehne of Kg54 had been a fighter pilot in the first war. Many men had experience of the Spanish Civil War. One of these was Adolf Galland. Galland was a Westphalian of Huguenot origin and before the war was over he would be made Inspector-General of Fighters. At the start of the Battle of Britain he had scored 17 victories and at the end of it he had 58. All told, he was an extraordinary character. In training he suffered a bad crash and severe facial injuries including damage to his eyesight. He was eventually passed fit to fly again because he gained admittance to the medical offices by night and memorized the eye chart. In Poland he flew a ground attack aircraft but he wanted to fly fighters so he persuaded a doctor to certify that his aircraft's open cockpit was giving him rheumatism. During the Battle of Britain he attended a conference with

Goering during which the latter was critical of the fighter force. Goering then asked Galland what single thing he would like to have that would improve the situation. Galland famously answered: 'I should like an outfit of Spitfires.' (This was not a serious request: it was simply a piece of insolence in response to what he saw as unjust criticism.)[ii] He was a keen cigar smoker but was banned by Hitler, who was vehemently opposed to smoking, from being photographed in public with a cigar. He obeyed this order but the cigar was in his hand at all other times. He even had his ground crew solder an ash tray into the cockpit of his aircraft so that he could smoke while flying.[iii] He was a colourful character but also a deadly effective fighter pilot.

Nowhere did the Luftwaffe's experience show to better advantage than in its fighter tactics. One of the keys to effective fighter patrols was flying in the right formation. During the 1930s the different air forces reached their own conclusions on this subject and they generally put neatness of appearance before combat utility. The R.A.F., for instance, usually flew in tight groups of three planes and had a series of choreographed moves for squadron attacks on formations of bombers. Fighting in Spain had taught the Germans that air combat was too fast moving and too disorganized for elaborate formation flying and their top pilot, Werner Moelders, had developed the best solution which was shortly to be adopted by all the major air forces. This was the so-called 'finger four', a loose formation of four planes composed of two leaders and two wingmen whose sole job was to watch the rear of the leaders so that the latter could concentrate their attention on hunting the enemy. The position of the planes roughly resembled the tips of the four fingers on your hand and they flew far enough apart that the risk of collision was minimal. This formation easily broke up into the basic unit of two planes. By contrast the tight groups of three forced each pilot to devote his attention to keeping formation and avoiding a collision and not to looking out for the enemy. Squadron attacks on bombers were simply free-for-alls because it was apparent that no real control could be exercised and all combats tended to break down into wild confusion. It should be emphasized that the preceding applied to fighter aircraft only. For bombers quite different considerations obtained. They needed to fly as close together as possible in order to derive mutual benefit from each other's defensive guns and achieve maximum concentration of their bombs on the target. Bomber pilots could concentrate on formation flying and leave spotting the enemy to their crew.

As a result of experience in the campaign in France and the Low Countries it was decided to concentrate all the fighter planes in each Airfleet under one single commander to be known as a 'Jagdfuehrer', usually shortened to 'Jafu'. Airfleet 2 appointed Theo Osterkamp to this post. He was a popular figure generally called 'Onkel' (Uncle). He had been a fighter ace in World War One and shot down two more aircraft in this conflict but he was really too old to fly a fighter plane in combat and this new staff post suited him. Airfleet 3 appointed Werner Junck, another World

War One pilot who was later to be the commander of Luftwaffe forces in Iraq during that country's brief war with Britain the next year.

The plan was simple: the R.A.F. would be attacked in the air and on the ground. Raids would also be launched against the aircraft industry so that lost aircraft could not be replaced. The bombing would start with air bases in the south of England and move north as the resistance weakened until airbases in the whole country had been blitzed. This operation would go into effect in August and the second half of July would be devoted to clearing British shipping out of the English Channel and drawing up the R.A.F. into attritional battles trying to protect it. The concept was much the same as that used against Poland or France without much thought being given to the different circumstances. The three most important of these were the presence of a large body of water between the Luftwaffe and its targets, the presence of radar and the existence of a large, well equipped and aggressive enemy fighter force. It must also be appreciated that Luftwaffe intelligence was very poor so that those who had to make the strategic decisions at bases in France were often woefully misinformed about such matters as the nature of particular targets or the effect of bombing raids. An outstanding example of this failing is that Spitfires were principally produced at one factory in Southampton but Luftwaffe intelligence thought this factory belonged to another company that made bombers so it was not a priority target.[iv]

Unlike the Luftwaffe, the R.A.F. had foreseen the present situation, or something like it, for a long time and had made careful preparations. It too, used the end of June and the beginning of July to bring its squadrons up to strength. The ill-fated Battle light bombers were retired wholesale and everything possible was done to increase the number of Spitfires and Hurricanes in the front line. By early July they could deploy 850 of them and the number was growing fast. The government had appointed a specific Minister of Aircraft Production. This was Lord Beaverbrook, a Canadian born newspaper magnate who was an outstanding administrator. His new-world enthusiasm and directness cut through British government red tape and achieved an almost miraculous increase in the output of Hurricanes and Spitfires from the factories. He had a very personal stake in this work since his only son, Max Aitken, was a Spitfire pilot. In July single-engine fighter production topped 500 planes while comparable German production was only a little over 200. This comparison also reflects the fact that Great Britain was not slow to realize that it was in a struggle for its very existence and had accordingly done everything possible to put its economy on a war footing while Germany did not fully mobilize its huge industrial capacity until much later in the war. Indeed, after the fall of France, Hitler had proposed a partial demobilization of the army. So efficient did British fighter production become that the Battle of Britain had scarcely started before it was apparent that the R.A.F.'s problem was going to be a lack of pilots rather than aircraft.

Because of Trenchard's work between the wars Great Britain had a network of well-built and well-run air bases so placed that fighters could reach any part of the country in a very short time. This was of particular importance in the southeast where the principal threat was correctly perceived to lie. Britain is not a very large island and if a bomber crossed the south coast heading for London it would arrive within fifteen minutes. This did not allow enough time for a force of fighters to be alerted, take off and climb to the height of the bombers. What was needed was an early warning system and that was what radar provided. By using radar the R.A.F. could spot enemy formations while they were still forming up over the coast of France and get their fighter squadrons into the air in time to intercept.

The radar scanners took the form of a chain of tall towers along the south and east coasts. They were very large and conspicuous. Even German radar, which was in a less developed state, used smaller and more efficient scanners. The scanners produced a picture on a cathode ray tube in a hut at the base of the tower. An additional device enabled friendly and hostile aircraft to be distinguished. The picture was a series of lines quite indecipherable to anyone untrained. The information gleaned from these pictures was telephoned to a control centre where it was married up with later sightings by an observer corps on British territory and the known information about R.A.F. formations to give a continuous unfolding picture of the situation in the air. This was presented in the form of wooden markers that were moved about on a very large scale map on a table. The moving was done by a team of female auxiliaries armed with long-handled pushers somewhat resembling a croupier's rake. A gallery above the table contained senior officers who could make operational decisions on the basis of the situation before them and controllers who were in radio contact with the R.A.F. squadron leaders in the air and could guide them to the nearest enemy formation. There were a number of these so-called 'Operations Rooms'. The master room was at the R.A.F.'s Fighter Command headquarters at Bentley Priory in north London and all information initially flowed there. Once it was confirmed as reliable, it was passed on by telephone to subsidiary operations rooms in each 'Sector'.

For the purpose of air defence the whole of Great Britain was divided into areas called 'Groups'. There were four of these: 10 Group in the Southwest, 11 Group in the Southeast, 12 Group in the Midlands and 13 Group which covered the north of England and Scotland. Ninety percent of the Battle of Britain was fought in the area of 11 Group. Each group was divided into sectors and each sector contained one 'sector airfield' that held an operations room. The operations room could set any squadron in motion with a single telephone call. Hence the famous order to 'scramble'. The squadron then got into the air as fast as it could manage and a controller then directed it to the nearest enemy formation.

The officer in charge of 11 Group was Air Vice Marshal Keith Park. Park was a popular and approachable officer who kept his own Hurricane in which he flew

A German Heinkel 111 bomber takes hits on its left wing during the Battle of Britain. The port engine has stopped. ©Imperial War Museum (CH 1830)

unannounced to his various airfields to talk to the men at the front line, always a sign of a good commander. He did this in white flying overalls that bore no indication of rank which led to him landing at one airfield and being reprimanded by a humble sergeant for parking his aircraft in the wrong place. If Park had a fault it was that he could be too abrupt and abrasive. Visiting 222 Squadron during the battle and talking to a group of its pilots he spotted that an Irish pilot had a small Irish flag painted on his Spitfire. The dumbstruck pilot was firmly rebuked in front of his colleagues and told to remove the flag immediately. As Park stamped off, all the pilots went back to their game of cards. The Irish flag remained where it was. He could display this kind of insensitivity even with senior officers and he was in due course to pay dearly for this failing.[v]

Park's superior was air Chief Marshal Sir Hugh Dowding, the head of Fighter Command. Dowding was an effective and experienced commander for whom the Battle of Britain was his finest hour. He was, however, personally aloof and distant and in the higher reaches of the R.A.F. command, where he was considered difficult and uncooperative, he was tolerated rather than liked. He had lost his wife some years before and brought up their only son alone and this experience had no doubt added to his prickly demeanour. Strangely he got on very well with Beaverbrook though the two could not have been more unlike in character. Perhaps this was because Dowding's son too was a fighter pilot. In any event it was a happy circumstance for the defence of Britain because they spoke on the telephone almost every day and developed a close understanding.

The pilots of R.A.F. Fighter Command were a thoroughly professional body and many of their members had now picked up a leavening of experience in France and over Dunkirk. The service attracted adventurous young men from all over the British Empire and even further afield. Paul Richey's Number One squadron was commanded by an Irishman and included pilots from America, Australia, New Zealand and Canada as well as Englishmen. One of the leading aces of the battle, Adolph 'Sailor' Malan, was a South African. His coolness under pressure was legendary. Over Dunkirk a Messerschmitt put a bullet through his gun-sight so he fitted a spare on the spot in the middle of the fight.[vi] Al Deere, another ace, whom we have met at Dunkirk, later described his experiences in a best-selling autobiography.[vii] He was a tough New Zealander who boxed and played rugby for the R.A.F. as well as flying. Of course the majority were English and men such as 'Ginger' Lacey, Bob Stanford Tuck and Bob Doe were to play a leading part. It is impossible to avoid mention of perhaps the most famous pilot of all, who embodied the idea of fighting on, whatever the odds. Douglas Bader joined the R.A.F. in 1928 but was dreadfully injured in a flying accident in 1931 when he lost both legs and had to retire to civilian life. When the war started the demand for experienced pilots was so great that he was allowed to sign up again and, despite artificial legs, soon proved himself one of the best combat pilots of all.

All these men and, indeed the whole country, had been galvanized by the intransigent defiance of the Prime Minister, Winston Churchill. They knew their backs were to the wall and that they were fighting for the survival of their homeland. Morale in Fighter Command was high.

There are two views as to when the Battle of Britain started. Some say that it began in August when Goering's Plan for the destruction of the R.A.F. within four weeks was put into action with raids on airfields, but the other view holds that it began in mid-July, specifically, on 10th because it was from this date that serious clashes between the two sides began over the Channel, or 'Kanal' as German pilots called it.

An obvious target for the Luftwaffe was British coastal shipping particularly in the Channel. Germany was well aware of Britain's dependence on seaborne imports and was beginning a campaign of attacks on British shipping by every means. In fact coastal convoys in the channel and around the south coast generally were not vital to Britain's commercial existence and when they were discontinued because of German raids much of their cargo was simply carried by rail. The Germans hoped however, that the R.A.F. would come up in force to defend the convoys and be shot down. On July 10th over 100 German planes, Do17s with an escort of Messerschmitts, attacked a convoy off Dover and were themselves attacked by a force of Hurricanes. Other, smaller raids were made on a convoy off the north Kent coast and on a small airfield at Raynham in Essex. In the day's actions, the Luftwaffe lost 13 planes and the R.A.F. lost 6. This day set the general pattern of actions during July. The 25th was probably the day that saw the fiercest action, with the Luftwaffe losing 16 aircraft and the R.A.F. losing 7. On 11th July, off Deal, Al Deere survived a head-on collision with a Messerschmitt and crash landed in a Kentish field in a burning Spitfire. He had to smash his way out of the cockpit when the hood jammed and was lucky to escape with only minor injuries.[viii] He had already been shot down over Dunkirk at the end of May as we have seen. These misadventures do not mean he was an ineffective pilot however. During this period he had also shot down five German planes.

The month cost the Luftwaffe 138 aircraft against the R.A.F.'s 70. This was a ratio of roughly two to one. In theory the Luftwaffe could afford this ratio simply because they had many more planes but the reality was that it was far from satisfactory. As we have seen, German aircraft production was substantially lower than British. The more meaningful contrast is in loss of pilots and here the Luftwaffe were at a big disadvantage because they were not fighting over their own territory. If they lost ten aircraft, that usually meant ten crews as well, though a few were saved by their very efficient air-sea rescue service. On the other hand the R.A.F. were fighting over home territory most of the time and this, crucially, meant that pilots shot down were often able to parachute to safety and were flying again the next day. Al Deere was a case in point. July was their worst month in terms of proportion of pilots saved because so much of the fighting was over water and at this stage R.A.F. air-sea rescue was very poor indeed. As the action moved to the skies above England this advantage came strongly into play. For instance, on 15th September, often regarded as the climactic day of the battle, the R.A.F. lost 25 planes shot down but only 13 pilots. As a general rule of thumb 50 percent of the pilots shot down lived to fight again. On the July figures the goal of wearing down the R.A.F. was going to take a very long time to achieve. The efficiency and fighting spirit of their English opponents was something of a shock to the majority of Luftwaffe pilots.

Already by the end of July certain other trends were becoming apparent. The Stuka was showing an alarming vulnerability in circumstances of less than complete air superiority. Likewise the Me110 was proving to be more of a liability than an asset. The R.A.F. were also finding that some of their equipment was not up to the job. It had two squadrons each of Blenheims and Defiants. The Blenheims were a fighter conversion of the light bomber and it was becoming clear that they had not the manoeuverability to compete with the single-engine fighters. It was not long before they were relegated to night fighting. The Boulton Paul Defiant was an aircraft that looked like a Hurricane but had a rotating turret behind the pilot manned by a gunner with four machine guns. It had no fixed, forward-firing guns. The idea was that it would have an all-round field of fire (except straight ahead) and would not be defenceless against the rear attack as were conventional interceptors. Indeed it proved to be quite effective against bombers because it could stand off to the side of them where their defensive fire could not reach. Unfortunately it was underpowered and slow and could not manoeuver adequately. At first German fighter pilots attacked it from the rear mistaking it for a Hurricane but as soon as they learned to be careful about their aircraft recognition the Defiant was slaughtered. On 19th July, 141 Squadron was jumped by Messerschmitts while patrolling nine aircraft strong. Five Defiants were shot down and the rest only saved by the intervention of a force of Hurricanes. When the survivors returned to base one crashed on landing and another was so badly damaged that it was a write-off. Seven out of nine aircraft had been lost in one mission which was unacceptable. 141 Squadron was promptly withdrawn from the battle.

In the early part of August the fighting died down because of bad weather. On the 4th, for the first time, there were no losses on either side. On the 8th, on the other hand, the weather cleared and the Luftwaffe attacked a convoy off the Isle of Wight in great strength. The result was the toughest day's fighting yet. The R.A.F. lost 20 planes and the Luftwaffe 30.

Goering's drive for the destruction of the R.A.F. was due to start on 13th August and on the 12th there were heavy raids on coastal airfields and on the radar towers along the coast by way of preparation. The Germans were by now aware that the R.A.F. had some kind of control system that allowed their fighters to appear at the right place at the right time and they knew the radar towers were something to do with it. It seems strange, in retrospect, that they never grasped how the whole system worked considering that they knew all about radar themselves and in a couple of years' time would have a similar fighter control system of their own. The radar towers were attacked by Me110s acting as fighter-bombers. They were very effective and several towers were put out of action but all except one were repaired in hours. Similarly three coastal airfields were heavily hit but were all back in full operation by the next morning. In the evening the Luftwaffe launched several probing raids to test the effect of their attacks on British fighter control. They were disappointed to find it apparently unaffected. These raids demonstrate, once again, a factor that was to bedevil bombing strategy by all parties throughout the war: the speed of recovery of a damaged target.

The 13th August was 'Adlertag', or 'Eagle Day', the first day of the offensive but it got off to an inauspicious start when poor weather led Goering to order a postponement until the afternoon. His order was not in time to stop some aircraft from flying including KG2 led by Johannes Fink. His bombers flew to attack targets in England without their escort and should have been decimated but, just to show that the Luftwaffe were not the only ones who could make a mess of things British radar operators somehow missed this formation and the observers on the ground reported it as being a small nuisance raid only. The result was that it bombed its targets and returned with the loss of only five planes. In the afternoon the 'go ahead' was given and the raids began in earnest with a major attack on airfields in the west of the country. From now on, for the rest of August and into September the fighting was intense except for five days of poor weather from the 19th.

This was the period that gave rise to the classic picture of the Battle of Britain: pilots sitting in deckchairs reading or playing chess in the bright sunshine and waiting for the command to 'scramble' that would have them racing for their Spitfires. In reality the strain was so intense that most of the pilots were exhausted and spent every spare minute asleep. They were on readiness every minute of daylight through the long summer days and every man knew that each day could well be the day of his death. In addition, during this time it became increasingly apparent that Fighter Command's ability to resist was slowly ebbing away. The strategy of attacking airfields was working. The most obvious result of bombing an airfield was the large craters that appeared in its runways but they were the easiest to repair and were almost invariably filled in overnight. Much more dangerous was the damage to communications. If an airfield's telephone lines were out of order it could do nothing because it could not receive orders. If its power was down it could barely function at all and damaged aircraft certainly could not be repaired. If its gas mains were broken all work had to stop until they were repaired for fear of an explosion. Hits on workshops and living quarters added to the problems. Manston airfield in Kent had to be abandoned because it was bombed so often and so effectively. The morale of ground crew there cracked and they retreated to an air raid shelter and refused direct orders to come out.[ix]

During this period the strain on the pilots reached its most intense. Al Deere shot down five aircraft during August but he was shot down himself on the 15th and though he was able to bail out he broke his wrist. He continued flying however and was shot down again on 28th. On 31st he was taking off with two other planes when a raid started and bombs exploded amongst them causing all three aircraft to crash. Deere's Spitfire turned over and slid along the ground with his head pressed into the earth. He was then trapped in his cockpit, upside down, with fuel dripping around him. One of the other pilots managed to free him though, himself injured and unable to walk. The third pilot appeared several hours later having come down in a river outside the airfield.[x] Despite losing part of his scalp Deere was flying again the next day now with one arm in plaster and a large bandage around his head. 54 Squadron's losses were so heavy that on 3rd September they were moved to the North of England to rest and refit in quieter territory.

The 15th August was the climax of this part of the battle with the Luftwaffe flying more sorties than on any other day in the campaign. Bombers in Norway joined in and attacked targets in the North of England. The distance they had to fly was too far for them to be escorted by Me109s and they suffered heavily from attacks by fighters of 13 Group. This came as an unpleasant surprise since German intelligence was sure that all the R.A.F.'s fighters were engaged in the fighting in the South. The bombers in Norway were thereafter transferred to France to join their colleagues. At the same time the decision was made to withdraw the Stukas from the battle. Their losses had become too severe to be born. The British regarded this as a great victory because the Stuka was the terror weapon that had blazed a trail for the Wehrmacht across Europe. In fact it should never have been used in the campaign other than to attack ships. Stukas were a short-range precision weapon that depended on local air superiority to survive and the whole point about the Battle of Britain was that the Luftwaffe did not have that superiority.

On 16th Fighter Command won its only Victoria Cross which was awarded to Flight Lieutenant J. B. Nicholson. Though wounded, he remained in his blazing Hurricane long enough to shoot down a Me110 before bailing out with severe burns. Dreadful burn injuries about the head and hands were all too common for R.A.F. pilots because the petrol tank in both Spitfire and Hurricane was situated just in front of the instrument panel and if it caught fire the flames streamed back into the cockpit. After the battle design changes improved the situation but fire remained a terrible hazard.

As the raids continued the defenders learned that the Spitfire performed better against fighters and the Hurricane against bombers and so, wherever possible, controllers sent their squadrons into battle in such a way as to take advantage of this fact. On 18th August the joint casualties of both sides were the heaviest of the battle and this date has become known as 'the hardest day.'

When bad weather enforced a break it was possible for both sides to review their position. The big problem for the R.A.F. was the shortage of pilots. Since the battle began they had lost 100 pilots killed or missing and another 60 sufficiently badly injured that they would take no more part in this particular battle. Replacements had amounted to only a third of losses. All kinds of expedients were now utilized to find more pilots. Men were transferred from the Fleet Air Arm, from Bomber Command and from army co-operation work. Moreover the considerable number of exiled Czech and Polish pilots were at last put into the front line. In fact this shortage was partly self-induced. Hundreds of trained pilots were carrying out administrative duties and there were many more, given basic training before the war and then released back into civilian life for lack of facilities for operational training. Moreover Fighter Command persisted with its policy of having more pilots on each squadron than there were aeroplanes. At times this worked well because a squadron could lose a few pilots and still have enough to fly all its planes but it also meant that every day many squadrons sent off twelve pilots on a mission while another three or four sat in the mess and read the newspapers.[xi]

The problems the R.A.F. was having were not apparent to the Germans. To them it seemed that there were as many British fighter planes as ever and their strategy was not working as expected. Goering held a conference to consider the situation at Karinhall, his estate near Berlin attended, amongst others, by Adolf Galland. Galland later recalled being lectured by Goering about the shortcomings of the German fighter arm at this meeting.[xii] He resented these strictures, feeling that the fighter arm was doing the very best it could. In conclusion it was decided to move the focus of the bombing to the inner airfields around London and to order the fighters to give the bombers close escort. Galland and others argued against the escort order but to no avail. The course of the war was to show that Galland was right in tactical terms. Fighters always did better if given the freedom to roam. On the other hand the effectiveness of Luftwaffe attacks over the next two weeks seemed to improve. The change of targets was a better move than Goering realized because the inner airfields around London were the sector airfields that controlled the defensive system.

On 24th August the weather improved and the battle was renewed. In the next few days Hornchurch, Biggin Hill and Kenley airfields all suffered severely. On 2nd September Biggin Hill was particularly badly damaged by a flight of eight Do17s from bomber wing Kg3 who were low level specialists and came in to bomb at hangar-top height. None of these key bases however, was actually forced to cease operations other than for a matter of two or three hours. The real damage was once again done in the air. On 31st August the R.A.F. suffered its worst day's losses of the battle so far with 39 planes shot down and 14 pilots killed. In the two weeks from 24th August 466 planes were lost while only 270 new and repaired ones were available to replace them. In the same period 103 pilots were lost.

At the start of September Dowding was forced to reorganize Fighter Command to accommodate its declining power. Up to now he had rotated squadrons out of the front line when they were exhausted and brought in fresh units to replace them. Now there were no more fresh units and he divided all squadrons into three classes. The first class units did the fighting, second class units guarded the rest of the country and the third class units became simply training organizations to provide pilots for the other two classes. In reality this was an admission that the number of squadrons could not be maintained. Moreover the quality of pilots was falling as the proportion of 'new boys' rose. A fresh pilot was next to useless until he had some experience under his belt and it was in those first few missions that he was at his most vulnerable. Meanwhile, during the first week of September no fewer than 750 bombers attacked airfields each day. Fighter Command was reeling from the punches.

The Luftwaffe was also reeling from its losses. That same week had cost them more than 100 bombers. August had cost them more than 600 aircraft in total. Morale amongst the pilots was waning and there was a well-known malady that began to afflict some of them known as 'Kanalkrankheit' or 'Channel sickness'. In effect this was battle fatigue. Luftwaffe intelligence had repeatedly said that the R.A.F. was down to its last few planes yet they rose to meet each new raid in seemingly undiminished numbers. The deadline for the invasion of Britain was drawing near and Goering was desperate to force a decision, so on 7th September he decided on a change of strategy. Bombing airfields was apparently not working so he would have to destroy the R.A.F. in the air. He would move to massed attacks on London and other crucial targets by his whole bomber force. These were targets that the R.A.F. would have to defend with all its power and the Luftwaffe would shoot its fighters down.

In fact this decision was a crucial mistake because it took the pressure off Fighter Command just enough to let it manage the situation and halt its relentless decline. Although September recorded the R.A.F.'s greatest loss of aircraft, the first seven days of the month made a disproportionate contribution. In very round terms it was losing an average of 20 aircraft per day in the first week and after the critical change of policy on 7th that figure dropped to 10 per day for the rest of the month. The Battle of Britain ended by some reckonings on 15th September and by others on 30th September or 31st October but whichever date is preferred, there was never any serious chance of the British losing after 7th September.

Naturally this was not apparent to anyone at the time and some of the hardest battles were still to come. On the 7th the Luftwaffe attacked London with three hundred bombers and every fighter it could muster: 648 of them. Goering himself stood on the French coast watching the armada pass overhead. On 9th September London was hit again and on 12th, London and Portsmouth. The 15th September was the climax of this part of the campaign and perhaps of the whole battle. It is now celebrated as 'Battle of Britain Day'. On this day there were a series of raids on London and intensive fighting once again. The Luftwaffe lost just over 50 aircraft, or 56 or 60 depending on the source you consult and the R.A.F. lost 26. One of the German losses was a Do17 that appeared to be attacking Buckingham Palace and was brought down by a Hurricane piloted by a young sergeant, Ray Holmes. When his ammunition ran out Holmes rammed the bomber which crashed in the yard of Victoria Station. Holmes escaped unhurt. The Dornier was, in fact, an unmanned cripple flying on autopilot whose crew had already bailed out.

There had been worse days for both sides but this one was decisive. The German commanders were depressed that after all their efforts the enemy seemed to be as strong as he was a month earlier; their campaign seemed to be as far from fulfilling its goal as ever. On the following day Goering summoned his senior officers to another conference at which recrimination was the order of the day and on 17th September Operation Sealion was postponed indefinitely.

The fighting did not die down for another six weeks when winter conditions made large scale operations impossible. At the end of September there was a flurry of substantial raids against the aircraft industry. On 25th September the Bristol Aircraft factory outside the city of the same name was attacked very successfully and put out of action for several weeks. 250 people were killed or wounded. The next day the Supermarine factory in Southampton was finally hit. 50 people were killed and the factory closed for a week. The output of Spitfires in October was less than half the figure for the previous month. The R.A.F. was fortunate this raid came toward the end of the campaign.

Hereafter the major raids in daylight ceased and small scale hit-and-run actions took over. These continued through October with some kind of action taking place almost every day. Some of these raids were carried out by a force of Italian planes sent by Mussolini to aid his German allies. For the R.A.F. pilots not much changed: they continued to fly and fight almost every day and to be constantly waiting for the terrifying 'scramble' call. The fighting was much the same for the average pilot in these smaller engagements as it was in the larger. The Luftwaffe's main bombing effort had now been switched to the night time. 544 R.A.F. aircrew had lost their lives repelling the German attack and 1,023 R.A.F. planes were shot down. The Luftwaffe lost 2,968 aircrew and 1,887 aircraft.

For Great Britain this was a famous victory that has now become a legend. Nothing the R.A.F. achieved in the rest of the war came close to matching it. Oddly enough there was recrimination in the higher circles of the R.A.F. despite obvious victory. During the battle there had been some bitterness amongst R.A.F. pilots that they always seemed to be fighting outnumbered by Luftwaffe planes. This was largely due to their commitment piecemeal against raids because of the shortness of the warning time available. Air Vice Marshal Trafford Leigh-Mallory who was the commander of 12 Group to the north of the Thames, had a theory that the German raids should be countered with large forces of British fighters which came to be known as 'big wings' and were designed to overcome this difficulty. The problem was the time they took to assemble and the difficulty of controlling them once assembled. They probably had their place in the scheme of things but were aggressively over-promoted by Leigh-Mallory. At the same time he had the task of covering 11 Group airfields while that group was fighting the German raids. In this task he several times failed and the airfields were bombed, usually because he was too busy assembling a big wing. This was, to all intents and purposes, disobedience of orders. His relationship with Park was consequently poor and this materially affected the conduct of the battle.[xiii] Before the war Leigh-Mallory sought the coveted position of commander of 11 Group but it went to Park instead. Given Leigh-Mallory's personality and conduct throughout the war, until his death it is hard to resist the conclusion that he put his personal interests above those of his country and was unsuited to high command.

One of Leigh-Mallory's pilots was Douglas Bader, probably the originator of the 'big wing' idea and certainly an ardent proponent. The adjutant of Bader's squadron happened to be a Member of Parliament who raised this tactical dispute in political circles. This was one reason for increasing criticism of the handling of the battle by Dowding and Park, criticism assiduously promoted by Leigh-Mallory. No sooner was the battle over than both Dowding and Park were relieved of command. Dowding was retired and Park was sent to take charge of training. Leigh-Mallory took over Park's job which he had coveted all along and the leadership of Fighter Command went to Air Vice Marshal Sholto Douglas previously Deputy Chief of the Air Staff and a Leigh-Mallory supporter. The man with ultimate responsibility for this decision was Sir Charles Portal the new Chief of the Air Staff. It was a decision that reflected ill on him and was not the only such which the war would bring.

Not long after the event the Air Ministry published a pamphlet giving the official history of the Battle of Britain. This contrived to make not a single mention of Dowding, prompting Churchill to comment: 'The jealousies and cliquism which have led to this offence are a discredit to the Air Ministry and I do not think any other Service Department would have been guilty of such a piece of work.'[xiv]

Shortly after taking over his new responsibilities Leigh-Mallory held a formal war game designed to vindicate his big wing theories. In fact it did quite the reverse and the umpires decided that Biggin Hill and Kenley had been bombed before Leigh-Mallory's big wing was even in the air.[xv] In actual practice during the Battle of Britain the big wing was ordered into the air 32 times but only made contact with the enemy on seven occasions.[xvi]

If the antics of the commanders add a darker tinge to the picture, the bravery of the pilots stands out undimmed. This bravery was famously saluted by Churchill speaking in the House of Commons.

'Never in the field of human conflict was so much owed by so many to so few.'

CHAPTER EIGHT

Convoy Protection and the Early Bomber Offensives

On 24th August 1940 the Luftwaffe bombed an oil refinery in the Thames estuary and some of the planes strayed too far to westward and their bombs fell on east London. As a result, and in retaliation, the R.A.F. raided Berlin the following night. It was a small raid and the damage was slight but that Berlin should be bombed at all was a shock to the German people and to Hitler in particular. With prompting from Goering he ordered that British cities be bombed night and day. Before the war Goering had boasted that if any British bomber reached the Ruhr '…you can call me Meier', (the point being that Meier is a very common German name and Goering is not).[i] These particular planes had gone a lot further and the boast now became a source of increasing embarrassment.

As we have seen, some of the early raids were made in daylight but from October the offensive went over to night bombing because bomber losses were minimal at night. British anti-aircraft fire at this time had no proper fire direction system which meant that, at night, the crew just pointed the gun at the sky in the general direction of aircraft noise and fired. Needless to say the chances of doing any damage were very small indeed. Confidentially it was admitted that A.A. guns were used primarily to boost civilian morale by giving the impression that something was being done to defend the ordinary citizen.[ii] Searchlights were inadequately powered so that they could not even pick out an aircraft much above 10,000 feet.

Night fighters were in a rudimentary state. When the war began there was a simple belief that any fighter plane could be sent up at night and it would spot bombers by the light of the moon or by the glow of their exhausts and shoot them down unbothered by escorting fighters. In fact it turned out that the bombers were extremely difficult to find by visual means and that flying a fighter plane by night was a challenge in itself. The key to night flying is cockpit instruments. Since the pilot can't see the world outside he has to rely on instruments such as an artificial horizon and a vertical speed indicator and he has to watch them with almost constant attention. Plainly he cannot do this and search the night sky for bombers at the same time. It soon became evident therefore, that night fighting required a larger aircraft with a two man crew. It also became apparent that small radar sets would provide the secret of detecting the enemy. Both the Blenheim and the Beaufighter were suitable aircraft for this job but in 1940, airborne radar sets were not available and so night fighters essentially had to do their best with ordinary human eyesight though there were experiments with dropping flares and attaching a searchlight to the fighter plane. The most severe raid in this period was one on London on 15th October when 400 bombers attacked. Night fighters shot down one.

From the middle of September London was attacked at night every night but one for two months. Other cities were also attacked from time to time. German bombers flying from France or Denmark or Norway could reach any of the large cities in Great Britain. This bombing campaign against London and other cities has become known as the 'Blitz' after the German word for lightning.

Early raids on London concentrated on the docks. The great daylight raid of 7th September set fire to miles of wharfs and warehouses and the flames were fed by the large quantities of stored rubber, paints and fuel. The attack was renewed that night and the fires were such that the attackers needed no navigational aids to reach their target. September 15th saw another heavy raid that caused 1,300 civilian casualties and put five rail termini temporarily out of action.

London, May 1941: firemen fight fires in the City after one of the heaviest air raids of the Blitz. Their efforts were severely hampered by broken water mains. Scenes like this were to become commonplace across Europe.
©Imperial War Museum (HU 1129)

From the second half of November to February the bombing spread to other cities and in that time there were eight major raids on London and 23 on provincial cities. On 14th November Coventry was heavily hit and its cathedral destroyed and on 29th December came one of the worst raids of all, when despite the interference of bad weather, the Luftwaffe managed a very concentrated two hours of bombing on London that virtually destroyed the old mediaeval City of London. Only by a miracle did St Paul's Cathedral escape destruction as whole blocks of houses and offices all round it went up in flames. In February 1941 the targets became Britain's sea ports but the defences were being improved and the Luftwaffe was beginning to take serious losses. There were increasing numbers of radar controlled anti-aircraft guns and an efficient system had now been devised for guiding night fighters to the bombers. Ground radar would detect a bomber and a controller would guide the pilot of the nearest fighter towards it by radio. At some point the small radar set now mounted in such fighters would 'see' the bomber and the radar operator would continue guiding the pilot until visual contact was made. This system was still in its early stages but it clearly had the potential to make night bombing almost as costly as its daytime counterpart. In May, the last month of the Blitz, the Luftwaffe lost over a hundred bombers. Even had it not been necessary for the bombers to take part in the invasion of Russia, losses would probably soon have forced a halt to the bombing in any event.

Meanwhile the Luftwaffe bomber force could still hit hard. Belfast suffered the worst raid outside London in terms of loss of life and on 10th May London was heavily bombed again and the Houses of Parliament hit. There were 3,000 casualties. A few days later Birmingham was bombed and then the attacks stopped as the German bombers flew east to new bases for their assault on the Balkans and Russia.

This campaign was the world's first attempt to implement the Douhet strategy of strategic bombing as a war-winning policy but it was applied in modified form. No one in the German air Ministry in Berlin really thought that it was going to force Great Britain to surrender, though there was certainly hope that it might force her to the negotiating table. Even if neither occurred it seemed reasonable to assume that a great deal of damage would be done to industry and to the morale of the civilian population and hence to their will to work hard to prosecute the war. Finally, as a matter of prestige it was essential for Germany to show that the Battle of Britain had not wholly defeated her bomber offensive. Bearing in mind the morale effects of fairly limited bombing in World War One, expectations about weakening morale were not wholly unreasonable. Certainly the American ambassador in London, Joseph Kennedy, did not think Britain could hold out.

Before the war the British government had considered what the effects of bombing might be and they too overrated its effectiveness. They estimated that as many as half a million people might be killed and took extensive though often unrealistic precautions. Gas masks were widely distributed and when the war started, half a million children were evacuated to the countryside. Much investment was put into anti-aircraft guns but little into air raid shelters because it was felt in official circles that they would encourage a defeatist mentality. Instead people were encouraged to build their own shelters according to a government approved pattern called an 'Anderson' shelter after the Home Secretary at the time.

The actual results of the Blitz were a surprise to all concerned. The effect on British industry was minimal. Bombing at night was too inaccurate and the weight of bombs dropped far too low to do lasting damage. Damage was certainly caused but no one had anticipated the resilience of industry. The psychological effect of the bombing turned out to be, if anything, an improvement in the national morale. There was a feeling that everyone was 'in it together' and a determination not to be cowed. Far from workers abandoning their jobs they took pride in appearing for work despite the greatest difficulties. It was soon clear that the civil unrest of the First War would not be repeated, to the Government's great relief. In fact the people of Britain had now had two decades to get used to the idea of aeroplanes and of bombing and were no longer inclined to panic. Churchill observed: 'I, like others, had often pictured the destruction becoming so overpowering that a general move and dispersal would have to be made. But under the impact of the event all our reactions were in the contrary sense.'[iii]

We will look at these issues again in more detail when we come to the Allied bomber offensive later in the war. This latter was on a completely different scale that made the bombing of London appear insignificant. In the whole war bombing (including V-1s and V-2s) cost the lives of a little less than 60,000 British civilians; it was to cost the Germans ten times that number but there was no collapse of morale and no collapse of industry. In the meantime the Blitz had the very positive effect for Great Britain of arousing sympathy for her throughout the world and particularly in the United States.

Night bombing provides testing problems of navigation and most of the successful means of overcoming these involve radio technology. Accordingly a technology battle developed between the two sides in this area that lasted throughout the war with first one side and then the other having the advantage. In 1940 the Luftwaffe developed a system of night navigation called 'Knickebein'. This was based on a well-known technique of broadcasting a narrow radio beam along which an aircraft could fly. To that was added a second beam that intercepted the first over the target. When the radio operator heard the signal caused by the second beam the bombs were dropped. Unfortunately for the Germans it was not too difficult to produce a false beam near the real one and lead aircraft off course and the British soon did this. The Germans then produced two further arrangements called X-Geraet and Y-Geraet. X-Geraet was really just a more complicated version of Knickebein and Y-Geraet reflected the radio beam back to the original transmitter which could judge how far away the plane was, according to how long it took the signal to come back. It was not long before the British learned how to jam these signals too and the bombers had to fall back on visual navigation by moonlight, when available. This was surprisingly successful because it is relatively easy to see a coastline from the air at night and nowhere in Britain is more than 15 minutes flying time from the coast.

Attacks on ports during the Blitz were designed to complement the U-boat campaign against British shipping and the Luftwaffe had another weapon that was used in a similar role in the early years of the war with results out of all proportion to the resources involved. The Focke Wulf Fw200 Condor was a four-engine bomber originally designed as a passenger aircraft for Lufthansa. It was fast for a bomber and had a range of 2,250 miles easily increased by installing additional fuel tanks. Its weaknesses were its small bomb load of 4,000 lbs and its light construction which rendered it unfit for strategic bombing. It was, however, ideal for use over the Atlantic as a reconnaissance aircraft and for attacks on ships far out to sea. For a year after the fall of France it filled this role virtually unopposed and Churchill called it the 'Scourge of the Atlantic'. In 1940 U-boats sank 2,200,000 tons of merchant shipping and aircraft sank 580,000. In 1941 the U-boats sank almost exactly the same tonnage and aircraft sank 970,000 tons, or almost half as much. Some ships were sunk by mines and others by surface raiders. The total was 4 million tons which indicates that roughly one ship in four was the victim of air attack. Not every ship sunk was sunk by a Fw200: Junkers and Heinkels also had their share but it was the Focke Wulf that was the king of this kind of warfare.

The British were desperate to counter this threat and were remarkably successful in doing so. During 1941 and 1942 they armed an increasing number of merchant ships with anti-aircraft guns. The key to successful bombing attacks on ships is to go in low but that makes the attacking plane very vulnerable to light anti-aircraft fire. The advent of the armed ship spelt the end of the easy kills for the Condors. A further development was the 'cam-ship'. This was a merchant ship with a catapult installed on which was perched a Hurricane fighter. When a Condor was sighted the Hurricane took off and attacked it. When the battle was over the Hurricane had to be ditched in the sea and was lost and the pilot baled out and was rescued by a lifeboat. This was a wasteful and dangerous procedure but surprisingly effective.

As from September 1941 the Royal Navy began to deploy escort aircraft carriers. These were small aircraft carriers built on the hulls of ordinary merchantmen. They sailed with convoys and were a deterrent equally to U-boats and Condors. At the same time the number of ships sailing outside convoys declined. The combination of these factors ended the Condor threat very rapidly. The Luftwaffe turned those that were left to co-operation with the U-boats acting as airborne convoy spotters.

Condors also acted as transport planes and were used to take supplies into Stalingrad. Some remained passenger planes as was originally intended. One acted as Hitler's personal transport plane. After the fall of France construction of Condors was switched entirely to a factory near Bordeaux. Naturally, after the loss of France,

Condors no longer flew over the Atlantic and their construction ceased. Only 276 of them were ever built.

However great the threat posed by Condors, the threat of U-boats was worse. The task of fighting them from the air fell to R.A.F. Coastal Command. From December 1941 the U.S. joined in but the great bulk of this work always fell to the British if only because they were closer to the U-boats' home. By the war's end there were six U.S. squadrons flying with Coastal Command, a rare example of U.S. forces directly under British control. Formed in 1936, Coastal Command was originally conceived as a coast-watching and reconnaissance force with shipping protection given only a subsidiary role because no one foresaw another battle with German submarines such as had occurred in the First War. As late as April 1940, a meeting at the Air Ministry in London still placed reconnaissance top of the list of Coastal Command priorities.[iv] But the U-boat threat soon changed all that and its defeat rapidly became by far the most important task for the coastal force. To achieve this, the R.A.F. needed the right planes, the right weapons and an efficient means of locating a U-boat.

Between the wars the Command was at the bottom of the heap as far as government funds were concerned and so at the start of the Second World War its equipment was poor. Moreover its role was seen as predominantly 'coastal' and therefore local, with the result that most of its equipment consisted of aircraft of modest range. The backbone of the force was the Avro Anson, a twin-engine monoplane of sturdy construction but unexciting performance and a range of only 500 miles. This aircraft equipped 14 of the 22 squadrons with which Coastal Command began the war. Only three squadrons of Sunderland flying boats had the range to provide truly oceanic coverage. Based on the Imperial Airways flying boats of the inter-war era the Sunderland was a large, four-engine flying boat of great beauty to an aviator's eye. Unfortunately it was very big and quite complicated to build. It included bunks, a galley and a small workshop for in-flight repairs. Its crew was ten or more. Its manufacturer, Short Brothers, was never able to turn it out in the numbers required. Only 750 were produced throughout the war despite the plane's usefulness in a variety of roles.

Even before the war began the need for greater range was apparent to the Air Ministry and the purchasing commission sent to the U.S.A. in 1938, was attracted by the Lockheed Company's design for a small passenger aircraft that could be converted to a light bomber and maritime patrol craft. The commission told the company what its requirements would be if this aircraft were to be so converted and were stunned when a full-scale mock-up was ready within 24 hours. In England such a model would have taken a month to produce.[v] The resulting bomber, the Lockheed Hudson, saw extensive service with Coastal Command and was an excellent stop-gap solution pending the acquisition of more long range heavy bombers. It replaced the Anson for anti-submarine work but the latter was such a useful plane of the 'runabout' kind that it continued to be produced in the thousands and was a familiar sight in the skies over Britain for years after the end of the war.

Coastal Command's great problem so far as equipment was concerned was that it continued to be last in the queue for suitable aircraft even when the U-boat war threatened Britain's very survival. Bomber Command bitterly resisted the loss of any aircraft transferred and relations between the two Commands were poor in consequence with results such as the refusal of Coastal Command to participate in the first 'thousand bomber' raid. Coastal Command became widely known as the 'Cinderella Service'.

In 1941 it was able to acquire some American PBY Catalinas. The PBY was a flying boat much used by the U.S. Navy and although it was old and slow it had the range necessary to patrol distant sea lanes and was very reliable. Reliability was a very important factor in maritime aviation. Survival chances for an aircrew forced to ditch in some remote part of the North Atlantic were next to zero. The turning point was the entry of the U.S.A. into the war which made available the big U.S. bombers, the B-17 Flying Fortress and the B-24 Liberator. Bomber Command had no use for these and so they were available in limited numbers for maritime work and it soon transpired that the B-24 Liberator was ideal.[vi] Its basic range was 2,800 miles but it had such a carrying capacity that it could be fitted with extra fuel tanks and still carry a full load of depth charges. The limiting factor for its patrols became not fuel but crew endurance. Air Marshal Joubert, commander of Coastal Command in 1942, decided that the normal patrol should not be more than 14 hours long, extending to 18 in emergencies.[vii]

As the war progressed air patrols extended further and further into the Atlantic until in May 1943 the whole ocean was covered. U-boat successes immediately declined sharply and the U-boat threat was never a serious issue again. Aircraft were particularly effective against U-boats even if they did not sink them. The threat of air attack was so serious for a U-boat that it had to dive as soon as it saw an aeroplane and once under water its speed was so slow that it was not in a position to catch any surface ships. Thus a U-boat stalking a convoy could have its entire hunt set at nought by the mere appearance of one aircraft. Often the aircraft would not even know what it had done.

At the war's beginning Coastal Command had to use an anti-submarine bomb that proved, in effect, useless. It then turned to depth charges but the only such available were those used by the navy and these were too large and heavy for easy aerial use. Only the Sunderlands could carry them and their explosion often damaged the aircraft.[viii] It was not until 1942 that a suitable smaller, 250 lb charge was perfected and armed with an efficient detonator. This then became a deadly weapon with the only proviso that it had to be dropped with great accuracy.

Finding U-boats started out as a matter of luck and good eyesight but they are tiny targets from the air and in the endless reaches of the ocean sightings were rare indeed. Naturally U-boats gathered round convoys and the chances of a sighting were always much better near one. The key to this particular problem however, as so many others, was radar. First available for use in the air in 1941 it was invaluable for detecting U-boats at night which was when they came to the surface to re-charge their batteries. When the Leigh light was introduced in 1942, aircraft at last had a means to find and kill U-boats with a measure of efficiency. The Leigh light was a searchlight attached to the nose of the plane which came on automatically at a certain distance from the target. It was directed in the same direction as the radar scanner. Because of the noise of the sea and of their engines U-boats often did not detect the approach of an aircraft at night and the light was their first warning of danger but it came too late for them to dive. In due course the German Navy developed a radar detector called Metox which warned the U-boat crew when they were being 'observed' by radar but in early 1943, Coastal Command began to use a wholly new kind of radar based on a centimetric wave length[ix] instead of metric and to this the Germans had no answer.

During the war aircraft sank 188 out of 785 U-boats destroyed and shared in the destruction of 21 more.[x] These figures, however, do not do justice to their contribution.

Great Britain maintained two bomber offensives. In the spring of 1941, with the return of reasonable flying weather the R.A.F. began offensive operations over France with its tactical bombers. There was also a strategic bombing campaign that had been in progress since the first day of the war. We will deal with the tactical offensive first.

The conclusion of the Battle of Britain saw Fighter Command growing stronger daily. On September 26th there were 569 aircraft available. On October 31st there were 684, the vast majority of them Spitfires and Hurricanes. In the new year there came into service a new version of the Spitfire with a more powerful engine and armed with two 20mm. cannon as well as four machine guns. This was the Spitfire V. More of this model of Spitfire were built than any other during the war. As a matter of policy, front line fighter squadrons in Great Britain were now all to fly Spitfires as and when sufficient of that type were available, while Hurricanes were relegated to overseas service and ground attack duties. A special version was produced for ground attack that was armed with four 20mm. cannon.

One of the ostensible reasons for the replacement of Dowding and Parke with Sholto Douglas and Leigh-Mallory was that the latter were supposed to be the more offensively minded duo and in the spring of 1941 they lost no time in trying to prove this estimate correct. The big wing idea was put into immediate effect with sweeps across northern France by three, four, five or more squadrons of fighters. These were ignored by the Germans since they did no harm. The British response was to use the fighters to escort small forces of bombers to attack targets in France or Belgium. This the Germans could not ignore and the result was large dogfights over the coastal regions just as the R.A.F. had wished. For a short time the British had the technical edge with their new Spitfire but then the Germans introduced a new model of the Me109: the 'F' model. This was a thorough redesign of the original aircraft with a more streamlined body and more powerful engine. All its armament was placed in the nose, giving it more concentration of fire. This was probably the best of the many versions of the Me109 that were produced during the war and it promptly removed the advantage of the Spitfire V.

In September 1941 R.A.F. pilots reported encountering a completely new kind of German fighter plane. This was the Focke Wulf 190 and it changed the picture again. The Fw190 was one of the finest fighter planes of the Second World War. It was designed by Kurt Tank who had been a cavalry officer in World War One but was devoted to aviation and made his career as a test pilot and designer. He had already attracted attention with a series of successful designs including the Condor when he was asked to create a new fighter plane as a successor and alternative to the Me109. He wanted to use the Daimler Benz 601 engine but that was in great demand for all the Messerschmitt aircraft and there was no prospect of the company producing enough engines to power another mass-produced plane. Accordingly he had to search for an alternative and his choice fell on the BMW 801. This was a radial engine, using which violated all the accepted principles of European fighter design at the time but it was a case of cutting your coat according to your cloth. Tank was a brilliant engineer who built on this inauspicious start to create a masterly design. The engine developed a massive (for the time) 1,700 horsepower which more than made up for the fact that it was less aerodynamically efficient. The faults of the Me109: its trickiness to fly and its delicate undercarriage were carefully addressed and the finished plane was given a massive armament of four 20mm cannon and two machine guns. The Fw190 was distinctly superior to the Spitfire V though it was not so very easy to fly despite Tank's efforts.

In May of 1941 the Luftwaffe was largely withdrawn from the Channel coast for the campaigns in the Balkans and in Russia. All that was left was two fighter wings, Jg2 and Jg26, amounting in practice to about 175 aircraft. They were top class veteran units and they spent the next two years fending off the whole R.A.F. daytime offensive.

In the middle of 1941 Sholto Douglas was already having doubts about the wisdom of this offensive but it ground on regardless. It was named the 'Non-stop offensive' and German propaganda promptly called it the 'Nonsense offensive' and not without some justice.[xi] By the end of the year it had cost the lives of 500 pilots, almost as many as the Battle of Britain and without any noticeable reward.[xii] A certain amount of sympathy is in order for the R.A.F. commanders responsible. There was always the possibility that the Germans would make another attempt at an invasion and even after the bulk of the Luftwaffe was engaged in Russia the possibility remained of a Russian defeat and that would have Hitler's eyes turning to Great

Britain again. Thus it was essential to maintain a strong defensive force of fighters in the U.K.. Moreover such a force could hardly be left wholly unemployed. Like any weapon an unused air force gathers rust. Then too, it was important from the political point of view to show the Russians that Britain was doing all it could.

On the other hand during 1941 first the Mediterranean theatre and then the Pacific sprang to life with their own pressing need for aircraft. Once the invasion of Russia began there was most unlikely to be enough summer left for Germany to defeat Russia and then turn to the invasion of Britain, so that a large part of Fighter Command could have been released for duty overseas. There were 78 fighter squadrons in Great Britain in the spring of 1941 but only three in the Western Desert and one in Malta. Moreover, the need to keep the aircraft of Fighter Command employed for reasons both of morale and of politics did not mean that they had to be wasted with the abandon actually employed and for no purpose. For the bombing missions undertaken were mere pinpricks and although the propaganda claim was made that this campaign was wearing the Luftwaffe down the reverse was true. Comparison of losses carried out since the war has shown that the R.A.F. was losing aircraft at the rate of three or four planes to every German loss.[xiii] R.A.F. pilots themselves were not oblivious to the pointlessness of most of these missions and bomber crews were resentful of the fact that they were being used as bait.[xiv] It must surely have been possible to devise a method of keeping the aircraft and pilots meaningfully employed without losing large numbers of both. It was claimed that they were tying down substantial Luftwaffe forces in the West, but the same forces would have had to be based in the West as a precaution more or less whatever the R.A.F. did or did not do.

In February 1942 the Germans decided that they needed to bring three large warships then in Brest harbour on the French Atlantic coast home to Germany for ultimate redeployment to Norway. Sailing them round the north coast of Scotland was not feasible because it would be to sail into the arms of the Royal Navy's Home Fleet. The alternative was to risk trying to sail through the Channel which had the advantage of being the more direct route, though also highly dangerous. On 11th February the ships set sail in poor weather, timing their run to start in darkness and take them through the Dover Strait in daylight. This was the reverse of what was expected and it wrong-footed the defence. A series of uncoordinated air and sea attacks were launched against the ships with conspicuous lack of success. The Luftwaffe had arranged for continuous air cover in an operation orchestrated by Adolf Galland and there were frequent running fights in the airspace around the ships which themselves reached Germany successfully, though one was damaged by a mine. British attacks cost 42 aircraft and the Germans lost 17 fighters. It was a humiliating defeat for the British who regarded the Channel as their own private property. The whole episode is perhaps best remembered for an attack by a flight of six old and slow Swordfish torpedo bombers that were wiped out. Their commander, Eugene Esmonde was posthumously awarded the Victoria Cross.

It should be mentioned that in May of 1941 Swordfish aircraft, launched from H.M.S. Ark Royal, had torpedoed the battleship Bismarck, then at large in the Atlantic and crippled her so that her destruction shortly thereafter had become inevitable. This showed that they could achieve results given the right circumstances.

In June 1942 the R.A.F. received the first of the new Spitfire IXs. These were a further improvement on the Mark V and were specifically intended to counter the superiority of the Fw190. Unfortunately production of them was slow and it would be a long time before every Spitfire squadron was equipped with them. Two years later on the eve of D-day the process was still not complete. The Mark IX was a big improvement on its predecessors: an even larger engine, improved cooling system, better supercharger etc. and it did go some way to redressing the balance. It has become a commonplace of aviation history that it was superior to the Fw190 but Eric Brown, the Royal Navy's chief test pilot, flew a captured 190 in 1944 and felt that it had a slight edge over the Mark IX.[xv] The explanation for this difference may be that the Spitfire flown by the average pilot was better, but the Fw190 flown by a veteran had the edge.

It was unfortunate that the new Spitfires were not yet widely available on 19th August when the Dieppe raid was launched. This was an attempt to take and hold a large port for a short time, partly to destroy its facilities but mainly to test the response of the defence given that by now, with the U.S.A. in the war, an invasion of the Continent was on the horizon. The raid was carried out by 6,000 troops, mainly Canadians and began early in the morning. It was given extensive air cover by the R.A.F., some 70 squadrons taking part, of which 56 were from Fighter Command. Leigh-Mallory was put in overall command of the air effort. The German fighter defence was Jg2 and Jg26 which, together, totaled the equivalent of some 14 squadrons. The raid was a complete failure and half of the 6,000 were lost as casualties, while in the air the Germans exerted a seemingly effortless superiority shooting down 119 British planes for the loss of 46 of their own.

In November of 1942, Leigh-Mallory replaced Sholto Douglas as chief of Fighter Command and was promoted to Air Marshal. In January 1943 he was knighted.

The second British bomber offensive was the strategic offensive that had been in operation since the opening day of the war. It had always been part of Britain's air policy to have a strategic bombing campaign in the Douhet mould. For the men on the Air Staff who ran the R.A.F. this was seen as the raison d'etre of their air force and the presence of large numbers of fighter aircraft a digression, forced on them by events. This was partly a matter of devotion to a theory but it was also a sensible reaction to geographical circumstance. Britain was an island and it was always likely that it would find itself fighting a continental adversary. Strategic bombing appeared to offer a way to strike a serious blow against that enemy without the necessity of invading with a large ground force; indeed many felt that an enemy could be brought to the point of surrender by air attack alone exactly as Douhet had predicted.

In 1939 the R.A.F. had 23 squadrons of bombers but six of those were Blenheims which were not strategic bombers and were to be used, or misused, for other purposes as we have seen. There were 17 squadrons of heavy bombers. They were not to be known as 'heavy' for long, for within two years the four-engine bomber was to make its appearance and then the aircraft we are considering, were re-christened 'medium' bombers. (And the Blenheims which were now 'medium', became 'light'.) The 'heavies' were disposed in three Groups along the east coast of Great Britain. 3 Group flew Wellingtons, 4 Group flew Whitleys and 5 Group flew Hampdens. All three types of aircraft had two engines and in peacetime they gave a similar satisfactory performance. The Wellington carried the biggest bomb load, the Hampden was the fastest and the Whitley was the favourite of the crews. Once war began it was soon apparent that the Wellington was much the best of the three. The Hampton had the smallest range and the least effective defensive armament. It was poorly designed from the point of view of the crew's comfort and missions of six to eight hours were a severe trial for them. (Empty beer bottles were much in demand.) The Whitley was slow and although it had a good range, the bomb load had to be significantly reduced to take full advantage of it. Moreover its ceiling, when loaded, was poor. It used Rolls Royce Merlin engines, already much in demand for Spitfires and Hurricanes, which required more maintenance than the rugged radial engines of the other two. The Wellington carried the biggest load and had the best defence. Its unusual geodetic construction was extremely strong, making Wellingtons great survivors. By early 1942 the other two types had been retired.

The officer in charge of Bomber Command when the war began was Sir Edgar Ludlow-Hewitt. Like all the senior officers of the R.A.F. he had had a distinguished combat career in World War One and had been much involved with training in the inter-war years. He was a scholarly man of great knowledge and penetrating intelligence. Arthur Harris, Bomber Command's most famous commander, thought Ludlow-Hewitt was the cleverest officer he had ever met.[xvi] Certainly he foresaw with great clarity precisely what the difficulties were that his force would face. He was worried that the bombers would not be able to defend themselves against fighters if they carried out raids in daylight and that their navigational capability was quite inadequate for night bombing.

When the war started, Bomber Command could dispose of some 200 aircraft for raids on Germany. This was a trifling number with which to confront a major power, but the plan was that the strength would be steadily increased over time and there were already designs drawn up for the offensive to employ much larger four-engine aircraft that would carry a greatly increased payload. The initial problem was the political decree that no civilian must be killed. This restriction effectively neutered the offensive in the early months of the war. It was limited to attacks on shipping, mine laying and dropping leaflets. These attacks were made in poor weather so that, frequently, not all the attacking planes found the target.

On 4th September an attack was launched against warships off the German coast in which seven aircraft were lost. The ships were only lightly damaged. Seven aircraft was 50% of those that found the target and was a foretaste of the terrible losses daylight bombing was to incur. On 29th September, a squadron of Hampdens was dispatched to the Heligoland area on a roving mission to look for ships and sink them. They found two destroyers and attacked them without effect. Due to a combination of weather and poor flying discipline by inexperienced pilots, the squadron became split into two groups. The Germans had tracked the raid with their coastal radar and sent fighters to intercept. The fighters found the second group of five Hampdens and shot them all down. However, during the autumn there were a number of other anti-shipping sorties that sank nothing but were unmolested. This encouraged a false sense of security and helped temporarily to obscure the lesson of the heavy losses. The truth was that if there was no shipping in the area for the bombers to threaten, the Germans simply did not bother to chase them.

On 18th December, 24 Wellingtons were dispatched to Wilhelmshaven looking for ships to bomb. Two planes turned back because of mechanical trouble and the rest circled the town in clear weather and saw several warships in dock, but they had to leave these alone because an attack might have imperiled civilian lives. This provocation was too much for the Germans however, and a mixed force of Me109s and 110s was sent up to intercept. Wellingtons had a tail turret with four machine guns and it was thought these would hold fighters at bay but the Messerschmitts were able to attack from other angles and escape the defensive fire. The result was devastating. Of the 22 planes, 12 were shot down and three more were so badly damaged that they could not make their home base. Losses on this scale were impossible to sustain and Bomber Command suspended daylight bombing.

Leaflet dropping had been carried out all over Germany at night since the war began. This work was done largely by Whitleys because of their long range and their slow speed which made them unsuitable for daylight work. The ease with which bombers could fly at night over the whole of the enemy's land quite unopposed contrasted sharply with the danger of daylight raids. Bombing by night was the obvious answer but the problems of night navigation were overlooked. With the aids then available it was next to impossible to navigate at night without a good moon and clear weather. In the two years before the war there had been more than 400 instances of forced landings in the U.K. by aircraft that had lost their way flying at night over the British Isles ![xvii]

Night operations with a ban on endangering civilians rendered the idea of strategic bombing farcical but everyone knew that the ban could not last and when the Germans bombed Rotterdam on May 14th 1940, with great loss of life, restrictions were lifted though Bomber Command was still told that its targets must not be indiscriminate but must be related to the prosecution of the war. During the offensive in the West and the Battle of Britain Bomber Command's Blenheim bombers continued to operate in daylight and to suffer heavy losses but the heavy bombers were set to attacking targets in Germany, and especially in the Ruhr valley, that were thought to make a direct contribution to the German war effort. Transport hubs were particularly popular for obvious reasons. The railway marshaling yards at Hamm, the largest in Germany, were a favourite target.

With the autumn of 1940 and the end of the Battle of Britain, the overall situation had changed. All of a sudden British strategic bombers were the only means for the country to strike blows against the Axis. Ludlow-Hewitt was replaced in April by Portal who brought a much more aggressive attitude to bombing policy. He was in favour of area bombing since he was realistic about the prevailing lack of accuracy and he wanted the number of targets reduced so that each could be attacked with larger forces. But the growth of the heavy bomber force had been slow. The Advanced Air Striking Force had returned from France, abandoned its Battle bombers and adopted Wellingtons. It reverted to its original status as 1 Group but this process of re-equipping and re-training was still ongoing. There was a steady leakage of planes and crews to the Mediterranean, to Coastal Command and to training duties. German bombing had interrupted the manufacture of Wellingtons. The result was that there were only 330 heavy bombers available, only a hundred more than when the war started. Now however, building up the force was to have priority and a faster rate of growth could be anticipated in the future.

In October, Charles Portal became Chief of the Air Staff and the job at the helm of Bomber Command went to Richard Peirse. Peirse seemed a good choice because he had been the Deputy Chief of the Air Staff with special responsibility for bombing policy and he was a man of great charm not to mention good looks. (In 1944 his career came to an abrupt halt when he eloped with a senior general's wife. This was an age when divorce was considered a serious matter.)

There followed nine months of complete unreality. Bomber Command would choose targets each night and dispatch bombers to bomb them. The targets would be specific factories or railway yards or refineries, the pilots would report success and the intelligence officers would cross that particular target off their list. In July 1941, the Air Ministry published an illustrated book on the campaign so far. It was entitled 'Bomber Command'. Clearly this was propaganda, but British propaganda did not knowingly go in for outright distortion of known facts. The book claimed, amongst other things, that 'One third of the town of Aachen......is in ruins,' [xviii]and, speaking of Hamburg: 'By May the damage to the city, apart from the harbour area, was severe.'[xix] All this was fantasy and wishful thinking. The odd bomb hit these cities but the damage was slight and quickly repaired.

There was growing unease about the results of the strategic bombing campaign because there were worrying signs, increasingly apparent to any intelligent observer, that the effects of the bombing were indeed not what was claimed. Photographic reconnaissance and intelligence reports from agents in Europe were at odds with any idea that the bombing was accurate. The result was that Lord Cherwell, Churchill's scientific adviser, set in motion an enquiry chaired by Mr. D. M. Butt, an official of the cabinet secretariat. The Butt enquiry examined a sample of ten percent of aircraft on typical raids. It looked at their operational reports and it looked at their bombing photographs. These were photographs taken automatically by each aircraft a few seconds after the bombs were dropped. The conclusion of the Butt Committee was that only one third of aircraft were dropping their bombs within five miles of the aiming point and, in the Ruhr valley, an area of industrial haze and heavy defences, this proportion fell to one tenth.

In practical terms this meant that almost no bombs at all were landing near the target and the whole campaign was, effectively, worthless. Indeed the story goes that there were days when the Germans only knew from BBC broadcasts that they were supposed to have been raided the night before. For Bomber Command this was the low point. Clearly the strategic bombing campaign must either be abandoned or completely re-thought.

CHAPTER NINE

The Balkans and the Eve of Barbarossa

With the conclusion of the Battle of Britain Hitler's eyes turned to the East. His crusade was the conquest of Russia and the elimination of Communism. His failure to subdue Great Britain did not unduly concern him: he considered that Russia could be conquered in a brief campaign and then he could reduce Britain at his leisure.

With the success of German arms in the West in the summer of 1940, the smaller countries of central Europe and the Balkans threw in their lot with Germany. In November 1940 Hungary and Rumania became allies and in March of 1941 Bulgaria joined them. From the point of view of air power the Axis made modest gains by reason of these developments.

Hungary was in the process of expanding its air force which was about 300 strong in the spring of 1941. Its weakness was that its equipment was second rate. Its fighters were largely Italian CR42 biplanes and its bombers Ju86s: a type already retired from the Luftwaffe when the war began.

Bulgaria's air force numbered approximately 250 aircraft. Most were Polish imports bought before the war and already obsolete in 1939, but there were 72 Avia B534s acquired from the defunct Czech air force via Germany. The B534 was one of the finest pre-war creations and though it was a biplane with a fixed undercarriage it was the very best of its kind. The R.A.F. had a very similar plane in the Gloster Gladiator but the B534 carried a similar armament and was 50 m.p.h. faster. (B534s were also used by Slovakia, the puppet Axis state that was all that was left of Czechoslovakia.)

Rumania was in a different class. Its air force numbered about 800 planes and some of them were up to date types including Hurricanes, Heinkel 111s, Stukas, Blenheims and Savoia-Marchetti SM79s. Moreover Rumania had its own small aircraft industry which principally consisted of the I.A.R. Company. This was Industria Aeronautica Romana, a government subsidized company set up in 1925 specifically to give the Rumanian air force independence from foreign imports. In this it was not successful but it did produce one capable fighter plane, the IAR80 which came into operation at the end of 1941. The weaknesses of this air force were its multiplicity of different types of imported aircraft and a poor ground organization supporting the squadrons which resulted in low serviceability rates.

It was, of course, essential for central Europe and the Balkans to be at least neutral before Hitler began his struggle with Russia. The last thing he needed was a second sideshow war going on at the same time in southeast Europe. There was already one of them. Italy had decided to invade Greece in October 1940 but far from winning an easy victory, the invasion stalled and the Italians were pushed out of Greece into Albania. Simultaneously the Italians had tried to invade Egypt but that plan went wrong too and the British had decisively defeated them. Even in east Africa the British were getting the better of them. Mussolini appealed to Hitler for help and Hitler felt obliged to give it. He was afraid that if Italian fortunes sank too low then Mussolini might fall from power and Italy turn from ally to enemy. Moreover, Greece and Britain now had common cause and there was a possibility of British bombers, based in Greece, raiding the Rumanian oil refineries at Ploiesti which were essential to the German war machine.

On March 25th 1941, Regent Paul of Yugoslavia joined the Tripartite Pact and now all the major countries of the Balkans were German allies except Greece. But powerful factions in Yugoslavia did not like this pact. Yugoslavia was a very odd country. It was created at the end of World War One essentially to reward Serbia for her steadfast support of the Allied cause. It consisted of Serbia itself, to which had been grafted various parts of the erstwhile Austro-Hungarian Empire, in particular, Croatia. These grafts were essentially Germanic in culture and origin and though they liked the idea of independence, they did not want to be forced into a union with the Serbs whom they regarded as ancient enemies. The result was that the country was schizophrenic, permanently at odds with itself and having two, mutually opposed, views of the world. The outcome was that there was a coup d'etat on March 27th by the anti-Axis elements and Peter II was declared King though technically still under age.

Hitler took this as his cue to launch an immediate invasion of Yugoslavia and Greece. This spring had already seen a massive movement of German military men and materiel to the east of Europe in preparation for the invasion of Russia. Parts of these forces, including 500 aircraft, were also moved south to Rumania and Bulgaria to be ready for a Balkan campaign. They were part of Airfleet Four under Alexander Loehr.

The Yugoslav air force was new and inexperienced. Its organization was poor and its integration into a national defence plan virtually non-existent. Its equipment was the usual mixture of imports from the major powers. Its fighters were mainly Hurricanes and Me109s and its bombers, a mixture of Italian SM79s, German Do17s and British Blenheims. There were also small numbers of its own indigenous Ikarus aircraft: the IK2 and IK3. The first was a fighter akin to the B534 and the second was similar to a Hurricane though, apparently, rather better. There were the usual problems of too many different kinds of aircraft from different sources resulting in poor serviceability. For instance, of 73 Me109s on hand only 46 were available for operations. The rest were in the workshops. Of 12 IK3s only 6 were available.

On 6th April the invasion began with the bombing of Belgrade. This was carried out over a period of two days and had devastating results. It was ordered by Hitler personally as an act of revenge for what he saw as Yugoslavia's perfidy. The bombing probably killed something in the region of 4,000 people though there have been suggestions that the casualties were as much as five times that number. From a military point of view it was very effective because so much of the military direction of the country was centralized in its capital city and the bombing dislocated communications and control. It is worth noting in the light of bombing campaigns yet to come, that when the war was over, Loehr was tried by the Yugoslavs as a war criminal for the bombing of Belgrade and executed.

The invasion brought a swift collapse of the Yugoslav will to resist, largely because of the divided spirit of the country as noted above. Its air force however, fought bravely. Pilots are something of a trained elite and tend to have an intense professional pride that prevents them from giving anything less than their best. More cynically, a pilot has no choice but to do his best if he wants to live. Certainly the Germans were surprised by the strength of the resistance over Belgrade where they lost 20 aircraft on the first day and calls went out for another 600 Luftwaffe planes to be assigned to the attack. They carried out their usual attacks on enemy airfields at the start of the campaign with the intention of destroying the enemy air force on the ground. This was a mixed success; the most effective raid destroyed one third of the 70 Yugolav Do17s at a blow. On the other hand widespread dispersal of aircraft prior to the invasion saved many planes though it led to a degree of administrative chaos and even poorer support services.

The Yugoslav air force was completely outnumbered and outgunned and its losses on the ground and in the air mounted rapidly. By the time an armistice was signed after 11 days of fighting, it had little resistance left to offer. It lost, in all, 50 aircraft in the air and 85 on the ground. Many more were lost in accidents or abandoned when damaged. 80 planes flew to sanctuary in neighbouring countries and some 300 were captured by the Axis and given to the newly formed state of Croatia, an Axis satellite.

The Germans lost 60 aircraft and the Regia Aeronautica 10.

The Greek air force was a tiny force of about 100 aircraft, mainly Polish PZL fighters and British Battle and Blenheim bombers. At the time of the German invasion this force was down to some 40 planes. Once the invasion began, the British provided some Gladiator fighters and some more Blenheims as replacements. More to the point, R.A.F. forces had been sent to Greece in the autumn of 1940 in response to the Italian invasion and were still there in April 1941. They consisted initially of three squadrons of Blenheims and two of Gladiators, a combat strength of about 60-80 aircraft. By the time of the German invasion this force had swelled to eight squadrons and included Hurricanes and Wellingtons. The Fleet Air Arm contributed a flight of the elderly Swordfish torpedo bombers. The total was now perhaps a little over 100 aircraft. This was quite a respectable force but they were far outnumbered by the Germans and Italians. Though they performed acceptably the ground war went badly and by 20th April the remaining aircraft were being evacuated to Crete. The Germans entered Athens on 27th April and the conquest of mainland Greece was complete on 29th.

An interesting feature of the fighting in Greece is the mystery of Squadron Leader Tom Pattle, killed in an air battle on 20th April. Pattle, a very gifted airman, originally went to Greece from North Africa in the autumn of 1940 with 80 Squadron. He later commanded 33 Squadron which he was leading when he was killed. In fact he had influenza at the time and a high fever and should never have been flying. He was a South African in origin and he had joined the R.A.F. before the war as a career officer. His progress therein was steady without being meteoric and he was apparently regarded by those who knew him as a thoroughly pleasant, if unremarkable, young man. It was universally agreed however, once war came, that he was an exceptional combat pilot. No one is sure how many planes he shot down because all the squadron records relating to the campaign in Greece were lost. The last certain figure seems to be 23 in March 1941 when he was awarded a Bar to the Distinguished Flying Cross (that is, he was given a second award of the medal). However, he undoubtedly shot down many more after that. Survivors from his squadron credited him with between 44 and 60 kills in total.[i] Since the officially

An informal moment for a German flak gun crew in Athens. The gun is the highly effective 37mm automatic weapon. ©Imperial War Museum (HU 39532)

recognized leading western Allied ace, Richard Bong, shot down 40, Pattle may well have passed him to become the number one. On the other hand these unconfirmed victory reports were notoriously unreliable so the exact number of his kills must remain a mystery. Was Pattle the greatest Allied fighter pilot of the war? The question will remain unresolved.

Flying for the other side was a young Italian called Ugo Drago from the little town of Arborio, west of Milan. He had been in Greece since the previous year when the 150th Fighter Wing, to which he belonged, had been posted there. Drago was to prove himself one of Italy's foremost pilots, fighting through the whole war, but his start was slow, probably because he was not flying the best aeroplanes. He started on the CR42 biplane and moved on in October/November 1940 to a Macchi 200, only a modest improvement, and shot down his first enemy on November 2nd. He was escorting bombers to Salonika when they were attacked by two Greek PZL24 fighters and Drago destroyed one of them. The 50th Wing remained in Greece until December when it was posted to Africa for ground support duties.

After the fall of mainland Greece the island of Crete remained in British hands. Its own garrison was swelled by a considerable number of troops evacuated from Greece so that its defenders numbered some 28,000 by the time of the German attack. On the other hand its air cover was non-existent. Immediately after the defeat on the mainland a rag-tag mixture of surviving R.A.F. aircraft flew there so that at the end of April there were on the island 12 Blenheims, 6 Hurricanes, 12 Gladiators and 6 assorted Fleet Air Arm planes. Only about half of these were serviceable and the infrastructure to support them was simply not there. Considering the overwhelming strength the Luftwaffe could bring to bear, the British sensibly decided that to use these aircraft in combat would be to lose them all to no purpose and so they were evacuated to Egypt. Thus Crete was left with no air cover at all. The nearest Allied air power was now in North Africa and that was too far away to interfere in any campaign on the island. There was a good argument for evacuating the ground troops as well but Churchill and the British war cabinet decided they must try to hang on there. They judged, correctly, that its capture would be no easy business even with complete control of the air because the Royal Navy had very nearly complete control of the sea.

The German attack plan was centered on two corps of Airfleet Four. 11th Air Corps comprised the Luftwaffe's paratroops that had been so effective in Norway and the Low Countries. It was supported by 8th Air Corps providing 280 level bombers, 150 dive bombers and 180 fighters. The plan was to make an initial attack with paratroops and follow that up with regular troops brought in by boat. It took some time to prepare the attack because several preliminary problems had to be overcome. First of all there were no available troopships in the area and so an armada of small coastal merchant ships and fishing boats had to be collected and prepared for service. Second, there was a shortage of decent airstrips within range of Crete and emergency action had to be taken to improve the facilities on those that existed. Third, there was a requirement for over 500 Ju52s and 100 gliders to carry troops, equipment and supplies but most of the Ju52s had seen heavy use in the Balkan campaign transporting supplies and were not in a fit state to undertake another front line task so soon. In a remarkable administrative achievement several hundred aircraft were flown back to Germany, refitted and flown south again.[ii] Finally, the operation would need over half a million gallons of aviation fuel and this had to be brought from Italy in a tanker. The tanker became stuck in the Corinth Canal where a bridge had collapsed into the canal and formed an obstruction. The bridge had in fact been captured intact during the fighting and then its demolition charges set off by accident. A special team of divers had to be flown out from Germany to clear the wreckage so that the tanker could get through.[iii]

The problems added up and there was a delay of almost a month before the attack was launched on 20th May. When it finally took place it was almost a failure. The Germans had underestimated the strength of the defenders and their determination and in particular, had no idea of the presence of the whole 2nd New Zealand Division. This was a costly intelligence failure because the New Zealanders were particularly aggressive and effective soldiers. The first wave of the attack went in at 7am and there were heavy casualties despite complete air superiority and heavy bombing at all strategic points by the aircraft of the 8th Air Corps. The Germans persevered however, and gradually gained the upper hand. In seven days the campaign was over and the surviving British forces were evacuated. In the course of the fighting, the Royal Navy had blockaded the island to prevent troops being brought in by sea and its ships had been furiously attacked by the Luftwaffe's bombers. Two cruisers and six destroyers were sunk thus finally making clear beyond doubt that aircraft could sink warships at sea, something that had been becoming increasingly obvious since Dunkirk. Strategically the capture of Crete was an important victory because it put the Axis in control of the whole of the north coast of the Mediterranean. It also showed what could be achieved by an airborne attack. On the other hand it demonstrated that paratroops attacking well-defended ground positions, held by reliable soldiers, will suffer very heavy casualties. 11th Air Corps lost almost 5,000 men and this was a particularly heavy blow because paratroops were elite soldiers. Because of this, Germany launched no other major parachute attack in the rest of the war.

With the Balkans subdued, German air units moved to the Russian border where the final preparations were being made for Hitler's gigantic invasion of that country codenamed 'Operation Barbarossa'. It has often been suggested that the Balkan campaign delayed the start of Barbarossa and thereby compromised the prospects of that massive operation. This seems unlikely since the weather was not suitable for the invasion until June that year and so, although the original start date of May 15th was revised because of events in the Balkans, the weather would probably have forced the revision in any event. The armoured units needed firm, dry ground for smooth running and the rivers had to be allowed to run off their spring surge caused by melting snow. Conditions were not right until the second week in June. Barbarossa's failure owed much more to mistaken strategic decisions taken by German leaders in the course of the 1941 campaign, particularly the delaying of the drive on Moscow to complete the encirclement of Kiev.

The shock of her poor performance in the Winter War against Finland led Russia to institute various reforms of her armed services. The principle shortcoming of the V.V.S., the Red Air Force, was outdated aircraft. Before that war had ended a specification for a new fighter plane was issued by the Soviet Air Ministry and aircraft engineers were invited to submit their designs. Three designs stood out and all were put into immediate production. The first was the I-26 created by Alexander Yakovlev. This was something of a surprise choice since Yakovlev had never designed a warplane before but his aircraft had the look of a thoroughbred with clean lines and excellent performance. It was soon re-named Yak-1 in line with the new, wartime policy of calling warplanes after the designer rather than the role they were designed to play. During the war the various models of Yak were built in enormous numbers and the Yak vies with the Me109 for the title of most numerous fighter of all time. More than 30,000 of each type were built. The Yak was such a sound design that it could be modified to carry all kinds of weapons and fulfill several different roles. Its biggest weakness was that it was under-armed. Most Yaks carried only one 20mm cannon and one or two machine guns and a very limited supply of ammunition.

The second design to be ordered into production was the Mig-3. This came from the new design bureau of Mikoyan and Gurevich whose post-war creations came to be almost synonymous with Soviet aviation. The Mig-3 was the fastest of the designs and the only one with a decent performance at higher altitudes but it was not very manoeuverable at lower altitudes and had a high landing speed making it hard to handle. It also caught fire easily if hit by enemy bullets.

The third design was from the bureau of Lavochkin, Gorbanov and Gudkov. Of the three of them it was Semyon Lavochkin who was the real force behind the actual designing. Their contribution was the Lagg-3. This was a fine, modern fighter not unlike a Spitfire to look at but made of a wood and glue mixture called 'Delta-drevsina' in deference to the shortage of aluminium in Soviet Russia at the time.[iv] This 'Delta' was very tough but very heavy too and the result was an underpowered aircraft. By way of comparison a Spitfire weighed 5,700 lbs on take-off while a Lagg-3 weighed 7,000 lbs even though it was a slightly smaller aircraft. The inevitable outcome was that its performance against German fighters was ordinary and it had a tendency to fall into a spin if handled too roughly. Because of its failings it fell out of favour in due course with the result that when its successor was produced it was called La-5 after Lavotchkin because he was the man responsible for it. Gudkov had left the bureau, not wishing to maintain a dangerous association with failure. For the sake of simplicity however, in this book all aircraft from this bureau will be called 'Lag,' which was the standard, if technically inaccurate, term commonly in use in the West at the time. If it seems odd that the successor to a '3' should be a '5' the answer is that all fighter aircraft in the V.V.S. were known by odd numbers and all bombers by even ones.

As we have seen, the Russians did not go in for strategic bombing and so had only one type of heavy bomber. This was the DB-3 which underwent a facelift between 1939 and 1941 and re-emerged as the Ilyushin Il-4. It now had a redesigned nose, better armour and stronger engines. It is little known in the West but it was a fine aircraft and served throughout the war. Around 7,000 were built which puts it on a par with the Avro Lancaster in terms of numbers, though it was only a twin-engine plane and therefore not really a 'heavy' bomber by the standards obtaining later in the war.

Somewhat smaller was the Petlyakov Pe-2 which we have mentioned before. This was a design originally intended to be a heavy fighter and some versions were used for that purpose but it was most successfully used as a light bomber.

Another light bomber was the Sukhoi Su-2. This was a single-engine monoplane of modern design with a retractable undercarriage intended as what the V.V.S. called a 'reconnaissance bomber', the idea being that it should carry out reconnaissance and then attack any enemy targets it saw. It had no armour of any kind however, and although it had a single rear-facing gun in a turret, the turret had to be rotated by hand, rendering it next to useless. The aircraft was not fast or manoeuverable and it carried only a modest 1,300lb bomb load. Once Germany invaded, this plane proved a complete failure in action. German fighter planes ate it for breakfast.

Because of this, it is difficult to find out how much of a role it played. The Soviet Official History of the V.V.S. in World War Two does not even mention it and until recently it was next to impossible to find out how many were made: estimates cautiously suggested 500 plus. Recent research suggests that a little short of 1,000 were built in all and that they equipped 15 bomber regiments and two separate squadrons.[v] To find out what role it really played some detective work is necessary and there are two clues. First, when construction of the Su-2 was terminated in 1942 its engine and nose were adopted for use in the Lag-5 and that aircraft was built in huge numbers from a standing start so there must have been plenty of engines and noses available. Second, when it was withdrawn from combat its place in the battle line was taken by the Il-2 and that was built in huge numbers too so it must have left a pretty large gap. Finally, Soviet newsreels of this time constantly feature the Su-2 in a prominent role which is a most unlikely situation if it was a rarity. In short it seems probable that the Su-2 was intended to be the main ground attack plane/light bomber of the V.V.S. in 1941 and there was then an attempt to write it out of history because of its failure.

Its place was taken by the Ilyushin Il-2 which was only just being delivered to the squadrons as the invasion began. This was one of the war's outstanding aircraft partly for its intrinsic genius of design but also for the way it was used and the way it became a symbol of national resistance. It was a single-engine, low wing monoplane with the enclosed cockpit and retractable undercarriage that was now the standard configuration for new planes. Its bomb load was similar to the Su-2 but it could also carry rockets, a weapon in whose technology the V.V.S. was more advanced than its western counterparts. Its most startling feature was its armour. The whole forward part of the fuselage including the cockpit and the wing roots was made as a single piece of armour to which the rest of the aircraft was attached. This made it extraordinarily resistant to ground fire but it also made it very heavy. The original plan was for the plane to have a rear gunner as well as a pilot but there was not enough power in the Mikulin engine to carry both and in the early versions there was only a pilot. This made the plane an easy target for German Messerschmitts and it suffered severely despite its armour. Although they managed to shoot it down German fighter pilots were horrified by the Il-2's toughness. Eventually the time came when the power of the engine was increased and a rear gunner could be added and this made the aircraft even more of a survivor.

As well as bombs and rockets the Il-2 was armed with two machine guns and two 23mm cannon which gave it a tremendous punch against ground targets. It was designed with ease of production and flying in mind and to that end it was kept as simple as possible. The cockpit had the minimum possible number of controls and the aircraft was docile in the air so that even the most callow pilot could handle it. Western visitors who saw it scoffed that it was primitive and laughed at the fact that instead of a gun-sight it had a circle and bead drawn on the windscreen. The truth was that the sight was often removed by squadrons at the front because of the number of accidents when a pilot crash-landed and his face smashed into the sight causing severe injuries.[vi]

In fact the Il-2 had a number of faults that were gradually rectified during the course of the war. They were essentially the result of trying to rush it into action too early. The story went that there were serious doubts about the design's future until Sergei Ilyushin, who was something of a favourite of the regime, stayed with Stalin at his summer dacha and thereafter immediate mass production was ordered.[vii]

All these aircraft with the exception of the Su-2 were only just coming into service as the German invasion started. The V.V.S. would have to meet the initial shock with the elderly aircraft verging on obsolescence with which it was overwhelmingly equipped. In addition it had no radar and its radio arrangements were primitive. Many regiments had no radio at all and, even where it was present, only the formation leader had a transmitter; all the rest of the flight had a receiver only. On top of these problems aircraft maintenance standards in the V.V.S. were lamentably poor and training was rudimentary. The general approach was that if a man could get an aircraft into the air and land it again then he was ready to fight.

The failings of the air force at this time are exemplified by the experience of 4th Ground-Attack Regiment. It was the first unit to receive the Il-2 but it only received its full complement of the new plane a week before the invasion. When it was ordered to the front from the Kharkov area five days into the war not a single pilot had carried out even one training flight carrying bombs, nor had anyone fired the new plane's guns. No one knew how to use the aircraft's sighting mechanism because the engineer from the Ilyushin works, who was supposed to demonstrate, it never arrived and mechanics had to learn by trial and error how to attach bombs because the aircraft used its own peculiar system for doing this, that nobody had bothered to explain to them. Even the flight to the front was delayed a day because the regiment did not have the paper needed for the pilots to map their route.[viii]

The German forces arrayed for the invasion were immense. There were 3.5 million German troops and another million Axis allies. There were also 600,000 vehicles and three quarters of a million horses. The front stretched from the Black Sea to the Arctic where the Finns had decided to join in, in order to avenge their defeat in the Winter War. It was the greatest invasion in human history, by some margin. The general plan of attack was a threefold drive into the heart of Russia supported by an additional attack on Leningrad (now St.Petersburg) by the Finns in the North. The northern arm of the German attack was aimed at Leningrad where it was hoped to link up with the Finns. The central arm was to drive straight toward Moscow, though Hitler undoubtedly hoped that the Soviet Union would collapse before it was necessary to take that city. The southern arm was to head southeast into the prosperous land of the Ukraine taking the Crimea on the way. Each piece of the offensive was supported by air forces.

In the Far North the Finns contributed some 500 aircraft. Gone were the Fokkers of the Winter War and the principal fighter was now the Brewster Buffalo export version. This was a fighter originally designed for the U.S. Navy who had found it unsatisfactory. The R.A.F. also used it to equip squadrons in the Far East and were not satisfied with it either but the Finns flew it with great success and seemed to have few complaints. They also used the Hawk 75 and the Fiat G50. Since two of these types came from countries that were to be their enemies from now on, they were faced with a problem in obtaining spare parts and replacement aircraft. As time went by their aircraft were slowly replaced by German models, a process that was completed in 1943. The Finnish air force was overwhelmingly equipped with fighters at this time. Partly this was due to a strategy that limited Finland's aggressive intent to recovering the land lost in the Winter War and partly it was a result of the country having limited resources which stretched much further with fighter aircraft than with bombers.

Supporting the Finns and operating from their territory was a German contingent drawn from Airfleet Five under General Stumpff whose principal area of responsibility was Norway. The Airfleet had some 240 aircraft of which about 75 were used for the attack on Russia and were based at Kirkenes in northern Norway.

The northern arm of the German invasion was supported by Airfleet One under General Alfred Keller. It comprised three bomber wings and one fighter together with some independent flights for a total of a little over 400 aircraft.

In the centre was Airfleet Two. This was the same Airfleet that took part in the Battle of Britain and it now had a dual responsibility for two different areas: one in the East and one in the West. Albert Kesselring remained the man in charge. This was the largest of the air fleets with some 1,500 aircraft in four bomber wings, three dive bomber wings and six fighter wings. One of the bomber wings was Kg2 'Holzhammer' which had the status of an elite unit and had fought in the Battle of Britain like many of the Luftwaffe wings now lined up against Russia. Johannes Fink was no longer in charge of Kg2; its new commander was Herbert Rieckhoff, a man of forty-three who had fought through the whole First World War, first in the infantry and then flying in a reconnaissance squadron. He followed a career in the police in the inter-war years but returned to flying in the sudden expansion of the Luftwaffe in the late 1930s. One of the Stuka wings was Stg2 'Immelman' and one of its pilots was Hans Ulrich Rudel. Rudel was a minister's son from Silesia whose poor academic record had left him with limited prospects until the expanding Luftwaffe gave him an unexpected opportunity. He was not everyone's cup of tea: sports-mad he neither smoked nor drank and his preferred tipple was milk. Since he was also, at least initially, a poor flyer he was not a favourite in the officers' mess and had so far been kept out of front line action. This was done ostensibly on the basis that his flying skills were not adequate but one suspects he was just an unpopular oddity in a very conformist service. On the eve of Barbarossa he was in Kottbus in Germany where he had flown a damaged Stuka for repairs. One would not have guessed at the time that a great future lay ahead of Rudel.

The southern arm of the attack was served by Airfleet Four under Alexander Loehr. This amounted to some 750 aircraft in five bomber wings and three fighter wings together with the usual extra independent flights.[ix]

The Luftwaffe at this time could muster a total of 4,300 aircraft of which 2,770 were waiting at the Russian border. Axis allies: Finland, Rumania, Hungary and Slovakia provided another 900. It is noteworthy that these figures are actually substantially less than the numbers available for the assault in the West a year earlier. The reason for this is twofold. First, the previous year had seen the Luftwaffe take heavy casualties in a series of campaigns that Germany's aircraft industry could not replace fast enough because it was still on a semi-peacetime footing. Second, the Luftwaffe now had the western front and the Mediterranean to cater for as well as Russia. The Luftwaffe forces poised to attack Russia were however, the best equipped in the world and comprised very largely veteran pilots of great skill. The Luftwaffe was probably now at its high-water mark.

By contrast the V.V.S. was at a low ebb. Most of its aircraft were old and outdated, its tactics were poor and its organization a model of inefficiency. Its rapid expansion since 1939 had led to poor workmanship in the aircraft factories[x] and many aircraft showed defects that had to be corrected before the aircraft could even be used. In the spring of 1941 it probably numbered in the region of 20,000 aircraft in all of which about half were available on the western border to resist the German attack. However, only slightly over ten percent were modern types such as the Yak-1, Lag-3 and the Mig-3. There were very roughly 5,500 fighters to 4,500 bombers. The western border of Russia and the Baltic coast was divided into 'Districts' for military purposes and aircraft were allotted to these various sectors, moving from north to south, as follows: Leningrad Military District 1,270 aircraft, Baltic Special Military District 1,211 aircraft, Western Special Military District 1,789 aircraft, Kiev Special Military District 1,913 aircraft, Odessa Military District 950 aircraft. In addition there was a Strategic Bomber Command of 1,332 aircraft under central control. The Russian navy had its own separate air force attached to individual fleets as follows: Northern Fleet 116 aircraft, Red Banner Baltic Fleet 707 aircraft, Black Sea Fleet 624 aircraft.[xi]

Of the fighters there were still plenty of the I-15 and I-153 biplanes at the front and the most numerous fighter by far was the I-16, also obsolete in 1941. The commonest bomber was the SB-2, another ageing model. The standard ground attack aircraft was the Su-2 whose failings have been discussed above. Introduction of new types was going ahead as fast as possible but had a long way to go and was attended by much confusion as the experience of 4th Ground-Attack Regiment testifies.

In many ways the V.V.S. in 1941 was a sacrificial lamb to be offered to the Nazi war machine. Its greatest asset was the unfailing bravery of its pilots.

CHAPTER TEN

The Invasion of Russia

The invasion of Russia was scheduled to start on 22nd June 1941 but for weeks before that date Luftwaffe reconnaissance machines had been flying over western Russia in blatant violation of Russian airspace. They were photographing every airfield, railway and defensive emplacement to facilitate the attack. Russian pilots were straining at the leash to get into the air and shoot them down but the official government attitude was that nothing must be done to affront the Germans whose intentions were presumed to be peaceful. That this view was mistaken was rapidly to become evident to everyone and that it was ever held at all is a matter for astonishment. Much has been written on this theme but politics is not the subject of this book so we will pass on after noting that in early June several senior V.V.S. officers made appeals to General Pavlov, Commander of the Western Special Military District, for permission to intercept German reconnaissance planes and were turned down on the basis that this would be to succumb to 'provocation'.[i]

The Luftwaffe's plan for the opening days of the invasion was the tried and tested blitzkrieg formula with improvements learned from experience in the West. It would start with an all-out assault on the Russian air force, follow up with attacks on bridges and communications targets with the object of isolating the front line and then move on to direct support of the armies on the ground. A last minute hitch arose over the precise timing of the attack's start. The army wanted to open the attack at dawn so that the troops moved off as soon as they could see what they were doing and the Russians were hit before they were fully alert and prepared for the day. For the Luftwaffe this meant that their aircraft must mostly take off at night and since formation flying at night was near impossible, it reduced concentration of attack and introduced a degree of disorganization. They wanted the attack delayed by several hours so that all aircraft took off at first light and were over their targets when the assault began but the army considered that this would cost them their bonus derived from dawn surprise, and it was the army who won.[ii]

The first Luftwaffe attacks were on airfields, all 66 of which in the border area had been carefully photographed by those reconnaissance planes. Airfields are excellent targets for aerial photography because they are large and very difficult to hide. They seemed particularly inviting targets because the Russians had taken no steps to disperse aircraft. On the contrary, on most airfields the warplanes were lined up in neat rows, all ready to be destroyed en masse. The reason for this was partly the political 'no provocation' ukase and partly a typical Soviet paranoia about counter-revolutionary spies and saboteurs who might attempt to harm the planes. Assembled in tight blocks, parked aircraft were easier to guard. There was also the little matter of 'proverbial Russian negligence' as a V.V.S. officer put it.[iii] The results were to be disastrous.

At 3.00 am on 22nd June hundreds of aircraft roared over the border into Russia aiming to reach their targets at 3.15 and after. The artillery that heralded the ground attack was to start at 3.30. The first attack of the whole Russo-German war was delivered by a squadron of heavy fighter wing Zg26, flying Me110s, on Alytus airfield near Vilna in Lithuania. Appropriately the squadron was led by Captain von Richthofen another relative of the Red Baron. The first wave of attacks hit 31 airfields: the rest were attacked later in the day. Russian aircraft were bombed and machine-gunned sitting neatly in their rows; the destruction was wholesale. News of what was happening filtered back to the machine shops at Kottbus where Hans Rudel grabbed the first serviceable Stuka he could find and flew back to his unit at the front where his wing was far too busy to worry about his eccentricities and

immediately cleared him to fly in a flight led by another unpopular pilot.[iv]

Heinz Knoke was a young lieutenant with the fighter wing Jg52. He took off at 5 am with his squadron to attack a complex of buildings identified as a Soviet headquarters. Knocke's Me109 had been specially modified to carry small fragmentation bombs. The flight to the target was uneventful: he saw no sign of the Soviet air force. Arriving at the headquarters he saw no hint of life until he dropped his bombs and then he described the scene as being like an overturned ant hill with soldiers in their underwear running for cover.[v]

Any suggestion that the V.V.S. did not fight back is, in fact, quite wrong. Wherever they could, Russian pilots took off and fought like devils against the German invaders. At one airfield the fighters were caught in the act of taking off by a fusillade of bombs and piled up at the end of the runway. Perhaps the first to make contact were the I-16s of 33rd Fighter Regiment who took off from Pruzhany airfield at 3.30 a.m. and met the Luftwaffe over Brest Litovsk on the border. When they returned they claimed six German aircraft destroyed.

A Dornier 17 bomber of Kg2 flown by Sergeant Stockmann was part of a flight attacked by I-16s and Mig-3s near Zambov. The inexperienced Russian pilots flew straight into the co-ordinated defensive fire of the bomber formation and three were shot down. Their leader, Senior Lieutenant Dmitry Kokorev, was determined to destroy a bomber however, and rammed Stockmann's aircraft which went into a spin and crashed. Stockmann himself was killed but two of his crew bailed out and survived. Kokorev was knocked unconscious by the concussion of the collision but recovered in time to crash-land his damaged aircraft. He was awarded the Order of the Red Banner for his actions.[vi] He continued his flying career and shot down another four German aircraft before he was killed in October. This episode on 22nd June was one of the very earliest examples of 'taran' or the deliberate destruction of an enemy aircraft by ramming. It was to become a common tactic of last resort in the V.V.S. particularly in these early days.

The Western Special Military District was at the eye of the storm and here the 122 and 127th Fighter Regiments flew a number of sorties during the day and claimed 35 victories in all. Lieutenant Zhukovsky, who was a squadron leader in the 127th, flew nine times that day and claimed four German aircraft shot down.[vii] These and other victories were against the run of play, as it were, and by the day's end the Western Special Military District had lost 738 aircraft: 528 on the ground and 210 in the air. This was a huge proportion of its 1800 available planes of all kinds in that district. Indeed, given the very poor Russian serviceability rates at this time it was probably the majority of its battle-ready planes.

Overall the Luftwaffe claimed to have destroyed 1,489 Soviet aircraft on the ground and 322 in the air on 22nd June for the loss of 61 of their own planes and 11 Rumanian. Even the official history of the Soviet Air Force admits the loss of 1,200 and the official history, written in the days of the U.S.S.R., is not prone to exaggerate Russian losses.[viii]

A German Junkers 52 transport plane about to take off in the snowy wilderness of Russia. Note the aircraft's winter camouflage. ©Imperial War Museum (COL 353)

Of the two, the German figures are probably slightly more reliable but exact numbers cannot be arrived at. Certainly a later survey of wrecks in the front line area ordered by Goering counted over 2,000.[ix] One of the difficulties of this kind of situation is the definition of a 'destroyed' aircraft. Taking an optimistic view, many destroyed aircraft are just 'damaged' and can be repaired. Thus statistics can be manipulated.

On the evening of 22nd General Hoffmann von Waldau, Chief of the Luftwaffe Operations Staff, wrote in his diary: 'the timing of the air attack was a complete success.'[x] It is worth noting however, that the Luftwaffe had suffered losses equal to their worst day in the Battle of Britain. The flights of 22nd revealed yet more Soviet air bases hitherto undiscovered and these were attacked the next day when another 1,000 Soviet aircraft were destroyed.

One of the strangest features of the early days of the invasion was the persistence of attacks by unescorted Russian bombers. The principal bomber involved was the SB-2 which was the mainstay of the Soviet bomber force though many Il-4s were also involved. These aircraft flew missions in formations of a dozen or two dozen bombers at a time. They met the Luftwaffe's Me109s and were slaughtered. Some of the top Luftwaffe fighter pilots shot down as many as five bombers in a single mission. The Germans were amazed at their easy pickings. It had been a clear lesson of the first 18 months of the war that bombers could not survive in daylight in the face of determined fighter opposition yet the Russians appeared not to have learned this lesson or to have ignored it.

The reality was that this strange attitude was a product of the contorted history of the V.V.S. . Yakov Alksnis, head of the V.V.S., had been shot in 1938 along with his deputy Vasily Khripin and the head of the Air Force Political Directorate, the head of the Air Force Academy and most of the area commanders. At the same time the power of political commissars in the V.V.S. was increased. The result was a complete absence of leadership coupled with paralysis born of fear. For a brief period of time a man called Loktionov was in command and then his place was taken by General Yakov Smushkevich who was a hero of Spain and the Nomonhan affair. Smushkevich was in charge during the Finnish Winter War when the V.V.S. made a very poor showing and as a result he was dismissed and Stalin chose a young man called Pavel Rychagov to take over. Rychagov, who was a veteran of the fighting in Spain and China was only 29 years old and had enjoyed a heady rise due to the deaths of competitors and his own undoubted administrative competence.

One of the failings of the V.V.S. in the Winter War had been the lack of co-operation between the army and the air force and this was addressed at its conclusion by the simple expedient of allocating most of the fighter aircraft and many of the bombers to the armies at the front and giving the land commanders control over their use. The result was that the battle orders for these air units were issued by generals who had no experience of air war at all and were in many cases barely competent because they were late replacements for men who had been purged. Most of the larger bombers were retained under central control in the Strategic Bomber Command. This organization however, had very few fighter planes under its control. The inevitable outcome of all this was that the individual armies jealously guarded their own fighters and used them purely defensively to act as an umbrella over the armies so that both they and the Strategic Bomber Command had to send their bombers into action without fighter escort. There was no one with the authority and the courage to challenge this way of doing things but even had there been such a one, it is far from evident that his challenge would not merely have resulted in his own death. These failings are evidence of the calamitous attempt by Stalin to create armed forces guided more by political criteria than military ones.

After the first couple of days the resistance of the V.V.S. on the central front had sunk to near zero. Losses in the air and on the ground had been too heavy to permit a reasonable level of sorties to continue. Moreover, since the Red Army was being defeated and falling back in increasing confusion the V.V.S. on the ground was caught up in the chaos just as had been seen in the campaigns in the West. The Luftwaffe's bombers struck at every possible target and shattered Soviet armoured counter-attacks before they began.

One target that did not easily succumb was the huge fortress at Brest Litovsk on the frontier. This was of modern design and was fanatically defended. There were no paratroopers available to take it by a coup de main and the effect of bombing was small. It did not surrender for nine days. This was a very minor foretaste of the problems that well-defended towns were to pose later in the war.

Hans Rudel, after his late arrival at the front, flew four missions that first day and then settled into a routine of flying from 3.30 in the morning to 10 at night. Every moment they were not in the air the pilots fell asleep under the wings of their aircraft. He described his targets as: 'always the same: tanks, motor vehicles, bridges, fieldworks and A.A. sites. On and off our objectives are the enemy's railway communications or an armoured train when the Soviets bring one up to support their artillery.' About the V.V.S. he was dismissive: 'their fighting power is small.'[xi] The Wehrmacht here on the central front was gradually pinning the main Soviet ground forces into a pocket in the Bialystock/Minsk area and there was little the V.V.S. could do to prevent it. The suicidal bomber attacks continued and the resultant losses were very heavy for little return. By 1st July the Western Special Military District was down to 374 bombers and 124 fighters of the 1800 aircraft it started with eight days before.

Red fighter pilots never quite gave up however and when the opportunity arose they fought with desperate bravery that could sometimes have unexpected results. On 1st July, near Minsk, Nikolai Terekhin of 161st Fighter Regiment was leading a flight of I-16s when they encountered a squadron of He111 bombers whose escort were too far away to intervene. Since he was already out of ammunition from earlier fighting he attacked one of the bombers with a skillful piece of flying whereby he closed from behind and used his propeller to saw off the Heinkel's rudder. The Heinkel was now without any lateral control and veered to the left into the next plane which, in turn, tipped over and hit a third bomber. All three planes dived down to explode on the ground and the I-16, propeller ruined, followed them. Half a dozen of the German crewmen were able to bale out, as was Terekhin. They all drew their pistols and fired at one another as they slowly descended under their parachutes. On the ground the Germans were quickly captured by local collective farm workers and tied up. A few minutes later Terekhin dramatically burst into the headquarters of General Zakharov's 43rd Air Division with pistol in one hand and in the other a rope with six trussed up German airmen on the end of it.[xii]

Despite the huge losses they were inflicting there were ominous signs for the Germans. For the first time they were faced with a country that was so large that their air force could only cover a small part of it. More than 90 per cent of the Soviet Union was untroubled by German planes and could therefore go about its business of preparing the defence unhindered. In particular the V.V.S. might have lost aircraft and air bases, but it had plenty left in rear areas and reinforcements could be moved forward judiciously. For instance in early July 401st and 402nd Fighter Regiments were moved up to the front from reserve. They were equipped with the Mig-3 and were manned by experienced ex-test pilots and instructors. These were some of the best units in the Soviet Air Force and it is a sign of the sheer size of Russia's war machine that after all its losses the V.V.S still had this kind of reinforcement available.

The Germans were beginning to realize that both in the air and on the ground they had underestimated the size of the Soviet armed forces and their willingness to fight. It was increasingly apparent that the defeats inflicted on them were due to command failures and other factors rather than any lack of fighting spirit in the average Soviet soldier or airman.

Although German aircraft losses were only a fraction of Soviet ones, nevertheless by the end of July they amounted in total to some 700 aircraft destroyed or damaged and it was beginning to be apparent that if the campaign lasted much longer, the strength of the Luftwaffe would simply bleed away.

On the northern part of the front the shock of the first few days completely disorganized the Baltic Special Military District. When the Germans overran Kaunas airfield in Lithuania they found 86 abandoned Soviet aircraft, most of them undamaged. General von Manstein's panzer corps was able to reach Daugavpils in Latvia by 26th June, a distance of 150 miles in four days. General Ionov the commander of the V.V.S. in this district was arrested. (He was shot in 1942.) For the Germans the only fly in the ointment was that Airfleet One did not have any Stukas and therefore their ground support role had to be taken by level bombers, principally Ju88s which were perfectly adequate for the task but were very vulnerable attacking at low altitude and accordingly took heavy casualties.

At this time there was something of a military reorganization on the part of the Stavka, the Russian High Command, which decided the Military Districts should be renamed 'Fronts'. Major General Novikov, the commander of the Northern Front was given responsibility for the Baltic Front as well. Novikov was a most able commander and he was able to put up a reduced but steady resistance to the Luftwaffe, albeit by transferring a number of aircraft from the Arctic far North. He gave his bombers escorts wherever possible and for the first time their raids had some effect. He was also aware that fighters must be more aggressive and not merely act as high cover for the ground troops. Despite the retreats the Russian army on this front had escaped any disastrous encirclement and much of the credit for this must go to Novikov and the V.V.S. .

German progress through the Baltic states was undoubtedly helped by the fact that those states, or at least Latvia and Estonia, had a substantial German population and had only recently been subjected to Soviet rule which they intensely disliked. The invading Germans saw the population as racially similar to themselves and therefore these countries were not treated with the savagery meted out elsewhere. Only the Jewish inhabitants suffered and it must be admitted that the rest of the population were generally indifferent to the fate of the Jews.

By the middle of July the German army had reached the Luga River which was the last significant defensive position before Leningrad. Airfleet One was down to barely 300 aircraft and was too weak adequately to support further advances.

The southern front was the one area where the air assault did not go entirely to plan: a plan which involved Army Group South driving southeast to cut off the Soviet forces facing the Rumanian border. Certainly the initial attack destroyed Soviet aircraft on the ground in large numbers but this was the front where the Kremlin's planners had placed the largest and best quality air contingent. Despite heavy losses the V.V.S. was always aggressive and made a real contribution to slowing down the German advance which, in this area alone, was limited and slow. Much of the credit for the stiff resistance in the air in the south must go to Lieutenant General, Yevgeni Ptukhin who was the V.V.S. commander of the Southwestern Front. This did not save him however, from the general bonfire of senior officers and on 1st July he was arrested and, some months later, tried and shot.

On 26th June three unidentified twin-engine aircraft carried out a raid on the town of Kosice in Hungary. One of the bombs dropped failed to explode and was subsequently identified as a FAB-100 of Soviet manufacture. This incident led to the declaration of war by Hungary on the Soviet Union which provided a very welcome addition to Axis forces both on the ground and in the air. To this day the Russians deny that the three aircraft were theirs and the suspicion arises that the whole affair was a sham engineered by the Germans to provoke just this declaration of war. Certainly they would have had no shortage of captured Russian bombs to use. The truth, however, must remain a mystery.

Slowly the Germans advanced but even by the middle of July, they were unable to take Kiev, the big prize in this theatre. On 10th July the Southwestern and Southern fronts, now joined in yet another new organization called the Southwestern Direction, received a new commander: Semyon Budyenny. Budyenny was an ex-Tsarist cavalry sergeant who joined the Communist Party in 1919 and became a close friend of Stalin. He was a colourful character with flamboyant moustachios but a calamitous commander in the field. In 1920 his incompetence was a large part of the Soviet defeat before Warsaw and in the Winter War he again held command with disastrous results. Now he was given even larger responsibilities and a further debacle could not be far away. The key to his survival was that close personal friendship with Stalin dating back to the early days of the Revolution. He was one of the very few people on earth whom Stalin felt he could trust, nor was Stalin disappointed, for what it was worth. Budyenny was an unfailing and uncritical supporter who finally died of old age in his bed in the 1970s.

On the central front the Germans drove on to Smolensk which was a little more than half the distance to Moscow from their starting points. Co-operation between army and air force remained close. Werner Moelders, the doyen of Luftwaffe fighter pilots became the first of them to score 100 victories. Albert Kesselring, commander of Airfleet Two, made sure that his own headquarters, contained in a series of trucks, was always close behind the front line and was in full operation twenty-four hours a day. The bombers' targets were troop concentrations, armour, rail hubs, motor transport columns, supply dumps, bridges, defensive strongpoints and A.A. installations. Their operations were so effective that it began to be apparent that the ground forces were becoming spoiled. Units increasingly delayed attacks until the Luftwaffe had bombed the target. Since the Luftwaffe had not the strength to be everywhere this increasingly caused a slowing of the advance, quite the opposite of what was intended. Moreover, the V.V.S. was recovering from its earlier trauma and fighting back hard. In July the Soviet Western Front received 900 replacement aircraft. They were used up and then replaced again. 410th Bomber Regiment arrived at the Western Front on July 5th with 38 brand new Pe-2 bombers and was at once thrown into the battle. By the end of the month it had only three left. 4th Ground Attack Regiment was down to ten aircraft, having been reinforced to 65 only two weeks earlier[xiii] and by the end of August it was further depleted and had to be taken out of the line.[xiv]

By the end of July the Luftwaffe claimed the destruction of 7,500 Soviet aircraft. This claim was undoubtedly exaggerated but even the Russians subsequently admitted the loss of over 5,000 up to October. On the other hand the Lufwaffe had lost 1,284 aircraft in the first month of operations. That was nearly half the force that started the campaign and was comparatively much more serious for Germany than Soviet losses were for Russia.

Now the stage had been reached where the Luftwaffe could no longer give the necessary support to the whole front. Airfleet Two, in the centre of the front, consisted of two Air Corps, the 2nd and the 8th. In early August, 8th was transferred to the control of Army Group North to help them breach the Luga line. It was assigned the area around Novgorod at the northern end of Lake Ilmen as Army Group North began the assault. The pilots of the 8th soon reported that the opposition they met was tougher here than on the central front. Nevertheless the offensive made steady progress and on 13th August German forces cut the railway line from Tallinn, the capital of Estonia, to Leningrad. Novikov fought back as hard as he could and brought up planes from the area south of Lake Ilmen to help in the protection of Leningrad. His command had been unwieldy ever since he took over the Baltic area and now his Northern Front was split up into a Karelian Front that covered the area being contested by the Finns and a Leningrad Front that encompassed the defence of that city.

At this time the career of Hans Rudel nearly came to an early conclusion. His squadron was part of 8th Flying Corps and his operations were now carried out in the Novgorod area and here, on one particular mission his squadron found the target obscured by a large and threatening thunder cloud. His leader turned away sharply and Rudel had to take swift avoiding action to avert a collision in the course of which he unintentionally entered the thundercloud and his aircraft was at once seized by the violent air currents and thrown around until it settled into a wild dive. Rudel struggled with the controls and finally pulled it back to level flight just as he felt a sharp bump. He climbed up again a little way for safety and when he emerged from the cloud it could be seen that a wing was damaged and carried, still attached, the broken branch of a tree. Rudel's colleagues were convinced that his conduct was the result, not of an accident, but a burning determination to get at the enemy, thunderstorm or no thunderstorm, and his stock rose accordingly.[xv]

In early September the final push on the city of Leningrad began. The air support came from Airfleet One and the 8th Air Corps and they applied a massive 'softening-up' operation on the eve of the attack. On the 6th September over 1,000 sorties were flown. There was very little fighter opposition from the Russians because the Luftwaffe had achieved an aerial ascendancy over the battlefield that even Novikov could not dent. Other attacks were launched on the city itself and amongst other targets, a warehouse was hit containing the city's entire sugar reserve which resulted in a mighty blaze.

On 12th September General Zhukov, who, as Russia's leading soldier, had been flown into Leningrad to direct the defence, ordered Novikov to throw in every last aircraft against German troops and airfields. This he did with surprising success because his aircraft were able to get in and out at low level often before the Luftwaffe's fighters could respond. On 14th September Zhukov launched a desperate counter-offensive that brought the Germans to a halt southwest of the city. Now the declining German fighter strength and the need for increasingly large escorts for the bombers had effectively reversed the balance of power in the air once again and given the ascendancy to the V.V.S..

One of the problems the Germans encountered operating near to the coast of the Gulf of Finland was that the defence was assisted by the ships of the Soviet Navy based at the island of Kronstadt outside Leningrad. A series of air raids was launched to neutralize these ships and on 23rd September the Stukas of the Immelman Wing sank the battleship Marat. The crucial hit that caused the battleship to blow up was scored by Hans Rudel who became a national hero overnight.

By Hitler's order 8th Air Corps was now transferred back to its parent Airfleet Two on the central front and with it went two bomber wings from the Leningrad front. Offensive operations before Leningrad were now over. The city was to be besieged but not assaulted.

On the southern front in mid-July Army Group South turned away from Kiev and pushed south to force the Russians holding the front against the Rumanians to withdraw. The retreat duly began and a portion of the Russian armies was surrounded at the town of Uman. Here the encirclement remained incomplete for some time because of the strength of the resistance, but the retreat of the Russians was rendered impossible by air power alone which brought rail traffic to a halt and made road travel by day hazardous in the extreme. Even as the Uman pocket was closed the Luftwaffe was forced to send 2nd Group of Jg 54 fighter wing home to Germany for rest and reinforcement. This fighter squadron had only half a dozen aircraft and exhausted pilots left, and was a spent force. It joined two bomber squadrons in withdrawal from the front for rest and repair.

The main strength of the Russian forces in this area lay with the 26th Army and this now retreated across the Dnieper in a well-organized operation that the Germans were not able to prevent. The key was the railway bridge over the river at the town of Kanev and despite its utmost efforts the Luftwaffe was unable to destroy it. The Stukas of Stg77 were used and it is significant that they had been transferred from the central front for the job. One German pilot recalled that: 'All previous air combat had been child's play compared with what we encountered above the Dnieper bridge at Kanev'.[xvi] So the Luftwaffe moved from a victory to a missed opportunity principally due to the decline in its front line power.

Now the bulk of von Rundstedt's Army Group South turned to the North to come round behind Kiev even as Guderian's panzer group from Army Group Centre came south to meet it.

The Russians prepared a counterattack under the command of General Yeremenko to stop Guderian and to support it he amassed a force of 460 aircraft. The Stavka had been carefully building up a reserve of aircraft and some of these were now released to help Yeremenko. The offensive halted Guderian and in the air there was intense fighting which went the way of the Germans, largely because the Russian reserves were pilots of little experience who were easy prey for the veteran German aces. One of those aces, Heinz Baer, shot down six planes in a day on 30th August bringing his victory total to 78, but the next day he was himself shot down and had to crash-land behind Russian lines. He sprained both ankles and had to lie in hiding for twenty-four hours while they recovered enough for him to start walking back to his own lines. He threw away his flying boots and turned his jacket inside out so that he could pass as a local peasant. He was successful in this and reached the German front line, but in doing so he aggravated the damage to his ankles so much that he had to spend two months in hospital.[xvii]

So intense were the Luftwaffe's attacks on the Russian forces that on 8th September the counteroffensive was cancelled and Yeremenko led his troops into a retreat.

Meanwhile the southern arm of the attack made good progress with little interference from the V.V.S. because the bulk of the reinforcements had been sent to Yeremenko further north. Von Rundstedt's panzers crossed the Dnieper at Kremenchug and pushed on to the North. In this area Airfleet Four was now able to give virtually complete air cover and almost no Soviet planes penetrated the screen of fighters. On 14th September the two arms of the encircling forces met and Kiev was cut off.

The Luftwaffe now turned its attention to pounding anything that moved within the Kiev pocket with negligible interference from the V.V.S. since Stalin had now written off the pocket and the forces within it. On 26th September the battle was over. The Kiev campaign had cost the Russians some 600,000 men. It also cost them about 1,500 aircraft.

Army Group South now rolled southeast across the Ukraine and south into the Crimea. Airfleet Four provided what support it could but its resources were running thin and its men were tired. It had to conserve its striking power and commit it only at intervals and where it would make the most difference. This led to inevitable complaints from the army that they were not getting the wholehearted support to which they were entitled. For the time being the Russians had few troops to bar the way and the burden of opposing the German thrusts fell largely on the V.V.S.

By the end of September the great city of Odessa had been cut off and besieged and the Soviet authorities came to the decision that they would do better to concentrate their defensive effort in the Crimea and therefore Odessa would have to be abandoned. A sea evacuation began in mid-October and was remarkably successful. The V.V.S. maintained constant air cover over the convoys entering and leaving the port and for some time the Germans did not even realize what was happening. When they finally grasped the truth they launched an attack on the next convoy with every available bomber, but it was an attack without escort as it was beyond the range of available fighters and the Russians were able to fend off the attack with almost complete success. Only one ship was sunk. 350,000 people were evacuated from Odessa in less than a week.

In the Ukraine the Germans soon found that the well of Russian resources was deep. Despite huge losses the V.V.R. was still very active and frequently delayed the German advance with well-judged bomber attacks. For many of the Russian pilots there was the galling experience however, of being re-equipped with planes that had recently been discarded as obsolete because these old veterans were all that was available at short notice.[xviii] Of course delay is not victory but it can be very important. When the Germans reached the factories of the big Ukrainian industrial towns such as Dnepropetrovsk and Stalino, they found them empty because the machinery had been loaded on trains and taken east to the Urals to resume operation undisturbed by the war. For a while trains became the main target for German bombers and Ju88s were equipped with cannon specially for train-busting missions, but this tactic was fairly easily thwarted by running the trains at night and in bad weather.

In the middle of October the rain and the consequent thick mud held up operations for both sides but it affected the Germans more because they were not used to it. Their attempt to blast through the Perekop Isthmus into the Crimea came to a complete halt. An independent Russian air command had been created in the Crimea and given some 500 aircraft scraped together from various places and set to a desperate defence of the peninsula. When the Germans brought in a fresh fighter group to support their attack the Russians carefully established the location of its base and then launched a dawn raid by several squadrons of Pe-2s. The result was freakish but successful. Not a single German fighter was destroyed but almost all were damaged and rendered unserviceable. The group was left with just six serviceable planes instead of 35.

Eventually strength told, however, and after a massive air attack on 24th October the Russian line crumbled and the Germans poured into the Crimea. 140 Russian planes were shot down that week. There is no viable defensive line in the interior of the Crimea so the Russians retreated to the fortress of Sevastopol and a siege began that was to last until July of the next year. There followed continuing clashes between the Luftwaffe and the Russian Black Sea Fleet. A cruiser was sunk and several destroyers damaged and on 7th November a great tragedy occurred when torpedo planes sank the steamer Armeniya with 5,000 people, wounded soldiers and refugees, on board. There were eight survivors.[xix]

All German resources were now concentrated on the drive for Moscow. By the end of September the Germans had lost 1,600 aircraft destroyed and another 1,200 damaged. Every possible plane was concentrated on the Moscow front. Reinforcements were drawn from the northern and southern fronts, two fighter squadrons were brought in from Western Europe and a Spanish volunteer squadron arrived. Despite these reinforcements the Luftwaffe's strength in serviceable aircraft was still only some 550.

It is uncertain what Russian losses amounted to by this time but the German claims amounted to 5,000 aircraft. The V.V.S. could muster a similar number of serviceable aircraft to the Germans but because of their low serviceability ratio they actually had rather more on hand. Moreover Russian pilots were gaining in experience and increasingly their squadrons contained new and improved aircraft types. One of the units before Moscow was the 11th Fighter Regiment, the first regiment to be wholly equipped with modern Yak fighter planes.

In the third week in September there was a severe frost and when that thawed there was deep mud. The offensive was launched on September 30th when the mud had dried. For three nights German bombers raided Moscow. The damage was moderate but the psychological effect was great. The Russians brought in aerial reinforcements of five bomber divisions drawn from other parts of the country and four regiments from the Stavka reserve in Moscow.

German armoured spearheads raced forward so fast that they were beyond the range of their fighters and suffered severely at the hands of Russian Pe-2s and Il-2s. In response the Germans took to using advanced fields for their fighters where transport aircraft flew in fuel and ammunition and the fighters flew to them early in the morning, flew in combat all day and retired back to their proper bases in the evening. Despite these difficulties the German army achieved another massive double encirclement at Vyazma and Bryansk on 7th October when the first snow also fell. On 9th, thick fog halted air operations for both sides but V.V.S. operations were not otherwise diminished by winter weather and they now concentrated on hitting German airfields. Such missions were made easier by the fact that the Russian pilots knew the target airfields well, having been based there a few days earlier. At Dugino airfield Russian bombers dived in to the attack just as Werner Moelders, now Inspector of Fighters, arrived for an inspection.

OKL, the Luftwaffe high command, now made the mistake of assuming the capture of Moscow was a foregone conclusion and sent 13 squadrons of the Moscow force to other parts of the front and two more to Germany for a brief rest and then a posting to the Mediterranean.

When the offensive was resumed the Germans found that far from collapsing, the Russian will to fight was redoubled. They established a new defensive line, the Mozhaysk Line, and brought in yet more reinforcements on the ground and in the air. The V.V.S. received 41st and 172nd Fighter Regiments fully equipped with Yaks and Lags and the 126th which was the first formation at the front to fly with lend-lease aircraft. It was equipped with American P-40s and its baptism of fire on October 12th was none too auspicious as its opponents, Jg51 claimed 14 victories for one loss.[xx]

On the northern flank the Germans reached Kalinin, 90 miles northwest of Moscow but had only the Spanish Blue Squadron of volunteers to support them. The Russians scraped together reserves from every source to cover this front including the 66th Bomber Regiment formed by impressing the personnel of a flight school, pupils, instructors and all. The Migalovo airfield became the epicentre of the fighting. Here Victor Talalikhin, hero of the Soviet Union, and 'night-taran' expert met his death. After shooting down two Me109s, a third one caught him. Junior Lieutenant Boris Kovzan brought down a German plane by 'taran' and then crashed behind German lines. Local people hid him until the Russians recaptured the area in December. When his plane was examined it was found that he had plenty of ammunition left and he was asked why he had resorted to ramming. He replied that he had never had any instruction in firing the guns.[xxi] Kovzan was not a pupil but a fully trained V.V.S. pilot. There could not be a clearer illustration of the low quality of Russian pilot training at this time (and indeed for much of the war).

On the southern flank the fighting approached Tula but progress was slow. On 23rd October there was a fierce air battle here and the score at the end of the day was 16 each: a sure sign that the V.V.S. was no longer the pushover it was in June and July. The German pilots remarked on the increased aggressiveness and determination of Russian pilots. The advance here ground to a halt because of mud and determined resistance.

In mid-November the winter started in earnest with heavy snow and temperatures of 20 and 30 degrees below zero. The Luftwaffe, which was quite unprepared for these conditions, was pole-axed. Least affected seemed to be its heavier bombers and on clear days strategic bombing missions were flown, but they were pinpricks in the Russian economy. Even had Germany possessed a fleet of strategic bombers it is doubtful if they could have made enough of a difference in the time available.

On 2nd December the German army made its last push toward Moscow and even penetrated the Moscow suburb of Khimki. However, Russian Il-2 Stormovik aircraft devastated its supply columns and the assault ground to a halt. The few German planes in the air could not protect their colleagues on the ground. Attrition and the weather had fatally weakened the Luftwaffe which now had fewer than 600 aircraft on this front against 1,300 Russians. The balance of power had finally tilted in Russia's favour and she had aerial superiority. The Soviet counter-offensive opened on 5th December and that was the end of German hopes of capturing Moscow.

In the far North German thrusts toward Murmansk had come to nothing and in the South, though huge areas of the Ukraine had been captured, no knock-out blow had been struck and the fortress of Sevastopol held out. Russian counter-attacks had re-taken Rostov and Airfleet Four was at the end of its strength. On this front too, the V.V.S. now held air superiority.

The Russian Air Force had been thrust into the furnace and had survived despite terrible losses. Though it had a great deal of fighting to do it would never face such a one-sided slaughter again. The V.V.S. had turned the corner but it came too late for its commander Pavel Rychagov. He was shot on 28th October.

CHAPTER ELEVEN

War in the Pacific

On the 7th December 1941 the Japanese attacked the United States Fleet in Pearl Harbour in the Hawaiian Islands and the Second World War became truly global.

From the start the Pacific War was quite unlike the war in Europe. The theatre of war was enormously larger and the aircraft fewer. Japan began the war with some 1,800 front line Navy aircraft and probably about 1,000 of the Army compared with Germany's 2,900 in 1939. In other words the Japanese Army and Navy Air Forces together were slightly less than the size of the Luftwaffe with a far greater area to control. Moreover, in the rest of the war Japanese industry built another 64,000 aircraft but Germany built nearly 90,000. The Japanese air forces began the war by attacking, amongst other places, the Philippine Islands 1,500 miles from Tokyo whereas the war in Europe began with an attack on Poland whose frontier was a mere 150 miles from Berlin.

The result of this was that the air war in the Pacific was less intense than in Europe, with the conflict bursting into life here and there as the strategy and the geography dictated, but with very few continuous battlefronts over which missions were flown day in and day out by large numbers of aircraft. China could have been such a battlefront but for most of the period 1941 to 1945 there was an undeclared truce on this front because it suited both sides not to fight: Japan had commitments elsewhere and the Chinese Nationalist government was content to let other people do the fighting for it. Thus air combat here was desultory and small-scale. There was a permanent battlefront in Burma but the air war there was sporadic since this was a low-priority theatre for both sides. There was intensive fighting over the Solomon Islands but only for 18 months. There was also intensive fighting over the home islands of Japan at the end of the war but only in New Guinea was there anything that approached the situation in Europe and even then, the similarity was limited.

The truth is that the Pacific always took second place to the European theatre in Allied plans because, in the long run, unless Germany won in Europe, Japan was never going to win in the Pacific. Japan's economic potential was simply not up to challenging the U.S.A. and doing so was always a gamble at very long odds. It was only ever undertaken by Japan's leaders because almost none of them except Admiral Yamamoto, Commander-in-Chief of the Imperial Navy understood the full implications of what they were doing. When the U.S.A.

entered the war President Roosevelt agreed that his country's first priority would be the defeat of Germany and the result was that the war in the Pacific became a large sideshow that never consumed more than 30% of U.S. military resources and some authorities say as little as 15%.[i] Yet within three and a half years the U.S.A., with only limited help from Britain and her Empire, had reduced Japan to impotence.

Such an outcome was a long way off in December 1941 and the months afterward, when the Japanese swept through Southeast Asia with fire and sword. The key feature in the Japanese onslaught was the Imperial Navy, because Japan was a collection of islands and any expansion had necessarily to involve control of the intervening seas. In this respect she was in much the same position as the United Kingdom which had always relied heavily on the capabilities of the Royal Navy. If Japan was to have an overseas empire she absolutely *had* to keep her sea lanes open and whatever fighting went on in that empire was always going to take second place to naval considerations. It is for this reason that all the crucial battles in the Pacific War are naval battles. Pearl Harbour set Japan on the road to expansion in the South Pacific. The Battle of Midway, in 1942, brought that expansion to an end and the Battle of the Philippine Sea in 1944, signaled the destruction of Japanese power. It is also for this reason that it is probably fair to say that though the air war may have been less intense than in Europe air power was, at times, more important.

It must be noted in passing that Japan had considered a quite different expansion policy involving expanding to the North and doing battle with the Soviet Union. At one time this was the favoured policy but the Nomonhan incident changed minds. If Japan could be bested on land by the Russians in this trial of strength, it was a poor augury for a total war.

The Japanese Navy travelled a long way between 1939, when we last considered it, and December 1941. By the time of Pearl Harbour it had six large aircraft carriers and five smaller ones which amounted to the best naval strike force in the world. It was the six larger ones that attacked Pearl Harbour: Kaga, Akagi, Soryu, Hiryu, Shokaku and Zuikaku. Between them they carried 450 aircraft. Those aircraft were some of the best naval designs anywhere. Following what was now universal custom the carriers' complement of aircraft was split into thirds by type: fighters, dive-bombers and torpedo planes.

The Navy had a new fighter aircraft called the Mitsubishi A6M2 Type 00. Its American code name was 'Zeke' but everyone then and now has called it 'Zero' after the year of its first construction by the reckoning of the Japanese calendar. It was put into production in 1940 which was the Japanese year 5700 and so it was the 'Type 00' in accordance with Japanese custom. It had a maximum speed of 336 m.p.h. and was armed with two 20 mm cannon and two machine guns, thus it was not exceptionally fast nor heavily armed, particularly since each cannon carried only 60 shells. On the other hand it had a range of 1,900 miles and was one of the most manoeuverable aircraft ever built. For the pilot it was very light on the controls and virtually flew itself. It was a radial engine, low wing monoplane with retractable landing gear and enclosed cockpit and it was a design of great natural beauty which challenged the Spitfire for aesthetic appeal and, over the years, has nearly matched it for fame. The Zero was an outstanding aircraft and it was flown by some of the best trained pilots in the world. It is then, small wonder that it was to sweep all before it in the first six months of the war in the Pacific.

The Army had a very similar new fighter the Nakajima Ki-43 'Oscar' whose only important difference from the Zero was that it was armed merely with two machine guns which was quite inadequate armament for the tasks it would face.

The Japanese Navy's dive-bomber was the Aichi D3A1 Type 99 known as 'Val'. This was a somewhat older design and still retained a fixed undercarriage but it was a strong, stable aircraft and an excellent bomber. It had a single, radial engine and a low wing configuration. The torpedo carrier was the Nakajima B5N2 Type 97 'Kate' which resembled the Val in most important particulars except that it had a retractable undercarriage. Like all torpedo carriers it could instead, take a small bomb load. It was something of a rarity in that it had no forward firing guns, the idea being that its bomb load or torpedo was its method of attack. This deficiency was also symptomatic of the obsessive Japanese concentration on keeping weight down in order to make their aircraft good aerodynamic flyers and easy to manoeuver.

From this feature stemmed the great weakness of all these aircraft and that was their lightness of construction. They had no armour and their fuel tanks were not self-sealing with the result that if an opponent could score a few hits on them they were likely to burst into flames or break apart.

For shore-based operations the Navy had a new bomber. This was the Mitsubishi G4M1 Type 1 'Betty'. This was a fast, twin-engine bomber with an amazing range of 3,700 miles. But it could only carry 2,200 lbs of bombs and less than that at extreme range and moreover, it shared all the characteristics of weak construction and flammability displayed by other Navy planes.

The Japanese war plan called for the fleet to knock out the U.S. Navy in its base at Pearl Harbour while simultaneously invading Malaya and the Philippines. This was to be followed by the invasion of the Dutch East Indies (today's Indonesia) and an offensive into Burma (Myanmar). This would provide the Japanese with the raw materials that their home country could not provide. Indeed the immediate cause of the war was the embargo imposed by the United States on oil imports upon which Japan was entirely dependent. The embargo was imposed in an attempt to coerce Japan into abandoning its invasion of China but one must admit that just as the Japanese underestimated U.S. power so the U.S. underestimated the Japanese aversion to 'loss of face'. Two other considerations propelled the Japanese toward war. The first was that they knew the Americans were beginning a major naval building plan so that although their Navy was weaker than that of the Americans, the imbalance would only get worse with time. The second was that the war in Europe had presented them with a unique opportunity. French and Dutch Far East colonies had been cast adrift by the defeat of the home country and Britain was fully committed in Europe and unable properly to defend hers.

The attack on Pearl Harbour was the key because if it was successful then the U.S. Navy would not be able to interfere with the rest of the Japanese plan. It was a great undertaking that involved preparing the fleet in utmost secrecy and then sailing over 3,800 miles in the rough waters of the North Pacific to strike at Pearl Harbour without warning. The attack itself presented its own difficulties because the anchorage was so shallow that normal torpedoes would simply bury themselves in the mud when dropped by aircraft. Special torpedoes had to be designed that had fins so that they would not dive so deep when they hit the water. In addition detailed intelligence about the base would be needed and the pilots would have to drop bombs and torpedoes with extraordinary accuracy. The details of the attack plan were worked out by a brilliant young naval officer pilot called Minoru Genda.

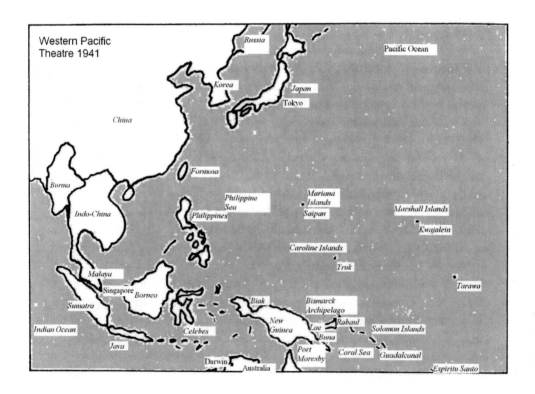

The whole operation was a great risk but if it came off then the U.S. Navy could be taken out of the equation and Yamamoto considered that Japan would have approximately a year of parity with the United States in which to achieve such victories that the latter would seek a negotiated peace. At the end of that year American industrial might would swing the balance immutably in her favour and the outlook for Japan would be bleak.

In French Indo-China, essentially that part of it that is now Vietnam, the Japanese Navy had based its 22nd Air Flotilla, part of 11th Air Fleet, to support the landings in Malaya. This consisted of 96 bombers and 40 fighters. On Formosa (Taiwan) there was the rest of 11th Air Fleet ready to strike at the Philippines. This was a force of 180 fighters and 190 bombers. The Japanese Army Air Force was available as backup. Its 3rd Air Division was also in Indo-China ready to support a move on Burma and could equally be used against Malaya. This amounted to another 300 front line aircraft. Its 5th Air Division was in Formosa with approximately another 150.

What power could the defenders muster to resist these attacks? The British in Malaya were well aware that a Japanese invasion was in the offing but they were indeed too heavily involved in the war in Europe to give Malaya the defence it needed. Pre-war it had been estimated that it would take 500 aircraft to provide adequate defence for the country but in December 1941 there were just 158 and none of those were the latest types. The fighters were Brewster F2A Buffaloes purchased from the United States and the bombers were the ubiquitous Blenheims. There were also some torpedo planes: Vickers Vildebeests. These were biplanes with open cockpits and fixed undercarriages that first entered service in 1928. In the whole of Malaya there was only one properly equipped aircraft repair shop and that was on Singapore Island.[ii] Not much could be expected of this collection of second-raters and one suspects that many of the pilots were not the best in the R.A.F. either. Certainly one of the Buffalo pilots was only in Malaya because he had volunteered for a posting to the Far East to escape an unfortunate romantic entanglement with a married woman in the U.K.[iii]

The U.S. Navy had its own carrier force but it was no match for the Japanese as of December 1941. It had six big carriers and in due course they would all be in the Pacific in the fight against Japan, but in December 1941 one was on duty in the Atlantic, another was on trials there and a third was undergoing a refit in the big Navy base at Norfolk, Virginia. A fourth carrier was also undergoing refit but in San Diego and the last two, Lexington and Enterprise, were at Pearl Harbour engaged in shipping planes and men to the base on the island of Midway. The Navy was in the last stages of re-equipping its nine fighter squadrons with the new F4F Wildcat fighter. (They had been flying Buffaloes.) The Wildcat was to meet the Zero head on across the Pacific and it must be said that the Zero came out of the contest the winner. However, the margin of superiority was not very great and in some respects the Wildcat was the better aircraft. It was very similar in that it had a single, radial engine, enclosed cockpit and retractable landing gear but it was not as manoeuverable as the Zero and did not have the same great range. On the other hand it was somewhat better armed with six .5 inch machine-guns and was much tougher. Part of the Zero's edge was in the extremely high quality of Japanese Navy pilots at the start of the Pacific War and as time went on and that quality declined the superiority of the Zero was less marked.

As noted, aircraft carriers all carried a mixed complement of fighters, torpedo planes and dive-bombers. The U.S. torpedo plane at this time was the Douglas TBD Devastator. It was a very old design and was extraordinarily slow and underpowered: its cruising speed was a mere 128 mph. It was due for replacement and the next year would see its place taken by the TBF Avenger, an infinitely superior aircraft that would stay in service through the 1950s and was, incidentally, the heaviest single-engine combat aircraft of the war. The dive bomber was the outstanding Douglas SBD Dauntless. Versatile, rugged and placid to fly, this aircraft was only replaced in late 1944 and even then, many felt that its replacement, the Helldiver, was no improvement.

The U.S.A. was unique among the major powers in having a third air force for its Marine Corps. This was much smaller than the other two and flew the same types as the Navy but always flew from land bases and never from aircraft carriers.

The beginning of the Second World War in 1939 had caused the U.S.A. to embark on a crash program of military modernization just in case they were to be drawn into the conflict at some point. This was nowhere more apparent than in the equipment of the Army Air Force where there was a complete clean-out of obsolete aeroplanes and introduction of new models. There was a new heavy bomber, the Consolidated B-24 Liberator, which first flew in December 1939 and was still only available in small numbers at the time of Pearl Harbour. It had a range of 2,000 miles with a full bomb load but if the bomb load was reduced it could fly an astonishing 4,000 miles and more and was a whole generation ahead of the Flying Fortress in terms of sophistication. More Liberators were produced than any other U.S. aircraft in World War Two.

Two medium bombers were put into production, the Martin B-26 Marauder and the North American B-25 Mitchell and there was a light bomber designated A-20 and called Havoc by the Americans and Boston by the British. We have already met this aircraft in the context of its sale to the French. It ended up being flown by almost every Allied country and in every theatre of war. It was extremely versatile and could be used not only as a light bomber but for ground attack purposes and as a heavy fighter. In all 7,400 of them were built and 3,000 of those went to the Soviet Union. Its design was so successful that an upgraded version, designated the A-26 Invader, was built which fought in the later stages of World War Two and then in Korea and Vietnam.

When it came to fighters the Air Force had a problem. The P-39 was something of a disappointment and the Lockheed Lightning was a long range twin-engine fighter. There can be no doubt that belief in the Douhet doctrine of the supremacy of the bomber had retarded fighter development. What was needed was a good, short range, single-engine interceptor. The only thing in the pipeline was the Republic P-47 Thunderbolt, but it was not likely that this would be ready until well into 1942. It was a sophisticated machine and it used a Pratt and Whitney radial engine for which there was already huge demand. The Army needed a simple fighter plane as soon as possible. The solution the Curtiss company hit upon was to take their existing P-36 Hawk which had been a good seller overseas and shown itself a capable fighter in China and elsewhere and upgrade it with a powerful new Allison in-line engine. This was the same engine that powered the P-39 Airacobra and it suffered from the fact that it had no supercharger so that its high altitude performance was poor. It was designed to work with a turbo-charger but there was no room for this bulky piece of machinery in a small fighter plane. The new aircraft was called the Curtiss P-40 Warhawk and although it was only a stopgap, it was surprisingly successful in a negative kind of way. It looked something like a Spitfire but had three times the range and since it had the radiator intake under the propeller in the nose, it had a 'shark-mouthed' appearance. It had an engine of approximately the same size as the Spitfire but it was a heavier plane and had a noticeably smaller wing surface and so was not very manoeuverable but it was tough and it was fast and it was reliable. For a plane with an in-line engine it was relatively easy to maintain. The result was that over 13,000 were built and it served in every theatre. It was never outstanding but it was good enough that no one was in a hurry to replace it.

American defensive strength in the Pacific was overwhelmingly centered on Pearl Harbour. That was where the fleet was and it was where nearly all the aircraft were too. The Army had some 230 planes there and the Navy 150. There were also another 150 Navy planes on the two carriers.

Elsewhere there was very little in the way of aerial defence on American islands. Wake Island had a Marine Squadron of Wildcats and Midway a handful of planes but Guam had no aircraft at all. The Philippines were the only American possession in the Far East and here there was based the Army's Far East Air Force. This was in the process of expansion at the time of Pearl Harbour and it only consisted of some 150 aircraft. Its backbone was represented by 35 B-17s and 80 P-40s. There were also some obsolete aircraft including a few P-26s, ancient machines dating back to the 1920s. This air strength was nearly all based at several airfields close to Manilla on Luzon Island. Many of the aircraft intended for the Philippines were in fact sitting at Pearl Harbour in transit at the time of the attack.

On the morning of Sunday 7ᵗʰ December 1941 the Japanese fleet lay 230 miles north of the island of Oahu and Pearl Harbour. The six aircraft carriers were guarded by two battleships and three cruisers. If the Americans had had any inkling of what was going on, they could have sailed out and overwhelmed this force. At 6.30 a.m. the first aircraft took off. The story of the next three hours has been told many times and there is not the space in the present book to tell it again in anything other than outline but it should be emphasized that treating the attack purely from a military point of view it was a masterpiece of planning and flying. The secrecy could so easily have been breached, the ships could have undergone any kind of misfortune on their long approach journey and a U.S. reconnaissance aircraft might so easily have spotted them. Weak resistance notwithstanding, the accuracy of the bombing and torpedo-launching was a tribute to the skills of the Japanese naval aircrew. Four battleships were sunk and three badly damaged; a number of other smaller ships were sunk or damaged. 100 Army planes and 80 Navy were destroyed. The attackers lost 29 aircraft in the attack but many more crash-landed on return to their carriers because of battle damage or the increasingly rough seas that were making the landing decks tilt alarmingly. 55 Japanese airmen died. Over 3,000 Americans died.

Very few U.S. planes managed to take off and fight the attackers in the air but those that did, gave a good account of themselves. Japanese pilots were taken aback by the aggressiveness of their U.S. counterparts; an ominous foretaste of things to come. And there was an obvious shortcoming in the Japanese victory: they had not even damaged a single aircraft carrier. This was not quite the disaster it has sometimes been made out to be. Aircraft carriers had virtually no defensive capabilities of their own, as ships, apart from their aircraft and there were frequent times such as bad weather and night when the aircraft could not operate. This meant that they needed an escort of battleships to carry out aggressive operations in enemy waters and that was no longer available. Moreover, had the Japanese attack caught the Lexington and the Enterprise and wrecked them, there were still another four U.S. carriers available. This being said, there was no doubt that the failure even to damage the U.S. carriers was a serious flaw in the victory.

When Pearl Harbour occurred, the Japanese invasion fleet was already bound for Malaya and British reconnaissance aircraft had already spotted it but could do nothing about it except watch. Within hours of the Pearl Harbour attack Japanese bombers were striking airbases in Malaya. At Alor Star a whole squadron of Blenheims was destroyed on the ground and much the same occurred at Butterworth where a squadron was in the act of taking off when they were hit. A Hudson bomber at Khota Bahru hit a Japanese transport off the beach where troops were landing and sank it, but apart from this small setback the landings on the Malayan coast went according to plan. Some of the ancient Vildebeests launched a torpedo attack against a Japanese cruiser in the middle of a tropical downpour but failed to do any damage.[iv]

Shortly before the outbreak of hostilities the Royal Navy had sent a battleship and a battle-cruiser to Singapore to strengthen the defence against just such an occasion as this. As the situation on the ground deteriorated they set sail to attack the Japanese beachheads and their guardian warships. The Prince of Wales was the Royal Navy's newest-but-one battleship, completed that same year; she was of 37,700 tons displacement, had a speed of 28 knots and a crew of 1,422. The Repulse was an older ship, launched in 1916. She was 27,650 tons, could make 30 knots and had a crew of 1,240. The original plan had been that these two mighty ships would be accompanied by an aircraft carrier to give them air cover but the ship earmarked for the post had been damaged and was not available. Admiral Phillips, in command of the ships, hoped that the land-based fighters in Malaya would be able to give him cover, but that proved not to be possible either, partly because they were fully engaged with the Japanese already and were taking heavy losses and partly due to poor co-ordination. The original mission of the ships was cancelled when they were spotted by the Japanese and they turned for home, but on the way they received a signal about another Japanese landing at Kuantan and went to investigate. Admiral Phillips did not tell Singapore of this change of plan nor request air support because he feared a radio transmission would reveal his position to the enemy. In fact at least a squadron of fighters was available.

Japanese bombers, which had been searching for the ships, now found them and proceeded to sink both in a little over two hours. In the middle of the battle a request was sent for air cover and a squadron of Buffaloes was sent from Singapore but they arrived too late. This patrol was commanded by Tim Vigors, the same man whose Irish flag upset Air Vice Marshal Park during the Battle of Britain. His squadron had been waiting for the call the whole time the ships had been at sea![v]

Two mighty battleships had been lost and with them went the last of the battleship age. These were the first battleships to be sunk by aircraft while at sea and under way. It was now quite clear that no ship could survive long in the presence of aircraft without its own air cover. General Billy Mitchell had been proven absolutely right. The Royal Navy, and indeed the whole of Britain, was stunned. Of the men on Prince of Wales, 327 were lost and of the men on Repulse, 444. Admiral Phillips was amongst the dead. He was the most senior British officer to be lost in combat in the war.

On land the campaign went from bad to worse and the air force, such as it was, was steamrollered by the Japanese. The 59th Wing of the Japanese Army, alone, claimed 11 victories in the air and 13 on the ground for the month of December. The Japanese ace Saburo Sakai later said: 'The Buffaloes were rough, inferior aircraft. They never stood a chance against our Zeros.'[vi]

On 12th December Tim Vigors was shot down over Kuala Lumpur. He was badly burned and was months recovering, first in Java and then in India. He never flew in combat again.

The crew of the battleship Prince of Wales abandon ship. Her sinking proved aircraft could defeat the mightiest ships. ©Imperial War Museum (HU 2675)

The Japanese attack on the Philippines was under way even as the raid on Pearl Harbour finished. Navy planes flew to attack airbases on Luzon from Formosa. This was a distance of 500 miles or a round trip of 1,000. Given that a fighter aircraft must be ready to dogfight when it reaches its target, this implied a potential flight of 1,200 miles. For the bomber pilots distance was not a problem but for the Zeros it was at the very limit of their range and practice flights were made in advance in order to reduce petrol consumption in flight. The record for low consumption was set by Saburo Sakai.[vii]

Sakai was a most interesting figure. His exploits in China had already made him something of a legend. He ended the war with 64 victories and was for a long time thought to be the highest scoring surviving ace. In recent years that particular distinction has been thrown in doubt but he was certainly a national hero and after the war he wrote his autobiography which is a unique source of insights into Japanese military attitudes and behaviour.[viii] He came from a poor farming family but a relative gave him the chance to study at a leading school in Tokyo. There he misbehaved himself and was sent home in disgrace. He then joined the Imperial Navy to seek redemption and soon showed that he was an outstanding pilot.

Sakai was one of the Zero pilots escorting the bombers from Formosa as they struck the U.S. airbases on Luzon. General Brereton, commander of the Far East Air Force, had been warned that raids were coming and wanted to send out his own attack on Formosa using his B-17s, but such a course was forbidden by General MacArthur who was in overall command of U.S. forces in the Philippines (and who later, implausibly, denied this.) Apparently MacArthur felt that this would be a provocative act. Since the attack on Pearl Harbour had already taken place this explanation was nonsense and, at first sight, inexplicable. Possibly McArthur wanted the Japanese to ignore the Philippines, or at least strike first so that the Philippines should feel the same sense of outrage as the continental U.S.A.. He had a long association with the Philippines and had been military adviser to the Government prior to being appointed the local U.S. commander so that his approach was overly political and he saw himself as Philippino as much as American. That such conduct made a mockery of his duty as an American officer would not have bothered him: his egotism and arrogance were world-class. If there is no such political explanation MacArthur would appear to stand indicted of one of the worst pieces of incompetence in U.S. military history.

As it happened, the U.S. air force was largely caught on the ground by the Japanese and destroyed. One squadron of fighters that became airborne was torn to shreds by the Zeros, only two of its twelve planes escaping. The raid of which Sakai was a part destroyed 44 aircraft on its own. As he flew over the airfields of Luzon and witnessed the quiet scene he could not believe the Americans were not up in the air to the last plane and ready to fight: 'Pearl Harbour had been hit more than five hours before; surely they had received word of that attack and expected one against these critical fields!'[ix] At the end of the raid he finally encountered five P-40s in the air and shot one of them down. By 10th December the number of U.S. fighters had been halved but even less were in a position to fly active missions. The surviving B-17s did manage to fly several anti-ship missions but without success. This was high level bombing and the Americans were finding out that that does not work against ships. They must be bombed and torpedoed at low level. On 17th the surviving 14 B-17s were evacuated to Australia.

By now Allied air power in Malaya and the Philippines had been destroyed but the Japanese attack rolled on and they made landings on Borneo on 11th December and then on other islands in the Dutch East Indies. To defend their East Indies possessions which stretched for 2,000 miles east to west, the Dutch could muster 200 planes which were the usual collection of second division equipment. The best were some P-40s but there were many P-36 Hawks and Buffaloes and Martin B-10 bombers, a kind long retired from the U.S. Army Air Force. There were also a few planes that had retreated here from Malaya and the Philippines. By the end of the month this number was down to 150.

In January 1942 there were landings on New Guinea. On 22nd the Japanese reached Rabaul on the island of New Britain. Aerial resistance now centered on Java, the most populous Indonesian island and reinforcements and supplies came in from Darwin on the Australian coast further south. New Britain, New Ireland and Papua New Guinea were Australian possessions largely covered in jungle but rich in minerals and there were numerous small mining settlements there which were now evacuated by air using every available plane that could be found.

On 19th February the Japanese carried out a major raid on Darwin with 125 bombers and 18 Zeros. Ships were sunk, port facilities were devastated and 18 planes destroyed. Darwin was no longer viable as supply base for Indonesia. In fact this was only the first of a long series of raids on the town that went on until January 1943.

Also on 19th, 23 Zeros were dispatched from Balikpapan in Borneo on a search and destroy patrol to Surabaja in Java. News of their approach was radioed to the town and more than 50 Dutch and other Allied fighters were waiting for them. But numbers made no difference: the Japanese planes and pilots were simply too good. Saburo Sakai was one of the Zero pilots. He shot down two planes and would have had more except that he saw five others destroyed by his colleagues before he could get to them. It was something of a turkey shoot.[x] On 20th February the Japanese landed on Bali and Timor.

One of the few means of striking back available to the Allies was the use of B-17s based in Australia. Available planes had been flown in, in ones and twos from as far afield as Africa. Now they carried out raids on Japanese ships and landing sites across Indonesia. They were too few to make much difference but Japanese pilots were awed by the strength of these huge planes and their ability to soak up damage. The new 'E' model B-17 made its first appearance at this time. It was much better armed than previous models and when the first two were attacked by a squadron of Zeros the pair shot down six fighters.[xi]

Forty P-40s that had been assembled at Darwin as reinforcements were flown north to Java in stages. Bombs and breakdowns meant that only 26 of them were ever fit for action. On 28th February a convoy sailing for Java was hit by a force of Betty bombers just off the island's south coast. The U.S.S. Langley was sunk. She was an old aircraft carrier now used to transport aircraft and she took 32 P-40s to the bottom with her. In the same convoy was the Sea Witch with 27 P-40s on board in crates. She made port at Tjilatjap on 28th but the Japanese landed on Java the same day and the crates were destroyed for fear they would fall into the hands of the Japanese. Thus almost 60 fighters were lost without a single one ever getting in the air.[xii]

Resistance on Java collapsed. On March 3rd a collection of flying boats at Broome Harbour were surprised by Zeros in the middle of an evacuation and slaughtered both on the water and in the air.

By March 7th the fighting was over. On February 15th Singapore had fallen and though American forces on Luzon still held out, they were besieged on the peninsula of Bataan without any air support and it was only a matter of time before the final surrender came in May.

The only place where the Japanese tide of expansion received even a temporary check was at tiny Wake Island. This was an atoll on which a proper airfield had been built so that it could be a staging post for Pan American Airways' Pacific passenger service. The island had a Marine garrison and a squadron of F4F Wildcats. Air raids on the day of Pearl Harbour destroyed seven of the 12 planes but when a Japanese invasion force appeared it was beaten off by shore batteries and the Wildcats carrying small bombs which managed to damage two cruisers and sink a destroyer. By 22nd December the last Wildcat had been shot down and the garrison surrendered the next day.

Admiral Nagumo's fleet, which had administered the blow at Pearl Harbour, then sailed through the islands of Indonesia raiding Darwin amongst other places and in March 1942 it sailed into the Indian Ocean with the intention of repeating Pearl Harbour with the British fleet in Colombo and Trincomalee on the island of Ceylon (now Sri Lanka). The British were warned however and sailed out of the ports in time though the Japanese planes did severe damage to the port facilities. Later they caught two heavy cruisers on their own and sank them both in 20 minutes. Worse, they found the aircraft carrier Hermes, which had been evacuated from Ceylon without her air group and sank her too. The Indian Ocean had now been added to the South Pacific as zones of complete Japanese domination.

In three months the Japanese had not only conquered a large slice of the globe but they had demonstrated in amazing fashion the superiority of the aircraft over the ship. Large or small, in harbour or at sea, no ship was safe from the dangerous attentions of aircraft unless it had its own aircraft to take care of it.

The losses at Pearl Harbour meant that no immediate counter-offensive was possible for the Americans but they were determined to do something to strike back. The aircraft Carrier Yorktown was summoned from the Atlantic and the Saratoga from the U.S. west coast. No sooner had the Saratoga reached Hawaii than she was torpedoed by a Japanese submarine and severely damaged, but the U.S. Navy still had three carriers in the Pacific and carried out a series of raids, on the Gilbert Islands, Kwajalein in the Marshall Islands and Rabaul on New Britain which was rapidly becoming a major Japanese base. At the first two targets considerable damage was done and merchant ships sunk, but at Rabaul Japanese planes spotted the American task force and attacked it. The battle was indecisive but the Americans wisely withdrew. One U.S. pilot, Lieutenant Edward O'Hare of the carrier Lexington, shot down five Japanese bombers on one mission thus becoming the Navy's first ace of the war since five victories is the traditional mark of the ace. He was awarded the Congressional Medal of Honor but, sadly, was killed later in the war. His name lives on in the form of Chicago's principal commercial airport.

Japanese expansion plans were not over. They were planning to invade the south coast of New Guinea next and the invasion of Burma was already under way.

CHAPTER TWELVE

The Bomber Offensive 1942/3

In August 1941 the Butt report shook the faith of the British Government in the whole concept of strategic bombing. A large tranche of Britain's scarce resources was going into the bombing campaign and it was only common sense that if it was not producing a commensurate return, then those resources should go elsewhere. The army wanted more aircraft to support its campaign in Africa and the navy wanted more aircraft to help combat the U-boat menace. The navy's case was particularly strong since this was a time when the submarine war was not going well and defeat at sea would mean the collapse of the whole war effort. At the same time the workforce building heavy bombers was equal in manpower to the entire British army.[i]

On the other hand Churchill had faith in the bombers and, being by nature aggressive, he liked the idea of a weapon that could strike back directly at Germany. It was also important politically to be able to show Russia that Great Britain was taking her share of the strain while Russian casualties mounted into the millions. Winning the Battle of the Atlantic was vital to prevent Britain from losing the war but it was not going to win it. He was shaken by the Butt report however, and replied to a memo from Portal in September 1941about future bombing plans with the peevish observation that bombing was no more than 'a heavy…. annoyance' for the enemy.[ii] In his reply Portal artfully pointed out that strategic bombing was accepted to be a central plank of the British war effort and if it was now to be merely an 'annoyance' then something else must be given priority and the allocation of national resources re-arranged.[iii] This brought Churchill up short: he had no other weapon to promote and he could not face the admission that everything done hitherto for the sake of the bombing campaign was wasted.[iv] He assured Portal of his support and never wavered again. There was some criticism in the House of Commons[v] but once Churchill was on-side, the bomber offensive was never really in doubt.

That does not mean however, that it was yet to achieve anything very much. Air Marshal Peirse the commander of Bomber Command ordered a series of long distance raids on Germany during the autumn including raids on Berlin designed to raise the profile of the offensive. These culminated in a near disaster on the night of 7th/8th November. An all-out effort was made that night with one section of the bomber force bombing relatively close targets on the coast of Europe or in the Ruhr and the other taking on targets deep in Germany including Berlin. Total losses of aircraft were 37 which was more than nine percent of those setting out. Moreover the losses were all amongst the aircraft assigned the further targets who therefore suffered almost 14 percent destruction. Such losses were unacceptable. It had been calculated that for bomber command to wage a viable strategic bombing campaign, which had to include growing greatly in size, it could not afford to suffer losses in the long term of more than four percent, though it might accept five for short periods.[vi] Churchill and the Air Staff were unanimous that Peirse must be reined in for the time being until the better aircraft and improved navigational aids that were in the pipeline became an operational reality. He was accordingly told that he must conserve his force as a first priority but he was not happy about this. He felt that it was a rebuke and that it negated the point of his command. In effect, he was right on both counts.

Conservation duly followed but it was only partial because the navy made repeated requests for bombing missions against the battleships Scharnhorst and Gneisenau in Brest harbour and the U-boat pens in Brest and St. Nazaire, as well as the U-boat manufacturing and repair facilities in the ports on the German North Sea coast. Bombing the battleships was worthwhile and in due course they were obliged to leave the port and return to Germany, though we have seen that the RAF did not cover itself with glory when that happened. Bombing the north German ports was of marginal significance to the U-boat war because, for various reasons, U-boat construction was a very difficult target. The real waste was the assault on the U-boat pens which were built of reinforced concrete too thick for any RAF bomb then in use to penetrate. All parties knew this fact but the Royal Navy still insisted on the raids, which had no effect other than steadily to destroy the towns around the pens and kill French civilians.

Peirse did not last. He had plainly lost the confidence of his superiors and in January 1942 he was sent to India to head the Allied air forces there. After a brief interregnum his place was taken by Arthur Harris, one of the most interesting and controversial of all the war's military commanders. Harris was born in 1892, the son of a member of the Indian Civil Service. In his teenage years he was plainly a 'difficult' young man and the upshot was that he emigrated to Rhodesia (now Zimbabwe) under his own steam, aged 16 in 1908 and worked at a variety of jobs. In 1914 he joined the Rhodesia Regiment as a bugler and fought in German Southwest Africa (now Namibia). When the campaign was over he travelled back to the UK and joined the Royal Flying Corps with which he saw front line action. After World War One he decided to make flying his career and became a professional airman with the R.A.F.. During the inter-war years his rise was steady and included a period on the planning staff at the Air Ministry. On the outbreak of war he was appointed commander of 5 Group which he ran with the energy and enthusiasm that were his hallmark. In 1941 he was part of the R.A.F.'s delegation to the United States. Harris was realistic to the point of cynicism and blunt to the point of rudeness but he could inspire intense devotion and was one of those people who have the knack of getting things done.

Shortly after his appointment Harris gave an address in a film newsreel in which he said, inter alia: 'There are a lot of people who say that bombing can never win a war. My answer to that is that it has never been tried yet and we shall see.' It was clear that Harris was a disciple of Douhet and was wholeheartedly committed to area bombing and the destruction of the enemy's will to fight by means of terror from the air. His name is now forever linked with this policy but it was in no sense originated by him: he was merely a keen follower.

During February 1942 the Air Staff issued the Area Bombing Directive which authorized a return to full-scale operations with area bombing as its objective.[vii] This was really the only practical alternative now that it was clear precision attacks were not working. Moreover, in March Lord Cherwell, the chief scientific advisor to the government, presented a paper to Churchill and the cabinet to the effect that bombing should seek to cause the enemy's economic collapse by destroying the homes of workers and thus making it difficult if not impossible for them to do their jobs. Such bombing would, at the same time, bring about a severe lowering of civilian morale leading to demands for peace.[viii] The fact that it would kill a large number of civilians was carefully omitted from discussions. There was, of course, the objection that this had been tried on Britain in the Blitz without any of the predicted effects, to which the answer was that what was to be done to Germany was to be ten times worse. In fact the idea of smashing the enemy's cities had been an unacknowledged and unofficial aim of bombing ever since the Blitz and there can be no doubt that it had public blessing. In the Air Ministry's 1941 book Bomber Command the claim has already been referred to that one third of Aachen had been reduced to ruins.[ix] Here was a boast of the effects of area bombing put forward for public satisfaction before it was even official policy.

Harris set to his work with a will. The two essentials for reducing the cities of Germany to ashes were, first, more aircraft, (particularly large, four-engine bombers,) to increase the bomb load delivered and, second, navigational aids to get the attacking force to the right place. When he took command he stated that he could put in the air only 300 bombers of which a mere 50 were the new four-engine 'heavies'. Harris being Harris, these figures may be a little conservative but they were not far wrong. He at once began a series of raids to show what Bomber Command could do but he was careful to limit himself to missions well within the known capabilities of the force. He attacked the Renault factory at Billancourt outside Paris: it was poorly defended and was not far away. In a sense this was an unusual target in that it was a piece of precision bombing. The mission was a success and showed what could be done in that line if conditions were right. Then he attacked Lubeck and Rostock, much further away but both cities were on the coast which made them relatively easy to find. The aiming point for the bombs was now the centre of the town and

All factories were targets for bombers. This is the Renault factory outside Paris in ruins after a night raid of 3/4th March 1942 by the R.A.F.. In fact raids on individual factories were more commonly carried out by the U.S.A.A.F. ©Imperial War Museum (C 4642)

Lubeck was particularly amenable to this kind of attack because it had a mediaeval centre of close-packed houses of largely wooden construction. The city centre of Lubeck, ancient and beautiful, was burned down. The bombing theory was that if you aimed at the centre of a town and dropped enough bombs you would not only 'de-house' the workers but destroy all kinds of infrastructure as well, albeit by chance.[x] Bomb loads were a carefully selected mixture of high explosive bombs to smash roofs and blow out windows and doors and incendiaries to set fire to the interiors thus exposed. The navigation for these raids was still done by eye and the target marked with incendiaries or flares by some of the leading aircraft so that the rest would know where to drop their bombs.

What were the Germans doing meanwhile to protect their cities? They began the war with no defences against night-time bombing at all because they thought the war would be short and in any event any bombing would be by day and they would be doing it. In 1940, however, when they were bombing Britain by night and the first British raids were striking at German cities, it was natural to consider the defence of their own land. In April 1940 the task of creating a force of night fighters was given to an officer named Wolfgang Falck and in July that force shot down its first bomber. Also in July the task of creating an integrated night defence of Germany was entrusted to Josef Kammhuber, a distinguished senior bomber pilot and the same man who was shot down and injured over Paris in the French campaign. Kammhuber soon realized that he did not have the resources adequately to defend every city in the Reich so he concentrated on creating a belt of searchlights and flak guns along the coast of Europe from Denmark to the Low Countries. Behind it he defended only the obvious targets in the western half of Germany such as the industrial towns of the Ruhr valley and, of course, Berlin. By 1942 this defensive system was well established and had been enhanced by the use of radar. The radar worked much as had the radar of the R.A.F. in the Battle of Britain: that is a ground station tracked a bomber and guided the fighter to it. Then it was up to the pilot to spot the bomber visually. In late 1942 an airborne radar was developed to make the task easier for the pilot. The differences were that this was more precise work with one bomber and one fighter. There were many ground radar stations and each one was allotted a 'box' of airspace in which to search. The boxes were arrayed along the 'Kammhuber line' several rows deep.

At first the night fighter force used single-engine fighters for the job but they soon proved themselves unsuitable and twin-engine fighters or converted bombers were used. Before long the force settled down to using predominantly two types: the Me110 and the Ju88, the latter being converted from bomber to heavy fighter. Night fighting was quite different from its day counterpart in that no particular manoeuverability was required but the plane must have an observer/navigator and later, radar operator, so the pilot was free to concentrate on flying and shooting. The planes were very heavily armed and once they found a bomber they could quickly dispatch it unless the bomber's own gunners hit them first.

This defence worked well but it had an inherent fault that the R.A.F. under Harris was quick to exploit: each box could only direct one fighter plane at a time. In the early days of the war this did not matter much because bombers were free to take any route they chose to the target and operate to their own timetable. Harris realized that if the bombers were concentrated into a narrow stream and sent at more or less the same time, they would swamp the defence by passing through only a few boxes and presenting far more targets than the fighters could cope with. This concentration also had the advantage that bombs would be dropped on the target in a much shorter space of time and thus would overwhelm the defences on the ground. A fire brigade that might fight ten fires one after another could not fight them all at once. The disadvantage was thought to be the risk of collision between bombers, particularly over the target. Harris decided to take this risk and he was proved right. Collisions did occur but not with anything like the frequency that had been anticipated.

By May 1942 Harris had 400 bombers available. True, over half of these were Wellingtons, good aircraft but part of the old generation, but he also had 136 of the new, four-engine heavy bombers. These latter were of three types. The Short Stirling was the earliest to see service in numbers but was something of a disappointment. Although it could carry a large bomb load it had a low ceiling and was slow. The result was that it was very vulnerable. Fighters could catch it, flak found it easier to reach and it was at risk from the bombs released by planes flying higher up. The next into action was the Handley Page Halifax. This plane had a number of deficiencies when first sent to the squadrons, from leaky hydraulics to a serious stability problem. When these were put right it was a first class aircraft which was used not only as a bomber, but for transport duties, glider towing and anti-submarine duties. The third type was the Avro Lancaster, a very famous bomber and sometimes acclaimed as the best bomber of the war. Its big advantage was that it carried a bomb load almost 50% larger than the other two types and for the R.A.F.'s saturation bombing campaign, bomb load was the overriding consideration. It was also tough yet still sweet to fly. Its crews grew very fond of it. Arthur Harris was a big fan and by the end of the war it equipped two thirds of Bomber Command squadrons.

Mention should be made of the Avro Manchester, a hybrid design with two engines but the carrying power of the four engine models. It was, in effect, the same design as the Lancaster but with two less engines. Unfortunately its two engines were a new design from Rolls Royce that was unreliable and the Manchester was thus wholly unsatisfactory and was quickly withdrawn from service but there were a few on the roll at the time we are considering. Roy Chadwick, the chief designer at Avro had quickly changed his design to accommodate four engines and the result was the Lancaster.

The Lancaster was the backbone of Bomber Command in the later years of the war just as the Wellington had been in the earlier years. It overshadowed the Halifax though the latter, in its Mark III version with stability problems ironed out, had much to recommend it. It was faster than the Lancaster, climbed better and was tougher, if harder to fly.[xi] Some pilots who flew both types thought the Halifax responded faster to the controls and it was internally better arranged with crew convenience in mind. Its loss rate was almost identical to that of the Lancaster despite claims to the contrary.[xii] What is quite clear is that the survival rate for crews shot down flying the Halifax, was two or three times that for Lancaster crews, since the Lancaster was something of a death trap because of the poor design and placement of its escape hatch.[xiii] The hard fact of war however, was that an airman who parachuted to safety became a prisoner of war and was no more use to the war effort, just as if he had been killed. Accordingly, with those who made the important decisions, this advantage of the Halifax counted for little.

Harris decided that he needed some major demonstration of air power to convince doubters that resources put into the bomber offensive were producing some result. He hit on the brilliant idea of the 'Thousand Plan'. This was simply the idea of carrying out a raid using 1,000 bombers. If the target was well chosen a great deal of damage must be done even if the bombing was of indifferent accuracy and the use of the magic number of 1,000, which was more than double the size of any previous raid, was guaranteed to hit headlines around the world. Every effort was made to ensure the bombing was as accurate as was humanly possible. The mission was suspended until weather conditions were optimal and the target was carefully chosen to be easily found and identified. Several cities were considered suitable but in the event the choice fell on Cologne which was not too far away and which sat on the Rhine, easily identifiable from the air. Finally, a new navigational aid, called 'Gee', was used for the first time in a large scale raid.

Gee consisted of three radio stations each sending out pulses that the bombers could receive. By measuring the time difference between receipt of the first two pulses and the third, you could measure how far you were from each of the first two radio stations and thus plot where you were. In theory this was a near magical solution to the problem of navigation at night but there were distinct drawbacks. First, the system needed a skilled operator in the plane; second, there were only a limited number of Gee sets available; third, the range of the radio pulses only stretched a little past the Ruhr Valley so much of Germany was not covered and fourth, the radio beams could be jammed by a strong broadcast on the same frequency. In fact, as soon as the Germans discovered the existence of Gee they would undoubtedly do just that and so Bomber Command had to make good use of their new asset while they could.

Considering that Bomber Command disposed of just 400 first line aircraft, finding 1,000 for the raid was a major task but it was accomplished, largely by impressing most of the fleet of training aircraft together with transport and liaison craft. The Royal Navy showed itself in a poor light by promising to contribute Coastal Command aircraft and then changing its mind for no apparent reason at the last minute. Nonetheless 1,047 aircraft went on the raid. They were sent in a concentrated stream and the raid was all over in 90 minutes. Cologne was hard hit: 500 were killed and over 15,000 buildings were destroyed. The Germans were shocked at the extent of the damage but the centre of the town was not wiped out as in Lubeck because most of Cologne was of 19th Century construction, brick and stone and with wide roads. This made it hard for fires to spread out of control. Only 41 aircraft were lost and only two of those due to collision. The rest were mainly lost to flak. German night fighters were a limited threat because the tactics of using a concentrated bomber stream were working well. The losses were tolerable and the new approach was proving a success. As a result of the raid one pilot was awarded the Victoria Cross for bravery. He was Leslie Manser, pilot of one of the ill-starred Manchesters.

Even before the raid Manser's aircraft was misbehaving. When he flew an air test it would not rise to more than 7,000 feet, less than half of its proper ceiling. He decided to take part nonetheless, on the basis that he might not be noticed flying so low. This hope was in vain and he was caught by searchlights over Cologne and hit hard by flak. He dropped his bombs and turned for home but he was now down to less than 1,000 feet in height and decided to try to climb but the port engine then burst into flames. He could have ordered everyone to bale out but he wanted to get home so he turned on the fire extinguisher and hoped for the best. The fire went out but before long the starboard engine began to overheat and the plane became hard to control. He ordered the crew to bale out but kept at the controls himself to hold the plane steady while they did so. The Manchester was losing height fast and by the time they were all gone there was no time left and he died as his aircraft crashed.[xiv]

Manser's situation was far from unique. In the course of the war many brave pilots stayed at their controls to let their crew bale out, though they well knew that they were condemning themselves to death. The essential problem was that the automatic pilots in use at that time were rudimentary and could not deal with anything out of the ordinary. If the plane was seriously damaged it was liable to go into a spin if left to itself and the centrifugal forces inside a spinning aircraft would pin the crew where they were and prevent them abandoning ship. The pilot therefore had to hold the plane steady and often then ran out of time to get out himself. Sometimes the plane's instability was such that he could never hope to get out because it would go out of control the moment he let go of the control column. In such a case his last, forlorn hope was to crash-land but doing that at night, in a large and damaged aircraft on strange territory was close to suicide.

The success of the Cologne raid caused Harris to mount two more thousand bomber raids in the next month. One was on Essen and was not very successful, largely because of the industrial haze that hung over the city. This was still the age when industry was coal powered and industrial areas tended to be shrouded in an unhealthy smog much of the time. The last raid was on Bremen and was a fair success, but there was a great deal of unpredicted cloud that affected bombing accuracy and it was not the equal of Cologne. Both raids were in fact carried out by slightly less than 1,000 bombers. There were no more thousand bomber raids because of the disruption they caused to training. However, they had served their purpose.

Everyone was impressed by these raids and Bomber Command now had a breathing space in which to expand and improve its methods, but 1942 wore on and it began to be clear that nothing much had changed. The bomb tonnage dropped increased steadily but the German economy was still hardly being affected, as was increasingly apparent, even in England. Churchill and the cabinet were prepared to wait however. They were totally committed and there was very little by way of alternative. Moreover, there were encouraging signs that promised real progress in the future.

Techniques for finding and marking the target were refined. It was apparent early on that it would not be possible to equip every aircraft with every navigational aid. Not only was industry not up to such a comprehensive job, but training the necessary operators was too slow and so a system was developed whereby a small, elite force would do all the searching and identifying of targets and then drop coloured target indicators on them so that the rest of the bomber force could clearly see where it was supposed to drop its bombs. The target would be the coloured markers and not anything else the pilots might see on the ground. The markers were coloured flares dropped in bunches and designed to burn for as long as possible. The elite marker force was called the 'Pathfinder Force' and it was constituted in the summer of 1942 as a quite separate bomber group (No. 8 Group) with the pick of the bomber crews and its own uniform badge and extra pay. Its crews had to do 45 missions before they were rested as opposed to the 30 for the rest of Bomber Command. It should be born in mind that with losses of 4% or more on each raid, the odds were against any individual crew completing a tour of 30 missions, let alone 45.

Harris was initially opposed to the creation of a pathfinder force, as such, on the grounds that creating an elite force necessarily downgraded skill and morale in the rest of the Command. When it became clear however, that his objections would be overridden, he acquiesced so that he could retain the right to appoint its commander. In typical Harris fashion however, he ignored the obvious choice for command of the new force, a man called Basil Embry, and appointed instead an Australian officer who was, admittedly, one of the finest airmen of the time. This was Don Bennett, a man who not only could fly any plane, he could take it to pieces and then put it back together again. He was the second pilot in the world to win a Master Navigator's ticket. Unfortunately he was a cold, aloof man who was extraordinarily pleased with himself and was also twenty years younger than the other Group commanders and promptly fell out with them. It is hard not to feel that this was Harris's intention all along. No. 5 Group, run by a man called Cochrane, a sour Scot but a man always open to innovation, became the new testing ground for improvements in marking technique.

As from August 1942 the Germans began to jam Gee as had been foreseen. Efforts were made to counter-jam but Gee became progressively less useful and without it, target identification was back to the old hit-and-miss visual method, but at the start of 1943 there was a great leap forward with two new navigational devices. The first was 'Oboe'. This was similar to the system used by the Luftwaffe in 1940/41 over England and consisted of a radio beam which an aircraft followed by means of an audible signal. When it reached the target it encountered a second beam that gave another signal and the crew released the markers. This system was found to be remarkably accurate. Inevitably it had drawbacks: its range was limited (but was better than Gee), it could be jammed once the Germans found out about it, and it could only provide directions for one, later two, aircraft at a time.

The second invention was H2S which was, quite simply, airborne radar that scanned the ground beneath. This was a breakthrough invention for obvious reasons but there were the inevitable drawbacks. The first was that the quality of picture it gave was poor and so the target had to be near to some distinctive ground feature such as the coastline or a major river or lake to get satisfactory results from it. The second drawback was that the beam it emitted could be tracked and it was not long before German night fighters were equipped with sets that could pick up and follow H2S emissions and so find the bombers emitting them. On the other hand H2S could not be jammed, had no range limits and as time went on, could both be refined in its performance and provided to an ever increasing number of aircraft.

A useful addition to Bomber Command's armoury at this time was the De Havilland Mosquito. This was a comparatively small aircraft with two engines and constructed almost entirely of wood. It was extremely fast and could fly very high indeed. It was useful for a number of tasks such as night fighting, reconnaissance and ground attack but its main role was as a light bomber. It took part in some daring low level raids but its principal use was to form a secondary night bombing force at high altitude in which role it suffered negligible casualties even though unarmed. It was simply too fast to be caught and its wooden construction made it hard to detect with radar. It also carried 4,000 lbs of bombs which was a big payload for a small plane. It gave a useful boost to the operational use of Oboe by reason of its high ceiling in excess of 35,000 feet. The higher you flew, the further away you could receive Oboe signals (because the radio beams moved in a straight line rather than curving with the earth).

Throughout the period under consideration, indeed throughout the entire war, Bomber Command carried out mine-laying by air in the coastal waters around Germany and her satellite lands. To choose a night at random, 28th/29th November 1942 saw 228 bombers dispatched to raid Turin but it also saw 19 sent to the Bay of Biscay to lay mines outside harbours there.[xv] This mine-laying was unglamorous and often tedious but not without its share of danger. Despite the example given above, mines were most often dropped on nights when the weather was unfavourable for major raids on cities because of cloud. This cloud gave the mine-laying aircraft valuable cover as they went about their work. The result was that the mine-laying campaign could be carried on with very little interference with the main offensive. Its contribution to the war effort was considerable since the German navy had to devote a substantial part of its resources to clearing the mines and they still took a steady toll of merchant shipping. Over the whole period of the war 717 merchant ships were sunk in this way or one for every 16 sorties flown.[xvi]

During 1942 the U.S.A.A.F. began to arrive in the U.K. and flew their first mission, appropriately enough, on 4th July. For the U.S.A. to mount a heavy bomber offensive from Great Britain there was required a gigantic task of organization and logistics. The heavy bombers themselves, B-17s and B-24s, flew to the U.K. via Canada,

Greenland and Iceland, a long and difficult trip achieved with a remarkably low accident rate. Everything else had to come by sea. The build-up was necessarily slow and the crews had to learn the arts of precision, bombing in daylight and formation flying by starting with small and short-range raids on Luftwaffe airfields in France and slowly building up to more ambitious targets at greater ranges such as the U-boat bases on the French Atlantic coast.

The Americans were quite convinced that the route to an effective bombing campaign lay through precision daylight raids on targets of industrial importance. They eschewed the British area bombing philosophy and were undeterred by the R.A.F.'s heavy losses during daylight raids early in the war. They were quite convinced that large formations of heavily armed bombers could fight their way through any resistance, however severe, and bomb their target. They had a new bombsight, the Norden, that was the latest thing in the relevant technology and their heavy bombers were armed with anything up to 12 heavy machine guns.

The aircraft in England were designated the 8th Air Force. Their first commander was General Carl Spaatz, a strategic bombing enthusiast who was also the overall commander of U.S.A.A.F. forces in Europe but, ironically, had to spend much of his time in Washington that year dealing with administration. In December 1942 he was put in charge of the Air Force in the Mediterranean and the command of the 8th devolved upon its former bomber commander. This was General Ira Eaker. He was a tough native of Texas who was 44 years old in 1942. He had joined the U.S. Army in 1917 and learned to fly the next year. He was another disciple of precision bombing and was never going to accede to British suggestions that the Americans should fly at night like Bomber Command. He pointed out that if the Americans bombed by day and the British by night, there would be a 24-hour-a-day bombing offensive. His approach had the wholehearted support of the overall commander of the Army Air Force General Henry H. (Hap) Arnold and of the political powers of the United States. Although nominally part of the army, the Air Force had independence in all but name. The United States had the industrial resources to mount a strategic bombing campaign on the largest scale without prejudicing other parts of its war effort. Arnold and Eaker therefore had a somewhat freer hand than their English counterparts when it came to the timescale within which their bombing was to bring Germany to its knees. The leaders of both air forces believed that the war could be won by bombing alone and Harris in particular held the view that bombing would win the war without an invasion of Europe being necessary.

In January 1943 Churchill and Roosevelt met at Casablanca in North Africa to co-ordinate Allied strategy for the fight against the Axis. Many important decisions were taken but two in particular concern us here. The first was the insistence that the war would only end with the unconditional surrender of the Axis powers, a stance whose principal effect was to ensure that those powers fought to the bitter end. In particular it steeled the people of Germany to endure strategic bombing because they saw no honourable way of ending it. The second matter to emerge from Casablanca of vital importance to the aviation war was the 'Directive for the Bomber Offensive from the United Kingdom'. This set out the official objective of the strategic bombing offensive in straightforward terms:

'Your primary object will be the progressive destruction and dislocation of the German military, industrial and economic system, and the undermining of the morale of the German people to a point where their capacity for armed resistance is fatally weakened.'

Given the above as the overall objective, a list of specific industrial targets was then set out. These were: submarine construction, the aircraft industry, transportation and oil. None of this was especially new; it did little more than recognize the status quo. However it could be interpreted as giving area bombing the imprimatur of the highest authority.[xvii]

With the benefit of hindsight one can see a certain irony in setting the undermining of German morale as a priority while, in practice, strengthening it immeasurably with the unconditional surrender demand.

By early 1943 the Army Air Force was still feeling its way toward making really damaging attacks. Its build-up was slowed by the need to transfer large numbers of aircraft to take part in the invasion of North Africa but the R.A.F. was ready to strike hard. With the worst of the winter weather over and various new navigational aids now in use, Harris began what he called the 'Battle of the Ruhr. This was a series of raids designed to bring industry in the towns of the Ruhr valley to a halt. The first was an attack on Essen on the night of 5th/6th March 1943. It was carried out by 442 aircraft and with great accuracy. For the first time in the war the famous Krupps armament works was badly damaged. Nine months before, in the second of the thousand bomber raids, 956 aircraft bombed Essen and did very little damage. Now times had changed; in this raid less than half the number of aircraft dropped three quarters of the weight of bombs used in the earlier raid and dropped them with far greater accuracy. All the big towns of the Ruhr: Bochum, Dortmund, Duisburg, Duesseldorf , Bottrop, Krefeld were repeatedly bombed between March and July and now extensive damage was being done with almost every raid. Not every raid flown was on the Ruhr towns because the weather was not always suitable and other targets could not be ignored. There were periodic raids on the Biscay ports and on the other great cities of Germany such as Berlin, Munich, Stuttgart and Mannheim. Moreover, targets had to be varied as a matter of principle to keep the defence guessing.

In the middle of the campaign, on the night of 16th/17th May, Bomber Command carried out a raid of a completely different nature which is perhaps the most famous single bombing mission ever carried out, leaving aside the dropping of the atomic bombs. This was the 'Dams' raid, flown by a specially formed squadron, armed with a specially designed bomb and carried out at very low level at night by 19 aircraft.

The targets were three dams, the Moehne, Eder and Sorpe which lay in western Germany some miles southeast of the Ruhr. It was thought that the breaching of these damns would bring the industry of the Ruhr valley to a halt by reason of flooding and loss of electrical power. The raid involved extremely skillful flying and pinpoint accuracy in the dropping of the bombs which, in the case of two of the dams, had to skip across the water of the relevant lake to strike the dam's wall. These two dams, the Moehne and the Eder, were breached causing spectacular flooding. The third dam was differently built and was a more difficult proposition: it was not broken. Despite claims made at the time it is now clear that the practical effect of the raid was disappointing. There was flooding in the Ruhr but it was minor and short-lived and there was no long-term loss of electrical power because the unbroken Sorpe dam was able to act as a backup until the Moehne was repaired. The Eder dam controlled water levels in the agricultural land toward the city of Kassel and the flooding caused was unimportant from the point of view of war production. The raid killed 1,294 people, mostly by drowning and this was a record death toll for a raid on Germany to this time. Unfortunately 500 of the dead were impressed foreign workers. 8 of the 19 attacking aircraft were shot down so that the loss rate was far too heavy for attacks of this kind to be made a regular feature of the bomber offensive. The great success of the attack was in the public relations field and the raid was soon famous world-wide. Guy Gibson, who led it, received the Victoria Cross and was sent on a lecture tour to the U.S.A. .

In July 1943 Harris turned his attention from the Ruhr to a new target: Hamburg. This was the second city of Germany and conveniently located on an estuary so that its H2S signal was very easy to identify. The idea was to launch a short, sharp series of attacks on one city to try to destroy it utterly. The 8th Air Force agreed to launch its own raids at the same time, directed at the city's docks where U-boats were assembled. The four Bomber Command raids were launched on the nights of 24th, 27th and 29th July and the 2nd August with an average strength of 773 bombers. U.S. raids were carried out on 25th and 26th July by forces of 120 aircraft which did little serious damage. On the other hand the R.A.F. raids brought a new level of horror to modern warfare.

For these raids the R.A.F. used a new weapon for the first time. This was 'window' which consisted of bundles of tin foil strips that were thrown out of the aircraft and blinded radar because each strip returned a radar echo just like an aeroplane, so that radar operators were swamped with pictures of what appeared to be millions of aircraft. Fighter and flak direction was completely blinded and the bombers could do their work almost unmolested.

The first raid caused much damage, mainly on the western side of the city. The fires smouldered on for several days, principally because of the large stocks of coal amassed by the residents. Thus the whole city fire brigade was here when the 27th raid fell on the other side of the city. It was a hot summer night and the new fires spread rapidly. The fire brigade had to cross the whole city to reach them and was slowed by many blocked streets. The fires were thus given a head start and were soon out of control. They joined together into one super-conflagration whose flames reached 1,500 feet into the air and whose temperature reached 800 degrees centigrade or more. This firestorm required so much oxygen that howling winds of up to 100 mph raged through the city towards it. Trees were knocked down and people blown into the flames. The air was sucked out of the cellars where the citizens of the town were sheltering and they suffocated wholesale. Four square miles of the city were completely devastated and something over 40,000 people were killed. In the days following the raids another 1.2 million people, two thirds of the population, fled the city which was left paralyzed. It is a frightening fact that the death toll of a few days in Hamburg was two thirds of the total of bombing deaths in the United Kingdom for the whole war. Moreover most of the dead were killed in one night.

The last two raids added to the devastation but there was no repeat firestorm and the night of 27th remained the dark highpoint of the short campaign. It could be said of the 'Battle of Hamburg' that it fulfilled all the promise of a Douhet-style bombing campaign. Albert Speer, the German armaments minister said that another half dozen raids on this scale would knock Germany out of the war.[xviii] A news blackout was imposed on the situation in the city.

As it happened Hamburg was something of a freak result which was only repeated on the same scale once more in the whole European war (at Dresden). Dry weather, the advantage of 'window' and the situation of Hamburg on a coastline produced a concatenation of circumstances particularly favourable to the bombers which was not to occur again in the same way.

Two points should be noted. Though attacks of this kind directly damaged any industry that happened to be under the bombs, Harris was quite definite that this was an irrelevance. His aim was to hit residential areas where factory workers lived so as to damage industry indirectly. In practice most industry is not located in the centre of cities and therefore escaped much of Harris's bombing. Secondly, though this was a thoroughly unpleasant way to wage war, it could be, and was argued that if successful it would finish the war faster and save lives in the end. This was the basic Douhet stance. By the time Dresden was bombed it was clear that this policy had failed and that is why the bombing of Dresden falls into a quite different moral category.

There was no more talk of the bomber offensive not paying its way.

CHAPTER THIRTEEN

Russian Recovery

January 1942 saw the German forces in Russia under attack almost everywhere. Stalin had ordered a general offensive in the overoptimistic belief that the German army was at the end of its strength. It was not, but it was certainly under pressure. On January 10th the Luftwaffe in Russia could muster 1,713 aircraft of which only 775 were combat-ready. Airfields were deep in snow, temperatures were many degrees below zero and servicing aeroplanes was a Herculean task. To prevent engines freezing irreversibly they were run up for fifteen minutes every hour throughout the night. Despite such precautions serviceability levels fell to 30%. The V.V.S. faced the same conditions of course, but they were accustomed to them and had all kinds of tricks for combating them such as adding petrol to lubricating oil to stop it freezing. Around Moscow the Russians were now quartered in permanent pre-war airfields equipped with every facility to resist the effects of the cold.

The second half of 1941 cost the Luftwaffe 5,700 aircraft on all fronts and production of new aircraft was only 5,100. The shortfall was partly made up in Russia by keeping aircraft in service that ought to have been retired but this was only a limited solution. In addition Airfleet Two was transferred to the Mediterranean along with part of Airfleet Four and a number of individual units were withdrawn to Germany for rest and refit. Accordingly January 1942 saw 1,000 less aircraft available than six months before, when the invasion started. Taking all fronts into account the Luftwaffe had slightly over 5,000 aircraft available so it seems odd that the OKL, the Luftwaffe High Command, were content that only a third of their air power was dedicated to the most important theatre of war.

The Russian counteroffensive made ground in the South and, particularly, before Moscow. One of the results was that two pockets of German troops were encircled at Kholm and Demyansk northwest of Moscow. Hitler insisted the troops must stand where they were and thus the only way to keep them supplied was by air. At Kholm only 3,000 were involved but at Demyansk it was 100,000. It was calculated that it would need the full time efforts of 150 transport aircraft to do this and Airfleet One, within whose area of responsibility the pockets lay, did not have that many available. It was necessary therefore to transfer aircraft from other fronts and borrow further machines from training and transport duties in Germany in order to resolve the situation which was done with remarkable efficiency though with the loss of a number of the ever-useful Ju52s. The pockets held out until they were relieved but a baleful precedent was set in that Goering and the High Command of the Luftwaffe became overconfident about what could be done in the way of aerial supply. This was to have disastrous consequences at the end of the year at Stalingrad.

Russian offensives petered out in April 1942 with the thaw. In the areas such as Moscow and the southern Ukraine where they had made especial progress one of the other factors that brought progress to a halt, was the fact that the offensives moved beyond air range of Russian fighters. In order to continue to provide adequate cover, V.V.S. squadrons had to move to the makeshift and under-equipped bases previously occupied by the Luftwaffe.

One area where no offensive ever made much ground was the far North where the Russo-Finnish border reaches Norway and then the Arctic Ocean a little to the west of Murmansk. The capture of Murmansk was part of the Barbarossa plan in 1941 but the offensive toward the port never progressed very far: it was not given adequate resources to enable it to succeed over very difficult territory. Airfleet Five, whose aircraft had the task of supporting the offensive, was nowhere near powerful enough. It had a mere 250 aircraft to cover the whole of Norway and it had to give priority to guarding against a British invasion. OKL feared a repeat of the British intervention in 1940 without realizing just how unlikely such an eventuality was. Murmansk was the only ice-free port in northern Russia and British military aid to Russia came in overwhelmingly through this single doorway. It was estimated that in 1942 it accounted for approximately one half of all Russia's imports of war materiel. Murmansk was joined to the rest of Russia by one single railway line that led south to Leningrad and in the second half of 1941 Airfleet Five, flying from its base at Kirkenes at the northern extremity of Norway, attempted to destroy this line and indeed, cut it repeatedly but, as has been noted before, railway lines are easily repaired and the Russians stored spare rails and sleepers at intervals along the line and kept permanent camps of workers ready to do the repair work so that for all the German efforts the line was rarely broken for long.

In 1942 Airfleet Five abandoned its unsuccessful railway campaign and turned its attention to the British convoys that were sailing to Murmansk with increasing frequency and bringing in ever larger quantities of war materiel. Little could be done until spring was well advanced because of the long nights at this northern latitude and when the campaign started, it was, for a while, a hit and miss affair partly because of the inexperience of the German bomber pilots at air operations against maritime targets, and partly because of the frequent storms and fog that occurred in this locality. As the days lengthened the weather improved and the pilots of KG26 were sent in rotation to Italy to learn the secrets of torpedo bombing, a skill at which the Italians were much more experienced than their allies. In May an eastbound convoy was attacked and eight ships sunk of 35 sailing. Five of those eight were sunk by air attack. In June the next convoy sailed for Murmansk from the United Kingdom. It also contained 35 ships and its code name was PQ17. At this time the British were aware that the German battleship Tirpitz was in Norwegian waters and, due to a misunderstanding they thought it was at sea threatening the convoy which was then ordered to scatter: the correct procedure when attacked by surface ships but most unwise in the face of U-boats and aircraft. The convoy was slaughtered and 23 ships sunk. Of those, eight were sunk by aircraft and another eight crippled from the air and finished off by U-boats.

The Allies were not deterred and the next convoy was of 41 ships and included a small aircraft carrier as part of the escort. Thirteen ships were lost, ten to German bombers but Airfleet Five lost 44 aircraft in the process, which left it too weak to be a serious threat to further convoys. Moreover the British were now using long-range aircraft to provide some cover to the convoys as well as the increasing use of aircraft carriers. The Russians began a series of air raids on the German airbases in north Norway timed to occur when the convoys were passing and cause the maximum disruption to Luftwaffe torpedo bombers landing and taking off. In December a convoy got through to Murmansk unharmed because it had not even been spotted by reconnaissance aircraft. Other Airfleets were supposed to send aircraft to Norway for anti-shipping duty when a convoy was known to be passing and in the summer of 1942 this duly happened but increasingly the demands of the land campaign meant that it was no longer possible. In addition, the hard-won skills of the bomber pilots in operations against ships were in great demand in the Mediterranean to which theatre many of them were accordingly transferred. From 1943 an increasing proportion of the aid reaching Russia travelled via Iran and though Arctic convoys continued until the end of the war, they were of decreasing importance and the German air force was never able seriously to threaten them again. Germany simply did not have the resources to devote to what had increasingly become a sideshow.

April 1942 saw something of a lull in operations in Russia because the thaw and heavy rains produced weather that made warfare next to impossible. The grass runways of the great majority of airfields were soon reduced to a sea of mud if aircraft tried to use them. Further units were withdrawn at this time, both for refit and for transfer to the Mediterranean.

With the return of good weather the Germans prepared for their planned offensive of the summer. The extent of the front was now so great that there could be no question of attacking along its whole length and the plan accordingly was to hold position in the North and centre and attack in the South, aiming to conquer the Caucasus and with it the Russian oilfields. Capture of these fields, particularly the rich wells around Baku, would at a stroke solve Hitler's oil shortage and doom the Russian war effort. This was to be a critical campaign since it was, in effect, Germany's last chance to win the war before the superior industrial capacity of her enemies overwhelmed her. As a preliminary to the campaign the flanks had to be made secure and this meant the complete conquest of the Crimea. In the spring the Russian army was driven out of the peninsula save for the fortress of Sevastopol where it held out in force. To assist with the siege of Sevastopol, the 8th Air Corps was transferred from the central front to the South and became part of Airfleet Four. The 8th was the force commanded by the able General von Richthofen and was becoming something of a 'corps d'elite' specializing in support for the ground troops. Altogether 600 aircraft were amassed in the Crimea. For a week at the start of June these aircraft pounded the fortifications of Sevastopol and then the army attacked and overran the town in a brief time. The army's advance revealed, however, that the air attacks had been less successful than had been anticipated when it came to breaking down solid concrete casemates and other defensive works. This fact is an interesting confirmation of the ineffectiveness of the bombs of the time against heavy reinforced concrete structures, as already revealed in the attacks on the U-boat pens in France.

At the same time as the assault on Sevastopol, the Russians launched an offensive against the German line in the vicinity of Kharkov. This assault was rapidly repulsed but not before a large number of aircraft had been withdrawn from the Crimea to face it and considerable losses suffered. Although this defeat was a heavy one for Stalin, its effect was to delay the German offensive and use up vital summer weeks that the Germans could ill afford to lose. During May and June 1942 the German armed forces, and particularly the Luftwaffe, prepared for the big offensive. Stocks of fuel and ammunition were built up and aircraft were transferred back to Russia from Germany and the Mediterranean. The 8th Air Corps was transferred to the area around Kursk, making it the northern flank guard of the coming offensive. In June von Richthofen, its commander, was promoted to lead Airfleet Four and thus to command the whole air effort on the southern front. By the start of July the air strength of the Luftwaffe in Russia had been built up to 2,750 and thus equaled that at the start of the invasion the previous year. 1,500 of these aircraft were in the South, leaving only 600 on the central front, 375 around Leningrad and 200 in the Arctic North.

The Russians also were preparing and reorganizing at this time. In early 1942 there was a new Commander in Chief of the V.V.S., Pavel Zhigarev, who had a plan for the much needed streamlining of the air force command system but although he appeared a sensible appointment Stalin transferred him in April, to the Far East and appointed in his stead General Alexander Novikov. It must be admitted that Novikov was an outstanding choice for the job. He improved the performance of the V.V.S. in any number of ways. He achieved the command reforms that Zhigarev had proposed, most notably by abolishing the system whereby each army had control of its own mini-air force and returning that control to the central V.V.S. authority so that aircraft could be massed in large numbers where they were needed. Henceforth all aircraft were in one of 18 Air Armies initially of two to three hundred aircraft each. By 1945 some were ten times that size. He revolutionized tactics, most notably by increasing the emphasis on the use of ground attack aircraft and by making the 'finger four' or 'schwarm' the standard formation of fighter units in action (as it was in the West). Pilots at the front had been crying out for this change to be made. He made radio communications a priority; this was a field in which the V.V.S. lagged badly behind the Luftwaffe. His goal was to ensure that every plane carried a two-way radio and there was a network of ground stations to exercise guidance and control such as had been so great a benefit to the R.A.F. in the Battle of Britain. He also rationalized aircraft production and ensured that the new and improved types were used wherever possible and the continued manufacture of outdated aircraft such as the I-153 and the I-16 ceased. This latter might appear common sense but there was always a body of opinion that held the manoeuverability of the old planes still made them valuable assets on the battlefield despite overwhelming evidence to the contrary. There was also the question of inertia, every bit as prevalent in the Soviet Union as in western countries, whereby the management and workforce of a factory which was mass producing Plane A, were extremely reluctant to face the inconvenience and extra work involved in changing to the production of Plane B.

In July 1942 the grand offensive opened and in the air the Luftwaffe was used in the tried and trusted way, first to sweep away the enemy air force and then to support the advancing armies with attacks on the enemy's bridges, railway stations and supply dumps etc.. Allied to this was the increasing use of aircraft in the close support role attacking targets such as gun emplacements and troop concentrations sometimes only yards from their own soldiers. Bombers carried out attacks on communications far behind the Russian lines but always on targets that had some bearing on the immediate campaign. There was no true strategic bombing of towns beyond the potential threat of the advance. The offensive was a great success in terms of ground taken and the German army swept eastward into the great bend of the River Don. In the South the river was crossed and German forces pushed into the Caucasus. On the northern flank the city of Voronezh was captured and held and in the centre the spearhead made for the city of Stalingrad (now Volgograd) on the River Volga.

Where the campaign was less successful, was in destroying the Red Army which had now learned to retreat instead of being surrounded. An organized retreat also reduced the effectiveness of air attack in that targets such as airfields and gun emplacements were bombed, but the enemy never used them anyway. Moreover the front line steadily moved away from the attacker's airfields necessitating changes of base to new airfields inherited from the enemy and abandoned with destroyed facilities. Large numbers of Russian aircraft were destroyed but the relocation of much Russian industry to towns in the Ural Mountains, which had damaged production in the year before, was now beginning to pay dividends and the losses were made good with ease. Russia produced 25,000 aircraft in 1942 and they could all go to fight Germany. By contrast Germany produced 15,000 and had to share them between three active fronts. Between August and November the number of aircraft available to the Russians on the Stalingrad/Don front increased five-fold even though they lost 2,800 planes in the same period.

The 4th Ground Attack Regiment was now the 7th Guards Ground Attack Regiment. 'Guards' units in the Soviet armed forces were elite units given the 'Guards' title in recognition of their outstanding performance. This unit was almost completely destroyed in the offensive. One of its pilots, Vasily Emelianenko, a capable and experienced pilot, had been a student at the Moscow Conservatoire before the war, but gave up his studies to fly and was an instructor in the early part of the war. His plane was hit by anti-aircraft fire in a raid on the Luftwaffe airfield at Artemovsky near Rostov. He pointed his crippled aircraft toward the Russian lines but it came down short and crash-landed in no-man's-land. Emelianenko was unhurt but spent two hours crawling to the Russian lines on his stomach through machine gun fire. On the way a stone was smashed by a bullet in front of his nose and he put one of the broken pieces in his pocket as a souvenir and kept it for the rest of his life. He had pushed his flying goggles back onto the top of his head and he later found that these too had been smashed by a bullet.[i] From the Don area the 7th Guards retired into the Caucasus eventually coming to rest near Stavropol. At this time the regiment had just two planes left ready for combat out of the 60 it began the summer with.[ii] Many of its ground crew had been left behind at Rostov in the confusion and haste of the retreat. They reappeared weeks later having walked over 400 miles to get back to their unit.[iii]

As the offensive progressed to the South, crossing the Don and moving into the Caucasus, there were effectively two offensives but the majority of the air support remained in the North with the Stalingrad attack whose importance was beginning to overshadow the drive to the oilfields. This was partly because the capture of that city was really essential to guard the flank of the Caucasus advance and partly because it was, itself, a city of great strategic importance sitting on the Volga River, which was a vital north/south transport artery, not to mention its talismanic name. This bias of force contributed to a steady loss of impetus in the South until it became necessary to transfer aircraft to make up the imbalance. The result was that neither arm was adequately supported in the air because the distances involved were simply too great and the overall number of aircraft too small. At the same time the Luftwaffe forces were operating under increasingly trying circumstances. They had far outrun the airfields they built during the winter and were now operating from simple grass strips and they were at the end of a tenuous and extended line of supply so that deliveries of fuel and spare parts, not to mention replacement aircraft, were sporadic and unreliable. Ground attack planes were too few to meet the demands placed upon them with the result that pilots were regularly flying four or more missions per day. The concentration of strength in the Stalingrad and Caucasus area meant that other areas of the front were inadequately covered with the result that Soviet attacks, or threats of attack, caused the transfer of units hither and thither when they should have had a chance of rest.

The final drive for Stalingrad began on 23rd August when German armoured forces broke out of their bridgehead on the River Don and drove across the flat steppe toward the city. They reached the River Volga at the northern edge of the city the same day. Their advance was covered by an umbrella of Messerschmitts that prevented Russian bombers from interfering in any way. The Luftwaffe outnumbered the V.V.S. two to one in this area and not only protected their own troops on the ground, but bombed and strafed the Russians without cease. Beginning that evening the city was subjected to a bombing campaign that lasted for two days and devastated it from end to end. On 25th General von Richthofen flew over the ruined city in his personal Fieseler Storch spotter aircraft and pronounced it totally destroyed.[iv]

On the ground the soldiers of the German army were disconcerted to find that the devastation had in no way diminished the ferocity of the defence and the Luftwaffe now went over to close support of the ground troops, often flying missions whose targets were no more than a building's width from their own countrymen. In the sky intense air battles raged in which the Luftwaffe had every advantage and the V.V.S. suffered heavily. For instance the 270th Bomber Division, which flew Pe-2s, was down to 19 aircraft by 29th August when its full complement was 108.[v]

The Luftwaffe had sufficient domination of the skies that it was able to send aircraft roving deep behind Russian lines to attack targets of opportunity. On 30th August a single Me110 attacked the airfield at Novo Nikolskoye and destroyed no less than ten U-2 biplanes on the ground. A flight of German fighters caught seven Pe-2s taking off from the airfield at Stepnoye, shot down three of them and badly damaged a fourth, flown by the Russian commander, Colonel Bystrov. Bystrov crashed trying to land his plane but walked away from the wreck unhurt. This was the second time he had been shot down in a fortnight.[vi]

The V.V.S. had now lost 200 aircraft since the attack began and had less than 200 serviceable craft left available for action but there was no let-up. On 4th September air battles resulted in 23 Soviet losses to four German. On 8th September no less than 50 Russian aircraft fell. But the Russians fought on. By mid-September 270th Bomber Division was down to 11 planes.

When darkness fell the sky belonged to the Russians, as was the case throughout the whole campaign in the East. Their bombers were in constant action, not just the harassing aircraft that were a V.V.S. specialty, but substantial formations of large Il-4 bombers. Unfortunately for the Russians their night bombing suffered from most of the same accuracy problems that similar tactics encountered in the West and the results could not be said to have amounted to more than a serious nuisance for the Germans.

Despite Luftwaffe domination in the air, the battle on the ground had stalled in the ruins of the city. The German commander, von Paulus was summoned to Hitler's headquarters to explain himself and received a dressing down. Von Richthoffen apparently rang Goering to say that von Paulus was uninspiring and should be replaced.[vii] The result was not his replacement but a new offensive launched on 13th September that was intended to subdue Stalingrad once and for all.

The fresh aerial bomber offensive concentrated on specific targets rather than city bombing. It was directed at defensive positions in the city and artillery positions both in the city and on the east bank of the Volga River. The bombers were covered by a swarm of fighters that fell on any Russian planes that appeared. The air battles were some of the largest and fiercest to occur on the eastern front. The fighting raged till 16th September when bad weather forced a brief break and both sides used it to fly in reinforcements.

On 18th September the Russians launched a counter-attack at Kotluban, north of the city but it met an immediate response from the Luftwaffe and was brought to a halt during the day with the loss of over 100 tanks, of which 41 were destroyed by aircraft. The Luftwaffe claimed the destruction of 77 Russian aircraft without a single loss. The truth was less startling but sobering enough for the Russians for they lost 40 aircraft, making this one of the Luftwaffe's best days of the whole war. Among the casualties of the day was Senior Lieutenant Vladimir Mikoyan, a Yak pilot shot down and killed by a Me109. He was the son of Artem Mikoyan, lead designer of the Mig aircraft design bureau.

The fighting flared up again on 20th and the V.V.S. lost another 16 planes. One of the pilot casualties was Senior Lieutenant Sergei Dolgushin shot down for the second time in two days. He survived but was badly injured. During the next few days the air battles continued but the V.V.S. was running out of men and aeroplanes and the intensity of the fighting began to decline. Nevertheless the 23rd was the most successful day of his career for German ace Hermann Graf. In five sorties during the day he shot down no less than ten aircraft to bring his total score to 197. In his aircraft almost every minute of daylight, day after day, an exhausted Graf scored his 200th victory on 26th September. He was the first pilot to reach this magical score and was carried shoulder high round his airfield by his ground crew. (Fourteen other pilots joined him in the '200 club' in due course.) this combat on 26th was one of the very few that took place that day as the Russians had finally been forced to concede the daytime skies over Stalingrad to the Luftwaffe. At night they still had complete supremacy but despite over 11,000 sorties in the Stalingrad area during the autumn months, they still could not forge a decisive advantage from their night-time dominance.

The bombing of Stalingrad was relentless. On 14th October, for instance, 4,000 sorties were flown against the city. Stukas destroyed Soviet gun positions on the eastern bank and decimated the river traffic on the Volga including the vital ferries that kept communications open between the troops fighting in the city and the rest of the Red Army on the other bank. Bombing is said to have killed 40,000 civilians in the city itself which was reduced to a ghost town of ruins. As the war was repeatedly to prove, however, heavy bombing of a town did not make it any harder for ground troops to defend because ruins themselves make excellent defensive positions. Despite all the Luftwaffe could do, the Russians clung tenaciously to a slice of the city by the river bank. Since 12th September the 62nd Army in the city had been under the command of a new General, Vasiliy Chuykov. Though he drank like a fish and was not above losing his temper and punching his subordinates from time to time, he was an effective and charismatic leader whose ruthless determination rubbed off on his troops.

Hans Rudel flew one of the attacking Stukas. After the award of the Knight's Cross, Germany's highest award for outstanding military service and a stint as an instructor earlier in the year, he had been at the siege of Sevastopol and was then hospitalized with jaundice. Finding hospital not to his taste he discharged himself and reported back to his squadron claiming he was fully fit. On the way he 'lost' his medical papers. As he flew over the city he noted that the Russians: '... are hanging on like grim death to every scrap of rubble, they lurk behind every remnant of a wall.'viii

The German offensive to the gates of Stalingrad and beyond, had now produced a long bulge in the front line with an exposed and thinly held flank on the northern side. Along the Don River southeast of Voronezh, there was a stretch of some 300 miles covered by only 70 to 80 aircraft. Von Richthofen could see the danger in this and accordingly 1st Air Corps was transferred from the Leningrad front to bolster the defences in this area. It was not enough and when the Russian blow fell in November, the Red Army broke through here with comparative ease having chosen as their target a sector of the front manned by Rumanians and Hungarians who were neither as well equipped nor as determined fighters as the Germans.

The Russian offensive was carefully planned and the V.V.S. played an essential part in it. In the Stalingrad and River Don area General Novikov had amassed three Air Armies, 8th, 16th and 17th which, together with some independent units, amounted to 1,500 aircraft, outnumbering the Germans two to one. The force included 575 Il-2 Stormovik ground attack planes, a hitherto unheard-of concentration. In the area where the attack took place there had been relative calm for a month or so before it began and this gave Russian air regiments time to train their new pilots. V.V.S pilots always arrived at the front woefully short on experience and were expected to learn on the job with their unit. If the unit was in heavy action they were pitched straight into battle with resultant heavy casualties. A quiet spell was therefore priceless.

The air forces of Germany's allies were in the path of the attack but their military value was slight. The Rumanians fielded about 100 fighters on paper but actual serviceability at this time is a matter of conjecture and was certainly much lower. The Hungarians likewise had some 60 aircraft in theory but the reality was that in November they had just 9 old Italian Reggiane fighters fit for service. The Italians had some 100 aircraft in total but their difficulties with supplies and spares were such that they were not operational at all for much of the time.

The rapid Russian advance, matched by another counter-attack south of the city, threw the whole Luftwaffe coverage of the Stalingrad front into confusion because airfields to the East of the breakthrough had to be abandoned for fear of being cut off and the aircraft moved further west. Aircraft needing repair were left behind. The move took the fighters out of range of Stalingrad and that meant that the bombers could not go there either because they could not risk the dangerous skies over the city without escort. Moreover, winter now intervened and imposed conditions that always favoured Russian aviation. Simultaneously the big Allied offensives in Libya and Tunisia necessitated the transfer of more aircraft to the Mediterranean. By the end of the year German air strength in Russia was down to barely 2,000 planes of which only some 950 were properly operational. Needless to say, the skies over Stalingrad belonged to the V.V.S. once more, more or less by default.

During the last months of the year an attempt was made to keep Stalingrad supplied by air since it had been cut off by the Russian counter-offensives and with it the whole German Sixth Army. Goering had promised to do this and now had to make good on that promise. He had managed air supply at the start of the year at Demyansk but now he had to do it on a far larger scale. At Demyansk there had been 100,000 to supply but at Stalingrad 230,000 were counted in December together with another 20,000 auxiliaries and non-combatants. It was a wholly unrealistic undertaking. When five Soviet armies were surrounded at Kiev in 1941 the suggestion of supplying them by air was made to Marshal Budyenny whose perceptive reply was: 'Such a mass of troops cannot be supplied by air.'[ix] Budyenny was not a very able commander but the truth was clear even to him and it was certainly clear to von Richthofen but he was overruled by Hitler and Goering and the attempt was made.

The troops in Stalingrad needed 700 tons of supplies each day to function normally and the airlift promised 500 tons which would allow them to scrape by. The aircraft needed to deliver that tonnage were hard to find and bombers had to be used and aircraft flown in from other fronts. But the promise could not be met. The best day's delivery was 289 tons and the average was barely 100. Why was Demyansk a success and Stalingrad a failure? There were two main reasons: the distance that had to be flown and the improvement in the performance of the V.V.S..

At Demyansk the whole operation was carried out under an umbrella of fighter cover, but at Stalingrad that was not possible. Fighters could manage the journey, just, but not escorting a slow transport plane which meant they had to twist and weave and fly in circles in order not to leave their charge behind. Thus they flew much further than the direct distance and did so in a very uneconomical way from the fuel point of view. The distance also slowed the turnaround time and gave the weather a larger opportunity to interfere. But the worst interference came from the V.V.S. whose fighters took a heavy toll of the transport aircraft, principally Ju52s and He111s with a few Focke Wulf Condors thrown in. There were quite simply more and better Russian planes flown by more experienced pilots. Losses over Stalingrad in the autumn had been rapidly made good and with no Luftwaffe fighters to interfere, the Russians showed at their best. 500 transport planes were lost, over half of them the invaluable Ju52s, whose available strength on the Eastern Front was shrunk by a third. Many of the downed aircraft fell within the Russian lines and much of the cargo could be salvaged for the Russians' own use. For instance, on 5th December Pyotr Bazanov of the 3rd Guards Fighter Regiment, flying one of the new Lag-5s shot down a Ju52 virtually on his own airfield and there was much rejoicing in the regiment because the plane was loaded with bread, honey and cigarettes, all worth their weight in gold to front line soldiers on either side![x]

The last Axis resistance in the Stalingrad pocket ceased on 2nd February 1943. It was a signal victory for the Soviet Union and a critical defeat for Germany. It has gone into the annals of history as one of the great battles of all time and is often seen as the turning point of World War Two. From here on the story was to be one of unrelieved retreat for the German armed forces in Russia.

For the Luftwaffe there was little to take by way of consolation from the disaster, though the last year had seen a realization that it must abandon its narrow emphasis on the tactics of attack and accept that its role now included defensive fighting. The most obvious manifestation of this change of heart was the creation of units of Ju88 and Stuka aircraft dedicated to tank destruction and armed with large cannon for the purpose. Most Russian attacks were spearheaded by numbers of their excellent tanks which often broke through the front line with alarming ease. If they could be stopped at this point the position could usually be repaired and anti-tank aircraft were the weapon needed to achieve this.

For the V.V.S. the achievements of the year were many and the satisfying result was that it could now often outnumber the Luftwaffe, at least locally, and achieve air superiority. Of course, it had outnumbered the Luftwaffe when Barbarossa started but now it had aircraft of the quality to make its numbers count. Its contribution to the victory at Stalingrad had been considerable; the first time it had made a material difference to a soviet offensive. Its organization and tactics had made great strides forward, as noted above, and its equipment was improving all the time. The fact that it suffered heavy losses did not negate its contribution.

When Alexander Yakovlev designed the Yak-1 he designed a two-seat trainer to be used in tandem with it. It soon emerged that the trainer was as good as the combat version, if different. It was a little less manoeuverable but it was easier to fly and more sturdily built because it was designed to withstand abuse by students. Accordingly it too became a combat aircraft under the designation Yak-7. This aircraft was always something of a compromise and it was clear that improvements could easily be made. This was duly done: principally it was a matter of removing the rear cockpit, streamlining and building the wing structure of metal instead of wood, and the result was the Yak-9 which was built in greater numbers than any other Soviet fighter. It made its first appearance at the time of Stalingrad. In principle it was a match for the Me109 but in practice it was not so. It was under-armed and provided with insufficient ammunition and it suffered from the shoddy production methods prevalent in the Russian aircraft industry.[xi] Once in the field it was often poorly maintained or scrapped when it could not fly.

By contrast Russian pilots enjoyed flying lend-lease aircraft because they were luxuriously finished by the Spartan standards the pilots were used to. During 1942 1,900 lend-lease aircraft came to Russia by convoy to Murmansk alone (and that was probably about half the total). Many types of British and American aircraft were sent to Russia but the plane that stands out is the P-39 Airacobra. 5,000 of these were exported to Russia and 2,400 of its successor the Kingcobra (which was more than two thirds of the total production of the plane). By way of comparison 3,500 Mig-3s were built and 16,000 Yak-9s so that it is clear the Airacobra and its successor were a substantial part of the V.V.S's equipment. It is a curious fact that in the West both the U.S. and the British considered the 'Cobra a second-rate aircraft but the Russians loved it and it would be fair to say, in retrospect, that it ended up being built essentially for Russian employment with occasional use by other countries. Despite misconceptions to the contrary, due to the fact that most versions sported a massive 37 mm. cannon, it was not usually used as a ground attack plane but as a plain air superiority fighter. The key to its success was probably that almost all air combat in Russia was at low, to very low level, the heights at which it performed best. It equipped the 16th Guards Fighter Regiment, probably the outstanding Russian fighter unit of the war and the home of Alexander Pokryshkin, the country's number two ace who became known as the 'Richthofen of the V.V.S' .

The aircraft that probably did most to transform the prospects of the V.V.S. at the end of 1942 was the Lag-5. (Strictly this should be the La-5 as discussed earlier.) Its designer was Semyon Lavochkin who had fallen out of favour owing to the poor performance of his Lag-3. He was anxious to restore his fortunes but he now had a low priority for the allocation of scarce resources. The underlying problem of the Lag-3 had always been that it was underpowered: it was too heavy for its Klimov M105 engine. This engine, which developed 1,200 horsepower was in great demand for the various models of Yak and other planes. At the same time the cancellation of production of the Sukhoi Su-2 ground attack plane had left factories turning out large numbers of Shvetsov M82 radial engines for which there was no obvious employment. The factories could be re-tooled to produce another engine but that was a major industrial undertaking to be used only as a last resort. Lavochkin decided to try using the M82 engine in the Lag; not the least of its attractions was that it produced 1,800 horsepower and thus boosted his fighter's power by 50 percent. It was, of course, also more reliable than the in-line M105. The result was the Lag-5 and it was something of a 'lash-up'. It was not easy to fly and the engine leaked oil onto the windscreen and could easily overheat and even 'super-cool'. (This meant that if you reduced power suddenly after a lengthy period at high revs the engine cooled too fast and as its parts contracted, it ran rough or even failed completely.) On top of that, exhaust fumes had a tendency to find their way into the cockpit so that most pilots preferred to fly with the cockpit open whenever possible. They also kept the cowl flaps open to stop the engine overheating and both these habits greatly reduced the speed.[xii]

For all its faults the Lag-5 was an outstanding aircraft. Some of its deficiencies were ironed out as time went by and it rivaled the Yak-9. Certainly it was better armed, having two 20 mm cannon firing through the propeller. It is no surprise that most of the Russian aces flew Lags though the Yak remained the favourite with the regime. It would be fair to say that it was, like the Yak, the equal of German fighters in principle but a little less in practice. Later in the war a successor, the Lag-7, was produced that was essentially the same aircraft 'cleaned up' and it was clearly superior to its enemies.

One other technical improvement must be mentioned and that is the addition of a rear gunner to the Il-2 Stormovik. The plane was always designed to have a crew of two but early versions dispensed with the gunner to save weight. The result was that it was simply too vulnerable to fighters and so the argument for having a rear gunner became irresistible. He was placed behind the pilot facing backward, where he should have been all along. His added weight reduced the manoeuverability of the aircraft and some pilots maintained that they had been better off in a single seat plane, but it is clear that the additional defensive capability given by having a rear gunner, saved many aircraft that would otherwise have been shot down. One unfortunate feature of the new configuration was that the extensive armour of the Il-2 protected the pilot but did not extend to the gunner's position so that he was very exposed and many planes returned from their missions with a dead gunner in the rear cockpit. The death rate for gunners was seven times that for pilots. Vasily Emelianenko noted that some pilots would rather not fly with a gunner because it was so distressing to return with him lying dead in the back of the plane. It was better to be killed yourself than bring back a dead friend.[xiii]

A striking feature of the V.V.S. in 1942 was the introduction of female pilots. This was the result of a meeting between Stalin and Marina Raskova, a distinguished Russian aviatrix, early in the war when she persuaded him that women should be allowed to fight as pilots. The result was that three regiments of women flyers were formed, one fighter and two bomber, and went to the front in the summer of 1942. They retreated into the Caucasus with other V.V.S. units and later came north with the counterattack of early 1943 to continue flying for the rest of the war. The bomber squadrons flew very specialized night missions in slow U-2 biplanes. These flew up and down over the German lines dropping bombs at intervals, more for their nuisance value and the loss of sleep caused to German soldiers, than for any hope of doing serious material damage. In fact German sources testified that this was an effective, if indirect, form of warfare and it was practised to the very end. These female pilots were nicknamed the 'Night witches' by the Germans, a sobriquet they were happy to adopt. Rufina Gasheva, a navigator with the 46th Guards Bomber Regiment flew no less than 848 missions during the war and was made a Hero of the Soviet Union.

The fighter regiment fought at Stalingrad and included in its number Lydia (Lily) Litvyak who became an ace with 11 victories to her name and the much publicized face of wartime women's aviation in the Soviet Union. She was killed in action in 1943.

As well as the aircrew there were women in every branch of the air service to a much greater degree than in the West where the only service that used females to a marked degree in functions other than administrative and support, was the R.A.F.. In Russia they served as mechanics and ground crew in most regiments and Vasily Emelianenko noted that their presence boosted morale and led to a great improvement in the dress and grooming of male pilots. He said: 'Men's vigilance during sentry duty increased rapidly. If girls were sent on sentinel duty there were always plenty of volunteers ready to join them.'[xiv]

Alone of the combatants the Russians used female aircrew. This is Senior Lieutenant of Guards Rufina Gasheva, a navigator who flew 850 combat missions. ©Imperial War Museum (RUS 5179)

In early 1943 the Russians swept forward in the South and recovered most of the gains the Germans had made the previous summer. They reached Rostov and then the River Donets. Finally they were again at the gates of Kharkov. German forces in the Caucasus had had to execute a hurried retreat to avoid being cut off, leaving only a small force holding the area of land in the northwest of the peninsula, known as the Kuban. This force could be supplied from the Crimea across the straits of Kerch. Even as the retreat went on, it continued to suck in air units at the expense of other parts of the front. By early February the Don/Donets sector held 53% of the Luftwaffe's strength on the eastern front and since much of what remained elsewhere was second line units, the real imbalance was even worse. Thus the Luftwaffe, like the Wehrmacht as a whole, found itself approximately where it had been a year before, but now weaker and more disorganized.

CHAPTER FOURTEEN

Japan Halted

One arm of the Japanese advance in late 1941 and early 1942 was an attack on Burma, then a part of the British Empire. Japanese troops moved from Malaya and French Indo-China into Thailand, which was a Japanese ally, in December 1941 and in January 1942 the Japanese 15th Army struck southern Burma. One of its first actions was to capture the airfield at Point Victoria on the southern Burmese coast which effectively cut air communications between India and Malaya. The air support for the invasion was provided by 5th Air Division under the command of Lieutenant General Hideyoshi Obata.[i] This numbered in the region of 200-300 aircraft. To oppose this force the R.A.F. in Burma had just two fighter squadrons and one bomber squadron totaling 53 planes under the command of Air Vice-Marshal Stevenson.[ii] In the course of time three more fighter squadrons and one of bombers arrived but the Japanese always enjoyed numerical superiority.

On the ground the Japanese army made rapid progress being, at this time, more accomplished at jungle warfare than the British. It also consumed much less in the way of supplies which was an important consideration in a land with almost no railways and few and poor quality roads. Notwithstanding the odds were against them, the Allied air forces put up a strong fight and this was the only sector of the Far East theatre of war in 1941/2 where the Japanese were outfought in the air. In large measure this was due to the presence in Burma of one of the three squadrons of the American Volunteer Group. This force was based in China and was effectively an extension of the U.S armed forces though nominally an outfit of civilian mercenaries. Its pilots were a tough and experienced bunch who had already been fighting the war against the Japanese since considerably before Pearl Harbour. They flew P-40s with shark's jaws painted on the cowlings and were popularly known as the 'Flying Tigers'. One of their prime tasks was to protect the Burma Road, a vital artery driven through the most inhospitable country of northern Burma to join India with China. Along this road passed all the military aid from the United States to China. One of the reasons for the Japanese invasion of Burma was the aim of cutting this vital supply route. The A.V.G. were in Burma to protect it.

These colourful Americans were extremely effective, shooting down enemy planes at three times the rate of the R.A.F. pilots.[iii] The reason for this, apart from their much greater experience, was that their P-40s were faster than the Japanese Nate

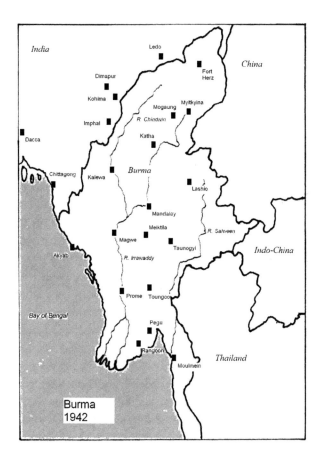

Burma
1942

and Oscar fighters and the Americans flew them in diving attacks using the vertical dimension and avoiding a turning fight which the Japanese would have won every time. If the P-40s were at a height disadvantage they simply ran for it and could not be caught. R.A.F. fighter pilots flying Hurricanes did not have that extra speed but flew an aircraft that turned well. They were used to using this turning facility to win dogfights and considered diving away to be a sign of cowardice. Unfortunately the Japanese planes turned even better and the British approach was a recipe for trouble.

Amongst the Americans was a future winner of the Congressional Medal of Honor, Gregory Boyington. Boyington was a rough, tough character from the Pacific Northwest. He was an extremely able pilot and had been a Marine Corps flying instructor. Unfortunately he was also a heavy drinker and a brawler and had had more than his share of disciplinary problems. He was based outside Rangoon and billeted at the luxurious villa of two wealthy, ex-patriot Scottish businessmen. At the end of each day's flying he would bed down his P-40 then drive to the villa for an evening of whisky-and-sodas under the stars: dinner was never served before ten o'clock.[iv] Boyington shot down several planes in Burma but he was still in the learning stage and his flowering was yet to come in the Solomon Islands.

Not only were British planes in Burma few in number but they had other drawbacks to contend with. A number of good quality airfields had been built in the country but in the wrong places. There was only one radar set in the whole India/Burma theatre and without radar British airfields had no warning of incoming raids. Setting up a network of observers on the ground was not easy since the countryside was covered in jungle and thinly populated, but it was done with limited success. All these difficulties were aggravated by the fact that the Burmese did not like the British and were correspondingly well disposed towards the Japanese[v] whom they saw as liberators.

Japanese bombers repeatedly bombed Rangoon, the capital and a major seaport. They did extensive damage but they paid a price. The Americans shot down over 100 aircraft for the loss of just 15 of their own. Japanese pressure was just too much however and Rangoon fell on 17th March 1942. Not only was this a blow in itself but it made the supply position for the Allies that much more difficult because they had relied on its port and now supplies had to come either through small harbours on the Burmese coast or on the long and difficult overland journey from India.

With Rangoon and its airfield facilities gone the British and Americans retired up-country. The Americans went to an airfield at a place called Magwe, but Japanese reconnaissance aircraft were watching and on 21st they raided this airfield with over 200 aircraft and wiped out the forces there. The Flying Tigers were left with just three aircraft. On 27th the Japanese raided Akyab on the coast where the R.A.F. survivors were now based. A great deal of damage was done and the British were left with no air force to speak of. The few surviving planes retired to India. Any semblance of organized resistance now ended and it was decided that the country must be abandoned, at least for the time being. The muddy roads were full of soldiers and civilians marching to the North to sanctuary in India minus their transport and equipment. By May Burma had fallen, the monsoon began and campaigning had to stop.

In April 1942 the Japanese Imperial Naval General Staff considered its next move in the light of the success, far beyond its expectations, that had come in the last few months. The obvious ploy was an invasion of Australia but the Army balked at this because they were already heavily committed in China and in Burma and a campaign in Australia would require a large number of troops which they simply could not find. As an alternative it was decided to strangle Australia by cutting off its sea link with the United States. This could be done by setting up a line of island bases through the Solomon Islands and on to New Caledonia, Fiji and Samoa. From these bases aircraft could destroy sea-borne traffic and Australia would be left relatively defenceless to be invaded later at Japan's convenience.

Several small bases had already been established early in the year on the north coast of New Guinea, in particular at Lae and Salamaua, and in April, in furtherance of the new policy, they were equipped with aircraft to carry out raids on Port Moresby, the capital of Papua New Guinea, which was on the south coast, just across the Torres Strait from Australia. It was Australia that administered the whole territory before the war. The centre of the island consisted of the Owen Stanley range of mountains that were 13,000 feet high and clad in thick jungle. It was some of the most inhospitable country on earth. Port Moresby boasted two airfields and these became the focus of the raids. The Japanese fighters based at Lae were from the Tainan Air Group, one of the best wings in the Imperial Navy Air Service and certainly the most famous. For four months constant raids and fighter sweeps were directed at Port Moresby which was defended by Australians flying P-40s and U.S. pilots in P-39 Airacobras. U.S. and Australian bombers would make counter-strikes against Lae and Salamaua.

This was 'happy hour' for the aces of the Tainan Group such as Saburo Sakai, Junichi Sasai and Hiroyoshi Nishizawa who amassed large scores against the Allied planes. Their standard mission was to escort Betty bombers over the mountains to Port Moresby where they would out-fly and out-shoot the P-39s and P-40s that rose to defend the base. Their feats must, however, be seen in context. The raids were normally conducted at 20,000 feet or more at which height the Allied planes, both powered by the Allison engine and not equipped with a supercharger, were sluggish performers. On top of that, the Zero was a better plane in most respects at any height and these Japanese pilots were veterans fighting beginners. This campaign, obscure and remote for Western readers, has a special place in the aviation lore of World War Two mainly because of Sakai's vivid memoirs that describe these events with great immediacy yet with a very human perspective.[vi]

The constant Japanese raids were, in fact, singularly ineffective. The Betty bomber, which was supposed to be the main Navy heavy bomber, could carry 2,200lbs of bombs. By comparison, the U.S. B-17, a heavy bomber often criticized for its small bomb load, could carry 6,000lbs, the Consolidated Liberator 8,000lbs and the Avro Lancaster 14,000lbs. Two Lancasters carried a bigger bomb load than a whole squadron of Bettys. During 1942 the British introduced their Typhoon fighter which could, if need be, carry 2,000lbs of bombs or very nearly the same as a Betty. It can be argued that the war in the Pacific required bombers to hit small targets such as ships and airbases and for this purpose a large bomb load was not necessary; what was needed was accuracy. But, as already noted, these raids were carried out at 20,000 feet or more, a height at which the required accuracy was quite impossible. The Americans and the Australians realized this and their bombers went in low and caused serious damage. No one seems to be sure why the Japanese followed this flawed bombing policy. It may have something to do with the vulnerability of the Betty bomber, of which its crews were very aware. Undoubtedly it was safer to bomb from a great height and that height, at least in the early days of the war, caught Allied fighters at their weakest. Japanese fighting men have never been known for a safety-first approach but higher officers were often very cautious: after all, they had no interest in seeing their planes and aircrew lost.

Before the 'strangulation plan' could be further realized however, the Americans scored a minor but important coup that was a warning to Japan of what U.S. enterprise and technology could achieve. Ever since Pearl Harbour President Roosevelt had been pressing his military leaders for a means of bombing Tokyo. There could be no possibility of doing any serious damage to the city at this stage of the war, but the mere fact of the raid would be a significant propaganda blow and put heart into the American public at a time when Japan seemed to be having everything her own way in the Pacific. After some delay the naval staff came up with a plan that the army also backed; (a rare example of co-operation between these two services.) This involved putting medium bombers on an aircraft carrier and taking them to within 500 miles of the Japanese coast where they could be launched and fly to Tokyo. They would be unable to land on the carrier again so the plan was for them to fly on after bombing and land at Nationalist bases in China. The plane chosen for the job was the B-25, which had never been flown from an aircraft carrier before and the man chosen to lead the raid was James Doolittle, an army test pilot, holder of several aviation flying records and a Schneider Trophy winner. After much practice it was concluded that the plan was practicable and on 2nd April 1942 the carrier Hornet sailed with 16 B-25s on board. They had to be launched prematurely because the Hornet was spotted by a Japanese fishing boat and it was feared that it had radioed to shore and surprise had been lost. In fact this was not so but the die had been cast.

The aircraft split up and bombed several other large Japanese cities beside Tokyo then flew on to China. Because of their enforced early start they had not enough fuel to reach the intended bases and the weather turned against them with low cloud and fog making proper landings virtually impossible. Most of the crews had to bail out or crash-land and returned home eventually with Chinese help. Three men were killed and eight captured by the Japanese. Of these, three were executed and one later died of maltreatment. The other four were released at the end of the war. One crew came down in Russian territory and were interned. It took them a year to find their way home via Iran.

No significant damage was done and all the planes were lost, which led Doolittle to think the raid was a failure for which he would take the blame, but the reverse was the case. The raid was a propaganda triumph and Doolittle was a national hero. The Japanese were horrified that they were so vulnerable and immediately increased the permanent garrison of aircraft in the home islands at the expense of the front line. This last fact alone made the raid a success quite apart from other ramifications.

At the start of May a task force set out from Rabaul in the Bismarck Archipelago north of New Guinea and sailed into the Solomon Islands to a small port called Tulagi on Florida Island. The island was occupied without combat and the Japanese began constructing a base there from which they intended to operate seaplanes.

Rabaul had become the headquarters for Japanese operations in this theatre. It was a depressing place on the north coast of the island of New Britain, overshadowed by an active volcano and periodically lightly sprinkled with ash. On the other hand it had an excellent harbour, was strategically well placed from the communications point of view and was geographically so sited that it could not easily be taken by surprise. The task force that went to Tulagi was guarded by the light carrier Shoho. She was a modern ship completed that year but was a hurried conversion of a hull intended to be a submarine tender and only capable of carrying 30 aircraft.

Hard on the heels of the Tulagi force came a flotilla of 14 transports carrying troops to execute 'Operation Mo', the capture of Port Moresby. Port Moresby, something of a glorified shanty-town, was, nevertheless, the centre of operations for Australian and American forces in the area and its capture would make the invasion of Australia a real possibility and at the same time make Allied interference with the Solomons operation and the 'strangling' of Australia that much more difficult. The Shoho joined the invasion force which headed for the Coral Sea on its way round the east end of New Guinea. Further east of it, the way was guarded by a task force including the Shokaku and Zuikaku, Japan's two newest and best large aircraft carriers together with cruisers and destroyers under the command of Admiral Takeo Takagi.

The Pacific War was a war of aircraft carriers. This is the U.S.S. Yorktown under attack by Japanese aircraft at the Battle of Midway. She was sunk shortly afterwards. ©Imperial War Museum (NYF 42432)

A factor now intervened to give the Americans a priceless advantage. This was the intelligence gained from cracking the Japanese naval code which allowed them to know exactly what Japanese intentions were. To counter the new thrust they sent a task force to the Coral Sea comprising the carriers Lexington and Yorktown and various escorts commanded by Admiral Jack Fletcher. Fletcher was an officer of modest talent from an old Navy family. The great American naval historian, Samuel Eliot Morison felt he did not have the ability for major fleet command.[vii] He was given responsibility for this task force ahead of several more senior officers because of his experience in command of large surface vessels. He justified the faith placed in him, just. The stage was set for the Battle of the Coral Sea, the world's first carrier battle and the first ever sea battle in which neither side even came within visual distance of the other: the whole battle was fought by aircraft.

The fight began early on 7th May 1942 when American search aircraft reported the sighting of two carriers. A strike of 93 torpedo aircraft and dive-bombers was immediately launched but found only two cruisers, no doubt misidentified by overexcited reconnaissance pilots. Where there were two cruisers there might well be other warships however, so the planes searched the area and quickly discovered the Shoho which was promptly attacked and rapidly reduced to a flaming wreck by bombs and torpedoes. The leader of the Lexington's dive-bomber squadron, Lieutenant Commander Robert Dixon radioed his ship: 'Dixon to carrier, scratch one flat-top!' [viii]This pithy remark was subsequently much quoted in the newspapers and made Dixon famous. The Shoho was the first major ship lost by Japan in the war.

Having lost their principal guardian and knowing American carriers were in the area the Japanese invasion force now turned around and returned to Rabaul. Takagi sent off a force of aircraft to find the Americans, but all they found was a fleet tanker escorted by a destroyer, which they promptly sank. At dusk another force was sent out and searched again. They found no ships but ran into some U.S. fighters and there was general melee in which the Americans came off the better. The planes then dispersed and made for home. One group of six Japanese planes found a carrier in the gloom and tried to land, but it was the Yorktown and they were all rapidly destroyed. In all Takagi lost 21 of the 27 planes he sent out on this mission.

When dawn came on 8th May the two sides were evenly matched. The Americans made the first move with a strike that found the two Japanese carriers. The Shokaku was hit by bombs and only saved by the fact that the nine torpedoes dropped by U.S. planes all malfunctioned. She was badly damaged and could not launch or recover planes. She withdrew from the battle. The Zuikaku was protected by a fortuitous rain squall and managed to get off a counter-strike that found the American carriers when most of their covering fighter force was on deck refueling. Bombs damaged the Yorktown, and the Lexington was crippled by multiple hits. At first it was thought the she might survive; she was able to move, if slowly, and began to crawl away to the East in the direction of Pearl Harbour. The Lexington had originally been planned as a

176

battle-cruiser and this had limited her plane-carrying capacity and reduced her value as a carrier somewhat, but it meant that she was very robust and, at 37,000 tons, was the largest aircraft carrier in the world (together with her sister, the Saratoga). The Yorktown, on the other hand, was only 20,000 tons but carried 50% more aircraft.

After several hours an accumulation of gasoline fumes on the Lexington ignited and she was gutted by a huge explosion. The decision was taken to abandon ship but she lingered on and had to be sunk by torpedoes from her own side to prevent the remote chance she might fall into Japanese hands.

Both sides now withdrew though Takagi wanted to fight on, and was only prevented from doing so by the fact that several of his ships were short of fuel. An order came from Tokyo for him to pursue the Americans but though he made an effort to comply, the latter had too much of a lead and he soon had to abandon the chase.

As already noted, this battle was historic in being the first completely air/sea conflict. The Americans lost a large carrier, another damaged and a couple of minor ships sunk and the Japanese suffered the loss of a small carrier and damage to a larger one so, on the balance of destruction this could be seen as a Japanese victory but, in fact, it was a defeat. They lost more aircraft than the Americans and they could ill afford the loss of their irreplaceable highly trained naval aircrew. Only a lucky squall and defective American torpedoes prevented the likely loss of both their best aircraft carriers. As it was, the Shokaku would be out of action for months while she was repaired and the Zuikaku also, because she had lost so many aircraft and crew she could not function. With the critical Midway operation looming, it was a grievous blow. American naval pilots had shown they were nearly the equal of their Japanese counterparts and in the future they could only get better, while the Japanese could only get worse as training times were shortened under the pressure of losses. The biggest victory was at the strategic level because this action foiled the Japanese attempt to take Port Moresby from the sea and it was never to be repeated.

A final footnote to the battle concerns U.S. torpedoes which were clearly defective and robbed their fleet of success. The problem with torpedoes had been noted from the start of the war but nothing had been done and the problem would not finally be resolved until 1944. The blame lay with the U.S. Navy Bureau of Ordnance that had conducted inadequate tests on the torpedo before the war and was inexplicably slow to remedy the faults once they were discovered. This delay prejudiced the effectiveness of American forces in battle and cost numerous lives. It was a disgrace but it does not appear that anyone was ever held responsible. This has been described by an American historian as 'The worst moment in the history of U.S. military technology'.[ix]

The Japanese now embarked on an enterprise that dwarfed the Port Moresby venture in size and daring. They planned to capture Midway Island some 1,300 miles northwest of Pearl Harbour and the Hawaiian Islands. This plan was the brainchild of Admiral Yamamoto and was aggressive to the point of foolhardiness. For this reason it was initially rejected by Admiral Osami Nagano, the Chief of the Imperial Naval General Staff, but then reluctantly accepted when Yamamoto threatened to resign. Yamamoto, alone amongst Japan's military leaders realized that Japan must win the war fast or be swamped by American armaments. In this context a policy of slow strangulation of Australia was not enough by itself. On the other hand the capture of Midway would be such a threat to United States power in the Pacific that there must be an immediate and violent reaction and this could lead to a climactic battle that Japan could win. Then there would be a negotiated peace. This was the trend of Yamamoto's thinking and to give it a chance of success, the operation must include the maximum force.

Accordingly almost the whole of the Imperial Navy was involved in a complicated plan that included a feint to the Aleutian Islands as well as the main assault on Midway.

The Aleutian operation can be swiftly dealt with. Although it was a feint, an attack on the Aleutians had its own purpose because their geographical position dominates the North Pacific and in this region, the distance between the U.S.A. and Japan, is at its smallest. The force that went there in 1942 included two aircraft carriers, the Ryujo and the new Junyo. On May 3rd they carried out a raid on Dutch Harbour, the only substantial town in the islands. They then captured the islands of Attu and Kiska without meeting resistance and occupied them for a year until U.S. forces recaptured Attu in a bloody battle and Kiska was abandoned as indefensible. The most important matter from an aviation point of view was that in the course of operations there, a Zero crash-landed on a remote islet and remained virtually intact though the pilot was killed. In due course the Americans found this aircraft and shipped it to the United States where it was extensively tested and provided U.S. aircraft designers with invaluable information.

The main Midway invasion force was divided into three parts. The leading section was the carrier force comprising the four carriers Kaga, Akagi, Soryu and Hiryu with escorting warships. There followed the occupation force with troops on transports ready to be disembarked on Midway, and some distance behind this and 300 miles behind the carriers, came the main battle force including seven battleships, one of which was the Yamato, the largest and most powerful battleship in the world. The Zuikaku and Shokaku were sorely missed although the crews of the four carriers present had always looked down on these two ships and their crews as inferior newcomers.

Once again the code breakers gave the U.S. Navy priceless information about Japanese intentions and they knew in advance that they had to counter a thrust aimed at Midway. The Japanese, on the other hand, thought that Yorktown had been sunk when it had not, had no idea where the U.S. fleet was and thought their Midway operation was a surprise when it was not. The Americans reinforced Midway both on the ground and in the air. The island's air garrison of 37 planes was reinforced to 80 together with 32 PBY Catalina reconnaissance planes. At sea Admiral Fletcher took station 200 miles to the north of Midway with the carriers Yorktown, Enterprise and Hornet. The

Yorktown's Coral Sea damage had been repaired by round-the-clock work at the Pearl Harbour shipyard though some of her boilers still did not work and she could only make a reduced speed. These were all the carriers the U.S. Navy had available: Saratoga was still undergoing repair and Wasp was serving in the European theatre.

The battle began on 3rd June 1942 when reconnaissance aircraft from Midway spotted the fleet of transports carrying the troops. A raid was promptly carried out by B-17s but it was a high altitude effort that brought no results at all. The following morning the U.S. fleet had reconnaissance planes out at first light. At the same time Admiral Nagumo, in command of the Japanese carrier force was launching a raid on Midway to be carried out by slightly more than a hundred planes. On Akagi, his flagship, the operations officer was Commander Minoru Genda, the talismanic officer who had planned and directed the Pearl Harbour raid. Genda was in the sick bay with a fever but came to the bridge in pyjamas to do his job.[x] Nagumo's fleet also launched a number of seaplanes to search for the American carrier force and one of these was spotted by a U.S. PBY flying boat that noted its course and promptly flew the reciprocal, that is, it flew in the direction the seaplane had come from. Before long it saw Japanese aircraft carriers and radioed its discovery to Midway. A few minutes later radar on Midway detected the force heading toward the island and the alert was given. All the aircraft on Midway promptly took off to avoid being caught on the ground by the incoming raid as had happened at Pearl Harbour.

The U.S. carriers now steamed toward the reported position of their Japanese counterparts intending to launch their aircraft as soon as they came within range.

Meanwhile the fighter planes from Midway met the incoming Japanese raid and took on the Japanese Zeros. The Americans were badly beaten and 17 fighters were shot down. The Japanese bombers duly raided Midway and caused a great deal of damage. The movie director John Ford was there and filmed it all, being injured in the shoulder by shrapnel while doing so. As the raid ended, the Japanese flight leader decided that he had not done enough and another raid was needed to finish the job.

Of the bombers on Midway, some found the enemy and an attack was launched by six TBF Avengers and four B-26 bomber aircraft fitted out to carry torpedoes. Only one Avenger and two B-26s survived and the attack did no harm to the Japanese. Nagumo knew these aircraft came from Midway and this seemed to underline the importance of carrying out another raid on the island, so he ordered the aircraft still on his ships loaded with bombs for another strike. They were carrying torpedoes and armour-piercing bombs for an anti-ship mission and they all had to be re-armed with high explosive bombs suitable for a land strike. All this time Japanese reconnaissance aircraft were combing the area looking for American aircraft carriers. Some of these aircraft came not from the carriers but from other large ships in the task force. It was the custom in all the major navies at this time for large ships to carry one or two scout planes that could be launched from a catapult. One of these aircraft, carried by the heavy cruiser Tone, had made a late start because of a fault in its catapult. This plane now radioed that it had found American surface ships.

At the same time further attacks developed from the Midway planes. 16 SBD Dauntless dive-bombers made the next attack but scored no hits. Defending Zeros shot half of them down. B-17s now attacked from high level and elderly Vindicator torpedo bombers came in at low level. Again no hits were scored.

The Tone scout plane now radioed that it had seen an aircraft carrier: for Nagumo the worst possible news at the worst possible moment. At the same time the aircraft that had raided Midway returned low on fuel and needed to land urgently. All the aircraft on the carriers' decks now had to be taken down to the hangars and re-armed once again for a naval attack while the Midway force landed on the decks above.

Admiral Fletcher and his staff made some careful mathematical calculations. They wanted to launch their aircraft at the earliest possible moment but the range must not be too great for them to find the enemy and return home, taking into account that the carriers would be moving while the mission was under way. They also wanted them to arrive shortly after the returning planes from Midway. They knew that if they did, they would catch the Japanese carriers with decks full of combustible aircraft not yet ready to fly again. Enterprise and Hornet launched their aircraft first because they were some miles ahead of Yorktown. The strike was an all-out effort and only a few Wildcat fighters were kept back as defence for the carriers. 68 bombers and 29 torpedo planes took part together with 20 escorting Wildcats. The last plane was airborne at 8.06 a.m. At 8.38, Yorktown launched her planes; 17 bombers and 12 torpedo planes with an escort of six Wildcats.

The various squadrons became split up in the course of launch and journey and consequently arrived at the Japanese fleet at different times. Because Admiral Nagumo had meantime altered course, some formations missed the fleet altogether.

The first to arrive were VT-8, the Devastator torpedo bombers from the Hornet. They had lost their fighter escort on the way and came in very alone. Their leader was Lt. Commander John Waldron, aged 42 at the time. He was an interesting mixture in that his father was from an old New Hampshire family and his mother was a Native American from the Sioux nation. He was a very experienced pilot who had spent much time as an instructor. Before the squadron set out, he told his pilots to do their utmost and that if there was only one man left he wanted that man to 'go in and get a hit'.[xi]

The Devastator was an old plane that flew slowly and in order to launch the poor quality torpedoes it carried with any chance of success, it had to fly very low and very straight as it approached the Japanese warships. The result was that VT-8 was an easy target for the defending Zeros and every single plane was shot down. Their torpedoes scored no hits. Only one man of the whole squadron survived. He was Ensign George Gay who was rescued from the sea the next day by a PBY flying boat.

Following VT-8, two more squadrons of torpedo bombers made their runs and the Zeros destroyed them too. Each squadron lost ten planes but scored no hits. Details of the Japanese side of this fight are hard to come by because most of the relevant pilots did not survive Midway. One who did, was Lt. Commander Iyozoh Fujita, a Zero pilot on Soryu who remembered that he tried a new tactic and attacked the torpedo bombers head on instead of stalking them from behind. His tactic was remarkably successful and he shot down four bombers and two fighters before he was caught by friendly fire and forced to ditch in the ocean. He considered himself lost and prepared to die but he was lucky and a destroyer picked him up after only a few hours in the sea. He survived the whole war and when it was over, flew for Japan Air Lines.[xii]

High in the sky there now arrived the aircraft of VB-6 and VS-6 the two bomber squadrons from the Enterprise in their SBD Dauntless dive-bombers under the command of Lt. Commander Clarence McClusky. These planes had been searching for the Japanese fleet for some time, confused by Nagumo's change of course. They too had lost their escort because the Wildcats had run low on fuel and had to turn back. This time the lack of escort did not matter because the Zeros were all down at sea level after their attacks on the torpedo bombers and first had to climb up to 15,000 feet where the Dauntlesses were.

Now the dive-bombers hurtled down into the attack with deadly accuracy. The very first bomb hit the flagship Akagi, smashed the deck and set her on fire. Her own bombs, lying around as the re-arming process was carried out, exploded violently and tore the deck apart. Another bomb hit parked aircraft and started uncontrollable fires. Nagumo transferred his flag to the cruiser Nagara and the Akagi was left to burn. Four more hits were scored on the Kaga which was also swept by fires and reduced to a hulk. Then the dive-bombers from the Yorktown arrived and scored immediate hits on the Soryu. Soon she too was burning fiercely as bombs ignited fuel and weapons stacked on deck.

Of the four Japanese carriers just the Hiryu was left untouched. She had been a little apart from the rest and was not spotted by the American planes. Admiral Yamaguchi on her bridge, who was Nagumo's second-in-command, ordered a counter-strike as soon as her planes were ready. At 10.18 am she launched 18 dive-bombers and six fighters who spotted some of the Yorktown's planes and followed them home to their carrier. Eight bombers got through the screen of fighters and anti-aircraft fire to drop their bombs and three hit the Yorktown which was badly damaged but still afloat and able to steam slowly. Yamaguchi launched a second strike and this time two torpedoes struck the Yorktown, leaving her dead in the water. A third strike was in preparation when the aircraft from Enterprise made another attack and hit the Hiryu with bombs before any planes could take off. It should be noted here that the U.S. ships had radar and the Japanese did not, so that the Americans always had warning of an approaching raid but the Japanese did not.

Hiryu in her turn was swept by fires and reduced to wreckage. When aircraft from the Hornet arrived they did not waste their bombs on her. On what was left of her deck, the 800 surviving crew paraded and were addressed by Yamaguchi who thanked them for their service and ordered them to leave on the vessels standing by to rescue them and continue the fight. Then he led them in three cheers for the Emperor. He and Captain Kaku remained behind by their own choice and went down with the ship.[xiii]

The next day Yorktown, inching her way back to Pearl Harbour, was spotted by a Japanese submarine and sent to the bottom. U.S. aircraft made a number of attacks on various ships in the Japanese fleet that was now in retreat, but without success until 6th June when they sank the heavy cruiser, Mikuma that had already been damaged in a collision. In all, the Japanese lost 275 aircraft and the Americans 132. Japanese pilot losses represented ten percent of the trained men the Imperial Navy had available and included a huge slice of their most experienced men.[xiv] All four Japanese carriers sank and with them went any slight, fanciful hope that Japan was going to wring a negotiated peace out of this war. From now on the only question was how long was it going to take the U.S.A. to defeat Japan and how many lives was it going to cost?

Most critical battles in World War Two lasted for days, weeks or even months but Midway was over in a morning. Winston Churchill said of Sir John Jellicoe, Commander-in-Chief of the British Grand Fleet in 1916, that he was the only man who could lose the war in an afternoon. Admiral Nagumo lost the next war in a morning. To be fair to him, if the critical defeat had not come at Midway it would have come somewhere else. That being said, he did make some serious mistakes. He should never have attacked Midway at all until he had some idea where the American fleet was and, having done so, he should have followed Yamaguchi's advice and launched a strike against the U.S. carriers with the bombs his planes were carrying and not risked having them all caught on deck.

A number of general lessons for aviation authorities were apparent from this most important of battles. The first was the extreme vulnerability of aircraft carriers. They were big targets and they were packed full of fuel, bombs and torpedoes; in a word, they were an explosion waiting to happen. Japanese carriers reflected the national refusal to consider anything even remotely related to a defensive mindset by having little regard to damage control either in their construction or their operation. By contrast American carriers were built to take punishment and their crews were skilled at fighting fires and limiting damage. As the war went on they grew even better. Much of the vulnerability could be avoided by having an armoured flight deck but this greatly reduced the number of aircraft a ship could carry. The Royal Navy had gone down this path and their carriers held, on average, about half the number of planes of their American and Japanese contemporaries. On the other hand they only lost one carrier to bombing during the whole war and that was Hermes, a very old ship whose armour was minimal. Moreover, she was caught at a time when she had no aircraft aboard to protect her.

The second lesson was the danger that land based aircraft posed to aircraft carriers. Although the damage at Midway was not done by the aircraft from Midway, the desire to make a second strike against the island was critical. Had Midway been another carrier the first Japanese raid would have sunk it. In the long run carriers could not win against land based planes and should stick to their strength, which was attacking other ships.

The third lesson, and this was of general application beyond the aviation sphere, was that a leader must have clarity of purpose and know what his priorities are. Nagumo was in a hopeless muddle as to whether he was to destroy the base on Midway or defeat the U.S. carriers first. If you were fighting against the enemy's aircraft carriers it was essential to get in the first blow as it might well be the only blow that was needed.

The fourth lesson was the vital importance of reconnaissance. This hardly needs stressing but in the case of a carrier battle, if you can't find the enemy's ships, you lose, however good your planes and pilots are. In this field the Americans had the priceless advantage of radar. Allied to this aspect is the question of intelligence and here again the Americans had a great advantage in their ability to read the Imperial Navy's coded messages.

One area where the Americans were at a disadvantage was the delivery of torpedo attacks. Their torpedoes were so unreliable as to render this arm of the carrier force second rate. In addition, most of the attacks made at Midway by U.S. torpedo planes were made by Devastators and they were obsolete. The new Avengers made a limited appearance without much success but the Avenger was, in fact, a fine aircraft though it too was to be handicapped until 1944 by the poor quality torpedoes. Partly as a result of this shortcoming the Japanese carrier squadrons were, on the whole, a more potent weapon than the American. It took only a handful of planes from Hiryu to cripple the Yorktown. This was the only Japanese ship-to-ship attack of the battle and had there been more, the result might have been quite different. As already noted however, Japanese air efficiency was on a downward curve as the Battle of Midway eliminated experienced pilots and U.S. Navy efficiency was on an upward curve as better aircraft appeared and training improved.

A final comment on the battle is that it gave rise to a new star in the U.S. Navy's galaxy of command. Fletcher's second-in-command Raymond Spruance, who had taken a major part in the conduct of the battle, was generally acknowledged to have put in an outstanding performance. In Morison's words: 'Spruance emerged from this battle one of the greatest fighting and thinking admirals in American naval history.'[xv]

Midway may have ended any chance of the Japanese striking the U.S.A. a knockout blow but it did not stop the policy of strangling Australia, and the next step in that campaign was the construction of an airfield on the island of Guadalcanal in the Solomon Islands right next to Tulagi where they had already established a seaplane base. For America though, the time for retreat was over and just as the Japanese engineers were putting the finishing touches to this airfield, the Americans invaded Guadalcanal and seized it on August 7th. There followed a six month struggle for this relatively unimportant island into which both sides were to throw their every resource.

CHAPTER FIFTEEN

Mediterranean Air War

Italy declared war on the Western Allies on June 10th 1940. She immediately joined the attack on France by invading across the Riviera frontier and she attacked Great Britain by invading Egypt and British Somaliland (now part of Somalia) in the Horn of Africa.

This was an ambitious program of conquest but Italy did not have the power to back it up. Of all the major powers involved in World War Two Italy had the weakest industrial base. Aircraft production is an example in point. In round numbers she produced 3,000 aeroplanes in 1940 to Germany's 10,000 and Britain's 15,000. So Britain was able to match Germany and still out-produce Italy at the same time. The result was that Italy's armed forces were poorly equipped and had little prospect of adequate replacement equipment arriving to make good losses as campaigns progressed.

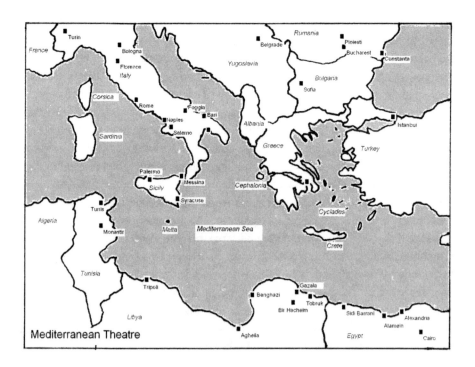

Mediterranean Theatre

A great deal of criticism has been directed over the years at the quality of the Italian fighting man in World War Two. Much of this criticism has been generated in the United Kingdom and was apparent even at the time. The larger part of it can be dismissed as propaganda, which must be seen against a background of consistent British defeats at the hands of the Germans and Japanese. Such defeats led the British to revel in the few victories that they could record, which were against the Italians. It is however, hard to resist the conclusion that the average Italian was not wholeheartedly behind Mussolini's dreams of conquest. There can surely be no shame in that however, and it must be recorded that the Regia Aeronautica's shortcomings can be put down to obsolete aircraft and irresolute command rather than lack of fighting spirit on the part of air and ground crew.

When she entered the war Italy had some 2,000 aircraft available but only some 1,000 were serviceable. Low serviceability rates were a constant feature of R.A. operations because of poor management of the supply of spare parts and the multiplicity of different types of aircraft in use. Of those 1,000 aircraft, 40 percent were Savoia Marchetti SM79 bombers but, typically, there were also small numbers of several other types that merely duplicated what the SM79 could do but, in most cases, did it less well. Design and tactics were better suited to the 1920s than the 1940s probably because that had been the decade when Italian aviation led the world.

The first action for the R.A. was against France and raids were carried out against French airfields, Corsica and shipping off the Riviera coast. The Italians quickly discovered, as other combatants had done, that high level bombing against ships did not work. They had no dive-bombers and so they set about using their bombers as torpedo carriers and in time they became very proficient in this work. A torpedo attack makes few demands on the aircraft but many on the pilot who must fly low, slow and straight into whatever A.A. fire the target can put up. The Italian pilots passed this test with flying colours.

Some of these early operations amounted to something like training sessions. 150th Fighter Wing, for instance, strafed the French airfield at Hyeres on 13th June 1940. A.A. fire was light and the Italians destroyed 14 planes on the ground and one in the air. One of the R.A. pilots was Ugo Drago. For him this was the first mission of a long and distinguished flying career. A further raid two days later on the airfield at Fayence provided stiffer opposition but the wing gave as good as it got. This wing was flying CR42s and at the end of the month it was re-equipped with superior Macchi MC200s which were monoplanes with retracting landing gear. The pilots did not like them however, and would not fly them and when the wing went to Greece in October, they did so still flying their CR42s.

The usual story in the air forces of this period (or any period) is one of pilots crying out for better planes and authority being slow to provide them. Here we have an extraordinary example of the reverse: improved equipment being rejected by the pilots themselves because of their innate conservatism.[i]

Of those 2,000 planes there were only some 400 devoted to the offensive in North Africa however, because of commitments in East Africa and an exaggerated emphasis on home defence. The invasion of Egypt, which began in September 1940, was a confused affair because the Italians had been fighting against France and therefore had to array their forces in Libya, with a view to defending their western border against French attack from Tunisia and not themselves attacking from the eastern border. A rapid change of plans was therefore necessary, with all the confusion that such a thing engenders. When one deducts reconnaissance and transport planes from the figure of available aircraft, the result is in the region of 300 combat planes though the sources are not certain. The best informed guess seems to be 282. The bombers were mainly SM79s and the fighters Fiat CR42s.

Against this array the British pitted 202 Group under the command of Air Commodore Raymond Collishaw, a Canadian and an ace from the First War who had scored 60 victories. 202 Group numbered 48 Blenheim bombers and 21 Gloster Gladiator fighters. But there were forces in other parts of Egypt reasonably close at hand and available for any prolonged struggle. These amounted approximately to another 12 bombers and 40 fighters. There were also various transport and army co-operation aircraft and two squadrons of the stately four-engine Short Sunderland flying boats based at Alexandria.

In general terms this force had second rate equipment because the best was kept at home for the defence of Great Britain. The Gladiator was a biplane like the CR42, which it resembled in many ways. It was armed with four .303 machine guns against the Italian plane's two 12.7 mm guns. The latter were, in theory, better guns because of their larger calibre, but these guns were the Breda Safat which was remarkably ineffective owing to its low muzzle velocity. When that was coupled with its high weight the result was one of the poorest guns in use in the air forces in World War Two. Both planes had engines of 840 horsepower but the Gladiator was somewhat lighter and therefore, perhaps, more agile while the CR42 was up to 30 mph faster depending on height.

The two principal bombers were more distinct. The SM79 was substantially larger, with three engines instead of two. It had a 1,200 mile range and carried 2,750 lbs of bombs. The Blenheim was smaller and faster, with a better range (1,400 miles) but its 1,000 lb bomb load was truly unimpressive. One would say that on balance, the Italians had the better bombers and the fighters were more or less equal.

When war was declared the Italians showed no inclination to initiate hostilities against the British and the R.A. remained inactive, largely because they were already carrying out the repositioning of forces that was plainly required as a result of the imminent collapse of France. It was the British who started active operations. On 11th June 1940 they sent a reconnaissance flight into Libya at first light and followed this up with a low level raid by eight Blenheims on the airfield at El Adem, near Tobruk. When they arrived they could see the whole staff of the airfield lined up on the parade ground and they immediately made strafing runs and sent the Italians running for cover. They then bombed the airfield and destroyed hangars and a number of parked aircraft. Meanwhile the Italian anti-aircraft gunners had manned their guns and their fire caught one bomber which burst into flames and crashed into the sea. Two others were damaged but managed to fly home, where one of them burst into flames on landing and its crew were incinerated before they could get out. The other, flying on a single engine, landed safely. The Italians on the parade ground had been listening to an announcement of the declaration of war on Great Britain: something of an irony in the circumstances.[ii]

The next day the R.A.F. raided Tobruk harbour. Some 29 aircraft were supposed to take part but there was a ground mist and plenty of cloud. This caused a number of the bombers to miss the target altogether. There were also more than the usual number of mishaps. Two aircraft dropped out of the mission because of mechanical troubles, two others crashed on take-off, one collided with a transport aircraft while taxiing and another scratched the mission after its observer/bomb-aimer walked into a spinning propeller. Only 17 aircraft reached the target where they hit the old Italian cruiser San Giorgio, which ran onto a sand bank to avoid sinking. Built in 1910 she was no great loss. She sat on the sandbank for the rest of war being used as a platform for A.A. guns by the successive occupiers of the port.[iii] In 1952 she was re-floated to be towed back to Italy but the journey had hardly begun when she was sunk by a storm.[iv]

These operations set a pattern for the early days of the war in North Africa and it was a pattern of aggressive flying by the R.A.F. against generally superior numbers. It was as well that the Gladiator proved a match for the CR42 or there would have been well-nigh insoluble problems for the R.A.F. because, after the fall of France, it was quite extraordinarily difficult to get replacement aircraft to Egypt. They could not come through the Mediterranean by sea or air because of the dominance of the Italian navy and air force. They had to be shipped to ports in West Africa and then flown by stages across the entire continent via the sub-Saharan lands and the Sudan. Another problem for the British was the fact that the SM79 was faster than the Gladiator and thus the Italians could conduct raids during which they could not be caught. It therefore became a priority to replace Gladiators with Hurricanes as quickly as could be managed. When a Hurricane finally caught some SM79s on 17th August, it destroyed three of them in short order.

When the Italian offensive into Egypt finally began in early September 1940 it made little difference to the air war which had already been conducted at a brisk pace for three months. Italian problems of supply and inadequate resources were not helped by Mussolini deciding to send gratuitous help to the Germans in their air assault on Great Britain. From September until early the following year a detachment of the R.A. operated from France against the R.A.F., achieving very little except to stretch Italian resources unnecessarily. In October he decided to attack Greece and the same strictures can be applied again and with increased force. Some 175 aircraft were sent to France and 360 to Greece.

The Italian offensive in Egypt rapidly turned into a retreat and it was a retreat that did not stop until the disorganized survivors reached the gates of Tripoli, Libya's capital, having lost the whole of Cyrenaica and seen the destruction of their North African army. During the whole of this period the R.A.F. maintained a general ascendancy in the air without ever coming close to destroying the R.A.. The British were simply too few in number and the Italians, despite having to do battle with increasingly inferior equipment, never gave up the fight. The R.A. suffered grievous losses in this period, probably in the region of 1,200 to 1,300 planes. The majority of these were captured on the ground as the British took the airfields where they had been abandoned. This is the major penalty for air forces that have to retreat in a hurry: any aircraft that cannot fly, even though this may only be for the want of one spark plug, must be left behind to be captured.

By January 1941 the Italians in Libya were utterly defeated and the way was open for the British army to advance and capture Tripoli and drive Italy out of North Africa altogether. Churchill ordered the army to halt however, because he was committed to sending substantial forces to Greece to aid the Greek army in its struggle against the Axis. With hindsight one can see that this was an unfortunate decision because a brief opportunity to strike a decisive blow was allowed to slip away so that another goal could be pursued which then turned to bitter defeat.

At the same time, as the fighting in North Africa was going on, there was another campaign being fought and it was one that attracted less publicity than almost any other area of combat in World War Two. This was the campaign in East Africa. Several points must be made at once about this campaign. The first is that the area in question was huge. At stake were Abyssinia (Ethiopia) and Somalia. The latter was, in those days, two countries: British and Italian Somaliland. Ethiopia and Italian Somaliland were both owned by Italy and known as Italian East Africa and together they were six times the size of Italy herself. The second point is that the whole area was wild and remote, wholly devoid of paved roads and with only two railway lines. There were mountains, deserts and scrubland for hundreds of miles on end. Airfields were of the most primitive kind. The third point to be made is that Italian East Africa was cut off from the homeland and therefore could receive almost no supplies or replacements, except tiny quantities flown in from Libya, whereas adjacent British Somaliland could be served by the Royal Navy and thus kept supplied at all times. The fourth point is that for both sides East Africa had long been bottom of the priority list for equipment. If second rate equipment went to North Africa, third rate equipment found its way to East Africa.

The British army in Egypt could not be supplied through the Mediterranean because of the aforementioned hostile Italian air force and navy and so all materiel came by the long route round the Cape of Good Hope, through the Gulf of Aden and the

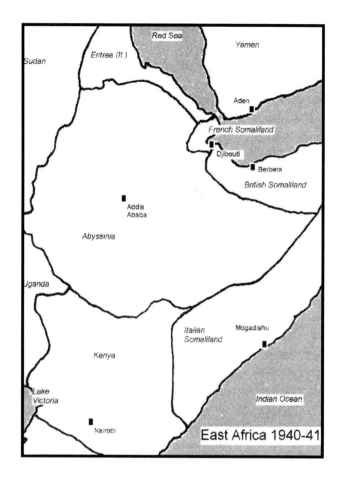

East Africa 1940-41

Red Sea and up to the Suez Canal. The Italians in East Africa occupied a large chunk of the coastline in the Gulf of Aden and the Red Sea and were thus potentially able to interdict the route. If they could do so effectively, the British must be defeated in North Africa and their whole presence in the Middle East jeopardized.

Despite the potential threat posed by Italian East Africa, Churchill's initial reaction was to leave it alone and subdue it by blockade. This sensible policy had to be abandoned when the Italians went on the offensive. In August 1940 they invaded British Somaliland and conquered it in short order. The Italians could muster some 200,000 men and 200 front line aircraft but the soldiers were mainly unenthusiastic local levies and the aircraft could not be maintained or fuelled for long. After the Italian defeat in North Africa in late 1940, Italian morale plummeted and the chance of reinforcement sank to nothing. The British counter-attacked from the Sudan and Kenya and, later from Aden in the Yemen across the sea to the Somaliland coast. The whole huge Italian territory was gradually conquered until, in October 1941, the British Middle East Command was able to declare that it was no longer a war zone.

The air war that was part of this campaign was fought by relatively small numbers of mainly obsolete aircraft and had more than a flavour of frontier adventure to it. Half of the Italian air strength consisted of Caproni CA133s. These were bomber transports of the generation before the Savoia Marchetti SM79. They were very slow, very vulnerable and carried a minute bomb load. There was just one squadron of SM79s which were probably the best planes in the whole theatre on either side. Nearly half the fighters were Fiat CR32s, the predecessor of the already obsolete CR42 which made up the balance of the fighter strength.

British air strength was divided up between the Sudan, Kenya and the Yemen. In the Sudan there were three squadrons equipped with Vickers Wellesley bombers. These were an obsolete single-engine, light bomber design, even more ancient than the Fairey Battle that fared so poorly in France. Wellesleys had been retired from use by the R.A.F. everywhere else. There was also a squadron of biplane fighters. In the Yemen, at Aden, there were three squadrons of Blenheims and a few Gladiators. To the South, in Kenya there was no R.A.F. presence but the South African Air Force could muster about 40 planes. There were some Hurricanes and some Hartebeests, (a predecessor of the Gladiator). The bomber element was made up of a few Battles and some Junkers Ju86s transferred from South African Airways and converted to carry bombs rather than passengers. Thus there was the irony of German-built bombers fighting on the Allied side. Altogether there were in the region of 100 Allied aircraft.

During the course of the struggle, which lasted a little over a year, the British were steadily reinforced, mainly with Hurricanes and Blenheims and the Italians managed to fly in some SM79s from Libya, but the numbers of aircraft involved was never very great. For the bombers the targets were strictly limited. There were no factories or railway yards to be bombed and vast areas of land contained no military targets at all. All efforts were directed toward hitting airfields and ships with intermittent strikes against infantry defensive positions and the odd supply dump. Mogadishu, Berbera and one or two other ports had rudimentary docks. For the fighters, the targets, as ever, were other aircraft. Air fighting died away somewhat in the later months of the campaign as Italian air strength evaporated.

Much of the struggle was against the conditions and the terrain. Poor equipment and poor maintenance took their toll. In June 1940, as the British sought to stem the Italian advance, a force of five Wellesleys of 223 Squadron took off from an airfield at Summit in the Sudan to attack targets on the Eritrean coast. One never made it into the air because flares stored in the aircraft ignited due to a fault and set the whole aircraft on fire as it tried to take off. Another plane crash-landed on the coast due to engine failure and another crashed on landing. One more was shot down by Italian A.A. fire so only one of the five survived but, of the losses, only one was unequivocally due to enemy action.[v]

In Western Europe, if a pilot was shot down he was almost always found immediately by civilians and taken to the nearest railway station from where he rode home to his base. In East Africa being shot down could be the start of a major adventure. Major Preller, commanding officer of the 11th South African Air Force Squadron, was shot down by ground fire on a reconnaissance mission over Mogadishu in Italian Somaliland. He was able to crash-land and all three of the crew survived unhurt. They set out to walk the several hundred miles to base with one water bottle between them. Air searches failed to find them and they were given up for lost until two weeks later an R.A.F. plane flying over the bush at low level, spotted a European on a camel. This was Preller who had left his crew at a water hole and set out alone to get help. They were quickly all rescued.[vi]

On 15th July 1940 an Italian bomber piloted by Junior Lieutenant Salvatore Suella was shot down over the Red Sea. Suella was killed but three of the crew survived and paddled in their life raft to an uninhabited island where they existed on a diet of bird's eggs. Eventually they decided their only chance of rescue was to paddle to the nearest inhabited island, but it took them several days to do so and more days waiting on the island when they reached it until an Italian ship picked them up. They returned to base three weeks after their flight.[vii]

Not every such story ended happily. In February 1941 an aircraft piloted by a Lieutenant Hamilton was shot down in Italian Somaliland and Hamilton was killed but his observer, Sergeant Dixon, managed to parachute and was taken prisoner. He was handed over by an Italian officer to a native soldier to be taken to headquarters but as soon as the officer was out of sight the soldier shot him.[viii]

It is hard to assess the significance of the aerial combat in East Africa because so few planes were involved and they were such antiquated models. It was a campaign that should have been fought half a dozen years earlier. It was also a campaign in which air power probably had less effect than most, but contemporary observers were well aware of that fact and would have committed more and better aircraft if they had had them available.

At the end of 1940 Hitler and the German Foreign Office took the view that they would have to help Italy or there was the danger that she would be expelled from Africa and Mussolini would fall from power. To this end the 10th Air Corps, under General Geisler, who had handled the invasion of Norway so well, was sent to Italy at the end of the year with an operational area of authority in southern Italy, Sicily and the southern part of Sardinia. By mid-January 1941 it had over 300 aircraft at its disposal. Its orders comprised three objectives: to neutralize Malta, to cut the British supply route to Egypt and to support Axis ground forces in North Africa.

A glance at the map reveals the strategic position of Malta. It is on the direct route between Sicily and Tripoli and it dominates the narrow gap between Tunisia and the mainland of Europe. In 1940 it was the only Allied base between Gibraltar and the British forces in Egypt. Aircraft based on Malta therefore threatened all movement in the central Mediterranean.

The Italians began bombing Malta as soon as they entered the war. On the 11th June 1940 there were three raids but Italy had so many theatres of war to prosecute at the same time in the second half of 1940, that she was never able to devote the weight of bombing strength that was required to close down the island as a military threat. It must be said that in the summer of 1940 Malta's threat was largely potential rather than actual. In June the air power of the island consisted of just three Gladiator fighters affectionately known by the R.A.F. personnel on the island as 'Faith', 'Hope' and 'Charity'.[ix] The poor state of its defences was due to a combination of lack of resources and the pre-war decision that it was indefensible and therefore any resources sent there were resources wasted.

It was the British, however, who struck the next significant blow. Their operations in the Mediterranean and North Africa were constantly threatened by the substantial Italian navy which included six battleships. The principal fleet anchorage was Taranto harbour and the British had devised a plan to attack it before the war began. This was now put into action and the aircraft carrier Illustrious sailed to a point off the coast of Greece where she released a force of 21 Swordfish torpedo bombers for a night attack on the harbour. At this time such an attack was unheard of and the Italians were taken completely by surprise. Three battleships were put out of action for the loss of a mere two aircraft and the whole fleet was subsequently moved north to Naples for safety. This attack was a classic example of imaginative use of airpower and was successful because of careful planning and faultless execution. The limited space in the harbour meant that the attack would have been impractical for faster aircraft but suited the Swordfish. A sea level torpedo attack against ships in harbour makes anti-aircraft guns very difficult to use because they cannot fire without endangering the town or other ships.

The Fairey Swordfish was an extraordinary aircraft. It was a biplane torpedo bomber that was obsolete when the war began and yet served throughout hostilities. For the first half it was the standard attack aircraft of the Royal Navy and for the second half it was used by Coastal Command for anti-submarine duties. The battles in the Mediterranean saw its apogee and Taranto was its finest hour. It was a canvas-covered mass of struts and wires, with an open cockpit and it was hopelessly slow and unwieldy, yet loved by its crews who called it the 'Stringbag'. It looked flimsy but was surprisingly tough and its single Bristol Pegasus engine was very reliable. It was simple and easy to maintain and very easy to fly. Its top speed was not much over 100 m.p.h. so that in many ways flying it was like driving a very stable fast car. For carrier pilots the most dangerous part of their existence is landing on their carrier's deck and the very low landing speed of the Swordfish dramatically simplified this tricky procedure. For all its cult status it was definitely an inferior warplane and the navy replaced it with the American Avenger as soon as they could. Its continued production thereafter may well be connected with the navy's desire to keep alive a sector of the British aviation business with expertise in designing aircraft for naval operations.

The 10th Air Corps began operations in January 1941 when they intercepted a British convoy bound for Malta, escorted by the aircraft carriers Illustrious and Ark Royal and other warships. Exact details are hard to come by but it seems that although a considerable air battle developed, only limited damage was done to the convoy which forced its way through to Malta. The Illustrious however, was hit by six bombs and severely damaged. There can be little doubt that had she been an American or Japanese ship, she would have been sunk but as it was, her armoured deck saved her. Even so she had to be sent to the United States for repairs and was out of the war for months. The following day Stukas sank the cruiser Southampton.

There followed a concentrated day and night bombing offensive against Malta by both the Germans and the Italians aimed principally at Valetta harbour and its installations and the airfields on the islands. Malta remained stubbornly resistant however, and the offensive petered out, principally because a large proportion of the available aircraft had to be sent to North Africa to support the Axis offensive there.

In March 1941 General Erwin Rommel arrived in Libya with a contingent of German troops that were soon to be known as the 'Afrika Korps'. He promptly launched an offensive that pushed the British back from El Agheila on the western coast of Cyrenaica all the way to the Egyptian frontier. In other words they were back where the Italians started in June 1940. Rommel's air support amounted to about 200 planes which had been flown in from 10th Air Corps in Sicily. They were principally Ju88s and He111s with a sprinkling of Stukas and Me110 fighters. They supported the German advance in the now familiar manner though the R.A.F., what little of it had not been sent to Greece, provided stiff opposition. For instance, on 18th February a squadron of Stukas was attacked by Hurricanes of 3 Squadron Royal Australian Air Force and eight were shot down.[x] Apart from anything else it soon became clear that the Luftwaffe force in Africa needed its own command and so an ad hoc headquarters known as Fliegerkorps Afrika was set up under General Stefan Froehlich.

This desert fighting had a romantic flavour of its own. Pilots, casually dressed for the extreme heat, sat about in shirts and shorts between missions and brewed up a cup of tea, or coffee, depending on the air force. Discipline was lax in all but the important matters. Conditions were hard but the desert was beautiful and the business of flying a sheer delight in the clear, vibrant air. On the other hand getting aircraft battle ready and keeping them so was a nightmare. Maintenance was a constant fight with the sand and the grit that got into everything and engines had to be fitted with special filters to keep it out. Shortage of spares was a constant irritant and fuel often had to be tipped into aircraft fuel tanks by hand from small cans, which was a backbreaking task.

At the end of March 1941 the Italian navy sortied to intercept the busy British naval traffic between Egypt and Greece. A British fleet intercepted them and the result was the Battle of Cape Matapan. The Royal Navy force included the Carrier

Formidable and her torpedo bombers heavily damaged a cruiser and a battleship. The cruiser was subsequently sunk by surface ships and the battleship, though it survived, was put out of action for months. Here was more evidence, if it were needed, that even obsolete torpedo planes could do great execution if resolutely flown and provided with effective torpedoes.

In April the fighter wing Jg27 arrived in Libya where it was to serve for the next eighteen months and with it came a young pilot by the name of Hans Joachim Marseilles. Marseilles was a gifted pilot with exceptional eyesight, but was also a handsome and charming young man from a sophisticated Berlin family whose first priority was imbibing cocktails and chasing young ladies. In his military career he was willful and disobedient and had already been thrown out of one wing. Its commander had had to leave him behind on more than one occasion because he was too 'tired' to fly as a result of his nighttime activities. The commander, Johannes Steinhoff, himself destined to be one of the Luftwaffe's foremost aces, finally decided that Marseilles was more bother than he was worth. Marseilles was transferred to Jg27 whose commander was more tolerant and could see the potential of the young man who had already shot down seven Allied planes in the Battle of Britain. Africa was Marseilles's great chance. There were no nightclubs or young girls to distract him in the desert and he could and did devote himself entirely to flying, with astonishing success.

Before his death on 30th September 1942, in an accident, Marseilles shot down 158 Allied aircraft making him the most successful German ace who flew solely against the Western Allies and at the time of his death, the leading ace of the Luftwaffe. His victims were almost exclusively R.A.F. planes. In fact there is some controversy about the exact number of his victories because there are occasions where the record of his claims exceeds the known Allied losses for the day in question. However, there can be no doubt that his tally was in the region of 150 and that he was a quite exceptional pilot.

On the other hand Marseilles was something of a two-edged sword. He was obsessed with increasing his personal score rather than achieving his unit's objectives. He was promoted to captain at age 22 and was the youngest captain in the Luftwaffe but he was really unsuited to command and turned his squadron into his personal sideshow, in which other pilots were expected to do nothing but protect him while he scored kill after kill. He ignored bombers to chase fighters because they were easier kills, but it was bombers that did the damage. On balance one has to wonder whether he was an asset to the Luftwaffe in Africa or a liability.[xi] To be fair, the arrival of this wing was a boon to the Afrika Korps because it provided Me109s for the first time and they were superior to any Allied fighters then in the theatre.

By late spring of 1941 the German advance had ground to a halt on the Egyptian frontier. The Afrika Korps stood at the end of a lengthy supply line and was exhausted. Reinforcement was unlikely in view of the total commitment of the

German war machine to the invasion of Russia. Moreover, the Italian Supreme Command, to which Rommel was theoretically answerable, had ordered him to stop and in this they had the backing of the German General Staff.

At the tactical level, Rommel could advance no further because of the resistance of the port of Tobruk. The town was subjected to constant bombing and was assaulted at the end of April without success. At the time this was seen as a significant setback for the German blitzkrieg philosophy, which indeed it was, but the war was to show that any kind of bombing had a limited effect on towns used as defensive strongpoints. The Germans were to discover this in Russia at Brest Litovsk and Sevastopol and the British at Caen, not to mention the crucial battle for Stalingrad. Ports were particularly resistant because they could be supplied and reinforced by sea. This was the case with Tobruk which the Royal Navy supplied at night. Indeed, in the autumn the garrison was virtually renewed *in toto* by this means.

On 12th May a convoy reached Alexandria carrying 50 Hurricanes. At the same time the trickle of aircraft reaching Egypt via the Trans-Africa route had swelled to a steady stream. From November 1940 to May 1941, 370 aircraft were sent on this route. That May, 328 more set out and before the end of the month the figure was 880. The quality was improving too. The Gladiators were gone and the R.A.F. and the South African Air Force now flew Hurricanes and Kittyhawks (the R.A.F. name for the American P-40E). There were still plenty of Blenheim bombers but there were now also some Wellingtons and some Marylands. This latter was another American design that was not outstanding but was definitely more impressive than the Blenheim and had double the bomb carrying capacity.

At this time there was a diversion because there was an Axis-backed coup in Iraq by a clique of army generals. Iraq was an independent country but Britain had a right to use its territories for military purposes and had a large air base at a place called Habbaniya not far from Baghdad. The rebels tried to lay siege to it and fighting broke out. There were 100 planes at Habbaniya, mostly old models used for training but they were still capable of fighting and were pressed into service. The British sent in reinforcements on the ground and a squadron of bombers in the air and the Iraqi air force was swept from the skies with ease. Thereafter the revolt was swiftly suppressed, the old regime restored and Iraq garrisoned for the duration. It was all over before May was out.

During the course of operations in Iraq it had become clear that the rebels had received help from the Vichy French regime that ruled Syria and Lebanon. In particular, German aircraft had flown in from Rhodes using bases in Syria as stopover points. The British decided to invade Syria and Lebanon and the assault began in June. The campaign lasted a month and the British were surprised by the ferocity of the resistance. The Vichy air force numbered around 100 planes, including some very capable Dewoitine D520 fighters. More aircraft were flown in from France and North Africa until there were nearly 300 present, but the primitive airfields in Syria did not have the facilities to cope with this number of planes. The countryside was flat and open and the bases lacked adequate anti-aircraft defences so that the planes made easy targets for the R.A.F. which destroyed them on the ground in large numbers. By the end of June, 180 had been destroyed and the rest were evacuated by way of Rhodes. It was a short and one-sided, if bitter, contest and an armistice was signed on 3rd July. Thereafter the Free French took over Syrian and Lebanese territory. The R.A.F. lost only a handful of planes: probably less than a dozen.

Churchill had grown increasingly dissatisfied with the R.A.F. Commander-in-Chief in the Middle East, Air Marshal Longmore and on 1st June he was replaced by his deputy Arthur Tedder. This was a most fortunate appointment for Tedder was to prove himself one of the ablest senior officers in any air force and from the moment of his appointment, his administrative capabilities enabled him to streamline command organization and increase efficiency all round. The result was a noticeable improvement in the R.A.F.'s operational performance and its morale.

In mid-June 1941 the British attacked Rommel's lines and the R.A.F. was sent in to carry out preliminary raids. At dawn on 14th June, six Hurricanes led by Flying Officer George Goodman, a veteran of the Battle of France and the Battle of Britain, attacked the airfield at Gazala hoping to surprise the defence and strafe German aircraft on the ground. The airfield was not surprised and the aircraft were blasted by flak. Three aircraft were shot down. One of them was flown by Goodman who crashed somewhere in the desert. Neither he nor his aircraft were ever found and his remains lie somewhere in the sands to this day.[xii] A raid on the same airfield later in the day was not a success either.

When the offensive began later that day the plan was that the air force should provide an air umbrella. It did this but was not able to stop German and Italian planes from breaking through to harass the ground forces. It took only three days for the attack to be stopped in its tracks and the stalemate to resume.

As a result of this fiasco, Archibald Wavell, the British commander in the Middle East was replaced by Sir Claude Auchinleck, a man with a reputation as an aggressive leader. At the same time Collishaw was retired and command of the Western Desert Air Force, as the Allied air force in North Africa was now named, was given to Arthur Coningham. Churchill was dissatisfied with Tedder and wished to dismiss him too but was faced with an ultimatum from the Chief and Deputy Chief of the Air Staff that they would both resign if he did so. In the face of a revolt of this magnitude Churchill backed down and it was well for Allied air power in the rest of the war that he did so.

It was clear that R.A.F. efforts to support the army so far had been deficient. There were many reasons for this but one of the most important of them was tactical and that was the policy of using British fighters as an 'umbrella' over the troops. This was a policy that Russian generals were indulging in at the same time and it did not work because of its passive and restrictive nature which was the antithesis of a fighter aircraft's strengths. The correct policy was one of aggressive attacks on the enemy's forces at all times: essentially the Luftwaffe policy. Tedder and Coningham realized this and set about changing British tactics. They were very successful and in due course were to repeat their achievement in the European theatre.

The British planned another major offensive in the desert but it took time to carry out the reforms discussed above and the summer of 1941 passed in relative calm.

In November the fresh offensive took place and met with immediate success. The Afrika Korps could only muster some 190 aircraft and the R.A. 320. Of these, probably little more than 300 were serviceable altogether. During the campaign another 100 German aircraft were transferred in from other parts of the Mediterranean. The Western Desert Air Force could call on some 650 aircraft of which 550 were serviceable. The Germans were bedeviled by supply problems, most of which stemmed from the British use of Malta to interfere with the transfer of supplies from Italy. In particular there was a shortage of petrol which severely curtailed Luftwaffe activity. There were also the usual problems of confusion attending a retreating air force that we have seen before. What supplies did reach North Africa had to be transported by truck some 500 miles along a primitive desert road. British and Commonwealth air support was now far better directed and thus, far more effective. Rommel abandoned the siege of Tobruk and retreated all the way back to El Agheila once more but the British attack petered out in the region of Sidi Barani because it was now their turn to be on the end of a long supply route and because, since they now had the larger army, their supply needs were proportionately greater.

Hitler and the German High Command reviewed the position in the Mediterranean at the end of 1941 and were frustrated by the fact that the year had passed without any conclusive outcome in this theatre. It was decided that additional resources would now be sent to the Mediterranean with a view to achieving a decisive victory. The first stage was to be an air assault on Malta followed by the invasion of the island and after this the Afrika Korps would sweep east along the North African coast, but this time it would capture Alexandria and the whole of the Middle East would lie at its feet. This would coincide with the German offensive in Russia which would drive into the Caucasus and approach the Middle East from the North.

The whole Mediterranean theatre was now placed under the control of Albert Kesselring, the commander of Airfleet Two which was transferred from Russia and the separate 2nd Air Corps was transferred to Sicily, so that Luftwaffe strength in the southern theatre grew to 650 aircraft. In North Africa a problem had developed in that relations between General Froelich, head of air operations, and General Rommel, who could be extremely aggressive and demanding, had broken down. Froelich was actually finding excuses not to meet Rommel. He was replaced by

General Hoffman von Waldau, a member of the Luftwaffe General Staff and an old-style aristocrat who was not intimidated by much and certainly not by a newcomer like Rommel.

In the new year of 1942 began the second big assault on Malta though it was initially low key and did not get into its stride till March. In that month there were over 400 German aircraft based in Sicily and devoted to the siege of Malta, which was relentlessly bombed for two months. Malta is a small island only 17 miles long and 9 miles wide. Its population at this time was 300,000. It suffered considerably more from bombing than any town in the United Kingdom. In the course of the whole war it suffered some 3,000 air raids and by this measure was the most bombed place in the Second World War. In the spring of 1942 the bombing was so heavy and effective that life there was virtually brought to a standstill. In April King George VI awarded the George Cross, the highest award for civilian valour, to the island as a whole for its bravery in the face of such adversity.

The R.A.F. on the island fought fiercely under near impossible conditions. Their airfields were under constant threat and aircraft on the ground were at almost as much risk of destruction as those in the air. There were three squadrons of fighters and a reconnaissance squadron, but they were under such pressure that most of the time only the equivalent of one squadron or less could actually take to the air to battle the attackers. The fighters were Hurricanes which were outclassed by the latest model Me109s. During this period great efforts were made to re-equip Malta with Spitfires. Some were delivered by ship and some were flown in from aircraft carriers at sea. Many were lost in transit however, or on the ground before they could fly.

The service community on the island was a relatively small one and adversity fostered a strong communal spirit of the kind that the British so much value. Undoubtedly the maintenance of high morale was of importance to the defence. Much like the desert, Malta was a refuge for the eccentrics and the misfits.

The most successful fighter pilot there was George 'Screwball' Beurling, (the nickname came from his frequent use of the word,) a Canadian who had been rejected by his own country's air force because of inadequate academic achievements and joined the R.A.F. instead. He was a brilliant pilot who shot down 27 planes in 14 days and was himself shot down four times. He did not smoke or drink and was a loner both in the air and on the ground. The normal teamwork of a fighter squadron was something he did not find easy but the madcap pressure flying of Malta suited him ideally. The last time he was shot down he was so badly injured that a long period in hospital followed and his Malta spree was over.[xiii] He survived the war and then joined the Israeli Air Force in search of more excitement. He was killed in an accident while ferrying a plane to Israel in 1948.

Another colourful pilot was Adrian Warburton, perhaps the finest reconnaissance pilot in the R.A.F.. It was he who flew the critical reconnaissance mission to Taranto harbour before the Swordfish raid which made the raid possible.

He seemed to have a charmed life because he took astounding risks and survived. On the ground he dressed in such a way that he was hardly in uniform at all and behaved as he pleased without regard to convention. He lived openly with a cabaret singer despite having a wife at home in England, conduct deeply shocking in the moral climate of the 1940s. In 1944 his luck ran out when he was shot down and killed over Germany.

The Germans had a plan to invade Malta by means of a paratroop landing, due to take place in August, but the idea was abandoned because the bombing appeared to have neutralized Malta and a new offensive in North Africa was going so well that there no longer seemed the need to risk the parachute drop. Hitler was very aware of the heavy losses sustained in the taking of Crete and did not want them repeated. In May 1942 the air raids were scaled back for these reasons and because many of the planes involved were needed in Russia for the summer offensive. The Luftwaffe did not have the resources to meet all its commitments and a full effort in one theatre was always at the expense of others. Though attacks on the island itself abated to a degree, attempts to supply it were met with undiminished opposition.

The tanker Ohio at the quayside in Malta which she reached barely afloat after numerous air attacks. She had been pulled into Valetta harbour by two destroyers lashed to her sides. Her cargo of oil saved the island.
©Imperial War Museum (A11498)

A major effort to resupply Malta occurred in June when convoys set out from Alexandria and Gibraltar simultaneously. The Alexandria convoy turned back when it was threatened by units of the Italian navy. The Gibraltar convoy of six merchant ships was strongly escorted by the Royal Navy but it was subjected to heavy air attack, mainly by the R.A. and only two of the six reached Malta.

The largest convoy of all sailed in August from Gibraltar. It contained 14 merchant ships escorted by three aircraft carriers and two battleships and a host of smaller warships. The aircraft carriers could put up 72 aircraft between them. After transferring all the reserves, they could lay their hands on the Germans and Italians could muster some 700 aircraft. There followed a five day running battle at the end of which nine of the merchant ships were sunk. Amongst the five that reached Malta was the tanker Ohio, that had to be towed into Valetta harbour in a sinking condition. It was successfully unloaded however, and discharged 11,000 tons of various petroleum products that were the saving of the island.

Meanwhile, in North Africa, Rommel launched an offensive in January 1942 and pushed the British back once more. That he was able to do this was the result of pressure on Malta already making it easier for Axis supplies to reach Libya from Sicily. During this offensive there were a number of heavy rain storms which reduced the primitive airstrips used by both sides to swamps and severely restricted air activity. The British army came to rest at pre-prepared defensive positions at Gazala, a little west of Tobruk. Once more the fighting died down due to the exhaustion of the attacker and his supplies. The great crisis in the North African campaign, however, was not now far away.

CHAPTER SIXTEEN

Strategic Bombing in Full Swing

After the immolation of Hamburg, in August 1943, Arthur Harris turned his attention to Berlin. He was convinced that he was now in a position to deal it such blows that the German will to continue the war would be fatally undermined by his bombing alone without any need for an invasion of Europe. R.A.F. Bomber Command was now a formidable force able to hit Germany hard if the conditions were right. It was Allied policy that from April of 1944 both U.S. and U.K. bomber forces would be subordinated to the commanders of the European invasion force so that they could be used to hit targets of an essentially tactical nature in France in order to facilitate the invasion. Until then Harris, and for that matter his American counterparts, had an eight month clear run to prove their theory that bombing alone could win the war.

It is often stated that the Battle of Berlin began in November or even later but this is not really so. Churchill had repeatedly urged attacks on Berlin for at least a year and after the devastation of Hamburg his pressure became even more insistent. On 21st August Portal, Chief of the Air Staff, informed Churchill that the attacks were about to begin.[i] It was, however, in November that Harris wrote his famous letter to Churchill in which he said:

'We can wreck Berlin from end to end if the U.S.A.A.F. will come in on it. It will cost us between 400 and 500 aircraft. It will cost Germany the war.'

This is the genesis of the idea that the campaign only started at that time. It was even later, in December, that Harris made his second startling claim, this time in a letter to Portal:

'It appears that the Lancaster force alone should be sufficient, but only just sufficient, to produce in Germany by April 1st 1944, a state of devastation in which surrender is inevitable.'[ii]

These claims may appear fantastical in the light of the fact that it took another year beyond that date and a land invasion to bring about the collapse of German resistance but one must remember what had just been done to Hamburg and what Speer said about another half dozen such disasters spelling the end for Germany. Had Berlin been subjected to such devastation in only a few nights, surrender might well have been a possibility though it is hard to see the justification for Harris's certainty about the matter. That was probably just a matter of him fighting his corner. One must always remember the importance of the time factor. A city destroyed overnight is a very different matter from destruction over a period of months or years. Berlin was indeed wrecked from end to end but it took until the spring of 1945 to do it.

Before looking at the campaign against Berlin it is necessary to glance at a controversy that was in its infancy at this time, but which grew to proportions that threatened to remove Harris from his post. It will be recalled that the Casablanca Directive not only called for strategic bombing in general terms, it also set out certain industries that were to be made specific targets whenever possible. Harris deplored any attempt to concentrate on particular industries which he scornfully called 'panacea targets'. As far as he was concerned the only way to proceed was to destroy cities by carpet bombing which would hit industry indirectly. In fact this did not stop him recognizing the necessity to strike at individual targets of high value from time to time if there was realistic chance of destroying them and he was so ordered. The Billancourt and Dams raid were examples, as was the Krupps works at Essen, though in this last case the town was built round the works so no change in normal operating procedure was required. These were however, exceptions and not part of his general policy.

Another of these exceptions happened at this time just before the Battle of Berlin began. This was the raid on the secret rocket research centre at Peenemunde on the Baltic coast. Harris was given a direct order to attack it that could not be dodged, though, as noted above, he was not against hitting specific targets if they were important enough. He did complain that his crews were not trained for precision attacks but they proved him triumphantly wrong. The raid took place on 17th August, was carried out by 596 aircraft and was unusual for a number of reasons. The bombers made a low level attack to achieve greater accuracy and they used a moonlit night which they usually avoided because of the night fighter danger. Part of the force bombed on a timed run rather than on the marker flares and the raid was controlled by a master bomber, the first experiment with an idea that was to see steadily increasing use. The master bomber, a senior and experienced pilot, circled the target throughout the raid broadcasting instructions and encouragement to the rest of the force. Needless to say, this was an exceptionally dangerous task admirably carried out at Peenemunde by Group Captain John Searby.

A diversionary raid kept the German fighters away from the Peenemunde attack until its end but in the clear conditions they found many targets when they arrived and the bombers lost 40 of their number, which, at over six per cent, was a heavy loss. The raid was a success however. Rocket research was set back months and the V-2 threat was permanently reduced in scale. This was the first occasion on which Luftwaffe night fighters used 'schraege musik' of which more will be said in due course.

By the middle of 1943 it was becoming clear that Harris was ignoring the Casablanca Directive except insofar as it could be said to support area bombing. This was becoming a matter of concern at the Air Ministry though Portal appeared content to give Harris a long rein. A relevant factor was Harris's personal relationship with Churchill. Bomber Command headquarters at High Wycombe and the Prime Minister's country residence at Chequers were a mere 15 miles apart and Harris was a frequent guest of the Prime Minister. The two men got on well and Churchill was a steady supporter of strategic bombing. There is no suggestion that they bypassed proper channels of command but anyone who sought to take on Harris must have known that he would end up taking on the Prime Minister too.

In June 1943 an amendment to the Casablanca Directive was issued as a result of the increasing fighter opposition that the U.S.A.A.F. was encountering over Europe. This was the 'Pointblank' Directive and it clearly set out the aircraft industry as the primary target for all strategic bombing from the U.K.. Harris cheerfully ignored this too but in the afterglow of his Hamburg success no one was initially too concerned. It should be emphasized that he was not openly defiant and always had excuses ready when challenged but it was clear to any informed observer that he was not complying with his instructions.

At this time Bomber Command was growing more powerful every day. The first of the Berlin raids took place on 23rd August and it was a 'maximum effort' which meant that every available front line bomber was used: that was a total of 719 made up of 335 Lancasters, 251 Halifaxes, 124 Stirlings and nine Mosquitos. Another eight Mosquitos would drop marker flares along the route as a guide to the main force and the remaining squadrons, comprising 62 Wellingtons, would carry out mining and leaflet dropping. The Wellingtons were no longer considered part of the main striking force and were being slowly phased out of operation altogether. There would be 788 aircraft aloft, just about every plane that Bomber Command could muster.[iii]

It is worth noting that the Berlin force of a little over 700 aircraft carried 1,800 tons of bombs while the 1,000 planes of the famous Cologne raid in 1942 carried 1,400 tons. Bomber Command's carrying capacity was rising steadily.

There was to be no firestorm however, nor anything near it. The markers did not identify the centre of the city correctly and marked the southern suburbs so that was where the majority of the bombs fell. This was an area of low density building where large fires were never going to develop but a surprisingly large amount of damage was done. A small part of the bombing force hit the centre of Berlin, more or less by accident and this may account for the fact that there were 850 deaths on the ground. The official city report on the raid said that (since this was the first really heavy raid to hit Berlin) many people did not bother to go to the air raid shelters and paid the price for their insouciance.[iv] 56 aircraft were lost which was nearly eight per cent of the attacking force and more than could be born on a continuing basis. For British night bombing to be viable, losses had to stay under five per cent as an overall average raid by raid. The raid was therefore a costly partial success.

Looking at the other side of the coin we find German defences in a period of

A Lancaster heavy bomber of the R.A.F. with the people needed to get it in the air for a mission. © Imperial War Museum (CH 15362)

transition and uncertainty in August 1943. The system based on the Kammhuber Line had been severely strained by the use of a tight bomber stream and the introduction of Window in the Hamburg raids caused a complete breakdown: the defence of the Reich had to be rebuilt from scratch.

There was a race to complete a new radar known as SN-2 which was in the course of development and which would be impervious to Window. This was promised for December. There was a scheme that had begun just before the Hamburg raids whereby single-engine fighters with no electronic aids of any kind flew over a city under attack and spotted bombers by eye against the background of fire and flares. This was known as 'Wild Boar' and was the inspiration of a bomber pilot called Hajo Herrman who saw it as a cheap way to augment the night time defences. It achieved some spectacular successes and Goering set up three new wings to specialize in these tactics. After the coming of Window, Wild Boar tactics were widely adapted by the regular night fighter force as a stopgap method of operation. 40 of the losses on 23rd August are thought to have been caused by fighters and this was almost exclusively a Wild Boar effort. Some radar operators also developed the difficult skill of spotting genuine radar returns from bombers amongst the mass of false ones generated by the foil strips. There was also the possibility of attacking the bomber stream before or after it was using Window and, of course, the slightest hint of moonlight made identification by eye possible.

It was soon found that a combination of these methods gave rise to a surprisingly effective defence of a new kind. The Kammhuber Line was now abandoned and the 'running commentary' defence system was born. With the introduction of the new radar this became the standard method of operation for the German night fighter force. It was colloquially called 'Tame Boar' and it became much more effective than the old system had ever been. Under the old system there were only enough directing radar stations to control a limited number of intercepting aircraft and many more were simply acting as spares and barely being used at all. The new system allowed all to be used although it was much more demanding of the pilot's flying skills because he might be sent chasing anywhere in the country. There is a distinct element of truth in the assertion that Window ultimately helped the Germans more than the British.

There had never been any difficulty in locating the general position of the bomber stream. For a start, German long-range 'Freya' radar was hardly affected by Window and numerous units on the ground could report the noise of aircraft overhead as there was no hiding the thunder of 500 bombers. As soon as a raid was known to be approaching the Reich, the fighters would take off from their airfields and assemble over a radio beacon of which there were a considerable number scattered around the country. From there they would be deployed against the bombers when it became evident where the bombers were heading. They would be guided to the bomber stream by radio, by controllers on the ground and when they got there they could pick out their own targets with their radar or visually. In this respect the route marker flares used by the R.A.F. were a great help until the British realized their unintended effect and stopped using them. The Luftwaffe also deployed their own bombers to fly above the British and drop illumination flares to light them up. Throughout the presence of the British over Germany, the ground controllers would keep up a running commentary to their fighters telling them exactly where the bombers were and vectoring them in to the attack and then home to base. The controllers were housed in underground headquarters remarkably like those used by the R.A.F. three years before in the Battle of Britain.

The R.A.F. tried what counter-measures it could. It made great use of 'spoof', or diversion, raids to confuse the defence. These were usually carried out by Mosquitos and were effective when first used, as during the Peenemunde raid, but the Germans soon became experts at telling a diversion raid from the main effort and were thereafter rarely fooled. Much energy was devoted to electronic counter-measures to interfere with the running commentary. These principally took two forms: either simple electronic jamming or the use of German-speaking Englishmen broadcasting confusing instructions to the German fighters on their control wavelength. Eventually a whole bomber group, 100 Group, was created that was devoted to counter-measures of one kind or another. There were some successes but, overall, the rise in German night fighting efficiency was not stemmed. By the spring of 1944 the night fighter had definitely gained the edge over the bomber.

One remedy that promised a fair degree of success was the use of Mosquito escort fighters to counter the German fighters. These Mosquitos were equipped with radar that could home on the emissions of the German SN-2 sets. As the war progressed more and more Mosquitos were used in this role but given the rate of bomber losses the increase was a case of too little too late.

Night fighting was an odd business. The biggest challenge for the fighter pilots was the weather and the sheer business of flying a relatively small plane in the darkness for hours on end. For many of them it was all that they could do to manage this, let alone fight anybody. But for a minority who could master the difficulties and were sufficiently offensively minded, great success beckoned. They took off night after night and the limits to their exploits were their ammunition and their fuel. The bombers fell in front of their guns like clay pigeons. At first their technique involved approaching a bomber from the rear, which risked the return fire of the rear gunner, if he was alert – and after many hours in a freezing turret many were not. Then 'Schraege Musik' arrived. This consisted of a pair of 20 mm cannon mounted at an angle in the fuselage so that they fired upwards. 'Schraege' means 'slanting' in German and 'Schraege Musik' was the colloquial expression for jazz. Using this new weapon a night fighter simply slid under a bomber where it had no defensive armament and opened fire. The usual technique was to fire into the wing: shooting at the fuselage risked igniting the bomb load in a mighty explosion likely to bring down the fighter with its victim.

Amongst these minority experts was Prince Heinrich zu Sayn-Wittgenstein, the son of a diplomat and a man of Russo-German descent whose ancestor was one of the Russian generals who fought Napoleon. He scored 83 victories before he was killed in January 1944, probably by a Mosquito. Like most German aristocrats Wittgenstein was no admirer of Hitler but fought for his country as he felt bound to do. As was the case with many of these night fighter aces he was a loner. Remembered as aloof, cool and a disciplinarian he was not greatly liked by his comrades.[v]

The greatest of all the night fighters was Heinz Wolfgang Schnaufer who shot down 121 bombers in total, including seven in one night, brought down within the space of twenty minutes. Schnaufer was from a family of wine merchants in Wurttemburg in southwest Germany. He was one of the regime's golden boys, academically accomplished and educated at an elite Nazi military school, though there is not much sign of him having any strong political views of his own. Tall and handsome he seemed to breeze through the war achieving apparently effortless success and surviving all dangers to return to the family business when the country was at peace again. Ironically he was killed in a car accident when on a wine buying trip to France in 1950.

There were six wings of night fighters by 1943, excluding the dedicated Wild

Boar units. At the time we are considering one was resting and refitting and one was still in formation, so four faced the bomber onslaught. The establishment strength of a wing was 100 aircraft but these wings were only able to put up about half that number. This was partly due to short supply of specialist equipment and partly for administrative reasons. In practice therefore, there were about 200 planes at a string of bases stretching from eastern France to Berlin. Of that number a tiny handful piloted by 'experts' did all the damage. It should be added that it was the deep penetration raids that suffered heavy damage. It took time to assemble the fighters and direct them and if the target town was somewhere that the R.A.F. could reach quickly, they could be there and gone before the Luftwaffe night fighters could catch them. Thus, on October 1st, a force of 243 Lancasters raided Hagen, a town in the Ruhr and lost just two planes.

Between August 1943 and the 24th March 1944 there were seventeen raids on Berlin. Naturally there were many raids on other towns. Berlin could not be the exclusive target for much the same reasons as were discussed when looking at the Battle of the Ruhr. The results of the raids varied widely. Some of the least successful were primarily wrecked by adverse weather conditions. The last of all was something of a fiasco with the planes encountering unforecast 100 m.p.h. winds and losing 72 of their number for small reward. The most successful night was 23rd November when the city was covered in cloud and the bombers dropped their bombs on the marker flares and headed for home with no idea whether they had caused much damage or not. In fact this was the worst raid to strike Berlin during the whole war; massive damage was done and there were several localized mini-firestorms.

One of the people who was on the receiving end of this raid was Princess Marie Vasiltchikov, an émigré white Russian working as a secretary in the German Foreign Office. After working late she walked home and was about to eat supper when the raid began and she spent the next hours in the cellar with her father and some friends as bombs fell all around. The cellar doors were blown in on them by explosions close by and a small incendiary bomb landed just outside which they managed to extinguish. A direct hit caused the house next door to collapse. Eventually, when the raid was over, she slept, exhausted, at 2 a.m. while fires raged nearby and threatened to engulf their house. But the fires abated and in the middle of the next morning she walked to work through the smouldering ruins past salvage teams working in the rubble, only to find her office destroyed.[vi]

Marie Vasiltchikov kept a detailed diary of her wartime experiences which was published in the 1970s to some acclaim. It is an extraordinary document: half death and danger; half high society social life.

At the airfields in England the bombers set off night after night and the losses mounted. The crews could see for themselves that they were unlikely to survive a 'tour' of 30 missions. Despite this fact, morale held up surprisingly well. Many men reacted to the poor chances of survival by regarding themselves as already dead. They continued to do their job with great dedication however, and often, extraordinary gallantry.

Flight Lieutenant Bill Reid flew a Lancaster to bomb Dusseldorf on the night of 3rd November 1943. He was attacked by a night fighter over Holland. Its fire shattered the windscreen and damaged the elevators. Reid himself was wounded in the face, shoulder and hands and could only keep the plane in the air by constantly pulling the joystick back. A few minutes later another attack killed the navigator, fatally wounded the wireless operator and injured the flight engineer. Reid himself was now wounded in the legs. Nevertheless he flew on in the icy wind and navigated to the target by looking at the stars. On the way back he was at the end of his strength and the bomb aimer and flight engineer had to hold the joystick for him. As they crossed the North Sea he passed out several times due to loss of blood and the aircraft nearly went out of control. He landed the plane at the first airfield they came to. As he did so he was half blinded by blood flowing into his eyes and the aircraft's undercarriage collapsed so that it slid along the runway on its belly in a cloud of sparks. Reid was awarded the Victoria Cross. He was later shot down and captured and survived the war.[vii]

The 24th March 1944 was the last raid on Berlin by the R.A.F.'s main force. It was however, repeatedly bombed by the increasing force of Mosquito light bombers and by the Americans right up to the end of the war. The result of the campaign against Berlin was not the collapse of Germany or the leveling of the city or anything like it and Harris' claims looked ill-conceived. The reasons for the failure are not difficult to find. The campaign required long nights so that the bombers could cross Germany and return in darkness but that meant winter and bad weather. Bomber Command's marking technique was still not good enough to give consistent results against a cloud-covered target. The key problem was that H2S did not give a sufficiently clear picture of the ground when the target was a city such as Berlin, that sprawled over a large area with no distinctive geographical features. It was also a city with no close-built mediaeval centre built of wood but wide streets, many squares and parks and constructed of brick and stone. Large-scale fires were correspondingly hard to start and each raid left burnt out buildings that acted as firebreaks when the next raid occurred.

The other side of the ledger was the constantly mounting losses caused by the increasingly efficient German night fighter force. In the first three months of 1944 771 bombers were lost which was almost a complete turnover of Bomber Command. There were an increasing number of raids in which losses were well over five per cent. In February a raid on Leipzig cost almost nine per cent and the period closed with a disastrous raid on Nuremberg on 30th March when little damage was done and 97 bombers were lost: 12 per cent of the attacking force. More airmen were lost on this night alone than in the whole of the Battle of Britain.

Harris grumbled that supporting the invasion from 1st April cost him the chance to bring Germany to her knees, but the truth was that it was his policy that was on its knees. Area bombing of German cities was close to being unaffordable and, as it was, the dream of ending the war by bombing alone was very dead indeed.

In the late summer of 1943 General Ira Eaker decided that the 8th Air Force was now powerful enough and experienced enough to begin raiding targets deep within Germany rather than on her coast. He began with attacks on Hanover and Kassel at the end of July. The losses were encouragingly small so on 12th August he sent 330 bombers against Bonn and targets in the Ruhr. 25 planes were lost which was 7.5 per cent of the force but the 8th Air Force was somewhat less sensitive to losses than Bomber Command and this was considered acceptable. Eaker now planned a major raid for the 17th August and it was to be the 8th's most famous raid of the war.

The plan was to bomb the Messerschmitt works at Regensburg in Bavaria and the ball-bearing factories in Schweinfurt using two forces of bombers that would strike within minutes of each other. The Regensburg force, of 146 planes, would strike first and then fly on to bases in North Africa which was now entirely in Allied hands. From there the planes could fly back to the U.K. at their leisure. The Schweinfurt force, 230 strong, would bomb its target 15 minutes later, the idea being that the defending fighters would attack the first force and would be landing to re-arm and re-fuel as the second force arrived.

The Regensburg plant produced approximately a quarter of all the single-engine fighters used by the Luftwaffe and so its destruction would be a devastating blow. Schweinfurt was the home of the ball-bearing industry and half of all the ball-bearings used by German industry were produced there. They were essential to the production of many types of machine including most engines. American intelligence saw these bearings as a key target because their use was so widespread and they were produced in a limited number of factories. This choice of specific military targets was quite alien to the British way of doing things and was only possible because U.S. raids were carried out in daylight.

At the war's very start Bomber Command had discovered how fiercely the Luftwaffe reacted to daytime raids and these raids would require long periods of flight deep within Germany and without fighter escort. There certainly was an escort: it consisted of more than 200 P-47 Thunderbolts but they had insufficient range to penetrate more than a short way beyond the German border. The whole rationale of the American strategic bombing program hinged on the ability of formations of their B-17s and B-24s to fight off the attacks of defending fighters without the help of an escort. Both Spaatz and Eaker were convinced that this could be done.

In fact, at this particular time the 8th Air Force was exclusively flying the B-17. All its B-24s had been transferred to the Mediterranean theatre to which it was thought they were better suited because they had the longer range. They were also somewhat less robust in construction than the older B-17 and it was thought that they would meet a lesser defensive effort in that theatre. B-24s reappeared in the 8th Air Force in 1944. There remains to this day a continuing dispute amongst aviation enthusiasts as to which was the better of the two aircraft. The B-17 was a graceful design and was easy to fly. It had a higher ceiling than the B-24 and it was a little bit tougher. Its very name, 'Flying fortress' has a romantic ring that has added to the lustre of its reputation. As a result it has completely outshone its rival in popular recognition. On the other hand the B-24 carried a larger bomb load further, faster. It was more modern and contained innovations such as bomb bay doors that rolled up inside the fuselage rather than hinging open, thus reducing drag during the bomb run. All its systems were electrically operated and it was generally more sophisticated all round. It suffered unduly when flying in company with B-17s because it had to keep formation with a much slower plane. It was also exceptionally versatile. It was the most expensive aircraft to build of any in the world to that date. It was also a completely utilitarian aeroplane whose design was functional to the point of ugliness and it was notoriously difficult to fly, particularly when trying to keep in a tight formation. One of its own pilots described it as 'a cantankerous, lumbering, draughty, unforgiving son-of-a-bitch…'.[viii] The last word however, is the undeniable fact that more B-24s were built than any other U.S. warplane ever; fifty per cent more than the B-17.

For the Germans it was vital, for obvious reasons, that raids of this kind be stopped or rendered too expensive to be continued. Serious damage to factories in either Regensburg or Schweinfurt posed a threat to the war effort of far greater immediacy than the destruction of the average provincial town centre by the R.A.F. The Luftwaffe had devoted a good deal of time and effort over the last year to developing ways of combating the huge and well-armed U.S. bombers. When they first encountered American heavy bombers in 1942, German pilots were at something of a loss as to how to tackle them. The conventional approach from the rear was very dangerous because of the bombers' heavy defensive fire. A single fighter approaching a formation of bombers thus was virtually assured of destruction as it faced literally hundreds of .5 inch machine guns. A single bomber was not invincible however, if it could be separated from its formation, but doing so was not easy.

During the course of the first half of 1943 the Luftwaffe took a number of steps that helped to combat the heavy bomber problem. The first one was simply to build more fighters. Between November 1942 and July 1943 production of single-engine fighters increased from 480 per month to 800 and when repaired aircraft were added in there were about 1,000 new planes available each month in the summer of 1943. The second step was radically to increase the number of single-engine fighters stationed in the homeland and the Low Countries. Numbers rose from 635 at the start of the year to 800 in July and 975 by October 1st. This increase was at the expense of other fronts which was, in itself, a victory for the U.S. bombing campaign.

Ground control of aircraft was centralized and improved so that the fighter wings were vectored to raids that were being tracked by radar in much the same way as was being done at night. There was an expansion of the ground infrastructure with many new bases being equipped to handle the fighters so that they could land to re-fuel and re-arm almost wherever they found themselves. This meant that a plane that had flown one mission against a particular raid in the spring could fly two or even three in the autumn.

A major problem for the defenders was inadequate armament. The Focke-Wulf 190 carried two or four 20 mm cannon depending on the model and production now went over wholly to the four cannon variety. A bigger obstacle was the weak armament of the Me109, the Luftwaffe's most numerous fighter, amounting to just one cannon and two machine guns which was quite inadequate to bring down a heavy bomber. Its wings were not thick enough or strong enough for additional guns to be fitted as permanent fixtures. A makeshift expedient was the provision of gun 'kits' that were sent to the airfields and fitted as needed by the mechanics. These kits contained a cannon in a gondola that could be screwed to the underside of the wing and unscrewed again when the mission was over. This was reasonably effective against bombers but made the planes ungainly in the air and difficult to fly. In this condition they were virtually helpless if they encountered an escort fighter. This 109 problem was never satisfactorily solved and the best solution, which was introduced in 1944 when all U.S. raids had a fighter escort, was to let the 109s tackle the escort while the 190s attacked the bombers.

A partial solution to the armament problems was the use of twin-engine fighters. There were plenty of Me110s and Ju88s available from the night fighting force and there were a limited number of the new Me410, an improved version of the Me110. These were all planes with at least two 20 mm cannon supplemented by four or more machine guns. Their greater range also meant that they could harry the bombers for longer. Their downside was their extreme vulnerability to escort fighters.

New tactics were needed and these were rapidly developed in response to the challenge. One, somewhat eccentric, approach was tried for a while whereby fighters flew high above the bomber formation and dropped bombs on it. This was the brainchild of Heinz Knoke whom we last saw flying over the Russian front in June 1941. This method achieved some minor success but its limitations were obvious and Knocke himself was the first to admit that it relied on a complete absence of escorts. Its use was fairly rapidly discontinued. On the other hand there was readily available a simple infantry weapon, a 21 cm rocket propelled mortar, that could be easily fitted to a fighter plane and fired into a bomber formation. Though direct hits were hard to obtain, they meant certain destruction of the target bomber when they occurred and the violent explosions of the rockets, caused confusion in the formations and helped to break them up so that the attackers could target individual bombers.

The key change, however, was the use of large formations to attack the bomber groups. This had the vital effect of splitting up the defensive fire so that each attacking plane faced much less. It also reduced the concentration of the gunners in the bombers who had a multitude of targets to fire at and the temptation to switch from one to another in rapid succession at the cost of accuracy. A further refinement was to launch attacks from the front because neither B-17 nor B-24 had any forward firing guns, at least not in the early models. They were added later but were not particularly effective and did not deter the head-on attack. Such an attack required careful organizing, skillful flying and a lot of nerve. The closing speed of the two formations was near to 500 m.p.h. and the effective firing time was less than one second. But a lot of damage could be done in that near second during which the engines and the cockpits of the bombers were exposed to fire. A few shells in the cockpit in particular, spelled the end for any bomber because they incapacitated the pilots. The sheer horror of the cockpit hit is, and was, not often understood because the plane crashed taking its pilots with it, but on rare occasions such planes reached home to reveal terrible scenes.

On 26th June 1943 Lt. Col. James Wilson was the pilot of a B-17 on one of the short range raids against a German airfield in France. He was attacked head-on by a Focke-Wulf 190 and shells streamed into the cockpit smashing the windscreen and taking off the co-pilot's head. Leaking oxygen bottles started a roaring fire which Wilson tried to beat out with his hands. The rubber in his oxygen mask melted onto his burned face. He could not put the fire out but had to try to fly the plane. With the skin burned off his hands and in extreme pain, he tried to work the control column with his elbows while other crewmen tackled the blaze and put it out. Fortunately there was, by chance, another pilot on the plane flying as a gunner and he was able to take over from Wilson. Without his fortuitous presence this plane would almost certainly never have reached home. As it was, the ex-gunner had to fly back to base in the teeth of an icy blast blowing in through the broken windows, in a blood-drenched cockpit with a headless corpse sitting next to him. When he reached base he landed the plane the wrong way along the runway so that it came to a halt near the boundary and far from the control tower. He did so because this was to have been the co-pilot's last mission and all his friends, and his fiancée, were gathered at the control tower to welcome him home.[ix]

August 17th 1943 was the great test of the Luftwaffe's new tactics, as it was of the U.S.A.A.F.'s belief in unescorted bombing. For a start the weather gods were on the German side. There was fog over England on the morning of the 17th which delayed the start of the Schweinfurt force so that it was three hours behind the Regensburg group. This meant that German fighters could hit one force, land and then attack the second, which was exactly what the plan had been designed to prevent. Eaker would have been justified in cancelling the whole operation but he was a 'press on' type in the best tradition and he knew cancellation would waste a great deal of preparation and would dent the reputation of the 8th Air Force.

The Luftwaffe attacked the Regensburg force even before it reached the limit of its escort's range and attacks continued all the way to the target. 15 aircraft were shot down and more crashed as a result of damage received as they made the long flight over the Alps and Italy to North Africa. Only 122 of the 146 aircraft in the formation reached North Africa safely and 60 more were damaged in varying degrees. Some could not be repaired in North Africa and so were write-offs. The leader of the Regensburg force was Colonel Curtis LeMay one of the U.S.A.A.F.'s outstanding officers who would later command the air assault on Japan and rise to Chief of Staff of the U.S. Air Force in the Cold War era. Brave to a fault and aggressive to the point of belligerence, LeMay was a chain smoker of cigars and was the Hollywood ideal of the brash and insensitive soldier. Indeed it is rumoured that he was the model for the eccentric air force general in the Cold War film 'Dr. Strangelove'.

When the Schweinfurt force entered German airspace in the early afternoon it was attacked by some 300 fighters with even more ferocity than the first force. The delay in the arrival of the Schweinfurt force had given these fighters the chance to land and prepare themselves for a second mission. The bombers duly reached Schweinfurt and dropped their bombs. They then had to fly the long route home through unflagging opposition that only faded away when they reached the cover of U.S. and British fighters in the extreme northwest of Germany. This force lost 36 bombers.

The experiences of Heinz Knoke that day illustrate the new Luftwaffe tactics. Based at Wunsdorf in northern Germany his squadron was transferred to a base in Holland during the morning. He first attacked at lunchtime carrying two of the new rockets under his wings and though he himself scored no hits, several of his squadron's pilots did so. His plane was damaged by defensive fire and so he landed at Bonn airfield. In the afternoon he led a second attack from Bonn at the head of a mixed formation of fighters from several different wings that had ended up there after the morning's fighting. He shot down a Flying fortress and was himself brought down by its fire and forced to crash-land near Bonn.[x]

In all 60 bombers were lost during the raid but many of the 160 damaged planes were subsequently written off. Altogether, the double raid probably cost near to 100 aircraft. These were not losses that could be sustained by any air force and it was apparent that the idea of bombing by unescorted formations had taken a serious blow. The Luftwaffe lost 40 fighter planes which was no small price to pay, but worth it, for the victory achieved.

The Messerschmitt factory at Regensberg was seriously damaged and production halted but by the exercise of great ingenuity and relentless labour, production was under way again on a limited scale within a month. Nonetheless it has been estimated that the total loss of production was 800 to 1,000 fighters, which was a major blow.

At Schweinfurt the picture is more confused. The damage was less though the industry as a whole was more vulnerable. Albert Speer said that the raid cost 38 per cent of production[xi] but a subsequent census of ball bearing stocks throughout

German industry revealed such reserves of bearings that even had production ceased completely, industry would hardly have been affected before production was restored.[xii] As it was, Speer was warned by the raid that the bearing industry was a target and he took steps such as the dispersal of production and the increase of capacity to ensure that the supply of bearings was not again threatened.

As a result of his actions during the raid one U.S. pilot was awarded the Congressional Medal of Honor. He was Major Gale Cleven of the 100th Bomb Group which came to be known as 'The Bloody 100th' and was part of the Regensburg force. During two hours of continuous air combat his B-17 was repeatedly hit. The electrical system was damaged, the hydraulics were destroyed, rudder control was lost, there was a large hole in the nose and one engine was on fire. One gunner was injured in the leg and the bombardier was injured in the head and shoulder. The radio operator died after his legs were torn off by gunfire. The crew would have been more than justified in baling out and the co-pilot asked Cleven for permission to do so. Cleven's reply was 'blunt' and there was an argument in which 'strong words' were heard. The outcome was that the crew stayed with the aircraft and, incredibly, completed the mission.[xiii]

It took time for the losses to be replaced and for two months the 8th confined itself to short range and French targets once more. There was one exception on 6th September when it went to Stuttgart and lost 30 bombers for no significant result. On October 14th it made another effort to bomb Schweinfurt. This time 300 bombers attacked and the scenario was a repetition of the August raid. 60 bombers were shot down, seven more written off as total losses on their return and 138 damaged. Such losses could not be endured and the unescorted strategic bombing policy was effectively dead. It was a policy upon which the leaders of the U.S.A.A.F. had insisted despite all the evidence that it wouldn't work and many young American airmen had died to prove them wrong. Eaker attempted no more deep penetration raids in 1943, though no formal admission was made that there had been any change in policy. It was now simply a matter of awaiting the arrival of a fighter plane with the range and performance to give the bombers the protection they needed throughout the whole of their flight. The necessary aircraft was in the pipeline and would soon be available in numbers so U.S. strategic bombing suffered only a temporary setback when seen as a whole.

For a while it had appeared that the solution might be the P-38 Lightning which had the necessary range and was a better dogfighter than most twin-engine planes but its engines could not come to terms with the cold damp conditions of northern Europe and were chronically unreliable. A whole bombing campaign could not be made to depend on this aircraft. It is a curiosity of war that it performed outstandingly in the Pacific theatre.

The fighter to solve the problem was the North American P-51 Mustang which vies with the Spitfire for the title 'Finest fighter of the war'. This aircraft was originally ordered by the R.A.F. in 1940 from the North American Aviation Company and was designed and produced in record time. It initially used the Allison engine which was designed for low level work and needed a turbocharger to be effective above 15,000 feet. The Mustang design could not accommodate a bulky turbocharger and so the plane was built without one. The result was that R.A.F. Fighter Command was committed to a large order for a fighter aircraft that was only one step away from useless, since its performance was poor at the altitude where all the fighting was done. In April 1942, during routine testing, the performance of the aircraft at low level was so outstanding that a Rolls Royce test pilot suggested that it might be a useful experiment to fit one with a Rolls Royce Merlin engine such as powered the Spitfire and see if that improved high level performance. The result was astonishing. Not only did the new engine improve high level performance, but it greatly reduced fuel consumption as well. Here, suddenly, was a high performance fighter with the range to escort bombers on raids anywhere in Germany. For longer missions it carried large external drop tanks and a tank behind the pilot was filled, with the result that the plane was one great big flying fuel container and was highly unstable. It had to burn off some of the fuel before it could safely engage in combat. The extraordinary test results were immediately conveyed to the Americans who were looking for a long range escort and they put the Mustang into full-scale production for the Army Air Force and called it the P-51. Because Rolls Royce was already working to capacity, the U.S. Packard Motor Car Company manufactured the necessary Merlin engines under licence.

On 5th December 1943 the 8th Air Force bombed targets in France and for the first time there were P-51s in the escort. There was only one fighter group of them amounting to 36 planes but the writing was on the wall.

There was also a command change for the 8th at this time. Ira Eaker was moved to take charge of operations in the Mediterranean theatre and Jimmy Doolittle became the new commander of the 8th Air Force in January 1944. The ostensible reason for this was that Eisenhower had just been appointed Allied Supreme Commander and he wanted to work with the team he was used to commanding in the Mediterranean. This meant that Carl Spaatz became overall commander of strategic air forces in Europe and Doolittle took over the 8th. Many felt however, that the move embodied an implied criticism of Eaker for the failure of the unescorted bombing policy. He was never promoted to the rank of full general while a serving officer, but was given it by a special act of Congress 40 years later.

In February the 8th was ready to begin a new round of combat. It was a more powerful force than the summer before, able to put up 800 bombers and 700 fighters. Its fighter arm now contained a substantial proportion of the vital P-51s and improved drop tanks greatly extended the range of the P-47 Thunderbolts that were still the mainstay of the escort force. Thunderbolts could now provide escort over the western half of Germany and P-51s could do so anywhere the bombers themselves could go. Doolittle changed the rules for the escort fighters who had hitherto been tied to the bombers at all times. He allowed them to break away and 'scavenge' for targets in the air and on the ground, particularly at the end of the mission when the Luftwaffe had exhausted its counter-attacks. This policy was surprisingly effective because it meant that no German ground installation was ever safe: a Thunderbolt or a Mustang might appear and begin strafing at any moment.

Between February 20th and 25th 1944 the 8th carried out an intensive series of raids on the German aircraft industry. These raids were informally named 'Big Week' and their aim was not just to damage the factories but to compel the Luftwaffe fighter force to fight back as hard as it could and thereby incur heavy losses in the face of the new strength of U.S. escorts. The damage done to the aircraft factories was not as great as it might have been, partly because of the poor weather conditions at this time of year and partly because of precautions taken by the managers of German industry such as the dispersal of manufacture. Nevertheless production of at least 1,000 aircraft was lost. The average number of bombers taking part in the raids was 720 and the average loss was 30, or just over four per cent which was definitely a bearable attrition. More aircraft were written off through damage, of course, even though they returned to base but their crews reached home safely and that was the important thing. The U.S.A could produce almost limitless bombers but not trained aircrews.

The Luftwaffe lost 260 day fighter planes in February. (In February 1943 they lost 25.) And the situation got worse and worse. In March they lost 340 and in April 540.xiv German industry was now under the direction of Albert Speer who worked wonders in terms of increasing output in the face of bombing but it was the loss of pilots that hurt. The skilled pilots were draining away and the new boys were just cannon fodder.

On March 6th the 8th Air force raided Berlin for the first time. It was their 250th mission. 730 bombers set out escorted by 800 fighters. 69 bombers were lost together with 11 fighters. It was the 8th's heaviest loss of the war but it could be afforded, just. The Luftwaffe lost 66 fighters. Tactically it was a good day for the Luftwaffe fighter arm but in every other way they lost the fight. Now American daylight bombers could go anywhere in Germany they liked. They could not be stopped and trying to stop them was becoming prohibitively expensive.

CHAPTER SEVENTEEN

The Kuban and Kursk

1943 opened with the German army in Russia more or less back where it was a year before save in the far South where it was still withdrawing its Caucasus spearhead across the Kerch straits. The Luftwaffe's strength in Russia had sunk to some 1,750 aircraft while the V.V.S. numbered around 5,000. The Wehrmacht not only still occupied the whole of the Crimea, but the Caucasus retreat stopped at the area known as 'the Kuban' around the river of that name in the Northwest of the peninsula where a substantial bridgehead was retained opposite the straits of Kerch. The Kuban enclave was retained partly to provide a jumping-off point for a second attempt on the Caucasus oilfields and partly as a buffer between the Soviet army and the Crimea. The Germans were very sensitive about the Crimea: not only was it rich country but if the Russians held it they could mount air attacks on the Rumanian oilfields. Rumanian oil was so important to the German war economy that this could not be allowed to happen even though, as we have seen, the Russian long range bomber force was not especially effective. The very same reasons made the Russians determined to eliminate the bridgehead as soon as possible.

The Russians had never lost control of the Black Sea. The Germans had no sea access to it and so ships could not be deployed there, other than a few Rumanian gunboats. The result of this shortcoming was that the 17th Army in the Kuban had to be supplied across the Kerch straits mainly by air even though the straits are less than three miles wide at their narrowest. The business of air supply had now been given to 8th Air Corps. The Corps set up a shuttle service taking fuel and supplies into the Kuban and bringing surplus soldiers and the wounded out. This exercise was a remarkable success, in stark contrast to the Stalingrad operation. It was possible to fly in 500 tons of supplies per day, a figure never reached at Stalingrad. The reasons were the short distance involved, better weather and plentiful fighter cover to ward off weak Soviet air attacks.

As the new year advanced, so did Soviet opposition. No effort was spared to drive the Germans back to the straits and out of the Caucasus, but the resistance was stubborn. General Novikov, commander of the V.V.S., assigned great importance to this front and gave it increasing resources. The 4th and 5th Air Armies were assigned to the North Caucasus front under the command of General K. A. Vershinin. Their total strength was about 900 aircraft. Against them the Luftwaffe's forces in the Kuban and the Crimea amounted to 800 though both sides could draw on additional help from aircraft on the main front north of the Sea of Azov. Russian aircraft were no longer inferior to German though their training standards remained woeful. 7th Guards Ground Attack Regiment, operating in the Caucasus, was re-equipped in the spring with the new two-seater Il-2 featuring a rear gunner. The gunners who arrived at their base however, who included one woman, had no training in the job at all and had to learn their trade from scratch in combat.[i]

In February the Russians made an amphibious landing on the coast near Novorosiisk at Mount Myshako. (The political officer with the troops was one Leonid Brezhnev). In April this became the storm centre of the fighting when the Germans launched an offensive to eliminate the bridgehead. They could concentrate 650 aircraft here, most of them flying from bases 30 to 60 miles away. The Russians could muster 500 but many of them had to fly over the Caucasus Mountains to make their attacks and the peaks of that range were 10,000 feet high and shrouded in cloud. Their approach route was 90 to 120 miles long. German bombers attacked in waves throughout the day. On 18th April the first Stukas took off at 4.45 a.m and the last landed at 6.30 p.m 20th April was the climax of the German assault and it was supported by every available bomber acting in a ground support role. The attack made slow progress and so, in the evening, raids were concentrated against Russian landing stages, barges and jetties. Stukas then made a night attack. This day was the crisis of the operation and during it Novikov released the Stavka reserve of aircraft to help with the struggle. These additional 400 planes turned the tide. After further prolonged struggle the German attack at Myskhako failed. The Luftwaffe had lost 180 aircraft and the V.V.S. less than a hundred. Here was the earliest example of a German offensive that was foiled by the Red Army, with the vital support of the V.V.S: it was to be a portent.

One curiosity of this particular campaign is that the German ace Gunther Rall remembered fighting Spitfires at Novorosiisk. They were, of course, lend-lease aircraft flown by the Russians.[ii]

On 29th April the Russians launched a counter-attack with the support of a massive air raid by every aircraft they could put into the sky. Success on the ground was limited but the pressure was kept up in the air and the fighting was heavy right through the summer months. During May the Luftwaffe in the Caucasus was forced to fly an average of 400 sorties per day when it should have been resting and building up its strength in preparation for the big summer offensive at Kursk. The drain on pilots and aircraft was steady. On 29th April alone the V.V.S. claimed 81 victories. By now the Soviet policy in the area had become one of attrition: this secondary front was being used to wear down the Luftwaffe with consequential effects right across the Russian front. The fighting in the Kuban in the first half of 1943 was some of the most intense seen during the whole eastern campaign.

7th Guards Ground Attack Regiment was sent to the southern Caucasus for rebuilding early in the year and once more reached its full complement of 60 aircraft.

It was then based near Krasnodar and in the thick of the fighting in the Kuban until its strength had sunk again, to 10 serviceable planes. Much of its fighting consisted of raids on targets around the straits of Kerch. The pilots were nervous about this because they spent long periods of time flying over water and the Il-2, should it have to ditch in the sea, sank like a stone because of the weight of the armour plating it carried. Junior Lieutenant Petr Vosgaev was the first to experience this particular fate when his aircraft developed engine trouble. He turned back for the coast but was not able to reach it and had to ditch in the sea. His aircraft sank in seconds and he barely had time to escape from it, but he had no life jacket and his prospects looked bleak. The coast was not far off but he was wearing a heavy flying suit and swimming was all but impossible. By good luck the water was fairly shallow and his plane came to rest with its nose on the bottom and the tail sticking out of the water. He clung to the tail and waited. At first it appeared that his reprieve was only temporary because the cold was slowly sapping the life from him, but then two other Il-2s appeared and began to circle him. Next he could see a rescue launch heading towards him but, unfortunately, it came from the German held coast. Then another appeared heading from Soviet territory. It was clear the German one would reach him first but the two Il-2s flew off and began strafing it so that it had to dodge about to avoid their fire and this slowed its progress sufficiently for the Russian launch to reach him first and rescue him.

After this, the 7th was issued with life jackets but the air pressure required to inflate them was greater than human lungs could generate so they were useless.[iii]

The outstanding 16th Guards Fighter Regiment was also much in evidence in the Kuban together with the inspirational Alexander Pokryshkin who commanded one of its squadrons. Pokryshkin, who was of very humble origins in Novosibirsk, was the number two ace of the V.V.S. after Ivan Kozhedub and scored 59 victories. He had been a mechanic in the V.V.S. for some years before the war and his repeated requests to transfer to pilot training were refused. Eventually he passed a flying course while on leave and his transfer to flying duties was then automatic. He began the war badly by accidentally shooting down a Russian aircraft and his victories were slow to come but simply surviving the first months of the war was an achievement in itself. He was at his best in the Kuban when his regiment had been equipped with the lend-lease P-39. Not only was he a brilliant pilot, but he was an outspoken critic of the poor equipment and outdated tactics employed by the V.V.S.. His criticisms got him into trouble more than once but Novikov was on his side and he survived by the skin of his teeth because he was right in what he said. While in the Kuban he was the architect of a revolution in Russian fighter tactics. He promoted the use of the 'finger four' formation in preference to the older arrangement of three planes or the line astern and he advocated the use of climbing and diving tactics in battle rather than relying on the tight turn. He was also responsible for what became known as the 'Kuban escalator'. This was a system of stacking formations of fighters in layers so that if the enemy attacked a particular layer, it was itself attacked by the layer above.[iv]

It was while he was fighting in the Kuban that Pokryshkin was expelled from the 16th by its commander, with whom he was on poor terms, stripped of his Hero of the Soviet Union award and threatened with a disciplinary tribunal. This was ostensibly because of his criticisms of the system but was, in reality, the result of malice harboured by his commander. Fortunately the regiment's commissar came to his aid and his name was soon cleared.[v]

The V.V.S. seems to have been prone to this kind of semi-personal, semi-political feuding which did nothing to help morale and discipline. Much of the trouble was caused by the unfortunate system of having political commissars in every unit to ensure the loyalty of the unit to the regime and instruct its members in Communist orthodoxy. They often had little or no military training and too much power. Moreover, their mere presence created a dual authority which is fatal to good discipline in any military unit. Coupled with this was the atmosphere of paranoia and suspicion left by the purges of the late 1930s. One of the worst examples occurred the year before in 19th Guards Fighter Regiment when one of the squadron leaders, Alexander Zaitsev, was accused of disobeying orders by his commissar. Zaitsev protested vigorously and the two were summoned before their superior officer to resolve the situation. In the ensuing argument, tempers became so frayed that Zaitsev pulled his revolver and opened fire on the commissar. Fortunately he missed. He was suspended from his post but allowed to continue flying pending disciplinary action. He was then unfairly blamed for the failure of a bombing mission and publicly rebuked before the regiment. Not long after this his aircraft was seen to dive into the ground killing him instantly. While a mechanical fault could not be ruled out, it seemed clear that Zaitsev decided he was in so much trouble that suicide was the only way out, for his family's sake if not his own.[vi]

One of the German units against which Pokryshkin and others fought in the Kuban, was the 52nd Fighter Wing, Jg52, which paralleled 16th Guards in being probably the most distinguished fighter unit of its side. Many of Germany's most prolific aces were members of this wing including Gerd Barkhorn, Gunter Rall and Walter Krupinsky. It also included the greatest of them all and the highest scoring ace of all time in any air force: Erich Hartmann who finished the war with an astonishing score of 352 aircraft shot down.

Hartmann began his extraordinary career in the Kuban. He was the son of a doctor from Wurttemberg and he wanted to be a doctor himself but the war intervened. In training he was a quick learner but showed no signs of being a genius in the making and his early days at the front were marked by only average progress, but as he found his feet he became a deadly combat pilot rarely returning from a mission without having shot down an enemy aircraft. Although his particular style was to get in very close to his target, in truth his method of fighting was nothing more than the application of a method employed by most of the great aces of this front. He was just the best at it. He himself described it as 'See, decide, attack, coffee-break'.[vii] By this he meant that he summed up the situation and only attacked if the situation was favourable. Then he got in and out fast. Also like most of the aces he had his share of luck. In training another pilot flew his plane at the last moment when he was confined to quarters over a disciplinary matter. The plane suffered engine failure and crashed and the other pilot was killed. In August 1943 he was shot down behind Russian lines and captured, but he escaped and made his way back to the German lines by night. There a sentry opened fire on him and a bullet passed through his trousers. For all his success Erich Hartmann was not a man who fitted easily into a military setting. Considering his achievements, his promotion in the Luftwaffe was slow. At the end of the war he became a Russian prisoner of war and spent ten years in various prison camps where he undoubtedly suffered because of his policy of non-co-operation and spent longer as a prisoner than he need have done. On his return to Germany he joined the post-war Luftwaffe and in due course was court martialed and forced into early retirement because of his outspoken criticisms of its policy.

As the summer progressed the fighting in the Kuban died down as it intensified elsewhere on the front. In September the Germans voluntarily abandoned the bridgehead because by now there was no realistic prospect of a return to the Caucasus in the foreseeable future.

Outside of the Kuban the first half of 1943 saw the last successful German offensive on the eastern front at Kharkov, despite the fact that a disproportionate amount of the Luftwaffe's strength was in the Crimea and the Caucasus. This was the counter-offensive of late February that re-took that city and once again saw the close co-operation between aircraft and ground forces that was the hallmark of blitz warfare. Airfleet Four was used en masse for this operation and was most skillfully handled by its commander General von Richthofen. By the end of March when the thaw stopped operations, the Germans had captured Kharkov and gone on to take Belgorod as well. This had secured their line in southern Russia and left the Red Army holding an uncomfortable salient north of Kharkov around the town of Kursk.

As spring advanced the Germans planned their main summer offensive as a campaign to pinch off this salient. It did not take the Russians long to divine this intention: not only were there the usual giveaway signs of massing troops and supply convoys, but any student of military strategy could see that this was the obvious place to attack. By the standards of the two previous years this was an offensive that was to be very limited in extent, but the forces amassed to carry it out were unprecedented. The late spring and early summer of 1943 passed in relative calm in Russia (apart from the Kuban) as both sides readied their forces for the trial of strength that everyone concerned could see was imminent.

During this period the Luftwaffe organization in Russia was tightened up and several semi-independent commands that had been created on an ad hoc basis over the last year were terminated and their operations brought within the ambit either of Airfleet Four in the South or the newly created Airfleet Six in the centre of the front. 8th Air Corps was relieved of transport duties and restored to front line duties in the Kharkov area. General von Richthofen left Airfleet Four to take command of Airfleet Two in the Mediterranean where a firm and capable hand was needed to restore Luftwaffe fortunes. His departure provoked strong protests from field Marshal von Manstein in command of the army on the southern sector of the front. The protests were overridden but they served to show what an able commander von Richthofen was. His place was taken by General Otto Dessloch, a capable man but not in the same class as his predecessor. The new Airfleet Six was placed under the command of Robert Ritter von Greim, a fighter ace of the First War and an enthusiastic Nazi, but by no means a fool.

During the quiet period prior to the summer offensive von Greim proposed the mass use of German bombers to strike at Russian armaments factories behind the front. OKL, the Luftwaffe general staff, accepted this idea and during June 1943 a number of raids were carried out against major industrial targets in towns east of Moscow. The targets were the tank factory at Gorky (now Nizhny Novgorod), the rubber works at Jaroslavl and oil depots and/or refineries at Saratov and Astrakhan. These attacks met with a surprising degree of success, particularly the raid on Gorky which brought the tank factory to a grinding halt. Before long however, the bombers were returned to their accustomed tactical role and sent against targets such as the rail centres in Kursk and Orel which were of direct relevance to the upcoming offensive. After the Battle of Kursk, command changes within the Luftwaffe meant that attention again turned to strategic bombing but nothing of significance was done because the Germans were forced to retreat far enough that worthwhile targets were now out of range.

At first sight the chances of seriously damaging the Russian war economy through strategic bombing might appear slight. After all, if the U.S.A. and Great Britain could not halt German war industry with 1,500 four-engine bombers, what chance had the Germans against Russia with 600 planes of half the range and carrying half the bombs? In fact the nature of the country and its industry made it more vulnerable than might be imagined. Soviet industry tended to be concentrated in a few massive factories and their locations were well known. It would not take very many well planned raids to do serious damage. For instance the fighter assembly plant at Gorky produced one quarter of all the fighters produced by Russia during the war. Moreover, the sparse population and poor communications made dispersal of production difficult. On top of this the factories had mostly been hurriedly constructed without thought to possible air raids. For instance there was much use of wood for buildings. At the Gorky tank factory such wooden buildings readily caught fire and burned down. The factories were also poorly defended with little sign of anti-aircraft guns and searchlights on the scale employed in Western Europe. The Russians were quick learners however, and if their failings were to be turned to advantage by the Germans it would need to be done fast. Moreover the Russian ability to recover from a blow was just as developed as that of any other country while the Germans still tended to think, quite mistakenly, that one successful raid meant the target was out of business for good. The Gorky plant was raided on 4th June but by 18th August it was back to full production.[viii]

For the coming battle the Germans intended to use Airfleet Four to the South of the Kursk bulge and Airfleet Six to the North. Between them the two fleets numbered 2,000 aircraft, nearly all those available on the eastern front. The majority were based on the southern side of the salient but that did not mean very much since the whole salient was only 120 miles across. A number of squadrons had been flown in especially from the West for the operation. Airfleet One on the northern sector of the front was left with just three hundred aircraft. The far South had essentially to be left to the Rumanians.

Russian forces comprised the 16th Air Army to the North and the 2nd Air Army to the South. Between them these organizations fielded some 3,000 aircraft. It must be born in mind however that the V.V.S. on all fronts numbered at least 8,000 of all kinds at this time so the rest of the front was not denuded in the manner forced on the Germans. One implication of this imbalance for the Germans was that the Kursk attack, known as Operation Citadel, could not be allowed to drag on too long without serious repercussions on other parts of the front.

The weather was hot and sunny with occasional thunderstorms. The fields were full of ripe grain awaiting the harvest. They were a golden sea undulating gently in the breeze. Like the Battle of Britain, Kursk carries with it the imagery of high summer and the picture of pilots waiting on their airfields, in their shirt sleeves for the call to take off, is part of the legend.

The two air forces were quite evenly matched despite the disparity in numbers because the Russian planes were, on the whole, barely a match for the Germans. The only model that was superior was the Lag-5FN which was the latest development of the Lag-5 design. The bulk of the Russian fighters were Yak-1s, Yak-7s and Lag-5s and they were not as capable as the Me109G, the latest offering from the Messerschmitt stable, though the real gap was in pilot quality. In the area of ground attack aircraft the Russians fielded large numbers of the excellent Il-2 Stormovik while the Germans mainly relied on the aging Stuka. They introduced an important innovation by modifying certain Stukas to carry two 37 mm cannon in pods attached under the wings. Hans Rudel was the pioneer and leading exponent of such aircraft. They were effective tank killers but only in the hands of an expert pilot and were themselves very vulnerable. Various other aircraft were pressed into the ground attack role such as the Me110 and the Ju88 but efforts to produce a quality replacement for the Stuka had resulted in failure. The first attempt was the Me210 which was a

Soviet Ilyushin Il-2 Stormovik ground attack planes in flight. 36,000 Stormoviks were built, more than any other combat plane of World War Two.
© Imperial War Museum (RUS 3479)

design disaster, having unsatisfactory engines and stability problems. The next effort was the Henschel He129 which was primarily used as a 'tank buster' and had a very limited bomb carrying capability. This aircraft was first produced in 1941 but production had been beset by difficulties and changes to the basic design and Kursk was its first trial in large numbers. It was very successful in that it is thought to have been the chief contributor to the figure of 1,000 Russian tanks destroyed from the air during the battle. Unfortunately the aircraft was underpowered, unwieldy and hard to fly with the result that it was very vulnerable to fighters and needed a strong escort to protect it and that was rarely forthcoming in the campaigns that followed Kursk. It was to remain a marginal influence.

In bomber aircraft the Germans really held the edge. They actually had more bombers in the area of the salient than the Russians and those aircraft, chiefly the Ju88 and the He111 carried heavier bomb loads than the Russian Pe-2s and Il-4s.

Earlier in the year the Luftwaffe had looked at means of increasing the supply of pilots, to little effect save that it realized the German allies boasted many experienced pilots hampered by flying inferior aircraft types. A program of replacement was immediately started whereby the Rumanian and Hungarian air forces received up-to-date German aircraft and this greatly increased their potential as combat forces.

The big difference between the two sides was in training and experience. The huge losses suffered by the V.V.S. in 1941 had forced it to cut its training program in order to turn out the large number of replacements needed at short notice. This was intended as a short-term measure but 1942 saw the loss of another 14,700 aircraft and an estimated 10,000 pilots. Accordingly short training times had to remain and the average V.V.S. pilot found himself at the front after just 15-18 hours of flight training. This was essentially nothing more than basic training: the moment a pilot could take off and land in an aircraft he was sent to the front. The result was inevitable, heavy losses which merely served to ensure that the policy had to remain unchanged. It was a vicious circle but it played to a Russian strength, namely, the size of the available population. By contrast German pilots received 70 hours training which meant that many more survived to become veterans. They were feeling the pressure though: pre-war training was 120 hours.[ix] It is interesting to compare these figures with those of the western Allies. In the R.A.F. at this time a pilot could expect 60 to 65 hours of flight training though it would be considerably more for specialist jobs such as piloting a heavy bomber.[x] In the U.S.A.A.F. the norm was 130 hours.[xi] Since the key to good flying and survival was plenty of experience these figures are very significant.

Although the Battle of Kursk as such began on 5th July 1943, the two air forces had been fighting a preparatory campaign for some two months before that. For both sides this had primarily taken the form of attacks against principle rail yards in the area. The V.V.S. probably had the better of this for, although they lost more aircraft than their opponents, their raids, coupled with extensive sabotage by partisans caused the Germans considerable anxiety over supplies, particularly aviation fuel.

The German plan for the battle was simple: there would be two thrusts led by armoured units against the two sides of the base of the Kursk salient. One was in the North and the other in the South and they were aimed at each other with the intention that they should meet in the middle, east of Kursk and cut off the city and its salient and all the troops in it. Of the two thrusts, the one in the South was the heavier.

Not only was this plan known to the Russians, but even the proposed time of its launch on the morning of 5th July and they duly launched a spoiling attack of their own just before it. To the South an armada of Il-2s headed for the German airfields around Kharkov where, even now, the German bombers were warming up for their own attack. The Russian bombers with their escorting fighters numbered in the region of 400. The German bombers remained on the ground while the fighters took off to intercept the approaching raid and their followed one of the largest aerial battles of the whole war. It was resoundingly won by the Germans. This was the territory of the crack 8th Air Corps. Many of their best pilots were in this sector and here was based Jg52, bursting at the seams with ace pilots. They made this day a field day. Captain Johannes Wiese shot down no less than 12 aircraft, Senior Lieutenant Joachim Kirschner, eight and many others scored multiple victories. There were some losses too. Walter Krupinsky, one of 52's leading pilots was forced to attempt a crash-landing at a nearby airfield after his aircraft was hit in the rudder and became hard to control. At the last moment he saw aircraft taking off from the runway and had to turn to avoid them. His plane immediately flipped over at low level and landed on its back trapping Krupinsky in his cockpit with fuel dripping over him until a rescue crew freed him. He was very lucky not to be incinerated but he was injured badly enough that he did not fly again for six weeks.[xii] The Russian bombers that got through were sufficiently dispersed that the raid achieved little.

On the north flank of the salient there was more bitter fighting as German Stukas attacked the Russian artillery positions and airfields. When the day closed the V.V.S. had lost 250 aircraft overall and the Luftwaffe 75, making this the hardest day's aerial combat of the whole war. These losses are three times those of the worst day of the Battle of Britain and greatly exceed the worst of the losses on American daylight raids. In the evening Stalin rang General Rokossovsky who was in command in the northern sector and enquired whether the V.V.S. had had won control of the skies. Rokossovsky had just received the report of General Rudenko, commander of 16th Air Army, to the effect that the Germans had resoundingly won that day's contest. His reply to Stalin was carefully worded: 'It is impossible to give a definite answer to that question. But tomorrow we shall resolve this positively.'[xiii] Telling Stalin the unvarnished truth was not always wise.

The next day the Russians intended a counterattack and to support it Rudenko planned to send his aircraft out in a mass attack at dawn. This was an unusual attack both for the number of planes used and for the choice of targets which were in the German front line rather than in the rear. The result was a major air battle in which the Russians achieved little while taking heavy losses. Their escort fighters were being used as close escort in large formations instead of being given their freedom. As the fighting died down a second wave of Red bombers attacked while the German planes were on the ground refueling and they did grave damage as a result. At the end of the day the situation on the ground was unchanged. The Russian counterattack had been halted. Despite their tactical victory the Germans were suffering from shortage of fuel and they had lost one of their leading aces, Reinhard Seiler. He had 99 kills and was chasing number one hundred, but failed to see an Airacobra closing in. He managed to bail out over his own lines but was so badly injured that he had to be flown to Germany for treatment and never fought again.[xiv]

On 7th July the Russians continued to pound the German ground forces, particularly their tanks and self-propelled guns. This time fighters were used more wisely in smaller groups and at different heights. The picture was much the same the next day save that deteriorating weather reduced the missions either side could fly. The Germans suffered more from this as they were the ones doing the attacking on the ground and they suffered heavy losses as a consequence.

On the southern flank the 6th July was a day of mixed fortunes. Poor weather grounded the Luftwaffe in the early part of the day and massed Russian fighter sweeps met little opposition. Later on, both sides launched bomber attacks and both took losses though the V.V.S. suffered the more. On the other hand the German advance on the ground was rapidly stalling despite resolute efforts by formations of Stukas in the now familiar fashion.

The following day General Krasovsky, commander of the 2nd Air Army sent out his Stormoviks in large formations instead of penny packets, with a corresponding reduction in losses, but his fighters were still under-performing and the German ground support aircraft did well: German panzer forces advanced further. On 8th July the German air effort was intensely concentrated on supporting the ground assault and Russian losses outran German ones, but the V.V.S. was learning fast and fighters were being urged to fly into German airspace and to operate in smaller groups at different heights: in effect Pokryshkin's escalator. The 9th began badly for the Germans when a morning weather reconnaissance flight of four Me109s became separated in the clouds and were all lost. One of them crash-landed in Russian territory, probably damaged by an unseen Russian fighter and the formation leader Senior Sergeant Edmund Rossmann landed to rescue the pilot but approaching Russian troops shot him and captured Rossmann before he could take off again.[xv] This was another day of heavy fighting and it included a symbolic clash when Ivan Kozhedub, Russia's top ace, shot down Gunther Rall, Germany's number three. Russian pilots' reports on the day's fighting noted a growing caution about the Luftwaffe: increasingly its planes did not attack unless the odds were in their favour.

At this time the attack on the northern front finally came to a halt. The German panzer forces could make no more progress. In the air the Luftwaffe was impressed by the fact that despite heavy losses, the V.V.S. was fighting as fiercely as ever and German fighter planes experienced great difficulty getting through the screen of fighters to hit the bombers. The whole battle of Kursk was a school room for the Russians who learned as they went along and had become very adept at doing so. They were now employing early warning radar and their network of radio ground control stations was growing in both size and efficiency all the time.

On the southern front the Germans had regrouped and on 8th July they made an all-out effort to break through the defences with a thrust toward the village of Prokhorovka. They were on course to collide with the Soviet reserves, in the shape of the 5th Guards Tank Army, moving forward. The result, on 12th, was the largest tank battle in history. It is often stated that a wild air battle took place above the fighting tanks but this is not strictly true. On this day there was less air combat than on most days of the battle and the reason was that while the Germans concentrated their efforts on the Prokhorovka area and had of necessity to leave other parts of the front bare, the V.V.S. spread its power more evenly and scarcely appeared over the tank battle because of the difficulty of telling one side from the other in a confused action of fast-moving tanks. The Luftwaffe was much better at this and used forward observers on the ground to keep their pilots informed of changes in the situation minute by minute. They did much damage to the Russian armour. The Henschel 129s were particularly effective and so was the ever-present Rudel who personally destroyed 12 tanks with his cannon-equipped Stuka.[xvi] The day of the Stuka was drawing to a close however. It had taken heavy losses in the battle and the decision was made to replace it. For want of anything better Stuka squadrons in Russia began to re-equip in the autumn of 1943 with Fw190s.

Despite the air support Prokhorovka is best described as a draw and in any event developments elsewhere were beginning to overshadow the struggle at Kursk. On the night of 9th/10th July the Allies invaded Sicily and Hitler summoned von Manstein and von Kluge, the other senior officer responsible for the Citadel operation to a meeting on 13th at which he announced the cancellation of the operation. Von Manstein persuaded him to grant more time, but it was to be only a few days and in that time the situation deteriorated. Even while the Battle of Prokhorovka was raging on 12th the Red army launched a major counteroffensive against the Germans in the Region of Orel. This was just north of the Kursk bulge and it threw the German forces on the northern flank of the bulge into a defensive stance. On 17th Hitler cancelled the whole operation and on 3rd August, the Russians launched another offensive south of the bulge in the area of Belgorod and Kharkov. This began a precipitate German withdrawal on the southern half of the front that was not to halt until the winter came and the Germans were deep in the western Ukraine close to Odessa and the foothills of the Carpathians.

The figures for aircraft lost in the battle give the impression that the Germans won. On the southern flank the Russians lost 677 planes and the Germans 220. On the northern flank the losses were 430 to 57. In fact this was a German defeat. Partly that is the case because the offensive on the ground failed and the air battle was only fought to support the ground battle. More important are the facts that the V.V.S. had stood its ground despite losses and that it could afford to take much greater losses in any case. Practically the whole of the Luftwaffe on the eastern front fought at Kursk, including all the leading aces, or 'experten' as the Germans called them. On the other hand the Russians only committed part of their air resources and that part was manned in large part by beginners. In the circumstances their performance was first class and it improved even as the battle progressed. Russian pilots were beginning to display a new confidence in their capabilities. Strategically Germany had been soundly defeated: their entire summer offensive had failed and the psychological impact of this was considerable. The German ace, Gunter Rall said: 'From then onward the Russian air force would only grow better and better while the Luftwaffe went into decline.'[xvii]

One immediate consequence of the Battle of Kursk was the suicide of Hans Jeschonnek, the Chief of the Luftwaffe Air Staff. Jeschonnek was an early follower of Hitler to whom he was devoted but he did not get on with Goering or Milch.

Kursk caused Hitler to lose faith in him and the other two were not slow to lay the blame for the Luftwaffe's failings at his door. The final straw was the events of 17th August when the R.A.F. bombed the Peenemunde research station and set back the rocket development program and the U.S.A.A.F. flew the length of Germany and caused great damage notwithstanding their heavy losses. On 18th Jeschonnek shot himself.

Jeschonnek's successor as Chief of the Air Staff was General Gunther Korten the commander of Airfleet One. Korten initiated a complete change of Luftwaffe policy, reducing the emphasis on army support and increasing that on defensive operations against strategic bombing. He also planned that the Luftwaffe would carry out its own strategic bombing campaign against Russia. The first part of this plan was inevitable if the Allied air attacks in the West were to be resisted but the strategic bombing was only marginally realistic. Bomber formations were withdrawn from the line in rotation to re-train in the techniques needed for strategic bombing, but this process was slowed by the opposition of the army who were understandably distressed to see their air support withdrawn. By the time the crews were ready, retreats on the eastern front had put the crucial Russian factories out of range of the Heinkel 111. There was then a further delay while squadrons waited to be re-equipped with the new Heinkel He177 four-engine strategic bomber.

This aircraft was a design disaster that had been used since 1942 sporadically in small numbers but was not available for Korten's plans until the middle of 1944, by which time a lack of aviation fuel in Germany precluded the opening of the strategic bombing campaign. The He177 was planned before the war to a specification that required it to have a dive-bombing capacity. This was absurd in a strategic bomber. The result was that to reduce drag and increase structural strength, the engines were mounted in tandem pairs, each pair driving one propeller so that the plane appeared to a lay observer to have only two engines. This arrangement caused endless technical problems that were never fully resolved. The aircraft was a vitally needed addition to the Luftwaffe's inventory that was a near complete failure.

The first result of Korten's change of policy was the transfer to the West in September of six fighter wings. Nominally this was over 700 aircraft (in reality it was probably around 500) and it stripped the East of most of its fighter power. From now on the Russian front had to make do with between three and four wings and the reduction ensured that the Russians would henceforth win air superiority virtually by default. In many ways this was a bigger blow than Kursk and it was the direct result of the daylight bombing campaign in the West, overwhelmingly that of the U.S.A.A.F..

The autumn was a tale of steady retreat for the Germans and their allies and advance for the Russians. First Kharkov and Belgorod were taken and then an attempt to establish a defensive line at the Dnieper River collapsed. The Russians took Kiev on November 6th. Though the Luftwaffe was compelled to disperse the concentration of aircraft that it had built up for the summer, the majority still flew in the southern half of the front with the result that the centre and north were grossly under-defended and there were consequential losses there too. Bryansk and Smolensk changed hands and very early in 1944 the siege of Leningrad was lifted. The intensity of the air fighting eased somewhat during the autumn because of the effect rapid movement always had on air operations: the disruption attendant on changes of base. For the Germans there was increased wastage of bombers and ground attack aircraft because they were no longer adequately escorted. Even in December they lost 200 planes. Of these 90 were lost due to causes other than combat and this ratio of accidents was by no means unusual: there was always a high wastage rate for both sides even before they started fighting.

Despite an increasingly threatening future the pilots of the Luftwaffe fought with undiminished exertion. Apart from anything else the big picture was not readily apparent to the individual pilot at his airfield whose thoughts were concentrated on his next mission and perhaps on the beer and cigarette to be enjoyed after it, if he survived.

The pilots of the V.V.S. had found a new confidence and their longstanding and, initially well-founded, inferiority complex in respect of the Luftwaffe began to dissipate. During this Russian offensive the 27th Fighter Regiment was honoured for its fine record by being designated the 129th Guards Fighter Regiment. One of its pilots, Evgeniy Mariinskiy, later wrote his memoirs and in them he described a successful battle fought with Messerschmitts in the Dnieper area at this time and his thoughts after the fight: 'I felt myself the victor although I hadn't shot down a plane. I hadn't even fired a shot but the feeling of supremacy over the Fascists didn't leave me. It didn't matter that it hadn't been my personal victory.'[xviii]

This was something new.

CHAPTER EIGHTEEN

South Pacific Battles

The seizure of the airfield on Guadalcanal by U.S. marines in August 1942 began a campaign against Japanese strongholds in the south Pacific that was to last to the end of the war. In many ways the whole affair was just a very large side-show. Japan was never going to be defeated in the Solomon Islands or in New Guinea: she was going to be defeated by American forces cutting her vital sea lanes. This could not be done until the U.S. Navy's wartime construction program bore fruit and that, in turn, was not going to happen until 1943/4. In the meantime Japan's army and navy had to be weakened as much as possible and her expansion brought to a halt. This was what the fighting in the South Pacific was all about. The islands that were fought over were of no intrinsic value: they were just on the way to somewhere else that *did* have value. All these islands were uncultivated and clad in jungle. They had no towns of any size and no economies to speak of. All the fighting, by land, sea and air was ultimately about airfields. The airfields were supplied by sea and therefore there were naval battles and air-sea contests aplenty but there was no strategic bombing and even the tactical bombing was against a very limited range of targets. It has been said that there were only four kinds of aerial mission for bombers in these campaigns:

1. Reconnaissance
2. Shipping strikes
3. Airfield attacks
4. Supporting ground troops.[i]

This is true enough and if one adds that for the fighters there was the usual mix of sweeps, escorts and intercepts, then the whole range of the air war is encompassed.

The conditions of climate and geography made the business of supply and maintenance particularly arduous. Everything had to be shipped in because there was nothing available locally. Heat, humidity and salt caused corrosion and rapid deterioration of mechanical parts not to mention food and even clothing. This was one of the reasons why aircraft in this theatre operated in much smaller numbers than in Europe. It was an additional reason why aircraft carriers were so important. They were a ready-made base for up to a hundred aircraft and carried their own supplies and workshops with them.

The main Allied base for the attack on Guadalcanal was the island of Espiritu Santo in the New Hebrides some 600 miles to the southeast. Here and at Noumea on nearby New Caledonia, large scale base camps were established and supplies amassed. Extensive facilities were built for the servicing of ships and aircraft. As of January 1943 the 13th Air Force came into being here and was the parent organization of all U.S.A.A.F. formations in the Solomons. Before that time all aircraft in the theatre, which meant all aircraft on Guadalcanal itself, were grouped together into the 1st Marine Air Division. At times this organization included aircraft from all three fighting services: army, navy and Marine Corps.

Their opponents were the Japanese aviators at Rabaul on New Britain Island beyond the west end of the Solomons chain. Here was based 11th Air Fleet comprising several assorted navy and army air groups totaling some 230 fighters and 180 bombers in theory but, in practice about half that number. At the end of 1942 the Imperial Navy ceded jurisdiction in New Guinea to the army's 12th Air Division and the army took over responsibility for the defence of that island against the growing Allied counter-attacks.

Without strategic targets there was no need for large fleets of heavy bombers filling the sky with their mass formations; though that does not mean heavy bombers were not important. Given the huge distances involved, they enabled airpower to be brought to bear on targets that would otherwise have been immune and they were useful for reconnaissance for the same reasons of range. They could also hit a target with a much greater weight of bombs than the smaller aircraft. Indeed Lieutenant Commander Mitsugu Kofukuga, commander of 6th Air Group of the Japanese Navy that fought in the Solomons, said: 'In my opinion, which is shared by many Japanese combat officers, the ability of the B-17 and B-24 to defend themselves and carry out their intended missions despite enemy fighter opposition was a deciding factor in the final outcome of the war.'[ii] The B-17 and the B-24 were heavily armed and Japanese fighters were lightly armed so that a single B-24 on a reconnaissance mission could very likely fight off any fighter patrol that attacked it. Moreover these planes flew at a great height and any Japanese plane taking off to intercept would tend to find its target long gone by the time it reached the height needed. By contrast with reconnaissance aircraft, heavy bombers on bombing missions tended to fly much lower than the 20,000 feet or more that was standard in Europe because of the problems with accurate bombing of small targets already noted. In the Pacific role it soon became apparent that the B-24 was better suited to heavy bomber tasks than the B-17. It was faster, had a longer range and carried a bigger payload. Its weakness: the fact that it was arguably less robust under heavy attack, meant less here than in Europe because it rarely had to face heavy attack.

Japanese bombing technique has already been commented on in the context of the early campaign in New Guinea and it has to be said that the tactics employed were woeful. High level attacks with small bomb loads could not have been better chosen to achieve next to nothing, yet the relevant authorities in the navy never seem to have learned any lessons in this respect. One gains the impression from circumstantial evidence that the army was more realistic, but not much.

The wealth of tactical and shipping targets meant that the South Pacific was a happy hunting ground for medium bombers. This was even more so because the terrain made it very difficult to move and deploy artillery so that aircraft had to stand in. At first the B-26 Marauder was used but in due course it gave way to the B-25 Mitchell. There were several reasons for this. The U.S. Air Force considered the B-26 the better bomber and therefore the European theatre had priority call on its services in accordance with the accepted strategic policy. As an aircraft it was very tough and very well armed but it was also complicated to service, hard to fly and needed long runways, all features that made its use in the Pacific problematical.

The Mitchell suffered from none of these drawbacks, though it was a lighter plane that carried a smaller payload. In the end it transpired that it fitted Pacific conditions very well.

The ubiquitous A-20 Havoc was also much in evidence. This was such a good design that it fitted in anywhere. Another excellent design, used mainly by the Royal Australian Air Force, was the Bristol Beaufighter. Originally developed to meet a pre-war requirement of the British government for a long range fighter, this twin-engine plane could fulfill a variety of roles and made an excellent torpedo bomber and ground attack plane. It too had heavy armament, including cannon, concentrated in the nose. This was another plane designed in Europe for perceived European requirements that performed at its best in other theatres, though its secondary role in Northern Europe was arguably due to simple under-utilization rather than any deficiency of design.

It was not long before there was a revolution in tactics. The accepted procedure with a medium bomber such as the B-25 was to approach the target in level flight at medium height, say 5-10,000 feet, and the bomb aimer would release the bombs at the right moment. As we have already seen it was hard to hit ships, or indeed any other small target of the kind the theatre offered in plenty, using this method. Pilots developed a new technique of making the whole attack at very low level. In Europe such an approach was fraught with danger: the ground defences were heavy and observers or radar would report the plane's coming long before its arrival. In the Pacific on the other hand, defences were generally much weaker and most of the time there was no one in the jungle or on the ocean to see a plane and report its approach, nor was there radar except in very rare circumstances. Attacking planes were therefore much more likely to avoid detection and anti-aircraft fire, at least until they reached the target itself, by flying low. The Allies in fact had a network of various civilians, largely ex-planters, known as 'coastwatchers', who did what their name suggests and provided some kind of early warning network, but it was of more use reporting naval movements than the appearance of aircraft.

At low level targets could be bombed with much greater accuracy. In the case of ships there was an additional refinement in that pilots discovered that if they dropped a bomb when they were going fast and very low over the water, the bomb would hit the surface and skip like a pebble thrown onto a pond until it hit the side of the ship. It was not long before the bombers were leaving their bomb aimers behind as superfluous: the planes were re-wired so the pilot could drop the bombs himself. At very low level he did not need the complicated bomb sight. The next step was to plate over the glass nose and fill it with a battery of 50 calibre machine guns whose concentrated fire was so devastating that it could tear vehicles apart and sink small ships.

These developments were an indication of the future of air warfare. In the post-war world the medium bomber effectively died out. Tactical targets were hit at low level by planes designed for the purpose and any level bombing of the old kind was done by heavy bombers at great height and in large numbers. This was facilitated by the development of small aircraft with a vastly greater load-carrying ability due to the ever more powerful engines, both jet and internal combustion, that were being developed. Shortly after the war ended the U.S. Navy received a new strike aircraft called the Douglas Skyraider which was built as a successor to the Douglas Dauntless carrier dive-bomber. It was a single-engine machine with a crew of one that could operate from a carrier but it could carry 8,000 lbs of bombs and/or rockets putting it at the heavy end of medium bombers in terms of weaponry. It could also carry a torpedo and it had a range of 1,300 miles. In fact it was a quite outstanding aircraft that was still in use in the Vietnam War and it made the old medium bomber superfluous.

The attack on Guadalcanal on 7th August 1942 was carefully planned. The landings were carried out by the Marine Corps and extensive air cover was provided by the U.S. Navy in the shape of the carriers Saratoga, Enterprise and Wasp. These could put up in the region of 100 F4F Wildcat fighters between them in rotation to provide a continuous air umbrella.

The same day as the seizure of the airstrip on Guadalcanal, the Japanese retaliated. They launched a strike of 27 Betty bombers and a handful of Val dive-bombers escorted by 18 Zero fighters of the Tainan Air Group imported from New Guinea. These planes flew from the base at Rabaul which was 600 miles away but was the nearest properly equipped airfield. The Japanese air effort in the Guadalcanal campaign was constantly hindered by this lack of adequate base facilities. The great distance from Rabaul had many disadvantages: increased fuel consumption, increased wear on aircraft, increased chance of becoming lost in poor weather, increased wear on pilots and almost no chance for damaged aircraft to reach home. The Japanese bombers dropped their bombs on the ships close to the island from a great height and hit nothing. The Zeros became involved in a whirling dogfight with the Wildcats and shot down seven of them and a Douglas Dauntless, though the Japanese were impressed by the relentless aggression of U.S. Navy pilots. At the day's end the Japanese had lost 13 aircraft in total.

Saburo Sakai was one of the Zero pilots and after shooting down two planes himself, for victories number 59 and 60, he approached what he thought were more Wildcats only to find at the last moment that they were Grumman Avengers (a type that he had never seen before) which had rear gunners who were watching him approach and in the next moment, opened fire. A bullet smashed Sakai's windscreen and hit him in the head, penetrating the brain. He passed out and only came to, just in time to stop his aircraft crashing into the sea. He was in a bad way: blind in one eye and paralyzed on the left hand side. He was bleeding heavily from the head wound that passed the length of his skull. After a long struggle he was able to stuff part of his scarf into the wound to staunch the blood and fly the plane with one hand and one foot in the face of a 200 m.p.h. gale coming into his face where the windscreen should have been. He then navigated the 600 miles back to Rabaul fighting agonizing pain, alternating with fits of drowsiness that would be fatal if he gave in to them. It was an epic achievement of human endurance. At the end of the journey, which took him over four hours, he managed to pull off a perfect landing at Rabaul and insisted on making his report to his commanding officer before he collapsed and was taken to hospital. It was two years before he was to fight again.[iii]

The next day the Japanese attacked again in similar strength and lost 18 planes without achieving anything of value to compensate. But the day after that they made up for it when a task force of cruisers arrived off Guadalcanal and defeated the Allied cruisers there in the Battle of Savo Island. The survivors had to withdraw and since the carriers had already departed to re-fuel, the island was left unprotected. All the supply ships had to leave because they had no idea what the Japanese would try next and they could not defend themselves. The key for the Allies was now to fly aircraft onto the island and use the captured airfield there to provide their own air cover. This they achieved on 20th August when the escort carrier, Long Island flew in a squadron of Wildcats and a squadron of Dauntless bombers to use the airfield now named 'Henderson Field' in honour of Major Lofton Henderson who had perished leading the Marine Corps torpedo planes at Midway. These squadrons had to face almost daily Japanese raids from Rabaul but they enabled the island to be supplied.

At the end of August the Japanese made another attempt to drive the U.S. fleet away and isolate Guadalcanal. They sent the two carriers Shokaku and Zuikaku with escorting ships from their main naval base at Truk Atoll to sail toward the eastern end of the Solomon Islands where Guadalcanal lay. A light carrier, Ryujo, was sent ahead to act as bait. The U.S. Navy, alerted, as ever, by their reading of Japanese naval signals, sent the task force of the three carriers to intercept. They sank the Ryujo but missed the main force whose planes badly damaged Enterprise in a classic attack carried out with great bravery and total professionalism. Enterprise was narrowly saved but both fleets withdrew. This is known as the Battle of the Eastern Solomons. On 30th August a Japanese submarine badly damaged Saratoga which had to limp back to the U.S.A. for repairs.

Like the Imperial Navy, the U.S.N. now had only two large fleet carriers active in the Pacific and then on 25th September another Japanese submarine sank U.S.S. Wasp outright. Now there was only one and at this stage the Americans were only holding on to Guadalcanal by the skin of their teeth. The waters around Guadalcanal by day were 'no man's land' and by night were Japanese.

The American presence on the island consisted of Henderson Field and a perimeter held by a force of marines. The Japanese held the rest of the island though 'the rest' did not amount to much more than many square miles of empty wilderness. It was the airfield that mattered. Guadalcanal was known over the radio by the code word 'Cactus' and so the aircraft flying from the island became the 'Cactus Air Force'. The men there flew and fought in primitive conditions eating monotonous tinned food, when they could get any food at all and suffering from malaria and a variety of other tropical diseases. Frequent tropical storms reduced the whole area of the airfield to a mud bath in which ground crews struggled to keep aircraft flying day after day with no prospect of getting clean or having a rest or a decent meal. Pilots had to fly almost every waking minute and at night Japanese naval bombardments and nuisance raids, often by single float planes, rendered sleep impossible. The Americans were fortunate that that first Wildcat squadron to land on the island, VMF 223, was commanded by Major John Smith, a first rate pilot and outstanding leader. Smith, a native of Oklahoma, ended the war as the second most successful Wildcat ace and was awarded the Congressional Medal of Honor but more important than his flying prowess was his inspirational leadership.[iv]

Towards the end of October 1942 the Japanese made another attempt to destroy American naval power in the area and isolate Guadalcanal. At the same time their army launched an attack on the defending Americans round Henderson field. They sent a fleet of four aircraft carriers and five battleships to patrol north of the Santa Cruz Islands in the hope of making contact with the U.S. fleet. That fleet was close by and consisted primarily of the two carriers Hornet and Enterprise, the latter having been rapidly patched up. The two fleets discovered each other and there was an exchange of air strikes between them. The light carrier Zuiho was hit and had to withdraw and the Shokaku received four heavy bomb hits on the flight deck and was severely damaged. Six months earlier this injury would probably have sunk her but the Japanese Navy was fast learning how to control damage on a big ship. Japanese planes found the Enterprise covered by a rain squall, so they attacked the Hornet which was left a flaming wreck that the Americans themselves later scuttled. There were then limited attacks on Enterprise but she suffered only minor damage.

The Battle of Santa Cruz was a marginal victory for the Japanese but at a terrible cost. One hundred aircraft and their veteran crews were lost. The crews were irreplaceable. The Americans had understood the value of naval anti-aircraft fire and their ships were increasingly festooned with AA guns that did grim execution amongst attacking planes.

The situation remained finely balanced but Guadalcanal was growing gradually stronger. At the end of August the Marine fighter squadron VMF 224 arrived with more Wildcats and a little later came the Air Force's 67th Fighter Squadron flying Airacobras. On 26th August one of the pilots of 223 was attacked while trying to land by a Zero that audaciously joined the landing circuit. The Wildcat pilot pulled up his undercarriage and conducted a wild dogfight with the Zero over the beach. He shot down the Zero which exploded violently to the delight of the watching troops. It is probable that this Zero was flown by Lt. Junichi Sasai, a talented young officer of the Tainan Group regarded with something near veneration by his men.[v] His loss was a severe blow to Japanese morale. The next reinforcement was a squadron from the damaged Saratoga that made Guadalcanal its home so that there were now aircraft from all three services present, though for command purposes they were all designated 1st Marine Air Division.

At the end of August work began on a second air strip on the island. Because it was a grass strip constructed in primitive conditions, the men knew it as the 'cow pasture'. Its presence was a great boon because there were now too many aircraft for one strip to handle economically. The more aircraft there were on Guadalcanal, the more difficult it became for the Japanese Navy to operate in the area.

After the Battle of Santa Cruz it became apparent to the Japanese that Henderson Field must be put out of operation or the island was lost to Japan. In November efforts were made to re-supply and reinforce the Japanese forces on the island so that they could mount another offensive and at the same time a task force including two battleships was sent to shell Henderson. It was now clear that shelling was a much more effective way of damaging the airfield than high level bombing by Navy Betties. The task force sailed on 12th and that night it ran into a U.S. force of cruisers posted off Guadalcanal to guard the numerous transports unloading off the beaches at Lunga Point by Henderson Field. A fierce fight followed and ships were sunk and disabled on both sides but the Japanese were compelled to withdraw without shelling Henderson and, worse, the battleship Hiei limped slowly away after taking heavy damage and when day came, was well within range of American aircraft of the Cactus Air Force and of the Enterprise which was making another appearance, having been patched up yet again. The attacks duly came in from Henderson Field and the Enterprise and Hiei was sunk. That night the Japanese sent a small force of cruisers and destroyers to Guadalcanal which shelled Henderson Field but without doing any serious damage. The following night the main task force returned but this time the Americans were ready and their fleet, with two battleships, defeated the Japanese and sank the battleship Kirishima.

Meanwhile a Japanese convoy of 11 troop transports sailed from Shortland Island at the other end of the Solomons chain making for the west coast of Guadalcanal to land 12,000 troops and fresh supplies so that the army could launch the decisive assault on the Henderson Field perimeter. American reconnaissance planes spotted this convoy on the morning of 13th and a ceaseless stream of air attacks ensued. Even heavy bombers from the far-off base at Espiritu Santo took part. By dusk six of the transports had been sunk and another disabled. During the night the survivors reached Guadalcanal and the admiral commanding the convoy decided to beach the remaining four ships to speed up the business of unloading, since he knew that with dawn the air attacks would be renewed. But the night was slipping away and it took time to get permission for this radical course. In the end there was just not enough time left. At first light the Americans returned and the four ships were still unloading. Japanese air cover was overwhelmed and the four beached ships and their human cargo were pounded. The sea was red with blood and choked with bodies and parts of bodies. Apparently the sight was so gruesome that some U.S. pilots were physically sick.[vi] In the end all the ships and supplies were destroyed and a mere 4,000 soldiers reached the shore alive, but without equipment so that they were useless as a fighting force and just became extra mouths to feed. The decisive assault on Henderson never took place.

These three days of combat, known as the Battle of Guadalcanal, were crucial in tipping the struggle for the island dramatically in favour of the Americans. Now it was the Japanese who had to try to sneak in men and supplies when they could, in the face of overwhelming air superiority. They tried to do this by night and on 30th November won a notable victory in the Battle of Tassafaronga when a force of destroyers defeated a more powerful US force. By December however, after several weeks of smuggling in supplies aboard destroyers and even submarines, they realized they could no longer win the struggle on the island and decided to evacuate their troops. In early February Guadalcanal was secure in American hands.

The air battle between August and February cost the Imperial Navy 893 aircraft and 2,362 naval airmen. The loss of aircraft was bad enough but the loss of airmen was literally irreparable. These were the men who had been trained pre-war and gained their early experience in China. The conditions no longer existed for them to be replaced. From here on the quality of Japanese naval pilots went into a steep decline. The whole balance of air power in the South Pacific had shifted and would never go back.

Before the month of February was out, the Americans had taken the adjacent group of Russell Islands with minimal opposition and there began a process of island-hopping along the Solomons chain. The process was based on the use of air power. On each new island that was conquered, an airstrip was immediately constructed and the aircraft based there were used to establish aerial superiority over the next island. U.S. engineers had become outstandingly skilled in airfield construction which could be achieved in as little as forty-eight hours. The key was a kind of chain link matting that was transported in rolls and unrolled on leveled ground to create a runway. The Japanese, whose own construction techniques were relatively leisurely, watched these achievements open-mouthed.

The Japanese Navy's response to the loss of Guadalcanal was to realize belatedly that it had been a prize not worth the fighting for. Horrified by the loss of ships in the campaign, it embarked on a policy of 'conservation' whereby its major warships would be kept safe in home waters while the army and the air forces fought the war. Accordingly there was no fleet intervention as the Americans fought their way along the Solomons, but only a last-ditch resistance on the ground on the island of Bougainville coupled with constant resistance in the air but the air war was now dominated by the Americans and the Japanese Navy took heavy losses in aircraft and crews to very little effect. Supplying their garrisons on the various islands became a nightmare for the Japanese because any transport vessel that showed itself in 'The Slot' as the central sea of the Solomons became known, was promptly sunk by U.S. planes. Supplies had therefore to be moved by night where possible and by barges and other small ships making short dashes from one island to another, usually heavily camouflaged with brushwood. Inevitably submarines were also used despite their very small carrying capacity.

In April 1943 it was discovered by American code-breakers that on the 18th of the month Admiral Yamamoto, the commander-in-chief of the Japanese Navy, would fly from Rabaul to Bougainville on a tour of inspection. The Americans arranged for a flight of P-38s to intercept the plane in which he was a passenger, and shoot it down. Yamamoto was killed and his death was a useful propaganda coup for the Americans and a serious blow to Japanese naval planning and morale. For some years after the war Allied code-breaking activities remained secret but this episode always aroused the suspicion amongst historians that there was more going on than met the eye. How, in the vastness of the Pacific sky did a flight of American planes just happen to be in the right place at exactly the right time to intercept this aircraft?

In June U.S. forces took the island of New Georgia and in August, Vella Lavella. On November 1st they landed on Bougainville, the largest of the Solomon Islands and the most westerly. Bougainville was scarcely 200 miles from Rabaul and at the same time as the landings on that island, a campaign of bombing against Rabaul was initiated. The first thing that U.S. forces did once they had a secure beachhead at Torokina on Bougainville was, inevitably, to build an airfield. At last the Japanese fleet decided to interfere and a force of cruisers and destroyers was sent from Rabaul to disrupt the landings. They were defeated at the Battle of Empress Augusta Bay and a cruiser and a destroyer sunk. The rest of the task force retreated back to Rabaul where further ships were gathering for a full strength sortie. Here, on November 5th they were attacked by American bombers and four heavy cruisers were severely damaged. The planned sortie was abandoned and the damaged ships limped away to Truk.

The Solomons campaign in 1943 marked a new stage in the Pacific War brought about by the first fruits of the mobilization of the U.S. economy for all-out war. The year saw the arrival in the Pacific of American military resources that gave them a permanent numerical advantage wherever they fought. The most obvious example of this was aircraft carriers. As we have seen, there was a time in the autumn of the previous year when there was only one fleet carrier available in the South Pacific. In the course of 1943 another seven became available together with nine light carriers. Beginning in the middle of 1941 the U.S. Navy had realized that it desperately needed more aircraft carriers and it began work on the new Essex class carriers of which 26 were planned and 24 eventually launched. These were ships of 35,000 tons capable of 32 knots and carrying 90 aircraft each.

At the end of 1941 the navy was worried that these carriers would take too long to build and so it commissioned nine light carriers to be built on existing cruiser hulls. These were the Independence class of 10,000 tons and capable of a similar speed. Each ship could carry 40 aircraft. As it turned out, U.S. shipyards were so efficient that the fleet carriers took little longer to build than their smaller sisters. In 1943, as noted above, seven of the big carriers and all nine of the smaller ones joined the fleet. Another ten Essex class carriers were commissioned before war's end. On top of this there were several designs of what came to be known as 'escort carriers' which were also light carriers, much slower than the Independence class but much the same size. They could carry 25-30 planes. All told, an incredible 90 of these were built and delivered either during or shortly after the war. In the same time frame the Japanese built a total of nine carriers of all kinds, not one of which could carry as many aircraft as an Essex class.

There were also new aircraft in early 1943. The Grumman Corporation carefully questioned pilots who had flown their Wildcats in combat about how the plane had performed and how it could be improved. By good fortune the Americans had captured an undamaged Zero in the Aleutians and tested it extensively to discover its strengths and weaknesses. The result of all this research was the Hellcat, a development of its older brother and specifically built to out-fly Zeros. Not surprisingly navy pilots were delighted with it. One is recorded as saying: 'I love this aircraft so much that if it could cook I'd marry it.'[vii] Another outstanding newcomer was the Vought Corsair reckoned by many to be the best U.S. fighter of the war. This aircraft was built with inverted gull wings like the Stuka: that, is they first angled down and then bent up halfway along. The reason for this was that the propeller was so large that it needed the extra clearance these wings gave it: without them it would have hit the ground. Although designed for use on aircraft carriers, it was at first considered unsuitable for that role because of the difficulty of landing it on a deck. Cockpit visibility on landing was poor because of the long nose housing the 2,000 horsepower engine. The result was that it was first used to equip the Marine Corps who flew from land bases and it made its debut flying from Guadalcanal in early 1943. Some of these planes were given to the Royal Navy who showed how to land them on a carrier by using a slanting approach so that the ship's deck was visible to one side until the last moment. The U.S. Navy then adopted them for carrier use though they were never flown from escort carriers whose deck was simply not long enough for them to take off, however skillful the pilot.

At the same time that these new planes were becoming available, supplies of P-38 Lightnings and P-47 Thunderbolts were reaching the Army Air Force. Their performance far outstripped the old P-39s and P-40s though their approach to fighting Zeros still relied on using speed and diving and climbing, The Zero remained the master of the turn but increasingly that was a worthless advantage as it faced much faster planes that did not need to try to turn with it and as the quality of Zero pilots declined. In 1943 the U.S.A. manufactured twice the number of aircraft produced by Germany and Japan combined.

The new Corsair was flown by, among others, Gregory Boyington. This colourful man had left the American Volunteer Group in the spring of 1942 and returned to the U.S.A. to rejoin the Marine Corps and resume his career. His application to rejoin was ignored and it took a personal letter to the Assistant Secretary of the Navy to get him reinstated. He put this down to malice in the Corps but given his record of boozing and indiscipline, it is quite possible that the Marine Corps simply did not want him back. Once reinstated in the ranks he was rapidly promoted to major because there was a desperate shortage of officers with combat experience. He was sent to Guadalcanal where he led a Corsair squadron for a month without any startling results, probably because he did not get the necessary opportunities. He was then sent on leave in Australia and when he returned, there was no flying post open for him so he spent the summer of 1943 doing various ground duties with increasing ill humour.

Eventually Boyington bullied his superiors into letting him put together a squadron with spare aircraft and pilots from the replacement pool. His squadron became known as the 'Black sheep' supposedly because they were an outfit of misfits whom nobody else wanted. In the autumn of 1943 he led this squadron to glory in the battles in the sky over the western Solomons, where they amassed a hatful of victories and he himself scored 26, which made him the joint highest scorer in the Marine Corps in the whole war. Because he was much older than the average pilot he was known as 'Pappy' Boyington. He was such a cool customer that he used to take a book along to read in dull parts of the flight between the battles. In January 1944 he was shot down on a mission to the Rabaul area and posted missing. It was thought he was unlikely to have survived the crash of his plane. But he *had* survived, though injured, and was rescued by a Japanese submarine. He spent the next two years in captivity and in March 1944 he was 'posthumously' awarded the Congressional Medal of Honor by a U.S. military who were convinced he was dead. The Japanese never informed anyone that they were holding him so his discovery, alive, in August 1945 was a surprise to all. One surmises that his unexpected survival put a few official noses out of joint.

Boyington's post-war career was blighted by his alcoholism but he wrote a best-

The use of paratroops was a novelty of the Second World War. Here Douglas C-47 transport aircraft drop paratroops on Nadzab in New Guinea.
© Imperial War Museum (EA 2759)

selling memoir of his wartime experiences[viii] and a television serial was produced about the Black sheep which made him a household name in the United States where he is probably the best known of all the U.S. aces the war produced.

At the same time as the fighting in the Solomons a parallel campaign was being conducted in New Guinea. Allied air forces consisted of the American 5th Air Force with headquarters at Brisbane in Australia and the Royal Australian Air Force. General George C. Kenney was the commander of 5th and also overall commander of Allied air forces in the southwest Pacific. Their principal base for operations in 1942 was the twin airfields of Port Moresby. These airfields, as we have already seen, came under repeated bombing attack by the Japanese based on the north side of the island principally at Lae. During most of 1942 a medley of Japanese units including the Tainan Air Group was based here and at other bases on the north coast but at the end of the year, in an administrative re-shuffle, New Guinea became the responsibility of the Japanese Army and the 12th Air Division was based here. From the middle of 1943 the area came under the jurisdiction of the new 4th Air Army with headquarters in Rabaul.

The Royal Australian Air Force, though a wholly independent body, shared the values and traditions of the much larger R.A.F.. In 1939 it consisted of just 12 squadrons. It flew a mixture of American and British aircraft: the British Beaufort and Beaufighter and the American A-20 Boston and P-40E Kittyhawk. The Beaufort was a torpedo plane similar to a Blenheim, which was made by the same company. Many Beauforts were in fact produced in Australia under licence along with a small number of an indigenous fighter plane called the Boomerang, made by the Commonwealth Aircraft Corporation. Despite its independence the R.A.A.F. had sent men to help out in the Mediterranean and European theatres. Some were on loan to the R.A.F. and others fought in Australian units sent to help out in those other theatres. When the casualties suffered by Bomber Command were totted up at the end of the war it was found that nine per cent, some 4,000, had been Australians. This commitment to other theatres meant that the Australian Air Force in the Pacific was not the force that it might have been. Nevertheless it played a significant part: in spring 1943 it contributed 33 of the 69 squadrons in action in the southwest Pacific. The toughness and fearlessness of Australian servicemen of all kinds was legendary.

'No one ever returns alive from New Guinea' was a common saying in the Japanese Army and it summed up the attitude of the average soldier and pilot to the 'green desert' in which whole units could disappear without trace.[ix] New Guinea was for the Japanese what the 'Russian Front' was for the Germans: a hell on earth which claimed the lives of most who ventured there. A typical New Guinea story is that of Captain Shigeo Nango. Nango was from a distinguished military family and his elder brother was a much respected fighter leader with the navy, killed in China in 1938. Nango himself went to New Guinea in July 1942 and fought there till his death in January 1944 while attacking a formation of B-24s. In that time he shot down 15 American aircraft, a considerable feat considering that for much of the time he was flying against superior aircraft in superior numbers. He was one of the few Japanese pilots whose victories were all won in New Guinea. He was so well thought of that at the time of his death he was about to be recalled to Japan to head the army's principal fighter school.[x]

One result of the bombing of Port Moresby, inaccurate though it was, was that it was difficult to base bombers there with any degree of safety. One must bear in mind that bombers require a great degree more care on the ground than do fighters and they make bigger and easier targets. The consequence was that bomber aircraft were often based in the Australian mainland and flew a shuttle run to Port Moresby before flying on to hit targets on the north coast. This may have saved aircraft but was a punishing regime for the crews. Moreover, in 1942 the lack of fighters with sufficient range meant that much of their work had to be done without escort.

After the Battle of the Coral Sea had ended hopes of a seaborne attack on Port Moresby the Japanese considered the possibility of getting to the south coast of the island by land. This involved crossing the rugged, mountainous, jungle-clad interior and there was only one place where such a crossing was feasible, though barely so. This was the Kokoda Trail which ran from the north coast at Buna to the south coast at Port Moresby. It was a foot trail through the jungle, running right through the Owen Stanley Mountains that formed New Guinea's backbone. At its highest the trail reached an altitude in excess of 7,000 feet.

Japanese forces landed at Buna on July 21st 1942 and began the march across the island. From the start they were harassed by Allied aircraft and attempts to bring in reinforcements from Rabaul were fiercely resisted. On July 29th a transport ship was sunk and on the 31st a whole convoy turned back in the face of the air attacks. Japanese fighters were unable to provide adequate protection. Gradually, mile by mile, the Japanese advanced along the trail. As part of this offensive the Japanese attacked the Allied air bases at Milne Bay on the eastern tip of New Guinea in August 1942. Geography made these bases very important because whoever controlled them controlled the sea for many miles in all directions. Their capture would seriously reduce Allied air power over New Guinea and offer the Japanese a chance of advancing to Moresby along the south coast. But the Australians had a much stronger garrison at Milne Bay than the Japanese realized and they were given outstanding support by the Australian Air Force, particularly two squadrons of Kittyhawks used to strafe men and ships. After hard fighting the Japanese called off the attack on 5th September.

It was also in September that the Japanese attack along the Kokoda trail came to a halt. The leading troops were only 25 miles from Port Moresby but this fact is deceptive, for the Japanese were exhausted and half-starved and in receipt of the merest trickle of supplies, while the Australians whose lines of communication had shortened with every mile they retreated, had been reinforced and were stronger than ever before. At this point Imperial Headquarters in Japan decided that it could not support major campaigns in New Guinea and Guadalcanal at the same time and that the New Guinea campaign must therefore end. This was a simple decision because a glance at the geography shows that defeat in the Solomons would isolate troops in New Guinea, however successful they were.

The Allies now went over to the offensive but the Japanese decision did not mean that resistance was at an end. The Japanese army stubbornly resisted the steady Allied advance right up to the end of the war. In November 1942 the Allies attacked Buna which they finally captured in January 1943 after a bitter struggle.

In April 1943 the Japanese decided to reinforce their bases at Lae and Salamaua which were the obvious next targets for attack. A convoy sailed from Rabaul for Salamaua consisting of eight transports and eight destroyers as escort. On board the transports were 7,000 troops. In a running battle lasting three days, swarms of Allied aircraft from both the 5th Air Force and the R.A.A.F. broke through the Japanese air escort with ease and sank all the transports and half of the destroyers. Of the troops only some 800 were rescued and landed without equipment at Lae. The battle ended with a prolonged attack by Allied aircraft and PT boats (small torpedo boats) on the survivors of the sinkings who were bombed and machine gunned in the water. This attack was contrary to all the laws of war.[xi] Attempts have been made to defend it on various grounds over the years, but there is no real justification save that the nature of the Pacific war was brutal. The Japanese themselves were guilty of many egregious breaches of the laws of war to put the matter at its mildest. Indeed one has to accept that western ideas about such laws were very difficult to apply in the Pacific.

Salamaua was duly attacked in June and Lae in September 1943. In early 1944 there were landings in the Admiralty Islands and on the southern end of New Britain itself, upon whose northern end stood Rabaul. By this time the Allied domination of the air in the area was near complete and Rabaul could be pounded in a prolonged air offensive with little opposition. In February 1944 the new Commander in Chief of the Imperial Navy, Admiral Mineichi Koga ordered all naval air forces to abandon Rabaul because their continued presence was achieving nothing but the destruction of large numbers of their own aircraft.

No account of the war in this theatre would be complete without mention of Richard Bong. By war's end Bong had shot down 40 Japanese planes which made him the leading ace of the western Allies. His tally began over Port Moresby in December 1942 and concluded in the Philippines in December 1944. Mild and shy on the ground, Bong was a killing machine once he was in the air. He was given the Congressional Medal of Honor and sent home to keep him safe. In a sad irony he became a test pilot for Lockheed and was killed in an accident on August 6th 1945.[xii]

CHAPTER NINETEEN

Africa to Italy

In May 1942 the German offensive in North Africa rolled forward. Although Malta had not been captured the air assault on the island in the first five months of the year had suppressed its offensive capabilities to the extent that adequate, though barely adequate, supplies were reaching Rommel in Africa. There had been a build-up of air strength at the front so that German and Italian air forces combined could put up 600 aircraft. Amongst the Italian pilots was Ugo Drago, now a veteran. On 9th June he claimed two Spitfires shot down above the island of Pantelleria. These were victories five and six and made him an ace. He was lucky to be still in business: in March he had attacked a truck that proved to be loaded with ammunition. The resulting explosion severely damaged his aircraft and it took all his skill to fly it back to his base where it was declared a write-off.

General Kesselring, commanding Airfleet Two, moved his headquarters to North Africa in order to be closer to the front and the move signaled the importance of this offensive which had Cairo and then the whole Middle East as its objective. Air support was as thorough as could be managed with most aircraft flying two to three sorties per day. It rapidly became apparent that the key to the battle of Gazala was a strongpoint at a place called Bir Hacheim which was manned by Free French units. This strongpoint held out for nine days and the whole force of Stukas was turned against it. The Axis offensive was successful and on July 20th 1942 Tobruk was taken.

From here on air support faded away and the reason was entirely a matter of supply. The Gazala battle had taken far greater toll of fuel stocks than had been expected and Allied strength on Malta was recovering from its battering. Moreover, every mile that the Afrika Korps moved to the east extended the length that supplies had to come. The capture of Tobruk did not relieve the problem because its harbour facilities were too devastated to handle more than a trickle of cargo and, once in German hands, it was a constant target of Allied air attack. The fact that Airfleet Two was now desperate to obtain adequate fuel and spare parts led Kesselring to complain that he was nothing but a glorified quartermaster.[i] After the Battle of Gazala there was a pause for recuperation by both sides and then Rommel launched what was to be the deciding attack toward Cairo at El Alamein (generally known as the Battle of Alam Halfa or First Alamein). At this stage the ability of the Luftwaffe and the R.A. to give support was very limited. Malta was back in full operation and aircraft based there were decimating Axis shipping trying to get supplies to Africa. It was apparent that the decision to forego an invasion of the island had been a bad mistake. Rommel's attack failed and another pause ensued while both sides gathered their strength.

On the eve of the great British offensive the Germans and Italians had only some 300 aircraft available in Egypt and very little fuel for them. They had another 400 in Sicily and Sardinia but these were too far away to have any influence on the battle. The Allies could muster 550 in the Western Desert Air Force which were mainly fighters and ground attack aircraft. On top of this there were another 650 aircraft under Egyptian H.Q. and the Middle Eastern H.Q. and these were either able to participate in the battle directly or were in a position to harry the extended Axis supply lines. Thus the situation was that the Axis forces were totally outnumbered and faced with an enemy who was not encumbered by supply shortages. In addition it must be remembered that the American landings in the west of North Africa were shortly to introduce a whole new air force. Allied aircraft types were no longer inferior to the German and in particular there was a wing of Spitfires somehow prized out of the hands of Fighter Command in the homeland. Most of the British pilots were now veterans and their junior leaders were men with years of experience.

An example is the commander of 260 Squadron which flew Kittyhawks. He was Squadron Leader 'Pedro' Hanbury who joined 602 Squadron at the outbreak of war, flew in the Battle of Britain and by this time had eight victories to his credit. His nickname was the result of his somewhat swarthy, mustachioed appearance but he was, in fact, as British as could be, being a member of the Hanbury brewing family educated at Eton College. He had been in Africa since 1941 and had been wounded in a dogfight over Syria. He had been decorated with the D.S.O. and the D.F.C.: there was not much you could teach this wily old bird about flying. He was constantly in action during the battle and in the follow-up advance. Finally he went home on leave to get married in the spring of 1943. On the trip back to Africa he was a passenger in a transport plane when it was shot down by a long range fighter and he was killed. He had been married ten days.[ii]

It is hardly surprising then that the Luftwaffe and the R.A. were not a significant factor in the battle of El Alamein which started on 23rd October 1942 and lasted into early November. To make matters worse for them one of the first acts of the battle was a series of raids on their airfields by the British which did heavy damage and seriously diminished such impact as they could have. Throughout the battle the Allies had complete air superiority. Rommel made a celebrated comment on the difficulty of trying to cope with such a situation: 'Anyone who has to fight, even with the most modern weapons, against an enemy in complete control of the air, fights like a savage against modern European troops, under the same handicaps and with the same chances of success.'[iii] Rommel found it hard to grasp that the Luftwaffe's failure was purely a matter of lack of supplies and relations between him and

Kesselring, never cordial, sank to a new low. With the end of the battle and the German retreat, the Axis air forces suffered from the usual collapse of air forces in retreat as ground crew and even slightly damaged aircraft were left behind and confusion reigned supreme in the precipitate withdrawal westward through Egypt and Libya. This was a time when Tedder and Coningham were able to hone the skills of their air force in the difficult science of air-ground co-operation.

On 8th November 1942 came the Anglo-American landings of Operation Torch. Allied troops landed on the Atlantic coast of Morocco at three places near Casablanca and at Oran and Algiers in the Mediterranean on the coast of Algeria. The Algeria landing was a mainly British effort with a small contingent of Americans to make it less offensive to the Vichy French. Air cover was provided from Gibraltar and as soon as an airfield was taken 332 Wing of Fighter Command, a unit of mixed Spitfires and Hurricanes, flew in to provide resident air protection. It was the first constituent part of what was to be called Eastern Air Command and was in due course to encompass the whole R.A.F. in Africa. The other two invasion sites were the preserve of the Americans and their air component for operations in Africa was the newly formed Twelfth Air Force. Its commander was Jimmy Doolittle of Tokyo raid fame.

At first air cover for the two Atlantic coast landings was provided by fighters flying from aircraft carriers that were part of the invasion fleet. There were five fleet carriers and seven light carriers accompanying the landing force which between them could field in the region of 150 fighter planes. This was the largest gathering of aircraft carriers the European war was to see. Of the major ships one, Ranger, was an elderly American veteran and the other four were from the Royal Navy: Argus, Formidable, Furious and Victorious. Each of the landing sites was specifically chosen to be close to an airfield and as these were taken, planes from the carriers were able to fly in and land there and both fighters and bombers flew in from Gibraltar and Great Britain as well. The two airfields near Oran were to be captured by paratroops flown all the way from Britain, but bad weather over Spain and the problems associated with operating at extreme range reduced the operation to confusion and most of the aircraft had to land in a dry lake bed some miles to the west of the target. The paratroops took the airfields none the less but would almost certainly have failed had they faced more resolute opposition. This was the first major Allied paratroop operation and it could only be considered a qualified success.

At Casablanca and Oran there was resistance from the Vichy French forces and French aircraft attacked the fleet, though without causing serious damage. French Dewoitine fighters also clashed with British Fleet Air Arm planes and gave a good account of themselves. But on the evening of 8th November an armistice was signed and fighting officially ceased though some French elements continued to resist for several days. During the afternoon of the 8th and again next day, small groups of German bombers attacked and sank one of the transports. The worst loss however, occurred on the 15th when H.M.S. Avenger, one of the escort carriers involved in the landings, was torpedoed off Gibraltar by U-155. The torpedo struck near where the bombs for the ship's aircraft were stored and the result was a violent explosion. The ship sank in three minutes and of her crew of over 550, only 17 were saved.

Operation Torch took the Germans completely by surprise. They had got wind of the preparations but had supposed that what was in the offing was either a major reinforcement of Malta or an attack on Dakar on the West African coast. It was too late now to contest Algeria far less Morocco but they immediately began a massive reinforcement of Tunisia with both land and air units. On November 8th 1942 there were 400 Luftwaffe planes based in Sicily and Sardinia and 500 Italian. Between then and December another 400 planes flew into the theatre and were based either at these two places or in Tunisia. This reinforcement was mainly at the cost of the Russian front though there was also a transfer of bomber formations from northern Norway that took much of the sting out of the German threat to Arctic convoys to Russia. Tunisia was made a separate Luftwaffe command and General Martin Harlinghausen was put in charge of it. Harlinghausen was an ace anti-shipping pilot who had sunk over 125,000 tons of Allied shipping in his career (at least 30 ships) and been awarded the Knight's Cross. He had been the Commander-in-Chief of the Atlantic front before his appointment to Tunisia. He remained in a command position in the Mediterraneean until June 1943 when he was removed for disagreeing with his superiors. A strong-minded and independent man, he crossed swords with Goering in 1944 and his career in the post-war Luftwaffe came to an abrupt end after another clash with the authorities.

By the end of the year the Allies were in the mountains of western Tunisia and the Eighth Army and the Western Desert Air Force were closing in on Tripoli, the capital of Libya. The Americans had founded yet another air force: 9th Air Force had its headquarters in Egypt from the end of November 1942 and operated in tandem with the Desert Air Force. The winter in this part of North Africa brings storms, heavy rain and floods and the primitive airfields in the area were universally waterlogged bringing air operations to a virtual halt until better conditions were brought in by spring weather.

In the spring the Allies opened a two pronged offensive against Tunisia with overwhelming force. On the western frontier the British and American air forces had some 600 aircraft and the Desert Air Force on the southern frontier had much the same, together with a similar number in rear areas. The Germans had under 200 aircraft in Tunisia itself, largely because of the lack of suitable airfields and they found themselves under remorseless attack by Allied fighter-bombers. One of the victims of those fighter-bombers was Claus von Stauffenberg fighting with the 10th Panzer Division. He was gravely wounded when driving between units in his staff car. It was he, of course, who led the unsuccessful coup against Hitler the next year.

German supplies and reinforcements all had to come from Sicily by sea or air and were now subject to interdiction by the numerically superior Allied air forces.

Allied superiority was such that scarcely a ship could make the crossing in safety. Some aircraft did so though it was a high-risk activity. At this time there came briefly to the front of the stage a strange German aircraft called the Messerschmitt Me323. This was the biggest transport aircraft used by any combatant in the war. It had six engines and a nose composed of double doors that could open up to admit vehicles. It was ideal for shifting large cargoes for short distances and therefore excellently suited to the Sicily-Tunis run. Being very large, very slow and having the manoeuverability of a bandstand, it was very vulnerable when attacked and on 22nd April a flight of 27 of these craft was intercepted by Allied fighters and 21 were shot down despite the efforts of the escort.

Assaulted from two sides and desperately short of supplies, the German position in Tunisia was hopeless. On 7th May 1943 Tunis was captured and six days later the fighting ceased as the surviving Axis troops surrendered. From the start of May the Luftwaffe had been flying men and machines out of Tunisia to save what it could. While taking part in this evacuation Lieutenant Ernst-Wilhelm Reinert, one of the 'experten' with over 100 victories to his name, shot down an Allied fighter plane while carrying two passengers in his single seat Me109:[iv] an extraordinary feat given that the only way to fit three people in an Me109 was to put one in the baggage compartment and the other on the pilot's lap. Some aircraft were saved but the last six months in Africa had cost the Luftwaffe the shocking total of 2,400[v]. Harlinghausen now wanted to give his forces a period of recuperation but the powers of the Luftwaffe would not permit this and when he complained he was removed from his post.

Harlinghausen was replaced by General Alfred Bulowius, a man who has left little mark on history. In fact the debacle in Tunisia led to a general reconfiguration of command in the Mediterranean, whereby Kesselring became overall commander-in-chief and the command of air operations in Italy and Sicily went to Wolfram von Richthofen who was transferred from Russia against his will. His comment on the move was: 'This is a theatre where I can lose my honour and my reputation.'[vi] This was part of a general housecleaning of the Mediterranean Luftwaffe whose performance in the last stages of the North Africa campaign had been ineffective. Various administrative reforms were made and control of units and operational planning tightened. Adolf Galland, now Inspector of Fighters, was brought in to monitor and improve performance. The remaining Stuka units, which had been found to be simply too vulnerable, were transferred to the Balkans. By July the Luftwaffe had a little over 1,200 aircraft available in the Mediterranean. The R.A. had another 1,200 or so but their value was limited because so many of them were outdated types and Italian morale was low.

The Allies' next target was, inevitably, Sicily. They now had 267 squadrons in the Mediterranean which added up to 3,400 aircraft. Not all were based within reach of Sicily and throughout the Mediterranean theatre serviceability rates were only in the region of 60 per cent so that there were in the region of 1,300-1,400 aircraft available to support the invasion. The same considerations diminished the Axis figure for available aircraft in the same proportion however, so that the Allies had a comfortable if not overwhelming superiority of numbers.

A major campaign of deception was undertaken to persuade the Germans that the next target was, in fact, Greece or Crete and not Sicily at all and this was very successful and resulted in the Luftwaffe dividing its forces so that resources were wasted in the eastern Mediterranean where there was, in reality, no threat at all.

The Luftwaffe and the R.A. were in a difficult position in that there were limited airfield facilities on Sicily and what there were, were heavily and constantly bombed by the Allies. To overcome this, the squadrons based there moved around but the result was that they were more or less permanently in a state of travel-induced disorganization and did very little combat flying. Other squadrons were based on Corsica or Italy itself but, for the fighters, this caused problems of distance. Fighters were what was needed over Sicily but fighters have the shortest range. Luftwaffe bombers were increasingly ineffective. There were enough of them to cause serious problems for the Allies but their performance was very poor. Such missions as were mounted suffered losses in excess of ten per cent due to poor navigation over long distances, let alone enemy action. The reason was the steadily declining quality of bomber crews due to months of heavy losses. The skills required by such crews are more complex and take longer to acquire than those of the fighter pilot.

On the evening of 9th July Luftwaffe reconnaissance planes spotted convoys heading for Sicily but when the troops landed the next morning under a huge air umbrella, there was no Axis opposition in the air at all. It was a triumph for Allied airpower though it must be admitted that it was more a triumph of numbers and the accidents of geography than of skill. Later in the day Axis bombers appeared but they faced overwhelming fighter opposition and 27 were shot down on that first day. Nevertheless they kept up their attacks despite constant heavy losses partly due to a lack of escorting fighters and their strength drained inexorably away. Von Richthofen devoted much of his time to long telephone calls to Goering and Jeschonnek to beg for reinforcements.vii He was surprisingly successful, most of the reinforcements coming from the eastern Mediterranean area where it was now clear they were not needed. On Sicily itself the Luftwaffe and the R.A. were soon reduced to extinction. By 18th July there were just 12 operational German aircraft on the island. To von Richthofen's relief Galland was recalled to Germany. Relations between the two men were not good and Galland's role as official gadfly was a recipe for discord.

It was unthinkable from a political point of view that Sicily not be defended but the Germans were well aware that an island in a sea dominated by the enemies' navies under a sky dominated by their air forces was a potentially deadly trap and they rapidly adjusted their thinking to concentrate on a withdrawal to the mainland after a brief show of resistance. This was achieved with extraordinary skill by ferrying troops across the Straits of Messina under an unprecedented umbrella of artillery sited on the shores and able to fire at attacking ships or aeroplanes. The straits at their narrowest are barely three miles wide and the guns could cover this short distance with considerable accuracy. For once air power was, at least partly, defeated. Low level attacks were suicidal. Heavy bombers could have pounded the ports on either shore very effectively and from a height at which they stood a chance of survival but, instead, the heavy bombers were used in raids against railway marshaling yards outside Rome. This was a politically inspired decision based on the hope that the arrival of the war on the capital's doorstep might induce an Italian capitulation. This hope was not immediately realized and the bombers' absence facilitated a near-magical Werhmacht escape act.

Nevertheless, for the Axis air forces the Sicily campaign was another disaster. The Luftwaffe lost 600 aircraft and the R.A. 400 and only some 40% of these losses were even incurred in the air. Most were aircraft caught on the ground by Allied bombers. And it was all to no purpose: Sicily was lost and the Allied air juggernaut was hardly inconvenienced. On top of this the pressure of Allied bombing on the western front led to the transfer of another 200 aircraft to northwestern Europe. The Luftwaffe was down to 880 aircraft available in the whole Mediterranean theatre and some 600 in the Italian area. Italy would never again be anything more than a secondary front as the American bomber offensive against the German homeland sucked in aircraft from all other fronts.

Even before Sicily was abandoned, the Germans were working to improve airfields and infrastructure in Italy to handle their aircraft. They guessed that there would be little pause before the Allies moved on from Sicily to attack Italy. Much of the far South of Italy was effectively 'out of bounds' because the attentions of British and American bombers rendered any improvements nugatory.

When the British invaded Calabria (the 'toe' of Italy) on 3rd September 1943 there was little German response however because their plan was to make their stand further north. There were some sorties by fighter-bombers but the main bomber force was held in reserve. When the Americans landed at Salerno near Naples on the 8th however, it was quite a different story. There was an all-out German effort to throw the Americans back into the sea and every available aircraft was thrown into the battle. This was a bigger effort than anything seen since the spring of the year before when Malta was under attack. A new weapon was used here: the radio-controlled bomb which was released in the normal way but then guided by the bomb-aimer to its target by line of sight through a radio receiver in the bomb which was able to receive signals from the aircraft and then send signals to alter the setting of the bomb's fins. This was a particularly effective weapon against ships and the main emphasis of the Luftwaffe attacks was on close support of the infantry on the one hand and anti-shipping work on the other.

The close support operations were not a success. Allied fighters kept up a constant patrol over the beachhead in three layers with Mustangs at low level, P-38 Lightnings at medium level and Spitfires at high level. Against such heavy defence the Luftwaffe could achieve little.

On the other hand the anti-shipping work was particularly effective. The battleship Warspite was hit and left dead in the water. It had to be towed away to undergo months of repair and two U.S. cruisers, Philadelphia and Savannah, were damaged. The worst blow however, was an indirect one. These losses and the appearance of the new bomb so worried the Allies that the whole aircraft carrier force of five ships was withdrawn from the battle as a precaution.

On land the Germans came close to throwing the Americans back into the sea. The main culprit here was the British Eighth Army which was supposed to move to the support of the landings but did so in such a dilatory and lackadaisical manner as to throw the success of the whole operation into doubt. The critical move was the decision to throw into the battle every aircraft that the allies could lay their hands on throughout the Mediterranean. All of these, including heavy bombers were employed in attacking the German army. Fighter-bombers roved up and down the lines without cease all day and bombers hit bridges and railway facilities behind the lines to prevent supplies and reinforcements reaching the front. Even the roads were bombed: 91 Wellingtons dropped 164 tons of bombs on a five mile stretch of road near the ancient ruins of Pompeii and left it completely unusable.[viii]

The weight of Allied airpower was finally equal to any setbacks and the landing was not repulsed. Not surprisingly the Luftwaffe effort cost heavy casualties and the concentration on the Salerno landings left Montgomery and the British relatively unmolested until their approach to the major complex of airfields around Foggia forced the Germans to abandon that excellent group of airfields. The Luftwaffe withdrew to positions north of Rome from which it was difficult to make much impact on the Salerno battle at the greatly increased range. But the Germans had a sound, prepared defensive position on the ground and the war in Italy was ready to stagnate for some months as the onset of winter added to the difficulties of campaigning.

During this period the Luftwaffe operated a policy of conservation and their operations were strictly limited. There was virtually no interference on the battlefield itself at all. This was not as serious a failing as might be imagined because the Wehrmacht was fighting a strictly defensive campaign in which its greatest ally was the rough nature of the country. There were no situations in which air power made no difference but this was as close to being an example of one as you were likely to find. The main effort was directed against shipping as it was considered, quite rightly, that an inferior air force must concentrate on a vulnerable enemy bottleneck and this was one such. Raids were conducted at night but were infrequent and inefficient with many planes not finding their targets. This, once more, was a direct result of the declining standard of training amongst bomber crews. There was one outstanding success however, on the night of 2nd December when 100 bombers, principally Ju88s set out to bomb the port of Bari, the most important landing point for Allied supplies. The bombers were aided by the fact that the dockyard lights had been deliberately kept on, despite the risk, in order to speed unloading. An additional bonus for the raiders was the fact that an ammunition ship blew up at its berth and added to the destruction. In all 17 ships were sunk and 34,000 tons of cargo destroyed. It was three weeks before Bari was back in full operation. Eisenhower described this raid as: 'The greatest single loss from air action inflicted upon us during the entire period of Allied campaigning in Europe.'[ix]

The Luftwaffe was not to repeat such a feat however because almost all the remaining bomber groups in Italy were now transferred to the western front to raid England, and Italy was left devoid of any significant force of medium bombers.

The end of the year saw a major re-organization of Allied command as Eisenhower, Tedder, Montgomery, Spaatz and Doolittle were all transferred to northern Europe in anticipation of the D-Day invasion. The new commander-in-Chief of the Mediterranean was Sir Henry Maitland Wilson, a man not noted for his grasp of air power. Fortunately that did not matter very much because Ira Eaker was his second-in-command and overall commander of air forces and he had a thorough grasp. The R.A.F. contingent was commanded by Sir John Slessor who had been in charge of R.A.F. Coastal Command. Slessor was a most impressive man. He suffered from weak legs as a result of childhood polio and was turned down by the army in 1914 but managed to join the Royal Flying Corps the following year by using family connections. He flew against the Turks in the Egyptian theatre where he was wounded and suffered the removal of a bullet from his thigh without benefit of anaesthetic, but after the consumption of large quantities of champagne and brandy. He later said of this episode that the operation was bad but the 'hangover was really awful'.[x] After the Second War he rose to be Chief of the Air Staff.

The invasion of Italy had led to her dropping out of the war in early September 1943. On the mainland the German response was simply to occupy the country and treat it as part of the German empire and this was easily achieved because there were large numbers of German troops already present but elsewhere in the eastern Mediterranean there were localities garrisoned by the Italian army that were at risk of seizure by the Allies. The Germans moved with great speed and efficiency to counter this setback. 100 aircraft, mainly medium bombers and Stukas, were transferred from Russia and used to support attacks on the islands of Cephalonia and Corfu and the town of Split with the intention of making the Adriatic secure and forestalling any Allied attempt to invade the Dalmatian coast. This was done outside the range of Allied fighters and it allowed the Luftwaffe to show, once again, just how effective it could be when it had control of the sky.

In the Aegean the islands of Leros, Kos Samos and Syros, which were part of the Cyclades, had passed into Allied hands. Kos and Leros were recaptured by direct assault with the Luftwaffe very effectively suppressing A.A. guns and other artillery and causing heavy casualties. Syros and Samos were then evacuated without a fight and the Aegean was once more securely under German control. Arguably this was the last wholly effective German offensive of the war and air power was the key to its success.

At the start of November 1943 the Allies separated out their heavy bombers and put them together into a new 15th Air Force based initially at the excellent Foggia airfields. There were some 400 of them at the start but they were steadily reinforced until by the middle of 1944 there were nine wings of heavy bombers totaling more than 1,000 aircraft. The great majority of the aircraft used were B-24 Liberators. For the rest of 1943 this force was under the command of the ubiquitous General Doolittle but at the start of 1944 the command went to Nathan Twining when Doolittle was transferred to northwest Europe in preparation for D-Day. Twining, from a military family of long standing, came from command of the 13th Air Force in the Pacific and was very much at home commanding a force of B-24s.

15th Air Force was the southern sister of 8th in England and it struck at strategic targets in the South of Europe as the 8th did in the North. Indeed attempts were made to co-ordinate the operations of the two air forces but they were not very successful except in the broadest sense because the communications of the time were not adequate to overcome the obstacle of distance. The power of 15th was not much less though its recognition does not compare with that of 8th. Historically it has always been treated as very much the poor relation, partly because of it being further from the perceived centre of the European war and partly because it never faced the same degree of opposition, though no one could claim that it had an easy existence. Between the last months of 1943 and the end of the war it bombed major targets as far apart as south Germany and Rumania, taking in Poland and Silesia on the way. In particular it made repeated attacks on the Messerschmitt factory at Wiener Neustadt south of Vienna which was too far from Britain for the 8th to reach and it also hit targets in Hungary and the industrial belt of Upper Silesia to which the same consideration applied. Perhaps its most famous and important target was the oil refinery at Ploiesti in Rumania.

The Ploiesti installation supplied at least a quarter of the oil products required by the German war economy. It was therefore exactly the kind of economic bottleneck upon which the Allies sought to concentrate their strategic bombing effort. During the war it was raided numerous times but it was not until 1943 that it was possible for it to be hit with sufficient force to do it serious damage. That summer a force of B-24s was brought together especially for the purpose and based at Benghazi in Libya where it trained extensively to carry out a low level raid on the Ploiesti refineries. The use of heavy bombers at low level was a novelty and a high risk policy but the thinking was, first that a low level attack neutralized the heavy flak guns which were designed to shoot high and, second, that the very considerable defences would be taken by surprise. It was accepted by General Lewis Brereton, in charge of the planning, that the raiding force might suffer as much as 50 percent casualties but the risk was considered worth taking in order to knock out an installation as vital as Ploiesti. It must be recalled that at this time the accepted thinking was still that strategic bombing could destroy industrial targets permanently with one attack.

The attack was made on August 1st 1943 by 179 aircraft. One crashed on take-off and two flew into the sea for unexplained reasons but presumably mechanical failures. Another was damaged early on in the flight by a German fighter and subsequently also ditched in the Mediterranean. The remaining 175 planes reached the target and bombed it. The scene over the refineries was like something from Dante's Inferno as dense smoke mixed with incessant explosions. The attackers took heavy casualties as they met a storm of fire from the flak guns. Despite the furious defence, the attack was pressed home with exemplary bravery such that five Congressional Medals of Honor were later awarded to crewmen of the bombers: more than for any other air action in U.S. history. Two of the posthumous recipients were Lieutenant Colonel Addison Baker and Major John Jerstad flying a plane called 'Hell's Wench'. (It was an Air Force tradition to name the bomber you flew.) Flak hit them as they approached the target and set the plane on fire. They could have attempted a belly landing in a field but instead kept on because they were the lead plane in their formation and it was their job to co-ordinate the bombing. They then climbed to gain enough height for the rest of the crew to bail out but lost control of their aircraft which dived into the refinery below.[xi]

Some 55 aircraft of the attacking force did not return home and of those that did, 56 had suffered varying degrees of damage. Such losses could not be sustained more than occasionally, much less on a permanent basis but they were less than Brereton had feared. On the other hand though great damage was done to the refineries it was far from fatal. The complex at Ploiesti consisted of ten separate refineries and the raid only hit half of them although it did strike the larger ones. Moreover most were working at less than full capacity for various reasons and could subsequently boost production to compensate for damage elsewhere. Above all, as we have already seen, the repair capacity of such targets was critically underestimated by planners on all sides in the Second World War.

The Americans were quick to realize that the job was not finished and repeated attacks were subsequently made on the refineries, almost all of them by heavy bombers of 15th Air Force flying in the conventional high altitude manner. In fact this was the best way to hit Ploiesti because it was a big target easily identified even from a great height. During the first nine months of 1944, no less than 24 more raids were carried out and when the Russians arrived at the refineries in September they found them completely ruined.

The Luftwaffe did what it could to combat the operations of the 15th Air Force and set up a special fighter district in the north Italian plain to co-ordinate aerial defence along the bombers' route over the Alps and into south Germany. But there simply were never the resources available for its sorties to make much difference.

For the crews of the 15th the principal enemy was flak together with weather and the very long distances they had to fly which took their toll of men and aeroplanes. Not every plane came down in the middle of heroic battle. On 27th May 1944 a mission was flown against Montpelier in France. One of the participating B-24s was 'Delayed Action' flown by pilot Ken Harrison and his crew. This was their first mission and as they approached the French coast one of their engines failed. They turned round to return to base and on the way home passed over the island of Elba where Harrison jettisoned the bombs, but they were hit by flak and the co-pilot was badly wounded. Two of the crew carried him to the radio compartment and there worked to stabilize his condition. Meanwhile the flak put out another engine and the aircraft began to lose height. The crew threw out everything moveable to lighten the plane but to no avail. Harrison knew he would never make his base and tried to put down at an emergency airstrip near Anzio. He and his men could have baled out: it was accepted procedure to do so if a B-24 lost two engines because it became hard to control. Their problem, of course, was that the wounded co-pilot could not bale out and they were not going to abandon him to certain death. Unfortunately Harrison lost control of the plane on the landing approach and it hit the ground, disintegrated and burst into flames. The co-pilot and the two men helping him were killed, two other crew members were injured but returned to duty within weeks and three men including Harrison were so severely injured they had to be taken back to the U.S. for lengthy stays in hospital, their military careers over. One man escaped unhurt and was assigned to another crew. On his very next mission he was drowned when his aircraft had to ditch: he was the only casualty.[xii]

The stalemate on the ground in Italy in late 1943 caused Allied commanders to cast around for a means of cutting the Gordian knot. They decided to launch a second invasion behind the German lines at Anzio, close to Rome. They considered that if it was well handled Rome must quickly fall.

The Germans were taken by surprise by this move because their strength in the western Mediterranean had sunk to a bare 300 aircraft in Italy and the South of France and their few reconnaissance aircraft led a highly dangerous existence constantly harried by Allied fighters. After their coming so close to throwing back the Salerno landing, they did not think that the Allies would try another landing and particularly not in the middle of winter. Fortunately for them they had troops on the ground near the site of the landing and the Luftwaffe reacted with its customary energy. Nearly 200 medium bombers were moved to Italy and the southern French coast brought from the Channel front and from Greece. They began immediate and intensive operations against Allied shipping using the new radio-controlled bombs. Such was Allied air superiority that the attacks had to be conducted by night and the new and under-trained Luftwaffe pilots were not up to the job. They suffered heavy losses but no significant damage was done to shipping.

The German army essayed three counter-attacks against the landing. The first was launched in poor weather and that explains the very limited performance of the Luftwaffe ground attack aircraft. The second was launched in the middle of February 1944 when the weather was favourable for flying and the Luftwaffe at first carried out energetic operations in support but after two days losses were such that the whole effort tailed off and when a third assault was launched at the end of the month, again in inclement weather, the Luftwaffe's contribution was zero. The landings were contained however, and the Allied dream of taking Rome by a quick coup evaporated. Though not very effective it must be admitted that German air operations contributed to the Allied caution and mismanagement that made this landing a failure and caused a resumption of the stalemate.

It might be mentioned that the tasks of ground attack and close support for

A B-17 Flying Fortress over Monte Cassino. Allied progress in Italy was slow despite air superiority.
©Imperial War Museum (IA 15552)

ground troops had by now been largely taken away from the Stuka which was, at last, wholly obsolete and could not live in an environment where the enemy had air superiority. Its place was taken by the Focke Wulf 190 fighter. This versatile aeroplane was adapted for ground attack work with the addition of extra armour. It could carry a 1,000 lb bomb and though its performance was much degraded in this role it was still vastly superior to the Stuka. However, pitted against large numbers of Thunderbolts and Mustangs its survival rate was not good.

With their attention fixed on Anzio the Luftwaffe did not have the resources to devote to the main battlefront further to the south. Here an offensive was launched to coincide with the Anzio landing and prevent the Germans from transferring troops. A feature of the German defensive line was a mountain known as Monte Cassino which had a monastery on its summit. This building was 14 centuries old and a jewel of western culture. The German defensive line deliberately ran just below the monastery and it is now agreed that there were no German soldiers in it. Nevertheless the Allies decided to bomb it just in case the Germans were to use it and on 15th February 1944 a mixed force of some 200 heavy and medium bombers blasted it to ruins. The Germans immediately occupied the ruins which became a very effective fortification. This was yet another occasion during the war when buildings were bombed to prevent them being used for defensive purposes only for the attacker to discover that the ruins made even better defensive positions than the undamaged buildings. We have seen it before at Stalingrad and we shall see it again at Caen in Normandy. You might think somebody would have learned the lesson.

The bombing achieved nothing and the war in Italy ground on.

CHAPTER TWENTY

D-Day and After

In the spring of 1944 the war was a very different beast from the local European squabble of 1939. Indeed the whole world of the 1930s had died away to be replaced by a new era of total war and mass mobilization. In England big country houses became hospitals and barracks and the officer corps of the armed forces now admitted men from a wide variety of backgrounds: there simply were not enough of the old officer class. In Russia shoulder boards with marks of rank had returned and political officers had been downgraded from executive to advisory duties. The revolutionary madness of the pre-war years gave way to the realities of a war for national survival. The U.S.A., that most pacific and isolationist of lands, had sent its young men to serve across the world from Iceland to the southern Pacific islands. In Germany the economy was finally geared for war and the population mobilized as it became plain that only a superhuman effort could save the country from Armageddon. In 1943 the Wehrmacht adopted a new uniform style of camouflage battle dress which would not look out of place in any army today. Japan perhaps changed least though, even there a man who had enlisted as an ordinary seaman like Saburo Sakai could end the war as an officer: enlistment to officer in eleven years – unheard of !

Early in 1944 Liberia and Peru joined the allied camp, the 38th and 39th countries to do so. The war now reached into every distant corner of civilization. Flying Officer C. P. Ross, a holder of the Distinguished Flying Cross, was killed taking part in a raid on Dusseldorf on 3rd November 1943. He came from the tiny island of Grenada in the West Indies with a population of 72,000 in 1939. 25 of its citizens joined the R.A.F. and three of them died in action; the dead are remembered on the war memorial in the island's capital, St. George's.[i]

Great Britain in early 1944 was one big armed camp and at the same time it was a stationary aircraft carrier loaded with many thousands of aircraft: all there to attack targets in Europe.

The main offensive arm of the R.A.F. was Bomber Command. In the notorious Nuremberg raid of March 30th 1944 it sent out 950 aircraft on the main raid and various diversions. Its American counterpart, the U.S. Eighth Air Force, sent out 1,600 planes, including fighters, on 27th March against assorted targets in France. Both forces were still growing.

In the summer of 1943 there had been a re-organization of the R.A.F. to create a new force called 2nd Tactical Air Force to provide air support for the upcoming invasion of Europe. This new body was formed partly by taking 2 Group, which consisted of light and medium bombers, from Bomber Command and partly by splitting Fighter Command in two and taking more than half its strength. The other part was retained in a force now known as Air Defence of Great Britain whose job was to do what its name suggests, that is, to defend the home country. 2nd Tactical Air Force received 60 squadrons and A.D.G.B. retained 39.

The Americans performed a similar operation whereby 9th Air Force, formed in the Mediterranean, was re-born in Europe in the autumn of 1943 and turned into their tactical support arm for the invasion. It did not bring its aircraft with it but had to be re-stocked in the U.K.. The first move was to transfer four groups of medium bombers from the 8th Air Force and from there on it was fleshed out with newly created formations. At the time of the invasion in June it numbered 11 groups of bombers and 20 of fighters. This was some 1,500 aircraft. Also attached to this air force was a troop carrier contingent with another 500 troop transport aircraft.

In all the Allies had some 6,000 front line combat aircraft ready for the invasion and many more in secondary roles such as training, supply, air-sea rescue, meteorology and communications. There was, too, Coastal Command which at this time consisted of some 600 aircraft. It would be fair to say that there were, in total, around 10,000 military aircraft at the disposal of the Allies in the British Isles in the spring of 1944.

The Allied overall commander was General Eisenhower and Air Chief Marshal Tedder was his deputy. The overall commander of the air forces for the invasion was Air Chief Marshal Leigh-Mallory, of the naval forces, Admiral Ramsay and of the ground forces, General Montgomery. Montgomery's command was strictly limited to the landings themselves and their immediate aftermath, following which, command of land forces would pass to Eisenhower. The strategic bomber forces in Europe were commanded by Carl Spaatz in conjunction with the British Air Ministry and the British force, led by Harris, was answerable to them jointly. These arrangements had their good points and bad. Eisenhower, though a general without battle experience, was an ideal negotiator and conciliator who could make the various different temperaments of his juniors function together most of the time though it was a hard task. He was working with two subordinates in Spaatz and Tedder who had been in the Mediterranean with him where they had made an effective team. On the other hand there were inevitable national rivalries: the British did not like the fact that the man in charge was an American and the Americans did not like the fact that all the individual heads of service were British. Both heads of strategic bombers did not think they should be involved at all and wanted to get on with the business of hitting strategic targets in Germany. The shared arrangement for overall control of strategic bombing was unsatisfactory and allowed Harris to go his own way as a kind of independent potentate.

The worst problem was Leigh-Mallory. Decribed as 'gloomy and hesitant' he could also be self-important and pompous. None of these senior officers respected him and nobody wanted to serve under him. The bomber commanders of both nations flatly refused to take orders from him and Spaatz was moved to urge U.S. commanders to put their own national interests first when dealing with him.[ii] This was deeply unhelpful but he was driven to this extreme position by the depth of the universal antipathy to Leigh-Mallory whom he could envisage wasting American lives through incompetence and vanity. The problem was circumvented by the fact that Tedder was extremely able and respected by all and increasingly stepped into the void to provide general direction of air strategy during the invasion. Leigh-Mallory kept up his lamentable performance by suddenly begging Eisenhower to cancel the American airborne element of the invasion at the last moment. He predicted that this parachute drop would end in disaster. Eisenhower ignored him as he had to do: he could not make major changes to the plans at such a late stage.[iii] There also can be little doubt that Eisenhower, who was a shrewd judge of men, had formed his own view of Leigh-Mallory. All this intervention achieved was to increase the burden on the shoulders of the Commander-in-Chief. The American parachute drop was, needless to say, a success.

One must ask why Leigh-Mallory was given this important appointment for which he was so ill-suited. Portal, the Chief of the Air Staff, was responsible and must take the blame. Portal had consistently backed him in all his posts since 1940 despite the man's doubtful competence and high-handed approach to his orders. This is not the only example of poor judgement of men by Portal and the reasons for the failing one can only guess at. Perhaps it was a function of the fact that all the senior officers of the R.A.F. had known each other well in the tiny inter-war air force and were too well acquainted to be dispassionate about each other. More important, perhaps, would be Leigh-Mallory's ceaseless self-promotion as the soi-disant hero of the Battle of Britain and his good fortune in being the younger brother of a then famous explorer who died on Mount Everest in the 1920s. The general public knew and admired him.

The first duty of the air forces supporting the invasion was bound to be ground attack in support of the land operations. For this reason the obvious choice as commander of the 2nd Tactical Air Force was Air Marshal Sir Arthur Coningham who had honed ground support to a fine art in North Africa with the Desert Air Force. He was universally known as 'Mary' which was a corruption of 'Maori' because he was a New Zealander and because he was the toughest and most masculine man imaginable.

The U.S. 9th Air Force was commanded by General Lewis Brereton, another of the team from the Mediterranean but more at home with command of heavy bombers and an odd choice for a ground attack role. Brereton was a highly capable but flawed man who had had problems with alcohol in the past and was notoriously difficult to get on with. Being a better administrator than soldier, most historians rate him as an average battle commander at best. Certainly he was slow to grasp and implement the requirements of ground attack in Normandy.

The aeroplanes available to the Allies for Operation Overlord, the invasion of Europe, were mostly first class though they did not have a great edge in quality on their German counterparts. The real advantage was in pilot skill since the Luftwaffe was forced to fill its ranks with increasingly poorly trained recruits. Some of the aircraft were not necessarily ideal for the job but they had to do however. The P-38 Lightning, which equipped seven U.S. groups, was ill-suited to cold, damp northern Europe because its engines did not perform at their best in that climate. There was nothing it could do that a Thunderbolt could not do just as well.

The 9th Air Force's bombing contingent was principally equipped with the Martin Marauder. This aircraft was very much a favoured child of the U.S.A.A.F. establishment but, even so, was nearly abandoned in its early days because of stability problems that caused frequent crashes on take-off and landing and caused pilots to call it 'the widow-maker.' Re-design conquered these problems but it remained difficult to fly and expensive to maintain. Its debut in the European theatre was disastrous when it was used at low level in a raid on Ijmuiden in Holland on 17th May 1943 and all ten aircraft involved were shot down. After that, it became exclusively a medium level bomber but with its substantial bomb load and seven man crew, (the same as a Lancaster), it was doing a job that could probably have been done better by heavy bombers. It is interesting to note that when the war was over it was one of the aircraft types that was retired from service in short order.

The worst example of unfitness for purpose lay in the Spitfire. This was an excellent aircraft but it was a specialist short distance interceptor and even external drop tanks could not extend its range very far. Moreover there were limitations to their use such as the fact that they had to be discarded before an aircraft faced any kind of danger. In 1944 the need was for aircraft with plenty of range in order that they could hunt deep into enemy territory and escort bombers. The presence of large numbers of Spitfires was, in fact, as much a hindrance as a help. For instance it restricted the choice of sites for the invasion since any such site had to lie within its limited range.

The R.A.F. had long been aware that it needed a fighter with longer range and had originally developed the Bristol Beaufighter to fill this role but it was unsatisfactory as a fighter plane for reasons already discussed. Hawker Aircraft was recruited at the start of the war to develop a new fighter with long range and good high level capabilities. Unfortunately the aircraft they eventually developed, the Typhoon, had very poor high level performance and so could not fulfill the role intended for it. It was also structurally unsound with a tendency for the tail to fall off if over-strained and for carbon monoxide to leak into the cockpit and asphyxiate the pilot. Once these problems were overcome, though the structural weakness was never wholly mastered, the Typhoon became an excellent ground attack aircraft. At this time its successor, the Tempest, was just coming into service. The Tempest was really only the Typhoon with the bugs ironed out and, indeed, it was originally called Typhoon Mark II. These aircraft were quite a handful to fly. The Typhoon weighed 11,400 lbs which was more than twice the Spitfire of 1940 and even more than the Blenheim, the R.A.F.'s early war medium bomber, but its massive 2,000 horsepower Napier Sabre engine gave it a top speed of more than 400 mph. Pierre Clostermann a French ace who flew with the R.A.F. made his first flight in a Typhoon at the end of 1944 and found it as much as he could handle, and he was a hugely experienced fighter pilot. 'My face was moist' was his comment on his condition at the end of the flight.[iv] The Tempest was a really outstanding aircraft that was to see extensive service lasting well beyond World War Two but at this time it only equipped two squadrons.

On June 6th 1944 the R.A.F. was still flying five squadrons of the early version of the Mustang which had no high level capacity and limited range. As previously noted, these were next to useless and could only be used for ground attack for which they were also less than ideally suited. There were already Typhoons and Beaufighters to carry out that task.

The story of R.A.F. fighter equipment and how it was put to use in the war years is really one of lack of foresight and mismanagement, though the glory of the Spitfire in 1940 tends to obscure this fact. One must remember that the Spitfire was a product of pre-war development and there followed a desperate search for a good fighter with decent range that ended up with the later model P-51 Mustangs which were powered by American built Rolls Royce engines while Rolls Royce itself turned out engines for more thousands of Spitfires that were surplus to requirements. The Spitfire was not an easy plane to produce and the British Government and aircraft industry had made a large investment to ensure its mass production. This was an industrial and financial juggernaut with such momentum that it was not easily turned aside.

Already by 1943 there were complaints that large numbers of fighters were being hoarded in Britain to no purpose when they could have been of great benefit in other theatres or in assisting the American daylight bombing offensive. There were approximately 96 squadrons based in the British Isles during 1943 and that meant 1,500 fighter planes. By way of comparison Hitler attacked Russia in 1941 with a force of barely 1,000 fighters. There was absolutely no threat of invasion in 1943 so what were they all doing? Their pinprick raids on targets in a strip of northern France and the Low Countries made no significant difference to the war at all. The Americans were understandably frustrated that their forces seemed to be fighting the air war by day all alone in 1943 while the British did not very much. John Searby, the leader of the attack on Peenemunde, and hardly an enemy of the R.A.F. later commented: 'After 1941 this Island was no longer under serious threat and yet hundreds of aircraft sat on lavishly equipped airfields from the Channel coast to the

Firth of Forth, with no real commitment.'[v] The problem was that Britain had to fight an offensive air war with defensive weapons. The responsibility for this state of affairs once again rested with Portal, together with the Air Ministry.

All these criticisms cannot detract from the fact however, that the air arm of the Allied invasion force was a mighty weapon and the greatest accumulation of air power ever witnessed. It was far beyond anything the Luftwaffe could hope to counter.

For the last nine months the Luftwaffe had increasingly been concentrating its fighter strength in northwest Europe to counter the American daylight bombing campaign. In early 1944 most of the bomber force followed in order to perform the mini-blitz on the U.K. that was ordered by Hitler as revenge for the bombing of Germany and as a tonic for home front morale. This was a puny effort compared with what the Allies were doing. The first raid, on 21st January 1944, was on London and was carried out by 270 bombers. Because of the poor quality of so many crews a system similar to that of Bomber Command was adopted whereby a pathfinder force of the best crews sought to mark the target for the rest to follow. This innovation was singularly unsuccessful and the bombs were spread all over southeast England. After this first raid the numbers of aircraft involved fell sharply and there were never again so many as 200 aircraft involved. Only a raid on London on 18th February could be called a real success when 175 tons of bombs were dropped on target. Thereafter navigation improved and half the planes found their target on each raid but the numbers involved were not very large and the campaign, which petered out in April, achieved nothing of note and certainly did not hinder preparations for the invasion. One should bear in mind that two days before the 'successful' raid of 18th February the R.A.F. had bombed Berlin with 891 aircraft and dropped 2,642 tons of bombs.

The Luftwaffe defence of northwest Europe was divided into two administrative areas: there was Airfleet Three which covered France and most of Belgium and Airfleet Reich which covered the rest of the Low Countries and the German homeland. Airfleet Three was commanded by Hugo Sperrle who had been in charge on this front since 1940. Lazy and cantankerous, Sperrle was no fool and as the war progressed he could see that the outlook was ominous and gloomy. Always something of a gourmet he turned increasingly to the pleasures of the table for consolation. Based in Paris he was ideally placed to indulge himself. Misogynistic by nature the increasing employment of women in auxiliary posts in the Luftwaffe irked him considerably and when a female voice answered the telephone he was liable to explode with anger.[vi] In 1944 Sperrle was a spent force and should not have held such a crucial post but he was an 'old fighter', had commanded the Condor Legion in Spain and was well regarded by Hitler.

Next door the commander of Airfleet Reich was Hans-Jurgen Stumpff. He was a careful and effective administrator who had served in the First World War and finished it in a junior post on the General Staff but had never flown. He had been

Chief of the Personnel Office for the Luftwaffe, Chief of Staff and commander of air forces in Norway. He prided himself on being a professional and non-political officer. He was tried for war crimes after the war but acquitted, the charges being related to the murder and ill-treatment of pilots shot down over Germany. The posts he held show that he was an able man if a somewhat uninspiring one.

On the eve of the invasion Airfleet Three mustered some 800 aircraft though they were spread out over the whole of France and Belgium. Only 170 were single-engine fighters but they were at least mainly based within striking distance of the Normandy beaches. There were 200 anti-shipping bombers but they were all based on the Atlantic coast or in the Mediterranean and the proficiency level of the crews in this most demanding of flying roles was no more than average. There were some 130 medium bombers comprising the remnants of the force that had been bombing England but they had recently taken heavy losses and were at a low level of effectiveness.

Reconnaissance was now also seriously inadequate since the Luftwaffe lacked a suitable plane to carry out this task in the face of the massive Allied air superiority. It needed something that could fly higher or faster than the enemy planes but there was nothing.

Airfleet Reich comprised at least 1,200 aircraft but they were too far away to fight the invasion without re-basing to airfields in France and technically the invasion took place outside their area of operations so a decision would have to be taken at a high level for them to intervene. In fact, that decision was rapidly taken when the time came because German command was always flexible in this way, (unless Hitler interfered), and the transfer of aircraft began almost immediately after the invasion. Where command fell down was in the failure to transfer ground attack aircraft from the East where they were held in large numbers to await the Russian summer offensive. The truth is, though, that those planes were needed in the East too. The Germans just did not have the resources to meet the power of their mighty adversaries.

Despite all the bombing and the recent 'Big Week', German aircraft production was in a healthy situation. Under the guiding hand of Albert Speer, the Minister of Armaments, production had been streamlined and speeded up and, most important of all, dispersed so that the number of large targets vulnerable to air attack was greatly reduced. Production concentrated on fighter aircraft which was what the situation demanded at this stage of the war, though that priority was a de facto arrangement by Speer and Erhard Milch, his predecessor and now subordinate, in the face of Hitler's insistence on the continued production of a large bomber force. German industry produced 25,000 planes in 1943 and 40,000 in 1944.

This large increase has sometimes been used as evidence for the argument that strategic bombing did not work, but that is far from the case. The truth is that without the bombing the increase would have been even greater. However the key effect of the bombing on the aero-industry was to hold back its quality. The increase was only achieved by concentrating production on a few aircraft types. In 1944 there was an obvious need for a new and better fighter aircraft. There were a number of designs in existence. There was the Dornier 335, a radical design with an engine at both ends but a raid on the factory where it was produced in March 1944 destroyed all the prototype machine tools for its construction with the result that it was only in the last days of the war that it flew in action. A similar fate struck the Me262 jet plane project whose production jigs were destroyed in the famous Regensburg raid of 1943. The Heinkel He219, a kind of German Mosquito and a very fine aircraft that could have wholly changed the bomber war, was made at a factory outside Vienna and raids on it in April and June 1944 did such damage that the 219 never reached the front in other than tiny numbers. (To be fair, it also suffered from the fact that General Milch took an irrational dislike to it and would not grant it the production priority it deserved.)

The Italians had produced an aircraft called the Fiat G55 which had a Daimler Benz engine and had been used in small numbers in the Mediterranean with impressive results: it could out-fly any Allied fighter plane. The Germans knew all about it but declined to build it themselves. Their difficulty was that the greatly dispersed aircraft construction industry on which they now relied, made the introduction of a new type of aircraft to the assembly lines a problem of almost insuperable complexity. The simplest expedient would have been to abandon production of the Me109 and go over exclusively to the Fw190 which had shown itself a better aircraft in the conditions of the western front. Even this was rejected as impractical because of production loss during any changeover. So the Luftwaffe soldiered on with the weapons that it had. By now they were barely adequate.

Pilot training was also in a healthy position as far as numbers were concerned; the shortage of new men reaching the front line units that the previous year had witnessed, was a thing of the past. The critical problem, as already noted, was quality. The training time had been cut to the bone and pilots arriving at the front had no chance to acclimatize themselves gradually but were thrown immediately into an uneven struggle where only the very skilled or the very lucky survived. Helmut Lipfert, one of the great Luftwaffe fighter aces of the eastern front was threatened with transfer to the West in May 1944 and his view was that it was 'a virtual death sentence'.[vii]

As an example of what it all meant in practice we can look at the case of Heinz Gehrke. He was a recently qualified pilot who joined a crack Fighter Wing in France, Jg26 'Schlageter', in the spring of 1944. He flew his first mission on 16th March when his squadron of the 26th intercepted 8th Air Force bombers returning from a raid on Augsburg. He was, by his own admission, very excited and when he got the chance to attack a lone B-24 he forgot all else and made three attacks on it before realizing that his colleagues had long gone and he was on his own. He saw some fighters in the distance and assumed they were his flight so hastened to join them.

When he got close he realized they were American Thunderbolts but it was too late and he was promptly shot down. He survived with only a bruised back. The Americans were part of the 356th Fighter Group and they were amazed that they appeared to have been attacked by a lone, fanatical Nazi plane. At least Gehrke was given credit for the destruction of the B-24.[viii]

By contrast, Heinz Knocke, an 'old hare' who had been at the front since the end of 1940 and who was transferred from Reich defence after the invasion, fought with ruthless and determined efficiency. 'I seem to have the instincts of a born hunter. I act calmly and deliberately.....Every time I have an enemy in my sights, he invariably seems to make some elementary blunder in tactics. I watch him crash coldly and dispassionately, without any sense of triumph.'[ix] He himself was barely recovered from a fractured skull suffered when he was shot down in April. All his friends had been killed and he was plainly a man existing on his last reserves both mentally and physically. His career ended in October 1944 when his car was blown up by Czech resistance fighters while he was transferring from one base to another across central Europe. He was very seriously injured and only emerged from hospital in the last days of the war. He never flew again.

The Luftwaffe's supply of men like Knocke was running out. Its great hope now

U.S. Consolidated B-24 bombers fly over the D-Day invasion fleet. The B-24 was much more widely used than its better known partner the B-17 and was built in much larger numbers (18,000 as against 12,000).
©Imperial War Museum (EA 25713)

lay with revolutionary weapons such as rockets and jet planes. Jet planes, as such, were not yet available for use at the front but a test unit was trying out the jet powered Me262 at Lechfeld in Bavaria. On the other hand pulse jets were very much to the fore in the shape of the Fieseler Fi103, better known to history as the V-1. This was a small, self-guiding aircraft packed with explosive and quite similar to the present day Cruise missile. It was driven by a pulse jet, a kind of engine halfway between a jet and a rocket. Air went in the front of the engine and was mixed with fuel and ignited. The resultant explosion blasted shutters, on the intake closed so that the explosive gases had to go out the back and thus create jet thrust. Air pressure then immediately opened the shutters again and the process was repeated over and over, 50 times a second. A simple gyro system kept the V-1 flying straight and level and a tiny propeller on the nose acted as a timer: after a pre-determined number of revolutions it activated a switch to turn the elevators down and the craft then fell out of the sky. These flying bombs were launched in large numbers from sites on the Channel coast with their timers set to cut out over London. They were unreliable and inaccurate and many fell to defensive measures but so many were fired that some had to get through. 10,000 of them were fired at London from 12th June until October 1944 when their bases were overrun and approximately 25 percent got through to cause great destruction and 6,000 deaths. Thereafter London was out of their range and Antwerp, with its extensive docks, was the target of a further 2,500 bombs. The Germans had great hopes of this weapon but in the end it was a disappointment: it represented another blitz on London but the British public bore it with stoicism and the course of the war was not changed one whit.

The British were well informed about the development of flying bombs and carried out a furious campaign of bombing against the launch sites which were hard to camouflage because the bombs required launch cradles not unlike a small ski jump in appearance. Once flying bombs were launched they flew at medium height and at approximately 350 mph and were vulnerable to both anti-aircraft fire and interception by the fastest fighter planes. Since they took no evasive action, they were relatively straightforward targets and suffered heavy losses. The new Tempest fighter was particularly effective against flying bombs being both fast and heavily armed.

The two months prior to the invasion were devoted to bomber operations designed to facilitate the landings. The main task was to isolate the battlefield and to this end a campaign of destruction was launched against the French transport network in northern France. It could not concentrate on the Normandy area without betraying the fact that that was the intended landing site and so targets were spread across the whole of northern France and were principally bridges and railway facilities particularly marshaling yards, repair shops, engine sheds and crossovers, not to mention the trains themselves. Locomotives were singled out for special attention.

The heavy bombers were employed in this task as well as the mediums though only under protest. Both Spaatz and Harris thought they would be making a bigger contribution by attacking the usual strategic targets in Germany. They disagreed between themselves as to how this was to be done but they were in complete agreement that they should be given independence to attack the enemy in their own way irrespective of any invasion and that the whole invasion was a mistake anyway. More specifically Harris claimed that his crews had no training in attacking the kind of smaller targets they would now have to contend with. Spaatz asserted that he was about to begin a campaign against oil production facilities that must go ahead at once. At a meeting in April he said: 'It is of paramount importance the Combined Bomber Offensive continue without interruption and the proposed diversion of 8th Air Force to support of Overlord is highly dangerous.'[x] However the High Command was tired of hearing exaggerated claims from the 'bomber barons' and no one was listening. Spaatz and Harris had to do what they were told. It was short-sighted of them not to be able to see that Britain and America simply could not rely on strategic bombing alone. Harris's claim turned out to be unfounded: his crews did very well against smaller targets. There was more in Spaatz's complaint. It was to emerge that his oil campaign was the key to German economic collapse.

The transport offensive in France was an outstanding success. The rail network was ruined across the land. As early as the beginning of May Colonel Hoffner, the head of rail transportation in France for the Wehrmacht, reported that the situation was critical. It took 100 trains a day to maintain the Wehrmacht in France and only 32 were getting through.[xi] There then followed further raids and the specific targeting of locomotives. The number of locomotives operating in the SNCF Region Nord which covered the whole northern part of France fell from 2,000 to 500. The rest were either destroyed or inoperative for want of repair. Rail traffic in France as a whole had fallen by 70 percent.[xii] Churchill had initially been hesitant about this campaign because it was estimated that it would cause 50,000 French deaths. In the event the figure was 12,000 and the French took this as the price they had to pay for liberation.

On the eve of the landings there occurred the largest parachute drop yet seen with strong forces dropped on both flanks of the target beaches. Extensive use was made of gliders which were towed across the Channel and then released over France. Many gliders broke up on landing and many paratroops were dropped wide of their designated drop zones but, overall, the operation was a success and secured the flanks. This was a most complex operation and it had definitely been a gamble but it must be said that the gamble paid off handsomely.

On D-day June 6th 1944 the invasion beaches were covered by an umbrella of fighter aircraft so complete that the Luftwaffe did not even try to intervene in force. Only very few aircraft arrived over the landings of which two made a strafing run along the shore. These were flown by the commander of Jg26 Josef 'Pips' Priller and his wingman Heinz Wodarczyk who sneaked up under cloud cover, made their attack and then ran for it.[xiii] Only highly experienced pilots such as these two could get away with something like this. Their attack was made famous by the film 'The Longest Day' in which there is a scene that grippingly portrays it.

For virtually the whole covering force the day passed quietly. On the eastern flank of the landings were placed some of the best pilots to be found because this was the area where the Luftwaffe was judged most likely to intervene. One of the units involved was the Tangmere Spitfire Wing commanded by Johnny Johnson, a superb pilot who was to finish the war as the top ace of the R.A.F.. He flew four missions in the course of the day covering the eastern flank and said that the biggest danger he faced was a collision with another Allied aircraft, so many were there in the air. Of the Luftwaffe he saw not a thing and he had time to marvel at the sea below, littered with ships of all shapes and sizes.[xiv]

As soon as night came, however, the available Luftwaffe bombers attacked, though this only amounted to 175 sorties. Some planes were lost to night fighters and some turned back in the face of the vicious Allied anti-aircraft fire. A few planes were lost to German flak in friendly fire incidents. The effect of the attacks was negligible. Friendly fire was to become an increasing problem for the Luftwaffe as their ground troops came to terms with Allied air superiority and simply assumed that any plane they saw must be an enemy. There was a bitter joke doing the rounds at this time amongst the soldiers on the ground to the effect that if you saw a plane and it was silver it was American, if it had camouflage it was British and if it was invisible it was a Luftwaffe plane.

During the next week 200 fighters and 110 bombers were transferred to France in an attempt to counter the Allied superiority: there were now roughly 1,000 Luftwaffe aircraft in France. This was the maximum effort that it was ever possible to make. Thereafter numbers inexorably declined. And it was still not possible to make any impact on the landings. British and American planes roved across France and repeatedly attacked airfields destroying planes and installations on the ground and making it increasingly difficult for the Luftwaffe even to get into the air. In particular, this tactic reduced already inadequate reconnaissance to vanishing point leaving the planners in the dark about the potential targets and their defences. An attempt was made to remedy the absence of ground attack aircraft by giving a proportion of the fighters that role. This was a mistake because it necessitated the conversion of fighters to carry bombs and the result was another failure since the pilots had no training in this kind of flying and achieved minimal results. On 12th June the Air Ministry in Berlin ordered that fighters must be used as fighters only and this was undoubtedly the right decision.

Bombers, operating at night, found that they simply could not penetrate the defences of searchlights, anti-aircraft guns and balloons that surrounded the beaches so they resorted to bombing from high level but they had not the accuracy to do serious damage and they soon realized this. They then turned to mining the sea routes to the beaches and this did cause a good deal of trouble and damage but in the end it did little more than inconvenience the Allies: there could be no question of their defeating the landings or anything near it. The Luftwaffe bomber force was simply not large enough or skilled enough to make a critical difference.

Allied air superiority made the Wehrmacht's job of fighting on the ground immensely more difficult. It became virtually impossible for troops to move by daylight on the roads and the railways were at a standstill. The crucial business of getting reinforcements to the battlefront was fatally undermined. One notorious example was the Das Reich SS Panzer Division which was stationed at Montauban in south central France when the invasion occurred. It could not be moved by rail so it drove by road some 300 miles to Normandy. On the way it was subject to much wear and tear and repeated attacks by French guerrillas, committing atrocities by way of reprisal. Its arrival in Normandy was delayed by a critical two weeks.

The months following the invasion were full justification of everything that had ever been claimed for ground support. If air power did not win the campaign in France by itself, it would be fair to say that the campaign could not have been won without it. In some ways it was a repeat of the fighting in France four years before but with the boot on the other foot. There was no collapse of the Wehrmacht because it was better trained and equipped than the French army of 1940 and more motivated but in the end it too was thoroughly defeated. In one sense there was nothing new about all this because the scale of what could be achieved by ground support aircraft had been apparent since Poland in 1939 and there had been hints of it in 1918. On the other hand Normandy in 1944 was confirmation that direct air support for armies remained a vital ingredient of warfare despite changing times and circumstances. On 21st July Field Marshal von Kluge, who took over command of German forces in the West after Rommel was wounded, wrote to Hitler: '...in face of the enemy's complete command of the air, there is no possibility of our finding a strategy which will counterbalance its truly annihilating effect, unless we give up the field of battle.'[xv]

There were also some new features. One of these was the widespread use of rockets against ground targets, particularly tanks and other armoured vehicles. The masters of this form of combat were the R.A.F. Typhoons armed with eight 60lb high explosive rockets slung under the wings or 25lb solid shot for armoured targets.

Another novelty was the use of the full force of strategic heavy bombers to hit the enemy troops on the ground. For two months after D-day the German defenders were able to keep the Allies penned in within a fairly small defensive perimeter. The heavy bomber force was used on a variety of missions in this time, from destroying enemy coastal gun emplacements to sealing the Saumur railway tunnel. The latter was done with a new bomb conceived by Barnes Wallis, the man who designed the Wellington bomber and the special bomb used in the dams raid in 1943. His latest design was a 12,000 lb bomb with a hardened nose that buried itself in the ground before exploding. It was colloquially called 'Tallboy' and was extremely effective.

The most startling use of the 'heavies' was in direct ground support raids on a massive scale. These were very effective in themselves but repeated errors of command and communication on the ground often frustrated their exploitation. On 7th July Caen was bombed by 467 heavy bombers but it turned out there were few Germans there and the city was reduced to ruins to no purpose. Once again it was to prove that a ruined city was actually easier to defend than a pristine one. On 18th July 1,000 British bombers and 850 American bombed the front southeast of Caen in preparation for Operation Goodwood, an all-out attempt to break through the German line. This was the largest such raid to be attempted during the war and its effects were truly terrible. The ground under attack was turned into a moonscape, tanks were tossed in the air like pebbles, the wounded screamed and men went mad or shot themselves.[xvi] But the Germans were extraordinarily resilient and the subsequent ground attack was poorly handled so that it petered out after three days.

There was always the danger with this kind of raid that even a small error of aim would result in friendly fire deaths and on 14th August a strike just in front of Canadian troops killed 80 of them and wounded many more besides doing much material damage.

On 31st July the Americans finally broke clean through the German defences at St. Lo and their forces spread out into northern France. The attack was preceded on 25th by an 8th Air Force attack of 1,600 bombers that devastated the defence line and stunned the defenders. Thereafter, with the front line becoming more fluid, it was impossible to mount this kind of attack. There might have been a resumption at the end of the year when the fighting became static again but by then the heavy bombers had been released to return to their strategic role from which they were not easily diverted.

Leading units of the American breakout forces headed east and raced across France south of the German defenders and before long those defenders were threatened with wholesale encirclement as the Americans in the south and the British in the North both aimed for the town of Falaise where they would link up. The German 7th Army and 5th Panzer Army raced to escape through the ever narrowing gap and as they did so, more and more troops were pressed into a smaller and smaller area in which military vehicles, both motor and horse drawn were crammed bumper to bumper. These made an ideal target for fighter bombers and destruction and slaughter followed on an horrific scale. This was the most startling example of the power of the ground support arm that the war in the West was to produce but it was the day to day work in the previous two months that had made the biggest contribution to winning the war.

Two points need to be made about the work of these ground support aircraft. The first is that though there was very little Luftwaffe interference ground attack planes suffered steady casualties from flak. On D-day itself there were seven squadrons of Typhoons engaged and they lost eight of their number. The next day nine Typhoon squadrons were in action and 14 planes were lost and one written off.

30 R.A.F. fighters were lost overall that day and 44 U.S.. So it continued day after day. The slaughter of the Fairey Battle aircraft of 1940 was soon easily surpassed but hearts were harder now and the losses were simply accepted without comment. Harder to bear were the inevitable friendly fire incidents which happened with great frequency. For instance, on 14th July 132 Spitfire Squadron was on patrol when it passed through a thin layer of cloud and emerged right in front of some American P-51s of the 361st Fighter Group who took them for Messerschmitts and opened fire. One of the Spitfires was shot down and two of the others then attacked the leading American plane and deliberately sought repeatedly to shoot it down in return. They followed it all the way back to England and landed behind it at its home base where the two R.A.F. pilots ran up to the American plane and threatened the pilot so aggressively that he drew his revolver to hold them off.[xvii]

The second point to be made is that ground attack planes in Normandy generally had a modest record when it came to attacking tanks. This is odd since tanks were one of their prime targets. During the German retreat in France panzer forces launched a counter-attack at a town called Mortain and after it had been repulsed a British research team studied the broken armoured vehicles left behind. The fighter-bombers had claimed 89 tanks destroyed. The researchers found 78 wrecked armoured vehicles but only nine showed clear evidence of destruction by air attack.[xviii] The truth was that it was more difficult to knock out a tank than it appeared and the pilots over-claimed wildly but in all innocence. Machine guns and cannon made little impact on tanks and the rockets were simply too inaccurate a weapon to be very effective except in the hands of a master airman. However their impact was always impressive with dirt thrown up and frequent pyrotechnics that gave the impression a tank had died when, usually, it was unaffected. It would have been interesting to see similar research carried out on the eastern front where Rudel claimed to be knocking out Russian tanks in large numbers. No doubt his claims were somewhat exaggerated but his attack technique was different, involving special ammunition and close range firing, and he most certainly was a master airman.

Another aspect of this conundrum is that tanks are much easier to attack when they are themselves attacking because they have to come out into the open and they leave their anti-aircraft protection behind. In Normandy German tanks were on the defensive ninety per cent of the time and in such a role they could hide under trees with flak guns close by or even be 'dug-in' whereby they were buried with just the turret above the earth. A tank in this position is a tiny and virtually invulnerable target.

The Allies were able to conduct their whole campaign in France with little interference from the Luftwaffe. Their supremacy was so complete that German fighters were increasingly used in June and July to defend their own bases and communication routes rather than for offensive purposes. Admittedly Luftwaffe priority was given to countering heavy bombers but it will be noted that the operations cited above were carried out virtually without interference from the air and that failure certainly was no part of the German plan. Poor weather for a few days in the middle of July gave the Luftwaffe some respite and they were able to achieve a 65 percent serviceability rate among their 450 aircraft available in France but in August the German defeat there and precipitate withdrawal to their own borders threw their arrangements into the familiar confusion attending retreats and by September the air opposition to the Allied armies was virtually zero. Poor Heinz Gehrke was shot down twice in this period but survived each time. On 13th June he was shot down by Thunderbolts at low level and his parachute opened only a second or so before he hit the ground. His plane fell on a French farmhouse and destroyed it and only the timely arrival of some Wehrmacht soldiers saved him from the vengeance of the local villagers.[xix] He was shot down again in July but his incredible luck held and he returned to his unit unhurt.[xx] One can only imagine what it was like for him to fly after each of these close calls and risk death yet again.

On top of their other woes the Luftwaffe High Command now had to contend with a desperate fuel shortage. In early July the 90 aircraft still carrying out anti-shipping duties in southwest France were withdrawn to Norway and the homeland

Three French boys stare at a wrecked German Panther tank in Normandy in 1944. Tanks were hard to hit from the air and pilots were often over-optimistic in their claims of tanks destroyed. ©Imperial War Museum (B 9665)

and shortly thereafter their operations were effectively ended by orders designed to save fuel. Even fighter planes were told to fly only against heavy bombers attacking Germany. The cause of their problem was an Allied campaign to target oil installations in Germany which was being carried on by Spaatz and the 8th Air Force. Despite their support for the forces in France the heavy bomber forces were still able to carry out sporadic strategic raids on Germany and the Americans were increasingly hitting oil targets. Here, at last, they had found the philosopher's stone of strategic bombing: a key industry whose destruction would bring a national economy to a halt. At the end of August 1944 Rumania changed sides and joined the Allies and her oil resources were thereby lost to Germany though production at Ploiesti had already been reduced to a trickle by bombing. Apart from a small quantity of oil imports from Hungary, Germany had now to rely on her own oil industry that produced oil from coal by a chemical process. This was done by a limited number of plants which it was not possible to hide or disperse and which were therefore at the bombers' mercy.

CHAPTER TWENTY-ONE

Russia Triumphant

On March 20th 1944 Hans Rudel, now commander of the 3rd Group of the 2nd Stuka Wing (Stg2) with 1,800 operational flights behind him and 200 destroyed Soviet tanks to his credit, flew the eighth mission of the day from his base at Rauchovka, 125 miles north of Odessa. During combat one pilot of his squadron had to land his damaged plane behind Russian lines and Rudel himself landed in a field with the intention of picking up the pilot and his gunner and carrying them back to safety. To his concern he found that the ground was so soft that the wheels of his plane sank in and he could not take off again. All four men ran from the advancing Russian soldiers for half an hour in full flying kit before they came to a cliff at the bottom of which lay the Dniester River, 500 yards across and in full spate with large chunks of ice floating past. They descended the cliff by jumping into the tops of trees growing on the river bank and sliding through the branches onto bushes at ground level and then they stripped to shirt and trousers and set out to swim the river. Three of them made it but Rudel's gunner was overcome by the cold near the far side and drowned.

They ran onwards on bare feet until they accidentally encountered a Russian patrol and were captured. Rudel however, made a break for it and got away though he was shot in the shoulder. He ran until he dropped with exhaustion and then escaped a Russian search party by sheer luck as they passed close by, but failed to see him lying inert in a ploughed field. When the coast was clear he staggered on until nightfall and then found a peasant hut where the owner and his wife gave him food and few hours rest. Then he continued, heading steadily southward toward the German lines and guided by the feel of the wind on his back which he knew was coming from the North. After 24 hours of travel, much of it spent running, he found a German patrol and was rapidly re-united with his command where he was greeted with great excitement and his superior officer ordered a period of leave at home in Germany. Rudel ignored the order however, and two days later was leading his group in action again, flying with one arm in a sling. His feet were so damaged that he had to be carried to his aircraft.[i]

His motto in life was: 'Only he is lost who gives himself up for lost.' He certainly lived up to it.

The feats of one man however, no matter how brave and capable he might be, could not be more than a flea bite in the drama of southern Russia in early 1944 in which millions were caught up. One scene in that drama was of more than usual significance to the big picture. That was the struggle in the Crimea. The Russian advance across the wide spaces of the Ukraine in the autumn of 1943 had cut off the Crimea and left it isolated, but kept in supply by sea and air shipments from Rumania. In April 1944 the Russians launched a major offensive to liberate it. The Crimea was garrisoned by the German 17th Army with 230,000 men and it was Hitler's order that it must be held at all costs. The purpose of retaining it was unclear: true, it constituted a serious nuisance for the Russians, threatening their southern flank and it would make a good jumping-off point for a renewed German offensive in southern Russia. On the other hand there was no realistic prospect of a further German offensive in the foreseeable future and the Crimea kept nearly a quarter of a million men busy in a sideshow when they were sorely needed in the main theatre. The old justification that it could be used as a base for attacks on the oilfields of Ploiesti was defunct since Russian forces on the mainland were now closer to Ploiesti in any event.

From the point of view of the air war, this campaign was significant because the Russians fought it with complete air superiority from the start and were able to hone their air/ground co-operation skills and use air power against the Wehrmacht so effectively that it was a major cause of their victory. The achievements here were a dress rehearsal for the major campaign of the summer shortly to come.

The Russian attack was two-pronged: westward from the Kerch peninsula on which they had established a foothold and southward from the Ukraine across the Perekop Isthmus. The first attack was supported by 4th Air Army and elements of the naval air force and the second by 8th Air Army. Altogether they had 1,250 planes against some 200 German and Rumanian in an ad hoc formation known as Battlegroup Bauer. The teeth of this formation were a German group of Me109 fighter planes and two groups of ground attack aircraft. The fighter group was the 2nd Group of 52nd Fighter Wing (Jg52). This was part of the wing that had fought in the Kuban and at Kursk and included no less than ten men with 50 or more victories to their names. It was led by Captain Gerhard Barkhorn who had 250 victories and it was probably the best fighter unit on the eastern front. In terms of sheer numbers of enemy destroyed, it could claim to be the best fighter unit in the world but such a claim would be exaggerated. It was repeatedly shown that the conditions of different theatres favoured different kinds of flying and top aces from one theatre were often mediocre in another. Luftwaffe aces of the East frequently could not repeat their success when transferred to the West.

The air battle began on 7th April when the 8th Air Army sent out swarms of Il-2s escorted by fighters to attack ground targets. All the German fighters intercepted but had to spend most of their time fighting the escort. At one point they broke through and seven Il-2s were shot down in short order but this was not enough and the Stormoviks did serious damage to number of ground targets. Even the very best German fighter pilots were not able to make any difference to the outcome.

On 9th April a pinpoint attack on a target known as 'Hill 30.3' by Il-2s and twin-engine Pe-2s was so effective that the defences in the North on the Perekop Isthmus began to crumble and the Russians spilled out into the heart of the Crimea. The defenders on the Kerch Peninsula were now in danger of being cut off and began to retreat. The interior of the Crimea offers few good defensive positions and so the defence now rapidly collapsed and became a retreat to Sevastopol, the fortress port in the southwest of the peninsula. From here a sea and air evacuation to Rumania began. The retreating troops were remorselessly harried by the V.V.S. and there were scenes not unlike Normandy, with roads choked with wrecked vehicles destroyed from the air. Helmut Lipfert, one of the aces flying with Jg52 recorded how the base his flight was using was raided four times in one day by Soviet planes and six Messerschmitts were destroyed on the ground.[ii] The ships carrying out the evacuation, mainly Rumanian, were obvious targets and a number were damaged or sunk. On 18th April a flight of Russian lend-lease A-20 bombers attacked the steamship Alba Iulia and scored a hit on the deck packed with soldiers: 500 were killed.[iii] On 10th May two steamers called Teja and Totilla were hit by bombs while loaded with soldiers. Both sank and few men were rescued. It is thought that up to 10,000 soldiers were drowned in total, making this one of the worst maritime disasters in history.[iv]

On 9th May Helmut Lipfert was carried to safety in Rumania as a passenger in the luggage compartment of a fellow pilot's Me109. The pilot, a man called Van de Kamp, was a beginner and Lipfert should have flown the plane instead of him but Van de Kamp was a large man and could not fit in the luggage compartment. With this extra weight the plane flew badly and had a Russian fighter spotted them they would have been easy meat. They were lucky however, and reached Rumania safely only to crash on landing, coming to rest at the edge of a store of fuel drums. A few feet further and both would have been incinerated.[v]

Between the 7th April and his evacuation, Helmut Lipfert had shot down 26 aircraft over the Crimea and been shot down himself twice. His efforts were by no means unique but Luftwaffe 'experten' such as he were now far too few to make any serious difference to the course of the war in Russia – or anywhere else.

Having pushed the invaders back to the Rumanian border in the South it was obvious to any observer in the early summer of 1944 that the Russians would launch their main summer offensive against the German line in the central part of the front where a swathe of Russian territory was still in German hands. Most observers expected the attack to make use of the exposed German flank laid bare by the retreat in the southern half of the front and the Russians were careful to cultivate that idea but the vast Pripyet Marshes were in the way of any strike from the South and their soft going was unsuitable for armoured vehicles so, instead, the Russians determined to hit the German salient head on. This was to be their biggest offensive yet and was codenamed 'Bagration' after a distinguished Russian general of the Napoleonic wars.

Russian airmen laugh at some horseplay in front of an Ilyushin Il-4 bomber.
©Imperial War Museum (RR 844)

There was to be an overture to the Bagration offensive however, and that was an assault on Finland. The Finns had only ever joined Hitler's war to recover the land they lost in the Winter War and when they had done that, their aggressive stance faded away and their sector of the front became more or less quiescent. With the defeat at Stalingrad the Finnish government decided that the writing was on the wall and they should make peace with the Soviet Union on the best terms they could get. Stalin did not normally indulge in magnanimity towards the defeated, but his relationship with Finland was a thing apart and he seems to have felt a certain gratitude that that country had not fought harder. Leningrad would probably have fallen if it had. Negotiations were opened but by early 1944 they were deadlocked and the Russian government decided that it was time to strengthen its negotiating hand by putting on military pressure so at the start of June the Karelian front suddenly burst into life as the Russians launched an offensive against the Finns. This was supported by 13th Air Army with 1,600 aircraft and began with a major raid on 9th June by 200 bombers and 150 Il-2 Sturmoviks supported by 400 fighters. The tiny Finnish air force amounted only to some 200 aircraft (or 300 according to some authorities)[vi] and was completely overwhelmed. The situation was somewhat like a repeat of the Winter War. The Russian offensive made steady, if slow, progress and all commentators agreed that this was primarily due to their total control of the air.

As usual there was a small minority of able fighter pilots for whom these circumstances were nothing other than an opportunity to exercise their skills. Two Finnish pilots stand above others: Warrant Officer Eino Juutilainen with 94 victories and Captain Hans Wind with 78. Juutilainen in particular, was a quite remarkable pilot whose plane was not once hit by an enemy bullet in three years of combat and who never lost a wingman in that time.

The high morale of Finnish fighter pilots was not emulated in the army which saw heavy wastage through desertion. It was clear to the government that they had lost the war and must make peace, which they did in September but meanwhile the offensive had the side-effect of causing the Germans to transfer a wing of ground attack planes and a squadron of fighters from the main front to Finland on the eve of Operation Bagration.

The V.V.S. was to play a larger part in the Bagration offensive than any previous one and its quality was steadily improving. For the first time it could be said that it had superiority in equipment, if by a small margin. About one third of its fighter planes were Yak-9s, mainly the D model which was perhaps marginally inferior to its German opponents but in April the factories had begun production of the U model (U for ulushchenny or 'improved') which was marginally superior. Another quarter of the fighters were Lag-5s. The FN model of this plane, which was the latest, was definitely superior to the Messerschmitts and Focke Wulfs. 15 percent of the fighter force consisted of lend-lease P-39 Airacobras. These aircraft defied logic. Long abandoned by other countries as obsolete, the Russians could not get enough of them and scored victories with them left, right and centre. One is tempted to wonder about the psychological aspect when it comes to this anomaly. Were the planes better because they were simply flown better by pilots who thought they were wonderful? In the West the Airacobra had always had a bad reputation among pilots and a man who dislikes his aeroplane is unlikely to get the best out of it. The balance of the fighter force was composed of older versions of the Yak and small numbers of various other types including Spitfires and P-40s.

That summer a new Yak was beginning to be produced in quantity. This was the Yak-3. It was the same basic design as all the other Yak fighters but it represented an attempt to make the design as fast, light and manoeuverable as possible. Since no new engine was available this was achieved by improving the streamlining and taking every possible measure to cut down on weight. The result was an aircraft that was probably the best pure dogfighter of the war. Its drawbacks were that it was fragile and under-armed and its range was relatively short because one of the weight-saving measures had been to cut down on the fuel it carried. So dangerous was it that by the time of Bagration Luftwaffe pilots had been formally warned not to engage it.

Soviet bombers were nearly unchanged from the year before: the Il-2 and the Pe-2. Pe-2s were increasingly being built with metal wings which made them stronger and lighter. This was possible because of the recapture of the Donbass region of the Ukraine, with its mines, the year before. There was a new bomber in the Tupolev Tu-2 but its numbers were as yet small. It was a twin-engine plane not unlike the Pe-2 to look at but much faster and carrying a much greater bomb load. It was a favourite with the crews who flew it. Widespread use was also made of the American A-20 Havoc (or Boston) another lend-lease favourite.

The quality of V.V.S. pilots was on the increase at this time because there was no longer the pressure of enormous losses to force the training time down. Moreover, there were an increasing number of veterans as the improving quality of aircraft meant that talented pilots had a chance to survive and accumulate experience.

The Germans had no significant new aircraft to help them. Their only new development of any significance was the strategic bomber the Heinkel 177 but, as we have seen, that aircraft was a complete failure. The main significant improvement in their equipment was the phasing out of the Stuka and the introduction of a ground attack version of the Fw190 to fill the same role in the dive-bomber wings now renamed Schlachtgeschwaderen or 'battle wings' instead of Sturzkampfgeschwaderen 'dive bomber wings' since the FW190 was not a dive-bomber. This was very much a second best solution resulting from the failure to develop a proper successor to the Stuka but in the short term it turned out better than anyone had a right to expect. In the wider context it was now too late for even an outstanding new design to turn the tide of war.

The other area in which the Luftwaffe still held the edge in quality was the pilots who flew the planes. Notwithstanding what is stated above about improved Russian pilot quality, the Germans still held a margin of superiority though it was not what it had been and it was eroding every day. Both sides suffered horrifically from accidents. In 1944 one third of all Russian aircraft losses were incurred in accidents and in June 1944 the Luftwaffe's losses on the eastern front were 238 planes to enemy action and 194 to accidents. The causes of these extraordinary figures were bad weather, inadequate airfields and facilities and poor maintenance coupled with the fact that both sides were, of necessity, training their new pilots inadequately for the extraordinarily demanding job they faced.

In June 1944 the V.V.S. had available some 13,500 aircraft across the whole front and 5,300 were facing Army Group Centre, the target of Operation Bagration, grouped into no less than seven air armies. These were augmented by approximately 1,000 bombers and escorts of the centrally controlled long range bomber force. Facing them was Airfleet Six and this could muster just 500 aircraft of which only 100 were fighters. Another 400 or so bombers could fly in as support from other areas but their value was slight since, the moment they were used, Russian fighters would swarm around them and the Luftwaffe did not have the fighters to protect them. Such was the imbalance that there could be only one outcome of the impending air battle.

On 22nd June 1944, the third anniversary of Hitler's attack on Russia, Operation

Bagration was launched. The offensive began with an attack on the German forces defending the city of Vitebsk. There was no preliminary air assault until the night before, in order not to alert the defence to the impending attack but during that night 1,000 bomber sorties were flown against targets in the Vitebsk area. One of the units involved was 46th Guards Night Bomber Regiment, an all-female regiment. One of its pilots, Junior Lieutenant Raisa Zhitova-Yushina, later remembered aircraft taking off at three minute intervals like a conveyor belt and returning crews calling out to the ground staff to re-arm and re-fuel their planes so they could get back in the air as fast as possible. This particular young woman flew 535 bombing missions in the course of the war.[vii]

In the morning the troops rushed forward supported by the 400 Stormoviks of General Nicolai Papivin's 3rd Air Army. A new tactic was employed which consisted of sending infantry forward first under a blanket cover of air power operating in close co-operation with the ground forces. This was in contrast to the conventional pattern of attack by tanks first which was what the German defenders expected and were prepared for. Ritter von Greim, commander of Airfleet Six, at first assumed this unconventional attack was a feint and decided not to commit his limited resources. German aircraft shot down not a single Russian plane that first day.

The offensive unfolded over the next few days as a series of attacks on specific objectives and each was given overwhelming aerial support that stunned the defenders. The result was something not seen hitherto on the eastern front: roads choked with fleeing German vehicles and soldiers throwing away their arms and taking to their heels wholesale. It was a reprise of 1941 but with the roles reversed. Professor John Erickson in his history of the fighting in Russia says of the offensive that ground attack aircraft pounded German positions in numbers never before seen[viii] and the German historian Paul Carell goes much further: 'The decisive factor.... was above all the appearance of a superior Red Air Force which brought the decisive shift in the balance of power.'[ix]

The initial crumbling of the German defences gathered force until the whole central front was in retreat and troops were cut off and taken prisoner in large numbers. The German army in this region lost 400,000 men making this the biggest defeat it had ever suffered. In two months the front line was driven back to the East Prussian border and the gates of Warsaw: Russia was cleansed of the invader and the Luftwaffe could do nothing. Of course the airmen of Airfleet Six fought bravely and they caused losses but they were too few to make any serious difference. In strategic terms they were an irrelevance. Naturally, reinforcements were drafted in to try to stem the flood of Russian victory. One group of fighters was transferred from the West and another from Airfleet Four on the Rumanian border. Together these amounted to about 80 planes. The real need was for ground attack aircraft and to this end 85 were transferred from Italy which had already been stripped bare. This transfer effectively ended any German offensive capacity in that theatre. Another 40 were pulled out of Normandy which was a much wiser move since they could achieve next to nothing on that front against the massive air power of the Western Allies. 70 more came from Airfleet Four. Thus other fronts, already hard pressed, made sacrifices to help Army Group Centre but it was all in vain. These numbers were nowhere near enough to make a serious difference.

One question that must be asked, if only to be answered swiftly and put in the archives, is why the collapse of Army Group Centre in the East was so total from the start whereas in the West, in Normandy, the Wehrmacht fought bitterly for two months and hardly gave an inch before it finally allowed a breakthrough and had to retreat in chaos. One must bear in mind that in each case the German troops on the ground faced the same total air superiority of their enemy. Part of the answer is that the troops in Normandy included many of the finest formations in the German armed forces whereas the best divisions of Army Group Centre had been transferred elsewhere during 18 months of comparative quiet on its front. The main reason however, is simply one of scale. The Normandy invasion front was some 50 miles long and the Germans put 20 to 30 divisions into it while the front held by Army Group Centre was at least 200 miles held by 40 divisions. Readers can do the mathematics for themselves and see that the task in the East was much harder.

In the North Luftwaffe forces were sucked into the disaster occurring on their flank but this was one theatre where the Russians did not have things all their own way. This was the territory of Airfleet One, which included nearly 200 ground attack planes in veteran formations and in the Baltic states and south of Leningrad its fierce resistance slowed the Soviet advance to a crawl. An experienced Focke Wulf 190 group was transferred in from Finland and on the 26th July they achieved one of the Luftwaffe's last heavy aerial victories in the East when they intercepted a Russian bombing raid near Narva and shot down 11 bombers and two Stormoviks for the loss of one Fw190. Their commander, Major Eric Rudorffer, claimed six victories personally.[x] This was not a situation that could last however because the geography of the situation was such that Army Group North was threatened with being cut off owing to developments further south and therefore it steadily abandoned ground and retreated southwest toward the borders of Germany. The Russian advance was too fast however, and by the end of the year Army Group North was indeed cut off in the Courland Peninsula in Latvia together with what remained of Airfleet One.

With Army Group Centre defeated and retreating in confusion, the Red Army prepared its next blow further south. This was to be another major offensive toward the city of Lvov (Lemberg) in southern Poland past the town of Brody which was to be encircled. This operation would be carried out by the 1.2 million troops of the 1st Ukrainian front under Marshal Ivan Koniev. Supporting him was the 2nd Air Army commanded by Colonel General Stepan Krasovskiy. This single army alone contained over 3,000 aircraft.

Opposite them was Army Group North Ukraine and the 8th Air Corps. This corps had been part of Airfleet Four in the south but was transferred to Six in the centre of the front just before the offensive began. In reality this distinguished organization was nearly independent. Its commander, General Hans Seidemann was on top of his job and as soon as Bagration started he intensified reconnaissance flights in front of his own section of the front which soon detected a build-up of Soviet forces. This could mean only one thing and so he made an appeal for reinforcements and was given various units from the hard-pressed Airfleet Six amounting to 100 fighters and 100 ground attack planes. From the Rumanian front in the South came the crack 2nd Group of 52nd Fighter Wing now led by Helmut Lipfert: Gerhard Barkhorn had been shot down and was in hospital in Germany. These reinforcements pushed Seidemann's command up to some 600 planes but they were still, of course, outnumbered five to one.

The attack was launched on 13th July, two days earlier than intended because it was clear to Koniev that the Germans were improving their defensive position and there was no point in sitting still and watching that happen. With Stormoviks swarming above the front line the Russian infantry was able to achieve an immediate breakthrough. Seidemann was cautious about committing his force and the air combats on the first day were few. In one of them an experienced pilot named Mikhail Devyatayev was shot down and captured.

Devyatayev was sent to a prisoner-of-war camp near Koenigsburg (modern Kaliningrad) where Russian prisoners were kept in appalling conditions. He tried to escape but was caught and sent to Sachsenhausen concentration camp where he made another failed escape attempt and was sentenced to death. He survived by taking the identity of another prisoner who had just died and was then sent as a forced labourer to work at Peenemunde, the rocket base. There were German planes at the rocket base and on 8th February 1945 Devyatayev and several others were able to surprise the guards and steal one which he flew back to Russia. In Soviet Russia it was an offence to be taken prisoner and so, far from being welcomed home, he was arrested and sent to a penal battalion as punishment until his discharge after the war when he was effectively branded a traitor and struggled to find any kind of menial work in his post-war homeland. In 1953, with the death of Stalin, he was rehabilitated and in 1957 was a made a Hero of the Soviet Union. This award is mentioned in the Soviet Official History. The arrest and his subsequent treatment are not.[xi]

If 13th July was a quiet day as far as air operations were concerned, the next day was the opposite. On the ground the Germans launched a counter-attack at Brody and in the air they launched massive attacks including sorties by bombers flying from bases in the Airfleet Four area further to the south. Russian fighters were ready and large-scale air battles took place. At the end of the day the Russians counted 90 planes lost. German losses are uncertain but they were heavy. The battle for Brody was still undecided and the 15th saw more heavy fighting in the air and on the ground. Stormoviks and Pe-2s were in action all day and V.V.S. fighters struggled to keep the

Luftwaffe out of the battle area. One unit in the thick of the fighting was 129th Guards Fighter Regiment. During the day's combat it shot down six Stukas and two Fw190s for no loss. Only a year before, such a one-sided victory for Russian fighter planes would have been unthinkable. Evgeniy Mariinskiy, of that Regiment, whom we encountered musing on a feeling of superiority over the Germans, also flew that day escorting bombers but his force was not attacked and for him it was another quiet day.[xii] It should not be thought however, that Mariinsky did not do his share of fighting. By the war's end he had 20 victories and was made a Hero of the Soviet Union.

These two days of constant air assault decided the issue at Brody and by 18th July the town was surrounded and cut off. It surrendered a week later. On 23rd, Lublin fell and on 27th, Lvov. The Soviet army was marching to the Vistula in the heart of Poland and though there was still much fighting in the air, the pace of combat slackened as the inevitable corollary of air units changing bases. Evgeniy Mariinskiy complained that he could not find any German planes at all to fight. The 129th was transferred to an airfield at Sandomir on the Vistula and then quickly on to another airfield nearby. A pilot by the name of Gulyaev, a leading ace, placed his medals in a corner of the back of his plane's cockpit for safekeeping. His chief mechanic found them and thought they were not so safe as several aircraft had been hit by artillery fire while parked so he took them into his own custody. Shortly thereafter the regiment was transferred and when Gulyaev arrived at his new base and looked for his medals he could not find them. He was distraught and it was not until his mechanics with the ground convoy arrived some time later, that he recovered the precious medals and his composure. This was one tiny example of the confusion wrought on air units by change of base.[xiii]

The shortage of German aircraft was not surprising. German records for the period are incomplete and unreliable but it seems that in July Airfleet Six lost over 400 aircraft, in August another 350. This meant that it was virtually wiped out as an effective fighting force, at least for the time being. Moreover, all German air activities on all fronts were now increasingly being affected by lack of fuel. Bomber formations were used only in exceptional conditions because of their heavy fuel consumption and bomber pilots were increasingly being transferred to fighter units to make good losses. Flying a fighter plane is quite different from flying a bomber and even the most experienced of these men had, effectively, to start again as beginners.

Efficiency of administration and clarity of policy in the Luftwaffe were not aided by the confusion that followed when the Chief of Staff, General Gunther Korten was killed by the bomb that exploded on 20th July at Hitler's headquarters as part of the Stauffenberg coup attempt. His deputy, Karl Koller, took over briefly but Hitler disliked him and sought another candidate, his preference being for Ritter von Greim who was not only a capable commander but a convinced Nazi. Goering however, did not like Greim and so quickly appointed Werner Kreipe to the position to preempt Hitler. Kreipe was the man in charge of training for the Luftwaffe and had little command experience but he was another dedicated Nazi and an 'old fighter' who had taken part in the 1923 Beer Hall putsch in Munich. By October Kreipe's inadequacy in the post was obvious and his 'schoolmarm' manner annoyed Hitler. (He was known as 'Miss' Kreipe behind his back.[xiv]) He was replaced by Koller who held the position for the rest of the war.

In the spring of 1944 the bulk of the Luftwaffe's power was in the South of the front with Airfleet Four but by July that situation was reversed because of the steady flow of reinforcements northward and the South possessed barely 200 planes. Rumanian airpower, at around 500 aircraft, was considerable and its equipment, now largely German, was modern but its pilots were little disposed to fight an enemy whom they could foresee overrunning their country in short order and whom they were therefore reluctant to antagonize.

On 20th August Russian forces under Generals Malinovskiy and Tolbukhin launched an assault across the Rumanian border supported by 1,759 aircraft in two air armies. In response the Luftwaffe transferred 40 Stukas and 30 Fw190s mainly from the Baltic region but this was, of course, wholly inadequate. It was, however, in the political field that the major shock arrived. On the 23rd August, Marshal Antonescu, the Rumanian dictator, was arrested by his own officials and on 25th August Rumania declared war on Germany. A German attempt to take Bucharest with paratroops and restore a pro-Axis government was aborted because sufficient transport aircraft and trained crews could not be found in the time available. What had appeared a fairly stable front with a fair prospect of holding up the Russian advance, now collapsed in the familiar chaos and the German armed forces fled northward through Transylvania and on to the Hungarian plain. In this debacle the retreat was covered in the air by German planes fighting Rumanian ones and Messerschmitt fired at Messerschmitt and the retreating columns of the Wehrmacht were bombed by Stukas.

On September 6th Bulgaria also declared war on Germany and the whole of the southern and eastern Balkans were lost to Hitler's empire. Rapid movement of bases and lack of fuel soon reduced the Luftwaffe to near impotence in this area and on September 11th only 250 German sorties were flown on the whole front compared to more than 2,000 by the V.V.S.

The retreat in the Balkans left behind many thousand troops and German civilians stranded in Greece and her islands. Despite the war many people were able to find some excuse why duty forced them to spend time on a beach in the Dodecanese. On August 20th Hitler ordered an evacuation and a force of 100 transport planes was hurriedly assembled and flew until October carrying thousands to comparative safety in northern Yugoslavia or southern Hungary. There was little Allied interference with this operation at first. Stalin, for his part, had agreed with Churchill that Greece would be a British sphere of influence and so Russian forces took no part in its liberation. In due course the Western Allies realized what was afoot and attacked the transport aircraft, quickly strangling the operation which was abandoned at the end of October. 30,000 soldiers were evacuated from Greece together with an unknown number of civilians. 23,000 were left behind to spend the rest of the war marooned in Crete and the smaller islands.

By November the Russian army was approaching Budapest. Airfleet Four had by now swallowed up Southeast Command which had been the Balkan branch of the Luftwaffe but even so, and with such replacements as could be scraped up, that Airfleet only mustered some 600 aircraft and could do nothing to prevent the Red Army crossing the Danube north of Budapest on December 9th.

The veterans of the Luftwaffe fought on, putting out of their minds the fact that the struggle was now hopeless. Helmut Lipfert of Jg52 was now flying from an airfield outside Budapest and on 5th December he shot down a Yak-9 for his 159th victory. Unfortunately he made the beginner's mistake of watching it spiral down to crash and was himself hit by another Yak. His wingman destroyed the Yak but Lipfert's plane was too badly damaged to do more than glide back to the German lines while Lipfert searched for a flat place to land and settled on a race-course where he crash-landed neatly in the middle of the track. A staff car appeared and a German officer climbed out and greeted him. Before they left, the officer's driver siphoned the remaining fuel out of the aircraft's tank. Not a drop could now be wasted.[xv]

The summer of 1944 was one of unrelieved disaster for the German armed forces on the eastern front and the cause was primarily the new air superiority of the Russians. This was clear to all at the time and has since been routinely acknowledged by historians. What is not immediately so apparent is that the cause of that superiority was only partly the improvement in Soviet aircraft and crew training. The other major cause was the withdrawal of German fighter aircraft to the West in order to combat the Allied bomber offensive. In effect this meant the U.S.A.A.F. offensive, for two reasons. The first was that they bombed by day and therefore it was day fighters that had to combat them and day fighters were what the eastern front needed too. The R.A.F. bombed by night and it required specialized aircraft with specially trained crew to combat them. These aircraft would have been of use in the East too but there were fewer of them and they would have had to be modified for the ground attack role and their crews re-trained before they would have been of any practical value. Moreover, the most acute shortage was not of ground attack planes so much as single-engine fighters. The second reason was that the Americans were conducting a bombing campaign that was seriously damaging the German war economy including the production of aircraft and the British campaign, by and large, was not doing this to anything like the same degree.

288

CHAPTER TWENTY-TWO

Japan Overwhelmed

Once the might of U.S. industry had provided the ships, the U.S. Navy was ready to begin an advance through the middle of the Pacific Ocean which would cut to the heart of the Japanese Empire and pose a threat that invasions of remote south Pacific islands could never match. These two competing theatres and their different strategies were the fundamental dynamic of the U.S. war in the Pacific. The conflict between them was never really resolved. Their differences were reflected in the different characters of the two area commanders.

The south Pacific was commanded by General Douglas MacArthur, a colourful self-publicist with a gigantic ego for whom the whole war was one big career opportunity. He was excellent at fighting battles and after the war he was outstanding as the military governor of defeated Japan but we have seen his shocking negligence (or worse) at the time of Pearl Harbour and his career later ended abruptly when he was commander of the Nato forces in Korea and defied the authority of the United States Government. He was always hugely popular with the American public, a popularity which he was careful to cultivate.

The central Pacific was commanded by Admiral Chester Nimitz who was also in command of the U.S. Navy throughout the Pacific. Nimitz could not have been a bigger contrast to MacArthur. From a poor family in Texas, of German ancestry, he developed a love of the sea mainly because of his grandfather who had been a merchant seaman. A simple man who sought only to do his job well, he was extremely able and a fine commander. It is hard to find any serious fault with his conduct of American strategy.

The first objective of the 5th Fleet was to capture the Mariana Islands from which the Japanese homeland could be bombed. To do this the Marshall Islands had first to be taken and no attack on them could go forward until Tarawa Atoll on their southern flank was captured. Moreover Tarawa was close enough to the sea route from the U.S. west coast to Australia to pose a real threat to that vital artery. Tarawa was therefore the first target of the new U.S. 5th Fleet.

The 5th Fleet consisted of six large, Essex class, aircraft carriers and six of the smaller Independence class together with a large assortment of escorting vessels. It carried nearly 800 aircraft which was rather more than the whole of R.A.F. Fighter Command for most of the Battle of Britain and not far short of double the number that attacked Pearl Harbour. Ships and aircraft alike were now designed and equipped in the light of experience in real war and not just theory. The aircraft carriers were built so that dangerous components such as gasoline and bomb stores were given as much protection as possible and the crews were trained in efficient damage control, something that U.S. sailors did particularly well. All ships were now given a massive anti-aircraft armament, particularly of the shorter range quick-firing variety.

The aircraft were still divided between fighters, bombers and torpedo planes in roughly equal proportions but the fighters were now the excellent Hellcat that could best any Zero and the torpedo planes were the Grumman Avenger, which, after a poor start at Midway had shown itself to be probably the best carrier-born torpedo plane and light bomber that the war was to see. The bombers were still the Douglas Dauntless dive bomber though a replacement began to take over from it in November 1943. This aircraft was the Curtiss Helldiver and it was very controversial. It was much faster than the Dauntless and carried a bigger bomb load and it was larger and tougher but it had serious stability problems mainly due to the restrictions imposed by the limited size of elevators on aircraft carriers which led to the plane being designed with a body too short for the wings. This made it difficult and dangerous to fly and delayed its introduction into front line service where its performance was considered no more than adequate and the men who had to fly it disliked it. It did not take over as the main dive bomber for nearly a year after its first introduction[i] and even then the Dauntless was still widely used for the rest of the war. Both the R.A.F. and the Australian Air Force ordered Helldivers but when the first planes arrived and they actually flew them both air forces cancelled their orders. As a machine of destruction however, there is no doubt that the Helldiver was a step forward and the men who had to fly it were the U.S. Navy's carrier pilots who were about as well trained as pilots come and they overcame its vicissitudes though they may not have liked it. They called it 'The Beast' which neatly reflected their ambiguous attitude.

On November 20th Tarawa was stormed by U.S. Marines from a task force of 200 ships. The attack was preceded by a naval bombardment and raids by the fleet's air force together with land-based bombers from several distant islands. Observers thought that the bombardment was so thorough that no defender could be left alive but when the marines landed it was clear that many defenders had survived and were fighting fit. It took five days to subdue them. This is another example of the amazing ability of human beings to survive the most severe of bombardments.

There was an airfield on Tarawa. Indeed, as was usual in the Pacific, it was the most important feature of the island. It seems however, that at the time of the attack there were, at most, only a handful of reconnaissance planes using it. Certainly Japanese aircraft played no part in the battle.

On February 1st 1944 the Americans attacked their next target, Kwajalein in the Marshall Islands. The technique was the same and the result was the same. Kwajalein fell in a week even though it was a much bigger atoll. The Japanese defenders were not expecting an attack however, because the Americans had leapfrogged over several other islands. On February 17th Eniwetok on the western edge of the Marshalls was attacked and occupied in six days. The speed of these conquests should not be allowed to give the impression that they were easy. The defenders fought to the last man and the Americans suffered heavy casualties on each island. This is however, a book about the air war and so the fighting for these islands cannot be covered in detail.

Japanese air defence in the Marshalls was feeble. In theory fighter cover was provided by 252nd Air Group based at Roi Island (part of Kwajalein Atoll) and at Wake Island but the Marshall Islands cover 400,000 square miles and one air group was far too little for such a large area. The Americans knew all about these bases and bombed them heavily at the end of 1943. In one raid on Wake alone 16 Zeros were shot down defending their base quite apart from aircraft destroyed on the ground. After this treatment and given the poor serviceability rates in the Pacific islands there were not more than a handful of active planes to oppose the mighty 5th Fleet which rapidly reduced that handful to nil.

The way was now clear to attack the Marianas but there was a drawback. West of the Marshalls lie the Caroline Islands and here the Japanese had their largest base in the mid- and South Pacific at Truk Atoll. It was sometimes called 'the Gibraltar of the Pacific'. Assaulting Truk would be a task of a whole new degree of magnitude. Judging by the Japanese resistance on the islands just mentioned, the much larger and better equipped garrison on Truk would mean a major battle. Moreover there was a substantial fleet in the harbour there and an airfield with several hundred planes. The Americans adopted an alternative strategy: they decided to knock out Truk as a threat to their operations by the massive use of air power and then leave it alone. It did not matter how many thousand troops there were on Truk if they were effectively marooned there because all their ships had been sunk.

The same morning as the Eniwetok attack, Truk was raided by aircraft from the carrier force and the raids continued all that day and all the next. To the chagrin of the U.S. pilots there were no major warships present because the Japanese had anticipated an attack like this and moved most of their fleet to a safer anchorage further west. There were many other ships in the harbour however, and during the two days American planes sank the three Japanese cruisers: Naka, Katori and Agano, three destroyers and 26 cargo vessels, in all 200,000 tons of shipping. There were 360 aircraft at Truk and, taken by surprise, many of them rose to defend the base as the first fighter sweep came in at dawn led by Lieutenant Commander Ed Owens and his squadron from the carrier Yorktown, named after the ship lost at Midway. Owens described the scene as like a Hollywood film set with aircraft taking off, bursting into flames and crashing all around him. There were so many targets it was hard to concentrate on one long enough to shoot it down.[ii] Nevertheless 50 Japanese planes were shot down in the first 20 minutes. They were out-flown by the

Americans who now had the better planes and more experience. The days when Japanese Navy pilots were among the best in the world were long gone. By the second day the air opposition had vanished. 275 Japanese planes were destroyed and the Americans lost 25 of their own. Perhaps more important, the U.S. strikes devastated the base's infrastructure: oil tanks, workshops, dry-docks, barracks, they were all destroyed. It was a stunning demonstration of what air power could achieve.

Thereafter the U.S. air force sent its B-24 bombers based in the Solomon Islands to hit Truk again at intervals with the intention of preventing a recovery. In this they were not entirely successful and it soon became clear that the Japanese were building up a force of aircraft there for operations against the new American bases in the Marshalls so a second blow was ordered and the 5th Fleet's aircraft returned on 29th and 30th April and bombed anything that had survived the first attack. There were 104 Japanese aircraft at Truk at this time and the American raids on these two days destroyed 93 of them. Three were shot down by Lieutenant Hollis Hills who had flown for the R.A.F. in Europe and shot down the first ever plane to be destroyed by a P-51 Mustang, over Dieppe two years before.[iii] American losses were 26 but many of the pilots were recovered by U.S. submarines lurking in the area for just that purpose. Some were even rescued inside the lagoon itself. Truk was never a serious threat again.

The success of the first Truk raid encouraged 5th Fleet to raid other islands in March and April 1944. The Fleet concentrated on targets in the Caroline Islands: Palau, Yap and Woleai. The attack on Palau was a notable success with a considerable number of Japanese aircraft shot down or destroyed on the ground. U.S. pilots claimed 90 kills but even at the time that was considered an exaggeration. A novel feature of the attack was that specially adapted Avenger bombers dropped mines outside the island's harbour so that the ships there could not put to sea and could be destroyed at leisure in the harbour. In all 36 ships were sunk, though again, no major warships. Yap and Woleai yielded few targets and were not really worth the effort of the attack. Woleai, however, provided an extraordinary example of the skill and bravery used to rescue pilots. Ensign John Galvin's plane came down in the sea and he swam to a nearby islet. The submarine U.S.S. Harder was waiting nearby and sent a rubber dinghy manned by three volunteers to fetch him. They battled through crashing surf to get there but then they could not get back with the wind and the seas against them. Another seaman then swam 500 yards from the submarine carrying a line which was attached to the dinghy and the craft and all five men were winched back to safety. All this was done under rifle fire from the shore of the main island.[iv]

On May 27th American troops landed on Biak Island off the northwest coast of New Guinea. This was an operation of the southwest Pacific area and was therefore under the authority of General MacArthur who felt that the main thrust of the campaign against Japan should be directed via Indonesia and the Philippines. Nimitz felt it should be in the central Pacific. The final resolution of this dispute was to be an unhappy compromise that involved elements of both ideas. The Japanese were very worried by the attack on Biak because the island was uncomfortably close to the oil resources of Indonesia. The troops on Biak held out stubbornly and several attempts were made to reinforce and assist them. One of these involved sending a convoy of troopships to the island on June 3rd but the convoy was forced to turn back by the ferocity of American air attacks.

When Admiral Yamamoto, the Japanese naval commander-in-chief was killed the year before, he was succeeded by Admiral Mineichi Koga and it was he who had astutely removed the main fleet from Truk before it was raided, but on 31st March 1944 he was killed in an accident when the flying boat in which he was travelling crashed in bad weather. He was in turn succeeded by Admiral Soemu Toyoda who resolved that the time had come for the crucial naval confrontation with the Americans. Biak and its airfields featured in his plan for this battle which was known as Operation A-Go. He had already sent Japan's two super-battleships, Yamato and Musashi, to bombard the Americans on Biak when he received news that the main American fleet was in the Marianas and bombarding Saipan. This changed everything. He recalled the two super-ships and prepared for a major counter-strike in the Marianas, probably with a sense of relief.

The Americans landed on Saipan on 15th June after the usual bombardment and preparatory air attacks by the fleet. This was the largest amphibious operation in history so far with 535 ships and 127,000 soldiers. As usual great damage was done by the preparatory attacks including the destruction of over 100 aircraft which was a blow to Admiral Toyoda who had been counting on the contribution those aircraft could make to his impending operation. As usual too, most of the defenders survived and there began a fierce battle for the island.

Now Toyoda knew exactly where the main American fleet was, it was time to launch his decisive operation. His principle weapon was the Mobile Fleet under the command of Admiral Ozawa. The fleet consisted of almost the whole of the remaining Japanese Navy. Its core was the carriers Shokaku, Zuikaku, Taiho, Hiyo and Junyo and the light carriers Ryujo, Chitose, Chiyoda and Zuiho. They were escorted by the Yamato and Musashi and four other older battleships, 13 cruisers and 30 destroyers. The fleet could muster 475 aircraft. Its commander was one of the best admirals in the Japanese service. He was an intelligent man and a strategic thinker and he was calm and deliberate by nature. He was also very tall at six foot seven inches, which, for a Japanese, is tall indeed and very ugly so that he was nicknamed 'the gargoyle.'v

The fleet's fighter planes were the stalwart Zero. This was a new model with more ammunition, a more powerful engine and, at last, a modicum of armour. Unfortunately the Zero was now simply outdated and cosmetic changes could not alter that fact. The navy had new fighter designs in the pipeline but they were not ready yet. The old Val dive bomber and Kate torpedo plane were gone and in their place were the Yokosuka D4Y Susei, codenamed 'Judy' and the Nakajima B6N

Tenzan codenamed 'Jill'. These were better planes and potentially a real step forward but they suffered from the chronic Japanese fault of neglecting strength of construction in favour of manoeuverability and range. The real problem with Japanese naval aviation in 1944 however, was lack of training. The men flying these planes were raw replacements posted to their carriers to replace lost pilots after quite inadequate instruction. They had had between two and six months training whereas American carrier pilots had had two years training[vi] and plenty of vital battle experience on top of that. Shortly after the Mobile Fleet set sail for the Marianas there was an accident on the Taiho when the pilot of a Jill lost control as he came in to land on the deck and slid into parked planes. The result was an explosion and six aircraft were destroyed.[vii] The pilot concerned was not even competent enough to land his plane successfully.

The battle plan relied upon the fleet's aircraft being supported by up to 500 land based aircraft from various islands in the vicinity and upon the skillful use of the one tactical advantage the Japanese possessed which was that their lighter aircraft had a longer range than the American so that if they could contrive to launch an attack when they were between 200 and 300 miles from the U.S. fleet the Americans would be unable to reply because their attack planes would not have the fuel to reach the attackers. Unfortunately for the Japanese both these factors turned out to be illusory. For a start most of the land based planes had melted away. Some had been on Saipan and were already scrap, some had been caught on Biak and many more on various islands in the Palau group had either been shot down by ranging American fighters or moved elsewhere to counter local threats. How many actually did join in the imminent battle is not clear but it was nothing like 500. The range advantage lost much of its force because the Americans chose to ignore it.

On June 18th a reconnaissance plane from one of the carriers found the American carrier force, known as Task Force 58, and news of the sighting was sent to Ozawa. Rear Admiral Obayashi, in charge of the light carriers which were in the lead, wanted to attack at once but there was not much light left and Ozawa decided the attack must come in the morning. Obayashi had to recall some aircraft he had already launched.

In the morning Ozawa launched every plane he could put in the air for a massive strike against the Americans who knew his position from intercepted radio traffic but could do nothing about it because the range was at least 300 miles. The Japanese strike was in four waves, each composed of bombers and torpedo planes escorted by Zeros. In theory Ozawa had now perfectly capitalized on his range advantage but it did him no good: his planes and his pilots could not exploit their advantage. The first wave of 71 planes took off at 8.30 a.m., formed up and disappeared to the east into the rising sun of a beautiful clear day. The second wave, 128 planes, took off just before 9 a.m.. As his bomber rose into the air from the deck of the Taiho, Warrant Officer Akio Komatsu spotted the trail of a torpedo in the water heading for his ship.

With great quickness of mind he turned his plane and made a suicide dive onto the torpedo. Plane and torpedo exploded in a fiery conflagration but the Taiho was not saved.[viii] A second torpedo struck her in the starboard side and water flooded in. At first the damage was contained but the torpedo had struck near the gasoline store and the shaft for the forward elevator began to fill with a mixture of gasoline and fuel oil. An inexperienced damage control officer ordered all ventilation ducts opened to clear the fumes but this action merely ensured that the fumes filled the ship which became a floating bomb just waiting for a spark.

The torpedoes were from an American submarine, U.S.S. Albacore, one of a number that had been arranged as a kind of picket line around the main fleet. A second submarine, Cavalla, torpedoed the Shokaku. It was a perfect attack and three hits were scored. Shokaku was rocked by explosions and it was soon clear that she was doomed. At 3 pm she rolled over and sank and a few minutes later the inevitable spark finally lit the fumes on Taiho which was blown apart by explosions and rapidly followed Shokaku beneath the waves.

Meanwhile the Japanese aircraft neared the mighty American fleet which included seven large aircraft carriers and eight light ones with a complement of over 800 planes. Task Force 58 was commanded by a very able and experienced admiral called Marc Mitscher who had been a distinguished pilot of seaplanes in the inter-war years and was the captain of the Hornet when she raided Japan in 1942.

American Hellcats fell on the Japanese force and destroyed it. The first pilot to attack was Lieutenant Commander C.W. Brewer. He shot down two bombers and then found a Zero on his tail. He shook it off and then shot it down too, and a few moments later destroyed a second Zero.[ix] In all 25 Japanese planes were shot down by the first American attack. After a brief pause a second group of Hellcats attacked and shot down 16 more. Only one aircraft got through to the fleet. It dropped its bomb on a battleship but the resulting damage was minor.

The second wave were still 60 miles out when the Hellcats hit them and shot down 70 planes. About 20 broke through to the fleet and attacked the American ships but they were met by a storm of anti-aircraft fire and most were shot down. They caused slight damage to several ships but nothing that reduced the fleet's fighting efficiency. In all 97 aircraft of this wave were destroyed. The aircraft of the third and fourth waves had been given the wrong co-ordinates for the American fleet (in the circumstances a criminal piece of negligence) and so posed little threat. Of the third wave of 47 aircraft, only 12 reached the American fleet at all. Seven of those were destroyed and the others scored no hits. The 87 planes of the fourth wave never found the fleet despite a long search, though one small group broke away to land on the island of Rota and found the Americans by chance. Its attack did no damage and only one Japanese plane escaped both fighters and anti-aircraft fire. The 18 planes from the Zuikaku became separated and were turned back by a force of Hellcats. The main party, when too low on fuel to return to their own carriers, tried to land on the island of Guam only to be ambushed by more prowling American fighters. 30 were shot down and the rest were thoroughly strafed once they landed. 19 planes landed but all were damaged in varying degree and in the evening Mitscher sent a bomber raid to Guam that finished them off together with many other aircraft on the island. One of the escorting Hellcats was flown by Lieutenant Commander Brewer. At one point defending Zeros sprang a trap of their own and Brewer and two other pilots were shot down and killed.[x]

As darkness came down Ozawa withdrew to the northwest and prepared to launch a further attack with his remaining aircraft the next day. The exact position was unclear to him. He did not know of the slaughter at Guam and many of his pilots reported fanciful victories and tales of carriers sunk.

Mitscher, now uncertain of the position of the Japanese fleet, again headed west during the night to chase it. Unfortunately this was the wrong direction. It was not until 3.40 p.m. on 20th that Ozawa was found and he was 275 miles away. It has to be said that if the American fleet had a weakness it was its poor reconnaissance. Mitscher had planes capable of night reconnaissance but did not use them. It is not clear quite why. One reason was certainly the fact that such missions were so dangerous as to be close to suicidal and the Admiral did not like ordering men to probable death.[xi]

It was late afternoon and the Japanese were really out of range but Mitscher decided to attack anyway and sent out a strike of 200 planes. They found the Mobile Fleet at the day's end and immediately attacked. Everyone who was present later remembered a scene of great natural beauty with the sun just touching the horizon and clouds stained with bright colours.[xii] There were 75 Zeros in the air and they, and anti-aircraft fire, shot down 20 U.S. aircraft but could not stop the attack. The carrier Hiyo was hit by several torpedoes and sank swiftly. Zuikaku was hit by bombs and badly damaged. The order to abandon ship was even given at one point though rapidly rescinded. The light carrier Chiyoda was also hit by a bomb and her flight deck ruined. The battleship Haruna was hit though not seriously damaged. In addition two tankers were sunk.

Now the attackers faced the return trip in the dark and, for many of them, the prospect of inadequate fuel which would mean no hope of reaching their carriers. For some the situation was hopeless. Lieutenant George Brown had sworn before the mission that he would 'get a carrier' and he was responsible for one of the torpedo strikes on the Hiyo but his plane was repeatedly hit, his crew baled out and he turned for home so badly injured he could not fly straight. Another plane guided him for a while but lost him when night fell. Brown was never seen again.[xiii] Mitscher, well aware of the desperate situation, took the great risk of ordering his ships to turn their lights on so that returning pilots could see them and this action undoubtedly saved many lives though it risked many more by reason of submarine attack which, fortunately, never came. Nevertheless no less than 80 planes ditched in the sea or crashed on landing. Efficient pilot recovery efforts during the night and the next day meant that only 16 pilots and 33 crewmen were lost. And so the battle ended. It was, and remains, the largest carrier battle of all time.

These two days of fighting became known as the Battle of the Philippine Sea though to American pilots the whole affair was better known as the 'Great Marianas Turkey Shoot'. It was a decisive victory that saw three large Japanese aircraft carriers sunk and 475 aircraft destroyed, of which 425 were the irreplaceable carrier planes. This was the end of the Japanese Navy's aircraft carrier threat because although they still had some carriers left they had no more than a handful of crews. The Americans lost no important ship and only 120 aircraft of which most were ditched as set out above.

The Americans were not as delighted by the battle as they ought to have been, partly because they were not immediately aware how critical were the Japanese losses and partly because there was a strong feeling in some circles that Spruance should have ordered Mitscher to give chase to Ozawa and finish him off. Spruance however, had clear orders to keep his ships close to Saipan to protect the landings there and not allow them to be lured away for any reason. Shortly after the battle Admiral Ernest J. King, Commander-in-Chief of the U.S. Navy went out of his way to assure Spruance that he had done the right thing but the controversy took some of the lustre off the victory.

On the Asian mainland 1944 saw the first major offensive by the Japanese for two years. First however, we must take a brief look at what occurred in the intervening time.

By the late spring of 1942 Burma was in Japanese hands and the road to China had been cut. American supplies now had to travel by air and a difficult and dangerous route it was, angling across the eastern part of the Himalayas and colloquially known as 'the Hump.' The Japanese 5th Air division, which provided the aerial support in this theatre, went into a semi-operational status in the summer because of the monsoon and many of the machines and their pilots were transferred on a rota basis to Malaya for training and exercises. The Division numbered about 200 planes of all types at this time.

With Burma lost, the front line now ran more or less along the Indian border and the British had to base their operations within that huge country and avail themselves of its infrastructure. From the point of view of military aviation that infrastructure was virtually non-existent when the war began. There were only 16 all-weather airfields in the whole country and not a single radar station. There was a primitive observer network but it was all set up to cover the northwest frontier on the other side of the country from the Japanese threat. In March of 1942 a plan was put into action to remedy these defects and by the end of the year there were 83 all-weather airfields and numerous second rate ones mainly with earth runways. There were also 50 radar stations and a new observer network based on Calcutta. The British Air Ministry made a study and concluded that this theatre needed 64 squadrons![xiv] Such a target had an element of pie-in-the-sky but at least a start was made. Two squadrons of Wellingtons were sent and there was a steady trickle of Hurricanes since they had largely been replaced by Spitfires in Europe. There were also no less than six squadrons of an aircraft called the Vultee Vengeance, a two-seater dive bomber of American origin ordered by the British Purchasing Commission which was sent to the U.S.A. in 1940. The Commission was impressed by the achievements of the Stuka and thought the R.A.F. should have a dive-bomber of its own so Vultee Aircraft designed one to fill the British requirement. By the time the Vengeance was delivered the Air Ministry had decided that dive bombers were not such a good idea after all, in the European theatre at least, where they had now seen Stukas shot down in large numbers by Spitfires. Vengeances were therefore all dispatched to the Pacific where it was anticipated, rightly, that they would face less intense opposition. As well as the R.A.F. the Australians used large numbers of them. Although it is generally known as second rate, if known at all, the Vengeance was, in fact, an excellent aircraft of its kind.

In early 1943 Richard Peirse was made Commander-in-Chief of air forces in India and began a complete reorganization of the command structure. When he arrived in Delhi he was shocked by the large size and poor quality of the headquarters staff and set about rectifying the problem. Since he had himself been removed from command of Britain's strategic bomber force because he was seen as not equal to the job, one may permit oneself a wry smile at this point. In fact the overall Commander-in-Chief in India, Archibald Wavell, had been removed from command of the Middle East in similar circumstances. Indeed this whole theatre was openly regarded as of the lowest priority for equipment and a repository for second rate soldiers.

Second rate or not, Peirse did a good job, often fighting pig-headed bureaucracy. For instance he saw at once that the location of the HQ in Delhi 800 miles away from where the fighting was going on, was madness and relocated it in Calcutta on his own initiative. When he informed London what he had done he was told that he had exceeded his authority and the transfer was quite unnecessary. The matter was not resolved until a senior officer observer had been sent from London to report on the situation and completely vindicated Peirse.[xv]

In the middle of 1942 the American Volunteer Group in China, the Flying Tigers, were incorporated into the U.S. air force and became, after an interval, part of 14th Air Force whose area of operations was China. The volunteer pilots were offered commissions in the U.S.A.A.F. but few accepted. Instead they dispersed to a variety of jobs, mainly of an aviation nature, all over the Pacific. Gregory Boyington, for instance, rejoined the marines as we have seen. The 14th Air Force was expanded by the creation of a, so-called, 'Composite Wing' using U.S. equipment and a mixture of U.S. and Chinese personnel. Its overall strength rose to some 200 fighters and 50 bombers (B-25 Mitchells) and it fought in China till the end of the war.

In the spring of 1944 the Americans began to fly the new and revolutionary B-29 bomber into India and then over the Himalayas to China by the route known as 'the

Hump'. The original plan was for a large force of these aircraft to bomb targets across southeast Asia and Japan but the logistics defeated even the Americans and in the end barely 100 planes operated from China as XXth Bomber Command and every gallon of fuel they consumed and every bomb they dropped had to be flown in from India. Their first raid was made on June 5th 1944 by 98 planes and was against targets in Thailand. Five aircraft were lost though not to enemy action. The B-29 experienced much mechanical trouble in its early flying days. On 15th June 58 aircraft raided Japan and though they caused little damage, the effect on Japanese opinion was electric since this was the first raid on the homeland since the Doolittle attack of 1942. Such were the supply problems, however, that this force could only mount two attacks per month and by the new year the whole campaign was abandoned in favour of the bomber offensive from the Mariana Islands. XXth Bomber Command moved to India to assist the campaign in Burma and in March 1945 it was transferred to the Marianas.

Another reason for the abandoning of this campaign was the fact that the presence of the bombers prompted the Japanese army to launch an offensive in China largely for the purpose of overrunning the B-29 bases or at least pushing them back far enough that they were out of range of the Japanese homeland. Thus the B-29s had turned a relatively quiet front into an active one, which did not serve the Allied purpose.

By the beginning of 1943 the R.A.F. and the Indian Air Force had some 2,000 planes of all kinds in India. However, this is an all-inclusive figure covering everything down to training aircraft and it covers the whole sub-continent. On the Burma front, facing the Japanese, there were some 200 fighters and 150 bombers, and given the problems of maintenance in a tropical environment the aircraft actually ready to fly on any one day would have been, by a margin, even less. The U.S.A.A.F. had sent the 10th Air Force to New Delhi in May 1942 but at that stage it was no more than a headquarters and during the year it received just two bomber groups to flesh it out: one of B-24s and another of B-25 Mitchells.

A word should be said here about the conditions under which the war was fought in India and Burma. In India the winter was the dry season but in the northeast of the country, which is where our attention is focused, it was not only dry but extremely hot to the extent that heatstroke was an everyday occurrence amongst the troops and in Calcutta local people died in the street. In Burma the situation was similar save that the atmosphere was more humid. Everything that was said about the tribulations of trying to run an air force in the islands of the south Pacific should be repeated in the context of Burma. Heat, rot, disease and poor and monotonous rations were the staples of life for aircrew and ground crew alike. Dysentery was endemic. The serviceability rate for aircraft was correspondingly low. On the Japanese side the men generally endured hardship better because they were used to a lower standard of living and because of an innate stoicism, but on the mechanical side the maintenance problem was, if anything, worse because Japanese military

A U.S. North American B-25 bomber roars over Japanese positions on Wotje in
the Marshall Islands. The B-25 turned out to be ideally suited to the testing
conditions of the Pacific air war.
©Imperial War Museum (NYP 17989)

transport left much to be desired and spare parts were always in short supply.

The dry weather brought a campaign of air attacks on Calcutta by the Japanese
which caused a panic evacuation of 1.5 million people. This led to the emergency
import of a squadron of night fighters who were so successful that they halted the
campaign in a few days for the loss of one Beaufighter whose crew bailed out and
landed in the swamps around the Hooghly River. They had to wade for three hours
in water up to their chests to find safety.[xvi]

The British now launched an offensive down the coast with the limited object of
capturing the town of Akyab and its airfields but Japanese resistance was stiff, air
support was inadequate and the attackers underestimated the mobility of the Japanese
army in jungle conditions. The British had much to learn about how to mount a
successful jungle offensive. There were also besetting problems in India where there
were riots and a savage famine, factors that required a large garrison to be retained
within the Indian borders. By May the offensive had run into the ground, the Japanese

had counter-attacked and the attackers were back where they started. An experimental exercise at this time was the sending of a column of troops to infiltrate the Japanese front in the jungle and cause damage to their lines of supply and communication. The column was led by an eccentric but charismatic officer called Orde Wingate and his troops became known as Chindits after a mythological Burmese winged lion. The column achieved some success at a heavy price but the most interesting thing about it from an aviation point of view was that it was entirely supplied by air with provisions dropped by parachute. This was a technique which, when perfected, would revolutionize combat in the Burmese jungle where there was one single railway line in the whole country and scarcely any roads amounting to more than a footpath.

In 1944 the Japanese launched a major offensive against India. Their reasoning was that the Indian people would rise up in their support to throw of the shackles of imperialism. Though this idea was undoubtedly fanciful they had some cogent evidence to back it: their friendly reception by the Burmese and the existence of an Indian nationalist army willing to fight at their side. The harder reasoning behind the offensive was the fact that they were coming under pressure from a Chinese/American offensive in the north of the country and Allied air power was beginning to make the supply of their forces in Burma impossible. A successful invasion of India would remedy all their problems at one stroke.

This supply problem was an example of the impact of air power used indirectly. Supply for the Japanese army in Burma had to come by sea either to one of the small ports on the west coast or to the port of Rangoon from where it was carried along the country's sole railway that ran north/south up to Myitkyina.

By 1944 British and American bombers were able to sink the ships and cut the railway. The Japanese decided, early on, to join up the rail network of Thailand and Malaya with that of Burma by building a link line from Thailand across the border to Rangoon. This would enable ships to unload at Bangkok or Singapore, well out of the range of Allied aircraft. Supplies could then travel the rest of the way by rail. As we have seen, damage to railways caused by bombing is normally relatively easily repaired but the railways in question were in rough and inaccessible country and included many vulnerable bridges. The link line itself was a poorly constructed single track section in mountainous land which never carried a great volume even when running at full capacity, which was rare. It was built with slave labour, including Allied prisoners of war, working under inhuman conditions. In the region of 100,000 workers died of disease, malnutrition and mistreatment to realize the project which was completed in October 1943. So terrible was this episode that the phrase 'death railway' came into being to describe this scene of the most terrible human suffering.

The Japanese offensive developed into a struggle for the two towns of Kohima and Imphal. 5th Air Division provided the air support as usual though it was weakened by the withdrawal of units to fight in the Pacific theatre. Exact details are hard to find because of the loss or critical records. Allied air power had by now swelled to major proportions. Many of the British Hurricanes were replaced by Spitfires which at last gave the R.A.F. a fighter plane that could best the Japanese fighters. Their biggest drawback was their lack of range which was a crucial failing in a theatre of such huge distances.

The American presence in particular had grown out of all recognition. 10th Air Force now included three fighter groups equipped with a mixture of Lightnings, Thunderbolts and the excellent P-51 Mustang. 5th Air Division took heavy losses during the battle. On 27th March 1944 alone the Americans claimed 26 victories and four 'probables' for the loss of two aircraft. Ground troops later found 22 wrecks in the area of the dogfight. Given the fact that several planes probably fell further away and were never discovered, balanced by the tendency of all claims to be an exaggeration the reality probably matched the claim almost exactly. Japanese pilots did their best but they were heavily outmatched. For instance Warrant Officer Bunichi Yamaguchi was based near Rangoon and intercepted a night attack by B-24 Liberators. By the light of the searchlights he picked out one of the bombers and shot it down. It was quite a feat to shoot down a heavy bomber with a tiny, lightly armed Oscar fighter. Yamaguchi was presented with a citation for bravery by General Tazoe, commander of 5th Air Division, which was quite an honour in an air force that did not award medals. Two bombers were shot down that night but the raid was not stopped. In August Yamaguchi was transferred to the Philippines. By the end of the war he had shot down six four-engine bombers: an astonishing achievement.[xvii]

The troops in the Kohima/Imphal area were cut off for three months and in that time the Allied air forces maintained 120,000 men entirely by air. As well as supplies they took some 20,000 men into the pocket and 60,000 out. This was an outstanding achievement which invites comparison with the German achievement at Demyansk. The circumstances were very different of course, but Kohima/Imphal proved that a whole army could indeed be maintained from the air for a prolonged period of time. Naturally complete air supremacy was required and that the Allies had. 5th Air Division never seriously threatened it. Allied bombers were able to pound Japanese ground forces relentlessly though the jungle provides ideal cover from air attack. Fighter-bombers sought out specific targets such as airfields and carried out effective surprise attacks. For instance on 25th March Lieutenant Hampton Boggs, leading a flight of P-38 Lightnings, spotted a squadron of Oscars in the process of landing at Anisakan airfield. He was able to drop to treetop level and surprise them. He personally shot down three planes in quick succession and much of the Japanese squadron was destroyed on the ground or in the air. Two U.S. planes were lost.[xviii]

One can safely say that this was a battle that simply could not have been won without the contribution of air power.

With the conclusion of the fighting at Kohima and Imphal the monsoon effectively closed down campaigning until November 1944. During the break the Japanese army transferred away most of the strength of 5th Air Division and when the weather cleared there were no more than 50 Japanese aircraft ready for action in Burma. That was a trifling number and Allied air superiority from now on was total.

In November Air Chief Marshal Richard Peirse was relieved of command of the air forces in Burma as a result of perceived irregularities in his private life, as noted earlier and his place was due to be taken by Trafford Leigh-Mallory. When this officer was killed in an accident on his way to take up his appointment, the job was given to Air Chief Marshal Keith Parke. In view of Parke's ousting from the command of 11 Group by Leigh-Mallory in 1940 there was a certain irony in the situation.

At the end of November 1944 the great offensive for the liberation of Burma began. Since there were few landing craft available in this theatre, a major amphibious operation on the Burmese coast was ruled out and therefore the offensive must be overland from the borders of India southward the length of Burma. Since there was no viable infrastructure for supplying the troops in this jungle-clad land and the only railway had been comprehensively wrecked by bombing, the whole operation would have to be supplied almost exclusively by air. Once Rangoon was captured, with its capacious docks, supplies could be brought in by sea but Rangoon was in the South. It had to be captured by the start of May when the rains came because air supply could not realistically be counted on during the monsoon.

The campaign that followed was a triumph of military science. The British 14th Army was led by General Sir William Slim, one of the finest generals that the Second World War was to produce. He recorded that the army's officers at the crossing of the Irrawaddy River were loud in praise of the air support they were receiving. When a call for aid was sent aircraft appeared within a matter of minutes. They were particularly effective in silencing Japanese artillery and knocking out tanks.[xix] This was just one episode of many such. Slim was not always an unquestioning admirer of the R.A.F. however. At the battle for the town of Meiktila he wished to be flown to a newly captured landing strip to see front line conditions for himself but to his fury the R.A.F. refused to fly him there because it was too dangerous and he was too valuable. They would take one of his staff officers, he was politely informed, but not him. He had his way in the end by hitching a lift with a U.S. plane.[xx]

The army reached Rangoon in the nick of time arriving as the first rains fell. The whole advance was a triumph of air supply which brought in 74,000 tons a month to 14th Army and an astonishing 95,000 tons if all the Allied forces in Burma are taken into account.[xxi] Battle casualties were flown out as transport planes flew home. This means that 3,000 tons per day were flown in and it took over 1,000 transport aircraft to do it. It is worth recalling that the Luftwaffe could not manage 500 tons per day to keep the troops in Stalingrad supplied. The basic difference, of course, is simply a matter of resources: the Allies had the aeroplanes and the Germans did not. From the point of view of the history of aerial warfare, it is this extraordinary achievement that underlines the importance of the Burma campaign of 1945.

CHAPTER TWENTY-THREE

The End in the West

On the 17th September 1944 the Allied Supreme Command launched the greatest air assault ever seen to seize the bridges over the lower Rhine in the vicinity of the town of Arnhem. Over 4,600 aircraft took part. There were 1,000 transport aircraft and 490 gliders escorted by 1,450 fighters. 1,000 bombers went ahead to smooth the way by bombing airfields and known flak sites along the route. 73 aircraft were still shot down by the flak but not a single aircraft was lost to any attacks by the Luftwaffe who made no attempt to interfere at all. 15 Fw190s were seen near the town of Wesel but swiftly made themselves scarce and that was all.[i] The Luftwaffe was no longer a significant part of the German war machine able to affect the outcome of battles. It was still very much in existence and at this time was re-grouping and growing in strength but it would never again be able to make more than a marginal difference.

The failure of the Arnhem assault condemned all sides to another winter of war and in the West that winter was largely one of stalemate as the Germans tried to recoup their strength on the borders of their country and the Allies sorted out their system for the provision of supplies which had collapsed during their rapid advance across Europe.

In November Leigh-Mallory was killed flying to India. He had, inevitably, been relieved of his European command in August and appointed to run the R.A.F. in southeast Asia, the graveyard of careers. The plane in which he was flying crashed in bad weather in the French Alps. The crew warned him it was not safe to fly but he insisted.

The Germans were remarkably successful in making a recovery. They were able to mount a counter-offensive in the Ardennes at the end of the year and the Luftwaffe was rapidly regaining its strength. Its failure to attack during the Arnhem operation was partly a matter of policy because it was obvious to the Luftwaffe General Staff that they must not allow their remaining resources to be bled away by intervening in situations where they could not hope to make a material difference. Operations were now largely confined to defending transport and communication facilities close behind the front line because they had discovered in Normandy that Allied attacks here had been particularly effective and had, inter alia, prevented the easy supply of replacement aircraft. Every squadron was now provided with a good quantity of spare planes ready for use at its own airfield.

September 1944 was, despite Allied bombing, the best month of the war for

German aircraft production and during the autumn the front line fighter strength grew by 70 percent from 1,900 to 3,300. The figures mask two big weaknesses however. First the quality of the majority of pilots was inevitably poor and nothing could be done about that. Second there was an increasingly acute shortage of oil and oil products and in particular aviation spirit. The oil shortage was one of the most important features of the situation and more will be said about it in due course.

The expansion of the fighter force was achieved at the expense of the bomber arm. In the first nine months of 1944 25 bomber groups were disbanded and by the end of the year there was only a token force left. In the new environment the pressing demand was for fighters, and yet more fighters and bombers had become something of a luxury. Albert Speer's measures to overcome the effects of bombing such as dispersal of production and standardization of parts had the weakness that it worked better with simple machines than more complex ones and this made bomber production even more unrewarding. By disbanding bomber units a small but priceless supply of veteran pilots could be obtained though there is a world of difference between flying a bomber and a fighter and many of the new transferees never successfully made the transition and simply became yet more cannon-fodder.

The night fighter arm also grew modestly during the summer of 1944 and by the autumn there were some 1,000 fighters available in the front line. Crew quality in the night force had not declined as seriously as in the day arm because night fighter casualties had been much more moderate. There was, however, a general shortage of manpower such as was being experienced by every branch of the German armed services at this time and this was particularly apparent in declining standards of ground crew. Night fighters used complicated (by the standards of the day) electronic systems and therefore required many more skilled mechanics than day fighters. Night operations were being hampered by the British build-up of a large force of their own long range night fighters and intruders. This force largely consisted of the outstanding Mosquito aircraft and made operations for the German night force increasingly difficult. The Mosquitos could detect radar emissions from German fighters and used them as a means of tracking them down and intruders attacked aircraft landing and taking off at their bases. The use of any kind of visual beacon became virtually impossible. The universal lack of fuel was another difficulty but the biggest problem was the collapse of the early warning system brought about by the Allied presence on the continent. Previously attacking bombers had to cross the North Sea and/or the Low Countries to reach Germany and the defending fighters could be deployed while they did this. Now the front line was at the German border and bombers could emerge from behind it and be inside Germany in minutes. It was not possible to build radar stations all along a fluid front line.

The one ray of hope for the Luftwaffe and, indeed, for Germany as a whole, was the development of new weapons, some of them quite revolutionary. The most extraordinary of all was the V-2 rocket. This was the brainchild of a German genius called Wernher von Braun. The V-2 was a pilotless rocket 45 foot in length and nearly 14 tons in weight that could be fired from almost anywhere by means of a mobile launch pad, reach a height of 50 miles and then fall back to earth under the control of its own gyroscopic guidance system with a degree of accuracy adequate to land on a chosen city. It carried a warhead with 2,200 lbs of explosive. There was no defence against it whatsoever. A total of 5,200 of these rockets were built and were almost all fired at targets in Britain or Belgium, overwhelmingly at London and Antwerp. The first rocket was fired on 8th September 1944 and the last in March 1945. This was a fearsome weapon capable of wreaking terrible destruction. One hit on a cinema in Antwerp killed 560 people in that single explosion. V-2s were mechanically very unreliable and a good proportion of them either missed their target or exploded prematurely. The British secret service leaked false information back to Germany to the effect that V-2s were overshooting London and the result was that the guidance system was adjusted and many rockets now exploded harmlessly in the Kent countryside.

Research and production of the V-2 was carried out at a site on the Baltic coast and, as we have seen, it was devastatingly bombed by the R.A.F. in 1943 necessitating the shifting of the whole program, to caves in the mountains of Thuringia where they were produced by slave labour in conditions of appalling inhumanity. Without this raid and the consequent disruption of the program the V-2 threat would have been even more severe. It is very doubtful whether it could ever have been decisive however. The whole trend of the evidence of the air war was to show that weapons aimed indiscriminately at an urban area caused civilian suffering rather than significant, lasting damage to war industry.

Allied to the V-2 in the sense that it was powered by a rocket motor, was the Messerschmitt Me163. This was a tiny fighter plane that used its rocket motor to catapult it to 30,000 feet in under three minutes which was unheard-of at the time. For take-off the aircraft sat on a trolley which was left on the ground. The ascent used up almost all its fuel however, and it then had to glide, using occasional bursts of power, until it reached its target bombers. After the mission it glided down to earth and landed on a skid built into the bottom of the fuselage. Needless to say this whole procedure was difficult and dangerous. The rocket motor required two liquids as fuel which exploded violently when mixed. Even a bumpy landing could cause a fuel leak and consequent explosion, destroying the aircraft. Some blew up during refueling. Something over 300 of these aircraft were built and though they were a marvel of technology far ahead of their time, they were not practical and the number of enemy aircraft destroyed by them was in single figures.

Much more practical were jet aircraft. Piston engines in aeroplanes have a limit to the amount of power they can develop owing to the fact that propellers lose power as the tips of the blades rotate at a speed approaching the speed of sound. Moreover there are enormous stresses inherent in the conversion of the reciprocating motion of the cylinders into the rotation of the propeller shaft and there is a limit to what the available construction materials can stand. The idea of a gas turbine (which is what a jet engine is,) was being explored both in Britain and Germany between the two World Wars. By an odd coincidence an experimental engine was tested in both countries in 1937. In Britain the development team was led by Frank Whittle working for the R.A.F. and in Germany by Hans von Ohain working for a subsidiary of the Heinkel Flugzeugwerke aircraft company. The British then designed a working jet aircraft and by July 1944 had a front line jet fighter: the Gloster Meteor. It was used against V-1 rockets and at the end 1944 one squadron was moved to Belgium and used for ground attack. Its shortcomings were that it was scarcely any faster than contemporary propeller-driven planes, it was slow to accelerate and it was not very manoeuverable. In fighting terms it was a mediocrity. The Americans were given the engine design by the British and produced a fighter in 1943 called the Bell Airacomet but this was an even bigger disappointment and never saw active service.

The Germans fared much better. They developed a greatly improved jet engine and they had a much better understanding of the aerodynamics of jet flight. The result was two outstanding aircraft: the Messerschmitt Me262 and the Arado Ar234, respectively a fighter and a bomber. Both had two engines and were so fast that they could effortlessly out-fly contemporary propeller-driven fighters and so were virtually invulnerable in the air. The Me262 could fly at over 500 m.p.h. and was armed with four 30mm cannon whose fire could easily tear a heavy bomber apart. The Ar234 carried no guns but could carry 3,300lbs of bombs and was also ideal as a reconnaissance aircraft. Indeed it completely turned round the efficiency of Luftwaffe reconnaissance in the last months of the war. The main drawback with both planes was unreliable engines. Even the Germans had not fully mastered the new technology; moreover they were constrained by shortage of specialist metal alloys. However, these two aircraft were potential war winners, the Me262 in particular, having the capability of sweeping the sky clear of Allied bombers.

The Arado 234 was produced too late to have much impact and only 270 were ever built. The Me262 on the other hand was flying in 1943 and could have been available in substantial numbers that year had Hitler not personally intervened.

Albert Speer and Erhard Milch were at an armaments conference in 1943 when they received a personal telegram from Hitler forbidding further work on the plane which was even then being prepared for mass production.[ii] This was a great mistake and is a contender for the hotly contested prize of Hitler's worst decision. He had however, been right on occasions in the past when he had made decisions against the weight of expert opinion. He was just wrong this time. His reasoning was that he did not want scarce industrial resources wasted on what appeared to be a science fiction project of limited practical value. By early 1944 however, with Germany's situation deteriorating by the day, he had changed his mind and gave his full support to mass production. Meanwhile, Speer and Milch had, bravely, ignored his ban and started limited production anyway. Hitler now announced that the Me262 must be used only as a bomber. This was madness on a large scale. He was obsessed with staying on the offensive and repaying the Allies for their bombing of Germany but the Me262 could carry only a tiny bomb load and could make no difference to the course of the war at all as a bomber. On the other hand, as a fighter it could have gone far to reverse Germany's fortunes. Milch, Speer, Adolf Galland and others argued with him but to no avail. Thus was the world spared a terrible Nazi resurgence.

Galland did, however, manage to circumvent Hitler's authority to the extent of setting up an 'experimental' Me262 fighter unit named Commando Nowotny after the ace who led it and by October 1944 this unit was in action with 50 of the jets before any of the bomber version had appeared. Making the 262 a bomber required some re-design and the business of training the pilots for this wholly new bombing role was a lengthy one. It should be mentioned here that flying these aircraft was not easy: the engines needed delicate handling and the landing was at a much higher speed than pilots were used to. The landing was such a protracted and complicated business that Allied fighters took to hanging around near jet bases and shooting the jets down as they made their final approach with flaps and wheels down and at a speed the piston-engine fighters could match.

Hitler was not finally won round until March 1945 but by then it was far too late. The 262 was not used against U.S. bombers in large numbers until early 1945. On March 18th it showed what it could do when a force of 37 fighters attacked a large bomber force and shot down 12 bombers and one escort for the loss of three of their own number. 1,100 262s were built but only a small proportion of those saw action. The end of the war found them parked in rows on airfields and factory yards all over Germany, stranded for lack of fuel and pilots.

There were other jet designs in the pipeline when the war ended. There was the Heinkel 162 called the Volksjaeger, or 'people's fighter'. This was a design that went from first jottings on paper to mass production in an incredible four months. It was designed to be simple, easy to produce and easy to fly. Post-war investigation of the few examples built showed that it was a death-trap, probably more from poor construction methods than inherent design failings. A more promising, if unorthodox, design was the Horton 229 which was a flying wing with no fuselage at all. This had progressed no further than prototype stage when the war ended.

Apart from rockets and jets the last months of the war saw the development of several new or improved models of conventional aircraft. There was a new 'K' model of the Me109 capable of 450 mph but the 109 design was coming to the end of its useful life and the 109K had little new to offer other than its speed. There was a new 'D' model of the Focke Wulf 190 and this was a much more adventurous development. A new, in-line, liquid cooled engine was used giving the aircraft a whole new profile and its nickname, 'Longnose'. It could manage 440 mph but opinion was always divided on its overall merit: some pilots thought it the best

German fighter of the war and others that it was a step back from the 190A model with less manoeuverability and lighter armament. As the war ended yet another development of this design was about to make its debut: the Focke Wulf Ta152, reputedly even better.

The oddest latecomer was the Dornier Do335 which had two engines, one at the front of the plane and one at the rear acting as a 'pusher.' It also had an ejector seat for the pilot because baling out in the normal way was not possible due to the rear propeller. The Do335 was recorded doing 474 m.p.h. making it the fastest production piston engine fighter ever made. (Specially modified one-off planes have gone faster.) Only a few dozen were built and saw action in the last days of hostilities. The R.A.F.'s great French ace Pierre Clostermann was one of the few Allied pilots to encounter a Dornier 335 in action. When he tried to close with it, it flew away and effortlessly outran him even though he was flying a Tempest, the R.A.F.'s best fighter, capable of well over 400 m.p.h..[iii] Historically speaking however, this aircraft was just a curiosity though it was evidence that the German aviation industry could still produce outstanding aircraft even as the country collapsed in ruins about it.

If new aircraft were the Luftwaffe's great hope its nemesis was the campaign against oil production. Oil had always been a weakness of the German economy because the country had almost no natural supplies of its own. Before 1939 the Nazis prepared for war by building up stocks in reserve and this, combined with access to the output of the Rumanian oilfields at Ploiesti, kept problems at bay until 1943. The first part of the Luftwaffe's operations to feel the pinch thereafter was the training program. The problem did not become acute however, until the loss of access to Rumanian oil in the summer of 1944. Germany now had to rely on a quite inadequate supply from a small oilfield in Hungary and on its own coal conversion industry which had been greatly expanded during the war to solve the problem of lack of natural resources. The conversion industry extracted a perfectly acceptable oil substitute from coal, mainly by something called the Bergius hydrogenation process. This demanded large and sophisticated plants however, that were hard to conceal and impossible to disperse. Nearly a third of synthetic fuel production came from plants at Leuna and Politz in eastern Germany and the top seven plants produced 40 percent of the fuel. Beginning in May 1944 the Allied strategic bomber forces launched a campaign against these oil facilities and it was their biggest contribution to winning the war. Although support of the invasion was their first priority at the time, they were released periodically for oil raids which were now seen as the prime strategic operation, having taken over first place from raids on the aircraft industry.

In April 1944, with the strictest economies, the Luftwaffe used 165,000 tons of aviation spirit. In May German industry provided, from all sources, 156,000 tons. That dropped drastically to 54,000 tons in June and by September it had collapsed to 10,000 tons, stocks had virtually run out and the Luftwaffe was all but grounded.

Thereafter production recovered somewhat to almost 40,000 tons in November before subsiding again to virtually zero by February 1945.

On 12th May 1944 8th Air Force bombed several of the synthetic fuel installations. Two days later Albert Speer walked through the twisted wreckage at the Leuna works. He could see the writing on the wall and later observed: 'It meant the end of German armaments production.'iv On 21st/ 22nd June both 8th Air Force and Bomber Command raided fuel plants and the next day German production of aviation spirit had dropped by 90 percent.v Of course Speer made desperate efforts to repair the plants and resume production but Allied commanders were beginning to grasp the lesson that you had to hit targets again and again. So why did production recover in the last months of the year?

The answer to this is simple: Arthur Harris. Harris was still quite convinced that the only way to use strategic air power was to carpet bomb cities and that trying to hit any specific targets like oil conversion plants was a waste of time. He derisively called them 'panacea targets'. From mid-September Bomber Command was released from the duty to support the Allied ground forces in France and was able to return to full time strategic bombing. Harris could now choose his targets every day and by October he had 1,400 heavy bombers to hit them with. He therefore devoted as little of his resources as he thought he could get away with to bombing oil targets and concentrated on leveling the cities of Germany. Two points should be made here. The first is that R.A.F. bombing had a more lasting effect on oil plants than American bombing because the R.A.F. dropped larger bombs. 8th Air Force's armoury stopped at bombs of 2,000 lbs but the R.A.F. had bombs of 4,000 and 8,000 lbs and even ones of 12,000 lbs and 22,000 lbs (a 'Grand Slam') for special occasions. The second point is that R.A.F. aircraft carried a larger bomb load so that one raid by the Bomber Command main force delivered nearly twice the tonnage of a similar raid by 8th Air Force.

Harris's conduct did not escape attention and there was an acidic correspondence between him and his superior, Marshal of the Royal Air Force Sir Charles Portal. In the course of this, Portal made the interesting observation that the policy of carpet bombing cities had not worked. He also asserted that its continued use was only possible at all because of favourable conditions created by American bombing. This was an astonishing declaration by the head of the R.A.F. and came close to admitting that its bombing policy of the last three years had been a mistake and the American daylight, precision bombing policy was the right one.vi

Portal was privy to Ultra intercepts as Harris was not, and he knew just how vital oil (and transport) targets were and how ineffective was the policy of smashing cities. After much disingenuous protestation that he was doing his best, Harris offered his resignation but Portal, amazingly, backed off and declined to accept it. He actually knew that Harris's behaviour was impeding the war effort and yet he left him in place. To be fair, Harris did then mend his ways to some degree which is why German oil production collapsed again in the new year of 1945.

It is not fanciful to suggest that the war could have ended in 1944 and countless lives been saved had these two men behaved properly. Harris, though disobeying orders, at least genuinely believed he was doing what was best, and was not in possession of all the facts. Portal however, knew everything and failed to act. Admittedly he was in a difficult position. Harris was by this time a famous man and much loved by the public and his removal would have caused dismay in many circles.

The whole Air Ministry was also caught in a trap of its own making. The historian Martin Middlebrook, an expert on the bombing campaign, has pointed out that ever since the idea of area bombing was introduced in 1941/2 the Air Ministry had been practising a systematic deception on the British public. The impression was carefully given that the R.A.F. went out and bombed industry; there might be occasions when bombs fell on residential districts but this was collateral damage and unintentional. In effect this was the same position as that adopted by Spaatz and the Americans. But in the British case it was not true. Bomber Command did not set out to bomb industry except on rare specific occasions; its policy was to bomb residential districts with the intention that this would harm industry indirectly. It deliberately targeted the homes and lives of factory workers.[vii] Because of this dishonesty no convincing explanation could be given for Harris's departure without risking unthinkable revelations. Nevertheless commanders at the highest level of the armed services are chosen to make these difficult decisions and a failure to do so is a dereliction of duty. Even the British official history, 'The Strategic Air Offensive Against Germany,' no less, said that Portal should either have 'enforced his view or changed it.'[viii] The draft of that work apparently said that he had 'virtually abdicated his responsibilities' but Portal threatened to sue and the phrase was removed.[ix] The official history goes on to say: 'Nor was this dispute ever resolved and there can be no doubt that it diminished the effectiveness of Bomber Command in the final phase of the war.'[x]

It is often argued that the strategic bombing campaign kept a million men and a large piece of the German economy tied up in anti-aircraft and damage repair operations that otherwise would have been used to prosecute the war directly. This is quite true but several points must be made. First, most of the German effort would have been the same had strategic bombing been limited to precision raids on specific industrial targets. Second, many of those million were schoolboys, Russian prisoners of war, women and the medically unfit, all categories who were not available for front line service in any event. Third, there were over two million men in the U.S.A.F. and a million in the R.A.F. together with at least that many again involved in the production of aircraft and associated products. Roughly one third of war industry in both countries was devoted to manufacture for the air forces. Even though not all these men and resources were used in the strategic offensive in Europe one could easily argue that it was, on balance, the Germans who were tying up Allied (especially British) resources in a sideshow rather than the other way round. Only the introduction of the oil campaign made any real difference to that assessment.

From September 1944 to the end of the war, Bomber Command dropped more than twice the tonnage of bombs dropped in the whole of 1943. In the first four months of 1945 alone it dropped a larger tonnage of bombs than in 1943. (Only in 1945 did the U.S. 8th Air Force actually surpass the R.A.F. in tonnage dropped.) Bombing methods were steadily improved to increase accuracy, particularly in bad weather. No.5 Group, now virtually operating as a separate air force, developed a new and revolutionary marking technique whereby a handful of Mosquitos flew in at roof-top level and dropped flares precisely on the target. The main pathfinder force then followed and dropped more markers on top of these so that there was a mass of light in exactly the right place that the main force could not miss.

The Pathfinder Group was by now in something of an eclipse. 5 Group were the largest group and the most skilled. Harris had actually taken some squadrons from the Pathfinders and given them to 5 Group. It will be recalled that the Pathfinders were commanded by Donald Bennett, a most unfortunate appointment of a man unsuited to high command. Bennett had declared that low level marking would never work. He revealed his worst side when Leonard Cheshire asked to join the pathfinders. Cheshire was arguably the outstanding bomber pilot in the R.A.F., already a legend who was later awarded the Victoria Cross for repeated acts of bravery. Bennett told him he would have to be tested to see if he was good enough for the Pathfinders. Apparently Cheshire told Bennett he could 'keep it.'[xi] He then joined 5 Group and it was he who developed low level marking. At the war's end Bennett alone, of all the group commanders, was not given a knighthood.

Bomber Command could and did scourge Germany from end to end in these last months of the war. Not even towns of modest size were spared. This was gratuitous destruction of the most unattractive kind. Oil targets, and to a slightly lesser extent, transport targets, were the way to end the war but they took second place behind demolition of city centres because of Harris's obstinacy and Portal's weakness. What makes the whole matter worse in many ways is that Bomber Command had the skills and the equipment to make precision raids that caused real damage and did shorten the war. 617 and 9 Squadrons specialized in such work. They sank the Tirpitz, the last German battleship and they breached the Bielefeld viaduct and the Dortmund-Emms canal. In this last attack flight Sergeant George Thompson of 9 Squadron won the penultimate R.A.F. Victoria Cross of the war. Thompson was the radio operator on a Lancaster that was hit by flak and set on fire. He fought through the flames to rescue two injured gunners who were helpless and pulled them to safety. In the course of so doing Thompson was so badly burned about the face and hands, that when he reported to the pilot he was not recognized. The damaged plane managed to crash-land behind Allied lines and injured crew members were taken to hospital but, sadly, one of the gunners and Thompson himself, died of their wounds.[xii]

The issues raised by this period of bombing have always been exemplified by the attack on Dresden on the night of 13th February 1945. There was nothing exceptional about this raid from the attackers' point of view: it was just another area raid on a large city. It should be noted here that only on 15th January the Air Ministry had issued a directive re-emphasizing that bombing targets should be oil and transport, and cities only attacked when a raid on these kinds of targets was not feasible.[xiii] There had recently been discussion at the highest level however, prompted by Churchill, about the desirability of raiding cities in the eastern part of Germany with the general intention of helping the Russian army in its advance. Accordingly the Air Ministry sent Harris a directive on 27th January which called for attacks on cities where 'a severe blitz will not only cause confusion in the evacuation from the East but will also hamper the movement of troops from the West.' But such attacks were to be 'subject to the overriding claims of oil'.[xiv] These then were the objectives though Harris could be forgiven for asking whether he was supposed to attack these cities or not. Evacuation from the East was a matter of thousands of homeless refugees fleeing westward to avoid the Red Army and find a new life. Quite how the Allied cause was to be advanced by causing confusion amongst them is not clear. Preventing troop reinforcements however, was undoubtedly a perfectly legitimate war aim.

Urban devastation caused by bombing. This is Dresden in 1945 but it could be half a hundred towns that suffered a similar fate.
©Imperial War Museum (HU 44924)

The raid itself was in two parts. First 5 Group attacked using low level marking. This wave involved 250 planes and set the city alight. Three hours later 550 planes carried out a second raid. It had no aiming problems because the fires in the centre of the city could clearly be seen. The fires now developed into a firestorm of a size and ferocity not witnessed since Hamburg. Much of this ancient city, one of the most beautiful in Europe, was utterly destroyed. A vivid description of what it was like to live through that night is given by Victor Klemperer in his diaries. Ironically he was a Jew and the raid undoubtedly saved him because he was able to 'lose' his identity papers in the chaos and pass himself off as a gentile for the rest of the war. He managed to struggle from his lodgings to the Bruhl Terrace at the edge of the Elbe River, an elevated and open stretch of ground, on which he spent the night dodging the flames. 'To right and left buildings were ablaze, the Belvedere and – probably – the Art Academy. Whenever the showers of sparks became too much for me on one side, I dodged to the other. Within a wider radius nothing but fires.'[xv]

What troubled him most was that in the confusion he had become separated from his wife and did not know what had become of her. Fortunately he found her unharmed the next day. Many thousands of others were not so lucky. Just how many died has been a matter of fierce debate. The city council counted 22,000 bodies but this was nowhere near a complete catalogue, partly because the Russian occupation authorities ended the counting[xvi] and partly because many bodies were completely consumed or never found or buried by their own families privately. Almost everyone accepts 25,000 as a minimum figure but many suggest 40,000 or more. Wild claims have been made that 100,000 perished. We really can only guess.

311 American bombers arrived the next day to bomb the marshaling yards. Though this was unpleasant for the surviving, much-tried citizens of the city it was a perfectly legitimate raid against a target of military value and caused few casualties compared with the night before.

The reason that the Dresden raid commands public attention, is that various factors combined to make it the worst example of the needless slaughter and destruction that was the R.A.F. strategic bombing offensive in the last months of the war. It was a particularly beautiful city. Of course it had some industry: any city of half a million has industry, though compared with other cities of similar size it had remarkably little. In any event the industry was not the target except in the wide sense that burning the city indirectly harmed industry. Undoubtedly there was some truth in that, but not enough to make it a valid attack strategy any more, if it ever had been, and Portal and other senior figures were well aware of this.

Dresden was in a virtually pristine state. It had only suffered two minor raids so far, both by the 8th Air Force and both directed at the marshaling yards. The damage they did was trifling compared with what happened on 13th February. Even the anti-aircraft guns had been moved away to locations where it was thought they were more needed. The city's immunity up to this late stage is an indication that it was not seen

314

as a target of economic importance. Considering how close was the war's end the destruction of the city seems additionally tragic. The point is sometimes made that the end was not so apparent to the military leaders but this is simply not true: war industry was already winding down in all the major Allied countries. Any industrial output from Dresden would scarcely have had time to reach the front before the war's end.

As for damaging transport, both the main road and rail bridges were outside the city centre and were not targeted or hit. The main rail line was cut but was repaired in twenty-four hours. Apologists for the bombing claim that the city was full of troops on their way to the front, but this is patent nonsense. There was a large barracks in Dresden on the north bank of the Elbe but, again, it was not a target and was not harmed. There was no substantial body of troops in the city centre that night. Incidentally, both bridges and barracks could have been easily destroyed by a precision raid by 617 Squadron or one of the many Mosquito night bomber squadrons had there been a real desire to interfere with transport.

On the 23rd February Pforzheim was bombed and another firestorm developed and utterly consumed the city centre. Over 17,000 people were killed and 83 percent of the city's built-up area was razed to the ground. This is generally considered the third most deadly raid of the bomber campaign against Germany after Hamburg and Dresden.

On 28th March Churchill sent a memorandum to the Chief of the Air Staff (Portal) in which he finally let the cat out of the bag: 'It seems to me that the moment has come when the question of bombing German cities simply for the sake of increasing the terror, though under other pretexts, should be reviewed......The destruction of Dresden remains a serious query against the conduct of Allied bombing'.[xvii]

This is the truth of what was going on: it was pure terror bombing for its own sake and of negligible practical value to the war effort. Everyone in the upper reaches of Bomber Command and the Air Ministry knew this. The memorandum caused a storm of protest, not least because Churchill had long been one of area bombing's keenest protagonists, and he agreed to withdraw it but it remains on the historical, if not the official, record.

It is essential to the justice of the Allied cause that whatever terrible things were done, were done to win the war and were reasonably necessary to that end. Bomber Command's area bombing of cities in this period appears to fall tragically short of this requirement. Let the last word be with Albert Speer, the Reich Minister of Armaments: '...the war could largely have been decided in 1943 if instead of vast but pointless area bombing the planes had concentrated on the centres of armaments production.'[xviii]

While the R.A.F. bombed cities by night, 8th Air Force bombed oil and transport targets by day and the point should be made that many innocent civilians were killed by their bombs too. Indeed, to the man burying his wife it matters little whether the bomb that killed her was aimed at her or aimed at another target and killed her by mistake.

The human cost of it all: bodies laid out for identification under the Christmas trees in a gymnasium in Berlin after an air raid in December 1943.
©Imperial War Museum (HU 12143)

During the autumn the Luftwaffe devoted most of its resources to combating these daylight raids. It now had 900 fighters available for the defence of the Reich but they operated with steadily decreasing efficiency. For instance on 21st November 400 U.S. bombers raided the oil plant at Merseburg escorted by 268 fighters. 650-700 German fighters attacked but only 14 bombers and nine fighters were lost and at least one of the bombers was lost to flak. On 26th November 1,130 bombers attacked rail targets across western Germany. 800 Luftwaffe fighters were in the air that day but only 34 bombers were lost. The reasons for the decline were clear and simple: falling pilot quality and heavy U.S. escorts.

There was at this time a plan afoot, sponsored by Adolf Galland, for the Luftwaffe to launch a one-off attack against a chosen American raid with every aircraft available. The hope was that if one crushing victory could be achieved then the Americans might re-think their whole bombing policy. The right conditions for this raid never arose and the operation metamorphosed into a mighty ground attack on New Year's Day 1945 which we will consider shortly. However, the poor results outlined above suggest that even if the big attack had been launched the results would have fallen far short of crushing victory.

In December 1944 the Germans launched their major counter-attack in the Ardennes region and this was intended to split the Allied armies in two and destroy them. It was the last big military effort by the German army in the West. To support it aircraft were diverted from other tasks and three groups of Fw190 ground attack aircraft were transferred from the Russian front. Fully 1,770 single-engine fighters were used, leaving only some 400 to oppose U.S. strategic bombing. There was also an assortment of another 500 twin-engine fighters and ground attack planes and the last few bombers still in service. This attack was really a forlorn hope but if it had any chance at all it had to have effective air support.

The attack was launched on December 16th but air operations were impossible because of thick fog. In practice this hampered the Allies more than the Germans. The skies did not fully clear until the 24th when Allied planes came out in force. German air support rapidly petered out. The primary cause was the relentless attacks launched on Luftwaffe airfields which were kept under almost constant attack so that any aircraft left in the open were rapidly destroyed and not even a test flight could be made. Serviceability sank to low levels because mechanics were of poorer quality now and because they were trying to work in impossible conditions. Finally, the morale of the Luftwaffe was at last beginning to sag and pilots would seek any excuse to abandon a mission. Goering was even forced to issue an order threatening immediate court martial for pilots who turned back without proper justification.

On January 1st 1945 a mass dawn attack was launched against 17 Allied airfields in the Low Countries and northern France. 800 aircraft took part and because of the low navigational ability of the many green pilots, the columns of attackers were led by Ju88 bomber aircraft with veteran crews to show them where to go.

The attack was a success in that some 200 Allied aircraft were destroyed on the ground but they could easily be replaced from the huge stocks available and Allied pilot losses were small, being limited to some of the few aircraft that managed to take off and fight back. The Germans however, lost at least as many planes and mostly with the pilots too. Some of the last of the 'old hares' were killed such as Heinz Wodarczyk who had strafed the D-day beaches and Gunther Specht who had flown fighters in the West throughout the whole war despite several serious injuries including the loss of an eye. He flew his last mission in full dress uniform and medals[xix] suggesting that he did not intend to return, preferring to die in action rather than see Germany go down to defeat.

January 1st was the Luftwaffe's last effort in the West. In January 500 aircraft were transferred to the East to face the increasingly serious Russian threat and a renewed and terminal fuel crisis occurred and operations thereafter were limited to minor nuisance flights by a handful of aircraft. Such fuel as could be found went east. Night fighters struggled on a little longer. Top ace Heinz Schnaufer shot down his last three Lancasters on 7th March. They brought his tally to 122.

In Italy the spring of 1944 had seen the withdrawal of the bulk of the Luftwaffe presence there to boost defences in Northern Europe against the anticipated Allied invasion. By July there were just 300 aircraft left in the whole Mediterranean compared with four times that number a year before. In effect the Luftwaffe High Command had abandoned this theatre because it simply did not have the resources to be effective everywhere and the sensible decision was made to ignore one theatre in the hope of adequately defending the other two. In Italy the spring also saw the withdrawal of most of the remaining aircraft to bases in the north of the country to be ready to repel another Allied attempt to launch an amphibious operation behind the German front line. This was also a useful area from which to intercept the 15th Air Force's operations against targets in central Europe. July saw a further draining away of strength until there were just 50 fighters, 40 Stukas (used for night bombing – they would not have lasted five minutes by day) and 35 reconnaissance aircraft left. There was no higher headquarters in the whole theatre. These aircraft were given the official instruction that reconnaissance of Allied shipping movements in the Mediterranean was their principle duty. Otherwise they sporadically intercepted the fleets of heavy bombers or launched night harassing attacks on the front line until lack of fuel brought flying to a halt in early 1945.

During this period the Luftwaffe was joined by a small but determined band of Italian pilots flying for the ANR, the Aeronautica Nazionale Repubblicana, the air force of the fascist Italian state that was the successor to the Italy of Mussolini. Their small force numbered 58 fighters and 42 bombers in July of 1944[xx] and they fought alongside the Luftwaffe. One of the features of interest is that some of the fighter planes they flew were first class. The Macchi 205, and the quite outstanding Fiat G55, both using German engines, were two of the best fighters of the war. They showed what the Italian aircraft industry was capable of and it was fortunate for the Allies that they were so late coming. This band of pilots produced several aces amongst whom outstanding examples were Major Mario Bellagambi who scored 12 victories and Captain Ugo Drago with eleven. Adding his six from before the armistice gave Drago 17 victories which made him Italy's number six ace.

It is noteworthy that most of his victories occurred towards the end of the war when he was outnumbered and fighting very much against the odds, but flying in a modern German fighter plane. It is interesting to speculate what he might have achieved if he had had access to top class equipment throughout the war. After the war he emigrated to Argentina but returned to Italy in 1953 and began a long career flying for Alitalia.[xxi]

A rather larger number of pilots flew for a re-born R.A. now known as the Regia Aeronautica (Co-Belligerent Air Force) which joined the Allied side. At first officialdom ignored them and they had to scavenge their own aircraft and supplies from the manifold detritus of war to be found in Italy. They soon amassed over 300 aircraft but only 111 were fit for front line service. Allied headquarters plainly had little idea just what to do with them and did not wholly trust them. Because it was unwilling to employ them in Italy where they would inevitably end up fighting and killing their countrymen, they were assigned duty in the Balkans supporting the Yugoslav partisans. By the spring of 1944 they could field over 400 aircraft and were gradually equipped with modern aircraft types as used by other Allied air forces. They served faithfully and well but it must be said that their contribution was confined to an area that was a sideshow of a sideshow.

One final point that must be made about these late-war Italian pilots is that their choice of which air force they flew for was overwhelmingly dictated by which part of Italy they found themselves in when that country surrendered rather than any personal political convictions they may have had.

In the early months of 1945 Allied supremacy in the air was quite complete in the West. For the bombers the work was not yet finished for the German army still resisted on the ground. Bombing raids continued almost till the end of hostilities. 8th Air Force flew its last mission, a raid on targets in Czechoslovakia, on 25th April. As late as 20th April it flew a mission that involved over 1,700 aircraft. Bomber Command's last mission was a raid on an oil plant in Norway on the night of 25th/26th April. Only 100 aircraft took part but as recently as 22nd April, 767 bombers had gone to Bremen. Many of the fighters were now without work and bored pilots sat about and waited for the end. Such Luftwaffe fighters as appeared sporadically were always outnumbered and were generally understandably reluctant to fight.

On 22nd February Heinz Gerhrke was in one of four Fw190s that took off from Plantluenne airfield for a short flight to test their engines. This was the day when his luck ran out. Gehrke described being jumped by a Spitfire and fleeing into a cloud layer to escape. The cloud was too thin and he came out the other side right into the middle of a whole formation of Spitfires. There could be only one result and Gerhke was soon baling out again. Part of his harness caught on the aeroplane and he had to fight to free himself. His parachute opened a second or two before he hit the ground terribly injured. Local people called a doctor to treat him on the spot and then he was taken to hospital. He was badly burned about the face and hands and his legs were mangled by metal shell fragments. The war was six months over before he was released from hospital.[xxii] In fact Gerhrke was almost certainly shot down by Squadron Leader David Fairbanks of 274 Squadron flying a Tempest.[xxiii] To the War's end German pilots always liked to think it was a Spitfire that shot them down.

There was still plenty of work for some Allied squadrons, especially ground attack ones and the last weeks of the war were a bloody time for them. There might not be many Luftwaffe fighters but there was still flak and in greater concentrations than ever. Pierre Clostermann, who had escaped from France to fly with the R.A.F., flew a tour of duty in 1943/44 which turned him into France's leading ace. He was then given a safe desk job but insisted on a return to flying and began another tour of duty flying Tempests in the ground attack role on the western front. He flew to the war's end. On 30th April 1945 he was sent on a strafing mission against Schwerin airfield leading a flight of eight Tempests. It was known as a well-defended target and the Tempests were spotted approaching. They made a single strafing run across the airfield through a storm of fire. Closterman saw one plane hit the ground and another smash into a flak tower. When he rallied his flight after the attack only one plane responded to his radio call. Six out of eight had been shot down in 30 seconds.[xxiv] Investigation of the records suggests that only two pilots were actually killed[xxv] but they died just four days from the cease-fire of 4th May.

CHAPTER TWENTY-FOUR

The End in the East

In the late summer of 1944 the Russian offensive on the north European plain that was driving toward Berlin ran out of steam having progressed much farther and faster than the Russians could ever have hoped for. Russian troops were at the gates of Warsaw and the borders of East Prussia but there they stayed for several months. Only south of the Carpathian Mountains did the advance continue as Russian armies crossed the Hungarian plain to surround and besiege Budapest. This is a campaign that aviation historians have largely ignored: the Soviet official history does not mention it at all and any information is hard to find. The Luftwaffe was weaker here than on the Polish plain because the fighting in Hungary was less threatening to the German heartland.

In January 1945 the Luftwaffe in Hungary was represented by Airfleet Four. In terms of aircraft with 'teeth' this amounted to only 85 fighters and a couple of hundred ground attack aircraft. There were also 130 of what were described as 'night harassing bombers'. These were mainly Stukas and obsolete reconnaissance planes that could no longer survive by day. Their inclusion in the roster looked good on paper but their contribution was slight to negligible. Opposite them was 17th Soviet Air Army mustering approximately 1,000 aircraft. The numbers alone show that the German cause was hopeless. The days were finally gone when the Luftwaffe could rely on a wide gap in the quality of equipment and training to make up for lack of numbers, though the bulk of the German fighters did belong to Jg52, which was probably worth twice any other wing in terms of the damage it was likely to do. Back in September 1944 it celebrated its 10,000[th] victory. Now it flew in the defence of besieged Budapest.

The forces in the city were supplied by air in a major night operation that was one of the Luftwaffe's best air supply efforts. Six groups of transport aircraft, mainly Ju52s and He111s, amounting to some 200 in all flew in supplies for the troops and flew out the wounded. Because the Russians had captured Budapest airport the transport planes had to land on the city's wide boulevards or in the park of Buda castle. When Budapest fell this effort, with the aircraft involved, was switched to the besieged city of Breslau in Silesia and was carried on until 7th April when the Russian advance on the ground meant that there was nowhere left for aircraft to land. Thereafter supplies were dropped by parachute until 1st May. The Breslau operation was more testing than the Budapest one because it involved longer distances and it cost 165 aircraft over the two and half months it was in effect.

As already noted, Jg52 included some of the Luftwaffe's greatest aces: Eric

Hartmann, Gerd Barkhorn, Gunther Rall and Helmut Lipfert amongst others. These four alone shot down a total of over 1,100 aircraft during the war. For many years it was believed that these huge scores were fictitious, or at least exaggerated, given that the top R.A.F. ace, Johnny Johnson, shot down just 38 planes and the top American ace, Dick Bong, 40. Gradually comparison of records has increasingly supported their veracity however. There are several reasons for these big scores. One is that the Luftwaffe, unlike most air forces, did not share kills so every plane shot down was credited to one pilot even if several took part in its destruction. There was a tendency amounting almost to a policy to award kills to the best ace involved because the Luftwaffe encouraged the cult of the ace as being good for morale. On the Russian front there was the woefully inadequate training of V.V.S. pilots to be taken into account and until quite late in the war, this was allied to inadequate equipment.

The overriding reason for the success of these men, however, was simply opportunity. Allied pilots were rested from time to time and their flying careers deliberately terminated when it was felt that they had done enough. The Allies were winning and could afford to do this; the German's were losing and could not. In the Luftwaffe you flew until you were killed or forcibly retired by crippling injury or the war ended. Moreover, if you were outnumbered but you were a brilliant fighter pilot like Eric Hartmann, the extra enemy planes were just so many more targets, but if your side was in the majority the targets became fewer and fewer.

At the start of 1945 it is generally estimated that the V.V.S. outnumbered the Luftwaffe overall by about ten to one. That means that if the whole Luftwaffe were shot down to the last plane, there would be only one victory for every tenth Russian pilot.

Johnny Johnson in particular complained about lack of targets in France in 1944 and you can be sure that if the planes had been there he would have shot them down. He flew in combat for three years and amassed his score fighting veteran enemy pilots, often flying better planes. In all that time his aircraft was only once slightly damaged by enemy fire. Dick Bong spent extended periods of leave in the United States and from September 1943, was supposed to have a desk job but sneaked away to fly combat missions when he could. In January 1945 he was sent home for good and his combat days were over. Had he been allowed a clear run at fighting from 1942 to war's end he must easily have shot down 100 or more planes.

We have already looked at improvements in equipment used by the Luftwaffe at this time but what of the V.V.S.?

They were using increasing numbers of the new Tu-2 and Yak-3 but there were also two new aircraft, if they can truly be called that. These were the Lag-7 and the Il-10. Just as the Yak-3 was a modification of earlier aircraft of the Yak family, the Lag-7 was nothing more than a Lag-5 of the latest FN model given some further refinements. An effort was made to improve its aerodynamic qualities by removing the large air intake on the nose and having two intakes in the wing roots instead and the oil cooler was moved from its position under the nose to one further back on the belly of the plane where it interfered less with air flow. Weight was reduced by using metal and not wood for the spars in the wings and fuselage (though much wood was still used elsewhere in the airframe) and by reducing the fuel the aircraft carried. The result was, in effect, a new plane showing a startling improvement in performance and the Red Air Force found itself with one of the very best piston engine fighter planes of the war. So good was it that its successor the Lag-9, essentially the same plane but now all metal, was flying in the Korean War. The great British test pilot, Eric Brown, flew a Lag-7 after the war and described its performance as 'quite superb'. However he criticized the use of wood in its construction, thought the instrument panel primitive and the plane under-armed by western standards.[i] It also continued the long-established Lag fault of heat and smoke from the engine leaking into the cockpit so that pilots flew with the cockpit canopy open whenever possible. This aircraft was a big favourite with Soviet aces and though the best Luftwaffe pilots could hold it off, it cut a swathe through the ranks of the inexperienced.

The Il-10 was a development of the Il-2 Stormovik and was in many ways what the Stormovik would have been had its development not been so rushed. It was faster and much more manoeuverable than the old Il-2 and just as rugged. Rather oddly it carried a slightly smaller bomb load but both planes had always relied for much of their effect on the ability to fire rockets. Its one big failing was that where the Stormovik was easy to fly and land, the Il-10 was more demanding, particularly where landing was concerned. It saw action for the first time in February 1945 and was used only in limited numbers before the end of the war, though it remained in first line use in Warsaw Pact countries until the middle of the 1950s.

One might note in passing that the Russians never produced a jet combat plane during World War Two though they did develop a rocket fighter of which about thirty examples were built, but it had many drawbacks and after its test pilot was killed in a crash in 1943 the program was cancelled. It never saw front line action.

The pilots of Jg52 flew day after day over the snowy plains of Hungary and though greatly outnumbered, the best pilots added steadily to their scores. On 2nd January 1945, Helmut Lipfert shot down a Yak-9 and a Lag-5; on 4th he had a particularly good day and shot down four planes including two Il-2 Stormoviks. These were victories 167 to 172.[ii] It made little difference to the big picture however, and in mid-February Budapest fell.

The next step was the arrival of reinforcements both on the ground and in the air so that a counter-offensive could be launched with the object of recapturing Budapest and cutting off the Russian armies in the area. Airfleet Four grew in strength to 850 aircraft and there was a period of intense air fighting in late February and early March as the offensive rolled forward and achieved early success. The Russians brought in reinforcements from 5th Air Army but even so their numerical superiority was not very great. It is a particular reflection of the way the air war had changed on the eastern front that they never lost air superiority in this area despite numerical near parity and despite all the Germans could do, with the result that the German army suffered severely from the depredations of the ever-present Stormoviks. An interesting feature of the fighting was a certain Major Alexander Koldunov leading an elite squadron of veteran pilots in Yak-3s with a commission to range the front and destroy German planes wherever they found them. This was a significant departure from normal operating procedure for the V.V.S. whose tactics were normally strictly tied to supporting the operations of their own army on the ground. During the whole course of the fighting in the East the Luftwaffe had undoubtedly benefited from the Russian reluctance to target it directly. It might be added that only a successful air force can try this kind of arrangement. Koldunov shot down three Me109s on 8th March and a Focke Wulf 190 the next day. He shot down two more 190s on 13th March and another on 14th.[iii] By mid-March the offensive was over and had achieved little.

Alexander Koldunov was a colourful figure. In November 1944 he was involved in an air battle near Belgrade between Russian and American aircraft which occurred when a formation of P-38 Lightnings attacked Russian ground troops due to a navigational error. Koldunov shot down three Lightnings. By war's end he had flown 412 sorties and shot down 46 planes (not including the Lightnings). In later years he rose to be Deputy Defence Minister of the U.S.S.R. but was sacked in May 1987 as a result of the German Matthias Rust landing a private Cessna in Red Square.[iv]

The Luftwaffe in Hungary was gradually pushed back to the West through southern Slovakia towards Vienna. One of the duties of the fighter units was to escort the Fw190 ground attack planes on their missions; that was until Lipfert and one of the 190s had a race which was comfortably won by the 190. Thereafter the escort duties stopped: the escort was more of a handicap than a benefit.[v] Lipfert's last base was at Brunn (Brno) in what is now the Czech Republic. His last sortie was on 16th April and his final total of victories was 203; then he gave up soldiering and devoted the rest of his life to being a schoolmaster. Erich Hartmann was captured by the Russians and spent the next ten years in prison camps in Russia.

Further north, across the Carpathians the front stirred into action in January as the final Russian offensive began. On its northern, Baltic, flank the remains of Army Group North were cut off in the Courland Peninsula. They were supplied by sea and resisted all attempts to subdue them. They were still there when the war ended. Their air support, such as it was, was provided by Airfleet One: 85 fighters and 30 ground attack planes plus 100 of the egregious night harassment bombers. The fighters belonged to Jg54, the 'Green Hearts', another outstanding wing. One of its pilots, Otto Kittel, who was shot down and killed on 14th February 1945 when he had 267 victories, achieved the dubious distinction of being the highest scoring ace ever to be killed in air combat. At the end of the war the pilots of Jg54 flew in formation on 8th May, to Flensburg where they surrendered to the British. The wing's ground staff followed by ship.

By the last months lack of fuel reduced this section of the Luftwaffe to impotence. All its fuel had to be brought in by sea under attack by Russian bombers. Restrictions on the use of fuel reached ridiculous proportions. During the last, failed, Russian offensive in February, Lieutenant Norbert Hannig was at instant readiness one day sitting in his cockpit ready to fly at a moment's notice when he saw the green flare that was the signal to take off and duly did so. He was at once told by radio to land again. Puzzled, he obeyed only to be informed that the flare had been ignited by accident and therefore he was in the air without proper orders and so was officially deemed to be wasting fuel. This was so serious that a military judge was brought in immediately to conduct a court martial. Fortunately the judge could see how foolish was the whole business and rejected the idea that Hannig should have guessed the flare was unofficial because it was fired from the wrong place. Hannig was exonerated but the episode demonstrates the fear in which everyone in the Luftwaffe lived at this time.[vi] Even a slight breach of the rules could lead to a death sentence as discipline was tightened to murderous levels in the face of crumbling morale.

All the spare fuel that could be found in early 1945 went to Airfleet Six in the central front on the road to Berlin. Here was concentrated the bulk of the Luftwaffe strength. The official view was that such fuel as remained was better spent holding back the Russians than the British and the Americans who appeared relatively

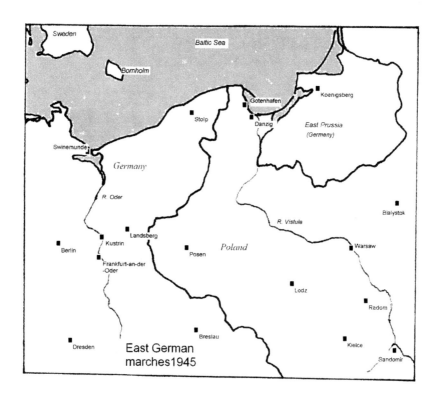

East German marches 1945

innocuous by comparison. On January 1st this Airfleet mustered over 1,000 planes and during the month reinforcements doubled that figure. These were overwhelmingly fighter and ground attack aircraft. The latter were now almost entirely the ground attack version of the Fw190, which had completely eclipsed the Stuka, save for small numbers of the anti-tank model Stuka. This latter was kept in service because it could fly low and slow enough to give a pilot a good, close shot at a tank. It needed a heavy escort to protect it however. The fighters of Airfleet Six were also about half composed of the fighter version of this same Fw190 so the one type dominated the scene.

Russian air power in the area amounted to over 8,000 aircraft divided roughly equally between fighters and bombers. The only twin-engine bomber present in quantity was the Pe-2 and it was joined by large numbers of Stormoviks and a profusion of lend-lease types. The fighters present in numbers were Yaks, Lags and Airacobras in that order.

Here the Soviet offensive began on January 12th in very poor weather. Snow and fog kept most aircraft on the ground at first but Russian artillery spotters took the risk of flying at low level over the front and the artillery was so effective with their direction, that the Russians tore a 20 mile gap in the German lines in the vicinity of Sandomir in southern Poland and their armour streamed through. German planes remained grounded for the most part throughout the day but the Russians, always better at

All aircraft need much maintenance and this unglamorous work gets little attention. Here Russian mechanics work on a lend-lease U.S. Bell P-39 Airacobra, an aircraft regarded as second rate in its home country but a favourite with the Red Air Force. ©Imperial War Museum (NYP 33951)

operations in unfavourable weather, put up 400 bombers and Stormoviks late on. They discovered columns of German tanks moving to the counterattack and smashed them. The next day they were flying again in conditions that had barely improved and continued to devastate German armoured formations. V.V.S. fighters in this area developed the very effective technique of keeping up a standing patrol over Luftwaffe airfields and instantly diving to attack any plane that tried to take off. Here, as in Hungary, we see the V.V.S. at last taking aggressive action aimed directly at the Luftwaffe.

The following day a Soviet attack was launched a little further north against East Prussia but here the Germans had some of their best troops and long-prepared defences. Moreover, crucially, the weather was so bad on this day, with blizzards sweeping the area, that neither side could use air power at all. The offensive here rapidly stalled and the next day it was the Luftwaffe who sent out its ground attack aircraft despite more bad weather. They did not achieve very much however and the Germans lost 19 planes to the Russians four. For the Luftwaffe this was an ominous pointer to the change in relative combat effectiveness of the two air forces.

On 14th January the forces before Warsaw attacked. Once again the weather made flying all but impossible and the attack took two days to gather momentum but on 16th the weather cleared and both sides made a maximum effort. The Luftwaffe flew nearly 600 sorties on this day but the 16th Air Army, which supported the Warsaw thrust flew 3,400. The Luftwaffe simply could not protect the forces on the ground and the Stormoviks had a field day. 300th Ground Attack Regiment, for instance, claimed 3,500 motor vehicles of all kinds destroyed in one day.[vii] This is plainly an over-estimate caused by excitable pilots exaggerating the effect of their attacks, but it is clear that they were achieving great success by any measure. On 17th January Warsaw was liberated and the German forces were, almost everywhere, streaming back in retreat. Lodz, seventy miles further west was entered by Soviet troops only two days later. Only in East Prussia, which was an ancient part of the German homeland, did the defenders stand firm. Here they fought with especial zeal and here the Russian army advanced only very slowly against fierce resistance.

Here too Captain Pavel Golovachyov, flying the new Lag-7 shot down two Fw190s on 16th January and four on 18th January when his 9th Guards Fighter Regiment intercepted a force of 25 of these aircraft. This took his score to 26 victories. His achievement would have been a rarity a year earlier; now it was almost commonplace. Golovachyov was a ferocious pilot. Only a month earlier he had run out of ammunition while attacking a Ju88 and brought it down by ramming, yet still managed to fly his damaged aircraft home to base. In 1942 he was knocked unconscious by enemy gunfire in mid-dogfight and came round to find his aircraft in a spin. He managed to regain control and level it out but the plane was badly damaged and a few minutes later the tail broke off and it plunged into the River Don taking Golovachyov with it. By some miracle he lived. He was twice made Hero of the Soviet Union and survived the war.[viii]

The central Russian spearhead was now heading toward Posen and Berlin at great speed. The Russians were using the method so successful for the Luftwaffe in France five years earlier of having ground attack aircraft on call to attack any resistance the spearhead tanks encountered. They were called in by radio and arrived in minutes. Radio communication in the V.V.S. had improved out of recognition in the last four years. One armoured unit advanced so fast that it was attacked by its own side because the men in the air could not believe the men on the ground could have travelled so far. 402nd Fighter Regiment was ordered to transfer to an airfield west of Warsaw and landed to find that one side of the field was still occupied by German troops holding out to the last. A German attempt to move forces to block this advance met severe difficulties in the form of air attack, particularly on stations and marshaling yards close behind the front.

On 20th January Airfleet Six flew 575 sorties and shot down 19 Soviet planes but it lost 24 of its own. One of the dead pilots was Senior Lieutenant Gustav Schubert. He had been in action since the first day of the war and had flown 1,100 combat missions. On 21st January, Ground Attack Wing 1(Schlachtgeschwader 1) lost its commander the veteran pilot Major Ernst-Christian Reusch. Also on that day Senior Sergeant Hans Ludwig died in an aerial collision. He was a tank-busting ace with 75 kills. His wing lost 18 aircraft on 20th and 21st January. The last veterans were draining away. As was so often the case with precipitate retreats, large numbers of aircraft had to be abandoned on their bases. When the Russians overran the Posen area at this time they found no less than 700 German aircraft abandoned on the airfields outside the city. When the Stavka, the Soviet High Command, heard these figures it did not believe them and sent a commission to establish the truth. The commission reported that the 700 planes were indeed there.[ix]

On the night of 23/24th January, advanced units of Rokossovskiy's Second Belorussian Front reached the Baltic coast between Konigsberg and Danzig. East Prussia was now cut off. Further south the Upper Silesian industrial area was overrun. Auschwitz was liberated and the Russian soldiers were shocked at what they found. Word of this horror spread and increased the Russian hatred of the Germans. Now that German soil was being invaded by the Russians, the latter were taking a terrible revenge for what had been done in their own land. In turn this led German soldiers to fight all the more fiercely. It was a bitter struggle with little mercy shown on either side.

On 26th January the Germans launched a counter-attack towards East Prussia in an attempt to rejoin it to the rest of the homeland. The aircraft supporting this blow suffered heavily. Jg4, an import from the Western front, lost nine aircraft on the first day and six the next. Many of the units now fighting in this last great battle had been brought from the West and had considerable difficulty adjusting to the different conditions that prevailed in the East. Erich Hartmann took over command of one such unit and found its pilots generally out of their depth. There were many reasons for this, for instance the lower altitude at which the fighting was done and the absence of heavy bombers. One of the problems was that the Western Allies rested experienced pilots and so the men at the front line tended to be mostly fairly inexperienced: well-trained, but inexperienced. In the V.V.S., like the Luftwaffe, as a general rule you fought till you died or the war ended so by now there were many highly skilled Russian aces at the front. German units from the West were not used to coping with such men.

By the end of the month the East Prussian counter-attack had stalled. Further south where the resistance on the ground had all but collapsed, the Luftwaffe was actually increasing in strength. On 27th January, 1,400 sorties were flown. The next day it could only manage half as many but the pilots claimed 800 Russian vehicles destroyed. The Russian advance was beginning to run out of steam. The roads of rural Poland were jammed with Russian transport for mile after mile and it made a fine target for German ground attack planes. Some of the major junction towns like Posen and Kustrin were still holding out and thus blocking vital traffic routes. At the end of January the Russian spearheads reached the Oder River, little more than 50 miles from Berlin and even established a bridgehead on the other bank. Needless to say this led to a fierce air battle over the river and the town of Frankfurt-an-der-Oder. In three days the Germans lost 107 planes here. On 2nd February alone, over 5,000 individual aircraft attacks were recorded by the Russians.

To make matters worse for the Russians there was now a thaw and their makeshift grass airfields became mud baths and were unusable. On top of this the rapid advance had had the usual effect of throwing air force ground units into confusion as bases were changed and changed again, ground crew were held up and consignments of spare parts went astray. On the other hand German units were able to fly from well-established homeland bases with concrete runways. At this time the Luftwaffe briefly reversed Russian air supremacy as the Russian offensive ground to a halt. The Russians were facing a greater concentration of German aircraft than anything seen in the West since 1940. In the first ten days of February the Luftwaffe flew 13,950 sorties in the central area and the Russians managed only half that.

Between the 12th January and 3rd February the V.V.S, on this central front lost 343 aircraft which is remarkably few considering the intensity of the fighting. Luftwaffe losses are uncertain but were undoubtedly far greater. The truth was that the air situation was like 1941 but with the roles reversed. Anything the Luftwaffe achieved was achieved at great cost but the failure to shoot down planes does not tell the whole story and it is certain that air attack was one of the main reasons for the halting of the Russian offensive.

The isolation of East Prussia led to a maritime campaign of evacuation to take the entire civil population and wounded soldiers back to the main German homeland. Ships sailed from many western Baltic ports to Koenigsberg, loaded up with passengers and returned. As the situation deteriorated they also called at Danzig and Gotenhafen (modern Gdansk and Gdynia respectively). This traffic was repeatedly attacked by Russian aircraft and submarines. Between the end of January when the evacuation started and the end of the war, a little over three months later, 161 merchant ships were sunk and 25,000 lost their lives. The worst loss was in fact one caused by a Russian submarine which torpedoed the liner Wilhelm Gustloff on the night of 30th January. The 25,000 ton ship went down in 45 minutes and of the 10,000 on board over 9,000 drowned in the icy Baltic waters. This was the worst maritime disaster in history in terms of loss of life. Another particularly tragic sinking was that of the hospital ship Posen set on fire and sunk by air attack on 12th April off Hela in the Gulf of Danzig. This ship had 115 beds but was grossly overcrowded and 300 lives were lost when it went down.

One of the few warships sunk was the old battleship Schlesien. This ship was obsolete when World War One was fought but took part in the Battle of Jutland. In 1939 she bombarded Polish coastal forts and by 1945 was little more than a floating gun battery. She too had participated in the evacuation but was also used to bombard Russian troops on the shore. She was attacked on 3rd May and hit a mine while trying to dodge bombs. Though she had to be towed to the port of Swinemunde and grounded in shallow water, her guns could still operate and so a final attack was launched the next day that reduced her to a hulk which remained in the shallows as a curiosity for ten years after the war.

Swinemunde was one of the main reception ports for the evacuation and it was raided by the U.S.A.A.F. on 12th March just as the merchant ship Andros was unloading 2,000 passengers. The town was devastated. The exact number killed is not known but was at least 10,000.

Despite these terrible losses the evacuation program, the largest ever undertaken by sea, succeeded in shipping out two million civilians and 500,000 soldiers by the war's end.

The Russian pause in February did not extend to the front in Silesia on the southern boundary of the offensive and on 15th February the city of Breslau was surrounded and besieged. Both sides lost heavily in the air battles over the city. Amongst other pilots the Russians lost Ivan Polbin, a legendary bomber pilot who had flown throughout the war and was responsible for developing dive bombing techniques in the V.V.S.. The Germans lost Hans Rudel, but only temporarily. His plane was hit by anti-aircraft fire and he managed to crash-land behind German lines. He was badly wounded and his right leg had to be amputated but nothing stopped this incredible man and he ran his air group from his hospital bed hearing lengthy reports and issuing orders by telephone. He was shot down on 8th February but was back with his group and flying again on March 25th. Using the rudder in most aeroplanes of that time involved pressing pedals with your feet. He obviously could not press the right pedal but he could wedge his remaining foot under the left pedal and lift it and this had the same effect. Before returning to the front he was summoned to see Hitler and the two men enjoyed a relaxed conversation during which it became clear that Hitler, not unreasonably, thought Rudel's fighting career was over. Rudel did not disillusion him fearing that it would lead to a prohibition on further flying.[x]

Rudel survived the war as the most decorated soldier in the whole of Germany. His score of over 500 tanks destroyed was a record. He was wounded five times and shot down or crash-landed 32 times. It is sad to have to record that he remained an unrepentant Nazi to his dying day.

Rudel is an outstanding figure of the air war in Russia but these last months of that war really belong to one man above all others and that man is Ivan Mykytovych Kozhedub. Kozhedub scored 62 aerial victories which made him by some way the leading Allied fighter ace of the whole war. He was casual about reporting victories and did not even bother with situations that might have led to a shared victory, so his real score is undoubtedly much higher. He himself thought it was probably over 100. He was born in a village near the town of Sumy in the Ukraine in 1920 and learned to fly at his local aero-club before the war. He graduated from military flying school in 1941 and was such a gifted pilot that he was retained there for two years as an instructor. In 1943 he was finally released to fly at the front and, after a slow start, showed himself an outstanding fighter pilot. Like all his kind he had luck on his side. On one mission his plane caught fire and as he was over German territory and did not wish to become a prisoner, he decided on a suicide dive into a gun emplacement but the dive put the fire out and he was able to fly home.

In the summer of 1944 Kozhedub, already a famous ace, joined 176th Guards Fighter Regiment who flew Lag-7s with a red nose and a white tail. He was promoted and became a squadron commander. In the autumn they fought on the Baltic front in and around Riga. In the new year 176th took part in the drive for Berlin, first around Warsaw and then ever further forward. On 11th February Kozhedub and his flight were on patrol over the Oder bridgehead when a force of 30 Fw190s attacked. A furious dogfight followed in which the pilots from 176th shot down ten 190s for the loss of only one of their own planes. On 19th February, again over the bridgehead he spotted a Me262 jet and was able to close with it using maximum throttle because the pilot did not spot him. He shot it down and joined the small band of pilots who could claim a victory over a jet plane. He shot down his last two enemies on 17th April. He was not at the front for the final days because he was summoned to Moscow to take part in the May Day celebrations. He was made a Hero of the Soviet Union three times.

Kozhedub also scored two victories that were never recorded. In April 1945 he saw an American B-17 under attack by a pair of German fighters. He attacked the fighters and drove them off and then a whole squadron of unidentified fighters appeared and the leader opened fire on him. Kozhedub dodged away and then came round to shoot down the last pilot in the formation. Then he did a half loop and shot down the leader and only at this point saw that these planes had blue and white stars on the wings. He flew home sure that his career was about to end in humiliation or worse and an international incident with the Americans. However, only one of the two American pilots shot down had survived and he landed amongst Russian troops to whom he reported that he had been shot down by a Focke Wulf with a red nose. This allowed Kozhedub's commander to pretend the whole thing had never happened and so he got away with his mistake without penalty.[xi]

As a student pilot Kozhedub's marksmanship was poor and his instructor told him he had to work on it which he did with such success that by the time his career ended he was noted as a crack shot. Unlike most of his kind he was not careful, cool and calculating but impetuous and a risk-taker who survived by brilliant flying and good fortune. Several times his life was saved by his wingman shooting down an enemy on his tail. He is such an important figure in the history of military aviation that it is a pity more has not been written about him and made available in the West.

The February lull was a remarkable period of calm, always excepting the siege of Breslau but it *was* only a lull and the final act was about to begin. The Russians were consolidating their position and could not supply a further advance on Berlin until they had captured the vital road junctions of Posen and Kustrin. Posen fell on 22nd February but Kustrin held out. Luftwafe activity was limited to sporadic raids on bridges that were part of the Russian supply line.

The bridge raids saw the employment of an eccentric Luftwaffe weapon developed as early as 1943 but now used for the first and only time in numbers. This was the Mistel or Mistletoe. It consisted of a fighter plane in a piggy-back arrangement on a bomber. Usually a Fw190 was used on a Ju88. The bomber had no crew and was packed with explosive. In some models the explosive was packed into the nose and constructed as a shaped charge designed to have great penetrative power. The pilot of this contraption sat in the fighter and flew close to the target then released the bomber which flew to the target under its own power, but guided by remote control. Like so many of the Luftwaffe's wonder weapons, the Mistel came too late to make any difference to the situation and its effectiveness is in substantial doubt in any event. It did, however, destroy the bridge over the Oder at Steinau at the end of March.

On 22nd March the final assault on Kustrin was launched and there was a flurry of air activity over the town. In two days the Russians claimed 110 victories, the Germans just 26. On 29th March Kustrin fell and the Soviet line of communications was clear. The final assault could begin.

Since the progress of their offensive had slowed at the end of January the Russians had been building airfields close behind the front as fast as they could go. They were now able to amass 7,000 aircraft for the final assault on Berlin. While the Germans had some 3,000 aircraft available in this theatre they had fuel for only one tenth of that number to be used in action.[xii]

The final drive for Berlin began on 16th April. As the artillery opened fire 668 bombers attacked the German lines and targets close behind them. All through the day waves of bombers attacked and German fighters attacked the bombers. German records for this period have largely been lost but the 176th Guards Fighter Regiment alone claimed 16 Fw190s for no loss. The Russian 3rd Fighter Corps claimed another 50 victories and 60 German pilots flew suicide missions on the Japanese pattern so there must have been in the region of 126 German losses. German claims amounted to 125 but a proportion of claims can always be discounted. Given the size of the Soviet air support, losses of this magnitude were of little significance. Heavy air battles continued for several days.

On 18th April the V.V.S. on the Berlin front claimed 151 German planes shot down; on 19th 112. On 20th occurred the last large-scale fight when a group of 15 Stormoviks with an Airacobra escort encountered 60 German fighters northeast of Berlin. A fierce scrap ensued in which five Fw190s were shot down for the loss of one, or possibly two, Russians. Total Russian victories for the day were 90.[xiii] On 21st April Russian victory claims amounted to only 11 planes. Luftwaffe resistance had finally collapsed.

The assault on Berlin began on 20th April and concluded on 3rd May. Russians on the ground had joined up with their western allies and most of Germany was in the hands of the victors. Well before then, German resistance had fragmented and organized resistance ceased but that did not mean the fighting was quite at an end. German planes still appeared in ones and twos and there were still dogfights though with decreasing frequency.

On 26th April Hitler summoned General Ritter von Greim, commander of Airfleet Six to his bunker in Berlin. Von Greim flew in with his fiancee, the noted aviatrix Hannah Reitsch and landed in the city in the face of ground fire from leading Russian units that wounded him in the leg. At the subsequent interview Hitler made von Greim a Field Marshal and put him in command of the Luftwaffe in succession to Goering whom he had sacked for treachery. At this late stage there was precious little Luftwaffe to command.

Yevgeniy Mariinskiy scored one of the last Russian victories when he was on patrol over the ruins of Berlin in early May. He was leading his patrol round the edges of the huge column of smoke that covered the centre of Berlin when he spotted a Me109 at low level emerging from the smoke and heading westward. He gave chase and slowly gained on it. His colleagues excitedly urged him on over the radio. Mariinskiy took careful aim and fired. The Me109 trailed smoke and flame and dived down to crash in the suburbs of the city.[xiv]

The last Luftwaffe victory of the war occurred on the afternoon of 8th May when Senior Lieutenant Friedrich Stehler, flying a Me262 jet, shot down an Airacobra.[xv]

The last air combat in the European theatre took place over Prague on 9th May when a German Fw189 reconnaissance aircraft was seen apparently photographing Russian ground troops. Captain Vasiliy Pshenichikov of the 100th Guards Fighter Regiment shot it down. The next day, 10th May, several missions were flown in the Prague area against German troops still resisting. These were the final missions flown in the theatre.[xvi]

CHAPTER TWENTY-FIVE

The End in the Pacific

After resounding victory at the battle of the Philippine Sea and the conquest of the Marianas, the Americans resolved upon the liberation of the Philippines. There were those who said that this was an unnecessary digression from the central business of defeating Japan and that an attack on the island of Formosa (now Taiwan) offered better prospects of a swift end to the war but there were political considerations to be taken into account, not least the firm commitment given by Douglas MacArthur to the people of the Philippines that he would return to set them free. In fact an invasion of the Philippines offered certain distinct advantages of its own. It would suck large Japanese forces into a grand sideshow campaign and it would clear out a nest of resistance which, otherwise, must sit in the Americans' rear area unsubdued. It took a meeting between MacArthur, Nimitz and Roosevelt to settle differences however.

As a preliminary to the invasion of the Philippines a major air attack on Formosa was planned. This would serve the double purpose of neutralizing the largest Japanese base in the area and at the same time suggesting that the island was to be the target of the next American strategic move though, in truth, the real identity of the next target was by now pretty clear.

From 12th to 14th October 1944 the aircraft of the U.S. 3rd Fleet pounded the airfields and docks of Formosa and B-29 bombers based in China joined in. After an administrative reorganization the 3rd Fleet under Admiral Marc Mitscher was now the carrier striking force of the U.S. Navy, though it still came under the authority of 5th Fleet of Admiral Spruance. It now comprised 17 aircraft carriers with numerous escorting ships and over 1,000 aircraft. As a preliminary to the Formosa raids the fleet had made air attacks on Okinawa and Luzon Island in the Philippines but the three days at Formosa were the centre-piece of the softening-up campaign. The Japanese Navy had 350 aircraft on Formosa but many more on Luzon, Okinawa and Kyushu, the homeland's southernmost island. In all there were perhaps 1,000 aircraft able to join in the battle. They were sent against 3rd Fleet in wave after wave but their efforts were fruitless. 500 Japanese planes were shot down or destroyed on the ground but the Americans lost only 125. The carriers Franklin and Hancock both suffered damage and the cruisers Canberra and Houston were more heavily hit but no ship was sunk. Admiral Fukudome, who commanded the Japanese air forces on Formosa commented that his planes were like 'so many eggs thrown against the stone wall of indomitable enemy formations.' [i]

It is appropriate to mention here the anti-aircraft fire of U.S. ships. We have already seen that aircraft had to make a low level attack to have a real chance of damaging ships and the best defence for a ship facing that kind of attack, apart from taking evasive action, was automatic anti-aircraft fire. By 1944 warships bristled with automatic anti-aircraft guns. Essentially these came in two kinds: the 40mm quadruple mounting and the single 20 mm. The first put out a hail of shells at a rate of two per second, on the shotgun principle that one or two would find their mark. The second was carefully aimed by its operator and attempted a precision kill firing seven rounds per second. An Essex class U.S. carrier carried eight 40mm quadruple mountings and 46 20 mm guns. If we assume that only half of the guns could be brought to bear at any one time, an attacking aircraft still faced a barrage of some 200 shells per second coming its way. And a carrier would be surrounded by numerous other ships all similarly armed.

Fukudome's pilots were largely beginners whose training had been cut short because of fuel shortages and they stood no chance against experienced and battle-hardened Americans in superior aircraft. The situation was much the same as in Germany though probably somewhat worse. The only pilots with a hope of doing battle on reasonably equal terms were the few of the old brigade who were left: the men like Sakai and Hiroyoshi Nishizawa who had been trained pre-war. As a contest between air forces the air war was so one-sided as to be virtually over: American aircraft destroyed Japanese aircraft in droves wherever they encountered them. There were just two circumstances in which the Japanese could hope to achieve anything of significance in the air. The first was with the use of suicide bombers which made their first appearance in the Philippines campaign and the second was where the tiny number of aforementioned aces made their presence felt.

As the war turned against them the Japanese realized that they must place increasing reliance on fighter planes for they found themselves consistently fighting on the defensive and facing fleets of U.S. bombers. The navy's Zero and the army's Oscar were now both hopelessly outdated and something new and better was desperately needed. Japanese designers had been at work on this problem and this late-war period saw the introduction of several new Japanese fighter planes of outstanding capabilities.

The army produced the Nakajima Ki-84 Hayate or 'Frank', which reached front line squadrons in April 1944. This aircraft looked much like a Zero with the cockpit set back somewhat but it had armour protection for pilot and fuel tanks (at last).

It was faster than contemporary American fighters and all-round was at least their equal. It was in great demand in the last months of the war and was numerically the most important army fighter during that time. About three and a half thousand were built in three different models. Potentially this aircraft was a serious threat to Allied air superiority but it had technical problems with its Homare engine and its landing gear was fragile. Both of these problems were due to use of poor quality materials, a direct consequence of the U.S. submarine war that was starving Japan of the raw materials it needed for its industry. The other insurmountable problem was that there were no longer the pilots to get the best out of it.

In 1945 the army produced a small number of the Kawasaki Ki-100 fighter which was produced more or less by chance when the supply of licence-built Daimler Benz engines used in the older Ki-61 'Tony' ran out. Since there was a batch of bodies already built, Kawasaki put some available Mitsubishi engines into the airframes and the result was the Ki-100 which turned out to be another outstanding plane. However, by the time of its creation Japanese industry was not in a state to produce it in any numbers: only 400 were ever manufactured.

The navy also produced two advanced fighters. The first was the Mitsubishi J2M Raiden (Jack). Originally designed in 1940, the prototypes revealed a host of problems and continued development delayed the operational debut of this plane until December 1943. It concentrated on toughness and good climbing ability rather than agility and in this respect was a new departure for Japanese aircraft design. It was almost exclusively used against U.S. bombers over the Japanese homeland and proved excellent at the job. Only some 500 were produced however, so its impact was limited. The second was the Kawanishi N1K Shiden (George) which was unique among fighter planes in being developed from a seaplane. This aircraft also underwent a long and tortuous design process: it also used the temperamental Homare engine. It reached front line units in the middle of 1944 and was first encountered by the Allies in the Philippine campaign. This was another fine aircraft similar to the Frank in appearance and performance but probably the silver medalist by a neck in any competition between the two. About 1,500 were produced in all and the modest production figures for these navy fighters make it plain that many pilots were still flying their old Zeros to the last day of the war.

On 20th October 1944 U.S. troops landed on the island of Leyte in the middle of the Philippine chain. The island itself was of little importance but it was strategically placed so that its capture would make the defence of the rest of the Philippines exceptionally difficult and it boasted an excellent bay with sandy beach, ideal for an amphibious landing. This was the largest Pacific operation yet. The fleet that steamed to Leyte was crewed by 50,000 sailors and carried 165,000 troops of MacArthur's 6th Army.

Capture of the Philippines would effectively split the Japanese empire in half and cut the homeland off from its sources of oil in Indonesia and rubber and tin in Malaya. This then, was a crucial battle. The Japanese army had troops in place on the islands but what was to be the navy's role? For some time now it had been navy policy not to risk ships unless there was a real chance that their use would make a significant difference. It was now clear that such circumstances were unlikely ever to arise again. The Japanese Navy numbered four aircraft carriers, seven battleships, two hybrid battleship-carriers and various smaller ships. The U.S. Navy in the western Pacific numbered 32 carriers, 12 battleships and many, many other, smaller ships. The Japanese did not have enough carrier-trained pilots left to equip more than half their carriers with aircraft. On the other hand what was the point of having a navy if it sat idly by while the crucial Philippines were lost? The Chief of Operations on the Naval General Staff pleaded that the navy be allowed to win the decisive victory or 'bloom as the flowers of death.'[ii] Accordingly a plan was prepared whereby virtually the whole of the remaining Imperial fleet would launch a desperate attack in an effort to wipe out the landing at Leyte. The result was the greatest air/sea battle ever fought and, by some criteria, the greatest naval battle of all time.

The fleet advanced in three separate task forces. Admiral Ozawa led the remaining carrier force from the North. The main task of this force was to act as a decoy so that U.S. forces would chase it and leave the landings on Leyte for the other two forces to attack. Ozawa's task force included four carriers and the two hybrids. The latter, which were supposed to carry seaplanes that would be launched by catapult and recovered from the sea in a crazy process of startling impracticality, carried no planes at all on this mission. It is often said that the carriers themselves had only a token force of aircraft but evidence suggests this is not strictly so.

Their capacity was only about 160 aircraft at the best of times and they seem to have had 110 on board. 75 flew to attack the American 3rd Fleet and the survivors of this force landed on Luzon so only the remainder were present to defend the Japanese carriers when they were attacked by American aircraft. This is probably the explanation for the assertion that the northern fleet had only a handful of aircraft. However many they had, it did them no good because the American naval aircraft sank all four carriers including the Zuikaku, the last survivor of the attack on Pearl Harbour. The two hybrids escaped. This force did achieve its objective however, of luring the American carrier force north, away from Leyte Island and the landings.

The southern task force approached Leyte via the Surigao Strait but it had been seen by American reconnaissance aircraft and attacked, though without result. This force consisted of two battleships, a heavy cruiser and some destroyers. On the night of 24th October it sailed up the Strait but the Americans were warned and a force of six battleships that had been bombarding shore defences was ready and waiting. The Japanese force was wiped out.

The central task force was the critical one and in terms of conventional ships it was much the most powerful. It was composed of five battleships, eleven heavy cruisers and accompanying lighter forces. Two of the battleships were the Yamato and the Musashi, sister ships weighing 62,000 tons and armed with nine 18 inch guns in a world where no other ship carried guns larger than 16 inches. These were, by some measure, the two most powerful fighting ships in existence. This force approached the Philippines from the West and headed for the San Bernadino Strait which would lead it to Samar Island just north of Leyte. On the way it was savaged by American submarines which sank two heavy cruisers, including the flagship, and so damaged a third that it was forced to turn back.

The next attack was by the aircraft of 3rd Fleet and it concentrated on the battleship Musashi. Though other ships were hit and damaged it was the assault on the Musashi that was the epicentre of the battle and that gives this action its place in history.

The exact location of the fleet on the morning of 24th October was determined by a reconnaissance plane at a little after 8 a.m. and the order to launch a strike was given by Admiral Halsey, in charge of 3rd Fleet, at 8.30 a.m.. The first planes arrived over the Japanese ships at 10.30 a.m. and waves of U.S. planes attacked the fleet until the mid-afternoon. Gradually the attacks concentrated on the Musashi as it became apparent that she was damaged. At dusk she was listing and dead in the water. She had taken 17 bomb hits and 19 torpedo hits. One must bear in mind that a normal ship, even a large one, could be sunk by two or three of either type of hit.

Lieutenant Commander Joseph Lawler led the fighter escort of the bombing formation from the carrier Enterprise. This group attacked the Musashi shortly after 2 p.m.. He remembered that as he approached the enemy ships what struck him was the white wakes they left in the tropical sea. His force split up to attack

Not even the mightiest ships were safe from aircraft. This is the I.J.N.S. Musashi under attack by U.S. Navy aircraft at the Battle of Leyte Gulf in October 1944. The Musashi (with her sister-ship Yamato) was the most powerful battleship in the world but she was sunk in this attack. ©Imperial War Museum (NYF 47538)

simultaneously from three angles. His plane was only armed with some rockets and he decided at the last minute to attack an escorting cruiser instead, on the basis that his puny rockets would not do much harm to a battleship. The cruiser was severely damaged and Lawler escaped the fierce A.A. fire to return safely to his ship.[iii]

On the bridge of the shattered Musashi Admiral Inoguchi, the man in command, summoned his surviving officers to the bridge and told them to abandon ship. He handed over his will to an officer for transmission to his family and announced that he would go down with the ship. The second in command, Captain Kenkichi Kato, asked for permission to join him. It was denied. He was told it was his job to save as many of the crew as he could. As darkness fell, the ship rolled over and sank.[iv]

During the battle Admiral Kurita, who commanded this fleet had radioed Manilla for air cover but the result was a derisory handful of Zeros because every plane that could be found had already been sent on a mass strike against 3rd fleet. These 180 aircraft were intercepted by the American cover force of fighters above the fleet and massacred but one single bomber got through and landed its bomb on the carrier Princeton which was seriously damaged and set on fire. The cruiser Birmingham pulled alongside to take off the wounded and to help with fire-fighting and was there when Princeton blew up. 200 men on the decks of the Birmingham were killed in scenes of appalling carnage. The flaming wreckage of the Princeton was scuttled in the evening.

The whole battle cost the Japanese 270 aircraft, 200 of them on this day when nine separate American pilots shot down five or more planes and thus became instant aces. One man, Lieutenant Copeland shot down three aircraft to bring his total of kills to six, each of a different aircraft type which is probably a unique achievement.[v] David McCampbell shot down an amazing nine on one mission[vi] and was awarded the Congressional Medal of Honor for the achievement. When he landed back on his carrier at the end of this mission, his fuel was all gone and the engine died as he rolled to a stop. McCampbell, a southerner born in Alabama, became the navy's leading ace of the war with 34 victories by the time it ended.

As a result of American attacks, Admiral Kurita who commanded the central fleet decided that with no air cover and having lost one of his finest ships, his only alternative was to withdraw. He turned round and steamed west, a fact which was spotted by the Americans and led to Admiral Halsey deciding that he could afford to sail north to deal with Ozawa and his carriers. Kurita was an unusual Japanese commander in that he did not believe in wasting lives in a useless fight to the end but during the night he changed his mind and turned his ships round again. The following morning they appeared off the coast of Leyte to find only a few destroyers and some escort carriers.

In fact there were 16 escort carriers in the general area and they carried a total of 450 planes though the number immediately available was much smaller than that. Nevertheless they began a series of desperate attacks on the Japanese ships in company with the destroyers. In a running battle three Japanese cruisers were sunk and Kurita decided to retreat despite having the U.S. ships and the landing beach with its many transports at his mercy. His only significant achievement was to sink the escort carrier Gambier Bay. This apparently inexplicable decision made sure that Leyte Gulf was a Japanese defeat when it could have been at least a partial victory. When he made this decision Admiral Kurita had been awake for three days, having his flagship sunk under him and having to swim for his life during that time. He thought the force he met was the whole of 3rd Fleet because that was what he was expecting and he thought that staying to fight it out would lead to total disaster. One must have some sympathy for an exhausted man trying not to lead his men to a meaningless death, but he remains yet another example of the curious caution and indecision that characterized Japanese admirals.

Another seminal event occurred on this day and that was the introduction of aerial suicide attacks or 'kamikazes.' the word means, roughly, 'divine wind'.

The idea of diving your aircraft into an enemy ship at the cost of your own life was not a new one in the Japanese air forces. It was frequently used by pilots who knew their plane was too badly damaged to get them home or that they were near death from wounds anyway. Saburo Sakai, wounded over Guadalcanal, contemplated such an end and only the fact that he could not find a suitable American ship dissuaded him. It was only in the Philippines in October 1944 however, that the kamikaze mission became official Japanese Navy policy. The idea was the brainchild of Vice-Admiral Takijiro Onishi the new commander of naval air forces in the Philippines. He was no butcher but a thoughtful man and a patriot who could see that his pilots could no longer hope to prevail with conventional tactics. Accordingly he formed a unit of volunteers to carry out suicide missions in the slight hope that they might inflict enough damage to halt the American juggernaut. (When the war was over Onishi committed suicide by ritual disembowelment.)

The first official kamikaze mission was flown on 25th October and the results were encouraging for the Japanese. The escort carrier St. Lo was sunk and six other small carriers damaged in varying degree. Five other ships were sunk. Encouraged by this success Onishi received the blessing of his superiors to expand the program.

On 26th October the Japanese Navy's greatest ace, Hiroyoshi Nishizawa, was killed. He had boasted that no American would ever shoot him down. In a sense he was right. He was a passenger in a transport plane flying to Luzon to pick up a new fighter when Hellcats shot it down. It is thought he had about 100 kills to his credit but accurate compilation of the scores of Japanese fighter pilots is an almost impossible task.

With the defeat of the Japanese fleet in the Battle of Leyte Gulf, the landings on Leyte were secure and the campaign for the liberation of the Philippines could begin. It was to be a slow and bitter struggle and the Japanese army was still holding out in northern parts of Luzon at war's end. On 20th November the U.S.A.A.F. transferred the HQ of 5th Air Force to Leyte and in their first two months of operations from bases on the island army planes shot down 314 of the enemy. 13th Air Force HQ followed in March 1945. After the battle for Leyte Japanese air opposition was reduced to nominal status save for the kamikazes. In January 1945 when landings were carried out on Luzon only 120 Japanese aircraft could be mustered in the whole Philippines to oppose it and they were beaten off without causing significant damage. Not so with the kamikazes which sank the escort carrier Ommaney Bay and various smaller ships and caused severe damage to two battleships and several cruisers including the Louisville, on whose bridge stood Rear Admiral Chandler when the kamikaze struck. He was dowsed in flaming gasoline from the aircraft's tanks. Dreadfully burned he continued to help to save the ship and took his turn with a fire hose. But his injuries, including scorched lungs, were too severe and he died the following day. These landings saw the U.S. Navy take its worst losses since the Battle of Tassafaronga during the Guadalcanal campaign in 1942.[vii]

After supporting the landings 3rd Fleet cruised through the South China Sea on a mission of destruction and sank 44 merchant vessels totaling 132,000 tons. There was no air opposition save at the end when the Fleet attacked Formosa again and the kamikazes appeared once more and damaged the carriers Langley and Ticonderoga. During January 1945, the navy destroyed 300,000 tons of shipping and 500 aircraft at a cost of 201 American aircraft.

In the last week of January a British fleet sailing into the Pacific raided the major Japanese oil refineries at Palembang on Sumatra and caused severe damage. They also destroyed 68 Japanese planes in the air and on the ground but the raids cost 48 Royal Navy aircraft. This fleet was the British naval contribution to victory in the Pacific. The U.S. Navy needed no help and did not want the British taking part but Churchill was anxious that Britain be seen to take a role in the final defeat of Japan and President Roosevelt gave him his backing. The only significant contribution the fleet made was to play a small part in the operations at Okinawa but its record was less than stellar. Its ships were old and overworked and inadequately equipped for tropical operations. One aircraft carrier had to be sent home after repeated breakdowns. Most of the fleet's fighters were Seafires, Spitfires adapted for use on a carrier, and they proved to be too sensitive for the rigours of life at sea and suffered a very poor serviceability rate. Moreover the presence of two navies with different supply requirements made the whole business of logistics a great deal more complicated.

One advantage of British carriers was their armoured decks. Three of them, Victorious, Indefatigable and Formidable suffered kamikaze attacks but none was seriously damaged or forced to cease operations. The whole fleet however, had to sail back to Sydney for rest and refit at the end of May 1945 because of mechanical defects and accumulated damage. The contrast with American fleets that remained at sea for months on end and remained in top fighting condition was painful. The truth was that at the end of a long war Britain had neither the manpower nor the resources to maintain a major fleet on the other side of the world.

Further to the South the New Guinea and Solomons theatre had become a backwater but fighting rumbled on there between the Australians and isolated Japanese garrisons. The Japanese 18th Army was cut off in the Wewak area of northern New Guinea and operations continued against it and other isolated garrisons at Aitape, Hollandia and other settlements right up to the time of the Japanese surrender.

The same was the case with the Japanese base at Rabaul and their army on Bougainville in the Solomons. It has been calculated that trying to maintain Rabaul as a viable base cost Japan four submarines, 30 warships, 154 transports, 517 barges and 820 aircraft.[viii] By early 1945 there was no longer any opposition from the Japanese in the air. Lack of fuel and spare parts had long since grounded any aircraft that were in the region. When airfields in the Hollandia area were captured in April 1945, 340 destroyed or damaged aircraft were found on three airfields. Australian aircraft were now flying ground attack missions against enemy airfields and troop positions together with air supply and the inevitable reconnaissance. But the most demanding mission in terms of aircraft involved, was anti-submarine patrol. 25 squadrons, or some 400 aircraft were devoted to such work. All the ground operations on various Pacific islands ultimately depended on supplies brought in by sea and these were vulnerable to attack by submarine. Such attacks never threatened the success of land operations but were a constant thorn in the side of the planners. For instance in 1943 11 vessels were sunk off the Australian coast in 21 submarine attacks.

With New Guinea and Rabaul reduced to impotence by the summer of 1944 Allied forces moved forward in the south to assist in the reduction of the Philippines. The island of Morotai, halfway between Mindanao at the southern end of the Philippines and the west of New Guinea was chosen for assault and the Australian air force struck at Japanese airbases on nearby Ceram and Halmahera as well as on Mindanao and even at Balikpapan on Borneo. The actual attack was launched on 15th September and was a complete success. The island was rapidly secured though, as was so often the case, isolated bands of Japanese soldiers held out in the jungle until the end of the war.

Morotai now became the base for the newly formed Australian First Tactical Air Force which ranged over the whole Netherlands East Indies (today's Indonesia). The invasion of the Philippines drew the last Japanese planes from the East Indies to the battle at Leyte and so the Australians found themselves unopposed. They ranged across the East Indies sinking ships and wrecking airfields and docks. In this the aircraft at Morotai were backed up by a force of B-24 Liberators flying from bases around Darwin on the north coast of Australia. One of the specialties developed by the Australians was mine-laying for which they used their large fleet of PBY Catalina flying boats. The East Indies abounds in small harbours and narrow channels that are ideal targets for mining. The biggest hazard for pilots was now mechanical failure and the vast area they flew over rather than enemy action. For instance a Catalina of 42 Squadron suffered engine trouble while on a mission to Java on 14th January and had to land in the open sea. The landing damaged the hull which sprang a leak and the crew had to bail all night before another Catalina rescued them the next day.[ix]

By early 1945 the Japanese position was so desperate, particularly with regard to shipping, that after March 1st no more attempts were made to supply any post outside the home islands.[x] Thus the Australians were able to land on Tarakan on the coast of Borneo on May 1st with virtually no opposition. This was followed by landings at Brunei Bay in June and Balikpapan on 1st July where the Japanese defenders fought fiercely. Each of these landings was supported by the bombers of the R.A.A.F..

At the war's end the Australian Air Force had 85 squadrons amounting, at a conservative estimate, to some 1,400 front line aircraft. Training planes probably amounted to another 1,000; and yet the R.A.A.F. was, in terms of size, a second rank air force.

The capture of the Mariana Islands provided the Americans with a base from which the systematic bombing of Japan could be carried out. Previous bombing raids carried out from bases in China had been unsatisfactory because of supply difficulties and the fact that not all of the Japanese homeland was within range. Moreover the bases were vulnerable to Japanese ground attack. The Marianas presented none of these drawbacks and were rapidly converted into a giant military base with airfields on all three of the main islands: Guam, Saipan and Tinian. The aircraft in China and India were transferred and a strategic bombing campaign against the industries and cities of the Japanese homeland began in earnest, using the Boeing B-29 bomber. All the bombers were put under the command of a new 20th Air Force which was unique in that it was retained under the direct control of General 'Hap' Arnold the Commander-in-Chief of the U.S.A.A.F., rather than coming within the sphere of control of a theatre chief. The reasons for doing this were to prevent the B-29 force being used for tactical attacks and to avoid having to choose whether MacArthur or Nimitz would have control of it. In practice Arnold had too many responsibilities to be able to exercise daily control and so command of 20th Air force on the ground was given to Curtis Lemay, the veteran of the 8th Air Force in Europe.

The Boeing B-29 was the ultimate development of the piston engine bomber. It was a generation ahead of anything else in the field, boasting a pressurized cabin and 12 machine guns in remotely controlled gun turrets together with an ability to cruise comfortably at 30,000 feet. Its wingspan was 141 feet and its length 99 feet so that it was, in round terms 50 per cent bigger than a Lancaster and needed a crew of 11. It could carry 20,000 lbs of bombs, compared to the 14,000 of the Lancaster. (It is true that some Lancasters could carry 22,000 lbs but these were a tiny number of specially modified planes.) It was powered by four Wright Cyclone R3350 engines developed specially for the job. Unfortunately the engines had been developed too fast and all the bugs had not been ironed out: they were not really ready for use in the front line. The whole development of the aircraft had been pushed relentlessly to meet the Air Force's perceived need. 'Hap' Arnold had even placed an order for 1,600 B-29s before the prototype had flown: an unheard-of risk. There were constant problems with the engines including an alarming tendency to catch fire while the plane was in flight and these difficulties were never wholly overcome. Though the B-29 had an impressive theoretical top speed which was almost the same as a 1940 Spitfire, its realistic cruising speed was nearly 100 mph less and was slower than the B-24. Despite these shortcomings this was undoubtedly the best heavy bomber of the war by a substantial margin. It was also a beautiful plane to behold, as the greatest aircraft usually are. Its clean, streamlined fuselage and rounded glass nose were reminiscent of a cigar tube and all B-29s were left a shining, metallic silver, innocent of any camouflage paint. The problem with admiring the aesthetics of this aircraft, however, is that it was the deliverer of fire and destruction culminating with the atomic bomb and therefore its beauty is the beauty of the angel of death.

A Boeing B-29 Superfortress at its base in the Mariana Islands. This aircraft was the ultimate development of the World War Two heavy bomber and dropped the atomic bomb. ©Imperial War Museum (NYP 69366)

The first major raid on Japan was flown from the Marianas bases on 24th November 1944 when 111 aircraft, led by Brigadier General Emmett O'Donnell in 'Dauntless Dotty', attacked the Masashima aircraft factory in Tokyo. Because of the height at which they were flying the attackers lost only one plane to enemy action but conversely the height contributed to extremely disappointing bombing results. For the next two and a half months there followed raids by smaller numbers of aircraft on industrial targets across Japan. The disappointing results continued; the reasons for this were threefold. First, there was the weather and, in particular, cloud cover. Because the weather moved from west to east adequate weather information would have required meteorological flights over Japanese-held China. This was not practicable. Second, the great altitude at which the raids were flown exposed the aircraft to the strong winds of the jet-stream. These buffeted them violently and made bomb-aiming a nightmare. Third, the crews were almost all new and inexperienced. Though they trained hard, it was not enough.

A particular problem was the huge distances to be flown over the open sea. From the Marianas to Japan is 1,500 miles and an increasing number of aircraft were lost due to mechanical problems or battle damage forcing them down before they reached home. However, directly on their route, at the halfway mark, was the island of Iwo Jima. If this could be captured it would provide an emergency landing ground for the bombers. Moreover, the island was equipped with radar which gave the Japanese early warning of raids and it had its own force of aircraft which attacked the bombers intermittently.

Accordingly another massive amphibious operation was launched in February 1945 to take this island. The garrison resisted with the ferocity invariably shown by Japanese soldiers and it took a month to secure this tiny island of only eight square miles. The Americans were not to know this but they could have taken it in the summer of 1944 virtually at will. At that time it was raided and bombarded and amongst the defending pilots was Saburo Sakai, now back at the front despite the loss of sight in one eye. It was at this time that Sakai performed a legendary feat when he was surrounded by 15 Hellcats and survived. He made sure the one-sided, twenty minute battle drifted toward Iwo Jima until the Japanese anti-aircraft guns on the island could open fire and drive off the Hellcats. When Sakai landed it was found that there was not a mark on his aircraft despite thousands of rounds being fired at it.[xi] Word of this exploit spread in a service which did not have much to be proud about at the time. By the end of the war Sakai was the object of something near to worship. A mechanic could ask for no greater honour than to be allowed to service his plane. The competition to fly as his wingman verged on violence.[xii]

In March 1945, with an invasion of Okinawa Island in the Ryukyu chain in the offing, the U.S. carrier force launched a series of raids on Kyushu, the southernmost of Japan's main home islands. It was from here that the bulk of Japan's missions in defence of Okinawa must be flown. Despite massive losses there were plenty of

Japanese aircraft left because there had always been a policy of keeping a strong force in the home islands for defensive purposes. In fact shortage of aviation fuel was the principal restriction on Japanese operations but the Americans had no way of knowing just how severe was this impediment. The greatest worry for the Americans was the time from the invasion until they could establish their own airbases on Okinawa itself. On 14th extensive raids were launched on airfields in Kyushu but the Japanese were warned and most aircraft flew out of harm's way in time. Later in the day the Japanese launched a counter-strike which damaged the carriers Intrepid and Yorktown. On 19th March there was a repeat performance and this time the carriers Wasp and Enterprise were damaged and the Franklin reduced to a wreck, dead in the water. Eventually the ship was saved but it had to return to the United States and took no further part in the war. Over 1,000 of the crew were killed or wounded including the captain. Over the next two days the fleet took up a defensive stance and allowed the Japanese to attack while retaining its planes for defence of the ships. This was successful as a policy and the Japanese lost dozens of aircraft for no tangible success. During these operations the pilots of the U.S. Navy claimed over 500 Japanese planes destroyed. Japanese air power on Kyushu was temporarily neutralized by the losses and did not interfere with the initial landing.

On April 1st 1945 U.S. Marines stormed ashore on the beaches of Okinawa, an island that was part of Japan and only 340 miles from the mainland. It was intended for use as the base from which the invasion of the Japanese mainland would be launched. The landing was preceded by aerial and naval bombardment in the now well established pattern and the aerial bombardment later included the nearby Sakishima Islands where there was a large airfield. This part of the operation was carried out by the Royal Navy contingent. The invasion of Okinawa was the last and most massive invasion of the Pacific War. 430 transports were required to carry 183,000 men and their equipment and they had to be loaded at 11 different ports. The whole invasion armada amounted to 1,200 ships. The Japanese defenders were 100,000 strong and had built themselves impressive fortifications. Their plans for the defence included the use of suicide boats packed with explosive and the now inevitable kamikazes which had become the only effective air weapon left to the Japanese.

They even had a rocket plane called 'Ohka', or 'cherry blossom', which resembled the German Mistel and was carried near to the target by a bomber and released. It then glided to close range when the rockets were fired and the plane raced to its target too fast for fighters or anti-aircraft fire to catch it. 850 of these contraptions were built though only a fraction were actually used and they sank or damaged only half a dozen ships in all. Their main shortcoming was that the bombers carrying them were so burdened as to be slow and incapable of manoeuvering, thus rendering them helpless targets for American fighter pilots. The Ohka is little more than a curious footnote to history.

The struggle for Okinawa lasted until June 1945 and was slow and bloody in the extreme. From the point of view of the air war, there are two matters to be examined. The first concerns the battleship Yamato, sister of the Musashi sunk at Leyte Gulf. This mighty ship left Kure harbour on 6th April escorted by a cruiser and four destroyers. She carried only enough oil to get her to Okinawa but not to return so, effectively, hers was a suicide mission. She was to batter the many transport ships still anchored off the invasion beach. She was not given air cover because a major kamikaze strike was launched at the same time against the American fleet. Possibly she was being used as a decoy. If that was so, she achieved her objective because long before she reached Okinawa she was attacked by 280 aircraft of the U.S. fleet and repeatedly struck by bombs and torpedoes as wave upon wave of American planes attacked her over a period of two hours. She was beaten to a wreck and took in thousands of tons of seawater. When the end was near Admiral Ito, in charge of the fleet, shook hands with officers on the bridge of the battleship and then retired to his cabin to go down with the ship. Her captain, Kosaku Ariga tied himself to the compass binnacle to ensure he too was drowned. At last the great ship rolled over and sank, taking most of her crew of over 2,000 men with her.[xiii] The escorting cruiser Yahagi was also sunk. Her captain, Tameichi Hara, an old warhorse who had survived many close scrapes, went down with his ship but, having neglected to tie himself to her, bobbed to the surface again and was saved. From the water he watched the end of the Yamato and saw the planes swarming round her 'like gnats'.[xiv]

The second matter for consideration is the kamikaze attacks launched on the fleet at Okinawa. These began with a mass attack on 6th April by 900 Japanese aircraft, one third of them kamikazes. Three U.S. destroyers and two ammunition ships were sunk. The Americans claimed 249 kills. The following day there was another mass attack and a battleship and a carrier were damaged. On 11th and 16th there were further mass attacks. Various smaller ships were sunk or damaged but no major warship and the Japanese were taking huge losses of aircraft. The Americans claimed 298 kills on 11th alone. In between the big attacks small missions were flown by groups of 20 or so kamikaze planes almost every day. So concerned was Admiral Nimitz about the situation that he asked the army to use their B-29s to bomb Japanese airbases on Kyushu. From mid-April to mid-May these became their prime targets and gradually the raids had their effect and the kamikazes decreased in number but they did not cease. As previously mentioned there were attacks on the Royal Navy fleet off the Sakishima Islands and several aircraft carriers were hit but, having armoured flight decks, they recovered from hits that would have incapacitated an American carrier.

In May there were more mass attacks. On 11th the carrier Bunker Hill was hit twice and badly damaged. 346 men were killed and the ship, though it survived, was out of the war. On 14th U.S.S. Enterprise, a carrier that had fought through the whole war, was hit at the front of the flight deck and the elevator was destroyed. She too was out of the war and sailed for the U.S.A. for repairs. A number of smaller ships, particularly destroyers, were sunk. By the second half of the month however, the bombing of bases and the heavy loss of aeroplanes caused the Japanese to scale down the attacks with a view to building up their air capability to face an invasion of the homeland which now seemed inevitable. The last mass attack was made on 21st June but it was ineffective. Overall the Okinawa campaign was the most expensive of the Pacific War for the Allies who had lost 38 ships and 763 aircraft. Japanese losses are not known with certainty but one authority gives a figure for 5,000 airmen lost in the Kamikaze campaign overall.[xv] Given that many missions were flown by a pilot alone this probably represents the loss of around 3,500 aircraft.

At the end of February 1945 General Curtis LeMay decided on a crucial change of tactics. His high altitude precision attacks on Japanese industry were not working and the whole campaign was becoming an embarrassment. He was acutely aware that marines were fighting and dying on Iwo Jima to give him a further base but if he was doing no damage, what was the point? He decided to move to medium level night-time area attacks on Japanese cities using incendiaries. A whole mock Japanese town had been built in 1943 in Utah and used to find out what kind of incendiary was most destructive. The result was a napalm based weapon which was now available for LeMay to use. This tactic took advantage of the fact that the Japanese had no night fighter force to speak of and their cities were not protected by the automatic anti-aircraft weapons which were so effective against low and medium level attacks in Germany. It was planned to remove the guns from the B-29s except for the rear turret, in order to reduce weight and allow for a bigger bomb load but LeMay found that the effect on crew morale was too damaging so only the top guns were removed and the gunners flew anyway because the crews hated to be split up.[xvi] The crews still considered the new tactics suicidal and were in rebellious mood.

Tokyo was attacked on the night of March 9th/10th by 325 aircraft using the new methods and with spectacular results. Japanese cities were more inflammable than their European counterparts by the nature of their construction, which almost exclusively used wood and wood-derived products. Tokyo burned like a torch and a firestorm soon developed. The violent thermals threw bombers about like leaves. 16.8 square miles of the city were devastated and more people were killed than in any raid on a German city. The exact number will never be known but it lies between 80 and 100,000. Only 14 aircraft were lost which amounted to some 4 per cent and was no worse a casualty rate than on the conventional high level raids. So successful was the bombing of Tokyo that LeMay quickly followed up with similar raids on Nagoya, Osaka and Kobe where there was similar widespread destruction and heavy loss of life.

It may seem strange that the Americans should abandon the precision bombing that had served them well in Europe for area bombing that had been so ineffective there, but the circumstances were, in fact quite different. We have already looked at the reasons why precision bombing was not working and we have also to consider the nature of the targets. Japan was a mountainous country and the population was squeezed into the limited space on the flat coastal plains and into large cities thereon. These cities had expanded hugely in the decades before the Second World War and factories and domestic housing were mixed up together to a degree not seen in Germany. Indeed Japanese industry made use of hundreds of small sub-contractors in workshops spread throughout all the urban areas. Moreover whole cities were built of the inflammable material only found in an old Mediaeval city centre in Europe. Since Japan imported most of its coal and steel heavy industry was concentrated as close as possible to the docks for obvious economic reasons. What this meant was that in Japan, unlike Europe, area bombing of a city really did destroy industry wholesale. For instance, at Osaka the arsenal, a 150 acre industrial site right in the middle of the city, was burned out. Naturally the Japanese had plans for the dispersal of industry into the countryside and to various forests and caves but the destruction was too sudden and too overwhelming for the plans to be put into effective operation in good time.

After the incendiary raids LeMay went back to precision bombing but from lower altitudes. It was the middle of April before he hit the large cities again with incendiaries. After that the next big raid was in the middle of May but thereafter a major incendiary raid on a Japanese city was launched on average once a week.

The cities of Japan were reduced to ruins one by one. LeMay brushed off the cost in human lives on the basis that the Japanese themselves had done terrible things and deserved everything they got. It must be remembered that the Holocaust was not evident to Allied eyes in Europe until the last days of the war and on the western front the war had been fought in accordance with generally accepted norms of behaviour save for some lapses here and there on both sides. In the Pacific however, the fighting had been brutal and marked throughout by Japanese savagery. Even as the B-29s were making their early raids on the homeland Japanese troops were on the rampage in Manila where they killed in the region of 100,000 civilians in an orgy of rapine and slaughter.

Unlike Harris's bombing campaign in Europe the effect on industry was immediate and dramatic. Steel production fell by nearly a half and production of aircraft engines from 1,822 in August 1944 to 345 in July 1945.[xvii] It is fair to say however, that the decline shown by these figures is also partly due to the collapse of vital imports of raw materials in the face of the American submarine war. There were Japanese fighter planes in the air almost to the very end and though they could not turn the tide in any sense they caused a constant if modest stream of losses. They had their best night on 25th May when 460 B-29s raided Tokyo and 43 were lost. By the end of the month there were raids in daylight accompanied by P-51 fighters based on Okinawa and Iwo Jima.

On April 12th 20th Air Force's only Congressional Medal of Honor was won by

Sergeant Edward 'Red' Erwin. It was his job to push phosphorous marker flares into a release tube from which they fell from the aircraft and illuminated the scene. A flare stuck in the tube and ignited as he tried to free it. Burning at 1,300 degrees Fahrenheit. it roared back up the tube and hit him in the face and then fell to the floor and started burning through the floor to the bomb bay. If it reached the bomb bay the aircraft was doomed. Erwin, who had been blinded and had his nose and an ear burned off picked it up and felt his way to the nose where he pushed it out of a window in the cockpit while the flare burned all the time. The plane then turned for home to get medical treatment for Erwin as soon as possible.[xviii] It landed at Iwo Jima where doctors doubted that he would survive his terrible burns. The paperwork necessary for the award of the Medal of Honor was rushed through so that it could be presented to Erwin before he died. But he lived and after three years in hospital and 40 operative procedures recovered much his sight and the use of one arm.

By the beginning of July organized resistance on Okinawa had ceased and the carrier force sailed to Japan and spent the rest of the war patrolling off the coast while its aircraft attacked anything that moved on shore. The last surviving ships of the Japanese Navy, hiding in small harbours and inlets, were hunted down and sunk.

On 6th August 1945 an atomic bomb was dropped on Hiroshima by a B-29 and the city was flattened almost instantly. 70,000 perished. On 9th August another bomb was dropped on Nagasaki, killing 35,000.[xix] The death toll was much less because hills shielded much of the city. These figures are approximate because of the inherent difficulty of making a comprehensive count and the continuing deaths long afterwards still attributable to the bombs. It is worth stressing that these two bombs together did little more damage than the March 10th raid on Tokyo.

Also on 9th August the U.S.S.R. declared war on Japan and invaded Manchuria. In terms of front line planes there the Japanese Army Air force was minute. Peace negotiations had been in train for some time but had shown no tangible result. Now the Emperor, horrified by the effects of bombing on Japan and the hopelessness of her position, accepted an unconditional surrender on 15th August 1945 and the Second World War on the ground and in the air, was over.

It took some days for the news to reach Japanese forces in Manchuria so it is hard to say when the last air battle took place. Saburo Sakai certainly fought one of the last in the homeland theatre when he attacked a bomber over Tokyo.[xx] In his memoirs he asserts that this happened on the night of 13th August though, in fact, it probably was several days later. He claimed to have destroyed the bomber but in fact it survived, unlike the empire he served so well.

Epilogue

Hardly had the guns fallen silent than the scrapping of surplus aircraft began. Naturally, in the countries that had lost the war, military aircraft were destroyed to the last plane but amongst the winners too there was now no need for the thousands of expensive aircraft that filled concrete hard-stands around the world.

The situation did not parallel that after the First World War in any way however. In 1919 the general assumption was that the so-called 'Great War' was the war to end all wars and decades of peace would ensue. In such a climate military budgets could be cut to the bone but after the Second World War the tension between the Soviet bloc and the West was such that a new war could be anticipated at any time. Accordingly most of the major powers retained substantial armed forces and research into military hardware continued apace. Naturally the whole military scene was dominated by the existence of nuclear weapons and the exact form that any future conflict would take was a matter for speculation, particularly once soviet Russia developed her own atom bomb. It was generally accepted however, that the aeroplane would play a major part in whatever manner warfare developed.

Technological advances in the decades that followed the end of the Second World War were so radical and so rapid that the military aviation scene changed dramatically. First the jet plane and the helicopter and then the guided missile, stealth technology, air refuelling and the digital age transformed the way air combat was conducted. The constant presence of the nuclear threat put all kinds of constraints on strategy. The result was that the Second World War in the air was rapidly turned into a museum-piece. It very soon came to represent the combat of a bygone age with little relevance to the modern requirements of war. Airmen who had remained in their country's air force after the end of hostilities had to learn new skills and get used to a new military environment.

Fighter combat was the first aspect of air warfare to mutate away from the accepted norms of World War Two. The speed of the new jet fighters and the use of air-to-air missiles rendered the dogfight obsolete. Twenty years after the World War, one plane could destroy another with a missile at ranges so great that the target was not visible to the attacker. Though the dogfight staged a brief revival in Vietnam, this occurred for purely technical reasons related to the design of the aircraft doing the fighting and the basic trend remained unaffected. In fact, so efficient were missiles that the bomber aircraft became little more than a target drone.

The existence of nuclear weapons rendered strategic bombing obsolete overnight: an atom bomb could do that job in the twinkling of an eye. But at the same time the use of such a weapon was unthinkable. Conflicts in the post-war world became limited affairs with no room for strategic bombing except in very specialized circumstances such as Iraq or Serbia.

The Douhet doctrine in its purest form was disproved by the Second World War itself but strategic bombing, it appears, can reduce a country to a state of prostration in which ground forces simply occupy the land against the feeblest resistance. The truth seems to be that the basic Douhet idea was correct but there are many variables that determine whether strategic bombing will be effective in any given situation. It helps if the bombing is swift and overwhelming and if the target nation is given some alternative short of total surrender and some prospect of a better life after the war. It is noticeable that all these features were absent in the case of Germany in World War Two. The example of Japan can support either side of the argument. Its economy was much smaller than that of Germany and much more vulnerable by reason of its concentration in a few urban areas and the flammable nature of Japanese building materials. The American strategic offensive was carried out in months rather than years and, once high level bombing was abandoned and area bombing adopted, cities were destroyed overnight, industry was devastated and production brought to a halt. Though the people did not demand peace the Emperor did, and so strategic bombing achieved its purpose. However, it can be argued that the surrender was brought about, at least in part, by naval blockade as well.

For many years after the war the accepted wisdom was that strategic bombing as an instrument of policy had failed despite the infliction of great suffering and in that climate of opinion there was no future for the strategic bomber other than as the bearer of atomic bombs, a job that did not call for large numbers of aircraft. The advent of the ballistic missile removed even that task.

Tactical bombing was undergoing a revolution even before the war ended. The medium bomber which was the mainstay of every air force in 1939 was being overtaken by the fighter-bomber. It had become clear that most targets were best attacked from low level and that this was best done by a small, fast aircraft. As the war progressed the range and carrying power of the fighter type single-engine aircraft increased enormously so that it began to eclipse the medium bomber. The only real limiting factor on this kind of attack was anti-aircraft fire: at low level it could be extremely accurate. The solution was to have the first wave of the attacking aircraft target the defences.

This kind of small, fighter-bomber attack plane had been used for ground attack duties at the front line since the First War and now its realm spread to take over the bombing of everything save strategic targets. It is hard to over-emphasize the advances made in this area. By the end of the war the Douglas Skyraider was about to enter service. It was a single-engine aircraft little larger than the fighters of the Battle of Britain and yet it could carry 8,000 lbs of bombs. That is the bomb load of a strategic bomber of World War Two. Aircraft like this rendered the tactical bomber obsolete.

The war also saw the passing of the dive bomber. It was an effective type in its time. It was conceived in the 1930s when the speed and weight of aircraft was low enough that the concept was practical but as they grew faster and heavier the structural problems inherent in the dive bombing technique became insurmountable. The Luftwaffe paid a heavy price for not recognizing this fact. In fact, what a dive bomber could do, a normal attack plane such as the Stormovik or the Typhoon could do just as well if properly handled and flown by an experienced pilot.

Most of the lessons taught by Second World War aviation were not new. The value of attack aircraft in support of troops, the possibilities of strategic bombing, the achievements of tactical bombing and the need for speed in fighter aircraft were all well-known factors between the wars and the Second War just served to underline them. One of the few areas in which the Second World War made a lasting and original contribution was air/sea combat. The ongoing debate about the value of the battleship in the air age was decisively resolved in favour of the aircraft and against the battleship which was effectively extinct by 1945. The vulnerability of all ships to air attack was made very clear and it is therefore no surprise that the only ship to come out of the war with its reputation enhanced was the aircraft carrier. Increases in the capabilities of carrier-borne aircraft coupled with air to air refueling now mean that there is virtually no part of the world that is safe from them.

Debate has rumbled on over the years about the ethics of strategic bombing. There does not seem to be much of an issue about the bombing of industry as such, even when it results in civilian casualties as a by-product. This is generally accepted as legitimate, though abhorrent and to be avoided if at all possible.

The big argument has been about the British policy of carpet bombing cities. A clarification is needed here because of the disinformation put out by the British government during the Second World War and still widely believed by the public more than half a century after the event. The general belief is that the R.A.F. bombed cities because the technology of the time was not such as to allow them to bomb industry only. That much is correct but the corollary is that they therefore bombed whole cities in order to hit the factories within those cities. This is not the case: cities were bombed in order to cause the maximum possible disruption to the lives of the people who lived there and thus indirectly to impede industry. Thus, not to mince words, the object was the wholesale slaughter of civilians.

The first point to be made is that this was not, in fact, the only policy open to the R.A.F.. They began the war making pinpoint attacks on industry only to discover that the methods used were so ineffective that the results were derisory. They then chose to pursue area bombing but there were other choices: they could have bitten the bullet and returned to limited daylight raiding of short range targets, perhaps at low level and in poor weather. Admittedly this would not have been an easy course. Secondly, they could have confined themselves to precision attacks but carried them out more frequently. There is no doubt that they were capable of doing this: the 'dams raid' is just one example of what could be achieved. Thirdly, they could have abandoned strategic bombing altogether, either for the duration of the war or until they had the technical aids to make worthwhile precision attacks. The bombers thus released, could have given invaluable aid to the army and the navy. Taking this course would have shortened the Battle of the Atlantic and the struggle for North Africa by a large measure.

That these courses were not pursued may be regretted but one cannot criticize the decision on moral grounds. British leaders made what they thought was the right decision in the circumstances to win the war as quickly and expeditiously as possible and with the least loss of life. It must be accepted that the men in command of the R.A.F. genuinely believed that killing civilians in large numbers would lead to a shorter war and thus save lives in the long run. The great majority of the British public supported the area bombing policy though this is a point of limited value since they were consistently misled by the government as to what the bombing policy really was. All this must be seen, of course, against the background of the bombing of England in 1940 and 1941 which cost Britain thousands of lives and hardened hearts.

One may however, note the fact that area bombing was not the first choice policy and the suspicion hangs over it that Britain had a strategic bomber force and supporting industry and needed a rationale for using them once it was clear that precision night bombing was not viable. If the R.A.F.'s leaders really thought area bombing was a war-winning weapon, why was it not used earlier than 1942?

The great problem arises with the conduct of the bombing offensive after the invasion of Europe. This invasion was supposed to have been rendered unnecessary by the bombing but the claims of the 'bomber barons' turned out to be fantasy and there is no doubt the war could not have been won without it. Area bombing had failed, yet it was continued right to the end of the war in the face of incontrovertible evidence that oil and transport targets were the route to shortening the war and could be hit with a reasonable degree of accuracy. Bombing city centres, it was now clear, was making little or no contribution to shortening the war.

The unfortunate truth was that the R.A.F. leadership was locked into a policy that they dare not abandon. To do so would be to make the implicit admission that it had been the wrong policy and that was an unthinkable course. After a major part of the national resources had been devoted to area bombing and 50,000 British and Commonwealth young men had died carrying it out, the leadership did not dare take any step that might even hint that a mistake had been made. That is why Harris stayed at his post and why area bombing continued to the end of the war. It must be noted that these were the considerations while the war was in progress. German deaths were not a major consideration because of the almost universal feeling that the Germans had started the war and deserved everything they got. Once the War was over and people realized the scale of the death and destruction visited on German cities a degree of public disquiet arose, reflected in the fact that Harris, alone amongst top level British military leaders, was not given a peerage.

It is important to recognize the difference between British and American strategic bombing policy. The Americans always believed that the way to win the war was to hit specific targets and that was what they sought to do. They were correct in this and so they were never confronted with a realization that they were on the wrong path though they certainly faced the possibility that their goal might be impossible of achievement. Certainly their policy also killed many civilians and at times the application of their approach was hard to distinguish from the R.A.F. area doctrine. The fact remains, however, that precision bombing was not only the less objectionable way to use a strategic air arm but also the more effective. The point is sometimes made that a bombing victim is just as dead whatever kind of policy led to their death and that is obviously correct. The key issue however, is the guilt or otherwise of the bomber. It is a fundamental of human justice that we look upon accidental killing with less condemnation than deliberate killing and that must surely be a proper attitude to take.

In the Pacific the Americans resorted to area bombing of Japan but the circumstances here were very different. The crucial point about this policy however, is that it worked: Japan surrendered, no invasion of the homeland was required and countless lives were thus saved.

On the other hand British area bombing did not work and was known not to work, yet was continued by reason of the obstinacy and desire for self-preservation of the people responsible. One sometimes hears that it was not realistic to expect Harris to be sacked or bombing policy to be changed but this is a specious argument: it assumes that a few careers and a certain degree of public disquiet are more important than thousands of lives. We certainly never took that view about the leaders on the other side.

There is always a tendency to believe that if your side does it, it is merely part of winning a just war but if the enemy does it, it is a war crime. This feeling is particularly, and understandably, strong amongst those who took part in or lost relatives in the area bombing campaign. Difficult as it is, we must put such considerations aside and recognize that R.A.F. bombing policy in the last months of the war was morally indefensible. This is the only true route to ensuring such horrors do not occur again.

APPENDIX ONE

Ranks and Organization

The air forces of the major powers in World War Two almost universally adopted the ranks of the army, the only important exception being Great Britain. Below are the commissioned ranks in the R.A.F. alongside the equivalent ranks in the army. Non-commissioned aircrew in the R.A.F. were sergeants.

Pilot Officer	Second Lieutenant
Flying Officer	Lieutenant
Flight Lieutenant	Captain
Squadron Leader	Major
Wing Commander	Lieutenant Colonel
Group Captain	Colonel
Air Commodore	Brigadier
Air Vice Marshal	Major General
Air Marshal	Lieutenant General
Air Chief Marshal	General
Marshal of the Royal Air Force	Field Marshal

Air force organization was, unfortunately, different in almost every country and often most confusingly so. For instance several air forces had an organizational unit called a 'Group' but they were not all the same size. I have set out below the organizational structure of the major combatants but it must be appreciated that there were often wide variations to suit the exigencies of operations or for other reasons. The establishment number of aircraft would rarely be exactly met in a combat situation.

Squadrons were divided into 'Flights' in all air forces. For the sake of clarity I have simplified what is a very complicated subject and the information given should be considered as guidance only.

U.S.A.A.F.

The United States Army Air Corps became the Army Air Force in 1941 and the United States Air Force in 1947. During the war people often spoke of the 'Air Corps' or the 'Air Force' when they meant the Army Air Force.

Air force: any number of divisions.
Division: any number of wings.
Wing: 3 or more groups.
Group: 3 or 4 squadrons.
Squadron: 6 bombers or 12 fighters.

U.S. Navy squadrons were designated either 'V' for aircraft or 'Z' for balloon, together with a letter to show their purpose ('F' for fighter, 'B' for bomber etc.) and a number, thus VF-10 was Fighter Squadron 10. The same squadron in the Marines would be VMF-10. Types of plane in the Navy were designated by the letter of purpose and a code letter for the manufacturer and a number if that manufacturer had provided more than one type for the same purpose. Thus the Wildcat fighter was the F4F because it was the fourth type of fighter provided by the Grumman company whose code letter was 'F'.

R.A.F.

Air force: any combination of smaller units.
Group: any number of wings or squadrons.
Wing: 2 to 5 squadrons.
Squadron: 12 to 20 aircraft.

V.V.S.

Air force: any number of regiments.
Corps: 2 or 3 divisions
Division: 3 regiments.
Regiment: 4 squadrons.
Squadron: 12 bombers or 15 fighters.

L'ARMEE DE L'AIR

Groupement: any combination of smaller units.
Wing (Escadre): 2 or 3 groups.
Group (Groupe): 3 escadrilles.
Squadron (Escadrille): 9 aircraft.

LUFTWAFFE

Air fleet: any combination of smaller units.
Air corps: any combination of smaller units
Air division: any number of wings.
Wing (Geschwader): 3 groups.
Group (Gruppe): 3 squadrons.
Squadron (Staffel): 12 planes.

The wings had different titles depending on their purpose, e.g.:

Kampfgeschwader – bomber wing – abbreviation Kg
Sturzkampfgeschwader – dive bomber wing – Stg
Jadtgeschwader – fighter wing – Jg
Nachtjadtgeschwader – night fighter wing – Njg
Zerstorergeschwader – heavy fighter wing – Zjg

These wings had a strong individual identity and names as well as numbers. Thus Jg2 was the 'Richthofen' Geschwader and Jg54 was the 'Green Heart' Geschwader.

REGIA AERONAUTICA

Division: any combination of smaller units.
Brigade: any combination of smaller units.
Wing (Stormo): 3 gruppi.
Squadron (Gruppo): 3 squadriglie.
Flight (Squadriglia): 6 aircraft but wide variations.

JAPANESE ARMY AND NAVY AIR FORCES

Air army/fleet: 2 air divisions (Hikoshidan).
Air flotilla (Navy): any combination of smaller units.
Air corps: any combination of smaller units. Discontinued 1942.
Air division (Hikodan): any combination of smaller units.

Air combat group (Hikosentai or Sentai): 3 squadrons.
Squadron (Chutai): 15 fighters or 10 bombers.

A Chutai was called a Hikotai in the navy.

APPENDIX TWO

Aircraft Production by the Major Powers

000s

	1932	1933	1934	1935	1936	1937	1938
Germany	0.03	0.37	1.97	3.18	5.11	5.60	5.24
Italy	–	0.39	0.33	0.86	1.77	1.75	1.61
Japan	0.69	0.77	0.69	0.95	1.18	1.51	3.20
U.K.	0.45	0.63	0.74	1.14	1.88	2.15	2.82
U.S.	0.59	0.47	0.44	0.59	1.14	0.95	1.80
U.S.S.R.	2.60	2.60	2.60	3.58	3.58	3.58	7.50

	1939	1940	1941	1942	1943	1944	1945
Germany	8.30	10.25	11.78	15.41	24.81	39.81	7.54
Italy	1.75	3.26	3.50	2.82	2.02	–	–
Japan	4.47	4.77	5.09	8.86	16.69	28.18	11.07
U.K.	7.94	15.04	20.09	23.67	26.26	26.46	12.07
U.S.	2.20	12.80	26.28	47.84	85.90	96.32	49.76
U.S.S.R.	10.38	10.57	15.74	25.44	34.90	40.30	20.90[i]

Aircraft Design and Air Combat

There are four forces acting on any aircraft as it flies. Gravity is trying to pull it down and the drag of air resistance is trying to pull it back. Lift from the wings is pulling it up and power from the engine is pulling it forward. For flight to be viable lift must exceed gravity and engine power must exceed drag. Lift is provided by air-flow over the wings, if that flow is fast enough. The engine provides the force to pull the plane forward and provide the air-flow.

In terms of physics the phenomenon of lift is fairly complicated and most of the short explanations of it are inaccurate. However, this is not the place for the long explanation. The two key factors are, first, that the wing is tilted slightly upward (this is called the 'angle of attack') and second, that it has a curve on the top surface. To see it in everyday terms imagine that you have a strong fan turned on and you hold a piece of paper in front of it by the two top corners. The pressure of the air-flow will push the paper up. Or consider water-skiing. If you stand still in the water wearing skies, you will sink but if a boat pulls you fast enough you stay on the surface and race along seemingly effortlessly. That is lift. Of course you only have water underneath your feet and not all round you. The secret is that the air is thinner than the water and so, as both move past you, the water is exerting a greater pressure on the bottom of your skies than the air is on the top. When you are flying, the curved shape of the wing ensures that the air flows faster over the top of the wing than the bottom which has much the same effect of reducing the pressure from on top. At higher speeds even the curved shape is not strictly necessary but such speeds are not in the realm of the 1940s aircraft we are looking at.

In a sense, overcoming gravity is the easy part. Once you know how to produce a wing you have lift and you are in business. The need for more, or more efficient, lift does not seem too pressing if you already have enough to make flight possible. The years we are considering did not see the research into the lifting quality of wings that it saw in other areas, largely because the phenomenon of lift was not wholly understood even then.

One big advance in this field however, was the 'Davis' wing. In 1937 David Davis, who was a freelance aeronautical designer, approached Reuben Fleet, President of Consolidated Aircraft, with the idea of a revolutionary new wing design that would transform aircraft construction of the future, so he said. He was given a chance to make a presentation of his idea to Fleet and his chief engineer Isaac Laddon but at the end of it Fleet and Laddon were not impressed and Davis was shown the door. Laddon could not get Davis out of his mind, however. Had they turned down one of the great inventions of the age? Eventually he persuaded Fleet to spend the money needed to test Davis's idea on a model in a wind tunnel. The results were extraordinary: the Davis wing was even better than its inventor had said. In fact it was so good that the suspicion arose that there had been an error in the testing. More tests were tried and eventually a full scale trial: everything confirmed that the new wing was indeed an astonishing advance. Shortly thereafter Consolidated designed and built the B-24 Liberator bomber using the Davis wing and the B-24 was a resounding success. More B-24s were built than any other U.S. military aircraft then or since. This aeroplane turned Consolidated Aircraft into one of the great corporations of America.

It turned out that Davis had, more or less by chance, discovered a near perfect shape for a wing in medium speed flight. Unfortunately, by 1945, the jet age was beginning and a whole new kind of wing was needed to cope with a whole new range of increased air speeds.

All aircraft wings work better at some speeds than others. There is a particular problem with very low speed flight. Most of the time warplanes in particular were trying to go fast but when they wanted to land, they needed to go as slowly as possible to minimize the shock of contact with the ground. But if they went too slowly the wings no longer generated lift and the plane dropped like a stone. The answer to this problem was 'flaps'. These were an extendable piece of wing that were kept hidden away in normal flight but when the aircraft needed to land, or go slowly for any other reason, were extended to the rear of the wing. In effect they made the wing larger and enabled the plane to go slower without stalling. They were often partially extended for take-off as well. They were such a good invention that they are still in virtually universal use today.

A great deal more effort went into increasing the power of engines and improving streamlining so as to defeat drag and make planes go faster carrying bigger loads. We have already seen that the Spitfire Mark I of 1940 had an engine of 1,000 horsepower; by the end of the war fighter planes were routinely powered by engines of 2,000 horsepower or more.

These engines came in two basic kinds. There was the 'in-line' engine and there was the 'radial.' The in-line engine was like the engine in your car, having the cylinders set in a line, or more usually, two lines inside a solid metal block. The vital business of cooling was done by a radiator, again, just as in a car and coolant was either pumped through tubes bored in the block or through a jacket placed over its top. The radial engine was designed so that the cylinders sat in a circle round the central crankshaft like the petals of a flower. The cylinders were exposed to the air and the air flow over them kept them cool. To aid cooling, the cylinders were covered with a mass of fins so that they had the maximum possible surface area because the speed at which something cools is proportional to its surface area. Motorcycles have an air cooled engine and the cylinder (they only have one, or at the most two) is covered with fins so that it looks not unlike a stack of plates. That is how the cylinders on a radial aircraft engine look. Both types of engine had to be extensively lubricated by oil and this needed cooling too, which was done by means of its own radiator.

Each type of engine had its own advantages and disadvantages. The in-line engine was more compact and was easily fitted into a metal covering, or 'cowling,' to give the front of the aircraft the best possible streamlining for maximum aerodynamic efficiency and hence speed . The Spitfire was an ideal example of this. In-line engines were intrinsically more resistant to damage and were more easily protected inside the shell of the aircraft which made them longer lived and more reliable. On the other hand they had a long crankcase with complicated drive arrangements that added weight so the power/weight ratio of an in-line engine rarely matched that of a radial. They might be tougher than radial engines in theory but they were more complicated and needed more maintenance and this gave more scope for something to go wrong. Worst of all they had to have a radiator that sat in the air flow somewhere creating drag. There was a trade-off here in that if the radiator was placed far back on the aircraft it least interfered with air flow but long, vulnerable pipes had to carry the coolant to and from engine and radiator. If it was placed right at the front by the engine you avoided the pipes but it caused maximum interference with the air flow so that you were losing most of the streamlining advantage of an in-line engine.

Two additional observations should be made. The first is that the coolant used was not water as in a car but one of various fluids related to alcohol, the most common of which was glycol, or a combination of this and water. The reason was that water has too low a boiling point, particularly given the fact that as you go higher the air pressure falls and as it does so, so does the boiling point of your coolant. Glycol has the advantage of a very high boiling point. The second observation is that, for convenience, most designers placed the oil cooler with the radiator and if you opted for the radiator-to-the-rear solution this doubled the piping required. Any leak in any of this piping would spell death for the aircraft through an overheated engine which would soon come to a dead stop.

The Spitfire is an example of the radiator-to-the-rear type having radiator and oil cooler at the trailing edge of the wings. The P-51 Mustang is another, with the radiator in the bottom of the fuselage behind the pilot. On the other hand the P-40 that gained fame as the 'Flying Tiger' earned the name because the radiator was right at the front with its big mouth below the propeller resulting in a look that resembled a shark with its jaws open. Generally the radiator had hinged flaps at the back so that when speed was not essential the pilot could wind the flaps open and increase the air flow through the radiator which made it cool more efficiently.

The radial engine avoided all the radiator problems by the simple expedient of not needing one at all, though it did need an oil cooler but that was much smaller than a radiator and could be accommodated without doing too much violence to the aerodynamic qualities of the aeroplane. As mentioned earlier, radial engines generally developed more power for the same weight than in-line engines and they were simpler and thus easier to maintain, particularly in difficult environments such as desert or jungle or at sea on an aircraft carrier. Their big drawback was that the cylinders were right at the nose of the plane arranged in a circle and this was a serious violation of streamlining creating a great deal of drag. All kinds of attempts were made during the years prior to and during the Second World War to design the noses of radial engine planes in such a way as to minimize the disruption to air flow, principally by cladding the engine in an aerodynamic cowling with the smallest possible amount of the engine exposed. Nonetheless radial engines could never entirely overcome the drawback of their drag. The cowling round the engine included several panels that could be opened by the pilot like gills to increase the air flow over the engine in the same way as was done with the radiator in the in-line engine.

There was also the question of the radial engine being more exposed to damage, though experience soon showed that it was surprisingly tough and engines were known to stay functioning with several cylinders shot away.

In general, in-line engines were reserved for fighters for which speed was critical. For bombers speed, though important, could be sacrificed to sheer power and ease of maintenance and so they were usually given radial engines. An interesting exception to this general rule was the De Havilland Mosquito which was designed for speed above all else even though it was primarily a bomber and was given two Rolls Royce Merlin engines (also used by the Spitfire) and built of plywood.

Wooden construction meant that factories outside the normal aircraft industry could build it. Moreover, such construction made the aircraft almost invisible to radar. In this sense it was an early version of the 'stealth' idea. Mosquitoes relied on speed for defence and most versions were unarmed. The wooden construction was not very robust but that did not matter if the enemy's fighters could not catch it. The Mosquito was a very successful design to which the Germans had no effective answer with the result that it suffered only very light losses.

Another important exception was the Avro Lancaster. This heavy bomber also used the Merlin engine, though one model was built with radial engines instead. The principal reason for using an in-line engine in this case was simply that it was available, of high quality and was being manufactured in large numbers.

By the end of the war the radial engine was in the ascendant. It had always had the edge with the Americans and the Japanese and aero-engines were now developing such power that the drag aspect was less important. It is significant that the British produced the Hawker Tempest fighter late in the war with an in-line engine in the first model but a radial in the second.

The end of the war also saw the introduction of the jet engine which worked on completely different principles. Air flowed in the front, was compressed by a spinning structure like a fan and then mixed with fuel and ignited, the resulting hot gases blasting out the rear of the engine and creating thrust on the principle of action and reaction. On their way out the gases also turned a second fan that drove the compressor at the front by means of a drive shaft. This was the engine of the future but the examples that saw service in the Second World War were relatively primitive and the aircraft driven by jets were an infinitesimal fraction of all those used in the war.

Whichever type of piston engine a plane used, it was going to encounter problems at high altitude due to the thinner air. Internal combustion engines compress air as an integral part of their function. That air is mixed with fuel and inserted into the cylinder which is where the compression and then the combustion take place. As the air grows thinner there is less of it to compress so the pressure goes down and so does the power produced by the engine. Since the amount of fuel in the cylinder is the same, it now exceeds the amount needed to get a good burn so there is incomplete combustion causing further loss of power and wear on the engine.

The answer is the supercharger. This is a small fan that compresses the incoming air before it reaches the engine. It is switched on when the aircraft reaches a height at which its engine begins to lose power. So the engine is again receiving air of the density it was designed for. The supercharger solves the excess fuel problem too but as the plane climbs higher still, there may again be a need for the amount of petrol in the cylinder to be reduced. This could be achieved by the pilot by means of a 'mixture' control in his cockpit. There was huge variation in the use of superchargers and mixture. Some aircraft had no supercharger and no provision for changing the mixture, some had one and not the other and some had both.

Subtly different from the supercharger was the turbocharger which did the same job but was driven by the exhaust whereas the supercharger was driven by the engine direct. The turbocharger was simpler, more rugged and more reliable but it was bulky. As a general proposition it would be fair to say that European aircraft designers favoured superchargers and Americans favoured turbochargers. In fact some planes had both.

Critical to the best performance from the engine is the matter of having a propeller the right shape. The blades of the propeller cut through the air like mini-wings and pull the aircraft forward. In the early days of flight propellers were two-bladed and carved out of a single piece of wood. By the Second World War they were growing more complicated because it had been realized that the angle of the blades made a big difference to performance. If the blades were set at a low angle they developed a lot of power but not so much pull. This was called 'fine pitch'. If the blades were set at a higher angle they developed pull but not so much power.

This was 'course' or 'rough' pitch. Fine pitch was needed for taking off and for combat but for cruising, rough pitch was much better because it used less fuel and put less strain on the engine. Any driver will recognize the similarity to the gears of a car. First a propeller was designed with adjustable blades that could be switched to either pitch and then came the propeller that could be set at any angle you wanted. By the middle of the war the variable pitch propellers were more or less universal. Two blades soon became three, four or even five. Three remained the most popular number however. In general terms the more blades you have the more efficient your propeller but it is also heavier and more complicated. At the hub, where there is limited space, each blade has to have the machinery to change its pitch. If you have more than three blades you cannot have an interrupter gear because the blades come past too fast for it to keep up. That means you cannot have guns shooting through the arc of the propeller. More blades mean the propeller can be of smaller diameter and this was an important consideration because there was only limited clearance between the propeller and the ground.

Controlling the flight of aircraft is done my moving the 'control surfaces'. As explained in Chapter One these are hinged sections on wings and tail that can be moved so that they stick out at an angle into the stream of air causing an obstruction that pulls the aircraft in that direction. On the tail plane are the 'elevators' that tip the aircraft up or down; on the vertical tail fin is the rudder that turns it from side to side and on the wings are the ailerons that roll the craft. The ailerons always work together, one going up and the other down so that they tip one wing up and the other down. In practice turning the aircraft is usually done using a combination of rudder and ailerons. All these controls are attached to the 'joystick', a simple stick that projects up between the pilot's knees and is pulled to the side to turn, to the front to dive and to the rear to climb.

Even if the pilot simply wishes to fly straight and level the aircraft may not oblige. There may be a number of reasons for this. For instance it may be that as fuel is used up the centre of gravity moves so that the aircraft is tipped up or down as the case may be. Many aircraft of this time would tend to pull up if flown at full power. Almost all had problems with torque. Torque arises from Newton's third law to the effect that every action has an equal and opposite reaction. Because the propeller is spinning in one direction the aircraft will try to spin in the other. The aircraft is much heavier than the propeller and not designed to spin so it just tries to roll gently and it does this all the time the engine is on. This effect can be countered using the joystick but it would be exhausting for the pilot to have to fly the plane trying to counter torque all the time as well as dealing with his other tasks and to solve this problem 'trimming tabs' were invented. These are a small version of the control surfaces mentioned above that are set into the wings and tail and left in permanent operation. If the aircraft rolls to the left because of torque the pilot sets the trimming tabs on the wings so that they are permanently tipping the plane to the right. The tabs are adjustable and the pilot moves the tabs to a position where they exactly balance the tendency to roll. Between them the trimming tabs can counter a tendency to move in any direction.

It should be mentioned here that torque was a particular menace for these propeller-driven planes on take-off. Take-off is carried out with the engine on full power and so creating maximum torque but before the aircraft is moving fast enough for there to be a significant air flow over the trimming tabs there is nothing to counter it. Since the aircraft is on the ground at this stage it cannot roll but because there is much greater downward pressure on one wheel than the other it will try to veer off to the side. To counter this, the pilot must apply the opposite brake and then opposite rudder as the plane gathers speed. This process was always a severe trial for student pilots.

Trimming tabs were designed only for fine tuning of an aircraft's balance and even the controls governed by the joystick had their limits. If the aircraft became too unbalanced it went out of control and crashed. Balance could be very easily disturbed. John Comer, a flight engineer with the 8th Air Force described how his B-17 nearly crashed on take-off because the tail would not lift off the ground. Only after bouncing in a field beyond the end of the runway did the aircraft finally climb to safety. The cause was found to be the tail gunner sitting in his turret during take-off with a load of spare ammunition.[i] That extra weight in the tail, amounting to a tiny fraction of the aircraft's overall weight, was enough to bring the plane to the brink of disaster. Because of this question of balance fuel tanks were placed as close to the aircraft's centre of gravity as possible and if there were more than one tank it would be standard practice to empty them all at the same rate and not use one and then another. It goes without saying that bomb loads had to be carefully stored so that the aircraft did not go out of control when the bombs were released.

Lateral balance was just as important as fore-and-aft. This was a particular concern for heavy bombers that often had fuel tanks in the wings and which might have one or more engine fail during flight. It was not unusual for four-engine bombers to lose two or even three engines and still reach home safely. In the middle of the war a number of Halifax bombers were lost when one or two engines failed on the same wing and they rolled over and dived straight into the ground whatever the pilot did. Since R.A.F. strategic bombers flew at night, no one saw this phenomenon occurring and the crews of the bombers concerned did not survive to report it. Once the problem was uncovered the tail of the Halifax was redesigned and there were no more difficulties of this nature.

Lateral stability is much affected by the positioning of the wings. The wings can be attached to the fuselage of an aeroplane at the top or the bottom or somewhere in between. This is known as 'high wing', 'low wing' and 'mid wing'. Each position has its advantages and disadvantages. High and mid wing positions are much more laterally stable than low wing because the centre of gravity is at or below the wings. If you rest a ruler with each end on your fingers and a lead weight tied to the middle you do not have to tip it much before the whole thing falls off if the weight is on the top of the ruler, but if it is underneath, it is much harder to shake the contrivance free. For this reason most bombers were of high or mid wing design though they faced the disadvantage that such a design inevitably meant the aircraft had a long and vulnerable undercarriage. The instability of the low wing design suits fighters on the other hand because it makes it easier for them to 'lean into' a turn as the centre of gravity is pulling the plane over. It is also unusual in bombers because, in the low wing design, the main spar that joins the wings takes up space otherwise available for bombs.

All these questions of design are a matter of trade-offs and horses for courses and even when the designer has decided exactly what he wants there are the constraints imposed by what his country's industry can provide.

When Kurt Tank was designing the Fw190 he wanted an in-line engine for it but all the suitable engines being produced were already earmarked for other jobs so he had to use a radial engine made by BMW instead. He still managed to produce one of the best fighters of the war.

Of course the pilot can use the joystick to put the aircraft through any manoeuvres he likes and the popular image of the aircraft of this era, particularly the fighter planes, is of them turning and twisting in the sky in wild dogfights. This did happen, but not very much. These kind of aerobatics are a terrific strain on the body. Tight turns and the action of pulling out of a dive cause centrifugal force to drain the blood out of the head causing the pilot to rapidly lose consciousness. As the war progressed and the planes grew faster these problems became worse and worse. Many pilots could not throw their planes around because they did not have the flying skill to do it. Jimmy Corbin, an R.A.F. fighter pilot who survived the Battle of Britain said that he couldn't do any aerobatics because no one had ever taught him how.[ii]

It is a commonplace that the great majority of aerial kills were achieved by attackers who were never even spotted by their victims. In this situation the victims were clearly not going to get the chance to take any kind of evasive action. Moreover air battles tended to be swiftly over. Time and again pilots described how they took part in dogfights that started with the sky full of dozens of aircraft and within a very short space of time they were on their own with no other plane in sight. Once an experienced pilot knew he had an enemy plane on his tail he was usually able to escape from it because keeping an enemy fighter in your sights long enough to shoot it down was no easy business. The problems began when he was outnumbered or flying an inferior type of aircraft. The problems were at their worst when the pilot was inexperienced and, inevitably, it was amongst the beginners that casualties were heaviest.

Clearly the turn was the first essential manoeuvre. The ability to make a tight turn would get a pilot out of many a dangerous situation. Next came the dive. All pilots could dive a plane but for escape purposes you needed a snap, vertical dive carried out as fast as you dared. You could not simply put the nose sharply down because centrifugal force came into play again, this time making the blood rush to your head which was not only extremely uncomfortable but could cause eye damage or even a stroke. In some early planes such a dive also caused the engine to cut out. To avoid all this, the pilot rolled his plane over onto its back first and then dived. As soon as he thought it was safe to do so he pulled out of the dive in any direction he wished. This manoeuvre was known as a 'split S' and was much used because it could be a life-saver but it was dangerous. You had to have enough height, when you started, to be able to pull out of the dive in time. There were numerous examples of pilots getting it wrong and simply diving into the ground. You also had to know your plane and how fast it could safely dive. Most planes had a speed beyond which they became uncontrollable and could not be pulled up.

The roll itself could be a good strategy. A clever pilot could roll his plane and change direction slightly at the same time. The result was a 'barrel roll' in which the plane moved in a circle as if it was rolling around the inside of a barrel. The advantage of this was that it took the plane out of the line of fire of an attacker behind. A roll could be executed faster than either a turn or a dive and so was a good remedy for a really threatening situation.

Most manoeuvres, even a gentle turn, result in a slight loss of height with the result that aerial battles between fighter planes tended to drift lower and lower. At the same time being higher than your adversary gave you an advantage because height can be turned into speed by diving and because your enemies conversely found it hard to get up to your level to attack you. Pilots were always looking, therefore, for an opportunity to regain some of the lost altitude but most climbing manoeuvres were close to suicidal. In a steep climb an aircraft slows right down which makes it an easier target and to make matters worse the lack of air flow over the control surfaces means that it is hard to manoeuver it as well. So climbing had to be done with great circumspection and preferably away from the centre of the fighting. One partial exception was the corkscrew climb which was an effective escape ploy in the hands of a veteran pilot. If you did not climb too steeply you did not lose too much speed and you made yourself a difficult target by turning at the same time. The enemy's aircraft had to be better at both turning and climbing to catch you. But this was an escape ploy rather than a means of gaining height.

Another problem with climbing is that if you overdo it, you stall. A stall is a situation where the airflow over the wing is not enough to maintain lift with the result that the aircraft starts to fall. The remedy is to point the nose down and let the plane gain speed until it flies naturally again. The worst kind of stall is a spin, in which, because the air over one wing reaches stall speed before the other, the plane begins to rotate around its fore-and-aft axis as well as fall. The escape method for a spin varies somewhat with the type of aircraft but the essential points are always to put the joystick in neutral and apply the rudder in the direction opposite to the spin.

Attacking planes tried to come in from higher and get onto the tails of their victims. If possible they would come from the direction that put the sun behind them because it made them particularly hard to see. The leading R.A.F. ace of the Battle of Britain, Adolph 'Sailor' Malan drew up a list of rules for air combat that was widely circulated amongst fighter squadrons and is of universal application.

1. Do not open fire until you are at very close range.

2. While shooting concentrate one hundred percent.

3. Always keep a sharp lookout.

4. Height gives you the initiative.

5. Always turn and face the attack.

6. Make your decisions promptly. It is better to act quickly even though your tactics are not the best.

7. Never fly straight and level for more than 30 seconds in the combat area.

8. When diving to attack always leave a proportion of your formation behind as top cover.

9. Initiative, aggression, air discipline and teamwork are words that MEAN something in air fighting.

10. Go in quickly – punch hard – get out.

Of course, all the above applies to combat between fighter planes. Combat between fighter and bomber was somewhat different; it was also a lot simpler. The battle tactics of bombers were to stick close together in formation and rely on their defensive guns to fight off attackers. There was no manoeuvering and the flying was simple (though not necessarily easy). Fighter planes attacked bombers from whatever angle was most appropriate bearing in mind the position of the target's guns. Early in the war there seems to have been a tendency for fighter pilots to underestimate the effect of defensive fire but this overconfidence, if it ever existed, evaporated with the appearance of heavily armed American bombers. The B-17 and B-24 were so heavily armed that conventional attacks from anywhere in the rear quarter against their mass formations were a recipe for disaster. Instead the Luftwaffe took to terrifying head-on attacks because the forward armament of these bombers was their weakest point and because, although there was not long to fire, hits could be scored relatively easily on the engines and the cockpit. Hits on the cockpit in particular, spelled a quick death for the pilots and hence, the bomber too.

One important use for fighter planes was to escort bombers and protect them from attack by the enemy's interceptors. Two problems arose in this field. The first was the question of range. All the major powers developed long range fighters before the war and they all found that those fighters could not match the short range interceptors they met in combat (with the partial exception of the American P-38). As escorts therefore, they were effectively useless. A partial solution was the use of external disposable fuel tanks that were jettisoned when empty or when combat threatened. For Britain and the U.S.A. the ultimate answer lay in one aircraft: the P-51 Mustang. This was a small, single-engine fighter not unlike a Spitfire but with a vastly greater range. It had the ability to hold its own with any other fighter and so solved the problem that had been holding back the whole daylight strategic bombing offensive.

Since the end of World War Two the Mustang has achieved iconic status and is often touted as the greatest fighter ever designed. Certainly it was very good but some of the claims made for it have been excessive. It had the advantage of coming into service just as the quality of Luftwaffe and Japanese pilots was collapsing but it did not seem to hold any terrors for the few remaining German or Japanese veterans.

Escort duty for fighter planes is slightly different from the straightforward dogfight because the primary object is to protect the bombers. If, in doing so, the escort shoots down the attackers that is all to the good but is not essential. Thus if an escort shoots at an interceptor and the latter dives away, the escort should never follow because its duty is to stay with the bombers and at the same time the interceptor is now no longer a threat. This brings us to the second problem which is the dispute that raged throughout the war about the respective merits of close or advanced escort. The close escort is within eyesight of the bombers and this has the advantage that the bombers can see they are being protected, which is good for their morale. It also means that the interceptors, when they appear, are concentrating on the bombers and are thus more vulnerable. The disadvantage is that a close escort rarely deters a determined attack completely and the escort loses its freedom of action. By contrast the advanced escort flies some miles ahead of the bombers and not within their view. It will catch the interceptors assembling for their attack on the bombers and disperse them after which few of them will find and attack the bombers. It was found that in general, the second method was more effective but the close escort could not be abandoned because the morale element was critical. If the bomber crews could not see the escort they could not see its good work and if any enemy fighters attacked them it seemed to them that they were getting no help from their escort at all. This problem of fighter aircraft being seen to do their job could be a serious matter. At Dunkirk the R.A.F. tried to intercept Luftwaffe bombers inland before they reached the beaches but this meant that when a few bombers broke through and dropped bombs, the troops saw no sign of the R.A.F. interfering. There was great resentment about this and it led to physical attacks on airmen by soldiers in England over the next few months.

The above relates to escorting level bombers, be they strategic or medium. Dive bombers present an extra problem, namely that the fighter cannot escort the bomber in the dive because the dive bomber has special air brakes which slow it up and the fighter does not. For this reason dive bombers usually made their own way home at low level after their attack while the escort stayed behind for a while to harass defending fighters.

Whatever the purpose of a combat flight it was commonly referred to as a 'mission'. There also existed the term 'sortie' which has a more technical application and means a mission by a plane but not any specific plane. Thus if a squadron flies ten sorties in a day these may amount to one flight by each of ten aircraft or ten flights by one. Missions are what matter to pilots and sorties are what matter to the people in charge.

In recent years there has been a tendency to talk about fighter planes of this period as 'angles' fighters or 'energy' fighters. The first refers to fighters that rely on their ability to turn sharply and the second to aircraft that rely on a combination of height and speed to make diving attacks because their turning ability is limited. This is a distinction that was unknown to the pilots at the time and is essentially artificial. What mattered was speed. Almost all the biplane fighters of the 1930s could out-turn either a Spitfire or a Messerschmitt but it did them no good because they were too slow. The faster plane chooses when to join combat and when to leave it and thus has the upper hand. An ability to turn sharply is essentially a defensive capability and useful to have but only if it is married to speed. The Spitfire is often praised for its manoeuverability but the key to its success was the combination of that agility with speed.

It is interesting to note that less than fifty per cent of fighter pilots ever shot down anything at all and barely twenty percent reached the magical figure of five victories which enabled a pilot to call himself an ace. Less than half of aces went on to shoot down ten aircraft or more. These figures were constant across all air forces and meant that almost all the damage was done by a small minority of the pilots and the rest were essentially crowd scene.[iii]

The first few months of war led to some small but vital modifications being made to aircraft by all combatants. The first was the introduction of the self-sealing fuel tank. In fact this was already under consideration in Britain before the war started. Bullet holes in fuel tanks not only resulted in the rapid loss of all the fuel but the leak represented a very dangerous fire hazard. To armour the tanks would make them too heavy and so another solution had to be found. The result was the self-sealing tank. This came in several varieties but the most common was to have two layers of casing with a soft rubber compound in between. When a bullet passed through, the leaking petrol met the rubber which was partially dissolved and oozed out to fill the hole.

The second was the widespread adoption of the tracer bullet. This is a bullet made of an alloy that heats red hot when fired. If every third or fourth bullet fired by a plane's machine guns is a tracer, they form a chain of red dots that show a pilot where his fire is heading. This is a great aid to the accuracy of gunnery.

The other modifications were to do with saving the pilot's life. It was soon evident that he was too vulnerable to an attacker's bullets. In fact, in the standard attack from the rear, if the attacker's fire was accurate enough to hit the target plane it was odds on that it would at least injure the pilot. The simple answer to this problem was a sheet of armour on the back of the pilot's seat. Likewise, a pilot attacking a bomber had to fly straight into his target's defensive fire and bullets had a tendency to come in through the windscreen and strike the pilot in the head. To overcome this, fighters were increasingly fitted with a large slab of armoured glass fixed to the back of the windscreen.

All three of these remedies added considerably to the weight of an aircraft and thus reduced performance. In western countries it was considered a sacrifice worth making where the safety of the pilot was involved but this was not the view everywhere. Many Russian aircraft continued to give their pilots only limited protection. Some of their fighters were thought unlikely to have to take on bombers and so were never equipped with armoured glass. The Japanese had a tradition of designing very light, agile aircraft of long range. Their performance would be seriously degraded and their range lessened by any major increase in weight and so, by and large, they ignored these lifesaving improvements. This was a stance that even the pilots supported. Japanese Navy pilots, for instance, were issued with parachutes but most preferred not to use them because they were heavy and uncomfortable to wear and they restricted the pilot's movement in the cockpit. The pilots' view was that if they were shot down over the endless stretches of sea or jungle in the Pacific theatre their chances of rescue were so small and the dishonour of being shot down so acute, that it was better to die quickly. The difference from western ideas could not be greater.

End Notes

CHAPTER ONE
[i] Masters: *Fourteen Eighteen* p.56
[ii] Traditional and from 'RFC Rhymes' in Popular Flying magazine via *'The Crowded Sky, an Anthology of Flight'* edited by Neville Duke and Edward Latchberry
[iii] Masters: op. cit. p.56
[iv] Jones: *Tiger Squadron* p.61
[v] Ibid. p137
[vi] J. E. Johnson: *Wing Leader* p.267
[vii] R. S. Johnson: *Thunderbolt* p.22

CHAPTER TWO
[i] Deighton: *Fighter* p.100; Boyne: *Clash of Wings* p.32

CHAPTER THREE
[i] Official History: *The Soviet Air Force in World War II* p.7
[ii] Maslov: *Polikarpov I-15, I-16 and I-153 Aces* p.7
[iii] Shores: *Finnish Air Force 1918-1968* p.5
[iv] Ibid. p.3
[v] Ibid. p.6

CHAPTER FOUR
[i] Hooton: *Gathering Storm* p.31
[ii] Deighton: *Fighter* p.42, Bekker; *The Luftwaffe Diaries* p.137
[iii] Harris: *Bomber Offensive* p.12
[iv] Gunston: *Fighting Aircraft of World War II* p.9
[v] Crouch: *Wings* p.231

CHAPTER FIVE
[i] Hooton: *The Gathering Storm* p.83
[ii] Ibid. p.85
[iii] Bekker: *The Luftwaffe War Diaries* p.42
[iv] Ibid. p.25
[v] Olson & Cloud: *For your Freedom and for Ours* p.51
[vi] Richards: *The Hardest Victory* p.13, Gibson: *Enemy coast Ahead* p.33
[vii] Hooton: *Blitzkrieg in the West* p.32
[viii] Smith: *Dive Bomber* pp.199-204
[ix] Ibid. pp.205-206
[x] Deighton: *Blood, Tears and Folly* p.360

CHAPTER SIX
[i] Hooton: *Blitzkrieg in the West* p.14
[ii] Deighton: *Blitzkrieg* p.221
[iii] Guderian: *Panzer Leader* p.102

iv Hooton op. cit. p.67

v Ibid. p.62

vi Collier: *1940 The World in Flames* p.89

vii Hooton: op. cit. p.65

viii Richey: *Fighter Pilot* pp.107 et seq.

ix Ibid. pp.137 et seq.

x Hooton op. cit. p.67

xi Ibid. p.72

xii Deere: *Nine Lives* p.59 et seq.

xiii Wikipedia Article: *R.M.S.Lancastria* 2.8.2011

CHAPTER SEVEN

i Liddell Hart: *The German Generals Talk* p.153

ii Galland: *The First and the Last* p.29

iii Deighton: *Fighter note to illustration* p.82

iv Ibid. p.204

v Vigors: *Life's too Short to Cry* p.183

vi Baker: *The Fighter Aces of the R.A.F.* p.142

vii Deere: *Nine Lives*

viii Ibid. p.90 et seq.

ix Ibid. p.127 and Deighton: *Fighter* p.232

x Ibid. p.142 et seq.

xi Deighton: *Blood, Tears and Folly* pp.377-378

xii Galland: op. cit. p.27

xiii McKinstry: *Spitfire* p.230 et seq. inter alia

xiv Churchill Papers, Personal minute M432/1 12.04.1941 quoted in Deighton: *op. cit. 2* p.386

xv Bungay: *The Most Dangerous Enemy* p.362

xvi Bishop: *Battle of Britain* p.210

CHAPTER EIGHT

i Shirer: *The Rise and Fall of the Third Reich* p.517 note

ii Churchill: *The Second World War* Vol. II p.303

iii Ibid. p.323

iv Hendrie: *The Cinderella Service* p.27

v Ibid. p.38 and quoting Harris: *Bomber Offensive* pp.27-28

vi Warnock: *Airpower versus U-boats* p.4

vii Hendrie op. cit. p.32

viii Ibid. pp.48-9

ix Ibid. p.107

x Wragg: *RAF Handbook* p.72

xi Caldwell: *Jg26 Top guns of the Luftwaffe* p.86

xii Oliver: *Fighter Command* p.179

xiii Caldwell op. cit. p.100

xiv Oliver: op. cit. p.177

xv Brown: *Wings on my Sleeve* pp. 58-9

xvi Harris: *Bomber Offensive* p.35

xvii Richards: *The Hardest Victory* p.24

xviii Air Ministry: *Bomber Command* p.121

xix Ibid. p.119

CHAPTER NINE
[i] Baker: *Fighter Aces of the R.A.F.* p.147
[ii] Bekker: *The Luftwaffe War Diaries* p.186
[iii] Ibid. p.187
[iv] Mellinger: *Lagg & Lavochkin Aces of World War 2* p.7
[v] Gordon and Kazanov: *Soviet Combat Aircraft of the Second World War vol. 2* p.77
[vi] Emelianenko: *Red Star against the Swastika* p.60
[vii] Ibid. p.13
[viii] Ibid. P.41
[ix] For German aerial strength see Air Ministry: *The Rise and Fall of the German Air Force* pp.165-166
[x] See e.g. Maslov: *Polikarpov I-15, I-16 and I-153 Aces* p.6; Mellinger: *Yakovlev Aces of World War 2* p.16
[xi] For Russian aerial strength see Bergstrom: *Barbarossa* pp.131-132

CHAPTER TEN
[i] Emelianenko: *Red Star against the Swastika* p.45
[ii] Bekker: *The Luftwaffe War Diaries I* p.219
[iii] Ibid. p. 219
[iv] Rudel: *Stuka Pilot* p.20
[v] Knoke: *I Flew for the Fuhrer* p.45
[vi] Bergstrom: *Barbarossa* p.17
[vii] Maslov: *Polikarpov I-15,I-16 and I-153 Aces* p.70
[viii] Wagner (editor): *The Soviet Air force in World War II* p.35
[ix] Bergstrom: op. cit. p.20
[x] Brookes: *Air War over Russia* p.26
[xi] Rudel: op. cit. p.22
[xii] Bergstrom: op. cit. p.28
[xiii] Ibid. p.47
[xiv] Emelianenko; op. cit. p.67
[xv] Rudel: op. cit. pp.28-29
[xvi] Bergstrom: op. cit. p.66
[xvii] Ibid. p.68 and Kurowski: *Luftwaffe Aces* p.56 et seq.
[xviii] Ibid. p.103
[xix] Ibid. p.104
[xx] Ibid. p.105
[xxi] Ibid. p.107

CHAPTER ELEVEN
[i] Overy: *The Air War* p.93
[ii] Campbell: *Air War Pacific* p.34
[iii] Vigors: *Life's too Short to Cry* p.196 et seq.
[iv] Campbell: *op. cit.* pp.34-35
[v] Vigors: op. cit. p.241
[vi] Sakaida: *Imperial Japanese Navy Aces* p.19
[vii] Okumiya and Horikoshi: *Zero* p.77
[viii] Sakai: *Samurai*
[ix] Ibid. p.51
[x] Ibid. p.63 et seq.
[xi] Caidin: *The Ragged, Rugged Warriors* p.285
[xii] Morison: *History of United States Naval Operations in World War II, Vol. III* p.359 et seq.

CHAPTER TWELVE
[i] McKinstry: *Lancaster* p.86
[ii] Ibid. p.65 quoting *The Portal Papers, folder 2* at Christ Church Oxford.
[iii] Ibid. p.66 quoting ibid.
[iv] Ibid. p.67 quoting ibid.
[v] Hastings: *Bomber Command* p.134
[vi] Webster & Frankland: *The Strategic Air Offensive Against Germany* Vol. IV p. 445
[vii] Ibid. Vol. IV p.143
[viii] Hastings: op. cit. pp.149-150
[ix] Air Ministry: *Bomber Command* p.121
[x] Harris: *Bomber Offensive* p.147
[xi] Richards: *The Hardest Victory* p.413
[xii] Middlebrook & Everitt: *The Bomber Command War Diaries* p.707
[xiii] Middlebrook: *The Berlin Raids* p.377; Merrick: *Halifax* p.40
[xiv] Barker: *The Thousand Plan* pp.163-166
[xv] Middlebrook & Everitt: op. cit. p.327
[xvi] Richards: op cit. p.395
[xvii] Webster & Frankland op. cit. Vol. IV p.153
[xviii] Speer: *Inside the Third Reich* p.284

CHAPTER THIRTEEN
[i] Emelianenko: *Red Star against the Swastika* p.85 et seq.
[ii] Ibid. p.117
[iii] Ibid. p.147
[iv] Bergstrom: *Stalingrad* p.73
[v] Ibid. p.73
[vi] Ibid. p.74
[vii] Ibid. p.79
[viii] Rudel: *Stuka Pilot* pp.62-64
[ix] Erickson: *The Road to Stalingrad* p.208
[x] Mellinger: *Lagg and Lavochkin Aces of World War II* p.33
[xi] e.g. Ibid. p.8
[xii] Ibid. p.8
[xiii] Emelianenko: op. cit. p.213
[xiv] Ibid. p.121

CHAPTER FOURTEEN
[i] Pearson: *The Burma Air Campaign* p.31
[ii] Slim: *Defeat into Victory* p.18
[iii] Ibid. p.51
[iv] Boyington: *Baa Baa Black Sheep* p.52
[v] Hata, Izawa and Shores: *Japanese Army Air Force Fighter Units and their Aces* p.49
[vi] Sakai, Caidin and Saito: *Samurai* p.76 Chapter 12 et seq
[vii] Samuel Eliot Morrison: *The Two-Ocean War* p.182
[viii] Costello: *The Pacific War* p.256
[ix] Bergerud: *Fire in the Sky* p.578
[x] Toland: *The Rising Sun* p.329
[xi] Ibid. p.334
[xii] Sakaida: *Imperial Japanese Navy Aces 1937-45* pp. 21-22
[xiii] Toland op. cit. p.340

xiv Sakaida; op. cit. p.22
xv Morison: *History of United States Naval Operations in World War Two Vol. IV* p.158

CHAPTER FIFTEEN
i Dunning: *Regia Aeronautica* p.146
ii Bickers: *The Desert Air War* p.22
iii Ibid. p.23
iv Conway: *All the World's Fighting Ships 1906-21* p.262
v Sutherland and Canwell: *Air War East Africa* p.34
vi Ibid. pp.35-36
vii Ibid. p.44
viii Ibid. pp.98-99
ix Sutherland and Canwell: *Air War Malta* p.1
x Bickers op. cit. p.55
xi Kaplan: *Fighter Aces of the Luftwaffe in World War II* p.171 et seq.
xii Bickers op. cit. p.60
xiii Baker; *The fighter Aces of the R.A.F.* p.21 et seq.

CHAPTER SIXTEEN
i Middlebrook: *The Berlin Raids* p.8
ii Ibid. p.2
iii Middlebrook and Everitt: *The Bomber Command War Diaries* p.425
iv Ibid. p.425
v Knott: *Princes of Darkness* p.104
vi Vassiltchikov: *The Berlin Diaries* p.106 et seq.
vii Wragg: *RAF Handbook* pp.293-294
viii Dorr: *B-24 Liberator Units of the Fifteenth Air Force* p.11
ix Miller: *Eighth Air Force* pp. 149-151
x Knoke: *I Flew for the Fuehrer* p.110 et seq.
xi Speer: *Inside the Third Reich* p.285
xii Searby: *The Bomber Battle for Berlin* p.72 quoting Sir Maurice Dean: *The Royal Air Force and Two World Wars*
xiii Freeman: *The Mighty Eighth War Diary* pp. 94-95
xiv Hooton: *The Luftwaffe* p.188

CHAPTER SEVENTEEN
i Emelianenko: *Red Star against the Swastika* p.213
ii Kaplan: *Fighter Aces of the Luftwaffe in World War II* p.65
iii Emelianenko: op. cit. pp.207-208
iv Brookes: *Air War over Russia* p.122
v Mellinger: *Soviet Lend-Lease Fighter Aces of World War 2* p.70
vi Ibid. pp. 58-59
vii Toliver and Constable: *The Blond Knight of Germany* p.46
viii Bergstrom: *Kursk* p.20
ix Ibid. p.23
x Wragg: *RAF Handbook* p.119 et seq.
xi Bowman *USAAF Handbook* p.80
xii Bergstrom: op. cit. p.34
xiii Ibid. p.40
xiv Ibid. p.48

xv Ibid. pp.67-68
xvi Rudel: *Stuka Pilot* p.85
xvii Bergstrom op. cit. p.121
xviii Mariinsky: *Red Star Airacobra* p.34

CHAPTER EIGHTEEN
i Bergerud: *Fire in the Sky* p.554
ii Ibid. pp.553-554
iii Sakai: *Samurai* p.145 et seq.
iv Styling and Tillman: *The Blue Devils* p.17
v Ibid. p19
vi Morison: *History of United States Naval Operations in World War II Vol.5* p.283
vii Toland: *The Rising Sun* p.499
viii Boyington: *Baa Baa Black Sheep*
ix Sakaida: *Japanese Army Air Force Aces 1937-45* p.52
x Ibid. pp.59-60
xi Corrigan: *The Second World War* p.380
xii Stanaway: *P-38 Lightning Aces of the Pacific and CBI* pp.84-85

CHAPTER NINETEEN
i Air Ministry: *The Rise and Fall of the German Air Force* p.143
ii Rhoderick-Jones: *Pedro passim*
iii Liddell Hart ed.: *The Rommel Papers* p.285
iv Hooton: *The Luftwaffe* p.143
v Ibid. p.143
vi Ibid. p.144
vii Ibid. p.145
viii Brookes: *Air War over Italy* p.30
ix Eisenhower: *Crusade in Europe* p.224
x Masters: *Fourteen Eighteen* p.72
xi Wolff: *Low Level Mission* p.101
xii Dorr: *B-24 Liberator Units of the Fifteenth Air Force* pp.55-58

CHAPTER TWENTY
i Author's discussion with staff at the Grenada National Museum and Brizan: *Brave Young Grenadians* p.59, p.94. Chorley: *Bomber Command Losses* p.234
ii Hastings: *Overlord* p.53
iii Eisenhower: *Crusade in Europe* p.270
iv Clostermann: *The Big Show* p.133
v Searby: *The Bomber Battle for Berlin* p.117
vi Hooton: *The Luftwaffe* p.228
vii Lipfert and Gerbig: *The War Diary of Helmut Lipfert* p.113
viii Caldwell: *JG26 Top Guns of the Luftwaffe* pp.218-219
ix Knoke: *I Flew for the Fuehrer* p.167
x Hastings: *Overlord* p.49
xi Wilmot: *Struggle for Europe* p.211
xii Ibid. pp.211-212
xiii Caldwell op. cit. pp.230-231
xiv Johnson: *Wing Leader* pp.221-222
xv Wilmot op. cit. p.364

xvi Beevor: *D-Day* p.314
xvii Foreman: *Fighter Command War Diaries Part 5* p.38
xviii Beevor: op. cit. p.412
xix Caldwell op. cit. p.235
xx Ibid. p.256

CHAPTER TWENTY-ONE
i Rudel: *Stuka Pilot* p.117 et seq.
ii Lipfert and Gerbig: *The War Diary of Helmut Lipfert* p.107
iii Bergstrom: *Bagration to Berlin* p.50
iv Ibid. p.52
v Lipfert and Gerbig: op. cit. pp. 110-111
vi 200: Bergstrom: op. cit. p.59. 300: Shores: *Finnish Air Force 1918-1968* p.11
vii Bergstrom: op cit. p.59
viii Erickson: *The Road to Berlin* p.217
ix Carell: *Scorched Earth* p.500
x Bergstrom: op. cit. p.77
xi Official History: *The Soviet Air Force in World War II* p.288. See also: Hastings: *Armageddon* pp.453-456
xii Mariinsky: *Red Star Airacobra* p.153
xiii Ibid. p.154
xiv Hooton: *The Luftwaffe* p.211
xv Lipfert and Gerbig: pp.150-152

CHAPTER TWENTY-TWO
i Campbell: *Air War Pacific* p.94
ii Styling and Tillman: *The Blue Devils* p.202
iii Ibid. p.203
iv Morison: *History of United States Naval Operations in World War II Vol. VIII* p.33
v Ibid. p.216 and Wikipedia entry for *Jisaburo Ozawa* 15th July 2011.
vi Morison: op. cit. p.235
vii Ibid. p.221
viii Toland: *The Rising Sun* p.500
ix Morison: op. cit. pp.266-267
x Ibid. pp.276-277
xi Ibid. p.286
xii Ibid. p.292
xiii Ibid. pp.295-296
xiv Pearson: *The Burma Air Campaign* pp.64-65
xv Ibid. p.64
xvi Ibid. p.70
xvii Sakaida: *Japanese Army Air Force Aces 1937-45* p.24
xviii Stanaway: *P-38 Lightning Aces of the Pacific and CBI* p.80
xix Slim: *Defeat into Victory* p.405
xx Ibid. p.435
xxi Pearson: op. cit. p.161

CHAPTER TWENTY-THREE
i Wilmot: *The Struggle for Europe* pp.501-502
ii Speer: *Inside the Third Reich* p.362

iii Clostermann: *The Big Show* p.187

iv Speer op. cit. p.346

v Ibid. p.350

vi Webster and Frankland: *The Strategic Air Offensive Against Germany* Vol. III p.89

vii Middlebrook: *The Battle of Hamburg* pp.343-344

viii Webster and Frankland: op. cit. Vol. III p.77

ix Richards: *The Hardest Victory* p.350 note

x Webster and Frankland: op. cit. Vol. III p.77

xi Bramson: *Master Airman* p.108

xii Wragg: *RAF Handbook* p.300

xiii Webster and Frankland: op. cit. Vol. IV p.181

xiv Ibid. p.301

xv Klemperer: *The Klemperer Diaries* p.837

xvi Irving: *The Destruction of Dresden* p.224

xvii Hastings: *Bomber Command* pp.414-415

xviii Speer: op. cit. p.280

xix Wikipedia entry: *Gunther Specht* 20.7.2011

xx Beal, D'amico and Valentini: *Air War Italy 1944-45* p.60

xxi Dunning: *Regia Aeronautica* pp.145 et seq.

xxii Caldwell: *Jg26 Top Guns of the Luftwaffe* p.336

xxiii Foreman: *Fighter Command War Diaries* Part 5 p.325

xxiv Clostermann: Ibid. pp.199-201

xxv Foreman: op. cit. p.421

CHAPTER TWENTY-FOUR

i Brown: *Wings on my Sleeve* pp.121-122

ii Lipfert and Girbig: *The War Diary of Helmut Lipfert* p.180

iii Bergstrom: *Bagration to Berlin* p.106

iv Mellinger: *Yakovlev Aces of World War 2* p.78

v Lipfert and Girbig op. cit. p.163

vi Hannig: *Luftwaffe Fighter Ace* pp.148-150

vii Bergstrom: op. cit. p.95

viii Ibid. pp. 96-97 and Mellinger: *Lagg and Lavochkin Aces of World War 2* p.77

ix Bergstrom: op. cit. p.98

x Rudel: *Stuka Pilot* p.208 et seq.

xi Mellinger: *Lagg and Lavochkin Aces* pp. 83-84

xii Bergstrom: op. cit. p116

xiii Ibid. pp.120-121

xiv Mariinsky: *Red Star Airacobra* p.158

xv Hooton: *The Luftwaffe* p.224

xvi Bergstrom: op. cit. p.124

CHAPTER TWENTY-FIVE

i Costello: *The Pacific War* p.499

ii Ibid. 501

iii Lawson and Tillman: *U.S. Navy Air Combat 1939-1946* pp.131-133

iv Toland: *The Rising Sun* pp.554-555

v Styling and Tillman: *The Blue Devils* p.242

vi Ibid. p.245

vii Morison: *The Two-Ocean War* p.483

viii Parnell and Lynch: *Australian Air Force since 1911* p.97

ix Ibid. p.121

x Ibid. p.121

xi Sakai and Caidin: *Samurai* p.205 et seq.

xii Ibid. p.7

xiii Toland: op. cit. pp.694-695

xiv Hara and Saito: *Japanese Destroyer Captain* p.299

xv Okumiya, Horikoshi and Caidin: *Zero* p.326

xvi LeMay and Yenne: *Superfortress* p.124

xvii Okumiya, Horikoshi and Caidin: op. cit. p.334

xviii LeMay and Yenne: op. cit. pp.137-138

xix Tillman: *Whirlwind, the Air War against Japan* pp.233, 236

xx Sakai and Caidin: op. cit. p.267 et seq.

APPENDIX TWO
i Overy: *The Air War* pp. 21 and 150

APPENDIX THREE
i Comer: *Combat Crew* p.135

ii Corbin: *Last of the Fighter Boys* pp.75-76

iii Holland: *Fortress Malta* p.384

Bibliography

The number of extant titles on the subject of military aviation in the Second World War is huge. This list is confined to books consulted in the research for, and writing of, this particular title and should not be considered in any way comprehensive.

Air Ministry, *Bomber Command*, H.M.S.O., 1941

Air Ministry, *Coastal Command*, H.M.S.O., 1943

Air Ministry, *The Rise and Fall of the German Air Force 1939-45*, The National Archives, 2008

Baker, E. C. R., *The Fighter Aces of the R.A.F.,* New English Library, 1962

Barker, R., *The Thousand Plan*, Airlife Publishing, 1992

Beal, N., D'Amico, F. and Valentini, G., *Air War Italy, 1944-45*, Airlife Publishing, 1996

Beevor, A., *D-Day*, Viking, 2009

Bekker, C., *The Luftwaffe War Diaries,* Da Capo Press, 1994

Bergerud E. M., *Fire in the Sky*, Westview Press, 2002

Bergstrom, C., *Barbarossa*, Midland, 2007

Bergstrom, C., *Stalingrad*, Midland, 2007

Bergstrom, C., *Kursk*, Chevron Publishing, 2007

Bergstrom, C., *Bagration to Berlin*, Chevron Publishing, 2008

Bickers, R. T., *The Desert Air War*, Leo Cooper, 1991

Bishop P., *Battle of Britain*, Quercus, 2010

Bishop, P., *Fighter Boys*, Harper Perennial, 2004

Bowman, M. W., *USAAF Handbook*, Sutton Publishing, 1997

Boyington, G., *Baa Baa Black Sheep*, Bantam Books, 1977

Boyne, W. J., *Clash of Wings*, Touchstone, 1997

Bramson, A., *Master Airman, A Biography of Air Vice-Marshal Donald Bennett*, Airlife Publishing, 1985

Brickhill, P., *Reach for the Sky*, Cassell, 2000

Brizan, G., *Brave Young Grenadians*, privately printed Trinidad, 2002

Brookes, A., *Air War over Russia*, Ian Allan, 2003

Brookes, A., *Air War over Italy*, Ian Allan, 2000

Brown, E., *Wings on my Sleeve*, Phoenix, 2007

Bungay, S. *The Most Dangerous Enemy*, Aurum Press, 2001

Caidin,M., *The Night Hamburg Died*, Ballantine Books, 1960

Caidin, M., *The Ragged, Rugged Warriors*, Bantom Books, 1979

Caldwell, D. L., *JG 26, Top Guns of the Luftwaffe*, Ballantine Books, 1991

Campbell, C., *Air War Pacific*, Crescent Books, 1990

Carell P., *Hitler's War on Russia*, Harrap, 1964

Carell P., *Scorched Earth*, Harrap 1970

Chesneau, R. (editor) *Conway's All the World's Fighting Ships 1906-1921*, Conway Maritime Press, 1985

Chesneau, R. (editor) *Conway's All the World's Fighting Ships 1922-1946*, Conway Maritime Press, 1980

Chorley, W. R., *Bomber Command Losses of the Second World War*, Midland Publishing, 2007

Churchill, W. S., *The Second World War*, Cassell & Co., 1948

Clostermann, P., *The Big Show*, Ballantine Books, 1951

Collier, R., *1940 The World in Flames,* Penguin Books, 1980

Collier, R., *1941 Armageddon,* Penguin Books, 1982

Comer, J., *Combat Crew*, Time Warner, 2003

Corbin, J., *Last of the Ten Fighter Boys*, Sutton Publishing, 2007

Corrigan, G., *The Second World War*, Atlantic Books, 2010

Costello, J., *The Pacific War*, Collins, 1981

Crosby, F., *The Complete Guide to Fighters & Bombers of the World*, Hermes House, 2006

Crouch T. D., *Wings,* W. W. Norton & Company, 2003

Currie, J., *Lancaster Target*, Goodall, 1997

Deere, A. C., *Nine Lives,* Hodder and Stoughton, 1959

Deighton L., *Blitzkrieg,* Triad/Granada, 1981

Deighton L., *Blood, Tears and Folly* Vintage Books, 2007

Deighton, L., *Fighter,* Jonathan Cape, 1977

Dorr, R. F., *B-24 Liberator Units of the 15th Air Force*, Osprey Publishing, 2000

Dunning C., *Regia Aeronautica*, Classic Publications, 2009

Dunning C., *Courage Alone*, Hikoki Publications, 1998

Eisenhower, D. D., *Crusade in Europe*, Heinemann, 1948

Emelianenko, V. B., *Red Star against the Swastika*, Greenhill Books, 2005

Erickson, J., *The Road to Stalingrad*, Phoenix, 1998

Erickson, J., *The Road to Berlin*, Widenfeld & Nicolson, 1983

Forbes, A., (editor) *Ten Fighter Boys*, Collins, 2008

Foreman, J., *Fighter Command War Diaries*, Air Research Publications, 2002

Forrester, L., *Fly for your Life*, Cerberus Publishing, 2002

Freeman, R.A., *The Mighty Eighth War Diary*, Arms and Armour Press, 1990

Freeman, R.A., *The Mighty Eighth War Manual*, Jane's Publishing, 1985

Galland, A., *The First and the Last,* Ballantine Books, 1957

Gibson G., *Enemy Coast Ahead,* Pan Books, 1955

Gordon Y. and Khazanov D., *Soviet Combat Aircraft of the Second World War*, Midland Publishing, 1998

Guderian, H., *Panzer Leader,* Futura Publications, 1974

Gunston, W., *Development of Piston Aero Engines*, Patrick Stephens, 1993

Gunston, W, *The Illustrated Directory of Fighting Aircraft of World War II,* Salamander Books, 1988

Hamlin, J. F., *Support and Strike*, GMS Enterprises, 1991

Hannig, N., *Luftwaffe Fighter Ace*, Grub Street, 2004

Hara, T., Saito, F. and Pineau, R., *Japanese Destroyer Captain*, Ballantine Books, 1961

Hardesty, Von, *Red Phoenix*, Smithsonian Institution Press, 1982

Harris, A., *Bomber Offensive,* Pen & Sword Books, 2005

Hastings, M., *Bomber Command*, Pan Books, 1981

Hastings, M., *Overlord*, Pan Books, 1985

Hastings, M., *Armageddon*, Macmillan, 2004

Hastings, M., *Nemesis*, HarperCollins, 2007

Hata, I., Izawa, Y. and Shores, C., *Japanese Army Air Force Fighter Units and their Aces*, Grub Street, 2002

Hendrie, A., *The Cinderella Service*, Pen & Sword, 2010

Hinchliffe, P., *Schnauffer, Ace of Diamonds*, Tempus Publishing, 1999

Holland, J., *Fortress Malta, an Island under Siege 1940-1943*, Phoenix, 2004

Hooton, E. R., *The Luftwaffe, a Study in Air Power 1933-1945*, Classic Publications, 2010

Hooton, E.R., *Luftwaffe at War: Gathering Storm 1933-1939,* Chevron Publishing, 2007

Hooton, E.R., *Luftwaffe at War: Blitzkrieg in the West 1939-1940,* Chevron Publishing, 2007

Irving, D., *The Destruction of Dresden*, Futura, 1980

Jackson, R., *The Encyclopaedia of Military Aircraft*, Parragon Books, 2002

Johnen, W., *Battling the Bombers*, Ace Books, 1958

Johnson, J. E., *Full Circle*, Cassell, 2001

Johnson, J. E., *Wing Leader,* Chatto & Windus, 1956

Johnson, R.S., *Thunderbolt,* Ballantine Books, 1959

Jones, I., *Tiger Squadron* W.H.Allen, 1954

Kaplan, P., *Fighter Aces of the Luftwaffe in World War II*, Pen & Sword, 2007

Klemperer, V., *The Klemperer Diaries 1933-1945*, Phoenix Press, 2000

Knoke, H., *I Flew for the Fuehrer*, Evans Brothers, 1953

Knott, C. R., *Princes of Darkness*, Chevron Publishing, 2008

Kurowski, F., *Luftwaffe Aces*, Stackpole Books, 2004

Lawson, R. and Tillman B., *U.S. Navy Air Combat 1939-1946*, MBI Publishing, 2000

LeMay, C. *Super Fortress*, Berkley, 1989

Liddell Hart, B. H., *The German Generals Talk*, William Morrow & Co., 1948

Liddell Hart, B. H., *The Rommel Papers,* Harcourt Brace, 1953

Lipfert, H. and Girbig, W., *The War Diary of Helmut Lipfert*, Schiffer Publishing, 1993

Mariinsky, E., *Red Star Airacobra*, Helion, 2006

Maslov, M., *Polikarpov I-15, I-16 and I-153 Aces,* Osprey Publishing, 2010

Massimello, G. and Apostolo G., *Italian Aces of World War 2*, Osprey Publishing, 2000

Masters, J., *Fourteen Eighteen,* Michael Joseph, 1965

McAulay, L., *MacArthur's Eagles, the U.S. Air War over New Guinea 1943-1944*, Naval Institute Press, 2005

McKee, A., *Dresden 1945*, Granada Publishing, 1983

McKinstry, L., *Hurricane,* John Murray, 2010

McKinstry, L., *Lancaster,* John Murray, 2010

McKinstry, L., *Spitfire, Portrait of a Legend*, John Murray, 2007

Mellinger, G., *LaGG & Lavochkin Aces of World War 2*, Osprey Publishing, 2003

Mellinger, G., *Soviet Lend-Lease Fighter Aces of World War 2*, Osprey Publishing, 2006

Mellinger, G., *Yakovlev Aces of World War 2*, Osprey Publishing, 2005

Merrick, K. A., *Halifax, From Hell to Victory and Beyond*, Chevron Publishing, 2009

Middlebrook M. and Everitt C., *The Bomber Command War Diaries*, Midland Publishing, 1996

Middlebrook M., *The Battle of Hamburg*, Penguin Books 1984

Middlebrook M., *The Nuremberg Raid*, Penguin Books 1986

Middlebrook M., *The Schweinfurt-Regensburg Mission*, Penguin Books 1985

Middlebrook M., *The Peenemunde Raid*, Penguin Books 1988

Middlebrook M., *The Berlin Raids*, Pen & Sword Books, 2010

Miller, D. L., *Eighth Air Force*, Aurum Press, 2007

Ministry of Information, *Front Line 1940-41 the Official Story of the Civil Defence of Britain*, H.M.S.O., 1942

Morison, S. E., *History of United States Naval Operations in World War II*, Naval Institute Press, 2010; volumes VIII and XIII University of Illinois Press, 2002

Morison, S. E., *The Two-Ocean War*, Naval Institute Press, 2007

Munson, K., *Fighters, Attack and Training Aircraft 1939-45*, Blandford Press, 1969

Munson, K., *Bombers, Patrol and Transport Aircraft 1939-45*, Blandford Press, 1969

Neillands, R., *The Bomber War*, John Murray, 2002

Okumiya M., Horikoshi J. and Caidin M., *Zero,* Corgi Books, 1958

Oliver, D., *Fighter Command 1939-45*, Harper Collins, 2000

Olson, L. and Cloud, S., *For your Freedom and Ours,* Arrow Books, 2003

Oughton, F., *The Aces*, Consul, 1962

Overy, R. J., *The Air War 1939-1945*, Potomac Books, 2004

Overy, R. J., *Bomber Command 1939-45*, Bookmart, 2000

Parnell, N. M. and Lynch, C. A., *Australian Air Force since 1911*, A. H. & A. W. Reed, 1976

Pearson, M., *The Burma Air Campaign 1939-1945*, Pen & Sword, 2006

Price, A., *The Luftwaffe Data Book*, Greenhill Books, 1997

Roderick-Jones, R., *Pedro, The Life and Death of Fighter Ace Osgood Villiers Hanbury*, Grub St., 2010

Richey, P., *Fighter Pilot,* Cassell & Co., 2001

Richards, D., *The Hardest Victory,* Coronet Books, 1994

Rudel, H. U., *Stuka Pilot*, Ballantine Books, 1958

Sakai, S., Caidin, M. and Saito, F., *Samurai!,* Ballantine Books, 1957

Sakaida, H., *Imperial Japanese Navy Aces 1937-45*, Osprey Publishing, 1998

Sakaida, H., *Japanese Army Air Force Aces 1937-45*, Osprey Publishing, 1997

Sakaida, H., *Imperial Japanese Navy Aces*, Osprey Publishing, 1998

Scutts, J., *Bf 109 Aces of North Africa and the Mediterranean*, Osprey Publishing, 1995

Scutts, J., *Mustang Aces of the Eighth Air Force*, Osprey Publishing, 1994

Scutts, J., *P-47 Thunderbolt Aces of the Eighth Air Force*, Osprey Publishing, 1998

Scutts, J., *Mustang Aces of the Ninth and Fifteenth Air Forces & the RAF*, Osprey Publishing, 1995

Scutts, J., *P-47 Thunderbolt Aces of the Ninth and Fifteenth Air Forces*, Osprey Publishing, 1999

Searby, J., *The Bomber Battle for Berlin*, Guild Publishing, 1991

Shirer, W. L., *The Rise and Fall of the Third Reich*, Book Club Associates, 1970

Shores, C. F., *Finnish Air Force 1918-1968,* Osprey Publications, 1969

Shores, C. F. and Thomas, C., *2nd Tactical Air Force*, Chevron, 2004

Slim, W. J., *Defeat into Victory*, The Reprint Society, 1957

Smith, P. C., *Dive Bomber* Casemate, 2008

Speer, A, *Inside the Third Reich,* Book Club Associates, 1971

Stannaway, S., *P-38 Lightning Aces of the Pacific and CBI*, Osprey Publishing, 1997

Stannaway, S., *Mustang and Thunderbolt Aces of the Pacific and CBI*, Osprey Publishing, 1999

Styling, S. and Tillman, B., *The Blue Devils*, Osprey Publishing, 2003

Sutherland, J. and Canwell, D., *Air War East Africa 1940-1941*, Pen & Sword, 2009

Sutherland, J. and Canwell, D, *Air War Malta, June 1940 to November 1941*, Pen & Sword, 2008

Tillman, B., *Whirlwind, The Air War against Japan 1942-1945*, Simon & Schuster, 2010

Toland, J., *The Rising Sun*, Modern Library, 2003

Toliver, R. F. and Constable, T.J., *The Blond Knight of Germany*, Tab/ Aero, 1970

Vassiltchikov, M., *The Berlin Diaries 1939-1945*, Pimlico 1999

Vigors, T., *Life's too Short to Cry,* Grub Street, 2006

Von Hardesty, *Red Phoenix*, Smithsonian Institution, 1982

Wagner, R., (editor) *The Soviet Air Force in World War II,* Doubleday & Company, 1973

Warnock, A. T., *Air Power versus U-boats*, Air Force History and Museums Program, 1999

Weal, E. C., Weal, J. A. and Barker, R.F., *Combat Aircraft of World War Two*, Arms and Armour Press, 1977

Weal, J., *Focke-Wulf Fw 190 Aces of the Western Front*, Osprey Publishing, 1996

Wellum, G., *First Light*, Penguin, 2003

Webster C. and Frankland N., *The Strategic Air Offensive Against Germany*, H.M.S.O., 1961

Williamson, G., *Luftwaffe Handbook 1935-1945*, Sutton Publishing, 2006

Wilmot C., *The Struggle for Europe*, Collins, 1952

Wolff, L., *Low Level Mission*, Panther, 1960

Wragg, D., *RAF Handbook 1939-1945*, Sutton Publishing, 2007

Yates, H., *Luck and a Lancaster*, Airlife Publishing, 2001

Websites

Wikipedia.com: entry for R.M.S. Lancastria, 2011

Ditto Jisaburo Ozawa, 2011

Ditto Gunther Specht, 2011

Index

Ukraine, 284, 284
Army Group South, 118, 121, 122
Army Group South (in Poland 1939), 49
Army and Navy formations, Japanese
15th Army, 170
18th Army, 342
Army and Navy formations, Soviet
1st Ukrainian Front, 284
26th Soviet Army, 121
2nd Byelorussian Front, 328
5th Guards Tank Army, 227
62nd Army, Russian, 163
Army and Navy formations, French
55th Division, 63
Army and Navy formations, U.S.
3rd Fleet US, 334, 337, 338, 340, 341
5th Fleet US, 289, 292, 334
6th Army US, 336
Arnhem, 304
Arnold, General H.H. 'Hap', 151, 343, 344
Artomovsky, 160
Astrakhan, 222
Athens, 103
Atlantic Ocean, 54, 57, 89, 91, 95, 131, 139
Attu, 178
Auchinleck, Sir Claude, 196
Augsburg, 267
Auschwitz, 328
Austria, 34
Auxiliary Air Force, 38
Avenger, HMS, 248
Avenger, see Grumman
AVG/Flying Tigers, 25,

170, 172, 298
Avia B534, 100, 101
Avro Anson, 90
Avro Lancaster, 40, 107, 146, 173, 201, 203, 207, 208, 263, 343, 364
Avro Manchester, 146
Bader, Douglas, 76, 83-84
Baer, Heinz, 122
Baghdad, 195
Bagration, Operation, 279, 281, 282-286
Baker, Lt. Col. Addison, 256
Baku, 157
Balbo, Marshal Italo, 31
Baldwin, Stanley, 39
Bali, 138
Balikpapan, 138, 342, 343
Ball, Albert, 11
Balthasar, Wilhelm, 69
Baltic Sea, 49, 54, 111, 202, 306, 324, 328
Baltic Front, 118
Baltic Special Military District, 111, 118
Bangkok, 301
Barbarossa, Operation, 105-111, 156
Bari, 254
Barkhorn, Gerd, 220, 278, 285, 322
Barratt, Air Marshal Arthur, 64
Bataan, 139
Batten, Jean, 15
Battle, see Fairey
Battle of Berlin, 201-209
Battle of Britain, 16, 41, 48, 70-84, 92, 98, 115, 135, 194, 205, 208, 226, 247, 289, 368
Battle of Britain Day, 82
Battle of Cape Matapan, 193
Battle of Empress Augusta

Bay, 239
Battle of Guadalcanal, 238
Battle of Hamburg, 153-154
Battle of Kursk, 223-228
Battle of Leyte Gulf, 337-340
Battle of Midway, 128, 178-183, 235
Battle of Santa Cruz, 236, 237
Battle of Savo Island, 235
Battle of Tassafaronga, 238
Battle of the Coral Sea, 174-177
Battle of the Eastern Solomons, 235
Battle of the Philippine Sea, 128, 293-297
Battle of the Ruhr, 152
Battlegroup Bauer, 278
Bavaria, 33, 58, 209, 269
Bay of Biscay, 150
Bayerische Flugzeugwerke, 20
Bazanov, Pyotr, 165
Beaverbrook, Lord, 73, 76,
Beijing, 23
Belfast, 87
Belgium, 59, 60, 61, 62, 66, 92, 265, 266, 306, 307
Belgorod, 221, 228, 229
Belgrade, 101, 102, 324
Bell Airacomet, 307
Bell P-39 Airacobra, 45, 133, 166, 173, 219, 226, 237, 241, 28, 326, 333
Bell P-63 Kingcobra, 45, 166
Bellagambi, Major Mario, 318
Benghazi, 255